A HISTORY OF WESTERN ARCHITECTURE

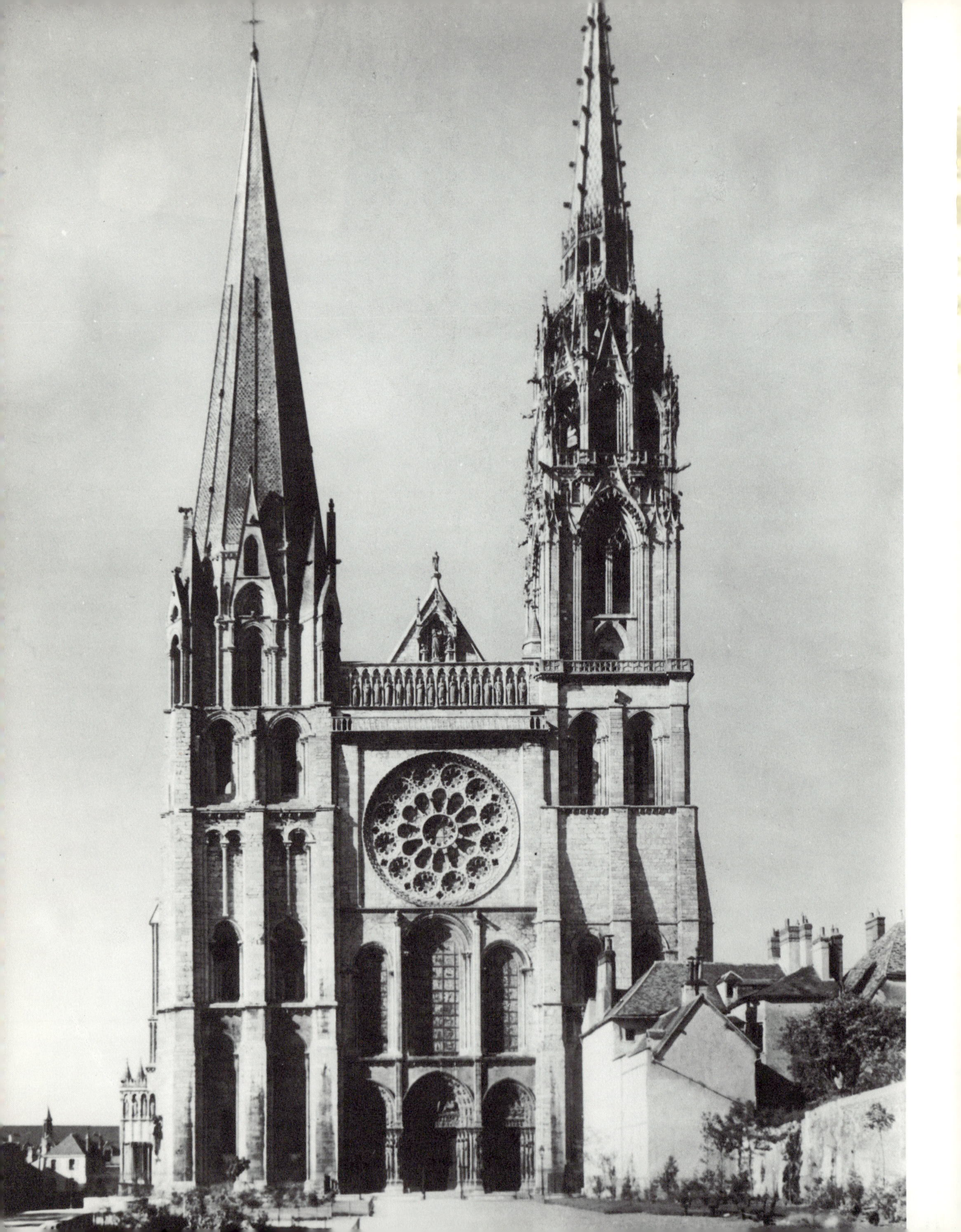

A HISTORY OF WESTERN ARCHITECTURE

Lawrence Wodehouse & Marian Moffett
UNIVERSITY OF TENNESSEE

MAYFIELD PUBLISHING COMPANY
Mountain View, California

Library of Congress Cataloging-in-Publication Data

Wodehouse, Lawrence.
A history of western architecture.

Bibliography: p.
Includes index.
1. Architecture — History. I. Moffett, Marian.
II. Title.
NA200.W64 1989 720'.9 88-13820
ISBN 0-87484-784-2

Manufactured in the United States of America
10 9 8 7 6 5 4 3 2 1

Mayfield Publishing Company
1240 Villa Street
Mountain View, California 94041

Sponsoring editor, C. Lansing Hays; production
editor, Linda Toy; manuscript editor, Loralee
Windsor; text and cover designer, Anna Post.
The text was set in 9/11 Palatino by Compset, Inc.
of Beverly, MA and printed on 60# Stora Matte by
W. A. Krueger Co., Inc.

Preface

This textbook, *A History of Western Architecture,* was written for students in introductory architectural history survey courses. Like many other teachers, we were raised on Sir Nikolaus Pevsner's *Outline of European Architecture,* with Sir Bannister Fletcher's venerable *A History of Architecture on the Comparative Method* looming in the background. For our students, these books, while still admirable, have become increasingly unsatisfactory. Their focus is inherently European, with particular emphasis on Britain, and their coverage of the nineteenth and twentieth centuries is less than what our students need to know.

We have written a straightforward account of western traditions in architecture, encompassing examples from prehistoric structures to the 1980s. For the period from 1750 onward, we have included American examples whenever possible so that readers may more easily identify developments on this side of the Atlantic. This book thus provides a solid foundation for a year-long course in architectural history and will be useful to students in architecture, art, and the humanities, or for interested lay readers.

Given the scale of the undertaking and the number of potential examples, choices had to be made, and not every well-known building is to be found in this book. We selected examples primarily for their contributions to the development of a style or building technique or for their illustration of cultural expression, in hopes of providing a coherent framework onto which individual instructors may add more detailed material according to their particular interests. We have tried to avoid current fashions or the slant of one particular theoretical approach.

Our aim has been to produce a readable and useful text that encourages student interest in architectural history. We have written in a manner comprehensible to undergraduates without presuming a detailed knowledge of European history or architectural terms and monuments. Because many architectural terms may be unfamiliar, they are presented in boldface and defined in the text when first used, then collected into a glossary. Maps at the beginning of the text identify towns containing buildings discussed in the text. To the extent possible, multiple photographs and drawings are used to illustrate salient features of major buildings. In particular, we have included numerous plans and sections to represent buildings in the convention of architectural language. A sixteen-page color photographic essay emphasizes the presence and impact of selected buildings through their historical connections, context, cultural influences, materials, and effects of light. All illustrations work with the verbal descriptions to aid students in visualizing the buildings and their settings. As an aid to further exploration of particular aspects of architectural history, we have provided a list of additional reading at the conclusion of the volume.

Many people have contributed to the realization of this book. We are grateful to our colleagues, Dorothy Habel, Connie Waltz, and Dale Cleaver, for reading and commenting on portions of the manuscript. Among others, Ted A. Ertl, University of Nebraska; Michael Fazio, Mississippi State University; Beverly Heisner, University of South Carolina; and J. William Rudd, Washington State University, read the manuscript at various stages and provided helpful criticism. At Mayfield Publishing, we found in C. Lansing Hays an editor who saw promise in the manuscript. Linda Toy has coordinated the myriad aspects of production with unfailing cheer, while Loralee Windsor has done a superior job of text editing. The book's design and appearance are a credit to Anna Post.

CONTENTS

Black Sea
Istanbul
Hattusus
Çatal Hüyük
Tepe Gawra
Khorasbad
Krak des Chevaliers
Samarra
Baalbek
Mediterranean Sea
Damascus
Babylon
Jericho
Jerusalem
Qusayr Amra
Uruk [Warka]
Bethlehem
Mshatta
Ur
Eridu
Giza
Saqqara
Dashur
Meydum
Beni Hasan
Tel-el-Amarna
Deir-el-Bahari
Karnak
Medina
N
Red Sea
Abu Simbel
Mecca

*Detailed maps of Italy, France, and Great Britain follow.

Grignasco
Milan
Vicenza
Maser
Venice
Malcontenta
Turin
Pavia
Mantua
Vallinoto
Ravenna
Marzabotto
Rimini
Poggio a Caiano
Florence
Pisa
Urbino
Siena
Perugia
Todi
Adriatic Sea
Cerveteri
Tivoli
Rome
Ostia
Pompeii
Paestum
Tyrrhenian Sea
N
Mediterranean Sea

N
English Channel
Bay of Biscay
Mediterranean Sea
Centula
Amiens
Laon
Jumièges
Beauvais
Reims
Caen
Poissy
St. Denis
Noisel-sur-Marne
Versailles
Paris
Garches
Vaux-le-Vicomte
Chartres
Sens
Germigny-des-Près
Ancy-le-Franc
Fontenay
Carnac
Ronchamp
Blois
Chambord
Vézelay
Chenonceau
La Charité
Cîteaux
Bourges
Autun
Tournus
Saint-Savin-sur-Gartempe
Cluny
Paray-le-Monial
Eveux
Angoulême
Périgueux
Conques
Nîmes
Saint-Gilles-du-Gard
Arles
Toulouse
Marseilles
Carcassonne
Canigou

N
Atlantic Ocean
North Sea
Helensburgh
Glasgow
Durham
New Grange
Irish Sea
Menai Straits
Southwell
Lincoln
Belper
Nottingham
Leicester
Ely
Earl's Barton
Cambridge
Woodstock
Greensted
London
Greenwich
Bexleyheath
Ramsgate
Wells
Twickenham
Canterbury
Salisbury
Sheerness
English Channel

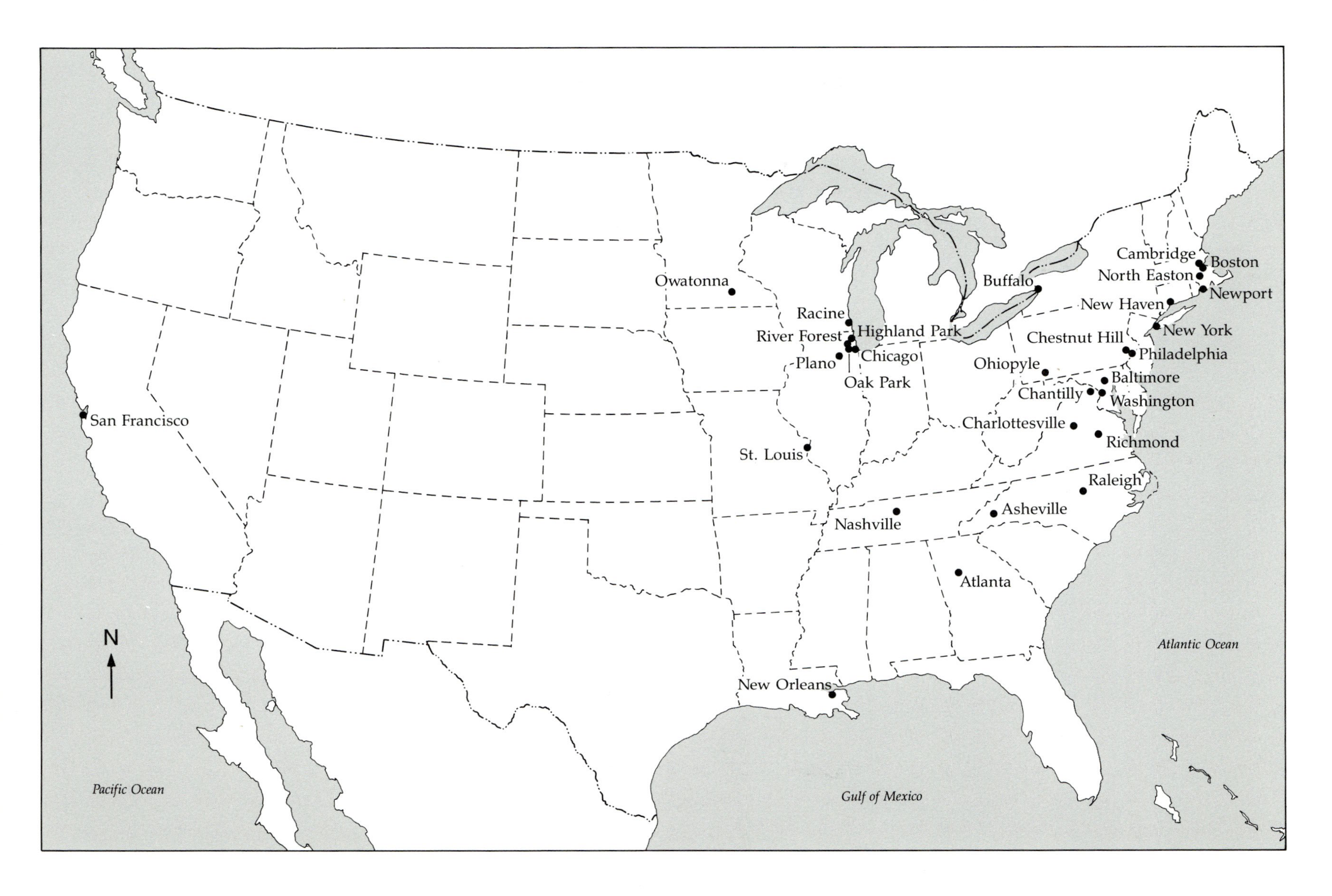
Owatonna
Racine
River Forest
Highland Park
Plano
Chicago
Oak Park
Buffalo
Cambridge
Boston
North Easton
Newport
New Haven
New York
Chestnut Hill
Philadelphia
Ohiopyle
Baltimore
Chantilly
Washington
Charlottesville
Richmond
San Francisco
St. Louis
Raleigh
Asheville
Nashville
Atlanta
N
New Orleans
Atlantic Ocean
Pacific Ocean
Gulf of Mexico

The exotic exterior of St. Mark's in Venice is matched by an equally lavish interior covered in gold mosaics. Venetian architecture has generally reflected influences from both Byzantium and northern Europe, and St. Mark's is no exception. Its plan was based on that of a now-vanished church in Constantinople erected by the emperor Justinian, and its façade is a Venetian interpretation of Gothic. Raised roofs over the domes, capped by elaborate crosses, contribute to the striking silhouette that makes this church the focal point of the Piazza San Marco, one of the most celebrated urban spaces in the world.

The warm yellow hues of the stone used in the Romanesque church of Sainte-Foy at Conques glow in the afternoon sun. Light enters the church from windows in the crossing lantern, illuminating the barrel vaults of the ceiling. This church, once a major stop on the pilgrim route to Compostela, was built to commemorate a twelve-year-old child who was martyred by the Roman legate during persecutions of the Christians. Her relics, contained in a golden reliquary dating from the tenth century, are still preserved in the church's treasury. ▶

The Queen's Apartments at the Royal Palace of Knossos flows out into a small courtyard which traps the brilliant Mediterranean sun while preserving privacy. Light reflecting off the walls bounces into the suite of rooms built into the hillside on which the Palace sits, providing adequate illumination. Earth insulation keeps the apartments cool in summer and the sunlit courtyard pleasant in winter.

The remote monastery of Saint-Martin is perched on a ridge of Mount Canigou in the Pyrenees and is still accessed only by a winding footpath. Far from worldly temptations, a small group of monks constructed these buildings around the year 1000, making this one of the earliest completely vaulted churches of medieval Europe. The stepped crenellations of the tower recall Islamic fortifications of neighboring Spain.

This view of the Great Mosque at Córdoba as seen from the tower shows the typical features of mosques throughout the Islamic world: an open courtyard (foreground) followed by a broad expansive prayer hall, here covered by parallel gable roofs. Most unexpectedly, the Mosque also contains a Christian church, the Cathedral of Córdoba which was built in the sixteenth century after the expulsion of the Moors from Spain, to symbolize the triumph of Christianity over Islam. ▼

The Court of the Lions at the Alhambra in Granada, Spain, is rich in architectural detailing and symbolism. The lions date from the eleventh century and represent beasts long associated with royalty. From their mouths pour water that flows into channels of the court and into the surrounding rooms, paralleling the Koranic description of Paradise as a garden below which rivers flow. ▶

This Romanesque church, Sainte-Madeleine at Vézelay, was constructed with semicircular arches spanning the nave between bays of groin vaults. These arches have since become distorted because of the great weight of the stone used in their construction. The alternate red and white stones set in the arches may reflect artistic influence from Islamic architecture, most likely from Spain, where similar polychrome arches were used in mosques.

Built just over a century after Sainte-Madeleine, Reims Cathedral shows how Gothic architects treated masonry construction, using the pointed arch, rib vault, and flying buttress to stabilize enormously vertical interior spaces. Windows much larger than anything possible in the Romanesque period were filled with colored glass that suffused the church with soft glowing light while also illustrating religious teachings in the scenes set in the windows. The vastness of the interior of Gothic churches must have contrasted sharply with the low and dark dwellings of ordinary people during the medieval period, and the effect of these soaring heights remains impressive even today.

The ethereal character of Go architecture is easily seen in these two photographs of Gothic cathedral vaults, the upper of Reims and the lowe Beauvais, the tallest French Gothic church ever attempte The builders of Beauvais experienced structural failur the high vaults of the choir collapsed shortly after construction, but they were rebuilt in a strengthened forn Even so, the entire project w never completed, leaving the choir, the transepts and one bay of the nave as ent witnesses to a much more ambitious design that was never realized.

The medieval citizens of Sien after winning the right to sel government late in the thirteenth century, chose to commemorate their independence by erecting an impressive city hal the Palazzo Pubblico, located at the focus of a new plaza, the Campo. The Palazzo is delightfully asymmetrical, punctuated by the soaring be tower visible from afar. Goth details and even crenellations from fortification design enliven the brick façade, making this an impressive monument to civic pride.

The centrally planned church of Santa Maria della Consolazione sits outside the ramparts of Todi, a medieval Italian hilltown. Constructed early in the sixteenth century, this church reflects Renaissance interest in simple geometries and domed buildings and may well have been influenced by sketches of church designs contained in the Notebooks of Leonardo da Vinci.

The east wall of S. Maria presso S. Satiro in Milan, as seen from the nave or central crossing, appears to be a coffered barrel vaulted chancel. It is an illusion, however, because the chancel is a painted moulded surface, as can be seen in this oblique view from the south transept. Donato Bramante, the architect, was utilizing the discovery of perspective in the early fifteenth century to maximum advantage.

The island monastery of S. Giorgio Maggiore, located at the end of the Grand Canal, is viewed here from the Campanile of St. Mark's in Venice. Palladio's design for the façade of the church sets a precedent in solving the problem of adding two superimposed classical temple fronts onto a basilica. This façade dominates the view from the Piazzetta leading from the Piazza San Marco.

This view is from the lantern atop Michelangelo's dome for St. Peter's in Rome, on foundations begun in 1506 by Bramante. It shows not only the extended nave of the church, leading to the façade of Carlo Maderno, but also the piazza of Bernini and the planning of Rome as formulated by Sixtus V and realized in the 1930s by Mussolini in the via del Conciliazione.

The churches of S. Carlo by Borromini and of S. Andrea by Bernini are located within a block of each other on the Via dei Quirinale in Rome and were designed and built within a few years of each other. Both designs rely on the oval plan capped by a coffered oval dome. There the similarity ends because Borromini logically places the entrance at one end of the oval and the altar at the other. Bernini, on the other hand, positions entrance and altar in the center of the long sides of the oval, a more difficult arrangement to achieve, but he does this through subtle organization and detail.

St. Paul's in London represents the masterpiece of Sir Christopher Wren, a mathematician turned architect, who many still consider to be England's greatest architect. In this church, he skillfully blended influences from Italian and French designs into an original composition, combining a longitudinal basilican plan with a tremendous domed central crossing. This view shows the massive piers necessary to transmit the weight of the triple-shell masonry dome down to the foundations.

Fallingwater is justifiably one of the most celebrated works of Frank Lloyd Wright. Designed as a weekend home for a wealthy family, the house artfully integrates architecture with the natural setting. By placing the house over the waterfall, Wright insured that the splash of water could be heard inside the house but seen only by going outside, where the horizontal cantilevered concrete balconies and rough textured vertical stone piers establish a splendid backdrop for the cascade, just as Wright intended. Few architects in modern times have equalled Wright in his ability to design with respect for the land.

A HISTORY OF WESTERN ARCHITECTURE

INTRODUCTION

Architecture has been defined in many ways: as the art and science of building, as the inescapable art, as frozen music, and as decorated construction, to name just a few. For some time architectural historians distinguished between *architecture* and *building,* that is, they separated imposing monuments designed by architects from utilitarian structures built by engineers or anonymous craftsmen. In this volume we have chosen to be less doctrinaire. We find the most suitable definition of architecture to be that of Marcus Vitruvius Pollio, a Roman practitioner active around 40 B.C., whose treatise, *The Ten Books on Architecture,* identified three essential qualities of architecture: *utilitas, firmitas,* and *venustas.* These have been rendered into English as convenience, durability, and beauty — or more memorably as commodity, firmness, and delight — and they provide as comprehensive a definition now as they did in Vitruvius's time.

COMMODITY

The term *commodity* reminds us that architecture is a purposeful art built to fulfill practical and symbolic human needs. The client and architect develop a program, or statement of practical functions, for an intended building before design begins. The program clarifies the activities the building will shelter and specifies the size and spatial relationship of the various rooms to be included. Thus the program for an apartment building would detail the total number of apartments and their sizes, the service rooms (mechanical equipment, trash, storage, mail, laundry), and the common spaces (lounges, lobby, and other rooms) to be provided for tenants. While the program outlines the basic aspects of a building, many possible designs can satisfy the same program, and it is this element of choice that makes the architect's job both frustrating and rewarding.

Drawings of the building's plan illustrate the functional relationships of a given design (Figure I.1). A plan is a diagram of the building seen as if it were sliced horizontally about 4 feet above the floor. The plan generally shows walls in solid black; windows as two or three thin lines connecting the solid wall sections; and doors as wall openings with or without arcs to indicate door swings. Particularly on vaulted buildings, plans often include fine lines within interior spaces that reflect breaks in the ceiling plane overhead. In one convenient drawing, a plan indicates the basic spaces in a given building and gives an indication of the project's size. In this book, we have tried to provide many plans to a common scale, so that readers can compare the relative size of important buildings.

Other scaled drawings commonly used by architects are elevations and sections. Elevations provide views of only one side of the building's exterior at a

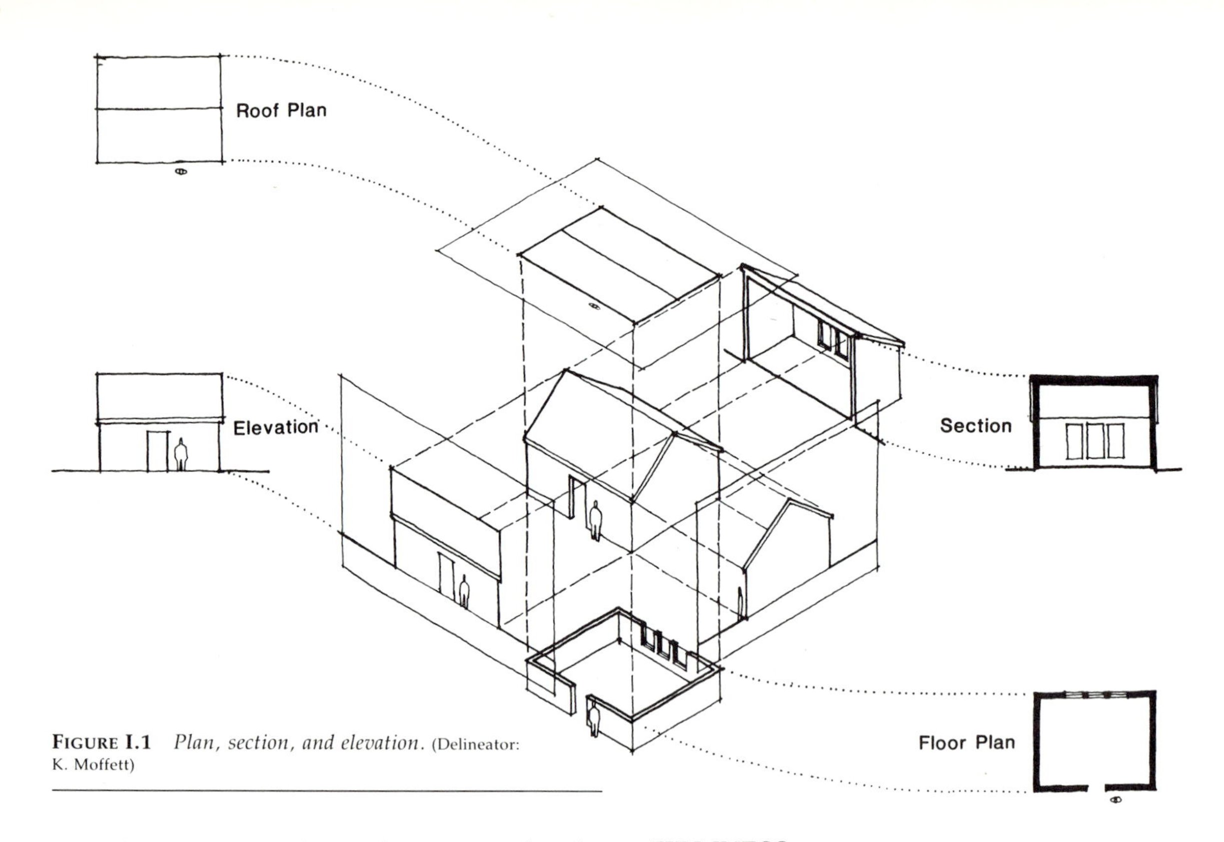

FIGURE I.1 *Plan, section, and elevation.* (Delineator: K. Moffett)

time. Sections are similar to plans, except that the slice made through the building runs perpendicular rather than parallel to the ground. Portions of walls or ceilings that were cut are generally shown as solid black areas.

Commodity involves more than functional considerations. Buildings are erected to meet human requirements, which include spiritual, emotional, and psychological needs. For some building types, such as industrial buildings, practical concerns dominate the design. In others, such as civic or religious buildings, symbolic considerations may greatly influence the practical functions. To most people, for example, a church should look like a religious building, not a gasoline station. The utilitarian functions of high-rise office buildings are tempered by the corporate image the owner wishes to project, and homeowners commonly modify their houses inside and out to accommodate functional demands and express individuality.

All architecture reflects the values and taste of the society that erects it; more money, finer workmanship and materials, and (often) better design are expended on buildings that shelter activities important to society. Thus for many periods religious buildings have endured, while residential architecture and commercial buildings have been more transitory.

FIRMNESS

Firmness is a basic requirement of architecture in that buildings must stand up. The elements of a building that primarily achieve firmness are collectively known as the structural system, and the forces to which they respond are called loads. The downward pull of gravity is responsible for the largest loads on the structure, from both the weight of the materials used in the building (dead loads) and the weight of people, furnishings, equipment, and the like that are contained in or on the building (live loads). Side or lateral loads created by natural forces such as wind and earthquakes also act on buildings. Only in the past 150 years has it been possible to quantify the direction and magnitude of loads and the ability of specific building materials to resist external forces so that designers can propose a structural system that can be demonstrated by calculations to be sound before being built. For the vast majority of buildings considered in this book, however, structure was a matter of trial and error, based on what had been successful in the past.

Structural systems can be classified in five types according to the geometric configuration of materials and the way in which loads are sustained (Figure I.2). These five structural types are post and lintel, corbel and cantilever, arch and vault, truss

FIGURE I.2 *Arch, corbel, truss, and post and lintel structures.* (From Viollet-le-Duc)

and space frame, and tension. Post and lintel systems, formed by vertical members (posts) supporting a horizontal element (the **lintel** or beam), are perhaps the most common type. The possible distance between posts is primarily determined by the spanning capability of the lintels. Under load, the lintels tend to bend downward, stretching (or putting in tension) the lower edge and contracting (or putting in compression) the upper edge. Certain materials, such as stone, can sustain large loads in compression but will break quickly if pulled in tension. Good materials for lintels should be equally strong in tension and compression, so wood, steel, and reinforced **concrete** are widely used.

Since stone was the most durable building material available to early societies, people found ways to overcome its inherent brittleness in tension and at the same time use it to span longer distances than was possible in post and lintel construction. The earliest method was through the **corbel.** Stone was laid in horizontal rows, with each row projecting slightly beyond the preceding one to form a corbeled **arch** or **dome.** This same principle was also used in cantilever construction, where a beam (often of wood) projects beyond its supports to form an overhang, such as an **eave** below a roof or an overhanging second floor (**jetty**).

True arches and **vaults** are composed of wedge-shaped stones called **voussoirs** laid on a temporary framework or centering until the arch is completed, at which time the stones push tightly against one another and become self-supporting. Such construction requires firm side bracing, as the arch exerts thrust, an outward, overturning force that must be counteracted if the arch is to remain upright. Properly built, a single vault can span over 100 feet using small stones. The profiles taken by arches vary considerably: semicircular, or Roman; broken, or pointed; horseshoe; and segmental arches are among the most important historically. All arches behave in a similar structural manner.

The **truss** method of spanning space connects short wooden or metal pieces in a triangulated framework. The Romans developed this technique for bridges, but their trusses were largely forgotten so the truss had to be reinvented in the nineteenth century. The names given to trusses invented then are those of the men who developed them; Warren trusses are probably the most common today. A truss frame repeated in a planar unit is known as a space frame, a twentieth-century structural development that is particularly useful for long, clear-span roofs.

Some structures are based on tension (Figure I.3). Simple nomadic tents are examples of tensile structures, as are suspension bridges. In both cases, the structural load is partly carried by thin fibers or cables woven or spun together. Early builders used animal or vegetable fibers—hair, vines, and sisal—to build tension structures, but their use was limited by the inherent weakness of the fibers and their tendency to decay. Tension construction has made great progress in the nineteenth and twentieth centuries as engineers have spun thin strands of iron or steel into cables to support the world's longest bridges. Cables are also used to suspend floors of multistory buildings.

The possibilities of these structural types are myriad, and some hybrid systems also exist, such as cantilevered and arched trusses. The selection of

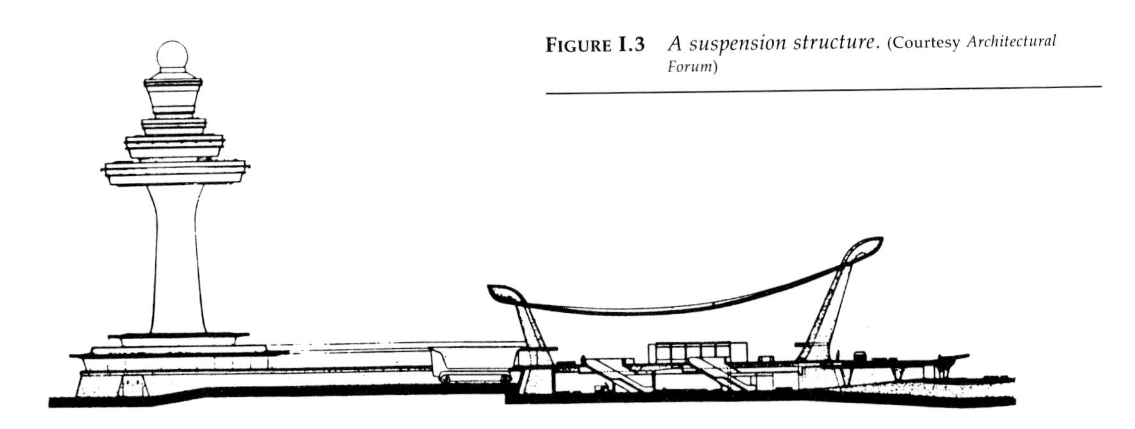

FIGURE I.3 *A suspension structure.* (Courtesy *Architectural Forum*)

any one of them for a particular building depends on available materials, economics, building requirements, and the aesthetic sensibilities of the architect or client.

DELIGHT

Delight is perhaps the most subjective of Vitruvius's three elements of architecture. It is the artistry with which functional concerns and structural requirements are so integrated into a single whole that nothing could be added or subtracted without detriment to the work. Delight encompasses questions of aesthetics (the philosophy of beauty), taste, and judgment on the part of the designer and the observer. Attitudes about beauty change from one period to another; what one age or group of people consider beautiful is not necessarily esteemed by people in other places or in other times. Aesthetic preferences are not evolutionary, that is, twentieth-century taste is not necessarily superior to that of the nineteenth century. Outstanding artistic achievements from any period are recognizable when the prevailing aesthetic canons of the time are clear.

Two major attributes for evaluating architecture deserve mention. One is the sense of organization in which all elements work together to reinforce the architectural concept of the building. The absence of organization is chaos, a condition that few people find pleasant; when presented with a confused jumble of items, most people try to find an underlying logic. The order created by the designer does not have to be immediately obvious, for there is sometimes delight in discovery, but there must be enough coherence in the scheme to communicate to the observer. Most buildings emphasize the important spaces within, and good designers carefully plan the sequence in which a visitor encounters them. Related to organization are the ideas of repetition and variation. Repetition of a structural unit, a decorative motif, or a detail sets up a sense of rhythm that can be satisfying but can also become monotonous if not relieved by variation.

As important as organization is the principle of contrast, which is indispensable in all the visual arts. The possible contrasts in architecture are endless: light and shade, smooth and rough, subtle and bold, soft and hard, concave and convex, low and high, delicate and heavy, straight and curved, wide and narrow, large and small, simple and complex, and open and closed, to name just a few. The play of contrasts within a building or cityscape gives richness to human experience by adding the elements of discovery and surprise.

Architectural monuments selected for inclusion in this book represent major examples from each historic period. Each work is significant because it contributes to the stylistic development of its time, embodies a new approach to design, or forms a transition link from one period to another. In presenting the major historical developments in western architecture, we hope that the reader will both understand the buildings of the past and observe the present with an increased appreciation of the continuing challenge presented by architectural design, that of providing shelter for human activities.

1.

THE BEGINNINGS OF ARCHITECTURE

The prehistoric era, that is, the period before the development of written language, begins as early as 35,000 B.C. and extends to about 3000 B.C. in the lands of the eastern Mediterranean and until after 2000 B.C. in western Europe. On the time scale of humankind, these dates correspond to the earliest years of "modern" human evolution from cooperative hunting-gathering societies into agricultural civilizations with a fixed settlement area and a priest-king class. In the absence of written records, archaeologists and historians must interpret the fragmentary remains of these ancient people — pottery, household implements and rubbish, burials, and tombs — in scattered locations in Europe, Africa, and central Asia. Twentieth-century science has assisted the dating of artifacts through radioactive carbon 14, thermoluminescence, and dendrochronological analysis, but both the methods and the hypotheses derived from them are subject to frequent revision as researchers discover new evidence and reexamine old ideas. The study of prehistory is still a very young discipline with many unanswered questions.

PREHISTORIC SETTLEMENTS AND MEGALITH CONSTRUCTIONS

Human settlement seems to have originated at the small clan or family level, with a sufficient number of people living together to provide mutual assistance in hunting and food gathering and mutual protection against enemies. Among the earliest huts to be discovered are those at Mezhirich, near Kiev, U.S.S.R., dated to about 14,000 B.C. Constructed of mammoth bones and pine poles with a lining of animal skins and a central hearth, the largest hut incorporated the skeletons of over a hundred animals in its framework. Excavators have found clusters of skin-covered huts dated to about 12,000 B.C. between Moscow and Novgorod. The largest of these huts, measuring about thirty-nine by thirteen feet in plan, was an irregular shape formed by three interlocking cones fabricated of inclined branches open at the top to allow smoke to escape from the three hearths.

Excavations of town sites suggest that larger communities were a much later development. The existence of urban settlements depends on an agricultural surplus that enables some people to assume specialized roles (priest, ruler, merchant, craftsman) not tied directly to the production of food. Two of the earliest known urban communities were Jericho, Israel (ca. 8000 B.C.) and the trading town of Çatal Hüyük (6500–5700 B.C.) [Figure 1.1] in Anatolia, part of present-day Turkey. Jericho was a fortified settlement, with a stone wall up to twenty-seven feet thick enclosing an area of about ten acres. Its earliest dwellings consisted of circular mud huts, which may have had conical roofs; the inhabitants were farmers and hunters who buried their dead below the hut floors. Çatal Hüyük appears to have been unfortified. The town was a dense package of dwellings without streets; residents gained access

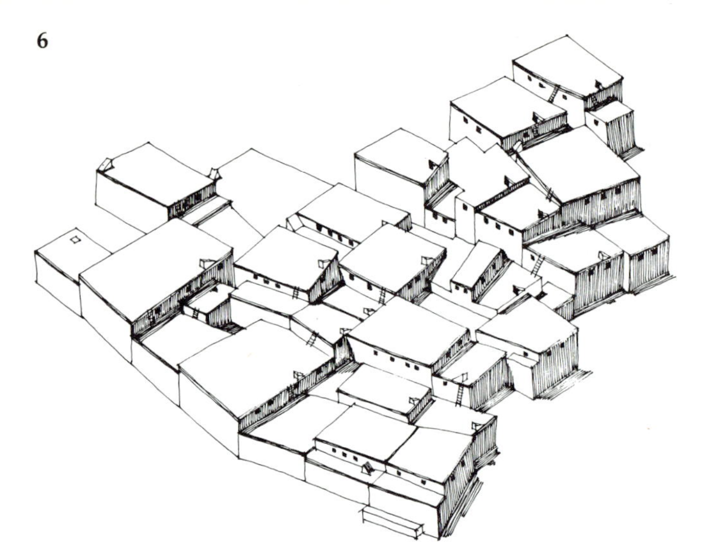

FIGURE 1.1 *Çatal Hüyük. Reconstruction view of urban dwellings, 6500–5700* B.C. (Redrawn after J. Mellaart)

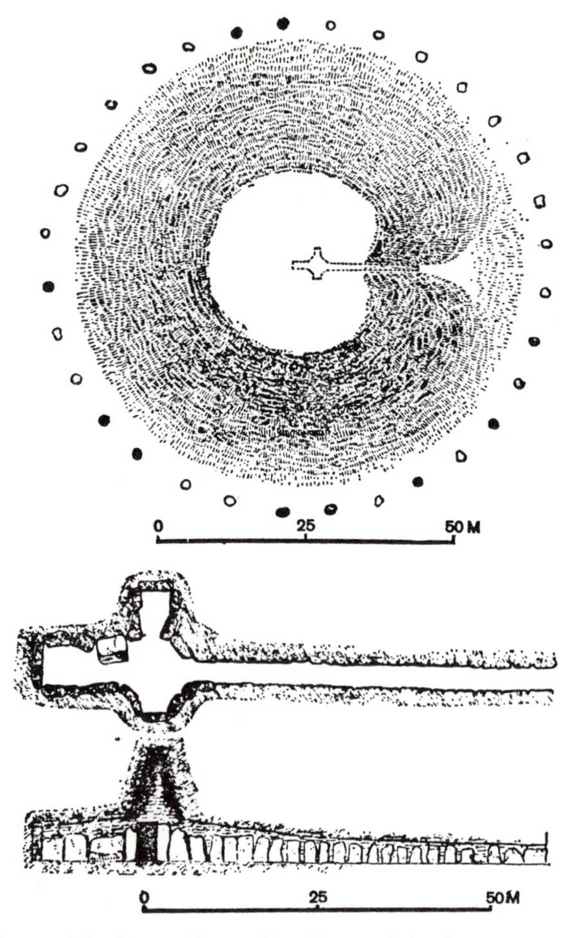

FIGURE 1.3 *Passage Grave, New Grange, Ireland, ca. 2450* B.C. (From J. Fergusson)

to the dwellings across roofs, while high openings in the walls were for ventilation. Mud-brick walls and a post and lintel timber framework enclosed rectangular spaces that abutted the neighboring houses so that the whole town automatically had a perimeter wall. Interspersed with the houses were windowless shrines containing decorative motifs of bulls and cult statuettes of deities. These seem to indicate that the themes of prehistoric cave art — hunting and fecundity — had not been discarded by this early urban society. The settlement at Çatal Hüyük is the precursor of more sophisticated communities that developed in the fertile valleys of the Tigris and Euphrates rivers at the beginning of the fourth millennium.

FIGURE 1.2 *Megalith tomb, Er-Mané, Carnac, 4200* B.C. (Redrawn after C. Renfrew)

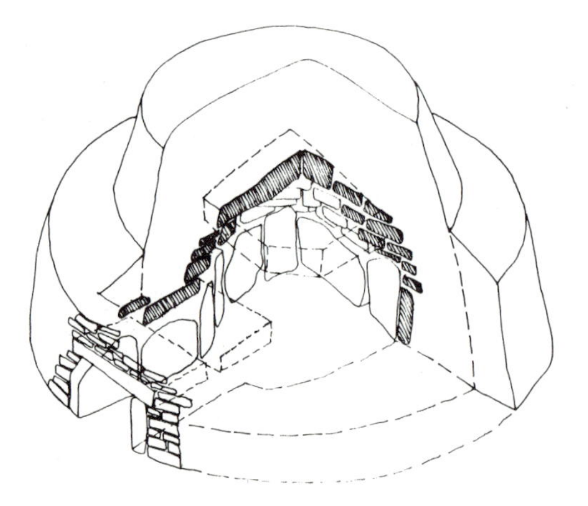

In western Europe the transition to urban communities was slower in coming, although the shift from hunting and gathering societies to larger agricultural groups under the direction of a priest-king was similar to the experience of societies on the eastern rim of the Mediterranean Sea. The significant architectural achievements of western Europe were megalith constructions, mostly astronomical observatories and communal tombs for the privileged class. Before 4000 B.C., chambered tombs of dry-wall masonry with corbeled roofs were constructed in Spain and France. These constructions are called megalith because they employ large stones or boulders and dry-wall because the stones are set without mortar. One of the earliest of the megalith tombs, dated to 4200 B.C., is at Er-Mané, Carnac, in Brittany (Figure 1.2). Nearly two thousand years later, the impressive passage graves at Knowth and New Grange in Ireland (Figure 1.3) were constructed on cruciform plans, with lintel-capped connecting passages and a beehive corbel ceiling on the main chamber. An earthen mound covers each tomb, with the weight of the dirt providing stability for the stone structure below. All three tombs represent a high level of construction skill, especially when one considers that the available technology provided nothing harder than copper or bronze tools for shaping stone. The organization of a work force sufficient to maneuver stones weighing up to five tons indicates that there was a trained class of building professionals. The New Grange passage grave has the additional characteristic of orientation to the winter solstice. On the twenty-first of December, at a few minutes past dawn, the rays of the rising sun are admitted through a small opening above the door lintel, shine down the passage, across the main chamber, and into the end chamber. This orientation was not accidental; it could have resulted only from careful astronomical studies on the site.

Megalith builders thus demonstrated their abilities to work large stones and to observe fundamental astronomical phenomena. These two skills were merged in the most celebrated of megalith constructions, Stonehenge, located on the Salisbury Plain in southwestern England (Figure 1.4). At least three distinct building phases can be observed on the site, beginning about 2800 B.C. and concluding about 2100 B.C. with the completion of a great circle of thirty sarsen stones (sandstone moved by glaciers) capped by massive lintels that encloses a horseshoe of trilithons (three stones arranged in a post and

FIGURE 1.4 *Stonehenge, 2800–2100* B.C. (Photo: Marburg)

lintel structure) at the center. Fifty-six chalk-filled holes form an outer ring approximately 300 feet in diameter. The purpose of Stonehenge has intrigued later civilizations, which have interpreted it variously as the work of giants, magicians, or people imported from the Aegean. The truth is somewhat more prosaic; archaeoastronomer Gerald Hawkins has demonstrated convincingly that Stonehenge was a great observatory for determining the solstices and predicting lunar and solar eclipses.

Stonehenge represents the culmination of megalith construction and scientific observation in the prehistoric era. Eighty-two of the dolerite bluestones in the monument were quarried in southern Wales and transported, largely by water, over 190 miles to the site. The larger sarsen uprights, which today form the innermost circle of thirty stones and the trilithon horseshoe, were quarried about 15 miles away and rolled or dragged overland. Knobs cut on the tops of the uprights fit into socket holes carved on the undersides of the lintels, so that the stones lock together in a mortise and tenon joint when correctly positioned. Both the distance involved in moving these large, heavy stones and the precision of their placement on the site demonstrate the capabilities of prehistoric builders in Britain. Experience gained in the construction and orientation of megalithic corbeled tombs enabled these people to erect one of the most haunting architectural works of all time.

ANCIENT MESOPOTAMIA

The distinction between the prehistoric world and historic times hinges on the development of written language, which was achieved by about 3500 B.C. by the Sumerians in the Middle Eastern lands of present-day Iraq and Iran. There, in the fertile lands between the Tigris and Euphrates rivers (named Mesopotamia by the ancient Greeks), the earliest literate civilizations developed in independent urban communities called city-states. Writing first developed as a means of record keeping (i.e., documenting governmental transactions) and only later was employed for what might be called literary purposes, reflecting the legends, glorious deeds, hopes, and fears of the people. In about 3000 B.C., perhaps as a result of contacts with Mesopotamia, another center of civilization emerged in Northeast Africa, along the banks of the Nile River in present-day Egypt. These two regions, Egypt and Mesopotamia, are thus considered the cradles of western history and architecture.

Mesopotamia encompasses an area about 500 miles long by no more than 300 miles wide. Its southern boundary is the Persian Gulf, the shore of which was about 130 miles farther north during the third millennium than it is today. The Tigris and Euphrates rivers flow separately into the gulf. The Euphrates originates in the mountains of eastern Turkey and meanders across the plains in its lower reaches. The more easterly Tigris rises in the same mountains but it develops into a more swiftly flowing stream because of its numerous tributaries in the Zagros mountains. As a result the Tigris was less navigable and did not have as great a unifying effect on settlements along its banks as the Euphrates.

Sometime around 4000 B.C., a nomadic people called the Al Ubaid, Indo-Europeans from the steppes of central Asia, migrated into southern Mesopotamia from the region east of the Caspian Sea. They settled in the fertile valley, mastered the arts of agriculture, and developed systems of irrigation to use the flood waters of the Euphrates. Their civilization, which lasted until about 2350 B.C., is known as Sumerian, and their typical settlement was the city-state, a political and religious center devoted to serving gods based on natural elements. These included the divine triad of Anu, god of the sky; Enlil, god of the earth; and Ea, god of water. They were supplemented by Nannar, god of the moon; Utu, god of the sun; and Inanna, goddess of fertility. The Sumerians believed that the sky and earth were two disks that had been blown apart and that all existence was governed by the gods, who represented the unpredictable elements affecting human life. They believed human beings were created from the alluvial silt deposits in the river valleys to serve the gods and relieve them of toil. Because the gods benefited from human praise, they had to remain in human favor. Thus there was a balance in the creative and destructive forces of the gods and a mutual need of people for gods and gods for people.

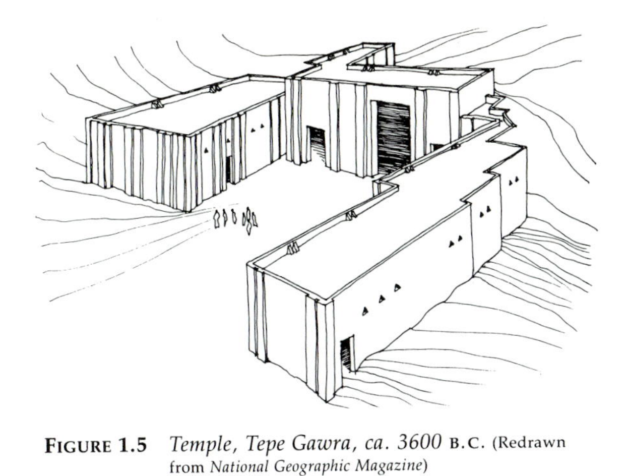

FIGURE 1.5 *Temple, Tepe Gawra, ca. 3600* B.C. (Redrawn from *National Geographic Magazine*)

Temple complexes of the Sumerian gods were at the heart of each city-state. The earliest level of Eridu, the oldest city, had a small chapel with a brick altar in front of a wall **niche,** possibly constructed to contain a cult statue. The elements of altar and niche were invariably found in all later Sumerian temples. Numerous rebuildings of this temple at Eridu successively enlarged the relatively modest original shrine; by about 3800 B.C., the temple of level VII stood on a platform. Its regularly buttressed exterior walls enclosed a rectangular shrine room surrounded by smaller chambers. At about the same time Tepe Gawra (Figure 1.5), nearly 500 miles to the north, featured an acropolis with two temples, a shrine, and dwelling houses. Archaeologists have found evidence of twenty rebuildings on the site, with the earliest Sumerian temple found at level XIII. Its major buildings formed a U-shaped open court around the North Temple, which measured forty by twenty feet. The temple had a central hall with side chapels, and its brick **façade** was articulated by **buttresses** and **pilasters** suggesting earlier wooden prototypes.

Uruk (the biblical Ereck and the modern Warka) was only fifty miles from Eridu and therefore was a considerable distance from Tepe Gawra. Nevertheless Uruk had a White Temple almost identical to the North Temple at Tepe Gawra but on a considerably larger scale (Figure 1.6). It differed from Tepe Gawra by being elevated on an artificial mountain rising forty feet above the surrounding plain. Dedicated to Anu, god of the sky, the White Temple was constructed of whitewashed, sun-dried brick. En-

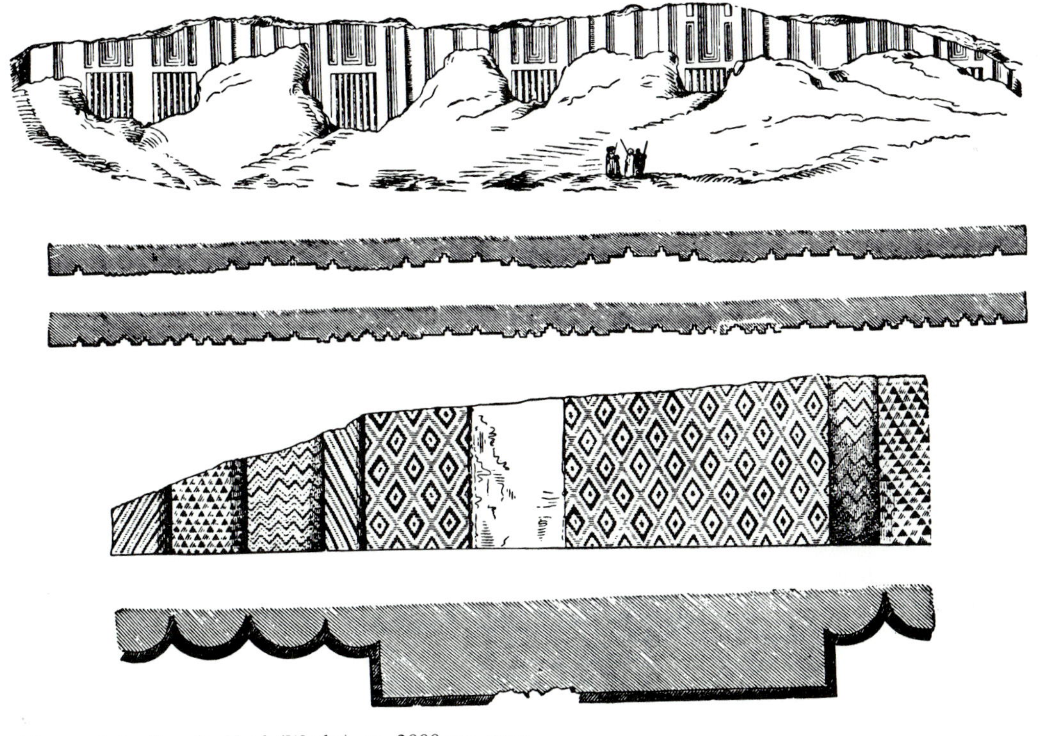

FIGURE 1.6 *Temple, Uruk (Warka), ca. 3000* B.C. (From F. Reber)

trance to the temple was from the long side, so that a "bent axis" led from the outside into the courtyard and end sanctuary. Contemporary structures excavated in the nearby precinct of Eanna (dedicated to Inanna) include two temples and a hundred-foot-long hall of eight **columns,** each six feet in diameter. Small terra-cotta cones ornament the column surfaces. The base of each cone was dipped in black, white, or red glaze, and then its apex was inserted into the clay of the column to form a polychromatic zigzag pattern with hundreds of circular elements.

The settlements of the Sumerians were disrupted about 2350 B.C. by the arrival of a new group of Semitic people from the steppes of central Asia. These new immigrants established cities in Sippar and Akkad; the period gets its name, Akkadian, from the latter city. Surviving evidence indicates that the Akkadians were a fierce people, governed not only by a priestly class but also by a warrior-king. Many aspects of Sumerian culture were adopted by the Akkadians, but their substitution of a king for city-state leadership was to be instrumental later in forging imperial states composed of many urban settlements.

ANCIENT EGYPT

The First and Second Dynasties

The geography of Egypt is dominated by one great river, the Nile, which originates in the highlands of present-day Uganda and passes through the Sudan and Ethiopia as it traverses more than 2000 miles before emptying into the Mediterranean Sea to the north. Within the 600 lower miles of the river valley, agriculture is facilitated by a warm climate and the annual flood deposits of organic silt, which renew the fertility of the fields. On the margins of the valley in dynastic times there were marshes and open lands rich in game. (Today the desert encroaches on these areas.) Outside the rather narrow fertile band bordering the Nile, great expanses of inhospitable desert provided security from outside invasion. The Egyptian culture that developed along the banks of the Nile was thus predominantly agricultural and peaceful, quite a contrast to the urban-oriented settlements in turbulent Mesopotamia. Egyptian life was modulated by the annual flooding of the river, and the cyclical rhythm of the seasons fostered a civilization that remained remarkably unchanged for more than 2000 years.

Historians continue to debate whether civilization emerged first in Egypt or Mesopotamia and which civilization dominated the other. Lower Egypt, the area around the mouth of the Nile where the river has created a delta, may well have had settlements predating those of Mesopotamia. In any event, two centers of Egyptian civilization, with differing cultural practices, arose in prehistoric times: Lower Egypt in the Nile delta and Upper Egypt in the rocky southern reaches of the river. The legendary history of Egypt begins with the union of these two by Menes, the king of Upper Egypt around 3000 B.C.

Menes may well be the King Narmer illustrated on the carved stone Palette of Narmer found at Hierakonpolis. The piece of slate, about twenty-four inches high, was a greatly enlarged version of the common implement used to mix a green eye paint applied for protection from infection and the sun. Its relief carvings on front and back provide the earliest record of the unification of Upper and Lower Egypt. By 3000 B.C., the Egyptians had also evolved a complex pantheon of gods derived from natural elements (sun, moon, and sky) and given animal form. Their king, who was god incarnate, was established as an intermediary between the people and the gods. The king had strong progenitive attributes: like a bull, he was successful in battle and responsible for the continued fertility of crops, animals, and people. The Egyptians created picture writing (hieroglyphs), a system using both pictorial and phonetic symbols to record information. In sum, the Egyptians forged the elements of a sophisticated civilization along the banks of the Nile.

Egyptian history subsequent to Narmer is divided into thirty dynasties, encompassing the period from 3000 B.C. to the conquest of Egypt by Alexander the Great in 332 B.C. The kings were known as pharaohs and were revered not only as temporal rulers but also as incarnations of Horus, the sky god, who would become Osiris, the god of the dead, after death. Egyptians believed strongly in eternal life. People's earthly existence was followed by an afterlife in which their eternal spirit, or *ka,* would move invisibly around the world, returning at times to inhabit the corporeal form. Preservation of the physical body after death was thus of great importance, as was the provision of household furnishings, servants, food, drink, and a suitable permanent chamber. The *ka* of an important person, especially the pharaoh, not adequately supplied with material for the afterlife would wander unsatisfied about the world and cause untold mischief for the living population. It was in society's interest to ensure that the pharaoh's body and spirit were well served; this goal lead to the construction of enduring tombs for royalty and the development of mummification to preserve the body. Tombs, not temples, became the most important religious structures.

Mastabas, the earliest tombs, were built as eternal houses for the departed and were in all likelihood based on the design of dwelling houses of the living (Figure 1.7). Ordinary houses were constructed of reed, thatch, and wood — materials wholly unsuited for a permanent dwelling — so the builders of mastaba tombs sought greater durability in brick while retaining characteristic details provided by the customary bundled reeds and wooden supports. The mastaba was a blocklike structure above ground containing a small chapel for offerings and another chamber (the serdab) for the body and a statue of the deceased. Worldly goods entombed with the dead soon attracted thieves, so an early revision of mastaba design was a deep shaft under the building. The mummified body was placed at its base, and the shaft was then filled with stone and rubble to deter would-be robbers. A later change toward increasing permanence was stone construction of the mastaba.

FIGURE 1.7 *Mastaba tomb.* (From G. Perret and C. Chipiez)

The Third Dynasty: Zoser's Step Pyramid at Saqqara

As the religious ritual prescribed by the priesthood changed to enhance the significance of the pharaoh, the mass of the mastaba was enlarged to a pyramid to reflect the importance of the king. At death the pharaoh accompanied the sun god on his daily journey across the sky, and he would therefore need to be lifted skyward in his eternal home. The pyramid, an upward-stepping form whose peak would catch the first rays of morning light, also makes symbolic reference to the annual rebirth of nature, for as floods recede, the first signs of plant life appear on the small hillocks. Thus the pyramid's form captured both daily and cyclical rebirth throughout eternity.

Imhotep, architect to the Third Dynasty Pharaoh Zoser (ca. 2700 B.C.), built the first pyramid at Zoser's funerary complex at Saqqara, outside Memphis (Figure 1.8). His was also Egypt's first monumental construction in stone, no small factor in its survival through 4600 years. The complex is a large rectangle in plan, covering thirty-five acres, surrounded by a wall thirty-three feet high and a mile long. There is only one entrance, a small door in the southeast corner that leads into a colonnaded processional hall. At the end of the corridor, one enters a main courtyard dominated by Zoser's stepped pyramid, which rises 200 feet above its 397-by-358-foot base (Figure 1.9). Begun as a mastaba, the pyramid was built up in several stages to attain its present shape, a mass rising in six steps (Figure 1.10). The exterior of the pyramid is faced with dressed limestone, while the courtyards and buildings surrounding the pyramid are representations of Zoser's earthly palace in Memphis, built here to last for eternity. The texture of the original materials is faithfully rendered in stone: reed-bundle and papyrus stalk columns, log ceilings, even a stone hinge for an immobile stone door. North of the pyramid is the temple in which the preburial ritual was

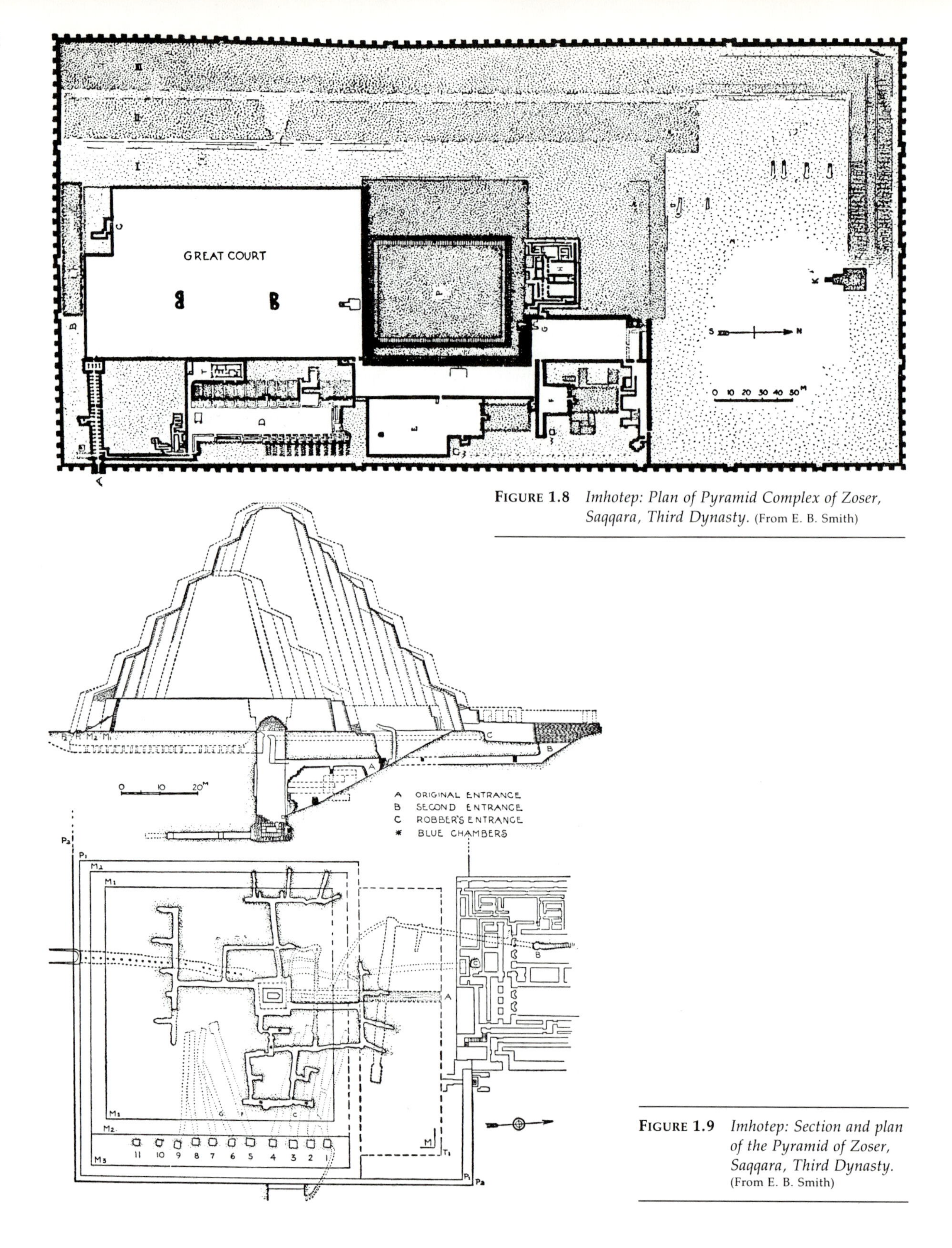

FIGURE 1.8 *Imhotep: Plan of Pyramid Complex of Zoser, Saqqara, Third Dynasty.* (From E. B. Smith)

FIGURE 1.9 *Imhotep: Section and plan of the Pyramid of Zoser, Saqqara, Third Dynasty.* (From E. B. Smith)

FIGURE 1.10 *Imhotep: Pyramid Complex of Zoser, Saqqara, Third Dynasty.* (Photo: Marburg)

performed; a statue of Zoser sits in the serdab, with a small aperture cut in the wall being the only access to the outside world. Incense could waft through the opening, and the statue is positioned looking outward.

Zoser's complex includes areas for rituals symbolizing the bond between Upper and Lower Egypt. The main courtyard was the scene of the Heb-Sed race, run by the king to ensure fertility of the fields. The course extended four times around the court in each direction, clockwise for half the kingdom and counterclockwise for the other half. Zoser had two burial chambers to symbolize his power and paternity over Upper and Lower Egypt. One chamber located beneath the pyramid contained his mummy in an alabaster coffin. The access passage was blocked by a stone plug six feet in diameter and weighing six tons, but this was inadequate protection against tomb robbers, who defiled the tomb before modern times. In 1928 excavators discovered the second chamber in the south side of the perimeter wall. Although it had already been plundered, the chamber had originally contained the embalmed internal organs of the pharaoh, emblematic of his fertility and defense and protection of Lower Egypt. Grave robbers could not steal the handsome blue faience wall decorations, all that remains of the interior. These tiles are set into horizontal and vertical stone members to represent rush matting between wooden slats attached to larger wooden supports. On one wall is a relief carving depicting Zoser running the Heb-Sed race. Wearing the white crown of Upper Egypt, Zoser is shown in the manner peculiar to Egyptian art with head, legs, and feet shown in profile and the torso shown frontally. In this one view Egyptian artists captured the essential features of the human body with great exactness, even though the pose is not a "realistic" or natural one.

The Fourth Dynasty Pyramids: Meydum, Dashur, and Giza

From its beginnings at Saqqara, the evolution of the true pyramid proceeds through at least three major projects before attaining the culmination of its form in the fourth dynasty tombs at Giza, outside Cairo. All three of these developmental pyramids were built or modified for one of the first kings of the Fourth Dynasty, the Pharaoh Sneferu (ca. 2625 B.C.), whose cult remained active for over two thousand years after his death. At Meydum, just south of Saqqara, Sneferu added an outer layer to the "Onion" Pyramid, which may have been begun for Huni, the last pharaoh of the Third Dynasty (Figure 1.11). It began with a stepped core of seven stages, which was transformed into a true pyramid with the addition of two overbuildings. As the third and final outer casing of limestone was being installed, there is evidence that the upper portions of the work collapsed because the steep angle of inclination of the sides was not braced adequately to prevent slippage. Even in its present ruined condition, the pyramid stands 214 feet high, its core rising above the rubble and sand surrounding the base. Entrance to the pyramid was through a sloping corridor opening off the north side, descending below ground, and then rising a short distance vertically to the burial chamber at the center of the pyramid's base. Corbeled construction in the vault of this chamber marks the first time this technique was employed in stone by the Egyptians, although it had been used earlier in brick.

The collapse of the Meydum pyramid had an impact on another pyramid of Sneferu's under construction at the same time at Dashur, about forty-five miles south of Meydum. There, a partially finished pyramid was transformed to create the so-called Bent Pyramid (Figure 1.12). Unlike the onion pyramid, the bent pyramid began as a true pyramid on a 618-foot square base with steeply inclined sides. Profiting from the difficulties encountered at Meydum, the builders at Dashur changed the angle of inclination from the original 54½ degrees to a lower angle of 43½ degrees when the pyramid was about half built. Eventually reaching a height of 318 feet, the Bent Pyramid gains stability from its firm limestone foundation, large blocks of inward-sloping stone casing, and its reduced angle at the top. These stabilizing design features were incorporated

FIGURE 1.11 *"Onion" Pyramid, Meydum, Fourth Dynasty.* (Photo: Marburg)

FIGURE 1.12 *Bent Pyramid, Dashur, Fourth Dynasty.* (Photo: Marburg)

from the first in the third pyramid of Sneferu, the Red Pyramid, also at Dashur. (The name derives from the reddish limestone of its core, now exposed since stone scavengers have long since removed the original smooth, white limestone casing.) From a base 728 feet square the Red Pyramid rises at a constant 43½-degree angle to its apex 344 feet above the ground. Its profile is thus relatively low, a testimonial to the conservative attitudes of its designers.

The trio of large pyramids at Giza (ca. 2600–2500 B.C.) (Figure 1.13) are the work of Sneferu's descendents, the Fourth Dynasty kings known as Khufu, Khafre, and Menkaure (or Cheops, Chephren, and Mycerinus in Greek transliteration). The largest pyramid, that of Cheops (Khufu), was built first and planned from the start to be a true pyramid of unprecedented proportions. The base is 767 feet on a side and covers 13.5 acres; the sides rise at an angle of 52 degrees to an apex at 479 feet. Most of the stone in the pyramid is limestone, although the large king's chamber in the center is made of granite. Nothing before or since has rivaled the Great Pyramid of Cheops as the largest construction in stone.

FIGURE 1.13 *Map of pyramids of Cheops, Chephren, and Mycerinus, Giza, Fourth Dynasty.* (From G. Perret and C. Chipiez)

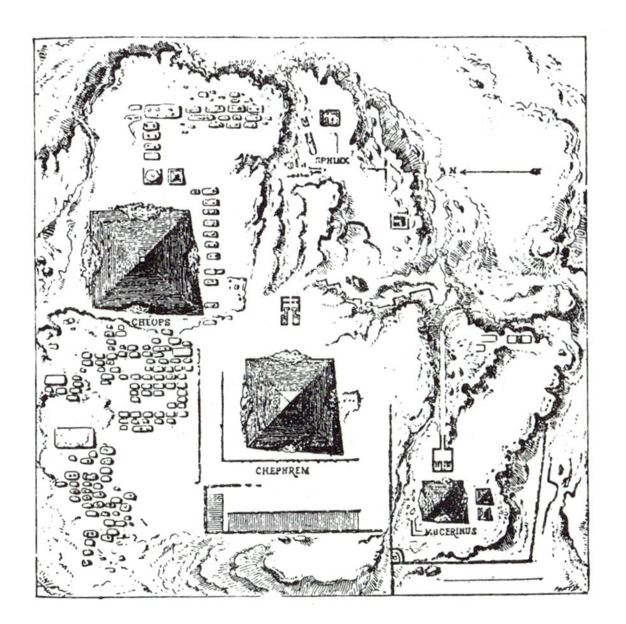

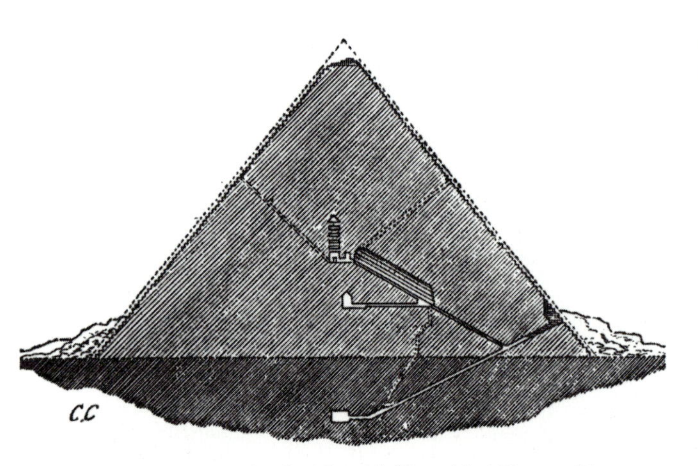

FIGURE 1.14 *Section through Pyramid of Cheops, Giza, Fourth Dynasty.* (From G. Perret and C. Chipiez)

Cheops's pyramid is not solid, however. Three burial chambers are built within it, one excavated out of foundation bedrock and the other two constructed as the stone mountain was erected (Figure 1.14). Egyptologists believe that these three reflect three changes made in the plan of the pyramid as work progressed, for as one rises in the pyramid each chamber is grander than the one below. All connect to a common entranceway (blocked and concealed after interment of the king) via sloping corbeled passageways. The uppermost, or king's chamber, still contains a granite sarcophagus installed during construction because it was too large to be carried through the corridors. To transfer the tremendous weight of the pyramid around the ceiling of the king's chamber, a gabled stone brace, with five horizontal slabs forming relieving spaces stacked underneath it, extends into the mass of stone above the chamber.

Next in sequence of construction and only slightly smaller in size is the pyramid of Chephren (Khafre), a son of Cheops by a secondary queen. Chephren's pyramid is 706 feet square at the base and rises at an angle of 52 degrees, 20 minutes to an ultimate elevation of 470 feet (Figure 1.15). In most photographs of the Giza pyramids, Chephren's tomb seems the tallest of the three because it stands on higher ground than that of Cheops; Chephren's monument is also readily distinguished by the substantial fragment of the original smooth limestone casing that survives at the apex. On the inside there is but a single tomb chamber in the center of the pyramid at the base level. A passageway in the north side provides access to the room, which, like all the tomb chambers in pyramids, was pillaged in ancient times.

The smallest of the Giza trio of major pyramids belonged to Mycerinus (Menkaure), and it marks the end of monumental pyramid construction. Containing about one-tenth the stone of Chephren's or Cheops's monuments, Mycerinus's tomb seems to have been erected hurriedly and with less care than its predecessors. Its dimensions — 355 feet square at the base, a slope of 51 degrees, and a height of 203 feet — maintain the general proportions established by the neighboring tombs. Mycerinus's successor, the last king in the Fourth Dynasty, chose not to have a pyramid burial, and although pyramids continued to be built during the remainder of the Old Kingdom, the quality and scale of the Giza trio were never exceeded.

Associated with each of the pyramids were ancillary temples now largely in ruins. Alongside the Nile was a lower or valley temple, where the boat bearing the pharaoh's mummy would land to disembark its royal cargo. A causeway connected the river temple to the upper or mortuary temple at the base of the pyramid itself. Here the mummy would receive a final ritual cleansing prior to entombment.

Of all the Giza valley temples, the lower temple of Chephren remains in the best state of preservation. Essentially square in plan, with massively thick limestone walls encased in red granite, its central hall is an inverted T shape. Red granite piers supported a roof with a **clerestory;** the windows were set so that sunlight coming through them illuminated the twenty-three statues of the king placed around the edges of the wall. Two levels of narrow storage rooms extended into the solid wall mass. Today the Temple stands without a roof or its outer stone facing beside the Sphinx, a man-headed lion 187 feet long and 66 feet high, carved in situ out of a natural rock ledge.

Chephren's Mortuary Temple is connected to the Valley Temple by a causeway running at an oblique

FIGURE 1.15 *Sphinx and Pyramid of Chephren, Giza, Fourth Dynasty.* (Photo: Egyptian Tourist Office)

angle from the river. The Mortuary Temple is rectangular in plan, with a series of axially disposed interior spaces. Its limestone structure was probably cased with a finer material; the floor was alabaster. At the center of the temple was a large courtyard surrounded by enormous pillars in front of which stood twelve large statues of the king.

Pyramids, especially the impressive Giza group, have long provoked two questions: How could ancient peoples, working with simple technology, have built such enormous structures, and why would they have built them? The question of how can be convincingly answered. Even though the Egyptians lacked metals harder than copper and made no use of the wheel for transport, they were not primitive. Their knowledge of surveying, necessary for reestablishing field boundaries after the annual flood, would enable them to lay out the pyramid's base accurately and orient the square to the cardinal directions. Cheops's pyramid deviates only 5½ minutes of arc from true north; its summit is only 1 foot off the center of the base; and there is only an eight-inch error in the length of one side of the base. The absence of wheeled vehicles was not a serious handicap, as much of the stone transport would have been over water or across sand where wheels would provide no real advantage over the boats and sledges actually used. Quarrying was accomplished by pounding balls of very hard rock along seams in the stone or by placing wooden wedges in notches, wetting the wedges, and letting the expanding wood split the stone.

Actual construction of the pyramids seems to have been done by large teams of peasants working

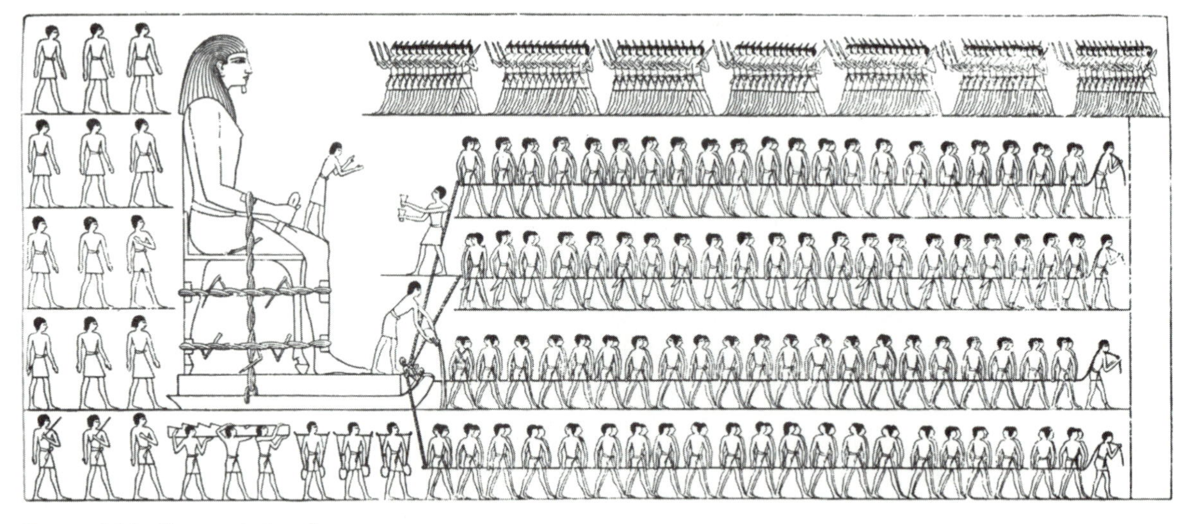

FIGURE 1.16 *Transport of a colossus.* (From G. Perret and C. Chipiez)

during the flood season when agricultural labor was impossible; the muscle power of men hauled the quarried blocks into place (Figure 1.16). A continuous earth ramp would be erected along with the masonry mountain to provide the inclined plane for dragging stone. Once the core of the pyramid was completed, the outer casing of finer limestone was carefully laid, with joints so tight that a thin blade could not be inserted between adjacent blocks. As the casing was laid from the top down, the earthen ramp could be removed systematically. The number of men required and the number of years needed to see a major pyramid through to completion are still a matter of scholarly debate, but in any event the ability to organize labor forces and professional quarrymen in the seasonal building campaigns remains a tribute to Egyptian engineers. Through careful marshalling of the tools and manpower at their disposal and with patient persistence through a sustained period of construction, ancient engineers were able to accomplish many works that still seem marvelous to modern eyes.

The question of why the pyramids were built has inspired more speculation and nonsense than the question of how they were constructed. Theories ranging from embodiments of standard measures (as defined in English units) to predictions of the Millennium have been offered to explain the configuration of Cheops's pyramid, but modern archaeology has overwhelmingly demonstrated that the pyramids were nothing more than tombs for the pharaohs. Why a society should direct so much effort to a seemingly useless project is harder to answer. The evidence that peasants, not slaves or prisoners, composed the work crews, has led some scholars to propose that pyramid building was devised to keep agricultural workers busy during the slack season and thus prevent tribal bickering and at the same time forge a national unity. The beginning of the Fifth Dynasty coincides with the ascendency of the cult of Ra, the sun god whose shrine was capped by a pyramid; the form may have been exploited for pharaonic tombs to reflect the king's divinity.

In terms of architecture, the Fourth Dynasty tombs represent a high point in Egyptian building during the Old Kingdom (Dynasties I–VI). The end of the Sixth Dynasty was marked by the First Intermediate Period, when various noble families claimed the throne of Upper and Lower Egypt. Around 2000 B.C. stability returned with the Middle Kingdom, and its architectural accomplishments are addressed in the next chapter, along with developments in Mesopotamia of approximately the same date.

2.

THE SECOND MILLENNIUM

We have seen how civilizations arose in both Mesopotamia and Egypt during the third millennium B.C. and how there was probable contact between the two centers, although exchanges cannot be documented with precision. Cross-cultural interaction continued during the next thousand years, and a third center of early settlement developed in the Aegean on the island of Crete and the Greek peninsula.

MESOPOTAMIA

The Akkadian dynasty, which had supplanted the Sumerian city-states around 2350 B.C., was in turn overthrown about 2150 B.C. by the Guti, a group of savage tribes from the mountain regions of present-day Iran. The military influence of the Guti weakened within a century of their invasion, and political allegiances reminiscent of the first Sumerian city-states returned in what is termed the Neo-Sumerian Period (ca. 2150–2000 B.C.). This period witnessed the development of Sumerian temple forms, particularly the temple elevated on an artificial mound or **ziggurat,** in cities. Commonly constructed of sun-dried brick bonded with bitumen, reed-matting, or rope, ziggurats were finished with a weather-resistant exterior of kiln-fired brick. From a rectangular base, the ziggurat rose with inwardly sloping walls in a series of stepped platforms, culminating in a high temple at the top. A flight of stairs set in the center of one side connected the temple to the ground. (Elements so placed in the center of a symmetrical form are said to be axial.)

The outward resemblance between the ziggurat and the Egyptian pyramids once led to speculation that the form was inspired by that of pharaonic tombs; after all, there were trading contacts between the two civilizations. There are, however, notable constructional and functional differences between ziggurats and pyramids. The pyramids were generally built of stone (a material not readily available in southern Mesopotamia), and they had internal chambers because they were used as tombs. The ziggurats, on the other hand, were built of brick and were fundamentally stepped platforms for elevating temples to the gods so that the gods might descend from the heavens and ensure the prosperity of the community. It is thought that the ziggurat represented the mountains whence the Sumerians came. To make their gods feel at home in the lowlands of the river valley, the Sumerians and their successors in Mesopotamia may have aspired to recreate their highland dwelling place. Raising the temple well above the elevation of the valley may also reflect the desire to protect the sacred precinct from flood waters; it certainly gave it visual prominence in the city.

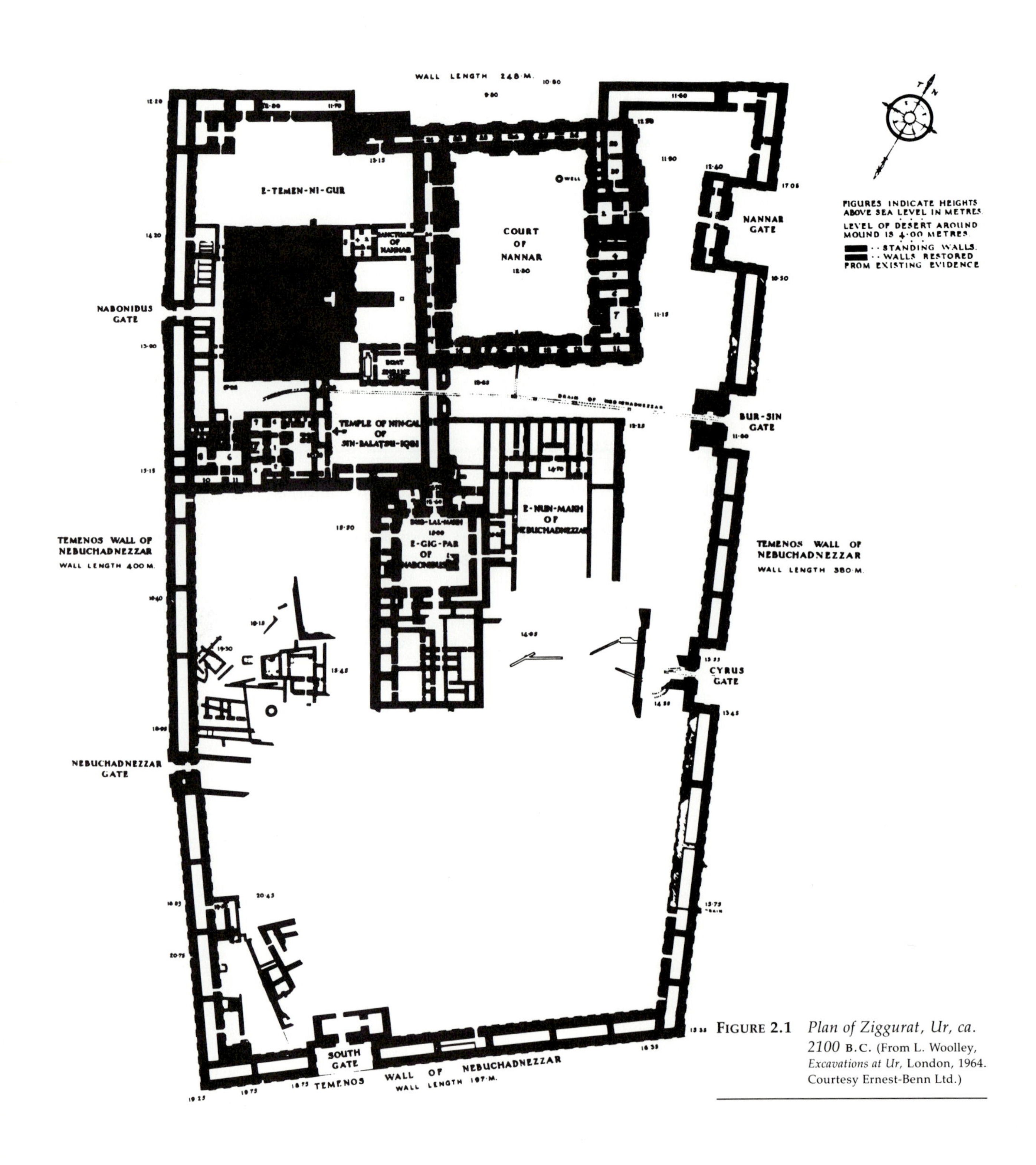

FIGURE 2.1 *Plan of Ziggurat, Ur, ca. 2100* B.C. (From L. Woolley, *Excavations at Ur,* London, 1964. Courtesy Ernest-Benn Ltd.)

FIGURE 2.2 *Gateways, Hattusas, ca. 1400–1200* B.C. (Photo: Turkish Ministry of Culture and Tourism)

FIGURE 2.3 *Gateways, Hattusas, ca. 1400–1200* B.C. (Photo: Turkish Ministry of Culture and Tourism)

Little remains of the ziggurats constructed during the brief Neo-Sumerian interlude. Sun-dried brick is not sufficiently durable to withstand the weather, and once the outer casing of kiln-dried brick was removed by scavengers, the earthen core of the ziggurat eroded considerably. Of those lofty man-made mountains that towered over Mesopotamian cities, only the ziggurat at Ur (ca. 2100 B.C.) remains with some of its features intact (Figure 2.1). In its ruined form, one can still distinguish the three long stairways that converged on a tower gate at the level of the first platform. Shorter flights led to the second and third terraces, which only the priests would enter. These upper levels, together with the crowning temple, have been reduced to crumbled heaps.

Dominance in the turbulent Mesopotamian region passed to the city-state of Babylon from about 1900 to 1600 B.C. There an exceptionally able king, Hammurabi, restored the Akkadian tradition of a central government leading diverse city-states. His lasting contribution was not so much military conquest as the first written codification of Mesopotamian law, the Code of Hammurabi, which was strongly reflected in the later Law of Moses.

About 1600 B.C. the Hittites, a vigorous Indo-European people from Anatolia, overran the First Dynasty of Babylon. After bringing down the city-states of Mesopotamia, the Hittites ruled northern Mesopotamia and Syria from their homeland capital, Hattusas, near the present city of Boghazkoy in Turkey. At the height of their empire (ca. 1400–1200 B.C.), the city covered 300 acres in a rather unconnected and asymmetrical plan. Within the town five temples dedicated to the weather gods were constructed around courtyards surrounded by well-lit ritual chambers. A small palace complex containing audience halls, archives, and granaries was situated in the upper city. The stone construction employed for its storage rooms made extensive use of parabolic corbeled vaults to enclose long, narrow rooms. Corbeled vaults were also used for the five city gates in the town wall. Two gates were flanked by sculptures of sphinxes or lions, guardian animals that suggest an Egyptian influence (Figures 2.2., 2.3). Documented contacts between the two civilizations remain, including the sending of a Hittite prince to marry the widow of King Tutankhamon and treaties between Hittite kings and Ramses II over territorial agreements concerning the coast of the eastern Mediterranean.

Invasions by other Indo-European tribes, notably the Thracians, Phrygians, and Assyrians, broke up the Hittite Empire about 1200 B.C., although its artistic influence continued in later Assyrian art and in the fortified gates guarded by beasts, especially lions, found in the Aegean settlements of the Mycenaeans.

EGYPT

The Middle Kingdom

The first six Egyptian dynasties, known collectively as the Old Kingdom, gave way to a period of upheaval when local feudal lords upset the unification achieved by King Menes. This era of interregional strife is designated the First Intermediate Period, and it was followed by a second period of centralized government called the Middle Kingdom (ca. 2000–1790 B.C.). The royal capital was relocated at Thebes, and the pharaoh's position was more that of a feudal lord over local vassals than an absolute and divine ruler in the Old Kingdom tradition. Royal tombs were still of major architectural importance, but either the resources or the skills required for monumental constructions were lacking, because the mediocre Middle Kingdom pyramids neither endured well nor intimidated grave robbers.

Variants on the traditional pyramid tomb were tried, however, most notably in the Tomb of Mentuhotep III at Deir-el-Bahari (Figure 2.4). Here the pyramid mass is but one part of the funerary complex, as temple, pyramid, and tomb chamber receive a more unified composition. The complex, approached by an axial route from the Nile, has two levels of colonnaded terraces supporting the diminutive pyramid, and the axis continues beyond this reception temple through a courtyard and **hypostyle hall** to the actual burial vault carved in the rock cliff. This integration of previously disparate elements into a compact group was a rare innovation in Egyptian architecture, and Mentuhotep's tomb would serve as a prototype for the more elab-

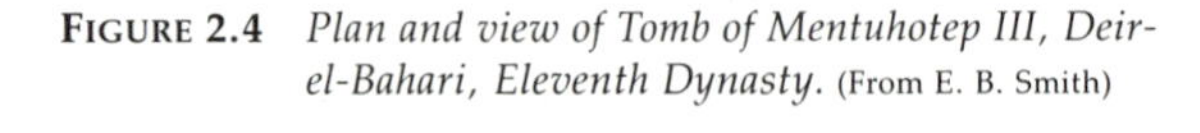

FIGURE 2.4 *Plan and view of Tomb of Mentuhotep III, Deir-el-Bahari, Eleventh Dynasty.* (From E. B. Smith)

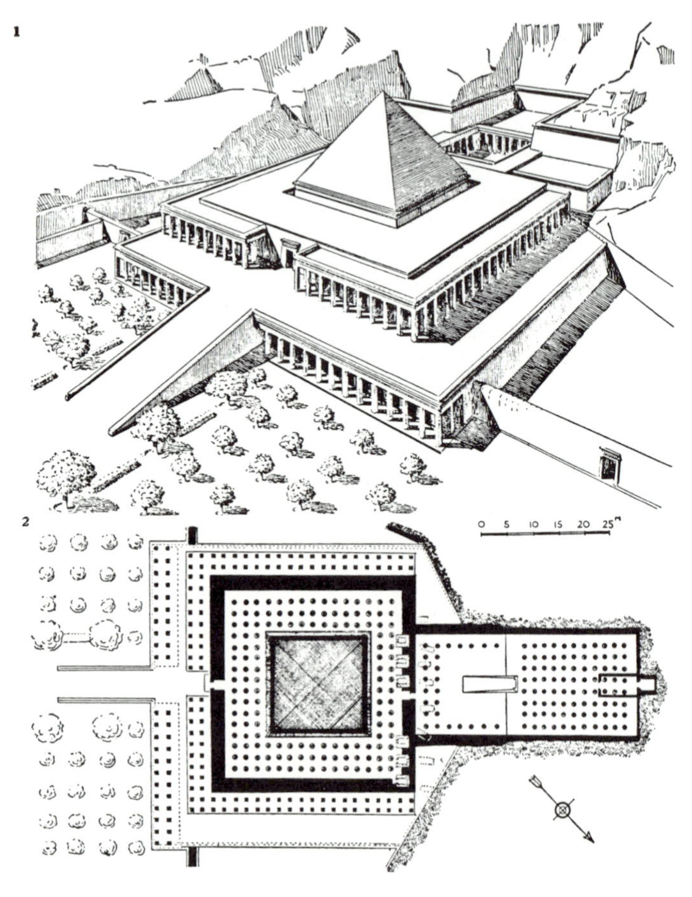

FIGURE 2.5 *Plan and section of rock-cut tombs, Beni Hasan, Twelfth Dynasty.* (From E. B. Smith)

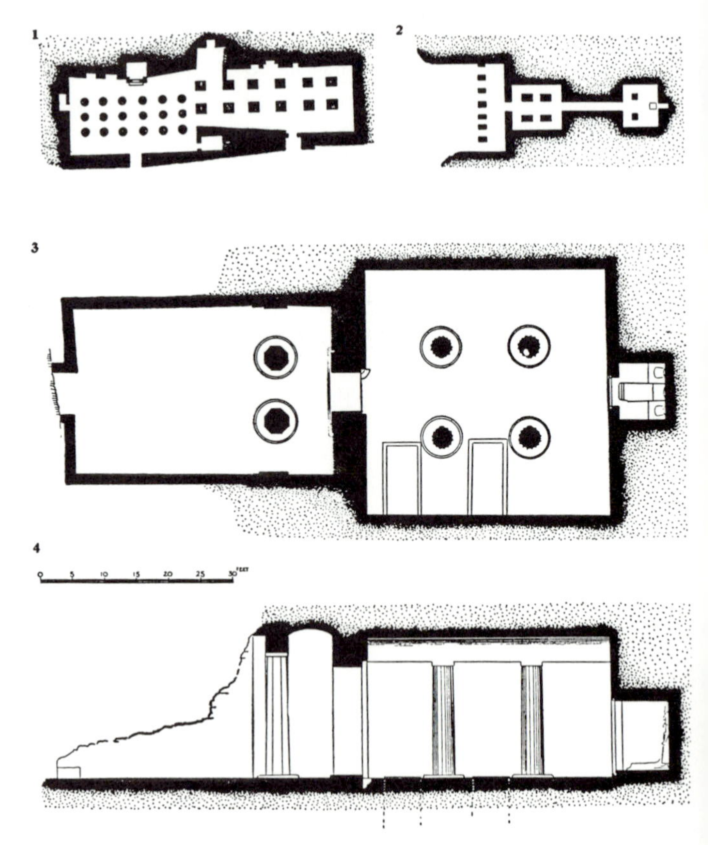

FIGURE 2.6 *Interior view of rock-cut tombs, Beni Hasan, Twelfth Dynasty.* (Photo: Marburg)

orate adjoining funerary complex built by the New Kingdom pharaoh Hatshepsut.

More typical of Middle Kingdom tombs are those at Beni Hasan, which are cut into rock cliffs and provided with sheltering **porticoes** (Figure 2.5). Reflecting the political importance of their builders, these tombs were constructed for minor nobles and court officials, who evidently commanded considerable influence and wealth. Most of the architectural character is created by excavation in the stone, and the builders replicated the spaces and details associated with ordinary dwellings, that is, wooden and plastered reed structures with slightly arched roofs composed of mats laid on the frame. As was the case at Zoser's complex at Saqqara, the stone has been carved to recreate nonstone materials, including palm trunks, bundled reeds, lotus flowers, and binding cords (Figure 2.6).

The New Kingdom

The Middle Kingdom was terminated by the arrival (ca. 1790–1570 B.C.) of the Hyksos, shepherd-kings who may have come from Asia. Whatever their origins, the Hyksos were the first successful invaders of Egypt in centuries. They introduced metallurgy, the two-man chariot, new deities, and new weapons to Egyptian culture, but their rule produced no lasting artistic innovations. With the expulsion of the Hyksos came the New Kingdom (1570–715 B.C.), which was characterized by an invigorated dynastic line of pharaohs who brought Egypt to new heights of political and cultural brilliance.

The Eighteenth Dynasty, first in the New Kingdom, continued the Middle Kingdom tradition of burial in rock-cut tombs, going a stage further by eliminating all suggestions of monumentality. It had escaped no one's notice that all the dynastic tombs had been successfully penetrated by grave robbers. The Giza pyramids were probably plundered during the First Intermediate Period. To preserve the worldly remains of the pharaoh and thwart the thieves, eighteenth-dynasty builders tried a new tactic: concealment. The Egyptian kings of the New Kingdom were interred secretly in the desert wilderness beyond Deir-el-Bahari, a region known as the Valley of the Kings, where very modest chambers were hewn out of the cliffs, and the entrances were hidden by dirt and sand. Spiritual nourishment for the deceased was provided at increasingly elaborate funerary temples, completely separate from the actual burial.

Among the most splendid of the Eighteenth Dynasty temples is the funerary complex of Hatshepsut at Deir-el-Bahari (ca. 1520 B.C.), notable both for its architecture and for the fact that its patron was a woman (Figure 2.7). (Succession to the throne passed through the female line, but the pharaoh was almost always male.) As was customary, Hatshepsut married her half-brother, who became the Pharaoh Thutmose II, but even during his reign she relegated him to a subsidiary role, and after his death she ruled for another twenty-two years as regent for his son, Thutmose III. Her consort was a commoner, Senmut, who was also the architect of her funerary temple. Hatshepsut was buried on the other side of the mountain range in the Valley of the Kings, so the temple complex was a mortuary chapel dedicated to the god Amon. Ramps lead up from the valley to three broad terraces, each defined by colonnades, which also serve as retaining walls for the next level up. The overall design was doubtless inspired by the neighboring temple of Mentuhotep, although Hatshepsut's temple is considerably larger and grander and completely lacks the pyramid. Columns in the north colonnade of the second terrace are faceted in a manner suggesting the flutes of later Doric columns. Relief carvings and wall paintings within the sanctuary spaces and in the great hall depict Hatshepsut's divine birth as the child of Amon and the activities of her peaceful reign, including trading expeditions to Punt (the Somali coast) bearing gold, ivory, baboons, and trees. Hatshepsut herself is always depicted as a man, sometimes as the god Osiris, wearing the apron and headdress of a pharaoh.

FIGURE 2.7 *Senmut: View and plan of the Funerary Complex of Queen Hatshepsut, Deir-el-Bahari, Eighteenth Dynasty. In the background is the tomb of Mentuhotep III.* (From E. B. Smith)

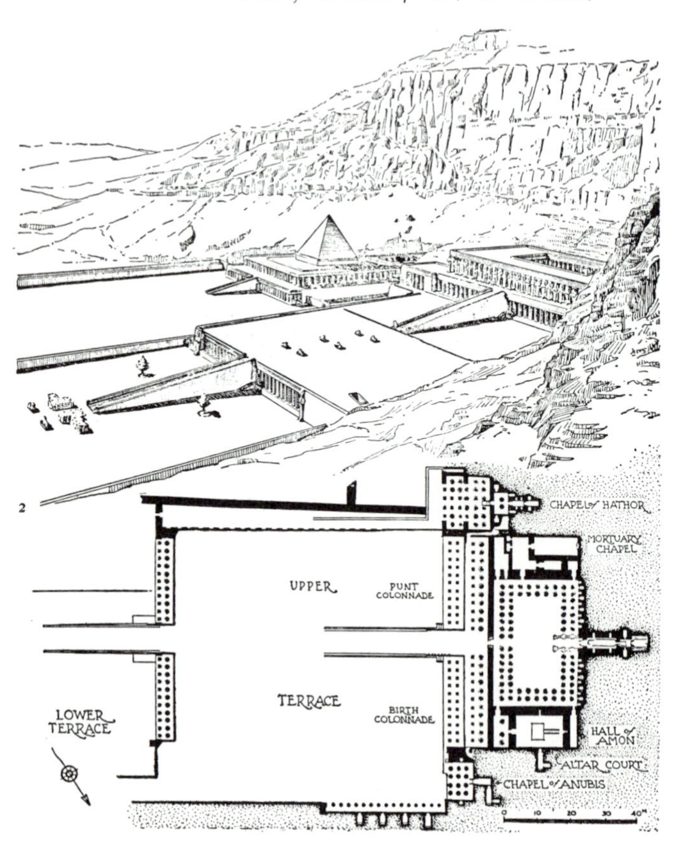

Today they are sand covered and barren, but in the Eighteenth Dynasty, the terraces of Hatshepsut's temple were embellished with thirty-two incense trees planted in earth-filled pits to create a garden for Amon's promenades. Buried pipes supplied water to sustain the trees, and priests placed tributes to the god beneath the branches in the shade. The entire setting of the temple, from axial ramp approach to the termination of the processional way at a false door painted on the wall of the final rock-hewn sanctuary, is a masterful blending of architecture into a dramatic landscape backed by rugged hillsides. Although Hatshepsut reigned and died peacefully, her successors did everything possible to eradicate her memory, erasing her name from inscriptions, smashing almost all of her sculptural representations, and desecrating the burial of Senmut, her architect.

In the course of the Eighteenth Dynasty, temple complexes built to honor both gods and pharaohs became more extensive and elaborate, aided by the establishment of a main "state" god and the increased power and influence of the priesthood. Several rulers in succession would add new portions or renovate older temples, creating a design whose chief attribute was grandeur, not coherence. The temple at Karnak, across the Nile from Deir-el-Bahari, is an example of this process (Figure 2.8). Begun about 2000 B.C., it was enlarged by Thutmose I (father of Hatshepsut) in 1530, enriched by **obelisks** given by Hatshepsut, and again expanded with a hypostyle jubilee festival hall constructed by Thutmose III for his own glorification. Yet another hypostyle hall, the largest of all, was built by Ramses II (Figure 2.9).

Hypostyle halls are large chambers created by rows of large columns placed closely together. The tight column spacing was necessary to support the stone lintels of the roof, while the large column diameter reflected the substantial height of the stone

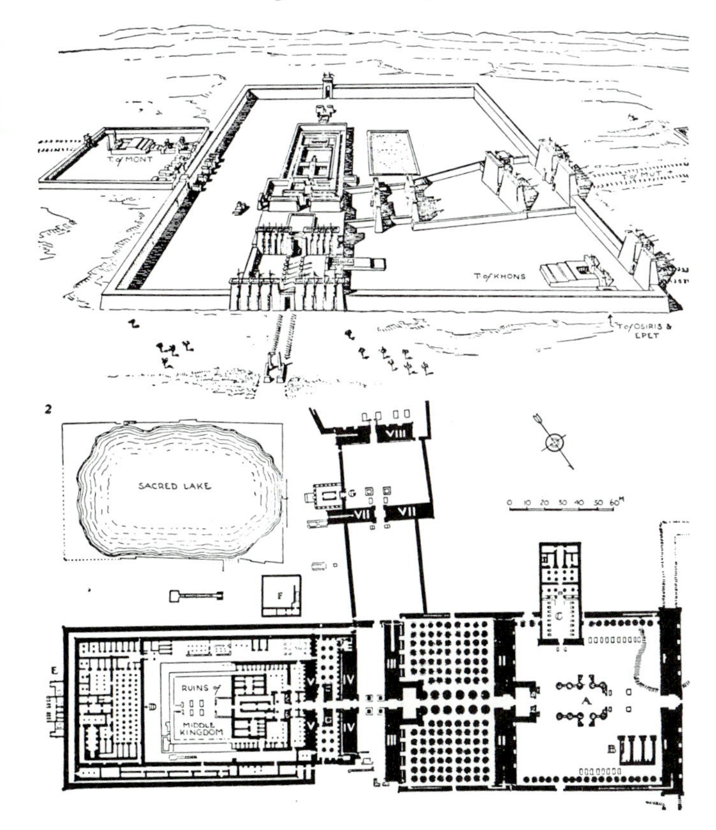

Figure 2.8 *View and plan of the Great Temple, Karnak, Eighteenth Dynasty.* (From E. B. Smith)

Figure 2.9 *Interior, Hall of the Great Temple, Karnak, Eighteenth Dynasty.* (Photo: Marburg)

FIGURE 2.10 *Detail of clerestory, Hall of the Great Temple, Karnak, Eighteenth Dynasty.* (From G. Perret and C. Chipiez)

cylinders. The net effect was a dim interior without a sense of spatial expanse. Daylight, admitted through slits in the stone clerestory grilles (Figure 2.10), filtered through the incense smoke and the upper volume of the hypostyle columns to create a sense of mystery, the desired setting for religious ritual. The temple was the habitation of the god, who was sheltered, clothed, and fed by the priests, by now a largely hereditary group. Each day the priests performed purification rites in the sacred lake within the temple precinct, dressed the statue of the deity in rich garments, and presented it offerings at the evening ritual. They carried some small statues in processions, and placed others in the sun for rejuvenation in special festivals, such as those marking the beginning of the new year. Monumental masonry entrance gates or **pylons** lined processional routes to represent the eastern mountains of Egypt through which the divine early morning sunlight emanated. Despite their rambling plans and numerous additions, New Kingdom temples maintained axial circulation spaces for the penetration of solar rays and the movement of priestly processions. The pylon gates were not only symbols of the entrance through which the sun was reborn each day, but also of the gates to the underworld through which the eternal spirit must pass.

Five generations after Hatshepsut, the Pharaoh Amenhotep IV made a major break with Egyptian religious tradition by disavowing the multitudes of deities and instituting a monotheistic religion devoted to the sun god, Aton. Changing his name to Iknaton (or Akhenaton), which means "all is well with Aton," Amenhotep abandoned the old capital at Thebes about 1370 B.C. to establish a new capital 300 miles to the north at Akhetaton (the modern Tell-el-Amarna). Akhetaton was a linear town nearly 7 miles long, bounded on the west by the Nile and on the east by mountains, and lacking a consistent overall plan. Transportation was facilitated by the waterway, and a river road linked the various residential sections of the town. Temples had altars set in open courtyards, and there were no segregated areas for the priesthood. Private houses were commodious, especially for the wealthy, with rooms grouped around open courts. The mud-brick walls were thick to modulate both heat and cold. No wall surrounded the settlement, protection being provided by freestanding guardhouses. To the east of the city was a worker's village, built on a grid plan similar to earlier construction camps like Kahun.

The Amarna period brought a change in artistic conventions. For a brief interval, stiff and highly stylized artistic canons were relaxed in favor of more natural approaches. This can be seen immediately in the portraits of Iknaton, who is shown with a deformed figure and distorted facial features.

(Medical specialists today speculate that Iknaton may have suffered from Froelick's syndrome, a disease of the bones.)

Innovative as they were, Iknaton's religious reforms eventually led to the downfall of the Eighteenth Dynasty. His preoccupation with Aton caused him to neglect the provinces of the Egyptian empire; repeated appeals from Syria for help in the struggle against the Hittites went unanswered. (The communications were found as archaeologists excavated Akhetaton.) In addition, the old deposed priesthood of Amon gained strength, so that at Iknaton's death in 1354 B.C. the cult of Amon was revived, and the former religious practices were reinstated. Thebes again became the capital as Akhetaton was deserted. The successor to Iknaton was his nephew, Tutankhaton, who renamed himself Tutankhamon to show his allegiance to the religion at Thebes.

There would be little to say about the brief and rather uneventful reign of Tutankhamon were it not that his burial in the Valley of the Kings remained virtually unplundered until its discovery by Lord Carnarvon and Howard Carter in 1922. The astonishing richness of the artifacts crammed into the two chambers of his tomb, in addition to the precious objects included with the mummy encased in a golden mask, adequately demonstrate why grave robbing flourished in ancient Egypt. If a minor king such as Tutankhamon merited such a lavish burial, imagine what treasures were entombed with an important pharaoh. The discovery of Tut's tomb greatly increased knowledge of Egyptian life, for the everyday objects — furniture, a wig box, camp bed, fire-making tools, and so forth — are as informative as the bejeweled objects are valuable.

Tutankhamon was the last pharaoh of the Eighteenth Dynasty; his chief military officer seized power after Tut's death and founded the next dynasty, of which Ramses II (1292–1225 B.C.) was the most outstanding pharaoh. In addition to his military and political accomplishments, including a peace treaty with the Hittites, Ramses II constructed a number of great monuments. His additions to the Temple at Karnak have already been mentioned. At Abu Simbel, he had two temples carved into the rock cliffs adjoining the Nile, thus exploiting ideas from the Giza Sphinx (monumental sculpture carved in living rock), Beni Hasan (rock-cut tombs), and the New Kingdom temples (pylon gates). The larger temple at Abu Simbel has four colossal statues of a seated Ramses II, each measuring sixty-five feet in height; these dominate the entrance face and continue the sloping contour of the cliff (Figure 2.11). Standing beside the pharaoh's legs are carved representations of family members, including his queen Nefertari. None of these secondary figures is as tall as Ramses's knee, which indicates their inferior status (Figure 2.12). Behind this sculpted façade is the temple proper, excavated into the rock for a distance of 180 feet. The plan is axial, with an entrance hall, colonnaded chamber, and shrine in the center flanked by long narrow storage rooms to either side. The interior surfaces are richly carved. The columns in the large chamber are composed of standing images of Ramses as Osiris, wearing the crown of Upper Egypt on the north side row and the double crown of unified Egypt on the south side row. The smaller temple is similar, with thirty-three-foot-high standing colossi representing Ramses and his queen set between buttresses that continue the slope of the rock face. Both temples have been repositioned today, the result of an inter-

FIGURE 2.11 *Plan of the Great Temple of Ramses II, Abu Simbel, Nineteenth Dynasty.* (From J. Fergusson)

FIGURE 2.12 *View of the Great Temple of Ramses II, Abu Simbel, Nineteenth Dynasty.* (From G. Perret and C. Chipiez)

national effort to save them from inundation in Lake Nassar, which was created behind the Aswan Dam. Their new locations on higher ground vary only slightly from the original orientations.

Later rulers of the Twentieth Dynasty did not eclipse Ramses's glory, but they maintained some of the same vigor as leaders. With the advent of the Twenty-first Dynasty (ca. 1085 B.C.), however, Egypt began a long slide into decadence and ceased to be a major influence in either art or culture.

THE MINOAN CIVILIZATION IN THE AEGEAN

During the second millennium B.C., invasions of Indo-European nomads into Mesopotamia displaced the trading communities of the Phoenicians, who had settled along the eastern shores of the Mediterranean Sea. In their search for new homelands some of the Phoenicians sought refuge on the islands of the eastern Mediterranean, especially Crete, about 2000 B.C. Their language was recorded in a script termed *Linear A,* a written form found only on Crete and still undeciphered by archaeologists. Until more is learned about these people, theories concerning their origins will remain unproven.

An examination of artifacts suggests strong influence from Mesopotamia as well as contact with Egypt. The religious practices of early settlers on Crete included cults of snakes and trees, a direct parallel with Sumeria. Since there are no snakes on Crete, the snake cult appears to be an imported practice, probably derived from the Sumerian water god, Ea, whose attributes included creativity, wisdom, magic, and slyness. Bull-baiting was a sport of the Sumerians, and it became a ritual game in

Crete. Lions are revered in both Mesopotamian and Egyptian royal symbolism, and they are used similarly in fortified royal settlements on the Greek mainland. Egyptian artifacts from the Eighteenth Dynasty have been retrieved from the harbor at Kairatos, Crete, and 1300 pieces of Aegean pottery dating from 1370–1350 B.C. were excavated from the rubbish heaps of Akhetaton.

Historians recognize two distinct civilizations in the Aegean during the second millennium: the Minoans, based on Crete ca. 2000–1400 B.C.; and the Mycenaeans, established at several sites along the coast of Greece ca. 1600–1100 B.C. The two civilizations share some artistic and cultural traits, including a reliance on trade with other communities in Egypt, Syria, Turkey, and Cyprus. The Mycenaeans traveled as far west as Britain, and Mycenaean sites were involved in the Trojan War (ca. 1200 B.C.) chronicled by Homer in the *Iliad*. Both civilizations contributed to the cultural patrimony of classical Greece.

The Minoans on Crete were named for the legendary King Minos, who was thought by later Greeks to have built the large palace at Knossos. Modern archaeologists trace the origins of Minoan settlements back to the Bronze Age (ca. 3000 B.C.), with a sophisticated civilization emerging prior to 1600 B.C., when the palaces built on the island were destroyed, possibly by an earthquake. Over the next 200 years, the Minoans rebuilt and greatly enlarged the palace at Knossos (Figure 12.13). Sometime around 1400 B.C. the complex was again destroyed by natural causes, most likely the eruption of Thera (present-day Santorini), sixty miles to the north. This volcanic explosion, one of the most powerful in ancient times (four times as large as the Krakatoa eruption of 1883), produced an enormous tidal wave and discharged volcanic gasses and ash over a large area of the eastern Mediterranean. Records in Egypt during the Eighteenth Dynasty tell of prolonged darkness, during which the sun appeared no brighter than the moon. Such an eruption would have been sufficient to capsize the Minoan fleet and drown the population in the tidal wave, while heavy deposits of volcanic ash would have filled the fertile valleys and destroyed the agricultural base.

Before the eruption, however, the palace at Knossos housed a refined and sophisticated court. The unfortified palace was set on a hill overlooking the harbor below. Nearly four acres of buildings surround a central courtyard measuring 170 by 90 feet. Immediately off the courtyard to the west was the throne room, approached through an anteroom. The wall paintings of eagle-headed lions flanking the alabaster throne symbolize the power and authority of the king through the eagle, monarch of the skies, and the lion, king of the beasts. On a lower level, opposite the throne room and separated from it by a low wall, was a sacred pool in which the king bathed for sanctification in ceremonies relating to the veneration of the Earth Mother, goddess of fertility.

Cleanliness and sanitation appear to have been important to the builders of Knossos, for they achieved a standard of indoor plumbing that would not be exceeded in western Europe until the nineteenth century A.D. Terra-cotta water pipes brought clean water through a series of settling tanks and siphons to supply baths located in the residential sections of the palace, and sanitary sewers carried off wastewater from basins and water closets. There may have been a supply of both hot and cold piped water.

A staircase around an open light well provided access to the royal chambers on the east side. The private apartments of the king and queen had balconies with outward-looking views across the valley of the river Kairatos. Off the northwest corner of the palace was the theater, connected to the palace proper by a sacred ceremonial road, but it seems that the large central courtyard provided the setting for theatrical ritual, including the ceremonial games involving acrobatic feats on running bulls. **Frescoes** preserved on some palace walls illustrate these amusements or rituals.

A detailed description of the palace at Knossos is difficult because of the multilevel complexity of the building and its collapsed condition. The Minoans employed wooden columns and roof beams, all of which have now disappeared, causing the upper walls to fall in. Archaeological exploration of the site, begun by Sir Arthur Evans early in the twentieth century, has led to the reconstruction of portions of the palace (Figure 2.14). Concrete columns,

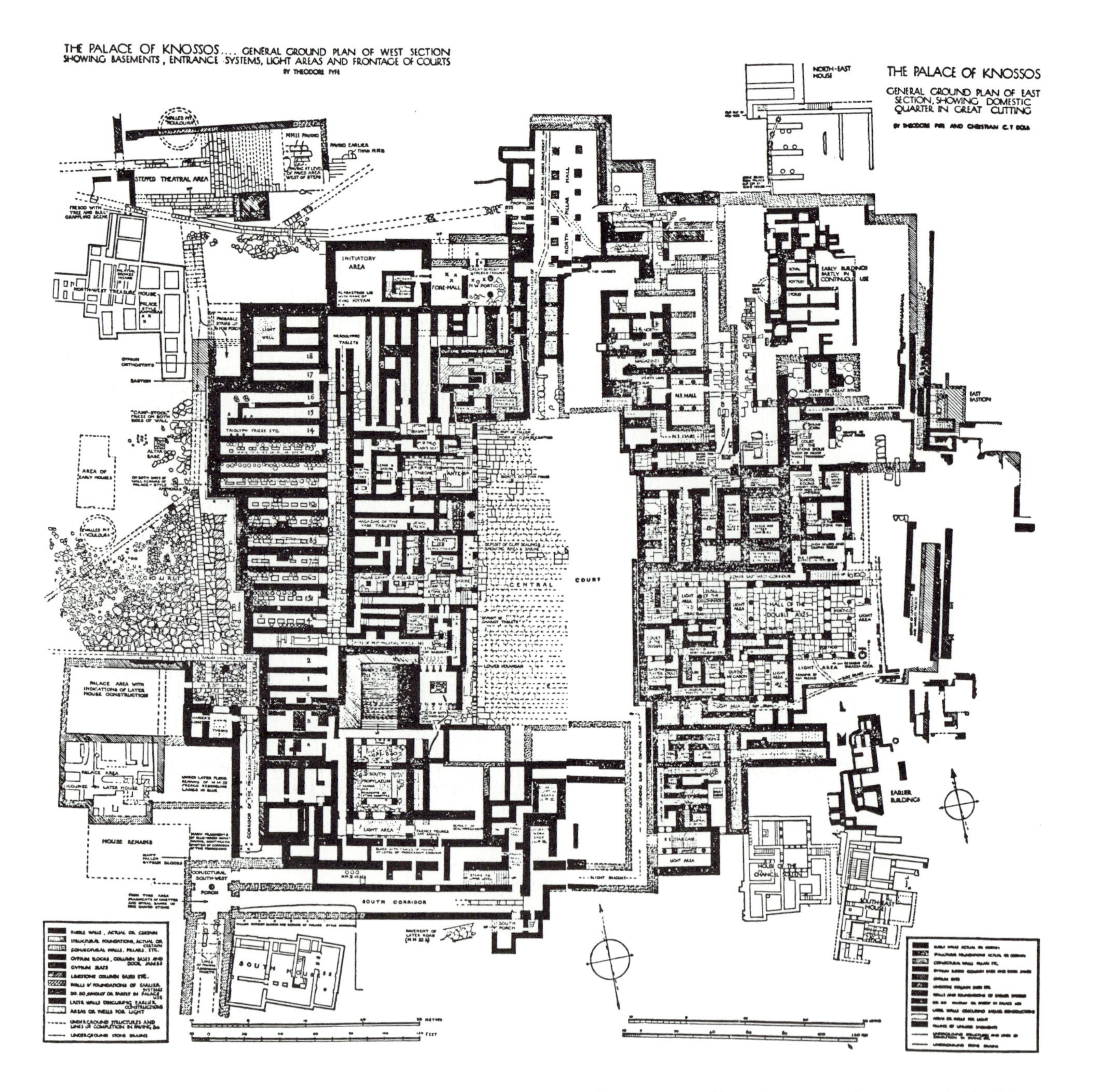

FIGURE 2.13 *Plan of the Palace, Knossos, ca. 1600–1400* B.C. (From A. Evans)

FIGURE 2.14 *View of the Palace, Knossos, ca. 1600–1400* B.C. (Photo: Marburg)

modeled after the timber ones found in Minoan art, have been inserted to support beams; these columns taper downward from a rectangular block and enlarged convex molding at the top. Nothing quite like them exists in contemporary civilizations, but at least a carved replica of a Minoan column appears ca. 1250 B.C. at Mycenae. Even after restoration, the uses of some rooms remain unclear. Storerooms containing pottery jars for wine, oil, olives, and grain are unmistakable, but the function of other sections, where several stages of construction can be detected, is still conjectural.

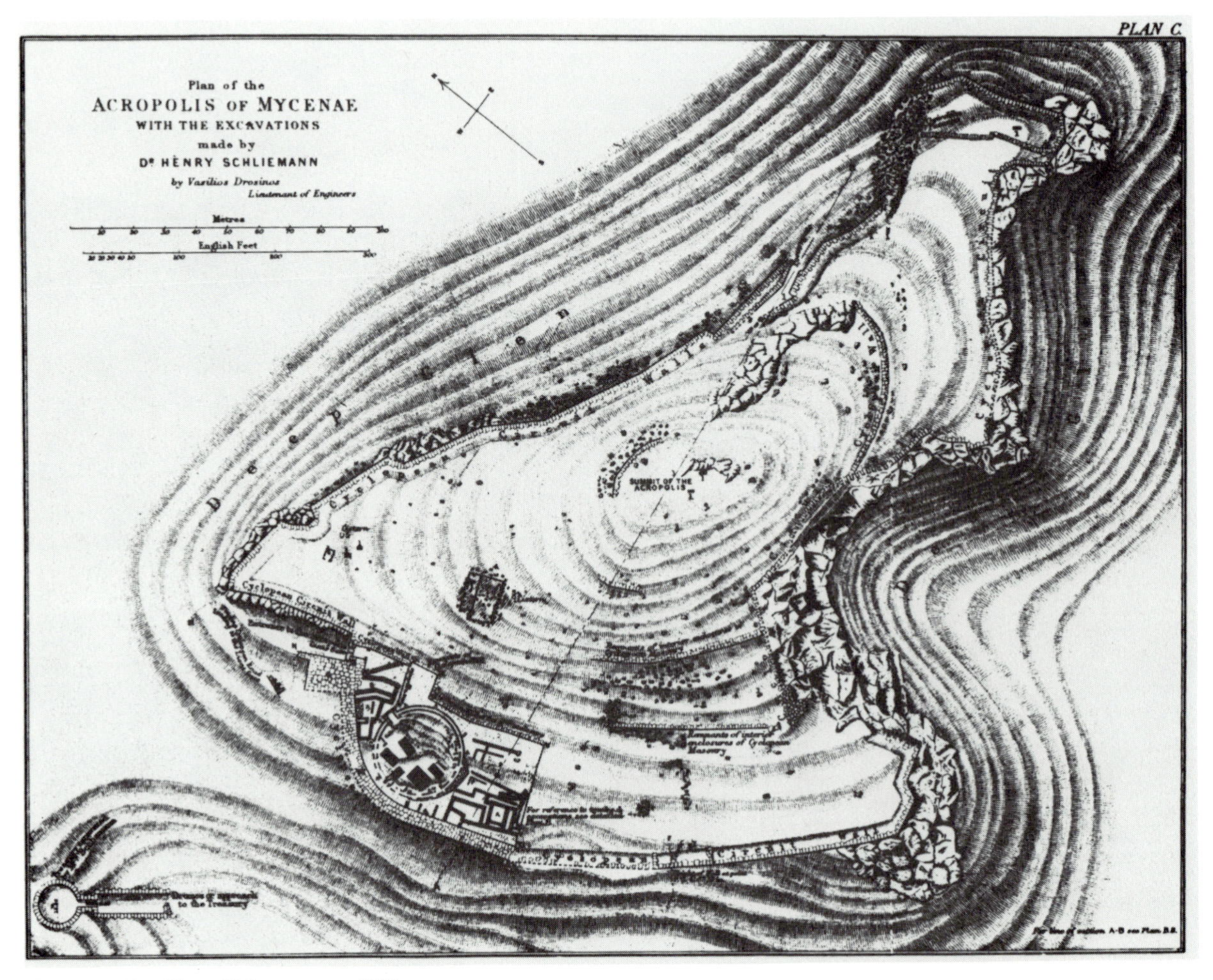

FIGURE 2.15 *Plan of Mycenae, ca. 1300* B.C. (From H. Schliemann)

THE MYCENAEAN CIVILIZATION

As was the case with Knossos, settlements at Mycenae date back to the Bronze Age. Mycenae reached its period of greatness after the destruction of Knossos (perhaps invigorated by the survivors of the Minoan palaces on Crete), although there have been significant archaeological finds dated from 1580–1510 B.C. in the Royal Grave Circle (Figure 2.15). The nineteenth-century excavator of ancient cites in Greece, Heinrich Schliemann, uncovered nearly thirty-one pounds of gold treasure — jewelry, face masks, and other decorative objects — in the graves there, indicating the wealth of this, the primary citadel of the Mycenaean trading civilization. Unlike Knossos, the entire citadel was built with a strong concern for defense. The site is on high ground, protected on the north by the 2650-foot Mount Prophet Elijah and enclosed on the other sides by a massive stone wall, eighteen to twenty-four feet thick and up to forty feet high. Stones in the wall are virtual boulders set in posi-

Figure 2.16 *View of the Lion Gate, Mycenae, ca. 1300* B.C. (Photo: Marburg)

tion with minimal shaping and no mortar. The later Greeks thought these walls were the work of giants, the Cyclopes, hence the adjective *cyclopean* to describe their construction.

Entrance to Mycenae was through the Lion Gate added when the citadel was enlarged about 1300 B.C. (Figure 2.16). The gate was positioned so that the approaching visitor had to pass through an increasingly narrow way parallel to the enclosing wall, allowing defenders inside the wall ample opportunity to attack hostile forces before they could reach the gate. The actual gateway is of considerable artistic interest. Single upright stones support an 18-ton lintel across the gate, above which is a corbeled arch. The space of the arch is filled by a triangular stone with sculpted reliefs of two lions with their forefeet on an altar bearing a column of the tree cult. The lions' heads are missing; they were carved separately and attached with dowels, the holes for which are still visible. Even in its damaged state, the Lion Gate indicates contact by its creators with the Minoan world, for the column of the tree

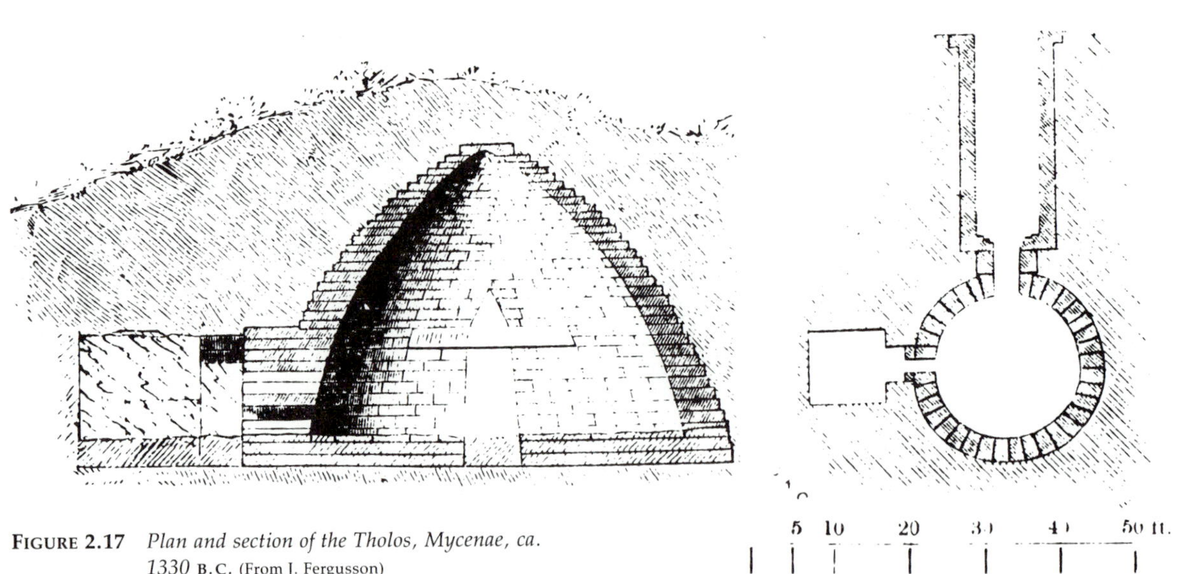

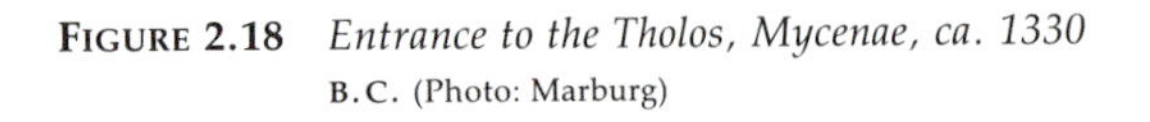

FIGURE 2.17 *Plan and section of the Tholos, Mycenae, ca. 1330* B.C. (From J. Fergusson)

FIGURE 2.18 *Entrance to the Tholos, Mycenae, ca. 1330* B.C. (Photo: Marburg)

cult is unmistakably the same as the columns used at Knossos.

Beyond the Lion Gate are the remains of shaft graves where Schliemann uncovered so much golden treasure. Originally these lay outside the citadel walls, but when the fortress was enlarged ca. 1300 B.C., the grave circle was carefully incorporated in the fortified area. The administrative and ceremonial spaces that lay beyond are now mostly ruined, and the residential quarters atop the hill are largely collapsed. From what remains it appears that the palace had many features derived from Crete, including entrance porches and megaron rooms. A **megaron** is a simple rectangular space, sometimes with an attached anteroom, having solid long walls without openings and an entrance in the center of a short side. It is an elementary house form still employed in Mediterranean countries, and it has been used by twentieth-century architects including Le Corbusier.

Outside the fortifications of Mycenae, about a mile to the southwest, is the *tholos*, or beehive tomb, commonly called the Treasury of Atreus (ca. 1330 B.C.) (Figure 2.17). It is a corbeled stone tomb rising 44 feet in thirty-three circular courses from a circular plan 48 feet in diameter. All the stonework, except for the stone-walled *dromos*, or entrance way, leading to the chamber, is covered by an earthen mound, whose weight adds stability to the dry masonry (Figures 2.18, 2.19). The construction technique is identical to that used by prehistoric megalith builders in northern Europe and by Egyptian masons as early as the Fourth Dynasty. Whatever the tomb contained in the way of bodies or goods for the afterlife was stolen long ago. Modern archaeologists have uncovered a few compact

FIGURE 2.19 *Interior view of the Tholos, Mycenae, ca. 1330 B.C.* (Photo: Marburg)

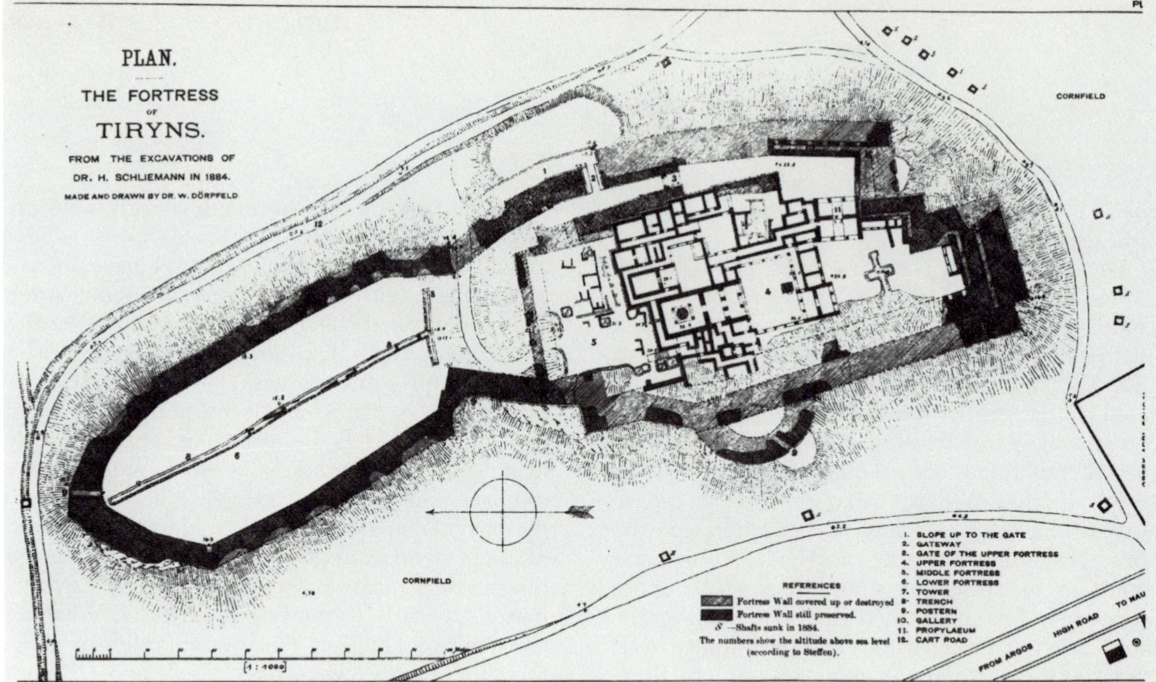

FIGURE 2.20 *Plan of Tiryns.* (From H. Schliemann)

skeletons in graves beneath the floor but no treasure.

A smaller citadel, better preserved than Mycenae, was located at Tiryns (Figure 2.20). It is sited atop a limestone ridge and protected by a massive wall of cyclopean masonry. Even more than the entrance to Mycenae, the approach to Tiryns led in an almost single-file passage beside and then between the walls, so attackers would be vulnerable well before reaching the first city gate. Even then, they had to traverse additional narrow passages before entering the palace area, which increased the opportunities for defense. Megarons were used for the major ceremonial spaces, and open courtyards organized the public and private sections of the palace.

Sometime around 1120 B.C., the Mycenaean settlements were overrun by successive waves of nomadic peoples from the east pushing down into the peninsula of Greece. The arrival of these nomads, known as Dorians, brought Mycenaean civilization to an end and plunged the Aegean into several centuries of cultural obscurity. Out of the confusion of this "dark age" rose the brilliant achievement of Greece's classical greatness, which will be discussed in the next chapter.

3.

The Greek World

In all three centers of western civilization established during the second millennium — Mesopotamia, Egypt, and the Aegean — the patterns of outside invasions, cultural continuity, and cross-cultural contact through military or commercial activity continued throughout most of the first millennium. New waves of nomadic tribes disrupted established city-states in turbulent Mesopotamia. The relative tranquility provided by Egypt's natural boundaries could not check internal feuding, as first priestly hierarchies and then foreign princes from Libya and Nubia usurped the pharaoh's throne, weakening the country where conservative tradition had maintained stability for so long. The rocky lands of the Greek peninsula were to have the most astounding development of cultural greatness, however, as Dorian and Ionian invaders merged with native populations to forge the Greece of classical antiquity. All three centers were joined briefly toward the end of the millennium in the sweeping conquests of Alexander the Great, a Macedonian who effectively subjugated the city-states of Greece by 337 B.C., conquered Egypt with no resistance in 332, and defeated the major Mesopotamian power, Persia, the following year. Alexander's dream of creating a world empire led him to initiate military expeditions as far east as the Indus River, which were curtailed only by his untimely death of a fever in 323 B.C., at the age of thirty-three.

MESOPOTAMIA: THE ASSYRIANS, NEO-BABYLONIANS, AND PERSIANS

When we last discussed Mesopotamia, the Hittites were ruling much of the western area from their capital at Hattusas, leaving the relatively ineffective Kassites and Mitanni to dominate the traditional southeastern centers around Babylon. The weakness of these rulers gave the Assyrians, a fierce people of northern Mesopotamia, an opportunity to gain a foothold in the fertile plains to the south. By 900 B.C., Assyrian might had established the Assyrian Empire, with capitals sequentially at Calah (present-day Nimrud), Dur-Sharrukin (Khorsabad), and Nineveh (Kuyunjik). Their relentless warfare and ruthless character are reflected in the strongly fortified citadels built for each capital.

Khorsabad, the royal city Sargon II built ca. 720 B.C., illustrates Assyrian architecture and planning (Figure 3.1). At the center of the city the twenty-five-acre palace occupied a plateau fifty feet above the level of the town (Figure 3.2). A rectangular order dominated the palace area, which was bordered by a sturdy wall heavily reinforced by watchtowers. Rising near the central axis was a seven-stage ziggurat, 143 feet square at the base, representing the cosmic order of the seven planets. (Despite the fact that they treated captured populations cruelly, the

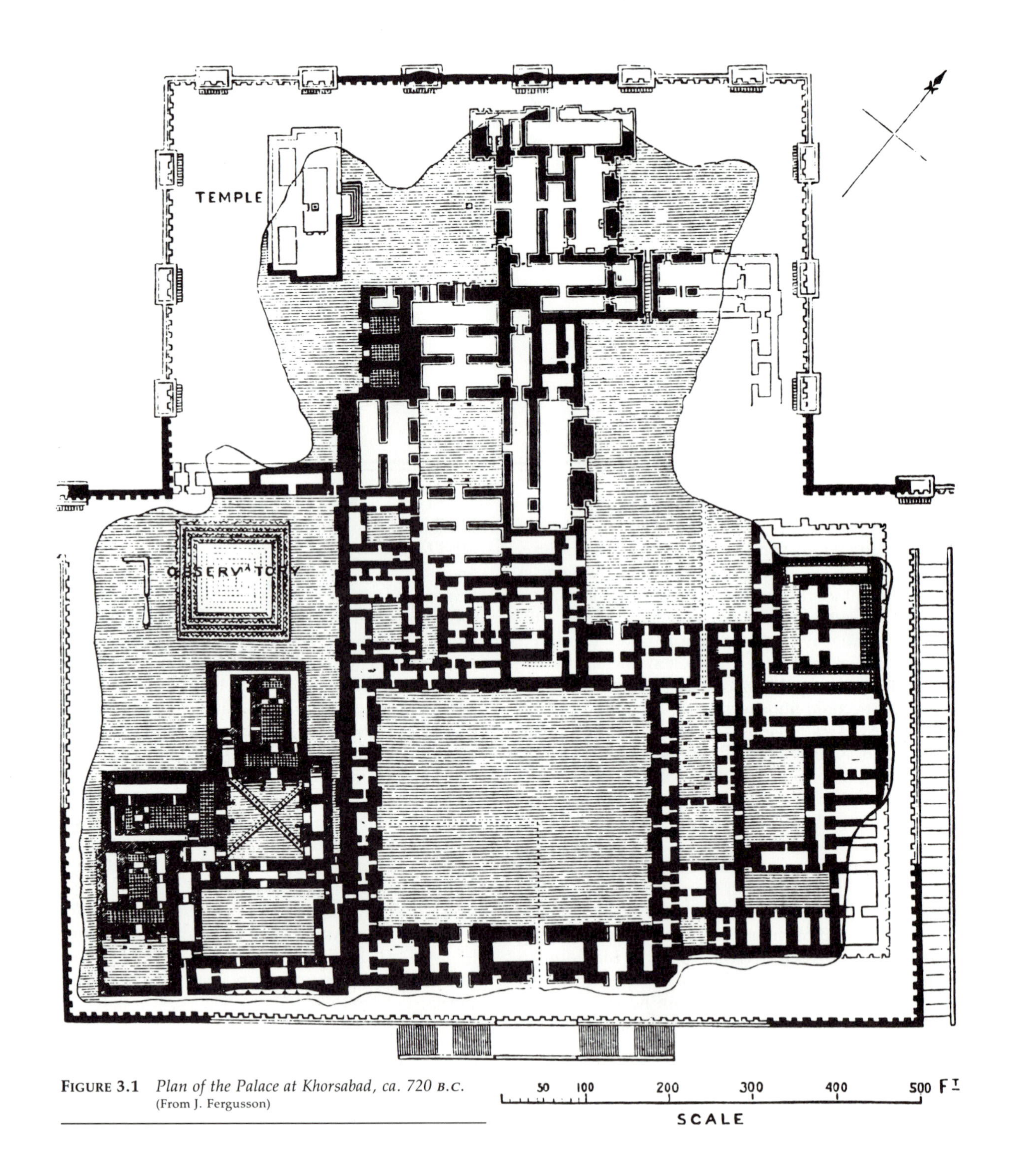

FIGURE 3.1 *Plan of the Palace at Khorsabad, ca. 720* B.C.
(From J. Fergusson)

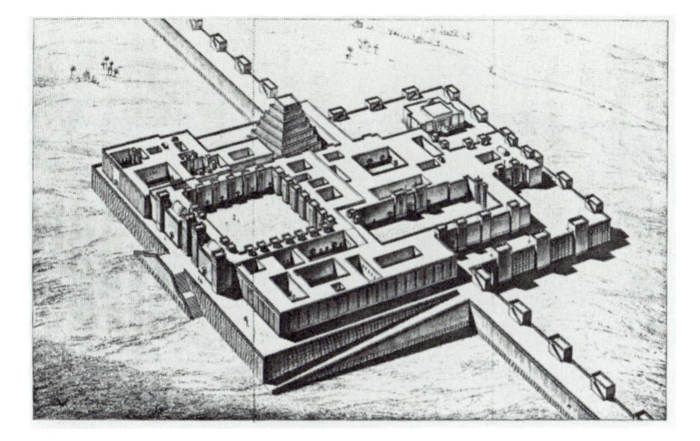

FIGURE 3.2 *View of Khorsabad.* (From G. Perret and C. Chipiez)

Assyrians adopted many of the religious and cultural practices of Sumeria and Babylon as their own.) The palace was organized around large courtyards surrounded by rooms, including the great hall and throne room. Man-headed winged bulls carved in high relief from thirteen-foot stone blocks guard the entrances to the palace. Seen from the front, these creatures stride forth with two front legs; viewed from the side, four legs are visible, so an oblique or perspective view of both side and front shows a beast with five legs. Bone and muscle are realistically represented, while feathers, hair, and beard are stylized, conveying with forcefulness the strength of the monarch: as man, the lord of creation; as eagle, king of the sky; and as bull, fecundator of the herd. Other relief carvings within the palace depict marching armies burning, killing, and pillaging to emphasize the folly of resisting Assyrian power. Without subtlety, Sargon II had the art and architecture of his palace communicate the overwhelming power residing in his person.

Perhaps because of its atrocities the Assyrian Empire lasted only 300 years before falling in 612 B.C. to the combined forces of the Babylonians and the Medes, which had both been fighting the Assyrians unsuccessfully for two centuries. Out of the Assyrian defeat came the Neo-Babylonian Empire (ca. 612–539 B.C.), which was distinguished architecturally by the rebuilding and enlargement of Babylon under Nebuchadnezzar II (604–562 B.C.). The city's processional way passed through the Ishtar Gate, a fortified portal clad in blue-glazed brick (Figure 3.3). Animals were modeled in shallow relief on the surface of the bricks, which were separately glazed and then assembled as the covering was laid in horizontal courses. The entire gate, now located in East Berlin's Pergamon Museum, recaptures the colorful splendor of ancient Babylon. Contemporary visitors marveled at the "Hanging Gardens" and designated them one of the Seven Wonders of the World. In all likelihood these were planted terraces not unlike modern conservatories, irrigated by water carried in buckets on an endless chain from a subterranean well. The Ziggurat at Babylon, now a crumbled ruin, was remembered in the Old Testament as the Tower of Babel.

Babylonia's greatness was eclipsed in 539 B.C. when it became part of the Persian Empire of Cyrus II. The Persians had previously overthrown the Medes, and they continued to expand outward from their capital at Susa (in present-day Iran) to conquer all of Mesopotamia, Asia Minor, and even

FIGURE 3.3 *Ishtar Gate, Babylon, sixth century B.C.* (Photo: Staatliche Museen, Berlin)

Egypt by 525 B.C. Within the next century they controlled territory from the Danube to the Indus, from the Jaxartes to the Nile, failing to subjugate only the Grecian peninsula.

The greatest architectural contribution of the Persians remains an impressive ruin at Persepolis, begun in 518 B.C. by Darius as a ceremonial capital to supplement Susa, the administrative capital, and Pasargadae as centers of court life (Figure 3.4). Lacking strong artistic traditions of their own, the Persians borrowed freely from the cultures they ruled. At Persepolis, there are echoes of Egyptian temple gates and hypostyle halls, Hittite audience chambers, and Mesopotamian sculpted royal animal motifs. The great palace, used primarily for ceremonies at the New Year and beginning of spring, occupied a terrace 1500 by 900 feet; it contained reception courts, banquet rooms, and audience halls in a rather informal layout (Figure 3.5). Xerxes's throne room was known as the Hall of a Hundred Columns (Figure 3.6), and this audience hall, begun by Xerxes and completed by Artaxerxes, was the largest enclosed space in the palace, able to contain 10,000 people within its 250-foot square plan. Most of the construction was in stone. Columns supported wooden roof beams resting on the unique double-headed **capitals** carved in the form of bulls

FIGURE 3.5 *General view of the Palace at Persepolis.* (From G. Perrot and C. Chipiez)

FIGURE 3.4 *Plan of the Palace at Persepolis, begun 518 B.C.* (From G. Perrot and C. Chipiez)

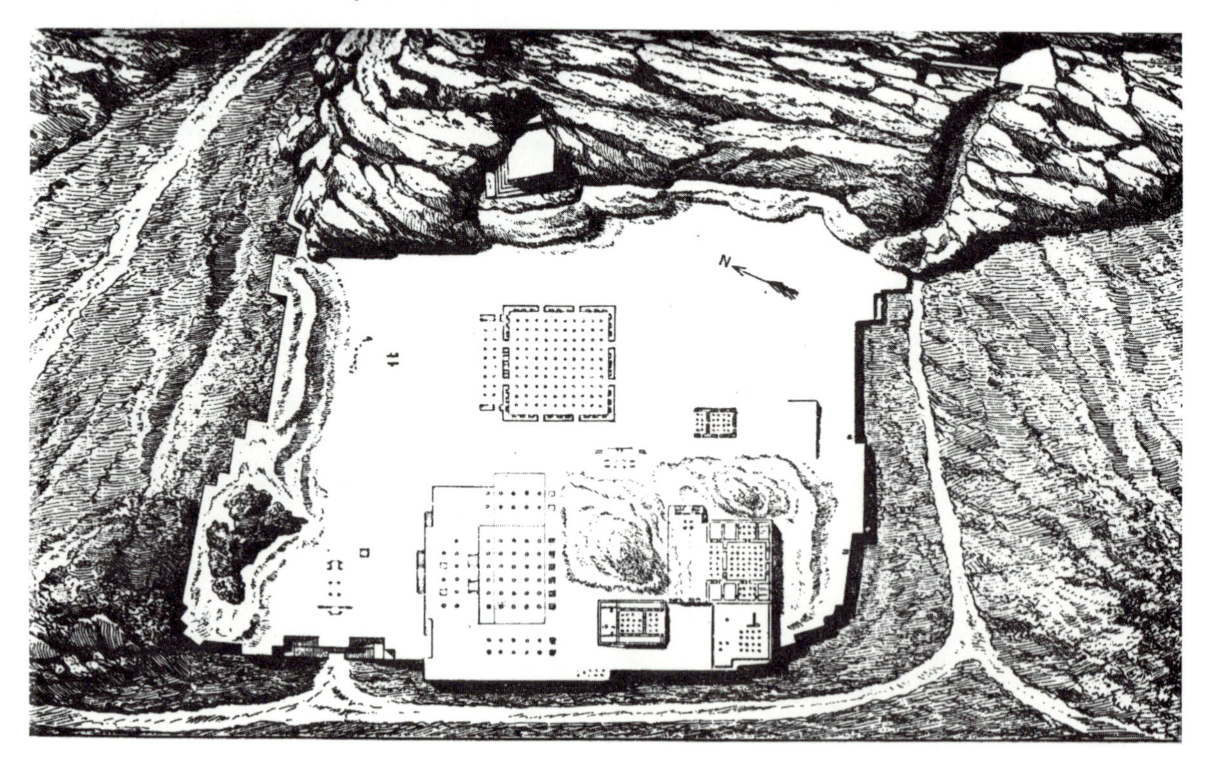

FIGURE 3.6 *View of the Hall of Xerxes in the Palace at Persepolis.* (From G. Perrot and C. Chipiez)

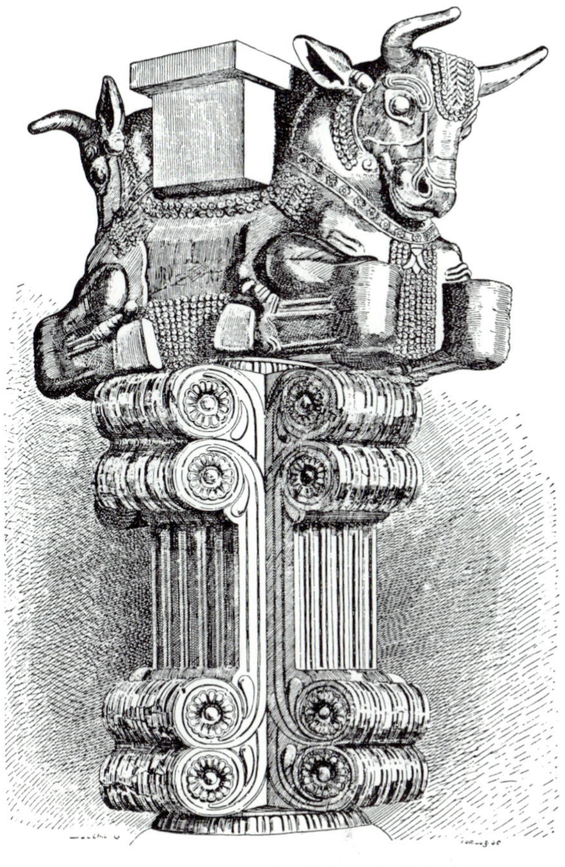

FIGURE 3.7 *Column capital detail from the Palace at Persepolis.* (From G. Perrot and C. Chipiez)

and lions (Figure 3.7). Access to the terrace was gained via a flight of stairs flanked by relief sculptures representing delegations from twenty-three nations bringing tribute to the sovereign. These stone figures, engaged in the same activity as real-life visitors, provided a foretaste of the pageantry and banquets awaiting in the palace above.

The conquests of Alexander the Great ended Persian dominance in 331 B.C. Alexander's armies eventually reached India, and Persian craftsmen appear to have accompanied them and remained there. They helped build the capital at Pataliputra (present-day Patna) for Chandragupta, where the many-columned halls and animal capitals recall Persepolis.

GREECE

The Archaic Period

Having accounted for the fates of Mesopotamia and Egypt during the first millennium, it is now time to chronicle events in Greece during the same period. The Dorians and Ionians overran the Mycenaean fortifications ca. 1120 B.C. Their military superiority, especially in the use of mounted cavalry with iron weapons, accounted for the defeat of the bronze-armed Mycenaeans. Several centuries of confusion followed, during which the invading tribes settled down, mastered the art of writing, and assimilated certain aspects of Mycenaean history and mythology as their own.

Within this time, the population began to exceed the limited agricultural possibilities on the peninsula, where only a relatively narrow strip along the coast and in the river valleys could be productively farmed. The mountainous center of Greece is rocky and sparsely inhabited even today, so the city-states began a program of colonization, establishing new towns around the eastern Mediterranean in Asia Minor, Sicily, southern Italy, and North Africa. These colonies were organized in advance and laid out with orderly plans, generally in rectangular blocks grouped around the market and temples at the center of the city. There were public facilities for bathing, recreation, and entertainment, and a protective wall surrounded the whole town.

In addition to grid plan towns, the major contribution to architectural history made by Greek architects and builders during the Archaic Period was the temple. Drawing on columned prototypes in Egypt and elsewhere, the Greeks evolved a characteristic temple form consisting of a small **cella** or shrine surrounded by a continuous colonnade that supported the roof structure. Greek temples were conceived more as houses for the deity than as accommodations for worshippers, so it is not surprising to note that the cella closely resembles a megaron, previously used by the Mycenaeans as a house form. The **fluting** of columns employed in the earliest temples can be traced back to Egypt, where extant examples are found at Zoser's funerary complex at Saqqara and at Hatshepsut's mortuary temple at Deir-el-Bahari. There is no precedent for the combination of megaron and colonnade, however, and the Greeks developed a highly stylized treatment for columns, capitals, and the supported members, the **entablature.** Later ages termed these elements the **orders** of architecture, recognizing three different modes in Greek work: the **Doric,** sturdiest of the three, based on the proportions of a man; the **Ionic,** lighter in character to reflect the proportions of a woman; and the **Corinthian,** slenderest of all with a highly decorated capital to suggest the form and proportions of a young maiden.

Each order has a particular combination of elements that belong to it alone. The Doric column has no **base** and has the simplest capital atop the fluted **shaft** of the column; its entablature consists of a plain **architrave** and alternating **metopes** and **triglyphs** in the **frieze,** which is crowned with a **cornice.** The Ionic has a base supporting its fluted column shaft and a capital with **volutes** (scrolls); its entablature is also composed of an architrave and frieze, both treated simply so as not to detract from the carved detail of the capital. A cornice with **dentils** concludes the order. In addition to these specified elements, there were general rules about proportions of the parts and overall height and spacing, rules that the ancient Greeks adjusted visually according to particular circumstances. (Italian architects 2000 years later codified the practice into a set of mathematical ratios based on the column's diameter at the base, but there is no evidence from measurements of surviving temples that the Greeks ever reduced temple design to a single formula.) The orders of architecture were thus at once specific and flexible, not a straightjacket for designers but an expressive medium for building.

The origins of the architectural orders remain obscure. The temples that have survived to the present day are constructed in stone, but some evidence suggests that the first Greek temples were built of

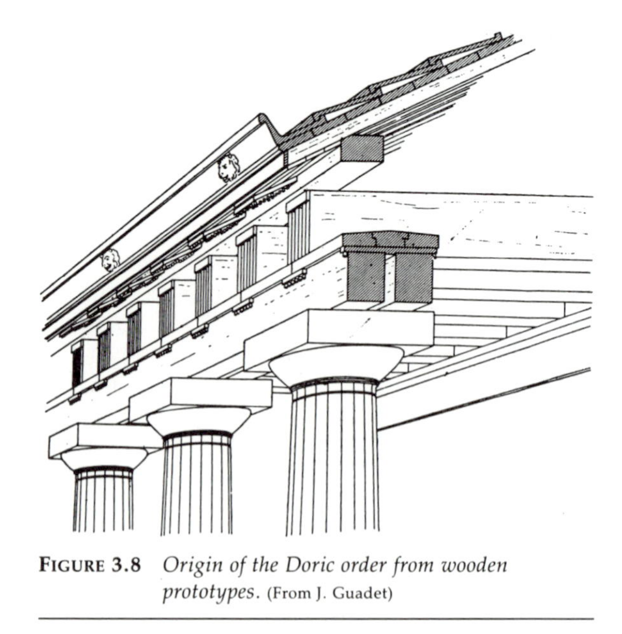

FIGURE 3.8 *Origin of the Doric order from wooden prototypes.* (From J. Guadet)

wood (Figure 3.8). Just as the earliest stone architecture of the Egyptians retained forms and details reflecting buildings in less permanent materials, the Doric order has generally been understood as incorporating details that originated in wood. Triglyphs, for example, are seen as the protective ends of wooden roof beams, and metopes the infill between. Each triglyph is aligned with the column support below. Once built in marble, the wooden end grain of the triglyph was stylized into vertical grooves, and the blank metope panel provided space for relief sculpture. In contrast, more recent studies have suggested that the Doric may have originated purely as a monumental decorative style using terra-cotta molded details with no particular reference to structural features in wood.

The refined proportions of classical Greek temples were developed during the Archaic Period, ca. 700–480 B.C., and some of the best-preserved works are at Paestum (in Greek, Poseidonia) in southern Italy, where a Greek colony was established in the seventh century B.C. Three temples at Paestum allow one to trace the increasing sophistication of Greek architects (Figure 3.9). The earliest is the Temple of Hera (ca. 550 B.C.), also known as the Basilica because some early archaeologists felt it was a civic building (Figure 3.10). Its Doric columns are squat and closely spaced, and there are nine columns across the short end of the rectangular plan, thereby placing a column in the center where there ought to be an **intercolumniation** space to accommodate the entrance axis on that side. A line of col-

FIGURE 3.9 *General view of the temples (left to right) of Ceres, Hera II [Poseidon], and Hera I [Basilica] at Paestum.* (From T. Major)

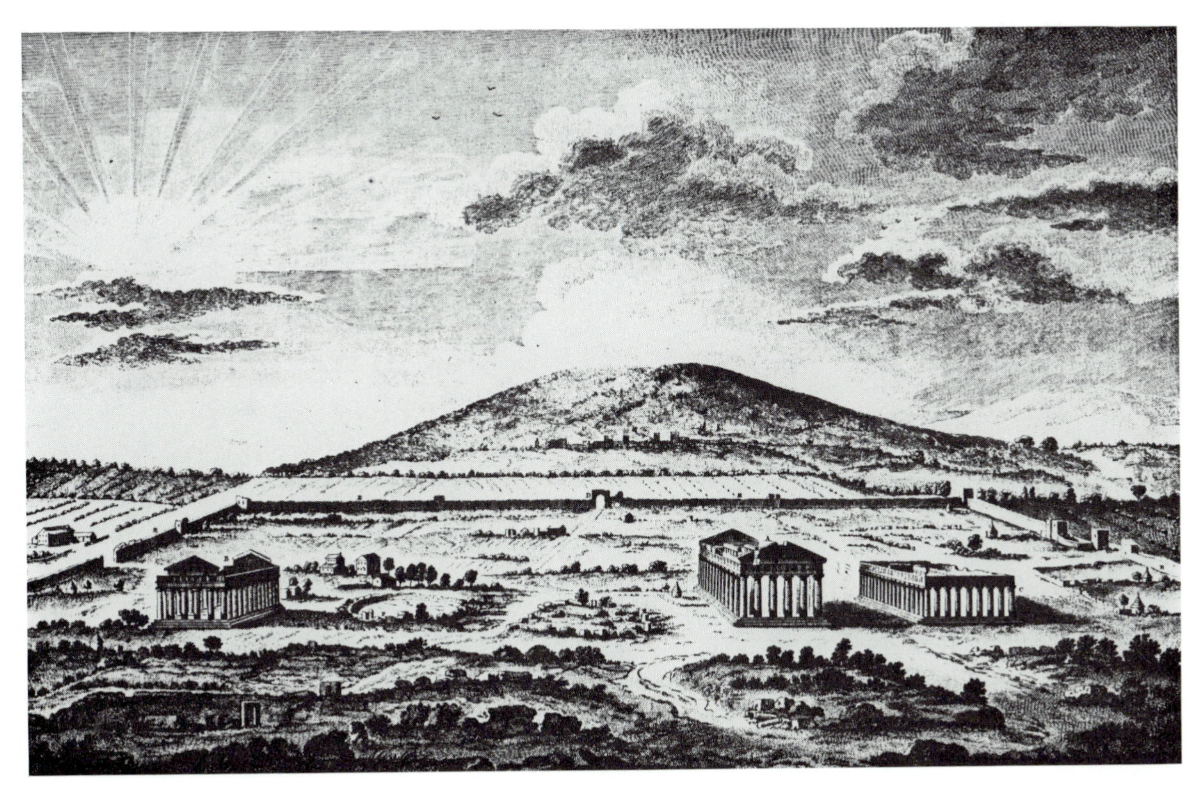

umns continues down the central axis of the cella to provide support for the roof beams, but the line obstructs the interior space. Looking more closely at the colonnade, one can see the fundamental elements of the Doric order. The shafts of the columns swell, then diminish, as they rise to the bulbous **echinus** molding that forms the capital. This change in column diameter is called **entasis,** and it was thought to be comparable to the muscular strength of an arm or leg, expressing visually the physical load sustained by the shaft. Above the capital is a flat square block, the **abacus,** which provides the transition from the cylindrical form of the column to the rectangular and linear architrave above. Joints between marble blocks are easily seen at Paestum, and the limited spanning capability of the stone is reflected in the close column spacing.

Somewhat more refined is the so-called Temple of Ceres, built around 500 B.C. (Figure 3.11). Its columns are more slender, but their entasis is still pronounced, and the echinus capital is rather flat. Here the architects placed only six columns across the

FIGURE 3.10 *Plan of the Temple of Hera I [Basilica] at Paestum, ca. 550 B.C.* (From T. Major)

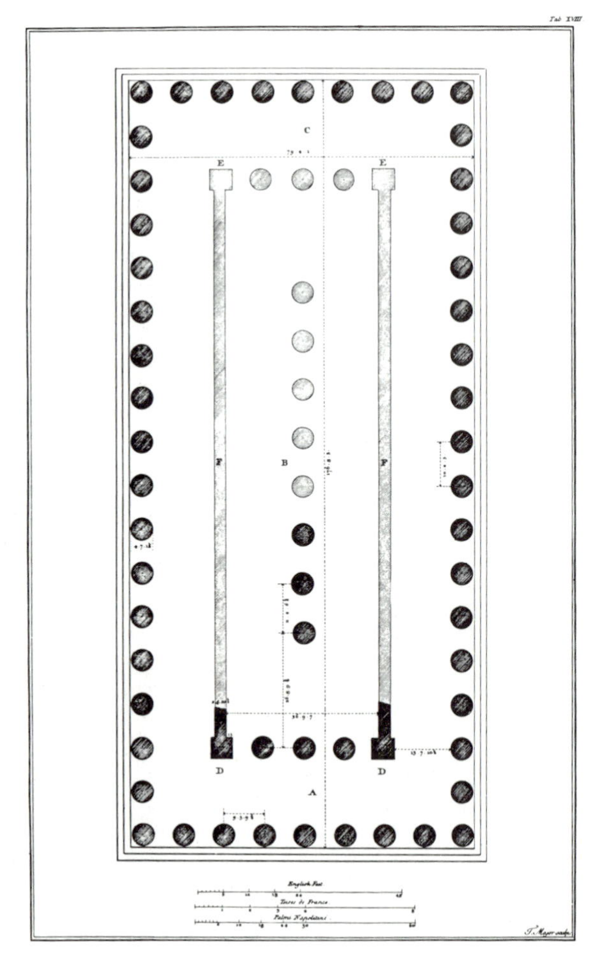

FIGURE 3.11 *Plan of the Temple of Ceres, Paestum.* (From T. Major)

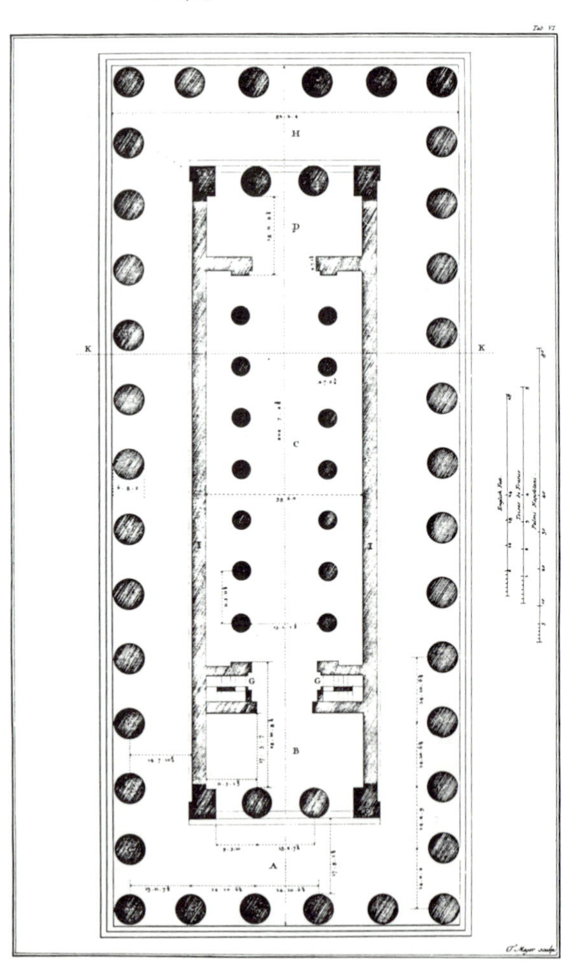

FIGURE 3.12 *Elevation of the Temple of Hera II [Poseidon], Paestum, ca. 450 B.C.* (From R. Sturgis)

FIGURE 3.13 *Plan of the Temple of Hera II [Poseidon], Paestum.* (From T. Major)

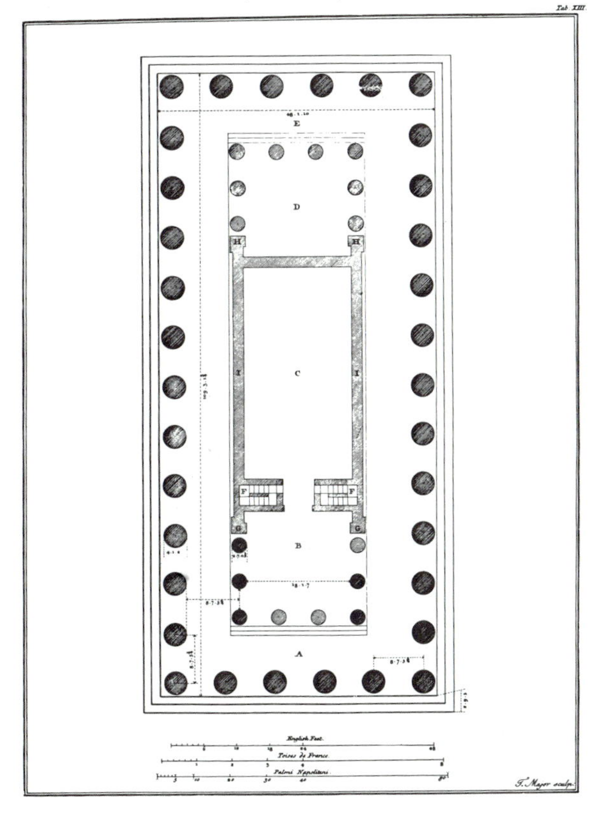

FIGURE 3.14 *View of the Temple of Hera II [Poseidon], Paestum.* (Photo: Alinari)

short end of the temple, so that there is a central space for entrance. The third temple at Paestum, once known as the Temple of Poseidon and now generally called the Temple of Hera II (ca. 450 B.C.), dates from the classical phase of Greek architecture, so it shows the mature Doric order in an unusually well-preserved temple (Figures 3.12–3.15). Its columns are skillfully proportioned, and the capital merges with the shaft so that the two elements appear as a logical unit. Much of the **pediment** (the triangular **gable** on the short end of the building) is

FIGURE 3.15 *Interior of the Temple of Hera II [Poseidon], Paestum.* (From R. Sturgis)

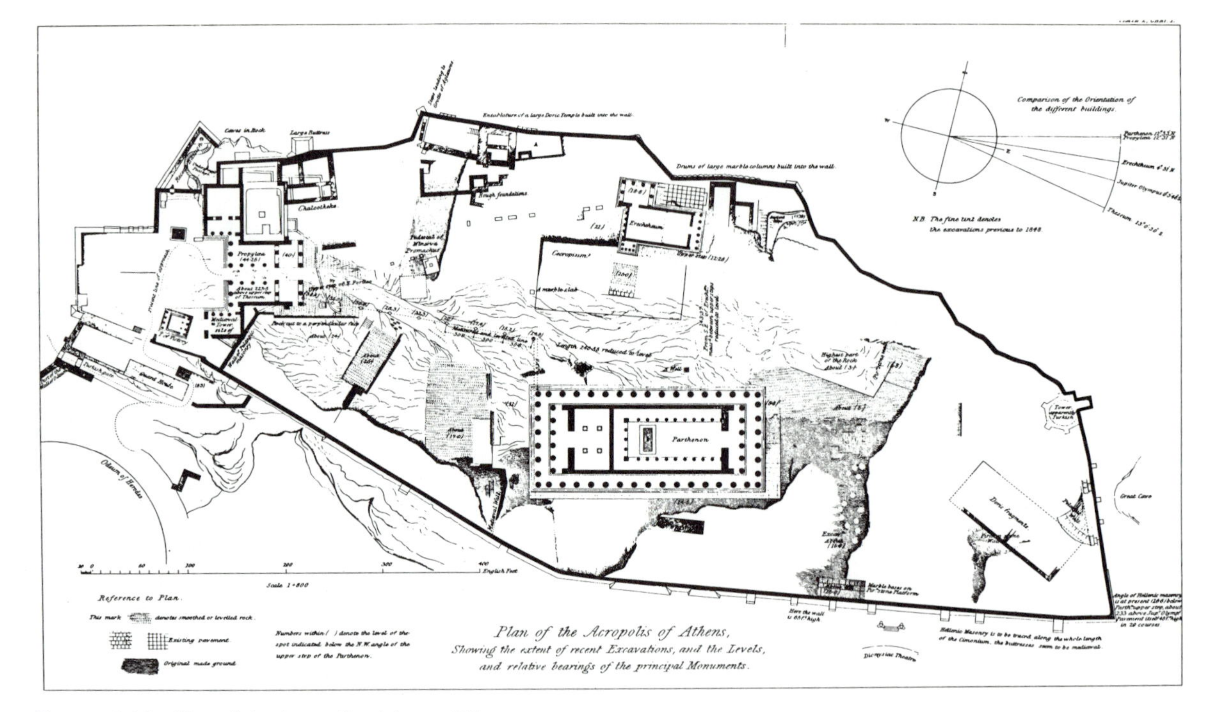

FIGURE 3.16 *Plan of the Acropolis, Athens, fifth century* B.C. (From F. Penrose)

intact, conveying the massing of the original form. All Greek temples had wooden roof members, none of which survive.

The Classical Period

During the Archaic Period the Persian Empire flourished in Mesopotamia, and Persian forces under Darius and Xerxes attacked the cities of Greece, both on the peninsula and around the Mediterranean. Ionian cities of Asia Minor had been under the Persian yoke from the middle of the sixth century. They had revolted and been reconquered, and Darius attempted an invasion of the mainland, where his army was defeated in 490 B.C. by the combined legions of Greek city-states at the Battle of Marathon. In 480 the Persians attacked again, devastating the region around Athens and sacking the city itself, but the Greek navy scored a decisive victory over the Persian fleet near Salamis. In 479 the Persians once again raided Athens and again were defeated in land and sea battles.

A period of relative peace followed these struggles, with Athens emerging as the leading city on the mainland. To prevent further incursions by the Persians, Athens united with Ionian cities to form the Delian League; its treasury was transferred from Delos to Athens, and a considerable portion of the money was spent to rebuild the ravaged Athenian **Acropolis,** which had been a military, political, and religious sanctuary since Mycenaean times (Figure 3.16). The four buildings erected there after 479 ushered in the mature phase of Greek architecture known as the Classical Period (479–323 B.C.).

Largest and most famous of these temples was the Parthenon (448–432 B.C.), a great temple to Athena, the patron goddess of the city (Figures 3.17, 3.18). An earlier temple on the site had been destroyed by the Persians. The new temple, designed by Ictinus and Callicrates, was constructed in the finest marble from Mount Pentelicus, employing the Doric order (connoting strength) with almost-Ionic slenderness (to reflect Athena's feminine traits), except in the western room, the Delian treasury, where four Ionic columns supported the roof. Entasis, which was rather obviously handled in the early temples at Paestum, is adroitly handled here to create a sense of repose. Minute adjustments in the horizontal and vertical lines of the structure enhance the perception of orthogonal geometry: the **stylobate** (the level from which the col-

FIGURE 3.17 *Ictinus and Callicrates: Parthenon, Athens, 448–432* B.C. (Photo: Marburg)

FIGURE 3.18 *Ictinus and Callicrates: Plan of the Parthenon, Athens.* (From F. Penrose)

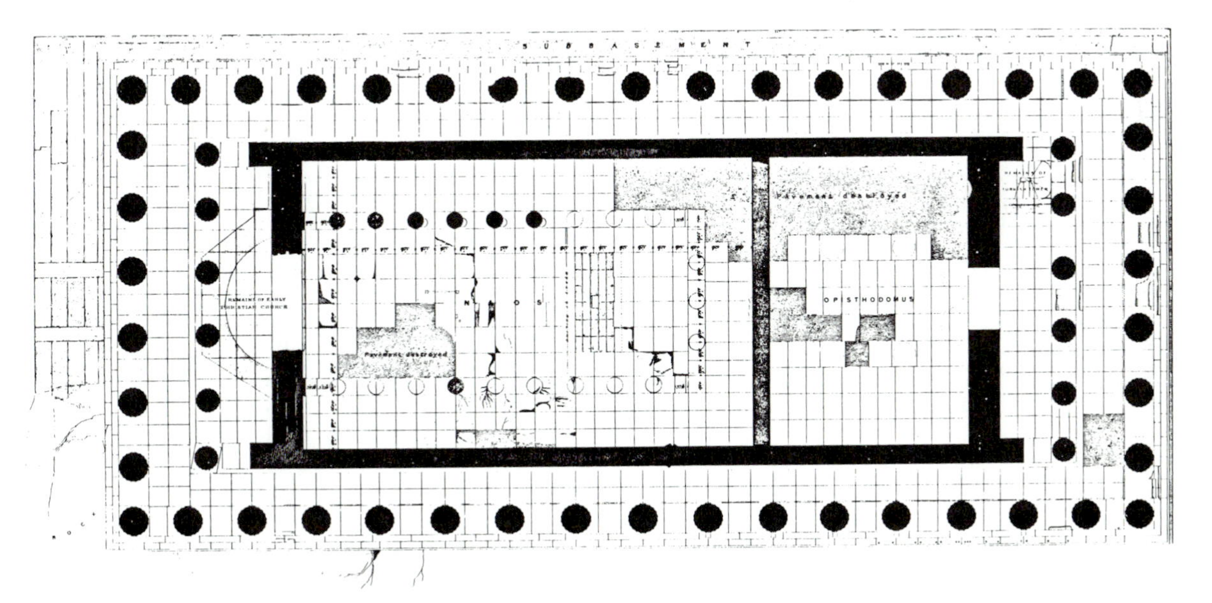

umns rise) is actually convex; the columns incline imperceptibly away from the viewer; and the central axis of each column is not vertical but radial from a point over 6800 feet above the ground. The columns are not the same diameter — the end ones are larger — nor are they equidistantly spaced — the corner ones are closer together. Even the use of eight columns rather than six across the gable end of the building reflects sophisticated understanding of visual phenomena. Most people see six or fewer objects as discrete numbers but perceive more than six as the uncounted "many."

Sculpture adorned both the outside and the inside of the Parthenon. The two end pediments were filled with over-life-sized figures representing, on the east, the birth of Athena witnessed by the gods and, on the west, the battle between Athena and Poseidon for the soil of Attica. The metopes contained relief sculptures depicting struggles between Greeks and Amazons, Greeks and Trojans, gods and giants, and Lapiths and centaurs (Figure 3.19). A continuous frieze ran around the cella walls inside the colonnade, portraying the triumphal procession of Athenians bringing gifts to Athena in the festival held every four years. The procession begins at the southwest corner and moves in both directions to meet again in the center of the east side, where Athena and other enthroned gods receive the offerings, including a specially woven cloth, the *peplos,* to drape an earlier statue of Athena. The sculptor Phidias served as artistic coordinator for the rebuilding of all monuments on the Acropolis, and he was responsible for the sculptural detail on the Parthenon, including the thirty-nine-foot-high cult statue of Athena. She was portrayed standing, with a goddess of victory in her right hand and a shield at her left side. The statue had a wooden armature finished with valuable materials. Ivory was used for all exposed parts of Athena's body; her drapery, armor, and helmet were represented in 2400 pounds of gold; and precious stones were used for her eyes and for decorating her robes and armor.

The cella of the Parthenon was one of the largest interiors built in classical Greece, and scholars still debate how the structure worked over such a wide span. Wooden beams must have been used, even though the Greeks did not understand truss construction. The relatively dark interior would have

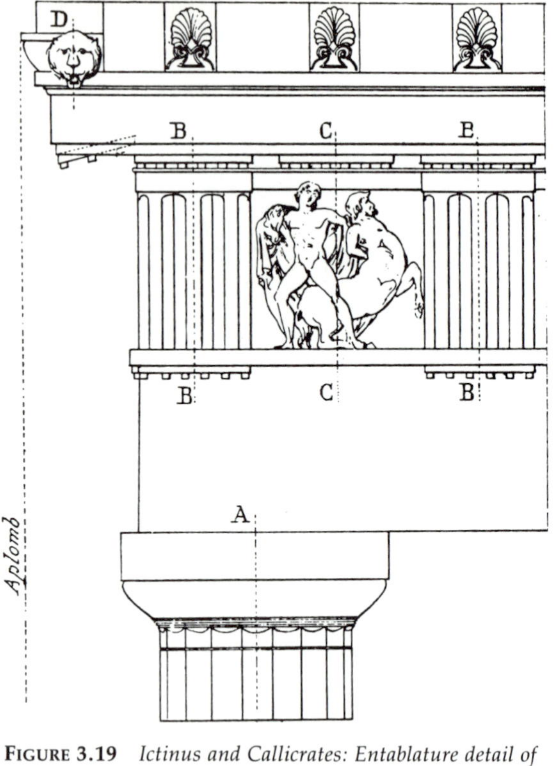

FIGURE 3.19 *Ictinus and Callicrates: Entablature detail of the Parthenon, Athens.* (From J. Guadet)

provided an appropriate setting for the dramatic image of Athena. The Parthenon was so oriented that the sun would penetrate the cella interior on the morning of her birthday, shining on the great chryselephantine statue.

Time and civilization have not been kind to the Parthenon. The statue of Athena was destroyed, probably for the value of its materials, by the second century A.D., and various adaptive reuses of the temple did little to preserve its best features. It became a Christian church, and after the Turks occupied Greece, it was for a time a mosque. By 1687 it was being used for gunpowder storage, at which time it was bombarded by the Venetians as they attacked the Turks. A direct hit caused an explosion that ripped out the cella wall and dislodged many sculptures. The victorious Venetians carried some off as trophies and others were left to ruin. Lord Elgin, the British ambassador to Turkey from 1799 to 1803, negotiated for the remaining sculptures, which he removed from the temple and shipped to England; his son later sold them (at a loss) to the British government. They are housed today in a climate-controlled wing of the British Museum. Well-meaning restorers in the nineteenth century

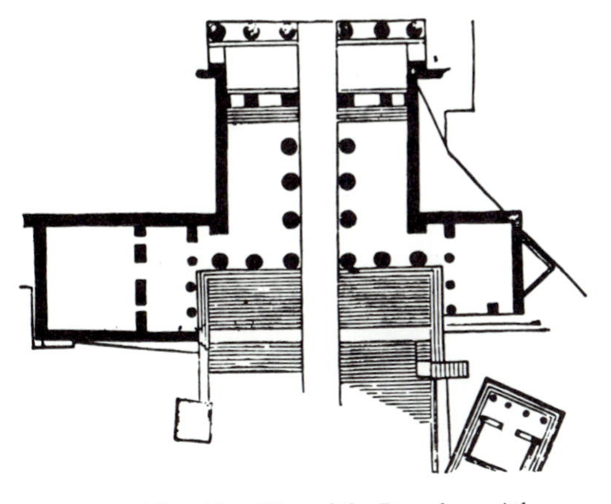

FIGURE 3.20 *Mnesicles: Plan of the Propylaea, Athens, begun 437* B.C. Common scale. (From F. Reber)

FIGURE 3.21 *Mnesicles: View of the Propylaea, Athens.* (From F. Reber)

FIGURE 3.22 *Mnesicles: Half section of the Propylaea, Athens.* (From J. Guadet)

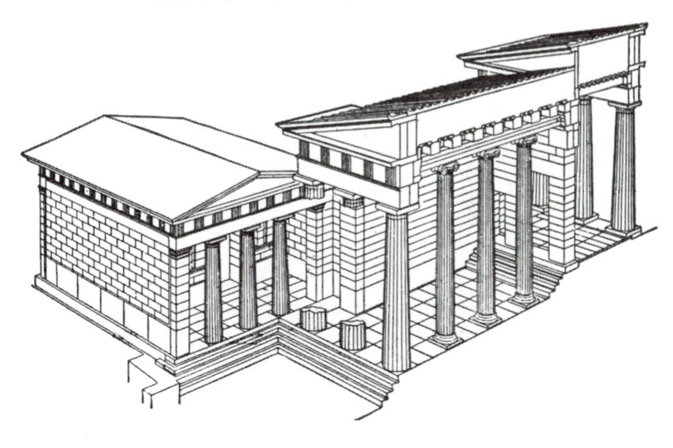

attempted to repair the Parthenon by using iron bars to replace the stolen metal clamps that had held the marble blocks in place. The iron has now rusted, causing structural problems for twentieth-century preservationists, who have had to remove the iron and replace it with stainless steel. Industrial air pollution is now the biggest threat. Sulfur dioxides combine with ever-present water vapor to form sulfuric acid, which is dissolving the marble.

The other buildings on the Athenian Acropolis are disposed in a manner that seems almost random yet is quite appropriate to the particular qualities of the site when experienced on foot. This emphasis on the individual character of each site is complemented by the proportions chosen for the temple itself. In the case of the Athenian Acropolis, the site is a plateau rising abruptly above the plain of the city below. From earliest times, the route of the Panathenaic Way from the civic and commercial center (the **Agora**) to the Acropolis traversed a winding, stepped path up the side of the escarpment. About 437 B.C. construction began on an appropriately scaled entrance gateway, the Propylaea, designed by the architect Mnesicles (Figure 3.20). Its plan had to accommodate several site restrictions: sacred sanctuaries on both sides, and an elevation change through the depth of the site.

The resulting design is asymmetrical, yet balanced, having a Doric portico flanked by projecting wings (Figure 3.21). The central intercolumniation is wider than the rest, reflecting the processional way that passed through the axial colonnaded space into the sacred precinct of the Acropolis itself. On either side of this walkway were three Ionic columns, used here because the rising ground level and scale of the space dictated the choice of a more slender column (Figure 3.22). A second Doric por-

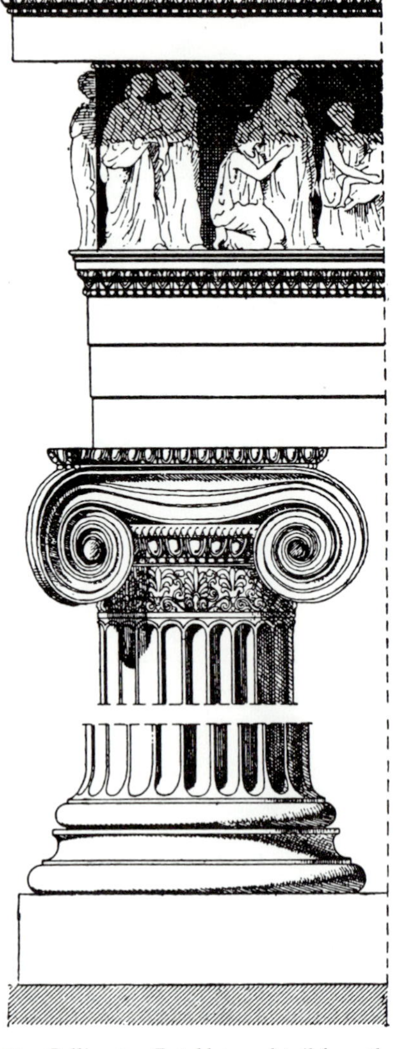

FIGURE 3.24 *Callicrates: Entablature detail from the Temple of Athena Nike, Athens.* (From J. Guadet)

tico terminated the Propylaea's central section. Its northern wing was the Pinacotheca or picture gallery, while on the south side was the small, freestanding Temple of Athena Nike.

A visitor coming onto the Athenian Acropolis would emerge from the eastern portico of the Propylaea to see a great statue of Athena close by, just left of center, balancing the majestic Parthenon, which rose farther back on the right side. Even though the entrance to Greek temples is placed axially, it was the intention of the architects of the Acropolis that visitors should first view the Parthenon from below, at an angle where the west pediment and long north colonnade presented the essence of the temple's volume at a single glance. One reached the sanctuary entrance by traversing a rising pathway running the length of the Parthenon and turning the corner to ascend the steps into the eastern portico. Only after experiencing the totality of the exterior would the drama of the interior be unfolded. Mnesicles's Propylaea both echoes the volume of the Parthenon and establishes the viewpoint that enhances the major temple on the Acropolis.

FIGURE 3.23 *Callicrates: Temple of Athena Nike, Athens, designed 448 B.C.* (Photo: Greek National Tourist Office)

Two other temples on the Acropolis deserve attention. The small Temple of Athena Nike (Athena Victorious) perches on the edge of the hilltop forward of the Propylaea (Figures 3.23, 3.24). It was designed ca. 448 B.C. by Callicrates as a simple sanctuary housing a wooden image of Athena holding her helmet and a pomegranate, the symbol of fertility. Four Ionic columns create a portico before the eastern entrance, and an identical set is placed at the western (rear) side, which is the elevation seen most clearly from below the acropolis.

Across from the northern side of the Parthenon is a more complex temple called the Erechtheum (Figure 3.25), begun ca. 421 B.C. on the site of the

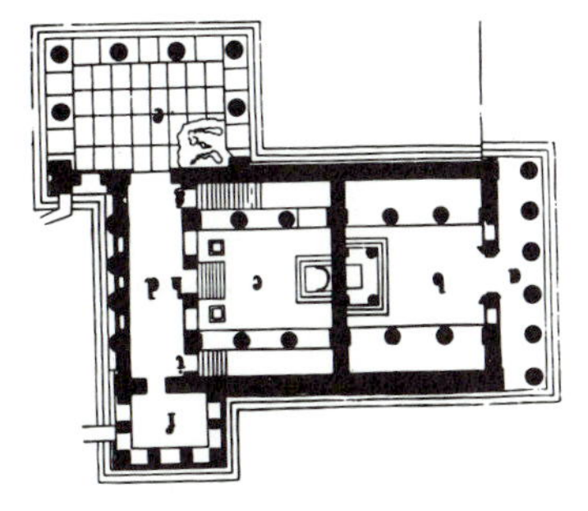

Figure 3.25 *Plan of the Erechtheum, Athens, begun ca. 421 B.C.* (From F. Reber)

Figure 3.26 *Corner of the north porch of the Erechtheum, Athens.* (From R. Sturgis)

Figure 3.27 *Caryatids from the south porch of the Erechtheum, Athens.* (From J. Guadet)

contest between Athena and Poseidon and of an olive tree sacred to Athena that had been destroyed by the Persians. Under the temple is the Sea of Erechtheus, a salt water spring that made the sound of the sea and had a rock bearing the mark of Poseidon's trident. The site was also sacred to Hephaistos and contained the tombs of ancient legendary kings of Athens, including Erechtheus. The temple is built on two different levels to accommodate the uneven ground. The eastern portico, distinguished by its slender Ionic columns, led to Athena's sanctuary, while the north porch, ten feet lower, gave access to Poseidon's shrine through an even more elongated Ionic portico (Figure 3.26). Four Ionic columns, partially engaged in the wall, extend across the western façade to the southern face, where the roof of the splendid porch facing the Parthenon is supported by six standing maidens, the **caryatids** (Figure 3.27). Their pose is graceful, with one knee bent slightly and drapery revealing the form beneath. As an example of the Ionic order,

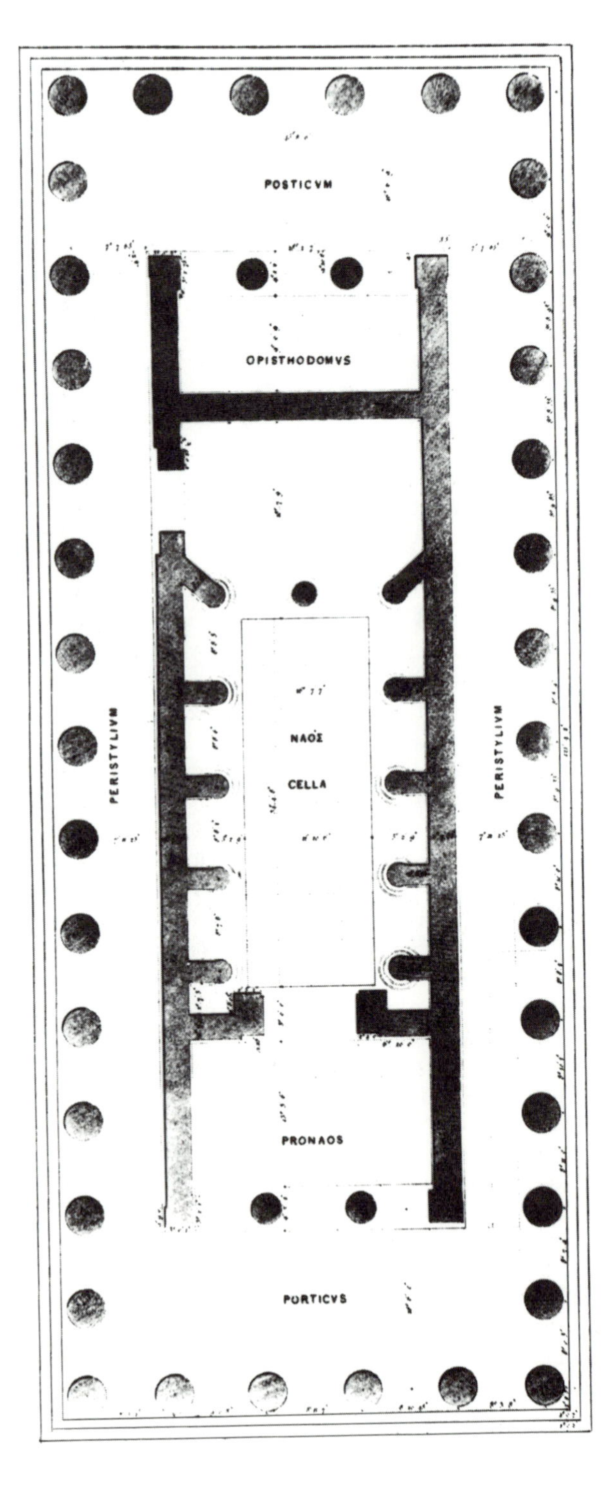

FIGURE 3.28 *Ictinus: Plan of the Temple of Apollo Epicurius, Bassae, ca. 450–425 B.C.* (From J. Stuart and N. Revett)

the elaborate detail of the Erechtheum has no equal in later Greek works, and the multiple complexities that have been united into a single temple are also exceptional in classical architecture. While its decorative detail may well have influenced the later Corinthian order, the form of the building was never repeated in antiquity.

Use of the Orders in Classical Architecture. The Doric order is intimately connected with the mainland of Greece. By contrast, the more ornate Ionic order reflects an oriental exuberance typical of its place of origin, the Ionian colonies along the western shores of present-day Turkey. After the fifth century B.C., there was a marked decline in the use of the Doric, possibly because of the meticulous sculptural ornamentation it required. For example, each flute in a Doric column has a precise edge, an **arris,** where the curved sections of adjacent flutes intersect, and these arrises must run absolutely straight up the shaft on every column. Doric also creates difficult design problems at external corners. The logic of the order is that triglyphs are placed above columns, with metopes in between. This works well until a

FIGURE 3.29 *Ictinus: Corinthian capital from the Temple of Apollo Epicurius, Bassae.* (From J. Stuart and N. Revett)

FIGURE 3.30 *Polykleitos: Soffit coffers from the Tholos, Epidaurus, ca. 360–330 B.C.* (Photo: Marburg)

corner must be turned, and the established rhythm would make two half-metopes intersect, an aesthetic impossibility. To avoid this, the final complete metope before the corner is generally elongated to allow the end triglyphs from both sides to meet at the corner. The Ionic and Corinthian orders overcome these problems by eliminating the troublesome features. The column flutes are jointed by flat **fillets** to simplify carving, and the frieze runs continuously without metopes or triglyphs.

The use of a particular order on the exterior of a building did not preclude the use of others within, as has already been seen in the Parthenon and the Propylaea. The Temple of Apollo Epicurius at Bassae (ca. 450–425 B.C.) (Figure 3.28), designed by Ictinus, employs all three orders: Doric for the external colonnade, Ionic for the cella side columns (which are connected to the cella wall by extended buttress-shaped **piers**), and Corinthian for the single axial column placed at the end of the cella (Figure 3.29). A statue of Apollo was set adjacent to this column so that it faced to the east through an opening in the cella wall. Among Greek temples, this one is unusual for its orientation, with the main entrance facing north, rather than east. The local limestone of which it is made has been finely worked to create a vigorous yet harmonious temple.

In classical Greek architecture relatively few buildings use the Corinthian order. One of the most celebrated is the Tholos at Epidaurus (ca. 360–330 B.C.), a circular temple approximately seventy-two feet in diameter. The external colonnade was composed of twenty-six Doric columns, and there were fourteen free-standing Corinthian columns in the inner circular colonnade fitted into a black-and-white rhomboidal flooring pattern. The ceiling had ornate **coffers** with floral decorations (Figure 3.30). An unused Corinthian capital found buried at the site shows the delicacy and grace achieved by Polykleitos, the architect of the Tholos. The corner volutes, derived from Ionic columns, are small, and their scroll form is complemented by the stylized curls of **acanthus** leaves that enrich the bell of the capital (Figure 3.31).

Equally famous (and in a better state of preservation) is the Choragic Monument of Lysicrates (ca. 334 B.C.) in Athens (Figure 3.32). This small cylindrical structure was erected to celebrate the victory of a chorus sponsored by Lysicrates in a song festival honoring the god Dionysus. Six Corinthian columns are built into the cylinder so that they appear as half-columns; the frieze they support illustrates the mythological story of Dionysus and the pirates of the Tyrrhenian Sea. There is no accessible interior space. Nineteenth-century American architects adapted the form of the Choragic Monument for quite varied purposes. It inspired the form of the Philadelphia Exchange and the cupola atop the dome of the Tennessee State Capitol in Nashville (see Figure 12.14), both works by William Strickland. Roman builders, who had a pronounced preference for elaboration, made extensive use of the Corinthian order, and they even invented a still-more ornate order, the Composite, for buildings where the Corinthian seemed too restrained.

When discussing the temples of ancient Greece, it is important not only to imagine them in a com-

FIGURE 3.31 *Polykleitos: Unused Corinthian capital from the Tholos, Epidaurus.* (From R. Sturgis)

FIGURE 3.32 *Choragic Monument of Lysicrates, Athens, ca. 334 B.C.* (From J. Guadet)

plete, unruined condition, but also to remember that the Greeks never saw their buildings as the bare stone sanctuaries we see today. Architectural and sculptural detail was always painted with gold and vibrant colors, and unarticulated walls may well have had murals to match. Traces of the original paint remain in protected crevices to confirm written accounts of the buildings' original appearances. If restored and repainted in authentic hues, Greek temples might well appear garish to modern eyes.

City Planning in the Classical and Hellenistic Periods. In discussing the buildings of the Acropolis in Athens, attention was paid to the experiential space that seems to have governed the placement and design of temples on the site. What appears in plan to be a haphazard arrangement unfolds before the visitor as a logical sequence in an ordered universe. The static poise of a colonnaded temple is enhanced by the subtle arts of the site planner, who has used surprise and a changing perspective to reveal the full drama of the architectural forms. A similar spatial approach was taken in the design of the Athenian Agora, the civic and commercial heart of the city, which developed around the Panathenaic Way that traverses the Agora along its diagonal as it extends from the city wall to the acropolis (Figure 3.33). On the west side of the Agora in classical times was the Doric Temple of Hephaistos, built ca. 449–444 B.C. on the side of a ridge overlooking the Agora and the Panathenaic Way (Figure 3.34). Civic structures, including a council house (**bouleuterion**) and a covered market (**stoa**), were built at the base of the rise, flanking the broad stairs leading to the temple above. Facing the diagonal path of the Panathenaic Way and set at right angles to the crest of the ridge was a longer market, the south stoa, which defined another side of the public space.

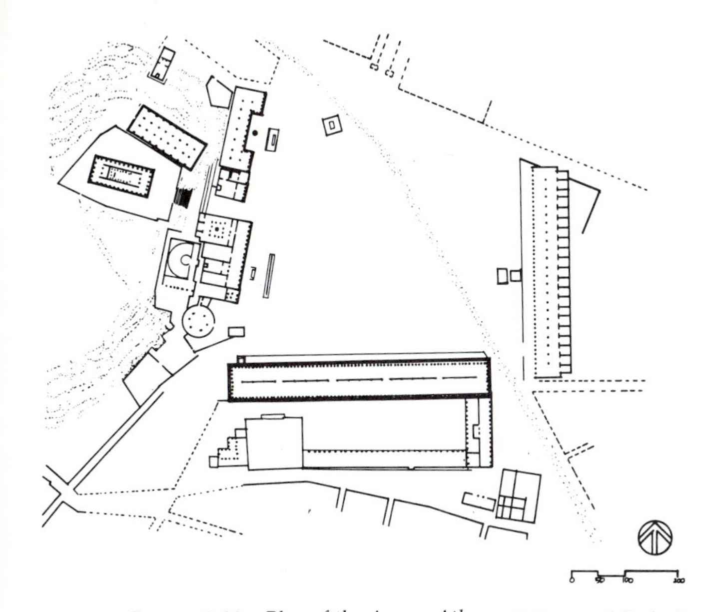

FIGURE 3.33 *Plan of the Agora, Athens.* (Delineator: P. Bushee)

FIGURE 3.34 *Temple of Hephaistos [Theseion], Athens, ca. 449–444 B.C.* The Parthenon is seen in the background. (From B. Taylor)

The Athenian Agora reached its full development after the conquests of Alexander the Great terminated the Classical Period in 332 B.C. During the period that followed, known as the Hellenistic era, Greek culture spread widely over the eastern Mediterranean and was assimilated into quite different artistic traditions as far away as India. In the Hellenistic period, some classical buildings of the Agora were modified, and other entirely new ones were constructed to create a more complete sense of spatial order and closure. The dominant Temple of Hephaistos and the axial approach established by it remained; the Bouleuterion was replaced by the more elaborate Metroön with an external colonnade fronting on the open civic space; and the south stoa was rebuilt on a shifted orientation with an additional middle stoa extending parallel to it in what had originally been open space. Across the Panathenaic Way, which remained unchanged, the Stoa of Attalos was erected at right angles to the middle stoa, and its southern end worked with the eastern terminus of the middle stoa to establish a narrow entrance, a contrast to the openness of the Agora beyond. From the colonnaded walkways of the stoas, one had a sense of shelter while at the same time being connected to the larger open space; the shadows of the covered space contrasted with the dazzling sunlight of the square.

Greek city planning was not always as asymmetrical and evolutionary in form as the Agora in Athens; the Greeks were perfectly capable of regular, orthogonal town plans and frequently employed them for colonial cities. Cities on the mainland grew rather organically over time, but colonies, planned in advance of settlement, were founded with a predetermined layout. In such cases, a grid design was both orderly and simple to lay out. Such was the case with Miletus, on the present-day coast of Turkey, in its day the leading city of Ionia (Figure 3.35). Its plan of rectangular residential blocks and an orthogonal Agora is credited to Hippodamus, a pupil of the great geometer, Pythagoras, but the idea of an orthogonal town probably predates Hippodamus. In the Agora at Miletus, Hippodamus created a formal arrangement of colonnaded stoas that complemented the right-angled residential districts while articulating the public space between the harbor and the undeveloped space beyond. Later expansions under Hellenistic and Roman direction became first more elaborate and finally more compartmentalized, but the basic rhythms established by Hippodamus survived through seven centuries of use and enlargement.

The layout of Miletus influenced that of Priene, even though Priene's site on the shores of Asia Minor was a hillside sloping diagonally across the grid of streets (Figure 3.36). These conditions provided good cross-ventilation through the narrow streets,

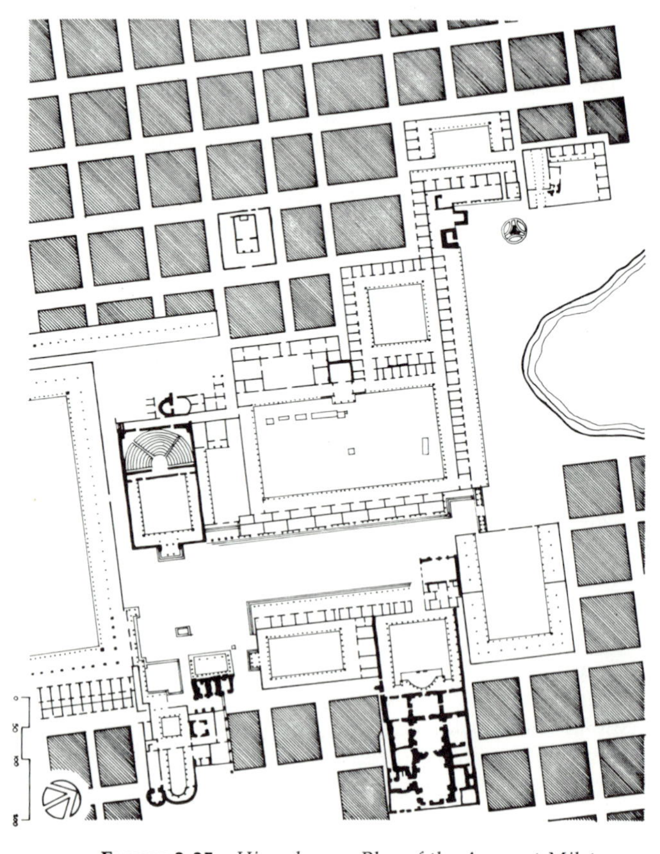

FIGURE 3.35 *Hippodamus: Plan of the Agora at Miletus.* (Delineator: W. Wheeler)

a not inconsiderable advantage considering the primitive sanitation arrangements. The Agora was defined on three sides by a continuous colonnaded stoa and completed on the north side by a raised stoa set parallel to the east-west street that entered the space. Above the Agora was the Temple of Athena, built on a promontory just northwest of the civic space and accessed by another major east-west street higher up the slope; this street also passed the theater. North-south circulation was achieved through narrower stepped streets following the contour of the ground. In contrast to the carefully designed public spaces, the residential blocks appear mundane, and the houses seem unremarkable, simply basic shelters for sleeping and eating. In this one can see the value Greek culture placed on public life. Free men in its democratic cities spent most of their waking hours out-of-doors in the company of others, and the noblest occupations were those involving the human mind: literature, philosophy, the arts and sciences, and politics. Manual work, although essential to society, was disparaged and relegated to slaves or other menials.

During the Hellenistic period, both architecture and city planning became more elaborate and theatrical, as can be seen in the design of Pergamon, where a large acropolis with temples and public buildings is set perpendicular to the outer edge of a theater constructed on the hillside. Originally the site was a fortress hill rather similar to the Athenian Acropolis, but in the second century B.C. it was embellished with monumental buildings to celebrate military victories over the Gauls. At the head of a wide flight of stairs there was a Great Altar dedicated to Zeus and Athena, and the high **plinth** on which the temple stood became the location for a frieze over 300 feet long sculpted with scenes of battles between gods and giants (Figure 3.37). Their intertwined wings, arms, and writhing snake bodies create a dynamic composition: even the hair on the gods' heads and beards falls in animated coils.

In the fourth century B.C. theater designs became increasingly sophisticated circular constructions set into hillsides to focus on the orchestra at the center below, where the drama took place, framed by the **skene** or backdrop building. Acoustics are particularly important in the theater, so special recesses were built behind the seating to trap unwanted reverberations and enhance the clarity of the human voice. In theaters such as that at Epidaurus (ca. 350 B.C.), where the original construction is largely intact, the acoustic system still works (Figure 3.38). Words spoken in a normal voice from the orchestra project intelligibly to all 5000 seats in the theater.

After the conquests of Alexander the Great, the independence and seclusion of city-states on the mainland of Greece stood in the way of any larger alliance for mutual defense, and the colonial cities were slowly lost to expanding powers in Italy and the Crimea. It was on the western side of the Italian peninsula, in Rome, that the next great culture was developing. The Greek mainland itself became a Ro-

FIGURE 3.36 *Plan of Priene.* (From W. Blaser)

FIGURE 3.38 *Theater, Epidaurus.* (Photo: Greek National Tourist Office)

FIGURE 3.37 *Temple of Zeus at Pergamon, second century B.C.* (Photo: Staatliche Museen, Berlin)

man colony in 146 B.C., but much of its artistic legacy had long since been transmitted to the civilized world.

ITALY: THE ETRUSCANS

During the first millennium, while Greek civilization originated and flourished on the mainland and around the eastern Mediterranean, an enigmatic people, the Etruscans, were settling and developing their own culture in the area of north-central Italy, presently known as Tuscany. The origins of the

Etruscans are not precisely understood; they are thought to have migrated onto the Italian peninsula from Asia Minor ca. 1200 B.C. From surviving inscriptions, art, artifacts, and architecture, it seems that the Etruscans drew on diverse cultural roots. Their language contained both Indo-European and non-Indo-European elements and was written in a script derived from Greek; their religion had much in common with that of Egypt; and their art shares with the Hittites carved reliefs of protective beasts at tomb entrances and with the Minoans and Mycenaeans naturalistic decorations depicting birds and dolphins. The Etruscan practice of reading omens from the entrails of animals follows that of Babylonia and Assyria, and their use of the arch and vault in monumental gateways indicates links with the architecture of Asia Minor. Despite all these connections the Etruscans were an original people whose accomplishments left distinct imprints on Roman civilization.

Etruscan settlements were loosely organized into independent city-states rather like those in Mesopotamia and Greece, and their economy was based on trade, especially in metals: tin from Britain, silver from Spain, and widely available iron and copper. Etruscan culture was well established by the eighth century B.C. and grew in influence for the next 200 years to encompass the area from the River Po in northern Italy to the region around Pompeii, south of Rome. Some of their cities, such as Marzabotto (Figure 3.39) near Bologna, had a grid plan, with the main streets running perpendicular to one another and intersecting in the center of town. The Romans, who would use similar plans for their military camps (*castra*), labeled the main north-south street the *cardo* and the east-west route the *decumanus*. The orthogonal plan may have owed something to colonial Greek cities; through trading contacts with the Greeks, the Etruscans were in a position to know of developments there.

It seems clear that the Etruscans borrowed the orders of architecture and the temple form from Greece, modifying both to suit their own purposes. Greek temples generally had a continuous colonnade surrounding the sanctuary at the center, with entrances on both gabled ends. In contrast, the Etruscan temple typically contained a three-compartmented cella oriented in only one direction,

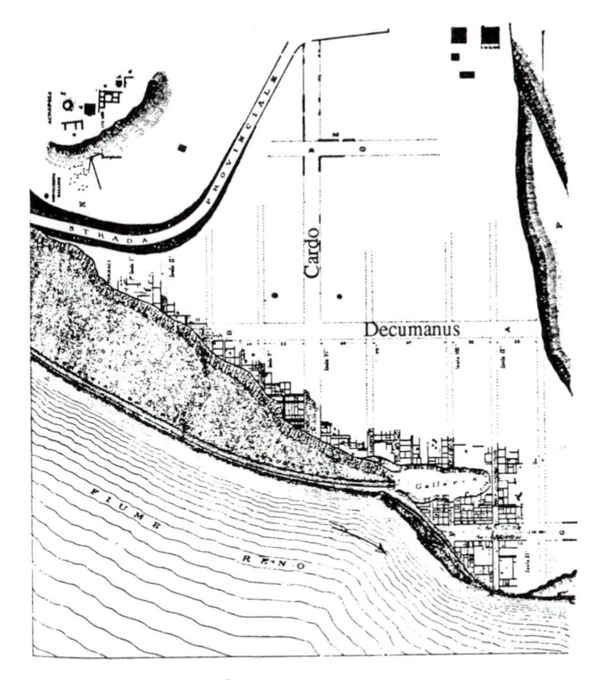

FIGURE 3.39 *Marzabotto.* (From P. Ducati)

FIGURE 3.40 *Etruscan Temple according to Vitruvius.* (From F. Reber)

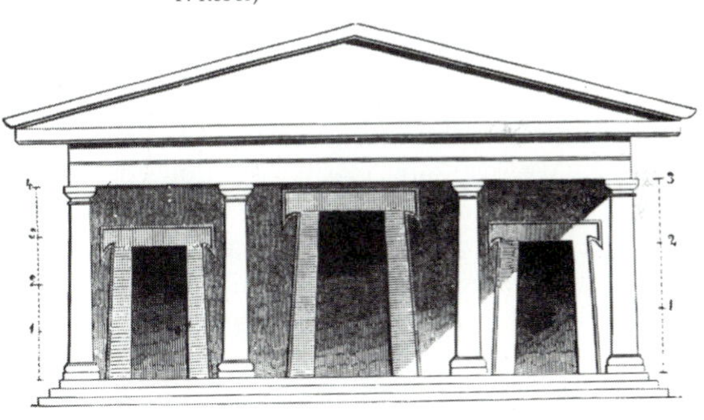

generally to the south. The temple was set on a high podium, covered with a gable roof, and approached through a double row of columns set at the top of a single flight of stairs (Figure 3.40). The intricate refinement of Doric and Ionic was forsaken for a greatly simplified original order, the Tuscan, which had the basic characteristics of Doric but no fluting on the column shafts or sculpture on the frieze. Intercolumnar spacing on Etruscan temples was

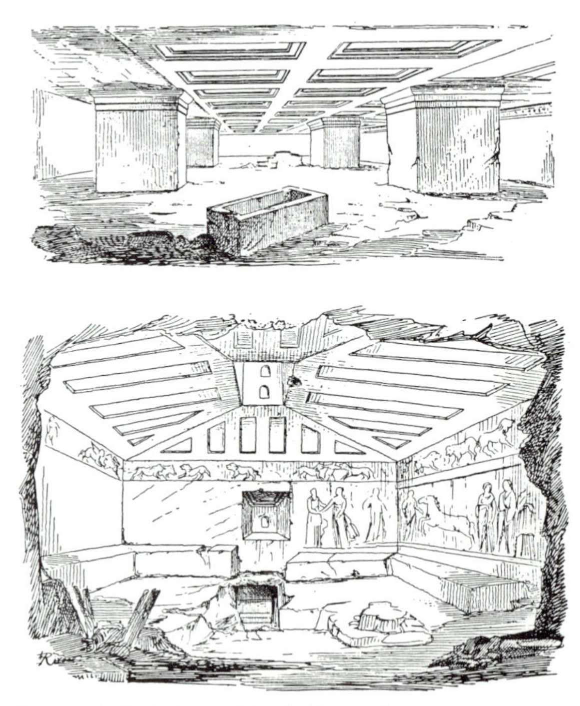

FIGURE 3.41 *Interior of tomb, Cerveteri.* (From J. Guadet)

FIGURE 3.42 *Gateway, Perugia, after 310 B.C.* (From J. Guadet)

markedly wider, the roof pitch considerably lower, and the eave overhang greater than on Greek temples, giving Etruscan work the general impression of squat proportions. Both the columns and roof structure were built of wood, while the walls were unbaked brick; terra-cotta was employed for roofing tiles, pediment ornamentation, and sculpture.

Because of their impermanent materials, no Etruscan temples survive, although literary and archaeological sources provide adequate evidence of their forms. Etruscan architectural remains are scarce, and much of what is known about residential designs has been deduced from tomb architecture and funerary urns made in the shape of miniature dwellings. Tomb excavations at Cerveteri give an impression of upper-class housing. The rooms, hollowed out of volcanic rock (tufa), are entered through a vestibule and grouped around an inner court, which suggests an **atrium** (Figure 3.41). In some tombs, the architectural features of doors, roof beams, and moldings have been reproduced, and furnishings, such as chairs, cooking utensils, and other household items, are likewise carved in stone.

At Perugia, which was the Etruscan city of Perusia, there still exists a monumental gateway (the so-called Arch of Augustus) illustrating Etruscan influence, although it dates after the fall of Perugia to the Romans in 310 B.C. (Figure 3.42). Above the double row of voussoirs forming the gateway arch is a decorative motif consisting of metopes and triglyphs similar to a Doric frieze. Circular shields fill the spaces of the metopes, and the triglyphs are actually short fluted pilasters with volutes at the top.

A relieving arch flanked by Ionic pilasters is set atop the band of Doric-inspired ornament. In borrowing from the Greeks, the Etruscans have used elements of the orders with originality, if not with understanding. Later the Romans would forge a coherent and powerful architectural style by employing the arch and vault for structure and using the orders to articulate and enliven the intervening sections of wall.

The Etruscans, together with native Italian peoples, the Latins and the Sabines, inhabited the hills that rose above the marshlands on either side of the Tiber River. Etruscan builders began to drain the marshes by digging the trench that later became the Cloaca Maxima, the major sewer of ancient Rome. According to legend the city of Rome was founded on these hills in 753 B.C. by Romulus, and it was ruled from 616 to 510 B.C. by members of the Etruscan royal house, the Tarquins. In about 500 B.C., the Latins overthrew the Tarquins and began the Roman Republic, which will be discussed in the next chapter. The expulsion of Etruscan rulers from Rome did not signal their disappearance from Italy, however; other city-states to the north continued to thrive even as Roman authority was growing. From 396 to 88 B.C. Roman forces gradually conquered the northern Etruscan towns, but not before many aspects of Etruscan culture were assimilated into Roman life. Their art and architecture merged into Roman work, and Etruscan customs, such as chariot racing and bloody gladiatorial contests, would continue in Roman society.

4.

ROMAN ARCHITECTURE

An account of the beginnings of Roman architecture might have been considered chronologically in the first millennium, for the civilization based in Rome was contemporary with those of the Greeks, the Etruscans, and the later Egyptians. Unlike all these cultures, however, Rome continued to grow in importance as the first millennium B.C. waned, reaching its apogee in the first and second centuries A.D. In time Rome absorbed the Etruscans, the Greeks, the Egyptians, and many lesser peoples and formed an empire with a remarkably homogeneous architectural style. Roman building practices, like Roman culture, were derived from many sources, especially Etruscan and Greek, but the forms of their architecture were in many respects original.

The Romans were practical builders. They constructed durable roads and bridges across the length and breadth of their empire; they brought clean water into cities through a series of **aqueducts;** and they carried away waste water in underground sewers. They also created impressive buildings, making extensive use of the decorative orders (most notably the Corinthian and Composite) on temples and other public structures and constructing some of the most awe-inspiring interior spaces in the western world. The Romans used their technical skills in building to provide comfort. They invented central heating under the floor for houses in colder climates, and they built large heated baths for public use in all their cities. They also enjoyed public amusements and spectacles, and their architects developed amphitheaters and stadiums to accommodate crowds for athletic events, gladiatorial fights, and pageants. The Romans built much and they built well, so that a surprising amount of their work survives in whole or in part for modern study.

BUILDING TECHNIQUES AND MATERIALS

The imposing quality of Roman construction derived from engineering skill applied to the problems encountered in everyday life. Roman construction exploited the arch, the vault, and the dome, building techniques developed by other civilizations but used in a very limited fashion. In Roman hands, however, these became the basis for hitherto unimagined structures with a freedom in plan not available with post-and-lintel construction.

A true arch consists of wedge-shaped stones (called voussoirs) set in a curved shape, generally a semicircle. Building one requires a temporary timber formwork or centering to support the voussoirs as they are laid, for the arch will not stand on its own until all the voussoirs, including the central **keystone,** are set in place. (Contrast this to the technique of corbeling, where each course rests on the preceding one. No centering is required, for the structure is always stable, but the form produced is not a true arch.) If the arch is continued horizontally, it produces a covering known as a vault; if the arch is rotated on its center, it produces a dome. By using arches, vaults, and domes, the Romans could enclose large areas with modestly sized stones cut carefully to shape. The space between supports, necessarily limited when stone lintels are used because the stone tends to crack under wide spans, could now be made much larger because vaulted construction carries the structural load primarily in compression, for which stone is well-suited. There is a price for this flexibility. The weight of the masonry in vaulted construction pushes downward and outward on the walls or columns on which it rests, and this overturning force or thrust must be countered by massive supports. Vaulted construction thus requires walls or piers that are much thicker than those used in post-and-lintel buildings.

The earliest Roman vaults were built for utilitarian structures. Mention has already been made of the Cloaca Maxima (Figure 4.1), the trench begun by the Etruscans to drain the Roman marshes. By the mid-first century B.C., it was vaulted with stone, and the construction still functions as one of the main sewers of Rome. Discharging wastes into the Tiber, however, made the river water unfit for human consumption, so fresh water for the city was brought from rivers or springs in the Sabine Hills beyond Rome. The water was piped in a gravity-fed system of aqueducts to city reservoirs, then distributed to fountains or other uses around the city. As much as possible, the aqueduct followed the contour of the land, but where it had to cross valleys, it became necessary to elevate the conduit above the land to preserve the constant slope of the supply line. The Romans erected handsome arched structures for this purpose. They completed the Aqua Appia in 312 B.C. and constructed three more aqueducts in the second half of the second century B.C. to provide water for the growing population of Rome. They added the impressive Aqua Claudia in 38 A.D., to bring water from Tivoli, some forty-five miles away; the aqueduct's great masonry arches, some over one hundred feet high, extended over the countryside for much of that distance.

FIGURE 4.1 *Cloaca Maxima, Rome.* (From F. Reber)

Perhaps the most spectacular surviving aqueduct span is the Pont du Gard (20–16 B.C.) outside Nîmes in southern France (Figure 4.2). Made of unmortared masonry (*opus quadratum*), the aqueduct strides 882 feet over the valley of the Gardon River on three tiers of arches, carrying the water channel 160 feet above the level of the river. Its design is deceptively straightforward: the two lowest arch levels are identical rows of semicircular arches, sixty feet in diameter except for the span across the river, which is eighty feet. The uppermost tier has arches set on twenty-foot centers, so that a unifying rhythm ties all three levels together. The projecting stones remaining for support of the centering and scaffolding add surface texture, and they were retained in case repairs were ever needed. Enclosed above the highest arches is the water channel, lined with mortar to prevent leaks. A roadway is carried above the lowest row of arches.

In Nîmes itself, the so-called Temple of Diana (ca. 80 A.D.) illustrates masonry construction applied to a building (Figure 4.3). The interior space was covered by a series of semicircular arches supporting intermediate stones to create the **barrel vault** (Figure 4.4); a thousand years later Romanesque church builders would revive this roofing system.

Relatively little of Roman vaulted construction is made in cut-stone masonry, however, for the technique was costly and required skilled workmen. The efficient Romans developed a more expedient building method by using a new material, hydraulic

FIGURE 4.2 *Pont du Gard, Nîmes, 20–16* B.C. (Photo: Marburg)

FIGURE 4.3 *Plan of the Temple of Diana, Nîmes, ca. 80* A.D. (From J. Guadet)

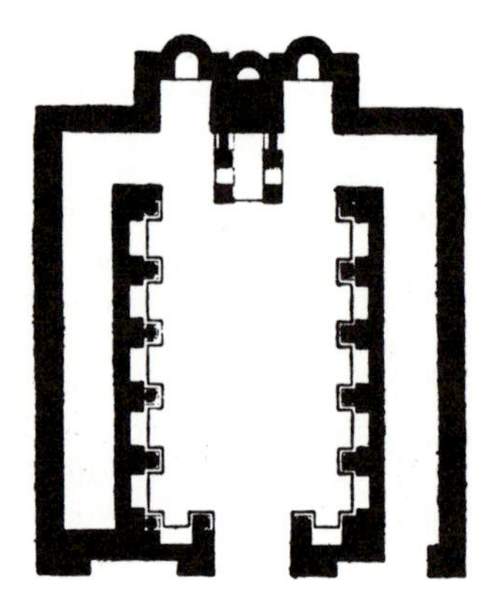

cement, derived from volcanic deposits first discovered around Puteoli (Pozzuoli) and named pozzolana. It was the naturally occurring equivalent of present-day manufactured cements, but the Romans did not use it in exactly the same manner as twentieth century builders do, although the principle is the same. The special quality of hydraulic cements that makes them useful in building is that, when mixed with water, they react chemically and harden to a stonelike consistency even if under water. The simple lime mortars known to the ancients had some bonding strength but were ineffective for the bridge and harbor foundations where Roman builders first exploited the superior strength of pozzolana.

The Romans also found uses for the artificial stone away from the water, and during the third century B.C. they gained experience in building with concrete. They placed a liquid mass composed of pozzolana, sand, water, and lime in horizontal courses over rough-laid rubble, which served both as aggregate in the wall and as an enclosure or form for the cement. The mixture solidified into a monolithic material that behaved like solid masonry. Curves and irregular shapes were of course much easier to obtain in concrete than in cut-stone work, but the resulting walls were generally not handsome, so the Romans became adept at nonstructural wall finishes such as stucco, **mosaic,** and marble veneer.

Because most buildings have lost their finish surfaces, one can see the underlying wall construction more easily today than Roman builders intended. Early concrete walls were composed of rough stones inserted into the concrete core (*opus incertum*), a technique later refined to shaped stones (*opus reticulatum*) which gave a more orderly exterior face. In imperial times (after 44 B.C.) the Romans increasingly used bricks as the concrete facing/aggregate (*opus testaceum*), laying their thin triangular shapes to present a smooth exterior and an irregular inner face for maximum bonding surface with the cement mixture (Figure 4.5). (Stamps impressed on the wet bricks in the factory have enabled archaeologists to date many Roman structures with reasonable precision.) After the second century A.D. concrete walls with stone rubble striped by horizontal courses of brick bonding every three or four feet (*opus listatum*) became common; the brick courses were both a horizontal tie and a leveling device to keep the work plumb and true. The strength, durability, and economy of concrete construction gave the Romans a versatile material for large-scale building, and by the middle of the first century A.D., they used it with rapidly increasing architectural sophistication.

FIGURE 4.4 *Temple of Diana, Nîmes.* (Photo: Moffett)

CITY PLANNING

City planning practices in ancient Greece and Rome had striking parallels. Both Athens and Rome, the cultural centers, grew without overall plans, while the colonial cities established by each were generally provided with orthogonal plans. Greek foundations might become Roman settlements later, as was the case with Pompeii (Figure 4.6), one of the best preserved examples of a Roman provincial town owing to its destruction in the eruption of Mount Vesuvius in 79 A.D. The fabric of the city, already shaken by an earthquake in 62 A.D., was engulfed by ash, lava, and mud, which preserved it until excavations begun in 1748 brought the remains to light.

Pompeii originated in the sixth century B.C. as a Greek settlement; it was later inhabited by the Etruscans, and by the time of its destruction, it had a population of about 20,000 people, encompassing great patrician families, middle-class merchants, and slaves. Its irregular grid plan covered about 160 acres within roughly oval town walls; the Roman civic center or **forum** was located in the southwest quarter, near the Marine Gate entrance. The earlier Greek center was two blocks to the east, on an acropolis with a Doric temple and a columned portico dating from the second or third century B.C. Streets ran approximately parallel and perpendicular from the Forum, their pattern being adjusted to the varying topography.

Public facilities were dispersed around the town. There were three baths, a large exercise facility (the

FIGURE 4.5 *Roman wall construction, with brick and stone facing a concrete core.* (From E. Viollet-le-Duc)

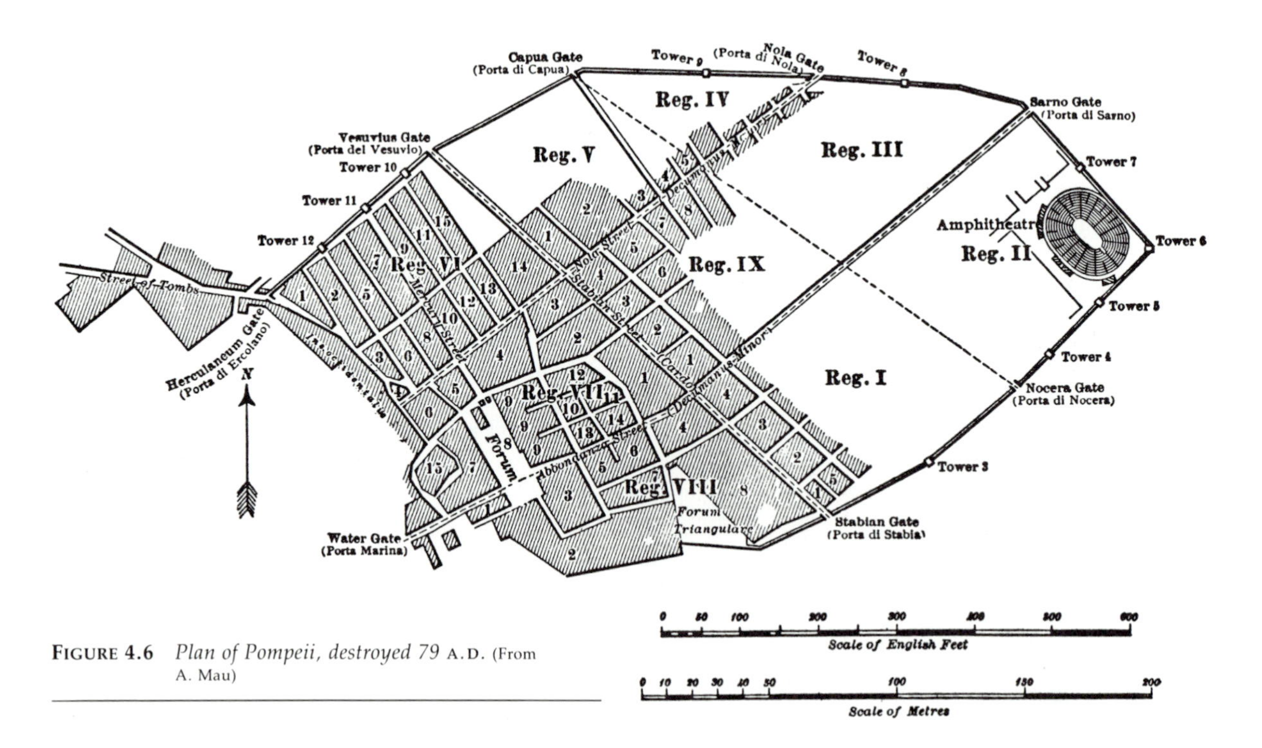

FIGURE 4.6 *Plan of Pompeii, destroyed 79* A.D. (From A. Mau)

palaestra) with a swimming pool, covered and open-air theaters, and an amphitheater capable of seating the entire population. Nine temples dedicated to various gods — Greek divinities, Roman deities, deceased Roman emperors, and the oriental mystery cults of Isis and Bacchus — indicate the diversity of religious beliefs in Pompeii. Cemeteries were located outside the town gates.

The Roman Forum in Pompeii was the focus of public life (Figure 4.7). A two-story colonnade surrounded its rectangular form, 510 by 125 feet, on three sides, the open fourth (north) side being occupied by the Capitolium, the center for state-sponsored religious observances (Figure 4.8). A triumphal arch marked the north entrance and prevented wheeled vehicles from intruding on the pedestrian domain. Buildings of various designs and uses flanked the Forum. On the east side were the Macellum, the meat and fish market; the Lararium, a temple for the patron gods of the city; the Eumachia building, containing guild offices of the cloth workers and dyers; and the Comitium, an open area where elections were held. The short southern side contained three halls used for governmental activities: offices for judges, public works officials, and the council chamber. On the west side, bordered by the road from the Marine Gate, was the large **Basilica,** where public assemblies for legal, commercial, and social purposes were held; it functioned much as the stoa in the Athenian Agora did, yet the space here was introverted and enclosed rather than being outwardly oriented, as at Athens. Beyond the Basilica were the Temple of Apollo, which dated from the earliest period of Pompeii; the vegetable market, one of the last buildings constructed on the Forum; and public lavatories. The use of colonnades linking most of the buildings gave the Forum architectural harmony. Conveying unity within such a diverse grouping of buildings constructed over three or more centuries is no insignificant accomplishment, and it indicates the high quality of Roman civic design attained even in provincial centers.

Some Roman cities began as military camps (*castra*) located in unsettled areas as a means of defense and of bringing civilization to new territories. For these, and for many colonial cities as well, the Ro-

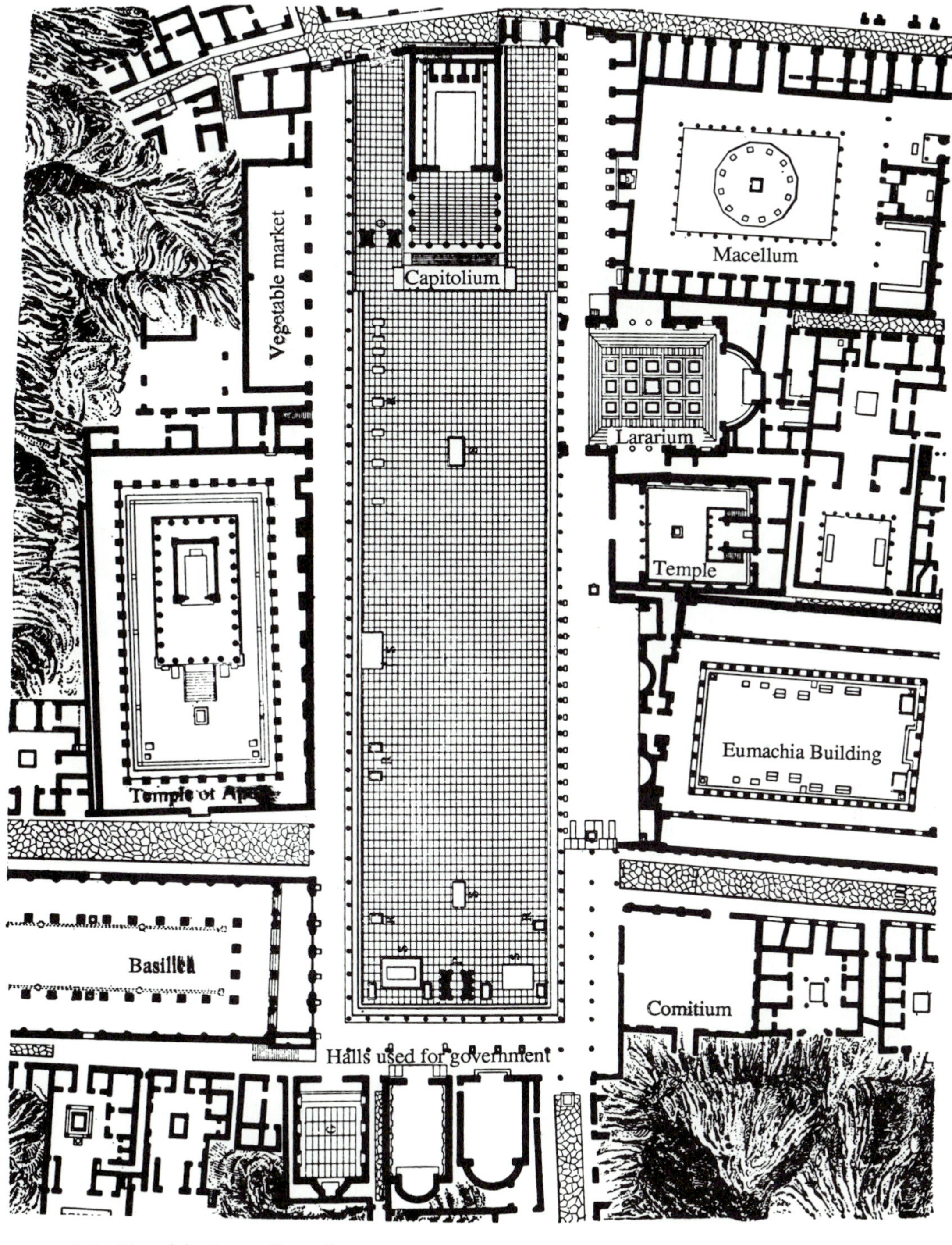

FIGURE 4.7 *Plan of the Forum, Pompeii.* (From R. Sturgis)

FIGURE 4.8 *View of the Forum, Pompeii, looking toward the ruins of the Capitolium.* (Photo: Special Collections Library, University of Tennessee)

mans had a standard plan, derived from the Etruscans and applied with consistency throughout their empire, from Britain to North Africa, Italy, and the eastern Mediterranean. The basic plan was rectangular or square, with two main roads, the *cardo* and the *decumanus,* crossing at right angles in the center of town. A wall surrounded the encampment, and the public spaces — the forum and military headquarters — were located, usually in one quadrant, at the intersection in the center of town. Residential sectors were laid out in square or rectangular blocks with land reserved for neighborhood markets and recreational facilities as the town grew. Streets could be numbered sequentially so that a stranger in town could find a given address easily. Large public buildings, such as baths and theaters, served the whole community.

This standard Roman plan underlies many present-day European cities, including Florence, Bologna, Cirencester, and Trier. Timgad in Algeria (Figure 4.9) is an example of one of these not overbuilt by a modern city; its major features can be seen even though it is a ruin today. Timgad was founded by Trajan in 100 A.D. for veterans of the Roman legions and became a thriving regional center until it was destroyed by native tribes in the seventh century. The city walls enclosed a square; the *cardo* and *decumanus* intersected in the center of town, with the forum to the south; and a large theater was set just south of the forum. (Because of the theater's placement, the *cardo* did not continue through the forum.) Entrances into the city were framed by triumphal arches, and continuous colonnades lined the major streets to lend dignity and shelter to the

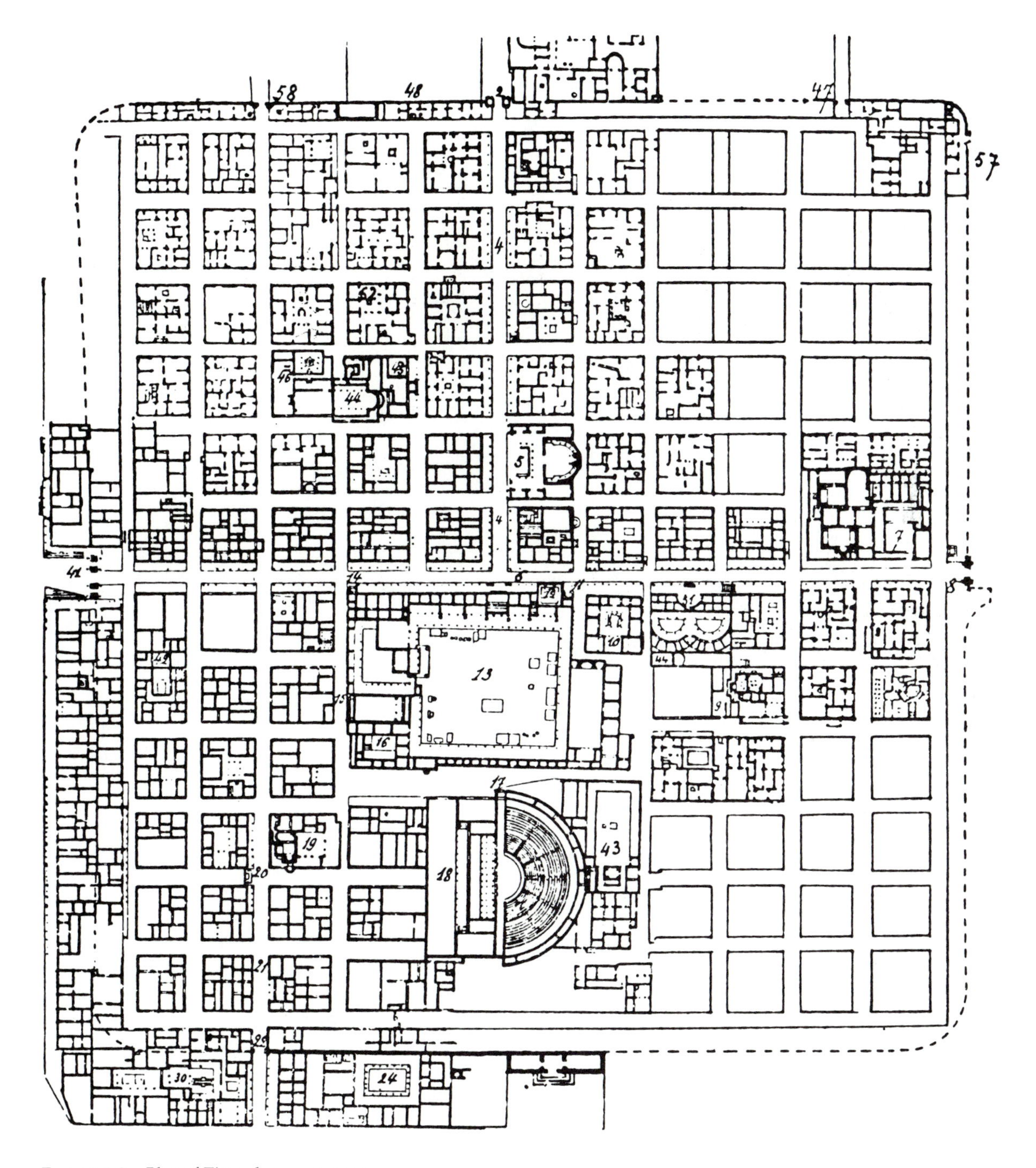

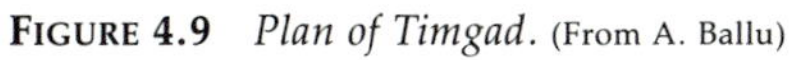
FIGURE 4.9 *Plan of Timgad.* (From A. Ballu)

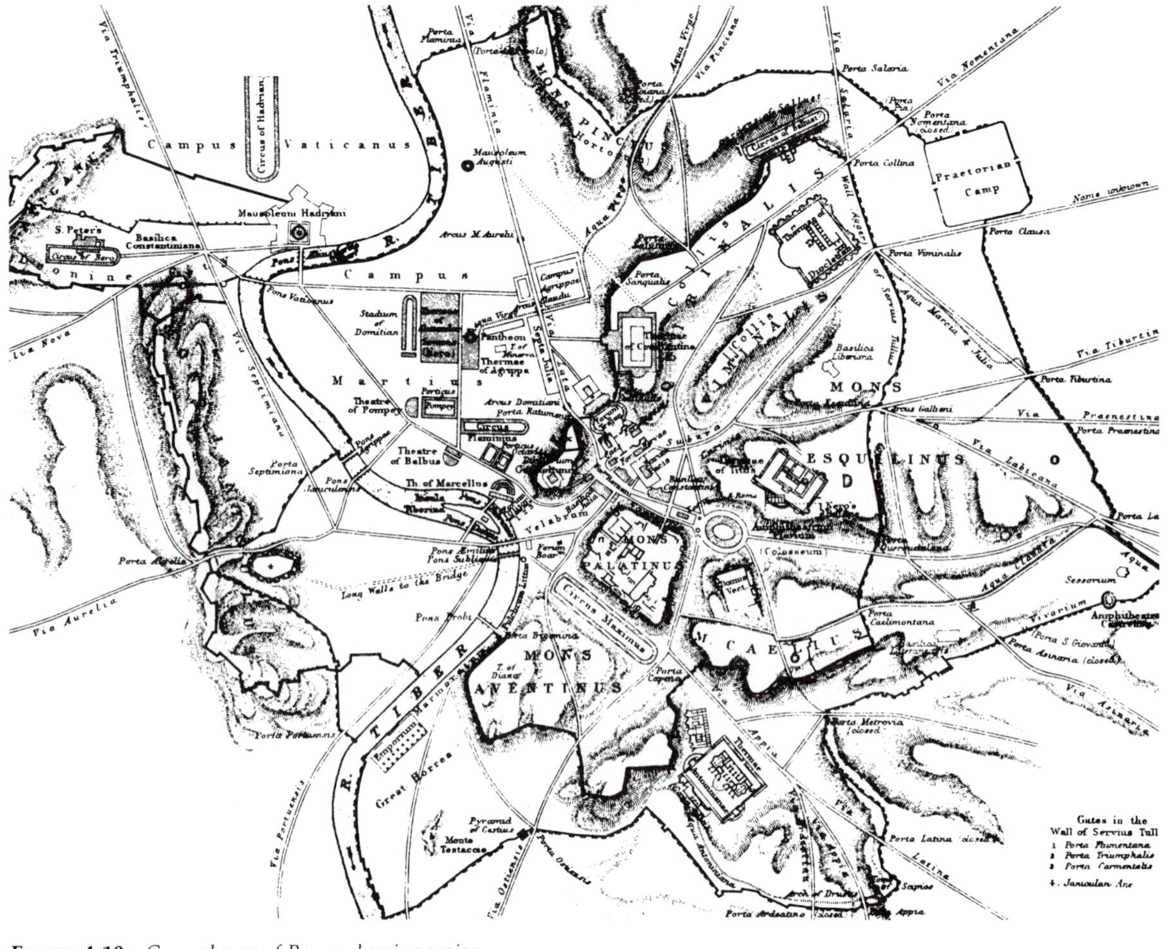

FIGURE 4.10 *General map of Rome, showing major monuments and aqueducts.* (From R. Lanciani)

sidewalks. Timgad prospered, having a population of perhaps 15,000 within a century of its founding, and in the third century it began to accumulate suburban developments along the approach roads to the north, west, and south. Large baths were built north and south of the walls, and markets and temples further served the expanding population outside the walls. None of the extramural growth conformed to the grid plan of the city proper.

Trajan is also remembered for the substantial contributions he made to the urban fabric of Rome itself (Figure 4.10). Civic life in Rome focused on the Forum Romanum at the base of the Capitoline Hill in an area drained by the Cloaca Maxima. Here the functions of commerce, government, law, and religion mingled, and with the growth of the city, the space became increasingly congested. From the middle of the first century B.C. onward the area expanded as new colonnaded forums were constructed adjacent to the existing fabric. Julius Caesar laid out a forum containing a temple and governmental chambers; Augustus constructed a forum at

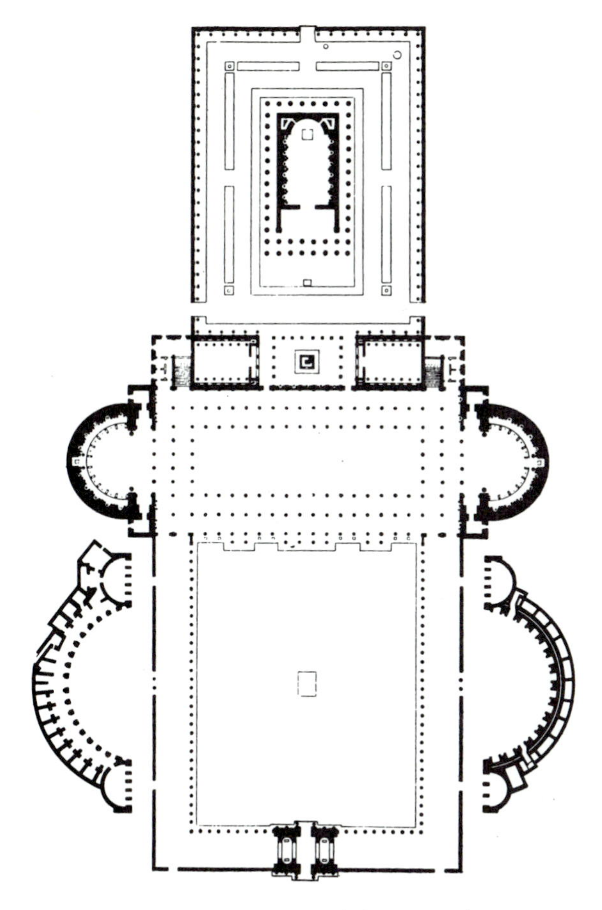

FIGURE 4.11 *Apollodorus: Plan of the Forum of Trajan, Rome, ca. 100–114* A.D. (From J. Guadet)

right angles to the Forum of Caesar to surround the Temple of Mars Ultor; and Vespasian built a forum around a library. Culminating these constructions was the Forum of Trajan (ca. 100–114), equal in size to all the others put together and built to designs of Apollodorus of Damascus, who had served with distinction as a military engineer (Figure 4.11). The site was north of the Forum of Augustus, where a ridge connecting the Capitoline and Quirinale hills was removed to provide a level area and improve access to all the forums from the north. Trajan's Forum was symmetrically planned, with a monumental entranceway from the Forum of Augustus leading into the forum proper, a court 330 by 375 feet defined by double colonnades and hemicycles set on a cross-axis. Dominating the center of the court was a large equestrian statue of Trajan. Opposite the entrance was the Basilica Ulpia, a magnificent judicial building with entrances placed on its long side. Beyond the Basilica was Trajan's Column, a marble shaft nearly one hundred feet high set on a fifteen-foot-high base and carved with a spiraling narrative relief illustrating Trajan's victories in the Dacian Wars; the spoils from the Dacian campaign were used to finance the forum's construction. The Column, which still survives, was flanked by two library buildings, one for Greek and one for Latin texts, now both gone. At the terminus of the axis was a temple, dedicated to Trajan and his wife by the later emperor Hadrian; the temple was set at the center of a curving colonnaded courtyard.

Needed commercial space adjacent to the Forum was carved out of the Quirinale hillside behind the northeast hemicycle. The buildings of Trajan's markets were set in a multistory semicircle with adjoining buildings, reflecting the hemicycle of the Forum below and becoming an arcaded complement to it (Figure 4.12). The markets contained over 150 shops, offices, and a vaulted market hall (Figure 4.13), all of which could be reached from the Forum and from streets on two higher levels. They were built of brick-faced concrete, a contrast to the marble and elaborate ornament of the Forum; durable

FIGURE 4.12 *Apollodorus: Trajan's Markets, Rome.* (Photo: Wodehouse)

FIGURE 4.13 *Apollodorus: Hall in Trajan's Markets, Rome.* (Photo: Wodehouse)

barrel vaults provided the basic structural module both for the individual shops and for enclosed walkways between them. Trajan's Forum and the markets, show at once the monumentality of great civic constructions and the ingenious adaptation of geometric forms to a fundamentally utilitarian project.

TEMPLES

Discussions of the Roman forums have indicated the locations of temples, which the Romans built largely on the basis of Greek and Etruscan precedent. Generally speaking, the Romans did not build temples as free-standing elements (as the Greeks had), but as axially approached buildings in an urban setting, like the temples of the Etruscans. The placement of the Capitolium in the forum at Pompeii and the Temple of Mars Ultor in the Forum of Augustus in Rome was essentially the same, and the temple designs were similar. Both were set on podiums, so that a flight of steps led up to the colonnaded portico of the cella space.

As the Capitolium and the Temple of Mars Ultor are largely destroyed, smaller Roman temples that have survived more completely provide a better image of temple architecture. In Rome the second-century B.C. Temple of Fortuna Virilis (Figure 4.14) superficially resembles an Ionic Greek temple until a closer look at the side elevation reveals that the columns are engaged in the cella wall and not free-standing. Expanding the cella to the limits of the surrounding colonnade provides a larger interior space and reinforces the axiality of the whole. This same theme is seen at the Maison Carrée at Nîmes (ca. 20 B.C.) (Figure 4.15), where the order is Ionic rather than Corinthian and the scale is larger, but the essential qualities remain. (Thomas Jefferson would later model his scheme for the Virginia State Capitol in Richmond on the Maison Carrée.)

Not all Roman temples were rectangular. The Greeks had built **tholoi,** and the Romans also constructed circular temples, but on a smaller scale.

FIGURE 4.14 *Temples of Vesta and Fortuna Virilis, Rome, second century* B.C. (Photo: Alinari)

Figure 4.15 *Maison Carrée, Nîmes, ca. 20* B.C. (Photo: Moffett)

One of the most striking is the Temple of the Sibyl (ca. 25 B.C.) in Tivoli. Set on a promontory, it seems akin to Greek precedent in both its design and siting. It is, however, distinctly Roman. The approach is axial, via a flight of stairs; the cella wall is constructed of concrete instead of marble blocks; and the ornamental frieze of the Corinthian order has Roman swags and ox skulls. Near the Temple of Fortuna Virilis in Rome is the so-called Temple of Vesta (see Figure 4.14), a circular plan temple of the first century B.C. that is similar to but slightly larger than the Tivoli example. Later modifications have changed its roof and destroyed the original entablature.

The greatest circular plan Roman temple is undoubtedly the Pantheon in Rome (118–128 A.D.), considered by many to be the most influential building in western architectural history (Figures 4.16, 4.17). Its size, the boldness of its design, and the technical accomplishment of its construction combine to make it a memorable work. As its name implies, the Pantheon was dedicated to seven planetary deities; it was constructed in the reign of the emperor Hadrian, who is reputed to have been its architect. The entrance is an enormous portico with twenty Corinthian columns supporting bronze roof trusses. (The truss appears to be an Etrusco-Roman invention.) This enormous portico is rather awkwardly joined to the circular cella, a space 142 feet in diameter and 142 feet high. The bottom half of

Figure 4.16 *Pantheon, Rome. 118–128* A.D. (Photo: Alinari)

Figure 4.17 *Plan and section of the Pantheon, Rome.* (From W. Blaser)

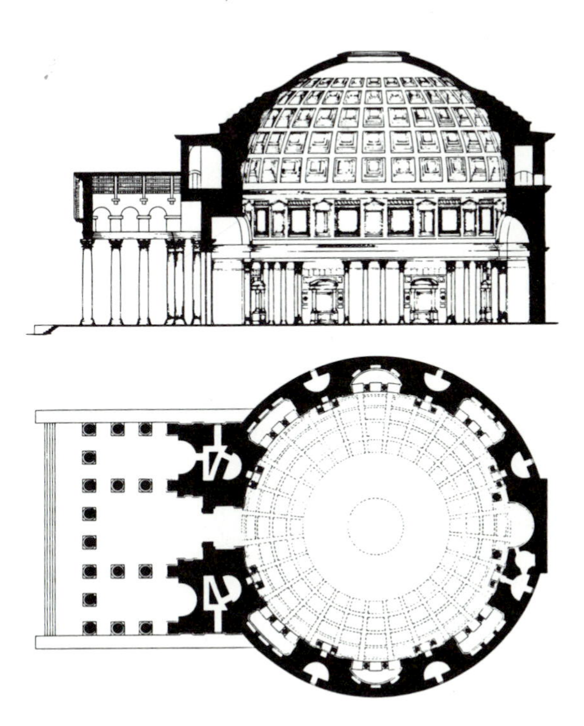

the cella is a cylinder on which rests a hemispherical dome, with an **oculus** twenty-seven feet in diameter at the top to let in light and air. The contrast of the interior to the exterior is breathtaking, even to twentieth-century senses, and it has not failed to inspire visitors since it was built.

The cylindrical cella wall is visually divided into two stories, a ground-level Corinthian order of fluted columns and pilasters supporting an **attic** story with rectangular openings resembling windows set in a patterned marble wall. The lower story is varied by niches, alternately semicircular and rectangular, set at quarter and eighth points around the circumference. Articulation in the dome is accomplished by five tiers of diminishing square coffers, designed with exaggerated perspective to add a sense of depth. The light pouring in from the oculus emphasizes the depth of both the ceiling coffers and the eight niches below. As one stands in the center of the Pantheon, the building creates the feeling that the space extends beyond the cylindrical **drum** and that the dome is much higher than its actual dimension.

The conceptual simplicity of the Pantheon's dome-on-drum design should not be mistaken for constructional simplicity. Behind the orderly interior columns, veneers, and coffers lies a technical masterpiece, a testimonial to Roman skill in building with concrete. The immense structural load of the dome is distributed to concrete foundations fifteen feet thick and thirty-four feet wide through drum walls that are up to twenty feet deep. Most of the constructional complexity is not visible on the interior. The first two rings of coffering conceal eight great relieving arches that work with a second set, likewise hidden, to concentrate loads on the wall sections between the niches of the ground story. Even these sections are not solid, but are hollowed by chambers accessible from the exterior to equalize contraction of the concrete as it dried and lessen the dead weight bearing on the foundations without compromising the stability of the whole. Aggregate in the concrete mix is progressively lightened to the top of the dome, from heavy basalt in the foundations to spongelike volcanic rock in the oculus ring.

Another significant circular plan Roman temple is the Temple of Venus at Baalbek in present-day Lebanon (Figure 4.18). Baalbek was a regional religious center before the arrival of the Romans, and under their leadership the existing sanctuary was dramatically expanded with some exceptionally large temples dedicated to Jupiter Heliopolitanus and Bacchus. In comparison to these, the Temple of Venus, dated from the third century A.D., is small indeed, but its highly original form illustrates well the theatrically ornate qualities of late Roman work. As with the Pantheon, the temple has a pedimented porch preceding the circular cella, but here the portico is wider than the cella, and the outermost columns on either side continue in a semicircle around the cella wall. The circular plan of the cella, truncated at the entrance, is crowned by a shallow dome built in stone. Its modest size — twenty-five feet in diameter — does not pose structural problems as extensive as those of the Pantheon, and the outward thrust of the dome is countered by a horizontally arched entablature supported on the external colonnade. Within the width of the cella wall are

FIGURE 4.18 *Temple of Venus, Baalbek, third century* A.D. (From R. Wood)

external niches (*exedrae*) that parallel the curved entablature above and podium below; both sets of concave curves respond to the convex shape of the cella interior in a manner suggestive of much later developments in seventeenth-century Italian Baroque work. Although the formal similarity is strong, there is no evidence that Baroque architects knew of the Temple of Venus, so it seems to be a case of similar results being arrived at through separate developments.

PUBLIC BUILDINGS

The Romans developed a number of public buildings for specialized functions: the basilica, a large assembly hall used for law courts; the bath, a many-chambered building containing bathing and recreational facilities; and the theater, a building type based on Greek prototypes that the Romans made into free-standing structures and enlarged to become amphitheaters for spectacular entertainments. Each of these building types posed spatial and constructional challenges, and each left its imprint on subsequent architectural developments.

The basilica on the southwest corner of the Forum at Pompeii has already been noted (see Figure 4.7). Dated ca. 100 B.C., it is the oldest known Roman basilica, though it was probably not the first. While legal activities were its main function, it doubtless also served as a gathering place for social and commercial functions, as did the colonnades of the Greek stoas. *Basilica* literally means king's hall in Greek. In plan it resembles a stoa turned inside out. The colonnades now line the interior rather than surround the exterior, consistent with the Roman emphasis on internal space. Entrance to the basilica at Pompeii was primarily from the short side adjacent to the governmental offices, but there were lesser entrances on both long sides. Set in a rectangular area in front of the end wall opposite the entrance was the tribunal seat of honor; it terminated the longitudinal axis established by the colonnades flanking the central space (**nave**). The stucco-finished brick columns probably supported a wooden gabled roof, no longer extant, in addition to separating the nave from the aisles on either side.

Trajan's Forum in Rome contained the more extensive Basilica Ulpia, which measured 200 by 400 feet excluding the apses (see Figure 4.11). Here the entrances were placed on the long façade because the basilica completes one side of the forum. On the interior double colonnades created two aisles on either side of the nave, and there were triple colonnades across the short sides in front of the semicircular niches (**apses**) there. Architectural restoration drawings show the interior with second-floor galleries over the aisles, with clerestory windows illuminating the nave; as at Pompeii, a gabled timber roof covered the building. Luxurious materials, financed by tribute money from the Dacian Wars, were employed in construction: marble on floors and walls, bronze gilding suspended from the roof trusses on the coffered ceiling, and Egyptian granite for the columns. Impressive size, rich finishes, and dramatic lighting combined here to create a setting fit for the dispensation of imperial justice. Of all this magnificence only rude fragments remain, but the basilica form would become the basis for Early Christian church designs.

Not all basilicas were timber-roofed. The Basilica Nova (also known as the Basilica of Maxentius and Constantine) in Rome (Figure 4.19), dated 307–315 A.D., had three great **groin vaults** over its nave, which were buttressed by three barrel-vaulted bays on each side **aisle.** The nave vaults are gone, but the grandeur of the original is conveyed by the surviving north side aisle vaults constructed in brick-faced concrete (Figure 4.20). The large size of each aisle **bay** creates a strong response to the corresponding aisle across the nave, thereby creating a spatial unit at right angles to the axis of the nave. From the straightforward linearity of Pompeii, the basilica form has been manipulated into one of dynamic complexity, with cross-axial interplay between aisles and nave.

The interior of the Basilica Nova owed much to the greatest vaulted Roman buildings, the baths. As the name implies, the Roman baths (*thermae*) were primarily hygienic facilities, but they also provided for exercise, relaxation, and informal socializing, activities more commonly associated with modern spas or health clubs than with twentieth-century baths. The Romans actually cleaned the body without soap by first anointing and then scraping the skin with spoonlike implements. Bathers induced perspiration in very hot rooms (rather like Finnish saunas) and then cooled down and relaxed in a se-

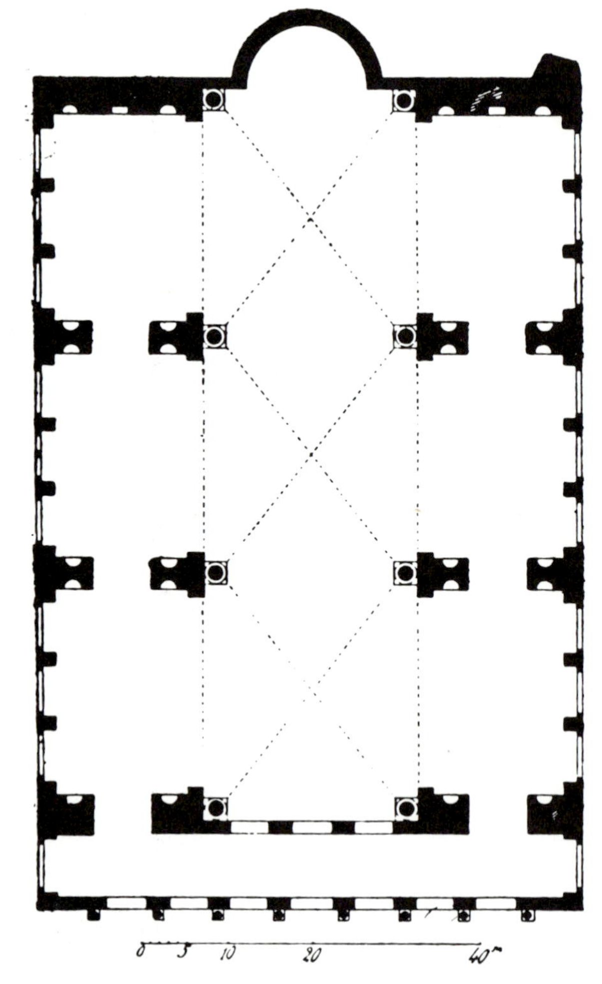

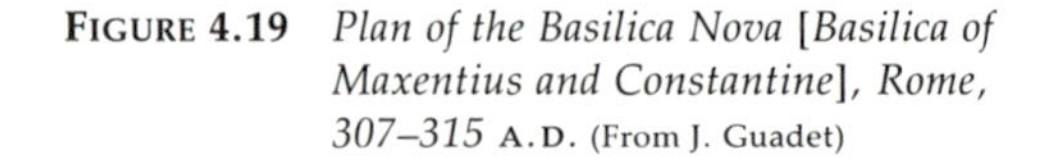

FIGURE 4.19 *Plan of the Basilica Nova [Basilica of Maxentius and Constantine], Rome, 307–315* A.D. (From J. Guadet)

FIGURE 4.20 *Basilica Nova [Basilica of Maxentius and Constantine], Rome.* (Engraving: Piranesi)

quence of temperate and cool plunges. They might extend their time at the baths by swimming, taking walks, enjoying conversation, or reading in the bath's library.

Such an array of activities required multiple spaces: rooms for hot, warm, and cold baths; exercise facilities; relaxing areas; and garden areas if possible. Adequate water supplies were essential. The Romans used mineral springs when available (Bath in England was one such Roman establishment) and heated the water if the supply was not naturally thermal. Because bathing was a healthful diversion for the large urban population, the later emperors vied with one another to build ever more elaborate bath complexes in Rome. Among the largest surviving ruins are the Baths of Caracalla (212–216 A.D.), a grand construction set in fifty acres of grounds in the southern sector of Rome (Figure 4.21). The building proper was essentially a symmetrical large rectangle, 702 by 360 feet, with a centrally placed extension housing the circular **caldarium** (hot bath) on the southwest side (Figure 4.22). Bathers had access to a series of changing rooms, latrines, and exercise facilities before entering the large-windowed hot rooms along the southwest façade; the coldest room, the **frigidarium,** was at the center of the complex, illuminated by clerestory windows (Figure 4.23). From it, the transverse axis extended south to the **tepidarium** (warm baths) and caldarium and north to the *natatio* or swimming pool. Symmetrically identical exercise courts lay at either end of the longitudinal axis. The scale was immense. For example, the caldarium's dome, 115 feet in diameter, rose higher than that of the Pantheon, and the frigidarium, covered by three groin vaults, measured 74 by 148 feet in plan. The interiors were finished with mosaic and marble, and the grounds were embellished with sculpture.

The Baths of Diocletian (298–306 A.D.), located in the northeast quarter of Rome, follow the basic disposition of rooms used in the Baths of Caracalla. The shape of some main spaces differs — the caldarium is rectangular with four apses, and the

FIGURE 4.21 *Aerial view of the Baths of Caracalla, Rome, 212–216* A.D. (Photo: Alinari)

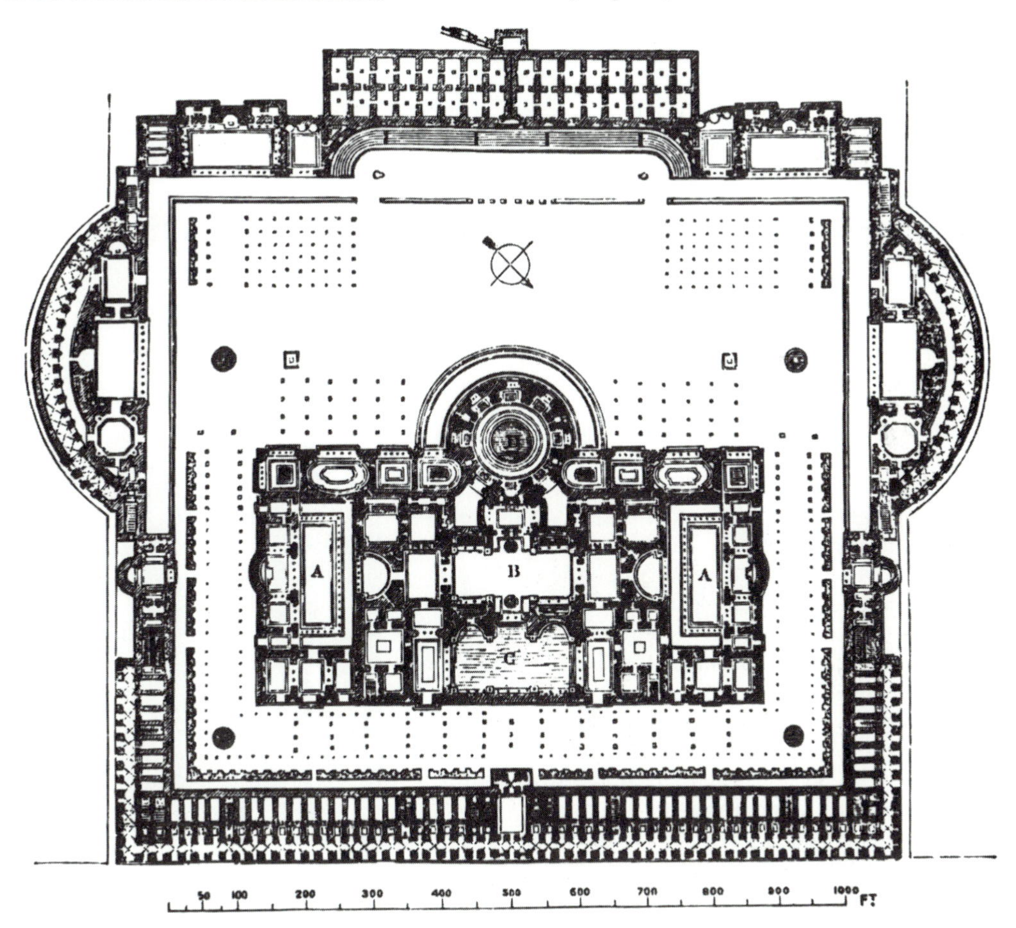

FIGURE 4.22 *Plan of the Baths of Caracalla, Rome.* (From J. Fergusson)

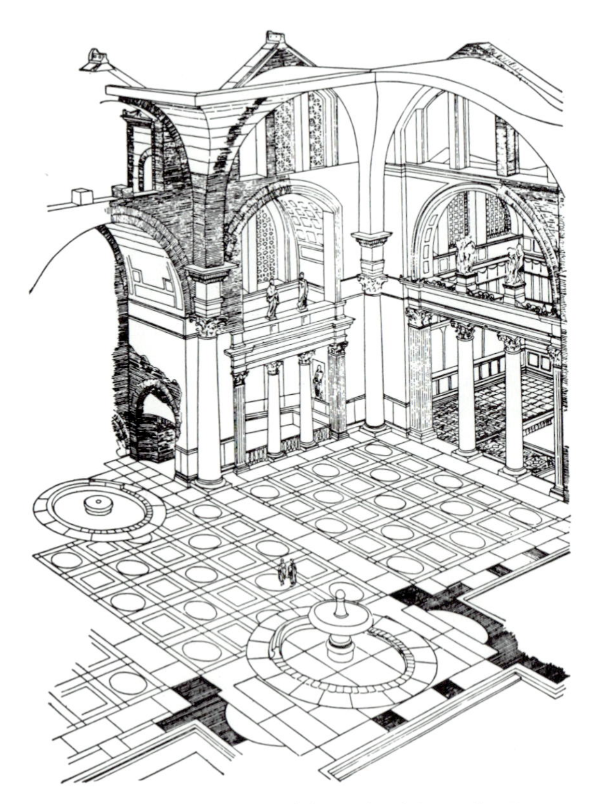

Figure 4.23 *Half section of the Baths of Caracalla, Rome.* (From R. Sturgis)

frigidarium is cruciform — but the general symmetrical design approach remains. The expansion of modern Rome has engulfed the grounds of Diocletian's Baths, but the frigidarium was remodeled by Michelangelo into the church of S. Maria degli Angeli in the sixteenth century (Figure 4.24), and one corner rotunda has been transformed into the church of S. Bernardo, so some substantial fragments remain intact to convey the vast nature of the entire scheme.

The baths of Caracalla and Diocletian were exceptionally large even in imperial times. Of ancient Rome's over 950 baths listed in a mid-fourth-century inventory, only a handful were this grand. One can appreciate the more common bath designs by looking at buildings that remain in provincial cities such as Paris, where the Cluny Museum incorporates part of a third-century A.D. bath, or Leptis Magna on the North African coast, where the so-called Hunting Baths (late second or early third century A.D.) are exceptionally well preserved. At Leptis the concrete barrel vaults and octagonally faceted domes are largely intact. The plan of the baths progresses logically from the caldarium rooms on the south end, through octagonal tepidarium spaces to the rectangular frigidarium on the north side; the whole facility measures thirty-six by eighty-six feet and occupies less than one-third the area of the frigidarium alone at the Baths of Caracalla. Hunting scenes depicted on its interior walls may indicate that the Hunting Baths were used by the professional gamesmen who supplied wild animals for gladiatorial fights in Rome.

Athletic competitions and dramatic performances were part of the culture of classical Greece.

Figure 4.24 *Interior of the Baths of Diocletian, Rome, 298–306* A.D. (From R. Sturgis)

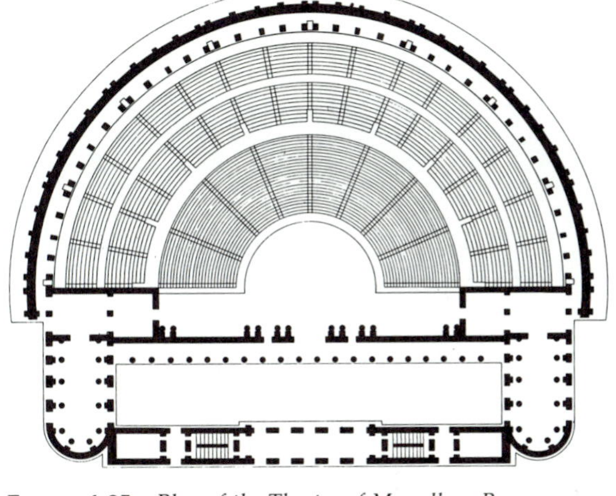

FIGURE 4.25 *Plan of the Theater of Marcellus, Rome, 13–11* B.C. (From W. Blaser)

FIGURE 4.26 *View of the Theater of Marcellus, Rome.* (Engraving: Piranesi)

The Romans, who inherited these traditions and added to them the bloodthirsty combats of the Etruscans, needed theaters and stadiums in which to stage these events. Greek building practice was to carve the shape of theaters or stadiums out of hillsides, thus adapting the natural setting for human use, but the Romans chose to construct their facilities whether the terrain was favorable or not, so they developed great vaulted structures to create the slope needed for spectator seating. An early result of this process was the Theater of Marcellus (completed 13–11 B.C.) in Rome, where a great semicircle of 11,000 seats rising in three tiers focused on a rectangular stage building that formed the backdrop for the drama (Figure 4.25). Enough of the theater's original construction has survived reuse first as a medieval fortress and then as a Renaissance palace to permit reasonable understanding of the structural ingenuity underlying the plan (Figure 4.26). Stacked radial barrel vaults made of cut stone and concrete extended outward to a massive two-level circumferential ring of barrel vaults containing entrances and internal circulation corridors. A third-story perimeter wall upheld one end of the timber supports for the highest tier of seats. Fragmentary remains of the exterior reflect the arched terminations of the radial barrel vaults. The arches were articulated by engaged half-columns and entablatures of the Doric and Ionic orders on the ground and second levels, respectively.

The design of theaters doubtless inspired that of amphitheaters, which were circular or oval in plan, with raked seating on all sides. The Amphitheater at Pompeii, dating from about 80 B.C. and the earliest-known surviving example, was sited so that seats at one end of the oval could be supported on rising ground (Figure 4.27). Later amphitheaters built in southern France at Arles and Nîmes were constructed almost entirely above ground level.

Greatest of all was the Flavian Amphitheater in Rome, more commonly known as the Colosseum, completed in 80 A.D. (Figure 4.28). Although the building's plan is the familiar oval and its structure is modeled on that of the Theater of Marcellus, the novel element here is size. The exterior of the oval measures 510 by 615 feet, encompassing seats for an estimated 50,000 people in a continuously rising tier with an additional upper seating band above (Figure 4.29). Except for this top level of seats, which rested on wooden supports, the entire building was masonry, a combination of cut stone and concrete resting on carefully laid foundations. Under the seating was an intricate network of structural supports, horizontal passageways, ramps, and stairs to accommodate the throngs attending spectacles in the building. The exterior was clad in travertine. Stacked half columns in the Roman Doric, Ionic, and Corinthian orders combined with arches of the supporting barrel vaults to create three stories of the façade. A fourth level of Corinthian pilasters without arches completed the elevation around the uppermost tier of seats. Attached to this wall were

FIGURE 4.27 *Amphitheater, Pompeii, 80* B.C. (Photo: Wodehouse)

FIGURE 4.28 *Colosseum, Rome, 80* A.D. (Photo: Alinari)

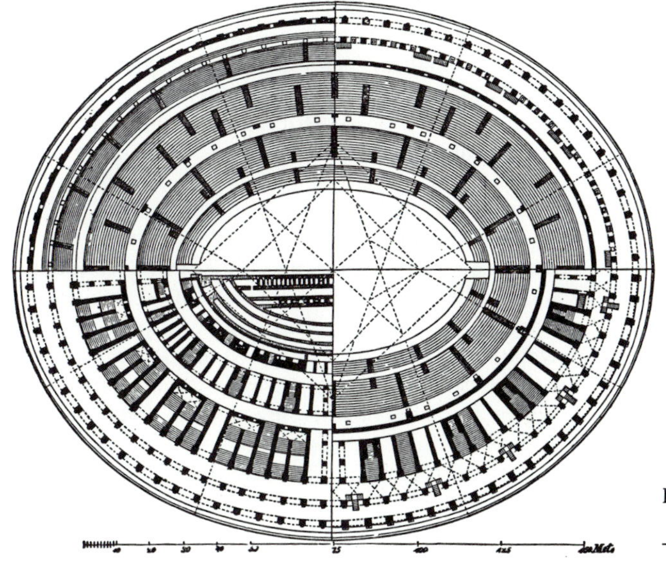

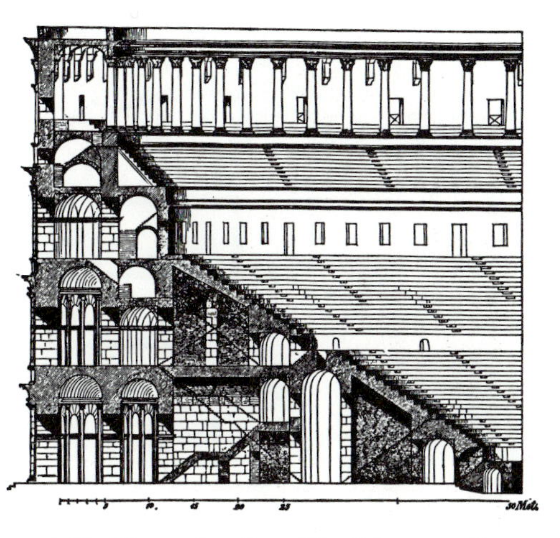

FIGURE 4.29 *Plan and section of the Colosseum, Rome.* (From F. Reber)

brackets for the poles that some historians believe to have been supports for a canvas cover (*velarium*) to provide shade for spectators. The area under the arena floor, an oval measuring 175 by 280 feet, was a labyrinth of passageways and chambers for gladiators, beasts, and hoisting machinery to service the spectacles staged above. The Colosseum is inextricably linked with savage and cruel entertainments, including the persecution of Roman Christians. During later eras the fine marble work was removed as the building became a source for ready-cut stone. It remains today as a partial ruin, but even in its crumbled condition, the Colosseum is a worthy testimonial to Roman construction skill.

RESIDENCES

To study Roman housing, we once again return to Pompeii, for the collection of ordinary dwellings, elaborate town residences, country villas, and farmhouses preserved there is the most complete record we have of the building designs in which people lived. The earliest houses there are built with atrium plans, an indigenous Italian type in which the principal rooms of the house directly adjoin an open courtyard for access and for light and circulation of air. Such a house presents a blank wall to the street on which it fronts without setback from the sidewalk.

The House of the Surgeon is the most ancient Pompeiian dwelling, and an examination of its plan reveals the typical features of atrium houses (Figure 4.30). The building is an irregular quadrilateral because it exactly fills the property on which it was built. On the street side it has three doors, two of which provide access to shops, one connected to the dwelling and the other forming part of a self-contained shop with living quarters upstairs. The center doorway, dignified by two entrance steps, was the principal entry to the house, and its location defines the axis of symmetry for the house proper. Passing through a vestibule, a visitor would next encounter the atrium, where a roof provided covering and shade except for a relatively small central area that was left open to the sky. Water running off the roof would fall in a catchment (*impluvium*) in the center of the atrium. On either side of the atrium were chambers generally used as bedrooms; straight ahead on axis was the main reception room (*tablinum*), flanked by large and small dining rooms. Beyond was a portico that opened onto the rear walled garden. Service spaces, including chambers for servants and the kitchen, were set in the wings

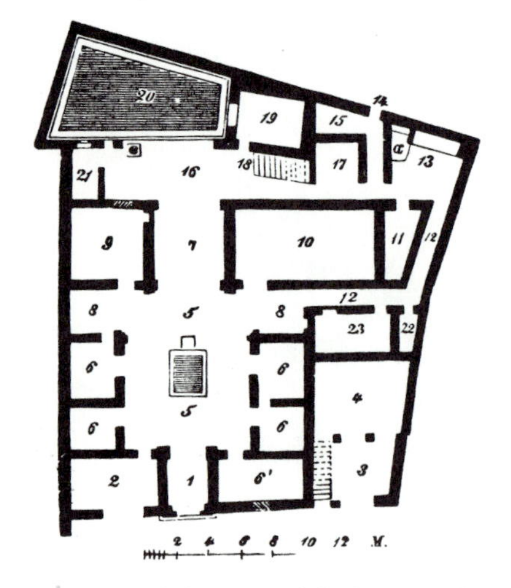

FIGURE 4.30 *Plan of the House of the Surgeon, Pompeii. Fourth to third century* B.C. (From A. Mau)

beside the dining rooms or tucked away in asymmetrical back rooms. All the internal spaces depended on the atrium or the garden for light, as the exterior walls were without openings. Only the tablinum, the most distinguished room in the house, had direct access to both sources; most of the remaining rooms must have been rather dim, even during the day.

The atrium plan had formal dignity combined with practical adjustments to living requirements. The owner could rent the frontage shop with second-floor living quarters to a tradesman or artisan and use the shop connected to the interior of the house as his own place of business. The functioning of either shop was independent of domestic activity, which was in turn isolated from street noise. The scale was ample. The private quarters in the House of the Surgeon covered about 5500 square feet, including the garden. Nevertheless, in the second century B.C. wealthier citizens were constructing expanded atrium houses. These newer houses might have more than one atrium, and the garden was greatly enlarged and surrounded by a colonnade to become a **peristyle.**

The House of Pansa at Pompeii is an example of the atrium-peristyle house that has been dated to the second century B.C. (Figure 4.31). It occupies one entire city block (approximately 27,000 square feet, over half an acre) and thus might have had windows on any of its four sides, but it has none, relying instead on an atrium, peristyle court, and a large walled garden for light and air (Figure 4.32). The entrance establishes an axial disposition of spaces similar to that at the House of the Surgeon. The small rooms around the atrium were used as bedrooms, with the dining rooms set adjacent to the peristyle. Beyond the peristyle, the axis passes through another reception room and portico to the walled garden, which occupied about a third of the site. Such a large house was uncommon. Most Pompeians lived in considerably smaller dwellings. Examples of three of these can be seen along the side street of the House of Pansa, where they were created out of the main house in a later remodeling. Lacking an atrium or internal court, these houses had windows for light and air, but they opened to the street, thus sharing the dust, noise, and smells of the public way. The two remaining sides of the House of Pansa contained shops; the oven of a bakery is clearly evident on the plan.

Inward-looking houses such as those at Pompeii presented a virtual wall to the street, an effect completely unlike the residential districts of American cities but not so dissimilar to the modern towns in Mediterranean countries. The streets in Pompeii were narrow, ranging from under eight feet to just over twenty-two feet. Major streets had raised walks on either side, and raised stepping stones at intersections enabled pedestrians to cross the street without sinking into the muck that often filled the roadway. These crossing stones also permitted wheeled carts to pass, carefully, and thus controlled traffic speed. The walls in most sections of town were covered with graffiti. Election slogans, public notices, advertisements for commercial establishments and public entertainments, and obscene remarks have all been found in the excavations of the city. On streets where tradesmen had shops, the walls sometimes contained murals illustrating the particular trade or product available within; their shop fronts opened directly to the street for the display of goods and were secured at night by wooden roller shutters.

Interior finishes in the houses at Pompeii have proven almost as interesting as the architecture. Art

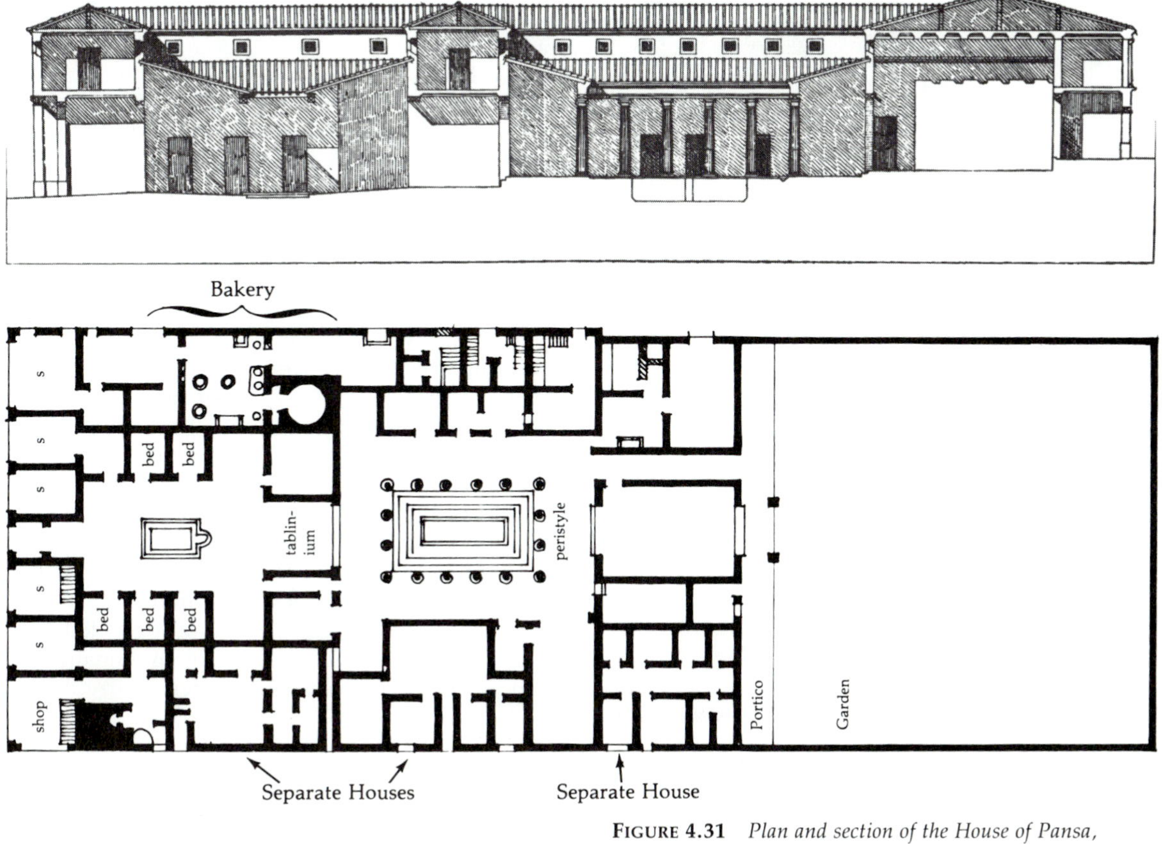

FIGURE 4.31 *Plan and section of the House of Pansa, Pompeii. Second century* B.C. (From J. Guadet)

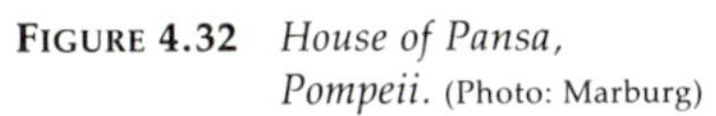

FIGURE 4.32 *House of Pansa, Pompeii.* (Photo: Marburg)

FIGURE 4.33 *Insula at Ostia.* (From *Monumenti antichi*)

historians have identified four styles of wall paintings at Pompeii; one of these, in which imaginary scenes were painted as viewed from high or low vantage points, seems a precursor of the elaborate Baroque creations that were used in the seventeenth century to expand the physical boundaries of walls and ceilings.

Stone and brick were the primary materials used in the construction of houses, although a surprising amount of timber was also employed, particularly for roof beams. In less-affluent housing, walls were often a wooden structural frame filled with rubble or brick, rather like the half-timbering construction of medieval Europe. Houses were originally one-story, but as the city grew and available land became more valuable, construction inevitably became multistory, and older houses were converted to apartments. By the time of Pompeii's destruction, in fact, many of the atrium-peristyle houses had been divided into multifamily dwellings as the wealthier families had moved to more spacious residences on estates outside the city.

For city residents, the dominant housing type after about 64 A.D. came to be the apartment block or **insula;** an inventory made in the fourth century of buildings in Rome counted 46,000 insulae, while there were fewer than 1800 single-family houses. The best surviving insulae are in the port city of Ostia (Figure 4.33). These apartment buildings, ranging up to six floors in height, occupied substantial plots of land and were designed around a central courtyard. Shops or commercial ventures were located on the ground floor street frontages, as was the case with single-family houses in Pompeii. Unlike the atrium houses, however, the upper-floor walls of insulae had windows out to the street, so that rooms could draw on both the courtyard and street for light and air; in middle-class districts, the windows would have glass panes to replace skin coverings for wintertime insulation.

Country residences were called villas, and at Pompeii, a fine example is preserved just outside the city wall. Known as the Villa of the Mysteries because of the wall paintings in one room that relate to the mystical cult of Bacchus, the villa grew gradually over a period of 300 years from a simple town house to a complex of sixty rooms (Figure 4.34). Elements from atrium houses remain in its plan, including the preference for axial symmetry, but the ordering of rooms differs. The entranceway led into the peristyle, followed by the atrium and finally the tablinum; extensive terraced gardens surrounded

FIGURE 4.34 *Villa of the Mysteries, Pompeii.* (Photo: Wodehouse)

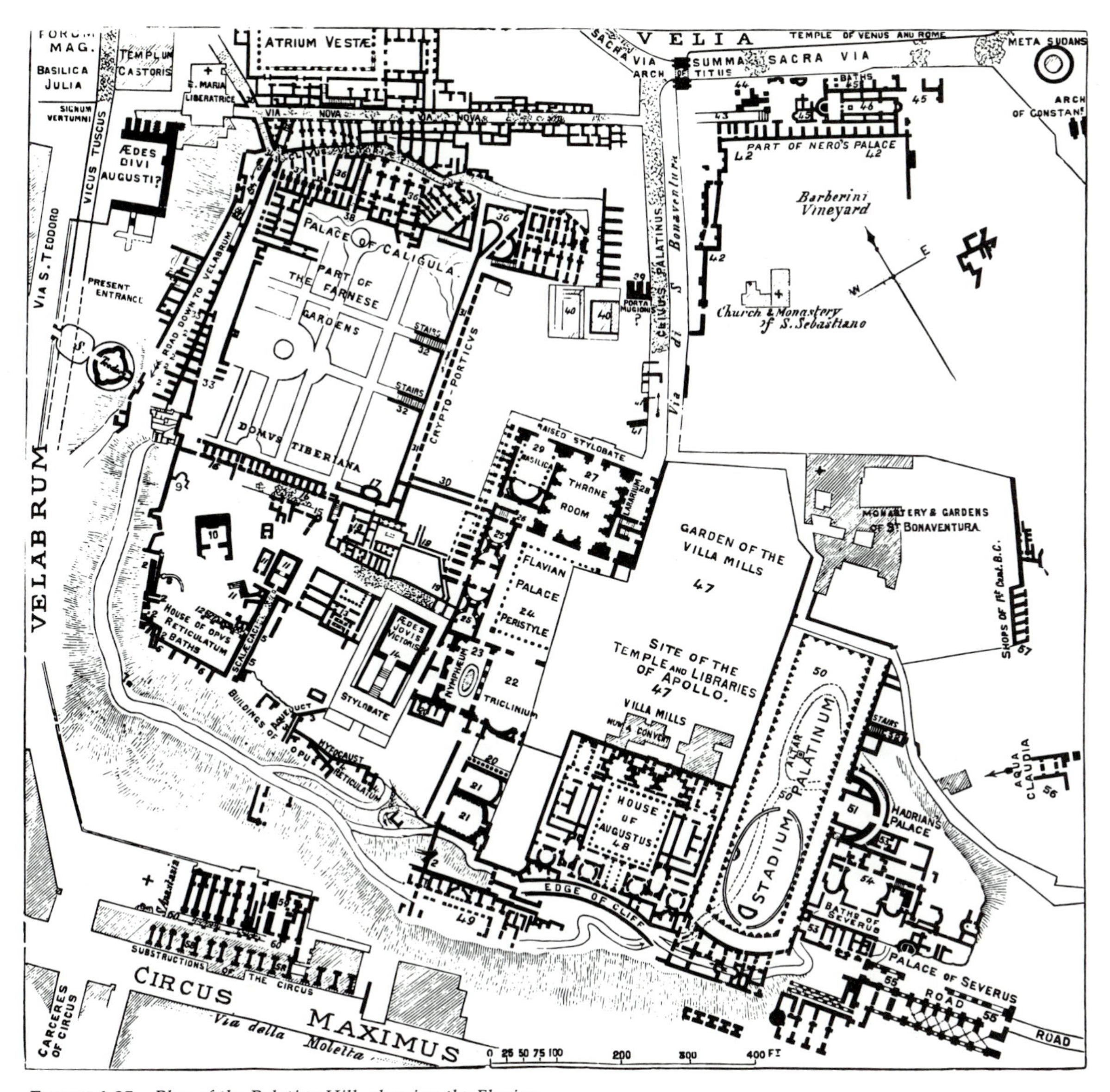

FIGURE 4.35 *Plan of the Palatine Hill, showing the Flavian Palace [Domus Augustana], Rome, finished* 92 A.D. (From J. Middleton)

the villa on the three nonentrance sides. From the original inward-focused house, the architectural developments at the Villa of the Mysteries seem to be leading toward a building in which the exterior elevations and their connection with the surrounding countryside were becoming more important.

Truly wealthy individuals, such as the emperor, had elaborate palaces in Rome, none of which survive. The ruins of the Flavian Palace or Domus Augustana (finished in 92 A.D.) on the Palatine Hill hint at the complexity of elements incorporated into an imperial residence, in which accommodations for public functions and private living had to be combined (Figure 4.35). The western section housed most state rooms, including a basilica, a large audience hall, a shrine for the emperor's family gods, and a large dining hall (*triclinium*) for banquets. The more intimately scaled private residence block was set on the south side, adjoining an elongated sunken garden known as the Stadium.

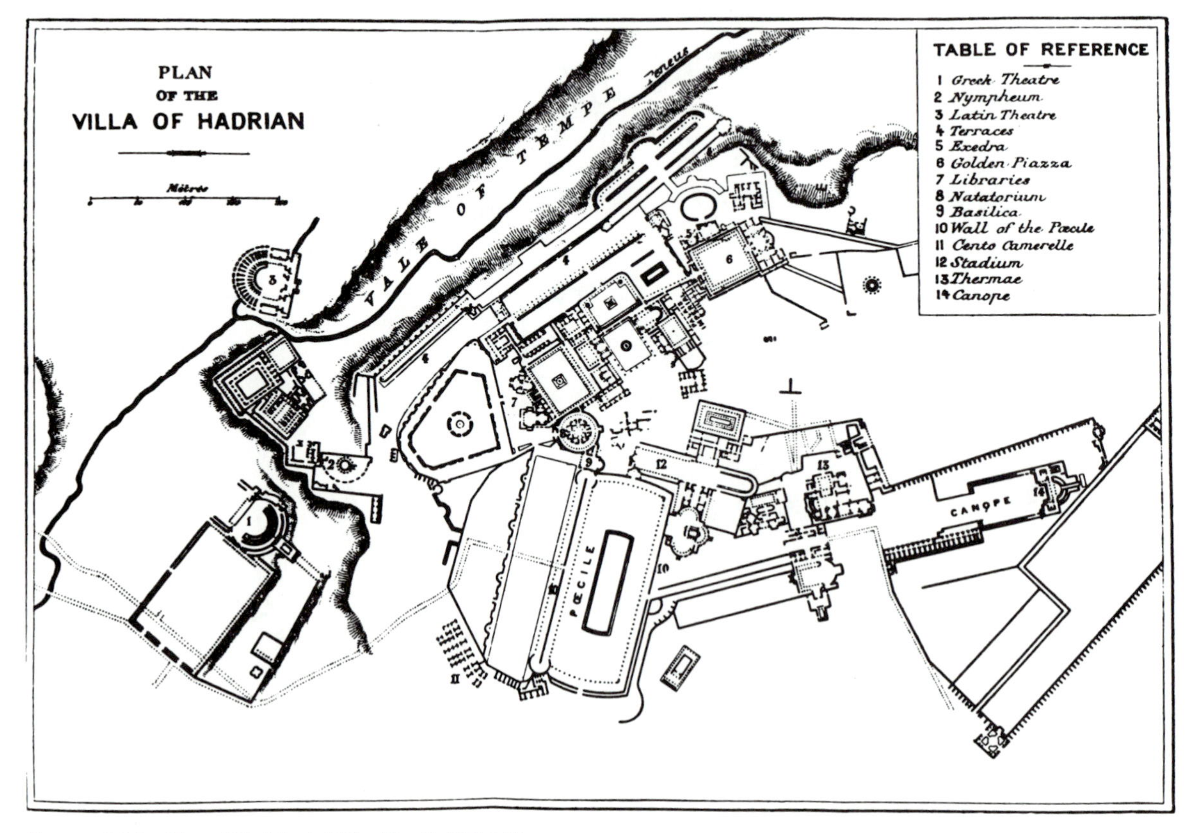

FIGURE 4.36 *Plan of Hadrian's Villa, Tivoli, 117–138* A.D.
(From G. Boissier)

In a better state of preservation is the imperial villa erected by Hadrian outside Tivoli, the result of his extensive travels and personal interest in architecture (Figure 4.36). Constructed from 117 to 138 A.D., Hadrian's Villa is a sprawling accumulation of geometrically controlled building groups sited to follow the landscape and linked to each other by a shifting set of axes and cross-axes. The many shapes incorporated in the buildings, including wondrously convoluted curves, exploit the design freedom afforded by concrete, of which virtually all the buildings were constructed. Hadrian intended that his villa should evoke architectural forms from all parts of the world, and the sheer variety of interior volumes and exterior vistas makes this a treasury of spatial sequences without precedent.

An enclosed garden built around a rectangular fish pond formed the percile, the largest single element in the villa. Here Hadrian could follow the advice of physicians and take gentle walks after eating, seeking shelter under the porticoed north wall from sun or rain. Below the western end of the percile were tiers of rooms for the palace guard and servants. To the east was a circular enclosed colonnaded area, the so-called Maritime Theater, which was not a theater at all but a solitary retreat for meditation or intimate meetings. Inside the enclosing wall and colonnade was a circular water channel that isolated the central circular building from the surrounding walkway. Access to the center was provided by a removable wooden bridge. Two libraries (one each for Greek and Latin manuscripts), various halls, and a guesthouse were grouped around the library court at the northern edge. Around the Piazza d'Oro (Golden Court) on the eastern side were some of the most inventive buildings in the villa (Figure 4.37). On its southern end, the piazza was dominated by a centrally planned building, which was probably domed. Eight piers set at the edge of the space support arches to carry the dome; between these piers are pairs of columns supporting a cornice that curves in and out, alternately concave and convex, around the space, creating a sensation of space extending beyond the concavities as did the niches around the Pantheon. The eight spaces from the central area lead into four recesses, two intermediate spaces, and an **exedra** opposite the entrance from the colonnade of the piazza. This building faces across the piazza to a smaller domed structure rising from an octagonal plan with alternate semicircular and square projections. The piers between each bay rise to form ribs of a "pumpkin" vault, where the dome segments between the ribs are themselves arched. Although Hadrian's Villa is in a ruined condition, many walls are of sufficient height to define areas and convey an impression of space. The free use of curves seen here and in other late Roman buildings provided inspiration for later architects during the Renaissance and Baroque.

Roman architecture as a whole encompasses so many formal variations that it is the single richest architectural legacy for later developments in the West. The Romanesque, Renaissance, Baroque, Neoclassic, and nineteenth-century classically derived styles, including the Beaux-Arts, have all found material in Roman building to generate form for buildings the Romans never imagined. Even twentieth-century Post-Modernism has looked back to the Roman Empire for inspiration, demonstrating the inexhaustible inventiveness of its architects and builders.

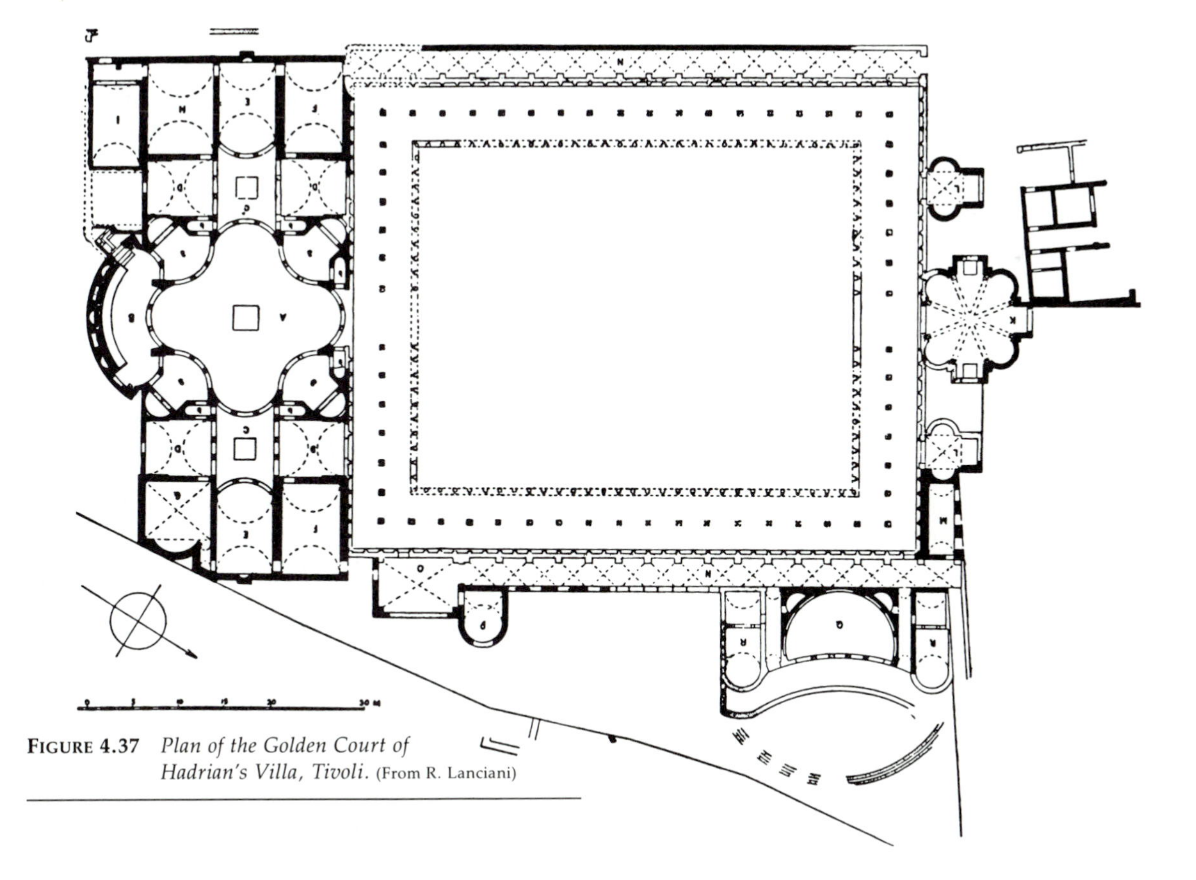

FIGURE 4.37 *Plan of the Golden Court of Hadrian's Villa, Tivoli.* (From R. Lanciani)

5.

Early Christian and Byzantine Architecture

The origin and spread of Christianity led ultimately to the development of an architectural style suitable to the requirements of a new religion. Christian influence grew in the first and second centuries A.D., but not until the emperor Constantine proclaimed toleration for all religions of the Roman Empire in the Edict of Milan in 313 did the Christians have authority to construct buildings for public worship. Prior to that time Christians held services in private homes, where common domestic rooms, most often the dining room, sufficed for worship. One table was used for the Eucharist and another for offerings, with participants in the service sitting on the remaining furnishings or standing. As the liturgy became more elaborate and the congregation grew, they needed a larger and more extensive set of rooms. In many cities Christians established community houses for worship and the distribution of alms to the needy in the neighborhoods, and organized separate Christian cemeteries to distance Christian burials from those of pagans. Christians disapproved of cremation, and if suitable land for a graveyard was not available, the Christian community developed underground cemeteries, generally begun in abandoned quarries, which became known as catacombs. Portions of the catacombs in Rome are among the oldest surviving Christian constructions, providing a glimpse of early Christian decorative art.

Christian architecture after 313 derived in large measure from Roman precedent, so Early Christian and Byzantine buildings continue certain aspects of classical antiquity. At the same time, stylistic developments in this period contributed to later buildings in the medieval period, thus forming the "hinge" between the classical past and what would become a distinctive architecture of western Europe.

EARLY CHRISTIAN BASILICAS

In giving official sanction to Christianity, Constantine became the sponsor of its early church-building efforts, most of which were based on the Roman basilica. Classical temples, with their pagan associations, were obviously unsuitable models for Christian worship, but the connotations of assembly hall and court of justice pertaining to basilicas suited the new religion much better. Basilicas could accommodate large crowds, an important consideration for a religion attracting increasing numbers of converts, as both priests and worshippers were contained in a common space for services. With relatively minor modifications, the Roman basilica form was adapted to Christian ritual. The altar was placed in the apse where the magistrate's seat had formerly been; entrances were set in the opposite

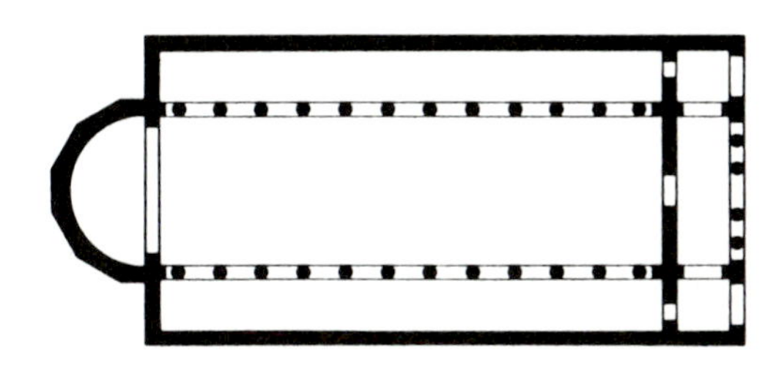

FIGURE 5.1 *Plan of Sant'Apollinare Nuovo, Ravenna, ca. 490.* (From W. Blaser)

short wall; and an atrium accommodated gatherings before services and was a place for the unbaptised to hear but not participate in the Mass. The longitudinal arrangement of atrium, nave, and apse created an impressive axis for processions, which terminated at the altar.

Constantine gave the Lateran Palace in Rome to the early church to serve as a residence for the bishop, and one of the earliest basilicas was built adjacent to the palace about 313. Much rebuilt and extended it stands today as St. John Lateran, and it is still the **cathedral** of Rome. The original building had paired aisles on either side of a lofty nave, which was concluded by an apse containing seats for the bishop (the cathedra) and priests. Clerestory windows high in the nave wall illuminated the central space, while smaller windows in the outermost aisle and above the first aisle colonnade provided light for the ancillary spaces. Open wooden trusses spanned the nave and aisles and were supported on the brick-faced concrete walls and marble columns salvaged from earlier Roman buildings.

A more vivid example of an Early Christian basilica is found at Ravenna in the church of S. Apollinare Nuovo (ca. 490) (Figure 5.1). Constructed of brick with single aisles flanking the nave, the church interior focuses dramatically on the semicircular apse (Figure 5.2). Above the nave **arcade** and below the clerestory windows on the intermediate wall is a brilliant mosaic of stately processions of female (north side) and male (south side) martyrs advancing toward the altar. In the highest sections of the nave wall above the clerestories are scenes representing the Passion story (south side) and the miracles of Christ (north side). This elaborate interior decoration not only communicated Christian teachings to a largely illiterate public but also symbolized the richness of the Kingdom of God to which the soul could aspire. On the exterior, the sober brickwork gives little indication of the shimmering golden mosaic work contained within.

MARTYRIA, BAPTISTRIES, AND MAUSOLEA

Basilicas were not the only religious buildings erected by early Christians. Among the structures raised to serve Christian purposes were **martyria,** buildings erected as memorials to commemorate saints or sites of special importance to the Christian faith. Celebrated martyria might attract large crowds for services and thus need to function as churches, but major importance was always attached to the tomb or shrine around which they were built. Old St. Peter's in Rome (318–322), predecessor of the present Basilica of St. Peter, began as

FIGURE 5.2 *Interior of Sant'Apollinare Nuovo, Ravenna.* (Photo: School of Architecture, University of Tennessee)

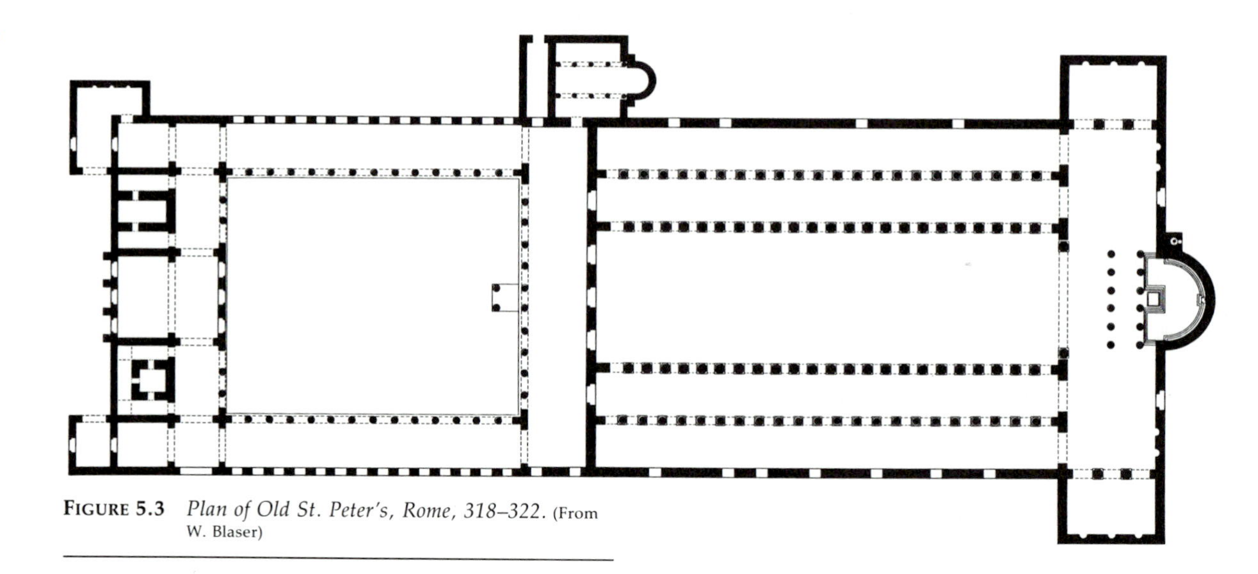

Figure 5.3 *Plan of Old St. Peter's, Rome, 318–322.* (From W. Blaser)

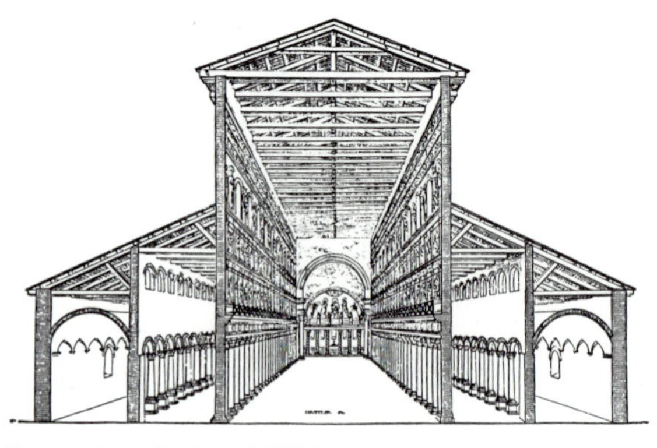

Figure 5.4 *Section of Old St. Peter's, Rome.* (From J. Fergusson)

Figure 5.5 *Axonometric of the Church of the Nativity, Bethlehem, ca. 333.* (After R. Krautheimer)

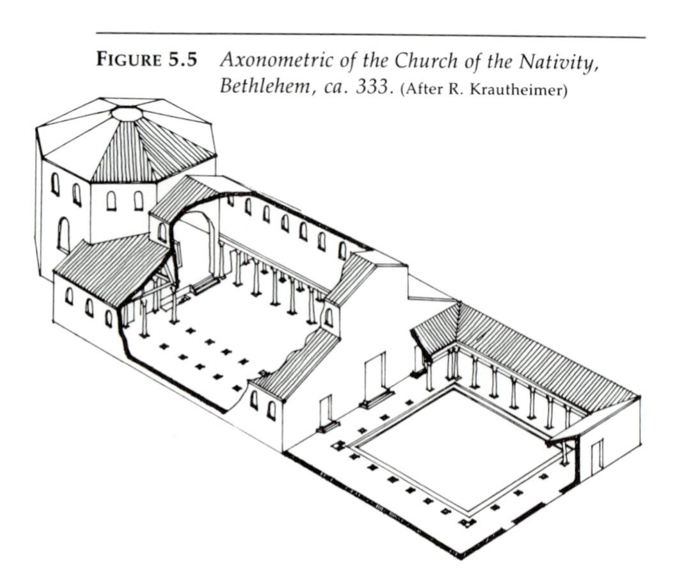

a martyrium marking the tomb of St. Peter and seems to have been used for several centuries as a place of burial for other Christians as well. Its plan is that of a basilica with double aisles on each side of the nave and a transverse element or **transept** projecting beyond the side walls and extending across the nave in front of the apse (Figures 5.3, 5.4). Centered at the junction of transept and apse was the tomb of St. Peter, surrounded by a railing and marked by a canopy rising on twisted spiral columns that reputedly came from the Temple of Solomon in Jerusalem. The transept spaces accommodated those coming to venerate the shrine, while the enormous nave (300 by 64 feet) and aisles functioned as a covered cemetery with space for burials and commemorative funeral meals. A spacious atrium preceded the martyrium, and the whole scheme provided the model for the church of St. Paul outside the Walls, built in 385 outside the city wall of Rome. In both cases the addition of transepts to the basilican plan was generated by the need for an area around the martyr's shrine.

A similar program influenced the design of the Church of the Nativity in Bethlehem (Figure 5.5), constructed under the patronage of Constantine about 333 over the grotto that tradition identified as the birthplace of Christ. As at St. Peter's, this building was a basilica preceded by an atrium, but rather than transepts and an apse, the Church of the Nativity had an octagon at the head of the nave. A passage around the octagon allowed pilgrims to circulate and view the grotto below through an opening in the floor; there may also have been stairs going down to the actual level of the shrine. The junction of a basilica with an octagon shows Early

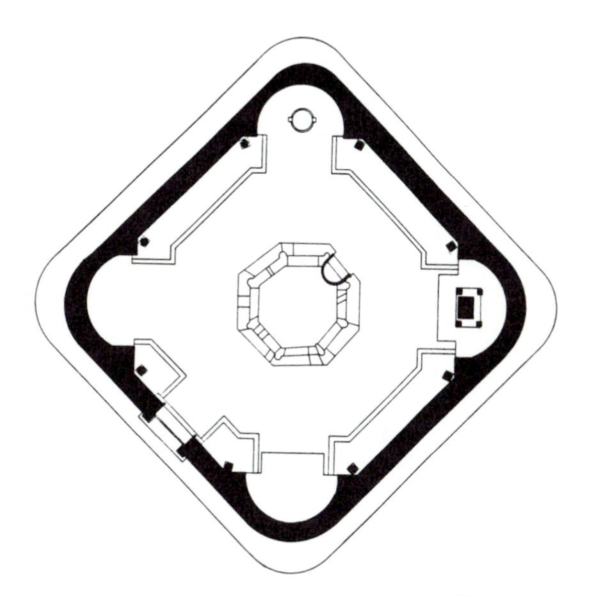

FIGURE 5.6 *Plan and section of the Baptistry of the Orthodox, Ravenna, ca. 450.* (From W. Blaser)

Christian willingness to explore new forms in the course of seeking appropriate and functional religious buildings.

Baptism is an important Christian rite, and in the Early Christian period, special buildings were often erected for this sacrament alone. Most were centrally planned around the baptismal pool, for at the time baptism was by complete immersion; and **baptistry** plans were frequently octagonal to reflect the number *eight,* which symbolized regeneration or the Resurrection since Christ rose from the dead on the eighth day after his entry into Jerusalem. The Baptistry of the Orthodox in Ravenna (ca. 450) is a domed octagonal volume surrounding the octagonal marble font (Figure 5.6). The central scene in the ceiling mosaic depicts Christ's baptism in the river Jordan, encircled by the twelve apostles and an outer ring illustrating altars in semicircular niches and empty thrones. As was the case with Sant' Apollinare Nuovo, the plain brick exterior, articulated primarily by eight arched windows and corbeled arches with pilaster strips, gives no hint of the sumptuous finishes inside.

Mausolea, buildings erected to contain the tombs of important people, were also in the repertory of Early Christian architecture. Following Roman practice these were often centrally planned, and they served as models for later domed churches. In Rome the mausoleum of Constantine's daughter Constantia was built around 350 as a circular monument with a cross section paralleling that of the basilica, having lower aisle spaces flanking the higher nave lit by clerestory windows (Figure 5.7). Constantia's mausoleum, now known as the church of S. Costanza, rotates the basilican cross-section about the center axis to create a circular building, rather than extending it longitudinally to form a basilica, and the resulting dome with encircling **ambulatory** focuses the visitor's attention on the sarcophagus originally placed in the center (Figure 5.8). Twelve paired sets of columns support the drum wall on which the dome rises above twelve clerestory windows. The aisle vaults are finished with mosaic, and the columns are of polished marble.

A smaller monument with even more elaborate decoration is the Mausoleum of Galla Placidia in Ravenna (Figure 5.9). Built ca. 425 on a Greek cross plan (that is, a cross having arms of equal length), it was intended to house the tombs of Galla Placidia and her husband and brother Honorius, the Western Emperor who moved the capital from Milan to

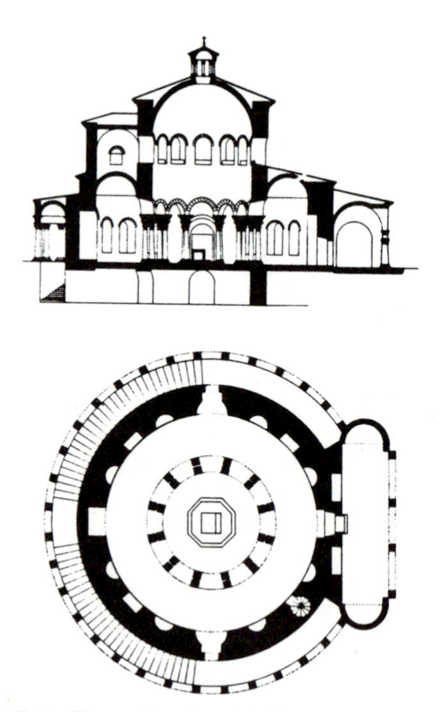

FIGURE 5.7 *Plan and section of S. Costanza, Rome, ca. 350.* (From W. Blaser)

FIGURE 5.8 *Interior of S. Costanza, Rome.* (Engraving: Piranesi)

FIGURE 5.9 *Mausoleum of Galla Placidia, Ravenna, ca. 425.* (Photo: Marburg)

Ravenna. The building also served as a memorial to St. Lawrence, the third-century martyr who is credited with helping to convert Rome. Behind the plain brick exterior, enlivened by blind arches and pilasters, is a rich and glowing interior created by marble floors and wainscoting with mosaic upper walls and vaults. The arms of the cross in plan are enclosed by barrel vaults, and the raised **crossing** is completed by a dome on **pendentives** (spherical triangles used to transform a square bay into a circle for the springing of a dome). Small windows admit light through alabaster glazing to shine gently on the mosaics. The small glass pieces or tesserae are intentionally set on a slight skew to the plane of the wall so that they do not all catch the light in the same way. This enlivens the surface and makes the inanimate material seem to glow. The ceiling vaults, covered with geometric stars derived from textile designs, are set on a deep blue ground and framed by decorative bands in brilliant colors, while the semicircular panels or lunettes formed below the barrel vaults at the end walls illustrate scenes of the Good Shepherd, the martyrdom of St. Lawrence, and the apostles. It is a stunning interior, reflecting imperial patronage and a high standard of workmanship.

FIGURE 5.10 *Sant'Apollinare in Classe, Ravenna, 532–549.* (Photo: Alinari)

BYZANTINE BASILICAS AND DOMED BASILICAS

The division between the Early Christian and Byzantine eras is generally made at the reign of Justinian (527–565) who, as Emperor based in Constantinople, put an end to factional disputes, reasserted imperial influence in portions of North Africa and Italy that had fallen to barbarian tribes, and engaged in a vigorous program of church building. Most of Justinian's architecture exhibits a clear preference for domes, and both basilican and centrally planned churches were covered with domes. Like the Romans, the Byzantines saw the dome as symbolic of the heavenly sphere, complementary to the earthly realm of floor and walls below.

Early Christian traditions were not entirely discarded, however. The church of Sant' Apollinare in Classe (outside Ravenna) (Figure 5.10), constructed under Justinian's patronage from 532 to 549, is an example of a wooden-roofed basilica without transepts (Figure 5.11). Its splendid apse mosaics are the glory of the interior (Figure 5.12). Sant' Apollinare guards a flock of twelve sheep (representing the disciples) grazing in a lush meadow. Overhead is a golden cross set in the starry blue sky. Rich marble

FIGURE 5.11 *Plan of Sant'Apollinare in Classe, Ravenna.* (From W. Blaser)

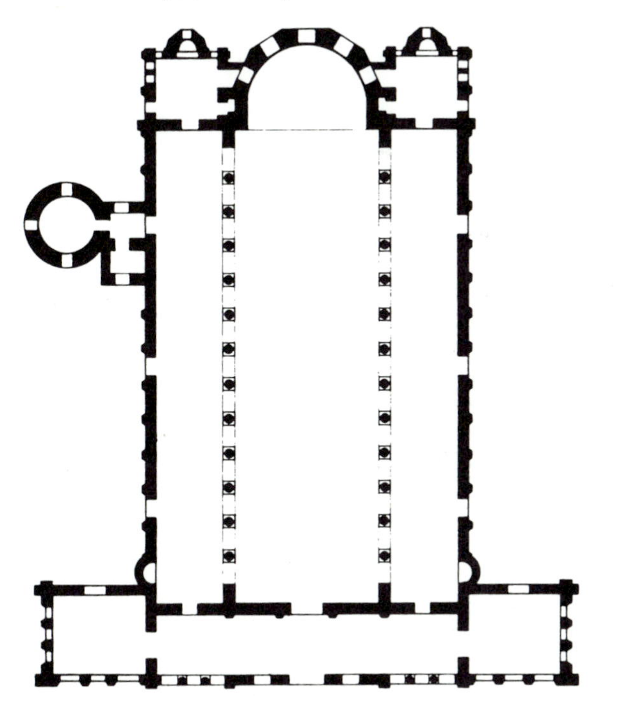

FIGURE 5.12 *Interior of Sant'Apollinare in Classe, Ravenna.* (Photo: School of Architecture, University of Tennessee)

FIGURE 5.13 *Plan of S. Irene, Constantinople, begun 532, remodeled 564, restored 740.* (Redrawn from B. Cichy)

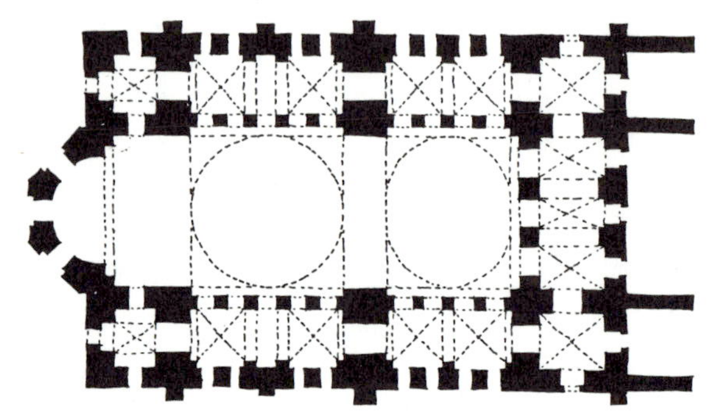

columns form the nave arcade, and above are restored portraits of saints set in roundel frames. In character and design the church is remarkably similar to the earlier Sant' Apollinare Nuovo. Other simple basilicas (the most common Byzantine church form in the sixth century) were constructed in Constantinople, but none survive.

The innovative domes of Justinian's churches are remarkable contributions to architectural history. In Constantinople two monuments that can be considered domed basilicas rose simultaneously and survive as models for the type. The smaller, S. Irene (begun 532 and remodeled in 564), has a rectangular plan divided into nave and aisles with a projecting semicircular apse (Figure 5.13). (The church seen today is largely a rebuilding after an earthquake in 740.) Two domes cover the nave, and their thrust is countered by massive rectangular piers, pierced by openings, and effectively strengthened by barrel-vaulted **galleries** over the aisles. The outlines of the aisle vaults articulate the exterior side walls, where tiers of arched windows admit light to the aisles and galleries. More windows are placed at the base of the dome and around the apse. S. Irene thus represents a new interpretation of the basilica, combining the liturgical logic of the longitudinal plan with the centralizing or heavenly qualities of domed construction. This same idea, on a much larger scale, was carried out at a contemporary church in Constantinople, Hagia Sophia, the Church of the Holy Wisdom.

Hagia Sophia (532–537) is one of the greatest buildings of all time, and it is without question the masterpiece of Byzantine architecture (Figure 5.14). We know the names and backgrounds of its architects — Anthemius of Tralles and Isidorus of Miletus. Both were mathematicians and scientists skilled in mechanics, geometry, and engineering. These talents were all needed to design and supervise the construction of the exceptionally large Hagia Sophia. In plan it is a basilica with a dome above the central space, complemented by two semidomes along the longitudinal axis (Figure 5.15). The 107-foot-diameter central dome, supported on pendentives, rises 180 feet above the floor and is flanked by two lower semidomes of the same diameter, a clear span of nearly 250 feet (Figure 5.16). In the description of the church written by Justinian's court historian, Procopius of Caesarea, the dome was seen to hover over the interior.

> [It] seems not to rest upon solid masonry, but to cover the space with its golden dome suspended from Heaven. All these details, fitted together with incredible skill in mid-air and floating off from each other and resting only on the parts next to them, produce a single and most extraordinary harmony in the work, and yet do not permit the spectator to linger much over the study of any one of them, but each detail attracts the eye and draws it on irresistibly to itself.

Aisles with galleries above range on either side, while a colonnaded atrium (no longer extant) and

FIGURE 5.14 *Anthemius and Isidorus: Hagia Sophia, Constantinople, 532–537.* (Photo: Turkish Ministry of Culture and Tourism)

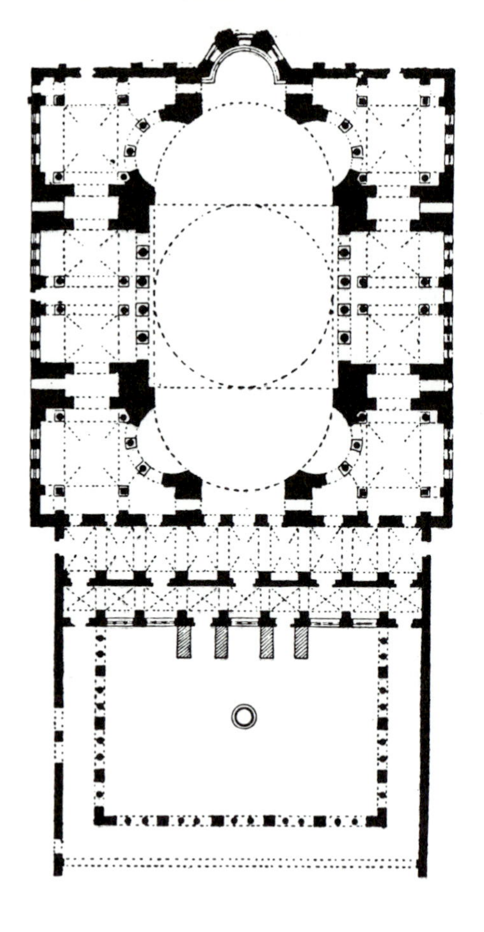

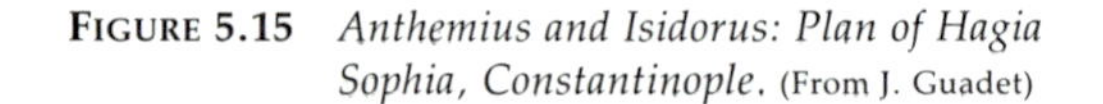

Figure 5.15 *Anthemius and Isidorus: Plan of Hagia Sophia, Constantinople.* (From J. Guadet)

groin-vaulted double **narthex** precedes the church proper.

The structural problems posed by such an audacious design were many, yet the necessary supports do not intrude on the internal space, creating the feeling that the dome floats effortlessly above the billowing interior volumes (Figure 5.17). Nothing could be farther from the actual case. While the brick used does constitute a relatively light construction material, and the vaults are amazingly thin to minimize both thrust and weight, the size of the building means that the gravity forces are large. The forty windows at the base of the dome are set between buttresses that stabilize the junction of dome and pendentives. From this point the load is transferred to four great stone piers, which are further buttressed by being extended above the gallery

Figure 5.16 *Anthemius and Isidorus: Section through Hagia Sophia, Constantinople.* (From J. Guadet)

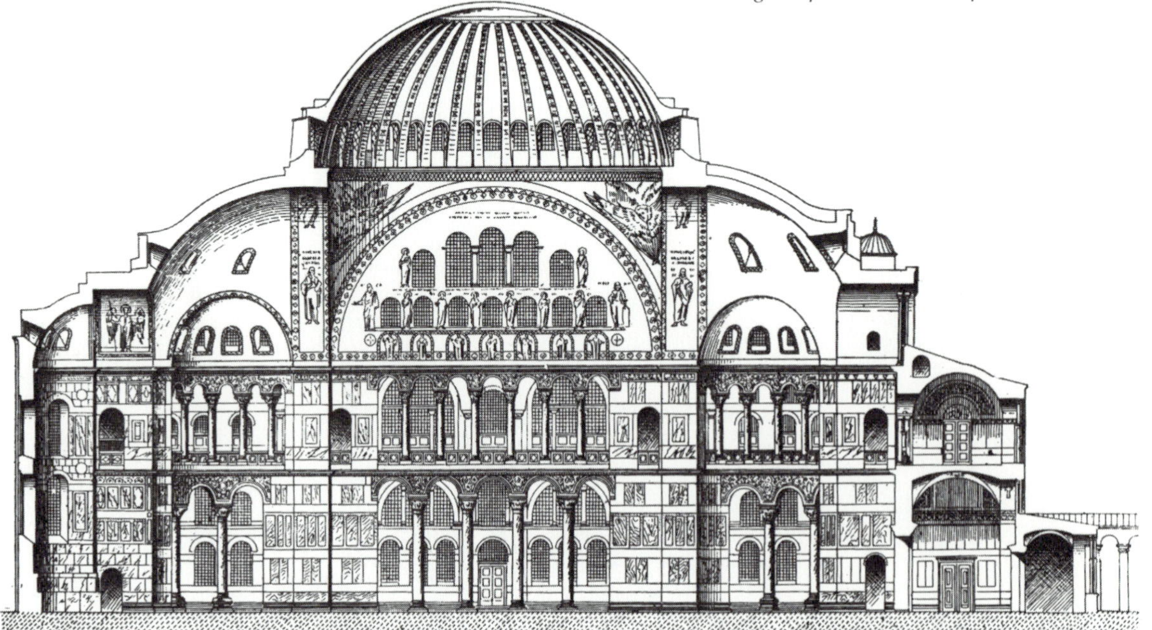

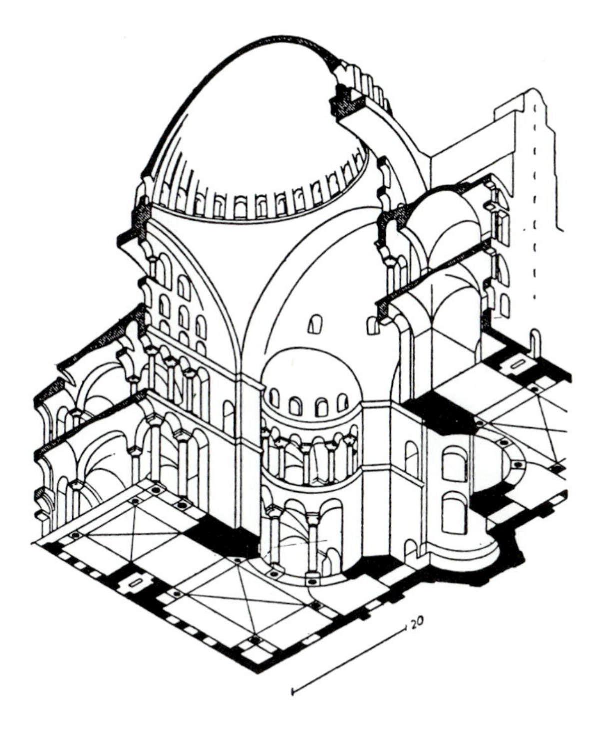

FIGURE 5.17 *Anthemius and Isidorus: Section axonometric of Hagia Sophia, Constantinople.* (From A. Choisy)

vaults to join in great barrel vaults along the sides of the church. The semidomes, which appear to brace the narthex and apse ends, probably contribute little to the structure's integrity, however satisfying they are visually. The masonry mass of the four piers is more obvious on the outside than internally. Anthemius and Isidorus's structural daring overstepped the physical limits of their materials, and the first great dome collapsed in 558. It was reconstructed with a steeper pitch and ribbed construction in 563, but the western half of the rebuilt dome fell in 989. Following repairs, the eastern half collapsed in 1346; the next dome built is the one on the building today.

Statics aside, the effect of the arches, vaults, exedrae, semidomes, and domes is ethereal. Light pours in from windows at many levels, playing over surfaces enriched by colored marbles and mosaic. From a position at the center of the nave, the repetition of curved forms reflects the great dome overhead and creates a pervasive harmony that is constantly varied. From the aisles and galleries, the view into the nave is dramatic, providing a partial perspective of the interconnecting layered spaces surrounding the interior volume. In the church ritual for which Hagia Sophia was built, the major space was reserved for two groups, the ecclesiastics and the retinue of the emperor. The clergy claimed the sanctuary space before the apse, while the imperial court occupied the region at the narthex end. The meeting of patriarch and emperor under the great dome marked a high point of the religious ritual. Ordinary people were relegated to the aisles and galleries, women on one side and men on the other, where they could observe the impressive ceremonial processions and symbolic joining of church and state in this magnificent setting.

CENTRALLY PLANNED BYZANTINE CHURCHES

Roman temples such as the Pantheon and Early Christian baptistries and mausolea had featured centralized plans. Not surprisingly, these precedents combined well with the Byzantine fondness for dome building and contributed to the development of the most characteristic Byzantine churches, which had circular or Greek cross plans. Justinian's churches again provide the dominant models for later centuries.

SS. Sergius and Bacchus (527–536) at Constantinople and S. Vitale (538–548) in Ravenna illustrate two variations on the theme of central plans. SS. Sergius and Bacchus (Figures 5.18, 5.19) is essentially a domed octagon surrounded by aisles and galleries encased in a square, whereas S. Vitale's octagonal dome is echoed by octagonal galleries and aisles. The strong centralizing tendencies of both churches are countered somewhat by apsidal projections opposite the narthex side, and the interior space is more fluid than that seen in S. Costanza, where a similar organizational idea is carried out in circular form. In SS. Sergius and Bacchus, the eight piers supporting the dome are interspersed with two columns, set alternately in semicircular and

FIGURE 5.18 *SS. Sergius and Bacchus, Constantinople, 527–536.* (Photo: Marburg)

FIGURE 5.20 *Interior of SS. Sergius and Bacchus, Constantinople.* (Photo: Marburg)

FIGURE 5.19 *Plan of SS. Sergius and Bacchus, Constantinople.* (From W. Blaser)

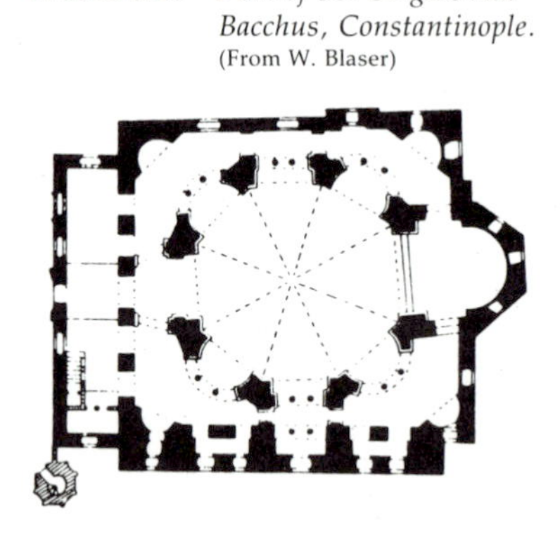

FIGURE 5.21 *S. Vitale, Ravenna, 538–548.* (Photo: Alinari)

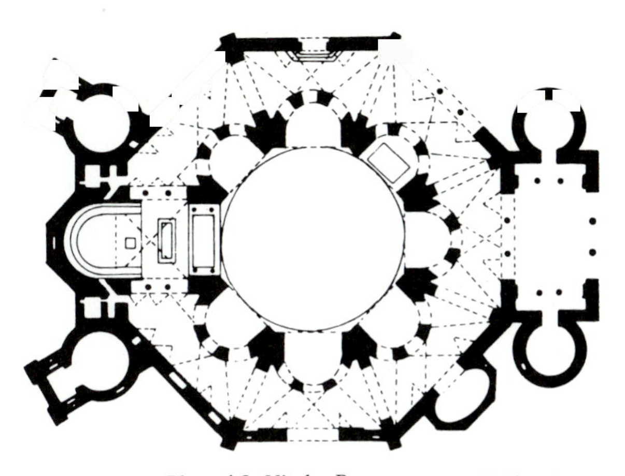

FIGURE 5.22 *Plan of S. Vitale, Ravenna.* (From W. Blaser)

straight alignments, so that the domed area penetrates the surrounding spaces (Figure 5.20). The sixteen-sided "pumpkin vault" dome reflects the alternating niches below in alternate straight and curved sections above its rather low drum.

Although the dome at S. Vitale (Figures 5.21, 5.22) is smaller, its design is more distinguished, with a higher drum and greater internal cohesiveness than at SS. Sergius and Bacchus. Clerestory windows illuminate the nave directly, and between the piers of the octagon, all the niches are semicircular, carving into aisles and galleries to borrow additional light from windows in the exterior wall (Figure 5.23). The proportions of the exterior are equally fine. Simple arched windows set in brick walls articulated by pilasters are capped by red-tile roofs in direct volumetric expression of the internal space. SS. Sergius and Bacchus has lost most of its original interior mosaic, but S. Vitale displays the beautiful products of imperial workshops in marble and mosaic. Carved capitals complete richly veined marble column shafts; book-matched marbles face the lower wall surfaces; and both geometric and figured mosaics complete arch **soffits,** upper walls, vaults, and floors. Mosaic donor panels set on the sides of the apse portray Justinian and his court across from the Empress Theodora and her attendants. The splendor of Byzantium glows throughout this handsome church.

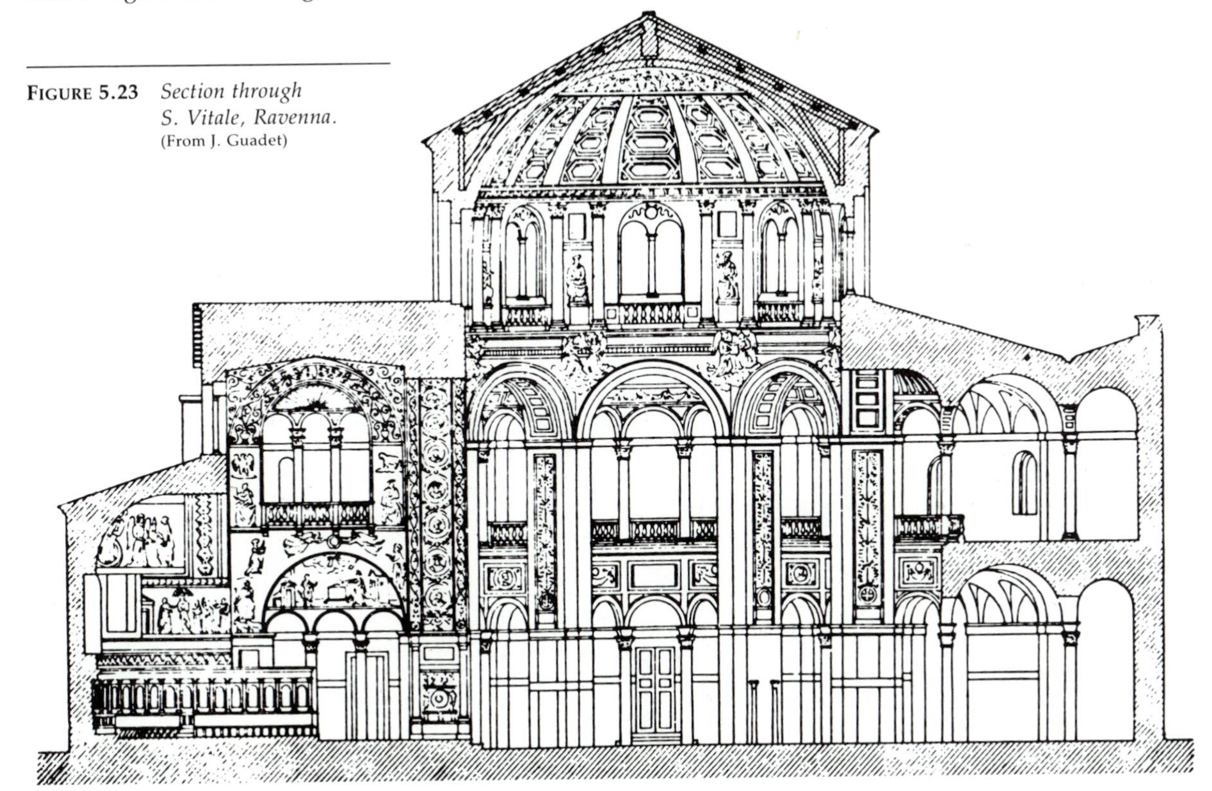

FIGURE 5.23 *Section through S. Vitale, Ravenna.* (From J. Guadet)

For the Justinian prototype of centralized churches on a Greek cross plan, we must rely on fragmentary evidence of the now-vanished Church of the Holy Apostles in Constantinople. Originally erected by Constantine as his own mausoleum and rebuilt by Justinian from 536 to 550, it was demolished in 1469 to provide the site for the Fatih Mosque. A standing church built on the model of Justinian's Church of the Holy Apostles is S. Marco in Venice, begun in 830 and rebuilt starting in 1063 (Figure 5.24). Hemispherical domes cover each arm of the Greek cross plan, and a central one crowns the crossing (Figure 5.25). All are set on pendentives with barrel vaults connecting the large pierced piers that sustain the downward thrust of the domes (Figure 5.26). Windows at the base of some domes illuminate the upper regions of the church and allow light to sparkle

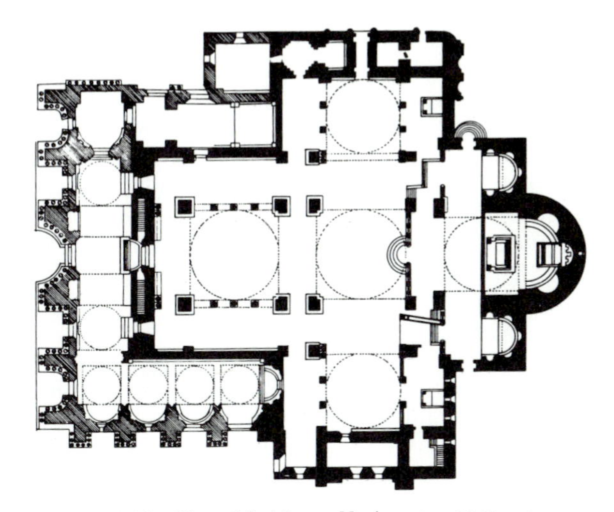

FIGURE 5.25 *Plan of S. Marco, Venice.* (From W. Blaser)

FIGURE 5.26 *Section through S. Marco, Venice.* (From J. Guadet)

◀ **FIGURE 5.24** *S. Marco, Venice, begun 830.* (Photo: School of Architecture, University of Tennessee)

across the gold-ground mosaics of the interior. While the basic design concept for San Marco stems from Byzantium, much there reflects other architectural traditions. For example, the present exterior portal hoods are fifteenth-century Gothic, and the external dome profiles, raised on a timber framework above the masonry work, reflect the shape of Islamic domes. Nevertheless, San Marco is substantially Byzantine, and it would become the model for Romanesque churches in France shortly after its completion.

The Greek cross plan became the most common one for later Byzantine churches in the lands of the Eastern Orthodox Church. Most often it was realized as a cross-in-square plan or a cross-domed plan on a rather modest scale, so the vaulting did not pose constructional complexities. The cross-in-square plan has nine bays, with the central one domed, and diminutive domes over the corner bays; all other sections are barrel-vaulted. In cross-domed plans, the arms of the Greek cross are reduced in length and covered with barrel vaults, which surround the crossing dome. Aisles and galleries enclose the church on three sides, and three apses complete the fourth side. Other variants, all encompassing centralized plans because these fit liturgical practice and symbolized the mystery of the Mass, were constructed until the fall of the Byzantine Empire in 1453, and they continue to inspire Eastern Orthodox churches of the present day.

6.

ISLAMIC ARCHITECTURE

As we have seen, Early Christians went through an extensive process to develop architectural forms suitable for and expressive of a new religion. Followers of the Prophet Mohammed underwent a similar evolution, but one leading to different results, as they created buildings to serve and symbolize the religion, called variously Muslim or Islam, that was founded by Mohammed.

Islam originated among the nomadic desert tribes of Arabia. In 610 the Archangel Gabriel appeared to Mohammed at his home in Mecca and expounded the revelation of Allah. These revelations were collected into a holy book, the *Koran,* which expressed in Arabic the message of *Islam,* a word signifying submission to the will of Allah and meaning "I hear and obey." Each Muslim accepted five basic truths or duties: to believe in the oneness of God as professed in faith in Allah and his prophet; to pray five times daily; to observe an annual fast during the month of Ramadan; to give alms to the poor; and to make at least one pilgrimage to Mecca.

Conversion of the desert tribes to Islam was accompanied by an intense awakening of Arab unity, and the courage and fighting skill of the nomads, previously exploited by the Sassanian and Byzantine empires, was turned against these masters in a fury of rapid conquests. By 661 Islamic armies had swept through Iran, Iraq, Palestine, Syria, and Egypt, and they then moved across the North African coast to enter Spain in 711. From Spain they pushed northward into France, where forces led by Charles Martel stopped their European expansion in 732 at the Battle of Tours. Muslim civilization remained in central and southern Spain until 1492, and Islamic armies continued to batter the southern borders of the Byzantine Empire until they finally conquered Constantinople in 1453. Through trade Islam made contact with China and India, where the Muslim religion would eventually follow. With military conquest came economic, social, and cultural dominance as surviving Roman practices were replaced by Islamic customs and Arabic language. Islamic policy toward conquered populations was generally one of accommodation; their rule was often preferred by the natives to that of harsh Byzantine governors.

EARLY SHRINES

Given their nomadic origins, the Islamic Arabs had few architectural traditions. For their earliest buildings, therefore, they assimilated techniques and forms from the civilizations they overran. Syrian and Christian influences are clear in one of the earliest Islamic shrines, the Dome of the Rock (687–691) in Jerusalem (Figure 6.1). Its site on Mount Moriah was sacred to the Jews both as the site on which

FIGURE 6.1 *Dome of the Rock, Jerusalem, 687–691.* (Photo: Israeli Government Tourist Office)

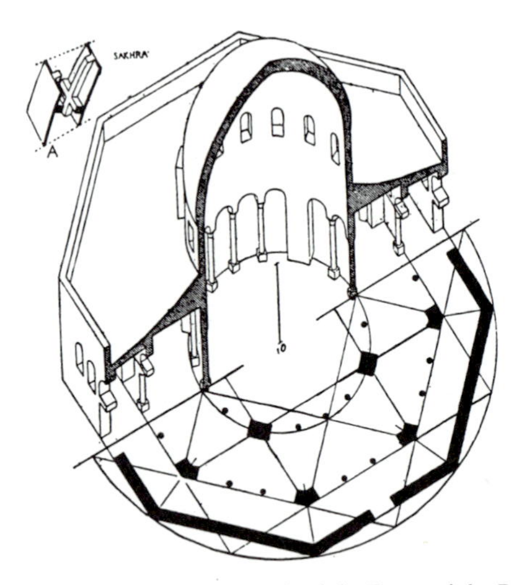

FIGURE 6.2 *Section axonometric of the Dome of the Rock, Jerusalem.* (From A. Choisy)

Abraham had offered his son Isaac as a sacrifice to the Lord and as the location of Solomon's Temple. To Moslems, it was the place from which Mohammed ascended in his Night Journey to Paradise, where he met Jesus, Joseph, Enoch, Aaron, Moses, Abraham, and Allah. At the center of the Dome of the Rock is a cave with a single opening. The shrine is carefully positioned around this rocky outcrop, the domed central portion enclosing the cave and a concentric aisle permitting circumambulation. The building's form was probably derived from Christian precedent. Constantine's Church of the Holy Sepulchre in Jerusalem had featured a similar rotunda, and there were many centrally planned domed churches throughout the Byzantine world. Unlike most Byzantine domes, however, the structure here is of wood; there is evidence that early Christian shrines also had wooden domes, although none have survived to the present day.

The dome of the Jerusalem sanctuary, sixty-seven feet in diameter, is constructed of a double-shell, each shell having thirty-two converging wooden **ribs,** and the whole rests on a cornice atop a masonry drum (Figure 6.2). The inner ribs are plastered and adorned with painted and gilded designs (fourteenth-century reconstructions); the exterior is sheathed with boards and finished with lead and gold leaf. The drum is supported on four piers, with three columns set between each pier. Between this inner ring of columns and piers and the outside wall is an intermediate ring of eight piers alternating with paired sets of columns, all supporting a circle of wooden tie beams overhead. The location of major elements in the plan is governed by a geometric figure contained in the circle circumscribing the octagon formed by the exterior walls. If two rotated squares are inscribed in this circle so that their corners are opposite the center of the octagon faces, the piers of the intermediate ring occur at the intersections of the lines forming the squares. Furthermore, the four innermost piers fit into the grid of lines drawn across the plan from the eight intermediate piers. Such a harmonic relationship would suggest that the architect had a sophisticated understanding of geometric order.

Rich materials covered both interior and exterior surfaces. Marble facings were used on some interior piers and walls, and elegant mosaics portraying stylized palm and acanthus plants finished other piers and vaulted surfaces. Windows had ornamental stone grilles based on Roman patterns, and the arches around the rotunda were set with alternating red and white stones, a technique called **poly-**

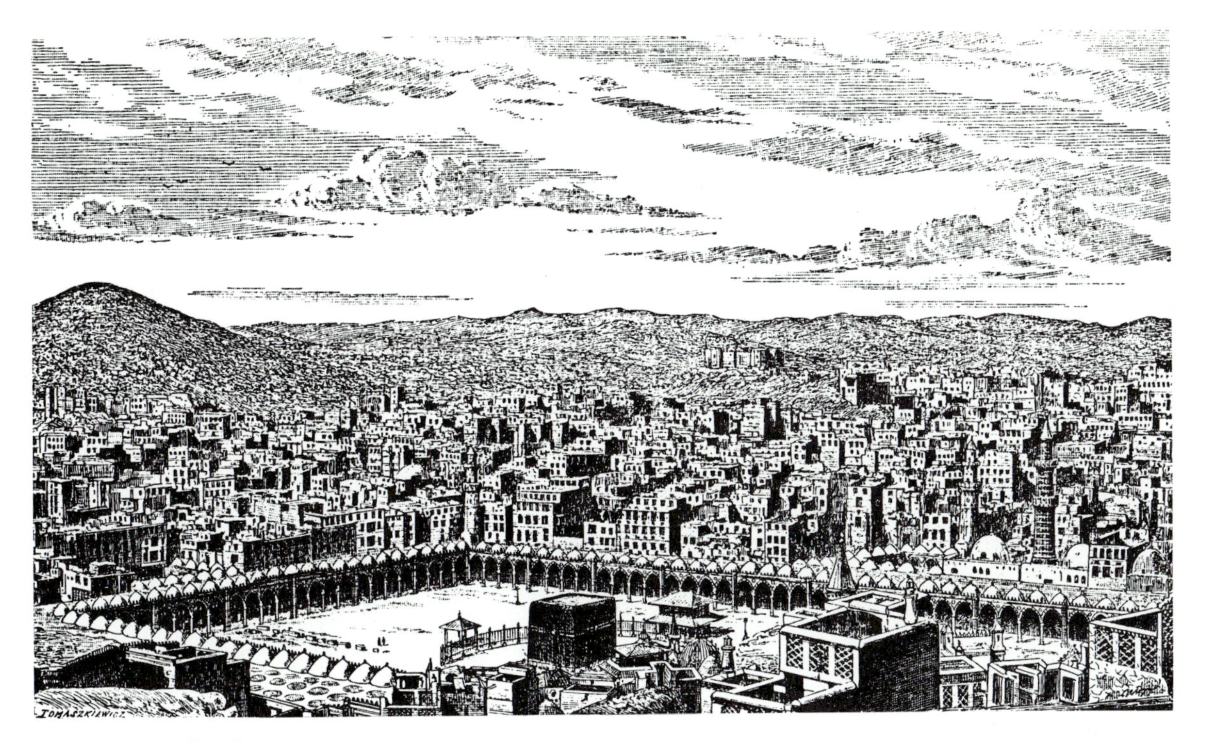

FIGURE 6.3 *Kaaba, Mecca.* (From G. Perrot and C. Chipiez)

chromy, which is seen in many later Islamic buildings. An inscription in Arabic characters at the base of the dome proclaims Islam as the true religion, the successor to Judaism and Christianity. In building the Dome of the Rock, Islam created a monument to rival the wealth and magnificence of other temples and churches, thereby providing a tangible symbol of the new religion's ascendency.

The general scheme employed at the Dome of the Rock, that of a central shrine around which the faithful could circulate, was used earlier at Mecca in rebuilding the Kaaba, the goal of Islamic pilgrimage (Figure 6.3). This shrine contained a meteorite that had been venerated in pre-Muslim times; Mohammed had destroyed the idols placed around it, and his successors cleared buildings from the vicinity in order to provide clear circulation space around the stone. At the Hajj, or annual pilgrimage, the devout process seven times around the Kaaba, stopping each time to kiss the Black Stone.

DESERT PALACES

Consistent with their nomadic roots, early Islamic rulers or caliphs preferred life in the desert to life in cities, and they constructed a number of desert encampments or palaces in the Middle East. About 711 to 715 (or as late as the middle of the eighth century), such a settlement was built at Qusayr Amra, about fifty miles east of Amman, Jordan, by Caliph Al-Walid or his successor, Al-Walid II (Figures 6.4, 6.5). The caliph's Bedouin followers would simply have pitched their tents in this desert resting place, but the leader merited more permanent buildings. Those that survive are an audience hall and a small private bath, both interesting for their vaulted construction. The audience hall is nearly square in

FIGURE 6.4 *Desert Palace, Qusayr Amra, 711–715.* (Photo: Jordan Information Bureau)

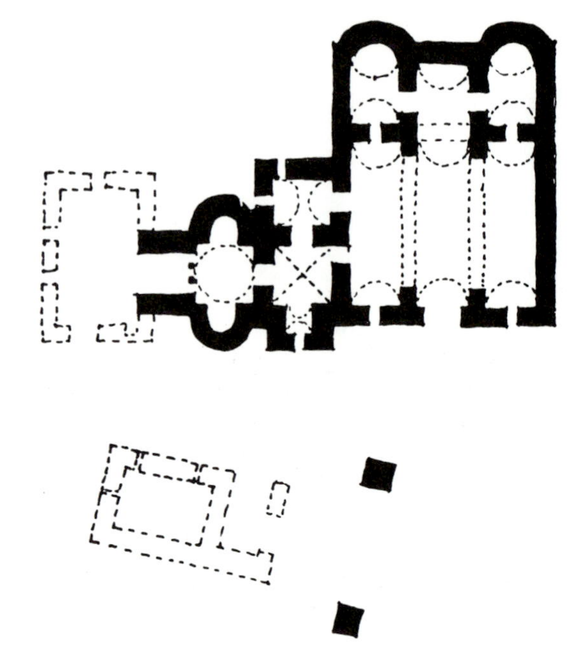

FIGURE 6.5 *Plan of Desert Palace, Qusayr Amra.* (Redrawn from K. Creswell)

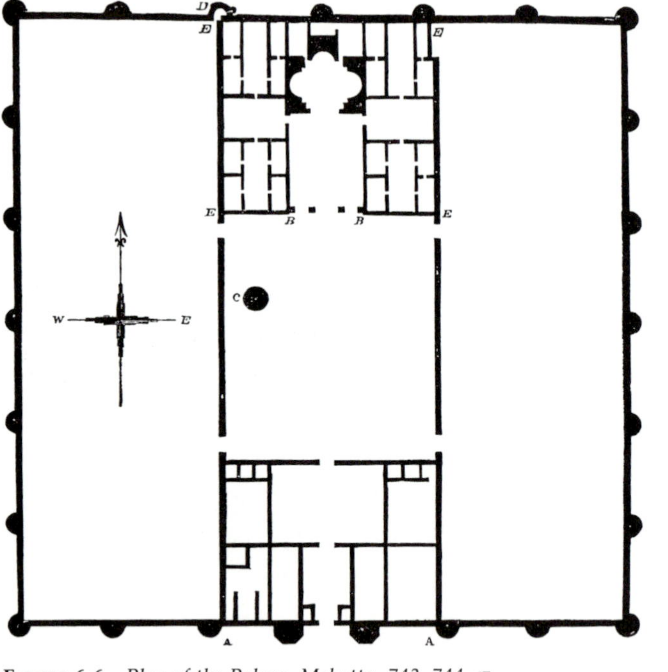

FIGURE 6.6 *Plan of the Palace, Mshatta, 743–744.* (From J. Fergusson)

plan, twenty-four by twenty-eight feet, with a central alcove on axis from the entrance flanked by side rooms. This division into thirds corresponds to the ceiling vaults of the audience hall, where two longitudinal arches support three transverse barrel vaults. Both arches are slightly pointed, making this one of the first places where this feature is found in Islamic work. It is thought to be of Syrian origin since pointed arches are unknown in Roman building. Attached to the audience hall are the three small rooms of the baths: a barrel-vaulted changing room, a groin-vaulted tepidarium, and a domed caldarium warmed by underfloor heating and supplied with piped water in the Roman manner. Interiors were finished with frescoes throughout, and the dome was embellished to represent the vault of heaven, with the northern constellations of stars and the signs of the zodiac. On the exterior, the articulated roofs directly reflect the vaulting patterns, and the massing of the whole complex is reminiscent of the Hunting Baths at Leptis Magna.

Other desert residences were based on the designs of Roman frontier forts combined with influences from Sassanian audience halls. Such was the case with the Mshatta Palace (Figure 6.6), located about twenty miles south of Amman, Jordan, and constructed in 743–744. Stone walls, reinforced by towers set at regular intervals, form the square enclosure, measuring about 475 feet on a side. There is only one entrance, in the center of the south wall, and it establishes the central axis through an entrance hall, a rectangular secondary court, the large square central court, and a concluding basilica hall terminating in a triple-apsed square chamber. Secondary rooms, including a mosque on the south side, complete the symmetry of the central section of the palace; the flanking side sections seem never to have been built, although tie courses in the stonework indicate that apartments were to have been constructed there. As with the Dome of the Rock, an orderly geometry underlies the plan, and reliance on Roman precedent is evident. The formal plan and central axis recall *castra* plans, while the entrance to the basilica hall is formed by a triple-arched gateway, with the central span being wider than the side spans in the manner of a Roman triumphal arch. Surviving decorations on the lower portions of the outer wall are set in a continuous frieze nearly fifteen feet high; they include a ground of stylized vines in intertwining geometric patterns, accented by rosettes set amid a great zig-zag projecting molding (Figures 6.7, 6.8). These form a novel scheme, demonstrating the same love of surface ornament found in the Jerusalem building, and presaging the intricate ornamental elaborations so characteristic of mature Islamic architecture.

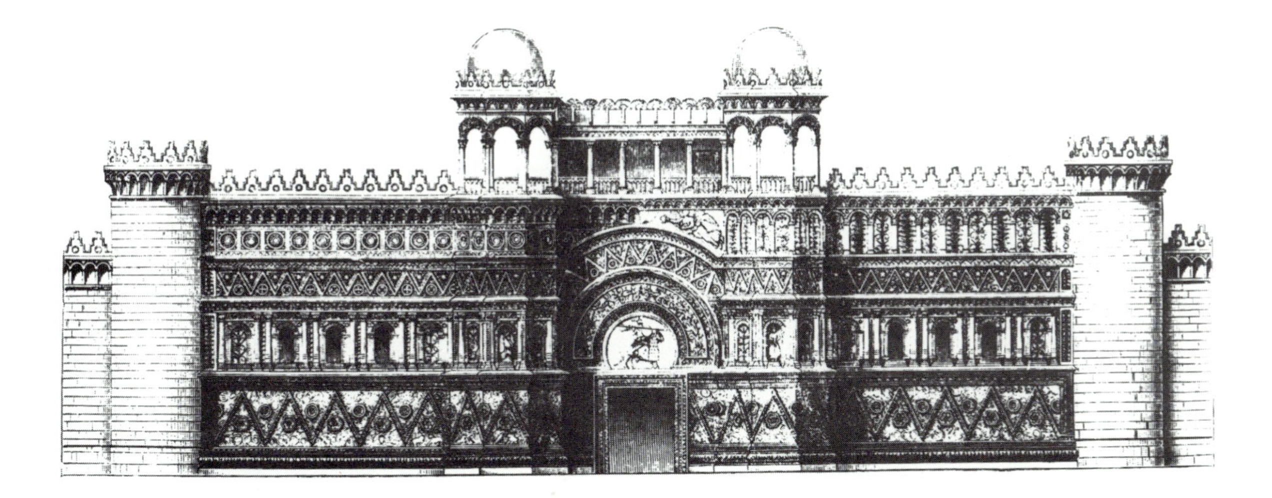

FIGURE 6.7 *Elevation of the Palace, Mshatta.* (From J. Fergusson)

FIGURE 6.8 *Elevation detail of the Palace, Mshatta.* (From J. Fergusson)

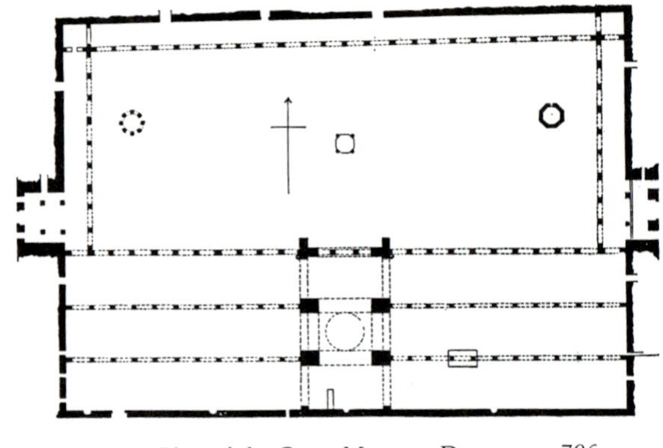

FIGURE 6.9 *Plan of the Great Mosque, Damascus, 706–715.* (From J. Fergusson)

DEVELOPMENT OF THE MOSQUE

The building type most closely associated with Islam is the mosque, the primary place of worship, which evolved from several sources, including the House of the Prophet at Medina (ca. 622), Christian churches, and perhaps the apadana halls of Persian kings. Beside Mohammed's house was a square enclosure, with small chambers set in the southeast corner for his living quarters. The remainder of the space was a partially open central court. Although constructed originally for domestic purposes, it also served as a gathering place for his followers to hear sermons and prayers, and after Mohammed's death, its form was imitated in simple worship facilities built in Islamic settlements. When territorial expansion brought the forces of Islam into established cities, readily available spaces, particularly Christian churches, were converted to mosques by removing Christian images and orienting the prayer wall or **qibla** to face toward Mecca. In areas formerly controlled by Persia, the remains of audience halls or apadanas were renovated to provide space for worship. The size of the mosque was proportional to the size of the community; the five daily prayers required of the faithful did not necessarily take place in mosques, but on Friday, all the men in the community were to assemble in the main mosque for prayers.

The Great Mosque at Damascus (706–715, with later rebuildings) illustrates the process through which the mosque form developed (Figure 6.9). The site was an ancient one on which had stood a Roman temple dedicated to Jupiter and a fourth-century Christian church dedicated to St. John the Baptist. For a time after Muslim conquest of the city in 635, both Christians and Muslims worshipped on the site, but in 706 the Christian church was pulled down and an impressive mosque, based in part on tripartite aisle-and-nave basilican church plans, was constructed under the caliphate of Al-Walid. The mosque's outline was determined by the shape of the Roman shrine, a walled irregular rectangle 1262 by 1004 feet, entered through a gateway in the center of the shorter east side. Four towers, once part of a Roman temple enclosure on the site, provided an elevated platform at the corners of the site from which a caller could summon the faithful to prayer. The general design of these towers, known as minarets, may have been based on earlier fortification towers or lighthouses, but with their incorporation at Damascus, they became standard features of subsequent mosques. Particularly important mosques could have multiple minarets; those in Mecca and later in Constantinople had as many as six.

Over half of the inner space was given to an open arcaded courtyard, the *sahn,* containing a domed fountain pavilion for ritual ablutions. The covered prayer hall extended along the entire long south wall. Two parallel rows of columns divided this hall longitudinally into thirds, near the center of which the arcades were interrupted by a broad transverse element similar to a transept, with a wooden dome over its central bay. The entrance to the transept from the sahn was through a triple-arched entry that historians believe was based on the design of the now-destroyed Chalki Gate of the palace in Constantinople. (That design also influenced the entrance to Justinian's palace in Ravenna, which is illustrated in the mosaics of S. Apollinare Nuovo.) The south wall being the qibla, there are three niches or **mihrabs** set into it to indicate the direction of Mecca; a raised pulpit or **mimbar,** from which Koranic readings, sermons, or official proclamations and addresses are given, is located to the right of the central mihrab. Extensive mosaics originally covered the upper walls and arches, and although little remains of them today, their subjects are known: naturalistic vegetation, as in the Dome of the Rock, together with a continuing frieze of villages, townscapes, and running water, the Islamic image of Paradise. The Great Mosque at Damascus was one of the glories of early Islamic architecture, and its features would influence later mosque designs.

Of later mosques the one begun around 785 in Córdoba, Spain (Figure 6.10), is most closely linked with the Great Mosque of Damascus, having been founded by a descendent of Al-Walid who brought Syrians with him to Spain. In the first construction period, the mosque contained ten rows of eleven columns to create an eleven-aisled sanctuary. Superimposed arches connect the columns, the lower arch being horseshoe-shaped and the upper one not quite semicircular (Figure 6.11). The effect of this work is light and delicate, and although the stacked arches of Roman aqueducts have been suggested as the inspiration for the superimposed arches, their treatment here is entirely original. Both arch levels are polychrome, composed of white stone voussoirs set alternately with red brick ones; the salvaged columns on which they rest are of various designs, some fluted and some plain, with Corinthian capitals. Since the ceiling above the sanctuary originally was flat, the builders facilitated roof drainage by a parallel series of gable roofs with sloping drains in the valleys to discharge water to the sides of the building. Each aisle opened to the sahn, where eleven horseshoe arches framed as many entrances to the sanctuary. The sahn itself was large, 240 feet by 197 feet, and its entrances were set in the midpoints of the wall enclosing the entire mosque.

FIGURE 6.11 *Interior arcades of the Great Mosque, Córdoba.* (Photo: Marburg)

FIGURE 6.10 *Plan of the Great Mosque, Córdoba, 785, 961–988.* (From J. Fergusson)

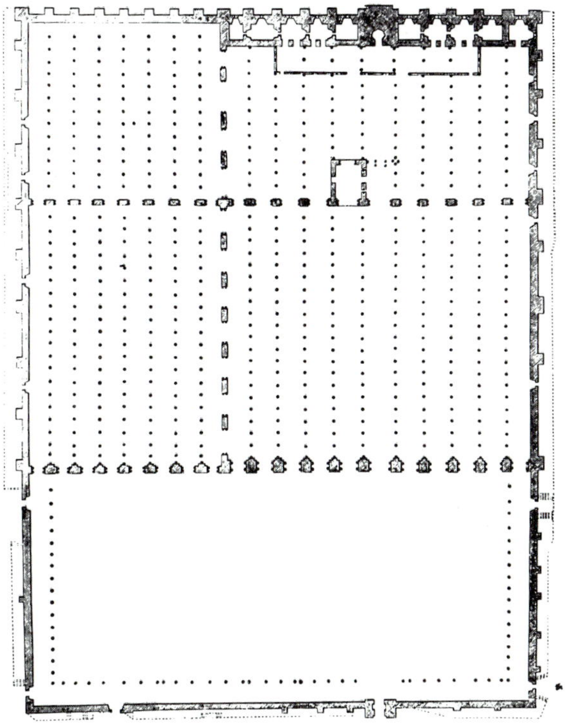

From 833 to 988, the Great Mosque at Córdoba was expanded in three separate building campaigns that enormously enlarged the prayer hall area by extending it both north and south of the previous space and building a further eastern extension to create an entirely new arcaded sahn with a new minaret in the northern boundary wall. The original eleven aisle sanctuary width and the design of superimposed arcades were maintained in the portions added from 833 to 848, although the original 110 freestanding columns became 180 and the surface decoration was even richer and more dazzling. In 965–966, the mosque area was increased by another 110 columns, and the qibla was extended southward. In the center of the new qibla was an elaborately domed bay in front of the mihrab, which rose above interlaced arches and was finished with

Figure 6.12 *Dome of the Great Mosque, Córdoba.* (Photo: Marburg)

glass mosaic from Constantinople. On either side were square bays crowned by vaults set in boldly interlaced arch ribs (Figure 6.12). Arches enclosing the *maqsura,* a screen surrounding the mihrab, were lobed and cusped, and its canopy was formed by open, interlaced arch ribs. The final extension of 987–988 was constructed on the eastern side, with another 319 freestanding columns. While sixteenth-century construction of a Christian church within the Mosque has destroyed its architectural unity, the imaginative design and ornamental magnificence of the original interior survive.

An Islamic center was established along the coast of North Africa at Kairouan (in present-day Tunisia) as early as 670, and its Great Mosque was rebuilt in 836 to substantially the design remaining today (Figure 6.13). The plan is essentially the standard one established at Damascus, with an arcaded sahn, a seventeen-aisled sanctuary, a central mihrab in the qibla (Figure 6.14), and a large imposing domed minaret copied from Syrian church prototypes (Figure 6.15). In contrast to the mosques at both Damascus and Córdoba, this mosque is comparatively plain. Much of the interior richness comes from the decorative columns and capitals reused from Roman and Byzantine ruins. The central aisle is the widest one and is given additional dignity by the use of paired columns on either side and two domes, raised on **squinches,** of a unique fluted masonry construction.

Figure 6.13 *Plan of the Great Mosque, Kairouan, 670, rebuilt 836.* (Delineator: C. Robbs)

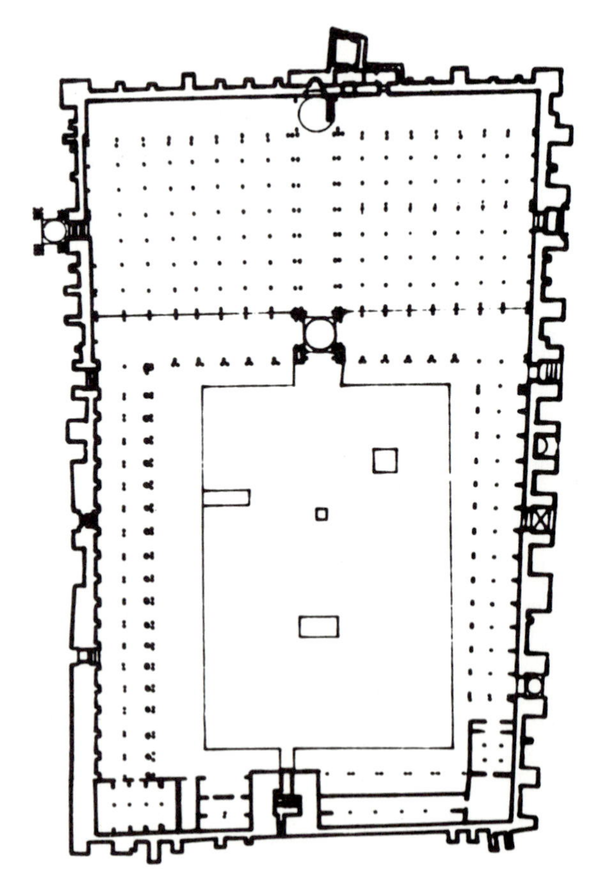

FIGURE 6.14 *Mihrab of the Great Mosque, Kairouan.* (Photo: Tunisian National Office of Tourism)

FIGURE 6.15 *Minaret of the Great Mosque, Kairouan.* (Photo: Tunisian National Office of Tourism)

In the ancient lands of Mesopotamia, factional disputes between Islamic leaders led to the establishment by the Abbasid caliphs in 836 of a new capital city at Samarra, about fifty miles north of Baghdad. The site was abandoned in 892, but not before an enormous mosque, the largest in Islam, was constructed from 848 to 852. The Great Mosque of Samarra was a walled rectangle, 784 by 512 feet, containing an arcaded sahn and a twenty-five-aisled covered prayer hall (Figure 6.16). Its central longitudinal axis was established by an impressive spiraling minaret opposite the northern entrance wall. The minaret and the mosque's enclosing wall are the best-preserved features of the building. All the interior supports and the roof have long since fallen to vandals, but it appears that the teak roof rested directly on octagonal brick piers flanked by four columns salvaged from earlier buildings. Fragments of

FIGURE 6.16 *Plan of the Great Mosque, Samarra. 848–852.* (Delineator: B. Schafer)

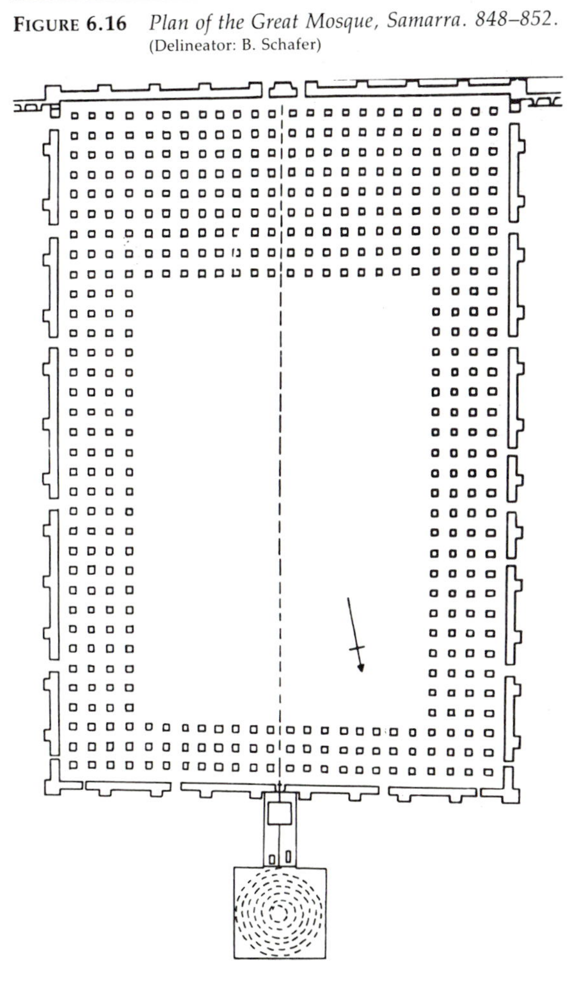

FIGURE 6.17 *Sinan: Sehzade Cami, Constantinople. 1543–1548.* (Photo: Marburg)

mosaic and wooden paneling hint at the interior decoration. Towering 164 feet over the ruins is the brick-built minaret, which rises from a square podium to become a ramped spiral that turns five times before reaching the cylindrical summit pavilion. Its form was probably inspired by Assyrian or Neo-Babylonian ziggurats such as the one in Babylon, which had a similar spiraling ramp to the top, although built on a square plan.

DOMED MOSQUES OF CONSTANTINOPLE

The end of the Byzantine Empire came in 1453, when the determined forces of the Ottoman Turks, led by Sultan Mehmet II, breached the walls of Constantinople and completed their conquest of the Balkans. Christian churches in the city were either converted to mosques, as ultimately happened to Hagia Sophia, or pulled down to make way for new buildings. Hagia Sophia, in particular, became a prototype for many later mosques, and domed construction became characteristic of Islamic building in eastern Europe and western Asia.

Among Mehmet II's additions to Constantinople was the Fatih Cami or Mosque of Mehmet II (1463–1470), an impressive structure with a sahn set in a still-larger courtyard surrounded by hostels, charitable foundations, a library, and sixteen theological schools. The axial plan recalls imperial Rome, and the domed prayer hall is clearly inspired by Hagia Sophia. On axis, its central dome, eighty-five feet in diameter, was followed by a semidome in front of the mihrab; the major volume was braced by flanking aisle vaults. This building collapsed in an earthquake in 1766 and was rebuilt along different lines. The sahn best retains the spirit of the first design, with a central fountain structure and cypress trees surrounded by polychrome arcades.

Islamic architecture reached its apogee with the long career of Koca Sinan (ca. 1490–1588), a distinguished engineer and architect who has been compared with his contemporary, Michelangelo, for the breadth of his contributions and the length of his career. Born to a peasant family of non-Muslim background, Sinan was recruited for governmental service as a youth and trained in the corps of Janissaries. After participating in military campaigns in Austria, Greece, and Mesopotamia, he served as court architect in Constantinople for fifty years, during which he designed and supervised construction of a large number of projects, including waterworks, bridges, and buildings. His first major architectural commission was the Sehzade Cami (1543–1548), a mosque composed of two joined squares (Figures 6.17, 6.18). One square contains the sahn, which has a central fountain and is surrounded by domed bays behind arcades. The second square is the enclosed sanctuary, where the central dome is complemented by four semidomes set at the sides, with smaller domes and half-domes filling the remaining spaces. The elegantly symmetrical geometry of the plan is matched by the balanced volumes of the interior space and the exterior massing (Figure 6.19).

A similar quality marks Sinan's most famous work, the Kulliye of Süleyman the Magnificent, begun in 1550 as a vast complex containing a mosque at the center with buildings of a theological university grouped at its sides (Figure 6.20). The site was

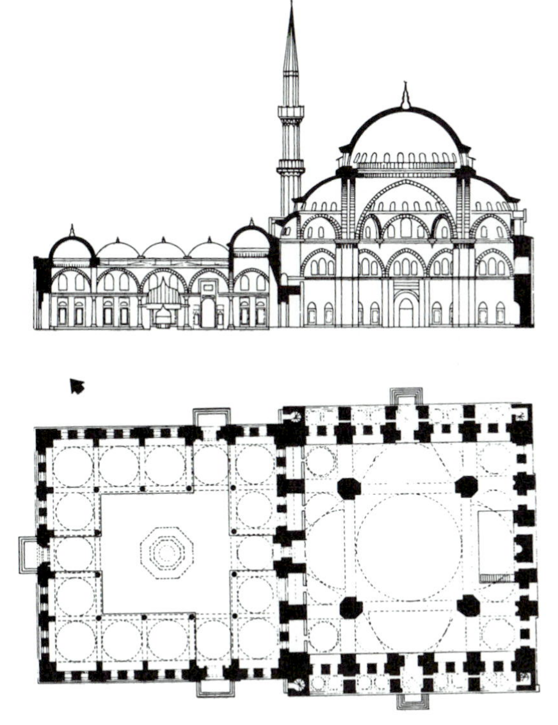

FIGURE 6.18 *Sinan: Plan and section of the Sehzade Cami, Constantinople.* (From W. Blaser)

FIGURE 6.19 *Sinan: Interior of the Sehzade Cami, Constantinople.* (Photo: Marburg)

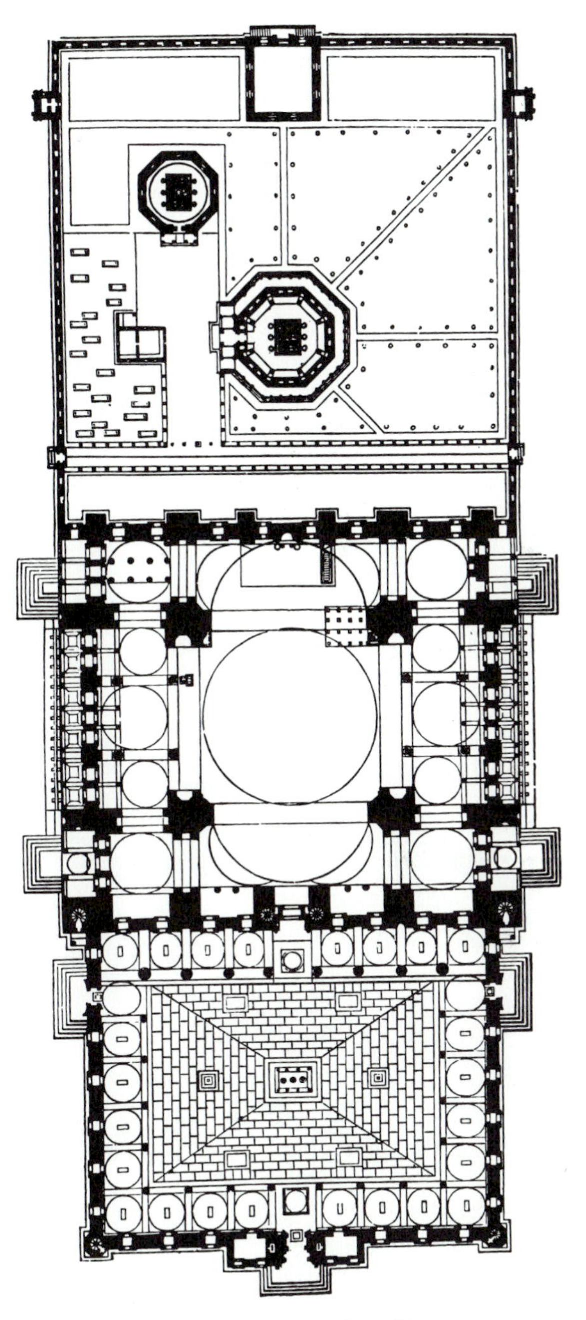

FIGURE 6.20 *Sinan: Plan of the Kulliye of Süleyman the Magnificent, Constantinople, begun 1550.* (From J. Fergusson)

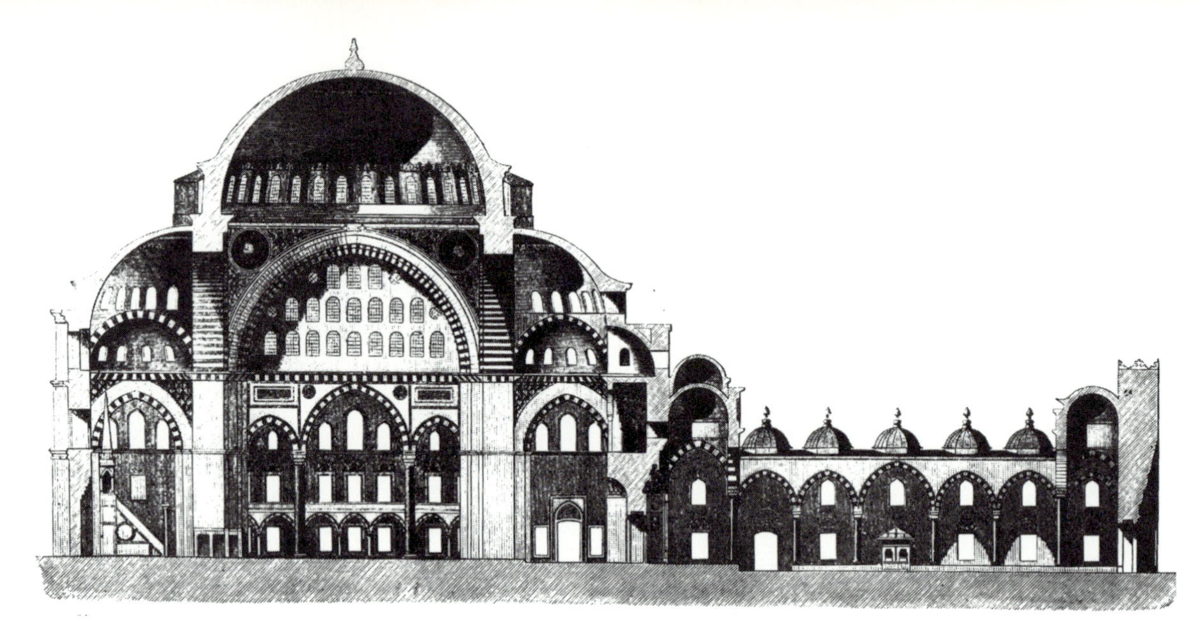

FIGURE 6.21 *Sinan: Section of the Kulliye of Süleyman the Magnificent, Constantinople.* (From J. Fergusson)

FIGURE 6.22 *Mosque of Ahmet II [Blue Mosque], Constantinople, 1609–1616.* (Photo: Turkish Ministry of Culture and Tourism)

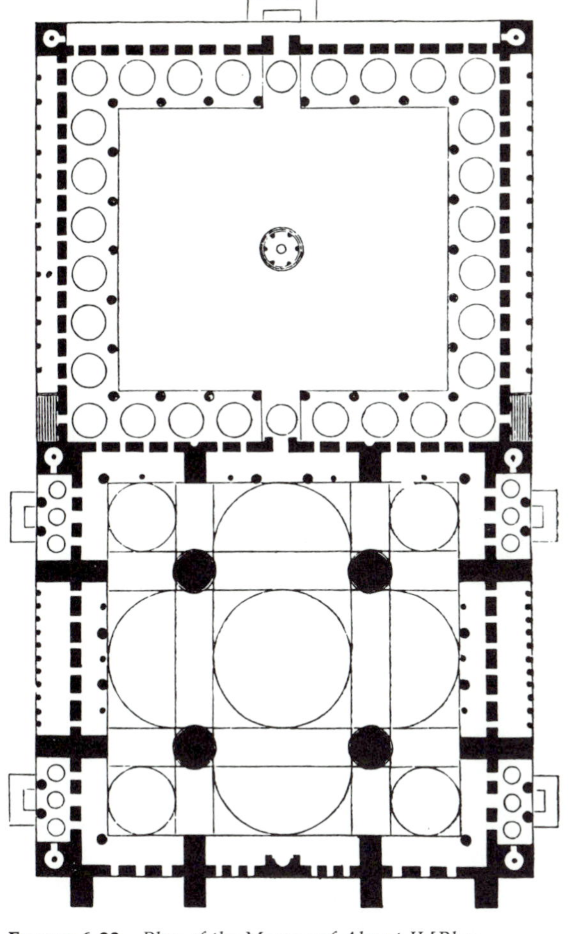

FIGURE 6.23 *Plan of the Mosque of Ahmet II [Blue Mosque], Constantinople.* (From J. Fergusson)

the sloping side of a hill fronting on the Golden Horn, and Sinan located the complex to reinforce the dramatic possibilities of the terrain. The Süleymaniye Mosque dominates the group (Figure 6.21). Its plan is familiar: an arcaded sahn, the domed prayer hall, and a walled tomb enclosure set on a linear axis. The prayer hall is a variant of Hagia Sophia, having a central dome flanked by two semidomes, but here the aisles, also domed, are so configured as to contain the entire building within a square. The whole presents a more consistent articulation, both inside and out, than was achieved in the Byzantine building. Buttressing elements, arches, vaults, and domes work together as structure and visual elements to create a satisfying architectural composition.

The general arrangement of the Sehzade Cami was used again in the Mosque of Ahmet II (1609–1616), the most prominent mosque built in Constantinople after Sinan (Figures 6.22, 6.23). Located across the ancient Hippodrome from Hagia Sophia, the Sultan Ahmet Mosque rivals the earlier building as a majestic presence in the cityscape and is distinguished by its six minarets, which rise from the corners of the domed prayer hall and the front façade of the sahn. Blue tiles adorn the interior, giving the mosque its popular designation as the Blue Mosque. Loads from the seventy-seven-foot-diameter dome are sustained in part by four great cylindrical columns, each over sixteen feet across. The fluting and ornamentation of these columns reduce their apparent mass (Figure 6.24). Multiple levels of windows in the exterior walls, along the upper galleries, and at the base of the dome and semidomes provide

FIGURE 6.24 *Interior of the Mosque of Ahmet II [Blue Mosque], Constantinople.* (Photo: Turkish Ministry of Culture and Tourism)

FIGURE 6.25 *Plan of the Alhambra, Granada, thirteenth and fourteenth centuries.* (From J. Fergusson)

FIGURE 6.26 *Court of Myrtle Trees at the Alhambra, Granada.* (Photo: Spanish Ministry of Information and Tourism)

FIGURE 6.27 *Court of Lions at the Alhambra, Granada.* (Photo: Marburg)

abundant interior illumination. This and other mosques built throughout the Turkish domains reflect the contributions of Sinan in handsome designs.

THE ALHAMBRA

Among the treasures of Islamic architecture is the fortress-palace of the Alhambra in Granada, Spain (Figure 6.25). The Alhambra was built in the thirteenth and fourteenth centuries by the Nasrid Dynasty, which governed the dwindling Islamic territories of southern Spain until being expelled in 1492 by Ferdinand and Isabella, the monarchs who also financed Columbus's expedition to the Indies in the same year. Some parts of the Alhambra are now ruined, and its site on a ridge overlooking the city is crowded by the later Palace of Charles V, but the primary ceremonial areas are intact. The most important chambers were grouped around two rectangular open courts: the Court of Myrtle Trees, which provided access to the Hall of the Ambassadors; and the Court of Lions, so named for an antique fountain at its center.

The Court of Myrtle Trees has a central rectangular pool fed by gently overflowing fountain basins at opposite ends (Figure 6.26). Arcaded galleries are set across the short sides and rows of myrtle trees parallel the pool on the long sides. At the north end is the Comares Tower which contained the square-plan Hall of the Ambassadors, a rather small room, thirty-six feet on a side, with a soaring sixty-foot ceiling. The Court of Lions is the more celebrated space. Its perimeter is set with slender-columned arcades and its center is divided into quadrants by shallow watercourses emanating from the lion fountain at the center (Figure 6.27). This layout symbolizes the Koran's vision of Paradise: a garden below which rivers flow.

The Alhambra's plan is enriched by the profusion of decorative detail that covers all surfaces conveying splendor, ineffable lightness, and the ethereal quality of a dream world. Marbles, colored ceramic tiles, and carved and gilded wood or stucco screens create changing shade and shadow as light reflects from water and polished surfaces or flickers through pierced walls and ceilings. Pattern and texture abound in both geometric arabesques and stylized plant forms embellished with flowing Arabic inscriptions; arches are lobed and cusped; windows have elaborate grilles; and ceilings feature stalactites of carved plaster. Behind the ornament, the underlying rubble masonry construction is not of the highest quality, as it was the effect of magnificence that was desired rather than the substance. Even without its interior furnishings and original courtyard plantings, however, the Alhambra's sumptuous character can still be appreciated today.

Although the Alhambra ends our discussion of Islamic architecture, it should be noted that Islam had a profound effect on buildings in Africa, India, and Asia, which lie outside the scope of this text because they have no direct bearing on western architectural history. Islam was also an important culture in the West, transmitting and extending arched construction from the Middle East to Europe. Polychromy became a part of Carolingian and Romanesque architecture; the pointed arch of Gothic work may well have originated with Islamic builders; and the domes of interlacing arches at the Great Mosque at Córdoba influenced late Baroque domes in northern Italy. The Moors were expelled from Spain, but their artistic legacy remained to inspire later architects.

7.

Early Medieval and Romanesque Architecture

While the Byzantine and Islamic cultures were flourishing in eastern Europe and around the southern rim of the Mediterranean, the portions of western Europe that had been part of the Roman Empire entered a sustained period of decline. From the first centuries of the Christian era, these outposts of the empire had been besieged repeatedly by waves of nomadic peoples migrating from central Asia. These tribes, called barbarians by the civilized Romans, eventually overran the frontiers established by Rome and occupied the city of Rome itself by 476. Many place names across Europe preserve the names of nomadic tribes. The Franks settled in what eventually became France, and the Burgundians in east-central France and the Lombards in northern Italy gave their names to Burgundy and Lombardy. The Goths and the Visigoths were memorialized in the architectural style called Gothic, and the behavior of the Vandals, who went everywhere, is remembered in the word *vandalism*. Gradually the nomads settled down, became converts to Christianity, and attempted to continue Roman governmental traditions, which they greatly admired although they lacked the expertise to administer them. In western Europe we call the period extending from the decline of Roman authority until the beginning of the Renaissance (approximately 400–1400 A.D.) the medieval period or the Middle Ages, because later historians saw it as a middle era separating antiquity from modern times.

Roman culture was based on city life and depended on a strong central government. In the chaos that accompanied the barbarian invasions, the basic skills required to maintain authority, such as literacy, virtually disappeared. Urban settlements and the money economy that sustained them were replaced by small agricultural units organized by local strongmen, who lived in fortified dwellings and controlled the surrounding land by force of arms. Peasants tilled the land in exchange for meager sustenance and the physical protection afforded them by the strongman's military might. Over the centuries this arrangement of mutual service and protection developed into the feudal system, embracing all levels of society from peasant to king in an intricate social, political, and economic order.

The barbarian invaders brought with them traditions that contributed to the development of medieval art and architecture. Their skill in wooden construction, using the abundant forest resources of northern Europe, can be seen in the few timber buildings and ships that survive from those unsettled times. Their smaller objects, including jewelry, ceremonial and household objects, and military regalia, are frequently adorned with intricate interlaced ornament, based on stylized plant and animal forms (thus its name, the Animal Style), an artistic tradition derived from the fierce Scythians who came from the steppes of central Asia.

ANGLO-SAXON ARCHITECTURE IN BRITAIN

The reintroduction of Christianity into Britain under the direction of St. Augustine was accompanied by the construction of churches. Like most Anglo-Saxon buildings, these were predominantly constructed of timber. Though not as durable as masonry, wood was abundant and frequently used throughout the medieval period. Vertical half-logs were used in some structures, such as the surviving Church of St. Andrew at Greensted (Figures 7.1, 7.2), while vertical timber frame with wattle and daub (woven reed with plaster infill) was used in others. Either wall system would have been capped with a thatched roof.

Parish churches such as that at Greensted were generally small, consisting of a nave and a **chancel.** In plan these churches were extremely simple versions of the Roman basilica, with the Roman semicircular apse often replaced by a square-ended chancel, the preferred Celtic plan. Construction of the nave was the responsibility of the local community, while the church authorities financed the chancel. Because of the difference in funding, English parish churches may have had different styles in the nave and chancel. The major entrance, protected by a porch, was usually on the south side rather than on the west end as in Early Christian churches. Towers to hold bells were built from an early date, and the free-standing **belfry** was soon attached to the church proper, where it also served as a watchtower. Interiors were dimly lit by small splayed windows with either arched or triangular-headed openings.

The best-known example of Anglo-Saxon masonry building is the tower of All Saints Church at Earl's Barton, Northamptonshire (Figure 7.3), which dates from about 1000. Although built of stone, with walls thirty inches thick, its exterior articulation suggests wattle-and-daub construction. The stone is set in vertical strips, with long and short work corners, giving the appearance of short wooden posts alternating with flat slabs of wood. The present battlemented **parapet** at the top of the tower is an incongruous later addition.

FIGURE 7.1 *Timber wall detail from St. Andrew, Greensted, 1013.* (Photo: Wodehouse)

FIGURE 7.2 *Plan and section of timber wall from St. Andrew, Greensted.* (From L. Dietrichson)

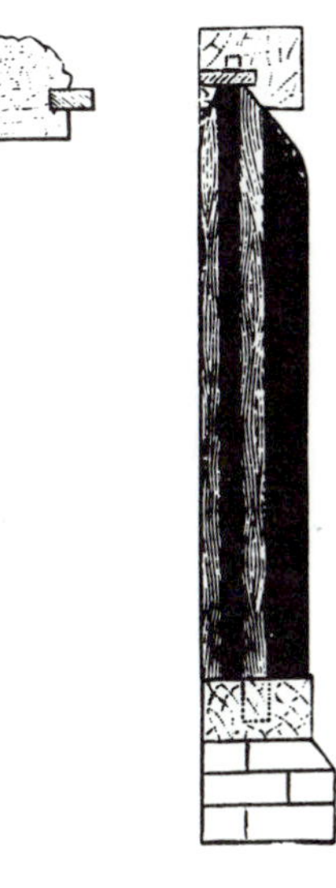

Figure 7.3 *All Saints, Earl's Barton, 1000.* (Photo: Marburg)

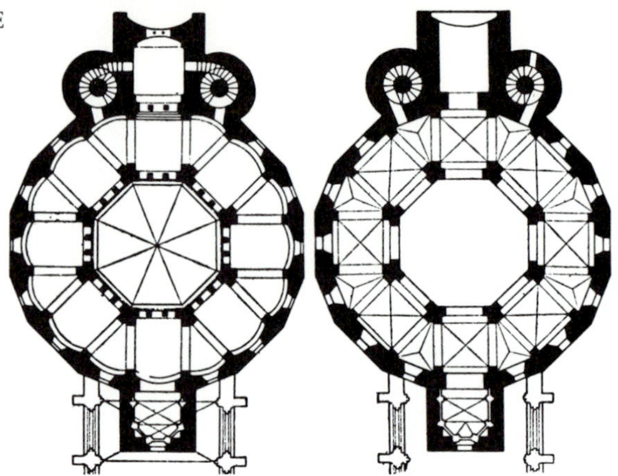

Figure 7.4 *Plans of the Palatine Chapel, Aachen, 792–805.* (From R. Sturgis)

Figure 7.5 *Section of the Palatine Chapel, Aachen.* (From R. Sturgis)

CAROLINGIAN ARCHITECTURE

On the mainland of northern Europe very little architecture has survived from 400 to 800 A.D. Between the chaos created by the barbarian invasions and the violence of Viking raids, western Europe experienced several centuries of unsettled life without the stability necessary to design and construct durable buildings. From the many strongmen who were leaders in the emerging feudal system came one man whose strength and military might enabled him to dominate his competitors. Known as Charles the Great, or Charlemagne, he was the grandson of Charles Martel, the Frank who had led assembled forces to victory over the Islamic army at the Battle of Tours in 732. During his reign (792–814) Charlemagne unified a large portion of the present-day countries of France, the Low Countries, and Germany through a series of successful military campaigns. Charlemagne's influence extended even to Rome where, on Christmas Day in the year 800, Pope Leo III crowned him Holy Roman Emperor. This illiterate descendent of barbarian chieftains had become the spiritual heir of the Roman Empire, the temporal equivalent of the Pope.

Charlemagne aspired to a renaissance of Roman times, including the excellence Rome had exhibited in government, literature, and the arts. He summoned the greatest minds to his court, established schools for the training of governmental administrators, and encouraged architecture by donating lands and money for the construction of churches and monasteries. The resulting buildings, termed **Carolingian** (from *Carolus,* the Latin name for Charles), are in many cases based on the Early Christian buildings Charlemagne visited during his travels in Italy. Such was the case with the palace complex built at Aachen. The overall plan is modeled on the Lateran Palace in Rome, with the chapel (792–805) (Figures 7.4, 7.5) derived from San Vitale at Ravenna (see Figure 5.22) and the audience hall being a Roman basilica. Much as Charlemagne and his architects may have admired Roman buildings, they lacked the technical construction skills necessary to achieve the desired result, so in comparison to their Roman prototypes, Carolingian buildings seem somewhat unrefined.

The Palatine Chapel at Aachen was designed by Odo of Metz and probably built by Lombard masons using stone salvaged from nearby Roman structures. Its central domed octagon was surrounded by a sixteen-sided aisle with a gallery overhead; its construction, including barrel and groin vaults and an octagonal cloister vault in the dome, reflects late Roman practice rather than the Byzantine techniques employed at San Vitale; and its plan simplifies the complex geometry of the Ravenna building. The main entrance is dominated by a **westwerk,** the western façade including the entrance **vestibule,** rooms at one or more levels above, and one or more towers. The addition of a westwerk to churches is one of the Carolingian contributions to western architectural traditions. Early Christian churches featured freestanding belfries, if they had towers at all. During the Carolingian period towers were often incorporated in the building scheme of the church.

The interior of the Palatine Chapel has a heavy effect, particularly in the eight great piers that support the dome, but the proportions of the arched openings at the ground and gallery levels are well-chosen (Figure 7.6). Polychromy is used in the semicircular arches of the main floor, while sixteen polished marble columns from the Palace of the Exarchs in Ravenna were hauled over the Alps to be reused in the arcade of the gallery. Locally cast bronze grilles of the balustrade and mosaics in the dome contributed to a rich interior. Charlemagne's throne room opened off the gallery level, and from this vantage point he could observe services being celebrated on the main level below. As the first domed building north of the Alps since the decline of the Roman Empire, the Palatine Chapel is comparable in scale, if not in elegance, to San Vitale, and it reflects Charlemagne's intense desire to revive classical ideals in architecture.

FIGURE 7.6 *Interior of the Palatine Chapel, Aachen.* (Photo: Marburg)

Of the monastery church at Lorsch, which was endowed by Charlemagne, only a small freestanding Gatehouse (Figure 7.7) remains. Its architectural precedent can be found at the Old Basilica of St. Peter in Rome, where a triple-arched **pavilion,** itself derived from the triumphal arch, marked the entrance to the atrium. The Gatehouse at Lorsch is articulated by arches supported with Corinthian columns, and the second-floor windows are surrounded by triangular frames in a decorative pattern derived from late Roman sarcophagi. One would never confuse the Gatehouse with an actual Roman building, however, for it features such ele-

FIGURE 7.7 *Monastery Gatehouse, Lorsch, ca. 800.* (Photo: German Information Center)

ments as a steeply pitched roof and decorative red and white tiling, which are distinctly nonclassical. The roof pitch was dictated by the rain and snow loads of its northern European climate, while the tiled designs seem to have been devised by local masons, perhaps influenced by Islamic polychromy or Roman *opus reticulatum.*

Another small building surviving from Carolingian times is the Oratory at Germigny-des-Prés (806–810) (Figures 7.8–7.11), which was built for Theodulf, Bishop of Orleans, Abbot of Fleury, and

FIGURE 7.9 *Plan of the Oratory, Germigny-des-Prés.* (From J. Guadet)

FIGURE 7.8 *Oratory, Germigny-des-Prés, 806–810.* (Photo: Marburg)

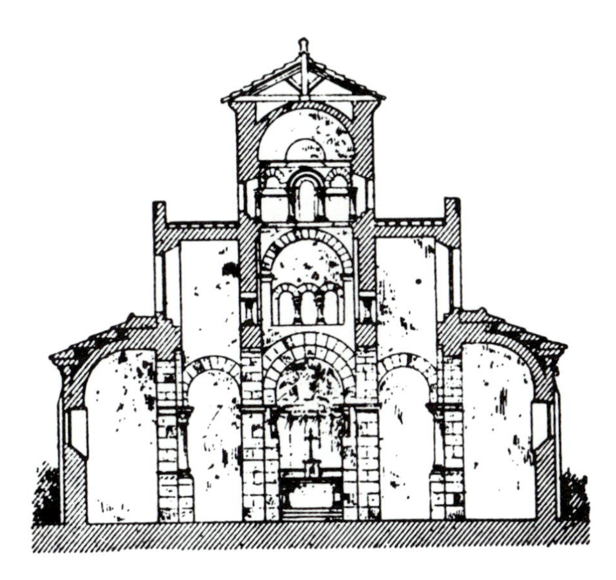

FIGURE 7.10 *Section and elevation of the oratory, Germigny-des-Prés.* (From J. Guadet)

FIGURE 7.11 *Interior of the Oratory, Germigny-des-Prés.* (Photo: Marburg)

close advisor to Charlemagne. Conceived as a private chapel for quiet reflection and prayer, the Oratory was designed with a Greek cross plan and a square central tower. Horseshoe arches are found in both plan and elevation. Together with the centralized plan, these suggest influence from Mozarabic churches in Moslem-dominated Spain. This assumption is made more plausible by the fact that Theodulf was from Septimania, the area between present-day France and Spain along the Mediterranean coast. Rather surprisingly, the Oratory also has a magnificent mosaic depicting the Ark of the Covenant in the eastern apse, the artistic technique and style of which both indicate artistic contributions from Byzantium. In these few surviving Carolingian buildings, one can thus trace elements from Roman, Early Christian, Byzantine, Islamic, and northern European civilizations, combined in what must be seen as the beginnings of an architecture unique to western Europe.

Monasteries

Charlemagne's empire did not long survive his death. His son, Louis the Pious, proved an ineffectual leader, and on his death in 843, the Carolingian empire was divided among Charlemagne's three grandsons. Governmental power in western Europe

FIGURE 7.12 *Monastery of St. Riquier, Centula, ca. 800.* (17th century engraving)

gradually reverted to the hands of local or regional lords. The one cohesive social institution that transcended regional groups was the Church, which organized medieval Europe into ecclesiastical dioceses, each administered by a bishop. The seat of episcopal authority was frequently a town that had been a Roman provincial center, and there was much of Roman governmental structure preserved in the organization of the Church.

Complementary to the town-based diocesan units were the largely rural monasteries. Their establishment had been encouraged by Charlemagne as a matter of practical policy for the settlement of conquered territories, in addition to their spiritual and educational contributions. Few institutions had as extensive an impact on the architecture of the medieval period as monasticism. Indeed, it would be difficult to discuss almost any aspect of medieval history or culture without considering the important role played by monks of the various orders. Medieval society was divided broadly into three classes: those who fought (the land-owning lords and knights), those who labored (the peasants), and those who prayed (the priests and monks). The work of each class was necessary for the well-being of all groups. The prayers of the monks were particularly necessary, it was thought, to provide a never-ending flow of praise to propitiate a God who was justifiably wrathful about man's sinful ways. Medieval people considered the Christian Lord to be as susceptible to flattery as his earthly counterpart.

The concept of monasticism, the withdrawal from the corruptions of everyday life in order to contemplate things spiritual, originated in fourth-century Egypt, where Christian hermits led solitary lives in the desert wilderness. At about the same time, the idea developed that groups of monks might live together communally, and both the eremitical and communal forms of monasticism spread rapidly from Egypt to the edges of the Christian world. Irish monks were active beginning in 432 until Viking raiders destroyed their settlements. The Rule of St. Benedict, endorsed by Charlemagne, came to be the dominant model for the organization of Western monasticism. (Hermits continued to be common in the Eastern church.) Under Benedictine rules, twelve monks and an abbot were sufficient to found a new monastery, and, in general, the monks chose remote sites with reliable water supplies for building. During the Middle Ages, these new foundations numbered in the thousands. The monks converted the countryside; their schools brought learning to every part of Europe; and their building and farming enterprises preserved and advanced the best in architecture, the arts, and agriculture. Medieval civilization throughout western Europe was achieved in no small measure through the spread of monasticism.

Reconstruction studies of the monastery of St. Riquier at Centula (Figure 7.12) convey some sense of the scale and arrangement of Carolingian monasteries. The exterior of the church was marked by towers, the major ones rising over the narthex as part of the westwerk and over the crossing, with minor ones enclosing staircases flanking the nave at the westwerk and the choir. An arcaded walk connected the main church with two smaller chapels, so the ensemble of buildings provided a triangular processional route for religious ritual. The nave and choir were completely occupied by altars at which the monks celebrated Mass, while transepts also given over to altars increased the available worship space. Medieval religious practice, which placed growing importance on the veneration of relics, required multiple altars to honor the individual saints. Laypersons who wished to attend services could observe from a chapel located over the narthex. As with other Carolingian basilicas, the roof was supported on wooden trusses, since vaulting major spaces was beyond the construction technology of the period.

Nothing remains today of the buildings of St. Riquier, but a surviving westwerk at Corvey on the Weser (Figure 7.13), built by monks connected with Centula, provides an idea of what the composition at St. Riquier may have been. Corvey's westwerk dates from 873 to 885. Its twin stair towers rise solidly beside the central entranceway, while the narthex and chapel above are contained in an almost-cubical solid. The towers terminate with pyramidal roofs rather than the cylindrical turrets shown on the old view of St. Riquier, but the spirit behind the designs is similar.

Charlemagne's interest in centralizing and standardizing affairs within his realm was also applied to religious institutions. After examining several models of monastic organization, he mandated that all monasteries should follow the Rule of St. Benedict, a flexible but rather specific set of regulations formulated around 550 for monks living communally under the direction of an abbot. The monk's life of prayer, contemplation, and manual work marked by poverty, chastity, and obedience was meant to emulate the example of Christ. In 817 abbots from leading Carolingian monasteries held a conference to resolve differences in interpretation of the Benedictine Rule. Out of its discussions came a document detailing a model layout for a Benedictine abbey. We know of this document through a copy sent to the abbot of the monastery of St. Gall, where, recycled as a book, the plan remained in the abbey's library until rediscovered in the eighteenth century. Known now as the Plan of St. Gall (Figure 7.14), this manuscript is the oldest surviving architectural drawing from the medieval period, and from it, twentieth-century scholars Walter Horn and Ernest Born have deduced much about monastic life and building practices in the Carolingian age.

The Plan of St. Gall clearly sets forth the major components of a self-sufficient religious community. The largest building was the church, a double-ended basilica in plan, with an enclosure for laypersons in the western hemicycle flanked by twin cylindrical towers. Inside the masonry-walled and

FIGURE 7.13 *Corvey on the Weser, 873–885.* (Photo: Marburg)

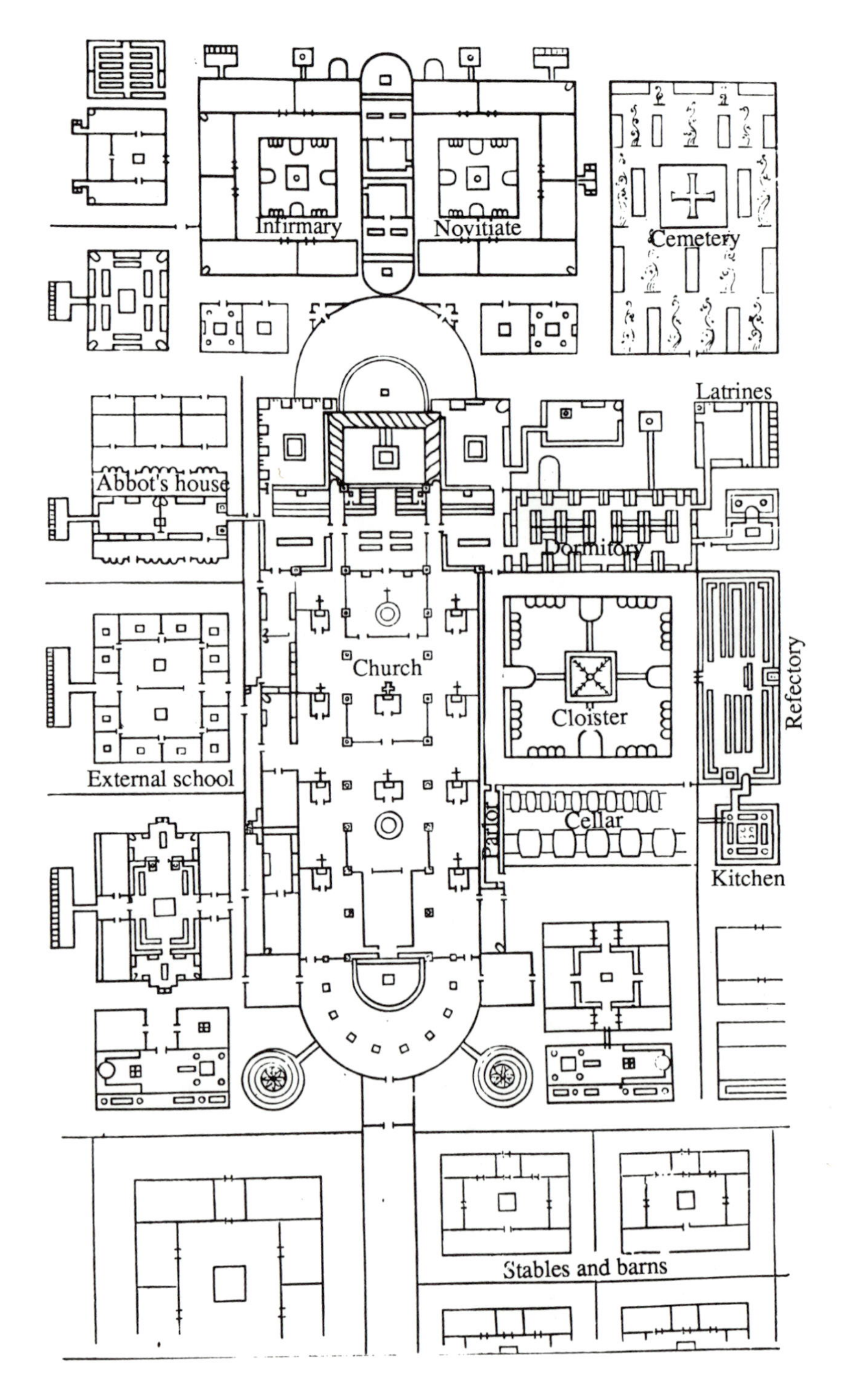

FIGURE 7.14 *Plan of St. Gall, 816–817.* (From E. Viollet-le-Duc)

timber-truss-roofed church was the worship space for the monks. Altars were located throughout the nave, transepts, and apse. On the south side of the church was the cloister, one hundred feet square, which was surrounded by a covered, arcaded walk connecting the major buildings on its sides: the **chapter house,** workroom, and warming room below the dormitory on the east; the refectory (dining hall) on the south; and the cellar or storeroom on the west. A stairway connected the monk's dormitory with the south transept of the church because the daily cycle of nine services included two celebrated during the night.

By counting the beds drawn on the plan, Horn and Born have concluded that the monastery was planned for approximately 110 monks. Around the cloister buildings were grouped the service buildings, staffed by an additional 130 to 150 workmen and servants necessary to provide for the monks' existence. A bake and brew house, artisan craft workshops, and a complete working farm, with pens or barns for goats, geese, pigs, horses, and cows, are indicated on the plan to the south and west of the cloister, although their actual arrangement on the land would doubtless have been adjusted to the location of fields and pasture. To the east of the church, the plan indicates a miniature double cloister to house the novitiate and the infirmary, together with a house for two physicians, a medicinal herb garden, and the cemetery. On the north side of the church was the abbot's house, connected to the transept by a passage. As the administrator and spiritual leader of the monastery, the abbot was responsible for the management of the monastery's life, and as its representative to the outside world, he was charged with public relations and hospitality for distinguished guests. Adjacent to the abbot's house were the external school, required by Charlemagne's decree to provide education for young men not intending to become monks, and the guesthouse and stables for high-ranking visitors. The more common lot of travelers would be cared for by the almoner at the cloister gate to the south of the church entrance.

Through its clear ordering of the practical requirements for a monastic community, the Plan of St. Gall encapsulates the high quality of functional planning achieved by Carolingian architects. While no monastery ever built precisely followed the Plan of St. Gall, its general disposition of monastic buildings was employed in Benedictine abbeys throughout the medieval period.

ROMANESQUE ARCHITECTURE

Early Period

The monastery of Saint-Martin at Canigou (1001–1026) (Figures 7.15, 7.16) remains as an example of the process by which monasticism spread, and its buildings illustrate architectural accomplishments of the First or Early Romanesque period. Its patron, the Count of Cerdana, landlord of this mountainous territory in the Pyrenees, endowed the monastery on a rocky outcrop to expiate his sins. Although the monastery of Saint-Martin never housed more than about thirty monks, its place in the history of architecture is assured because it has survived, with the aid of an entirely sympathetic twentieth-century restoration, as one of the earliest completely vaulted Romanesque churches. In plan the church is a basilica without transepts and with semicircular apses terminating the aisles and nave. The barrel vaults of the nave and aisles rest on ten supports — eight stubby columns and two grouped piers — and the solid exterior walls. The only natural light comes from small windows at the east and west ends, resulting in a dark interior. From the exterior, the entire monastery forms a harmonious composition. A square plan tower abuts the side of the church, guarding the entrance to the abbey, while the cloister and its related buildings form an irregular quadrangle on the limited building site. The stone construction is simple, articulated primarily by semicircular arches used over windows and also set as surface relief in horizontal bands. The stepped crenellations atop the tower recall Islamic fortifications found in neighboring Spain.

Saint-Martin at Canigou exemplifies the Early Romanesque style. As the name implies, Romanesque buildings have a certain affinity with Roman architecture, primarily because they tend to employ the semicircular or Roman arch. Beyond this simple generalization (which itself is not always true), it is difficult to characterize Romanesque buildings with

Figure 7.15 *St. Martin du Canigou, 1001–1026.* (Photo: Marburg)

Figure 7.16 *Interior of St. Martin du Canigou.* (Delineator: J. Desmond)

great precision. The style flourished from around 1000 to 1250. Romanesque buildings had to be massive and heavy for structural reasons and thus were dark inside because the windows were small. The construction problem that Romanesque builders set for themselves — efficiently supporting a roof made entirely of small stones — posed a real challenge and encouraged varied approaches according to the materials available, the experience of the architect, and the ambitions of the patron. It is perhaps easiest to understand the Romanesque as a great series of experiments to enclose and illuminate interior space, using incombustible masonry construction to reduce the chances of fire.

Medieval builders could not calculate structure as we can today. (Indeed the systematic study of materials and structural theory was not sufficiently advanced to be applied to ordinary buildings until about 1850.) Trial and error, based on knowledge of what had worked in previous projects, formed the basis of building practice. Yet within the span of 150 years the structural experiments of hundreds of Romanesque builders led to the refined masonry techniques that made Gothic architecture possible. It was a long process, however, for the semicircular arch is not a particularly efficient structural element. The Romans had employed it extensively for its aesthetic qualities and ease of construction (the arch scaffolding or centering is relatively uncomplicated to build), qualities that doubtless recommended it to Romanesque architects as well, even though the outward, overturning thrust generated by the semicircular arch caused problems, which were commonly resolved by building massive supporting walls. Since any opening cut in the wall weakened it, Romanesque builders used windows very sparingly to avoid impairing the structure's integrity. The semicircular arch, the barrel vault, and the groin vault (two barrel vaults intersecting at right angles) also imposed geometric constraints. Square or rectangular bays could be handled easily, while irregular or circular sections posed aesthetic and structural difficulties.

During the Early Romanesque period, large expanses of exterior wall were often articulated, as at Saint-Martin at Canigou, by decorative devices commonly used by masons in Lombardy. These so-called Lombard bands consist of vertical pilaster strips and corbeled arches set in shallow relief on the wall surface; arches on the Early Christian buildings of Ravenna, such as the Mausoleum of Galla Placidia, have been suggested as the origin of Lombard bands. Lombard work spread from Italy to the rest of Europe; it can be seen on the westwerk of Saint-Philibert at Tournus, a monastic church in central France (roughly contemporary with Saint-Martin at Canigou) that exhibits both traditional and novel features in its fabric. Carolingian architects had added towers and a westwerk to the Early Christian basilica of nave, aisles, and apse; the Early Romanesque made further elaborations at the east end to accommodate additional altars and processions.

Monks had come to Tournus to escape the pillaging of Norse raiders, only to find themselves attacked by the Huns in 937. Given this history it is not surprising that they wanted fireproof masonry churches. Work on the present building began about 950 with construction of the **crypt** or basement level under the choir (Figure 7.17). In plan the east end of the crypt had a central chapel for the relics of St. Philibert, surrounded by a passage recalling the ambulatory of Early Christian martyria such as the Church of the Nativity in Bethlehem. The difference at Saint-Philibert was the inclusion of three rectangular chapels radiating from the ambulatory; their plan is repeated in the east end of the church above, reflecting the need for circulation around the church and access to additional altars set in each chapel. At the opposite end of the church, the massive westwerk contains a narthex above which is a chapel dedicated to St. Michael. Stubby cylindrical piers at both levels support groin vaults in the narthex and barrel vaults in the chapel.

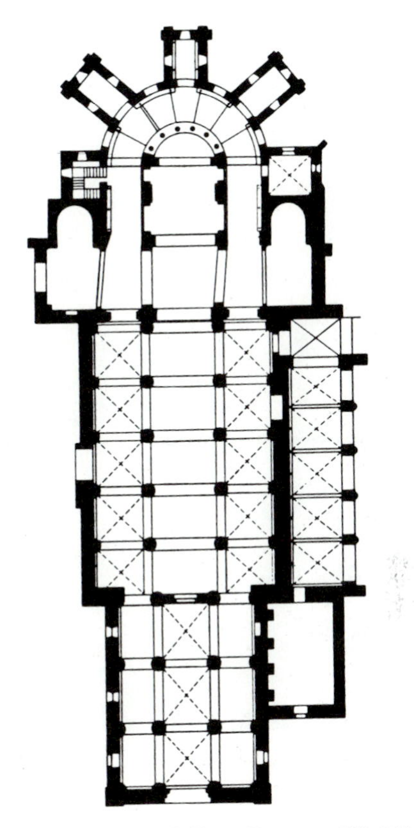

FIGURE 7.17 *Plan of St. Philibert, Tournus, 950–1120.* (From W. Blaser)

Similar piers in an elongated form extend the length of the nave as supports for a unique series of transverse barrel vaults over diaphragm arches defining each bay (Figure 7.18). The architects thus resolved several constructional problems. They reduced the clear span required of their barrel vaults to the width of each bay, which was less than the nave width; they countered the thrust of each barrel vault by that of its neighbor, ultimately anchoring the sequence with the mass of the westwerk and crossing tower; and they inserted relatively large clerestory windows in the enclosing walls at the ends of each barrel vault, thus obtaining direct light into the nave. These advantages were offset by an

FIGURE 7.18 *Interior of St. Philibert, Tournus.* (Photo: Marburg)

interrupted ceiling plane on the interior. The unity of the nave and its axial direction toward the altar were diminished by the vaulting, which may account for the fact that this solution was never repeated over a major space.

In its choir plan, its ingenious structure, and its unadorned construction, Tournus reflects the struggle between tradition and innovation faced by Romanesque builders. It also illustrates the Romanesque tendency to maintain discrete elements in plan as separately articulated volumes in the three-dimensional reality of the building. From the exterior, most Romanesque church features are readily discernible. The aisle roofs are lower than that of the nave; the westwerk is a distinct mass, as are the radiating chapels, ambulatory, choir, transepts, and crossing tower. With experience, Romanesque architects achieved remarkable compositions of these plan-generated elements.

Architecture of the Holy Roman Empire

The middle portion of Charlemagne's empire, corresponding roughly to modern Germany and northern Italy, eventually came under the vigorous House of Saxony, whose three successive emperors named Otto gained the title of Holy Roman Emperor in the course of their capable leadership. Their rule, termed *Ottonian,* extended from 936 to 1002, but its effects lasted nearly a century longer.

Ottonian architecture is in many respects an extension of Carolingian traditions; it is the German expression of Romanesque. An outstanding example is the Ottonian church of St. Michael at Hildesheim (1001–1033, now much restored) (Figures 7.19–7.21), which is a double-ended basilica with entrances along the side aisles like many original Roman basilicas. Its two apses also recall the

FIGURE 7.19 *St. Michael, Hildesheim, 1001–1033.* (Photo: German Information Center)

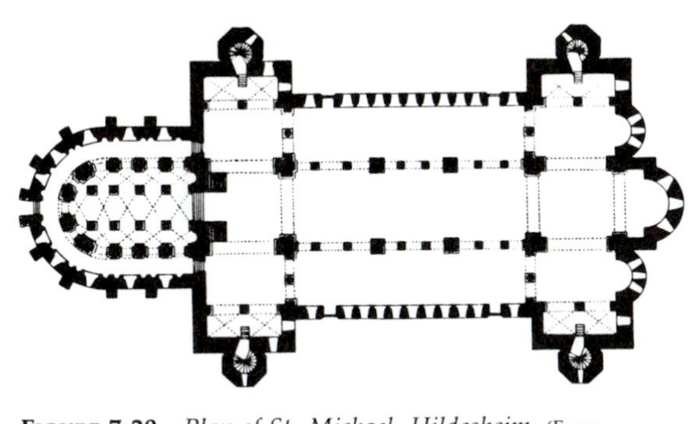

FIGURE 7.20 *Plan of St. Michael, Hildesheim.* (From W. Blaser)

general church layout indicated on the Plan of St. Gall. On the interior, the eastern apse contains the altar, and the western apse contains a raised platform for seating the emperor and his court. Illumination is provided by clerestories, simple punched openings in the unarticulated nave wall, while the supporting nave arcade has a subtle A-B-B-A rhythm established by piers alternating with two columns. Polychrome arches, derived perhaps from Islamic Spain; boldly carved column capitals suggestive of Italian examples; and an elaborately painted wooden ceiling enrich the interior.

FIGURE 7.21 *Interior of St. Michael, Hildesheim.* (Photo: German Information Center)

FIGURE 7.22 *Cathedral, Speyer, 1030–1182.* (Photo: German Information Center)

St. Michael's was built for Bishop Bernward, an enlightened patron of the arts. For this church the bishop commissioned a set of bronze doors ornamented with low reliefs depicting scenes from the Old and New Testaments; these doors are celebrated examples of the revival of sculpture as an architectural art. The well-traveled bishop knew the bas-relief carvings on the wooden doors of Early Christian churches in Rome, which may have been the precedent for the bronze reliefs at Hildesheim. The work of Bishop Bernward's artist displays a fine sense of proportion and detail in addition to an observant eye for expression and motion.

Slightly later than St. Michael's at Hildesheim is the spacious imperial Cathedral at Speyer (Figures 7.22–7.24), begun about 1030 and continued in three medieval building campaigns until 1182. It is a massive and majestic construction, extending over 425 feet from the thick walls of its imposing westwerk to the semicircular apse flanked by a pair of square-plan towers. The nave is wide, long, and tall, given stately dignity by the semicircular arches framing each bay. Covered at first by a flat wooden ceiling, the nave received groin vaults set over paired bays

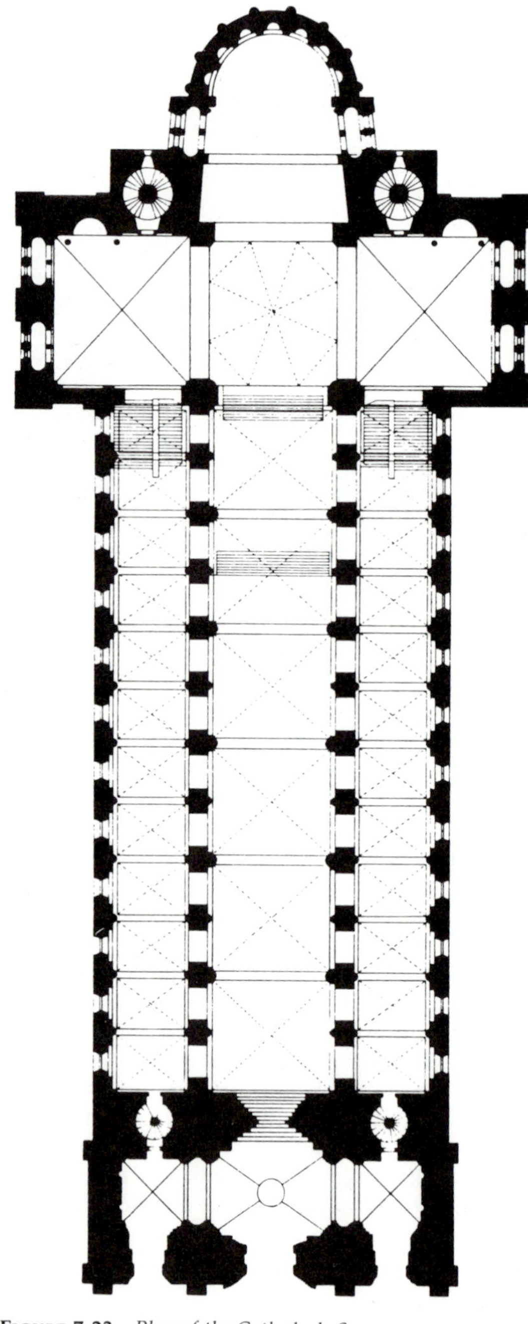

Figure 7.23 *Plan of the Cathedral, Speyer.* (From W. Blaser)

Figure 7.24 *Interior of the Cathedral, Speyer.* (Photo: German Information Center)

and separated by transverse arch bands in the course of building activity from 1082 to 1137. At 107 feet above the floor, these vaults rank as the highest built in the Romanesque and approach the accomplishments of Roman construction. Interior decoration is restrained, even severe, with the variegated warm yellow-to-pink hues of the stone enlivening the surfaces of walls and piers. Influences from Lombardy are seen in the cubiform capitals of the crypt and the corbel arch tables and pilaster strips of the exterior wall.

In the southern regions of the Holy Roman Empire, the classical heritage of Rome heavily influenced Romanesque architecture. Italian cities

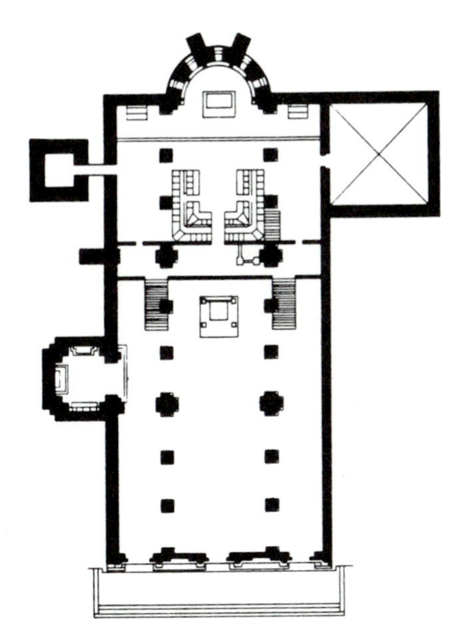

FIGURE 7.25 *Plan of S. Miniato al Monte, Florence, 1062–1090.* (From W. Blaser)

FIGURE 7.26 *S. Miniato al Monte, Florence.* (Photo: Instituto Italiano di Cultura)

FIGURE 7.27 *Interior of S. Miniato al Monte, Florence.* (From J. Guadet)

developed their own versions of Romanesque architecture, retaining a strong reliance on the classical past with little influence from northern Europe. In general the Early Christian basilica remained the standard church form, seldom having a westwerk or attached towers as in Ottonian architecture. The church of S. Miniato al Monte in Florence (1062–1090 and later) (Figure 7.25) is typical. A single pair of aisles flanks the transeptless nave, which is terminated by a simple semicircular apse. Its façade (Figure 7.26) is articulated on the ground level by five arches supported by Corinthian half-columns, with Corinthian pilasters and a gable defining the roof of the nave. Geometric patterns set in marble veneers enliven the essentially flat wall plane, and the entire elevation clearly follows the profile of the basilican space behind it (Figure 7.27).

FIGURE 7.28 *Cathedral, Pisa, 1063–1272.* (From J. Guadet)

FIGURE 7.29 *Plan of the Cathedral, Pisa.* (From W. Blaser)

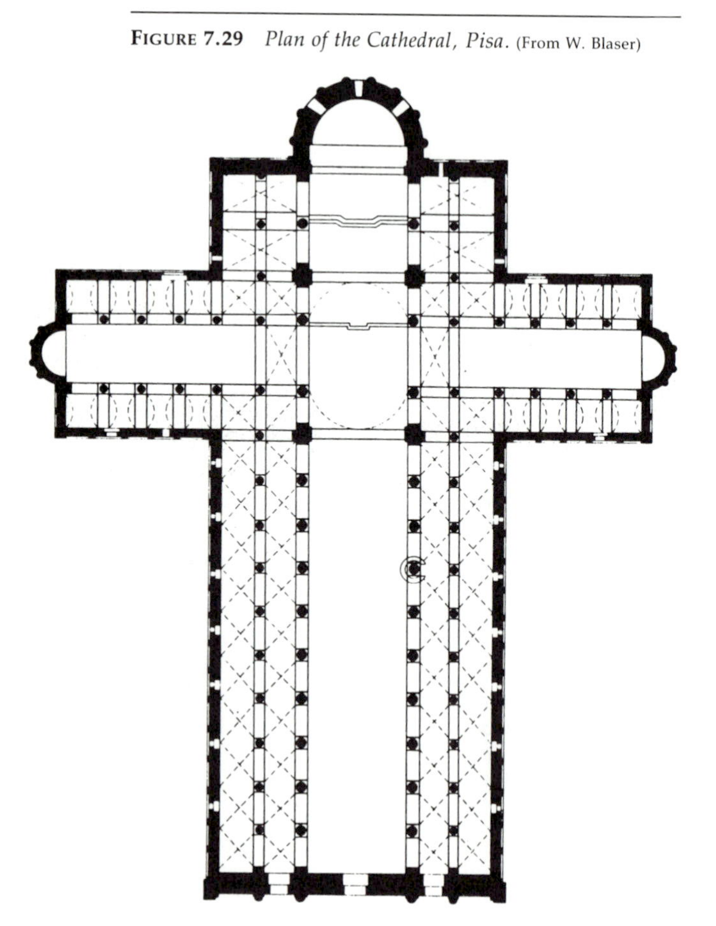

The freestanding Cathedral at Pisa (begun in 1063 and finished 1089–1272) (Figures 7.28, 7.29) is more elaborate, although still close to Early Christian tradition. In plan the basilica has a transept and double aisles and galleries flanking the nave and single aisles and galleries flanking the transepts. At the crossing, an oval dome is raised on squinches and shallow pendentives, recalling the centralized church plans of Byzantium, while the remainder of the church is roofed by wooden trusses. The exterior is sheathed in marble arcades, stacked row on row across the western façade and continuing around the church. The interior is marked by polychromy, in this case alternate courses of dark and light marble set in horizontal bands, and there are Byzantine mosaics in the apse. The Cathedral is complemented by two adjacent structures, a circular Baptistry and a cylindrical **Campanile,** the famous Leaning Tower of Pisa, now over thirteen feet out of plumb.

In the northern Italian region known as Lombardy, the outstanding Romanesque building is the abbey church of S. Ambrogio in Milan (Figures 7.30–7.32). The dates of this important monument are still a matter of scholarly debate. Research indicates that work on the present structure began around 1080, and the nave was begun after 1128. The dates of the nave vaults, thought to have been built about 1140, are interesting because the region around Milan had several churches that made early use of rib vaulting, here built over square bays. In plan S. Ambrogio conserves Early Christian practice. An arcaded atrium precedes the church proper, and the transeptless basilica is terminated by a semicircular apse and smaller semicircular chapels at the ends of the groin-vaulted aisles. Galleries over the aisles help buttress the thrust of the nave vaults, but they preclude the possibility of clerestory lighting.

The Great Churches of the Pilgrimage Roads

Along with monasticism, the medieval period was marked by another important religious phenomenon: the pilgrimage. To atone for sins, seek a cure, or assure salvation, medieval men and women trav-

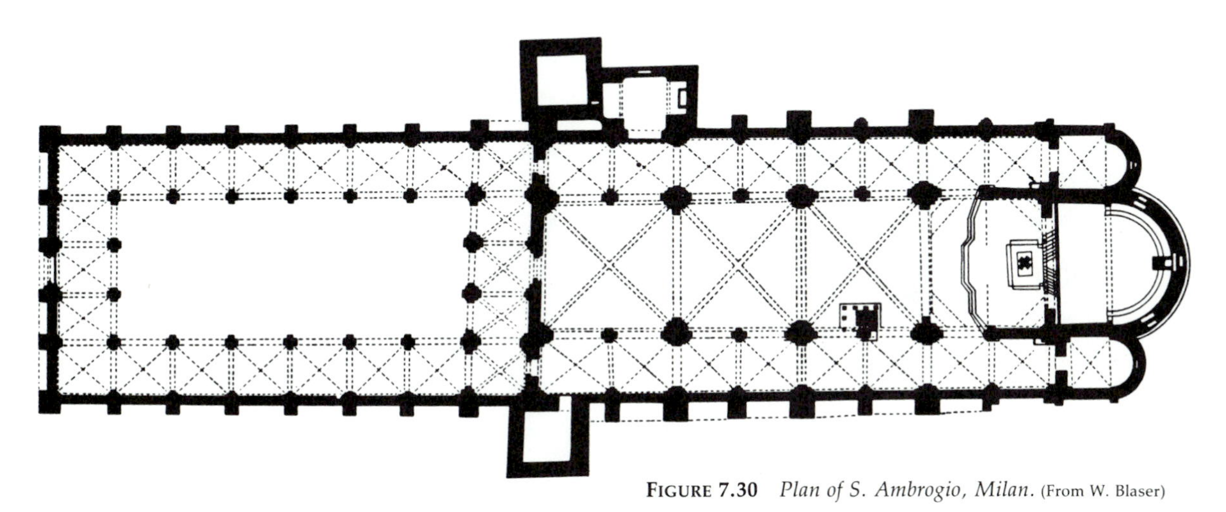

Figure 7.30 *Plan of S. Ambrogio, Milan.* (From W. Blaser)

Figure 7.31 *S. Ambrogio, Milan, 1080–1128.* (Photo: Alinari)

eled as pilgrims to shrines containing the relics of saints. As every church established since Carolingian times was required to possess relics as a condition for its existence, pilgrimages could be local, regional, or international. Jerusalem and Rome were the most celebrated of the major centers for pilgrims, but they were also the most expensive and hazardous for northern Europeans to visit.

Around the year 1000 a new center for pilgrimage arose to rival the popularity of Rome and Jerusalem. It was the Shrine of the Apostle James (Santiago in Spanish), located at Compostela in northwestern Spain. With considerable assistance from the Church, Santiago became the goal for thousands of pilgrims as stories of miracles wrought by St. James encouraged people from all parts of Europe to visit his tomb and pray for his assistance. Gradually an entire network of roads and hospices developed to support the growing tide of pilgrims traveling to Compostela.

Monasteries, the traditional centers of hospitality for travelers, found the increasing numbers of visitors disruptive to monastic services held in the church. The monks made architectural accommodation for pilgrims by modifying the basilican church plan to include an ambulatory, such as that found at Saint-Philibert at Tournus, which worked as an extension of the aisles to provide a continuous passageway around the entire church. At the east end, radiating chapels opened off the ambulatory, so relics placed there could be visited by pilgrims without interrupting the monks' services being sung in the choir.

Churches built in response to the pilgrimage are common on the major roads to Compostela. Five of the largest are so similar in plan, scale, and architectural detail that they illustrate strikingly the artistic communication that moved up and down the roads. Oldest of the five was Saint-Martin at Tours (now destroyed), where a rebuilding of the apse as early as 918 introduced the scheme of radiating

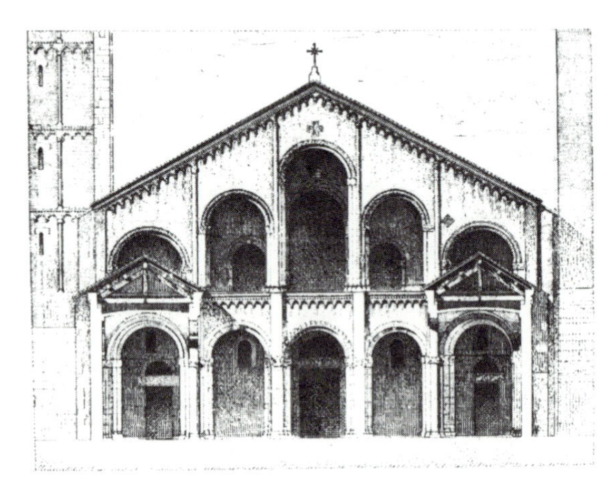

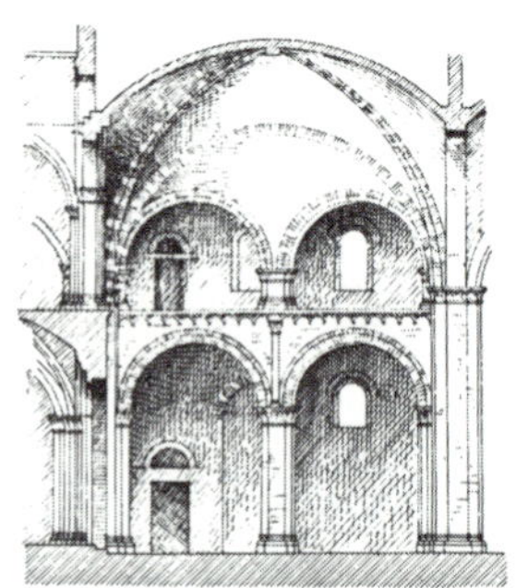

FIGURE 7.32 *Elevation and sections of S. Ambrogio, Milan.* (From J. Guadet)

FIGURE 7.33 *Saint-Sernin, Toulouse, 1077–1119.* (Photo: French Government Tourist Office)

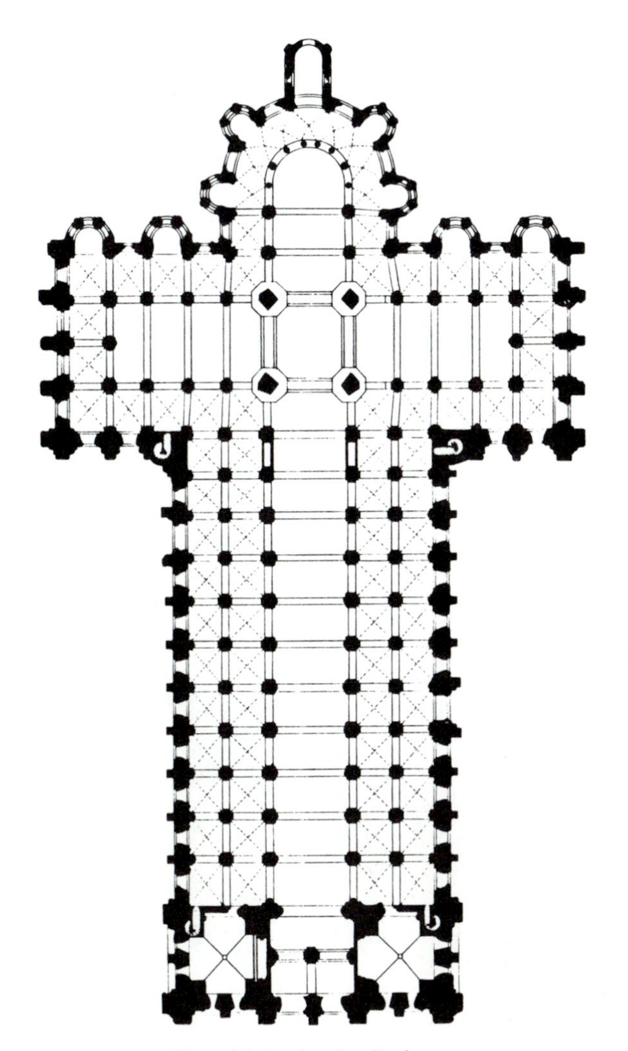

Figure 7.34 *Plan of Saint-Sernin, Toulouse.* (From W. Blaser)

chapels and ambulatory attached to a large nave and spacious transepts. By the middle of the eleventh century, this theme had been picked up by the churches of Saint-Martial at Limoges (now also demolished), Sainte-Foy at Conques, Saint-Sernin at Toulouse, and St. James at Compostela, producing a series of buildings with an unmistakable family resemblance.

The church of Saint-Sernin at Toulouse (Figure 7.33) clearly illustrates the group. Saint-Sernin remains a major monument of the Romanesque even though its west front was never finished, its crossing tower was greatly enlarged in the Gothic period, and the whole church sustained a largely unfortunate nineteenth-century restoration. Begun about 1077, the choir was consecrated in 1096, and the transepts and nave were probably complete, except for the vaulting, by 1119. In plan the church has paired aisles on each side of the nave, four chapels on the east of the large transept, and five radiating chapels around the apse (Figure 7.34). At nearly 360 feet it is a long building with a width of nave and aisles totaling about 100 feet. The banded barrel vaults rise about sixty-five feet and are braced by second-floor galleries over the inner pair of aisles. This gives the church a triangular cross section, but precludes the insertion of clerestory windows to light the nave. Windows at the east end and light from the windows in the crossing tower provide relative brilliance near the altar in contrast to the dim light of the nave. The harmonious exterior arrangement of chapels, ambulatory, and choir rising to the great crossing tower is deftly composed; the ensemble is enhanced by its construction materials, warm brick trimmed with stone.

Figure 7.35 *Interior of Sainte-Foy, Conques, 1080–1120.* (Photo: Marburg)

FIGURE 7.36 *Sainte-Foy, Conques.* (Photo: Marburg)

Other pilgrimage road churches remain at Conques and Compostela. Sainte-Foy at Conques in a remote region of central France is the smallest. In plan it has only a single pair of aisles and galleries flanking the nave, but its structural scheme is identical to that at Saint-Sernin (Figure 7.35). Sainte-Foy preserves on its **tympanum** (the semicircular panel created under the arch of a doorway) a magnificent sculpture (ca. 1120) of the Last Judgment, which provides for an illiterate public a vivid image of the hereafter according to teachings of the Church (Figures 7.36, 7.37). At Compostela the Church of St. James (Figure 7.38) still functions as a major pilgrim

FIGURE 7.37 *Tympanum from Sainte-Foy, Conques.* (Photo: Marburg)

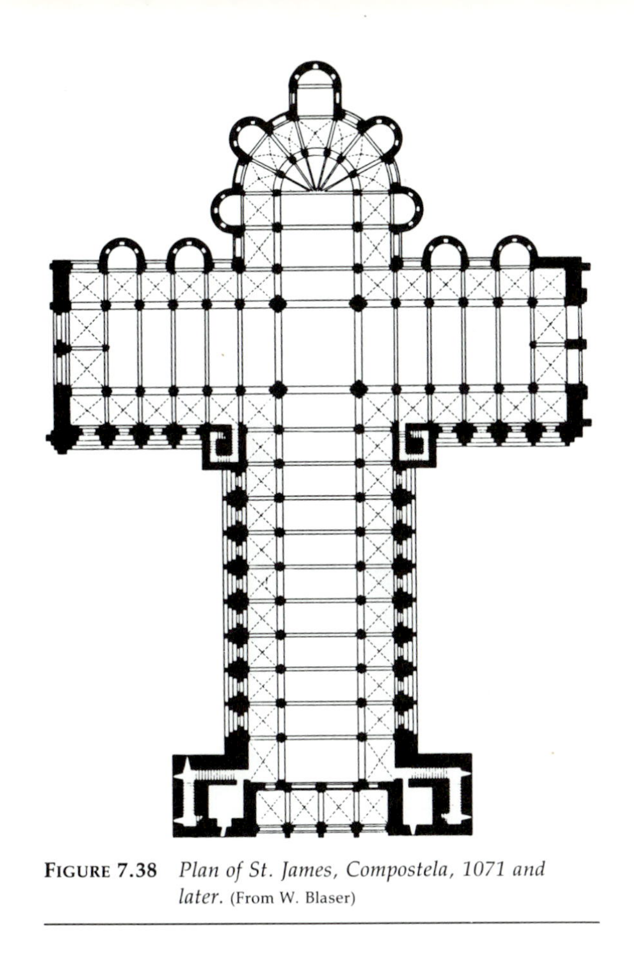

FIGURE 7.38 *Plan of St. James, Compostela, 1071 and later.* (From W. Blaser)

FIGURE 7.39 *Interior of St. James, Compostela.* (From J. Fergusson)

shrine. The church received an elaborate Baroque exterior in the eighteenth century, and while the majority of its medieval west front remains behind the added façade, centuries of rebuilding have resulted in the fragmented rearrangement of portal sculpture on the south transepts. On the interior the choir and crossing have been remodeled, but the transepts are relatively unchanged (Figure 7.39). There one can see the Romanesque character evident at Saint-Sernin and Sainte-Foy.

Architecture of the Order of Cluny

In 910 Duke William of Aquitaine, desiring to atone for his less-than-saintly life and seek divine favor, endowed a monastery on his lands at Cluny, where there was a Gallo-Roman villa or farm. Through an unusual provision in its charter, the new monastery was exempted from the jurisdiction of the local bishop and made directly responsible to the pope. Twelve monks, led by their abbot, Berno, came to Cluny seeking a stricter observance of the Benedictine Rule, and the monastery prospered. The exemplary life of its monks attracted more converts and bequests; its position in Burgundy on the route from Paris to Rome and its virtual independence from local religious authorities allowed it to grow into an influential organization with 1450 abbeys and priories all over Europe; and the exceptional leadership and longevity of its early abbots brought distinction to the Congregation and Order of Cluny. By 1088 the church and monastic complex (known as Cluny II), built after the original villa was outgrown, had also become too small, and a new church (known to historians as Cluny III) was be-

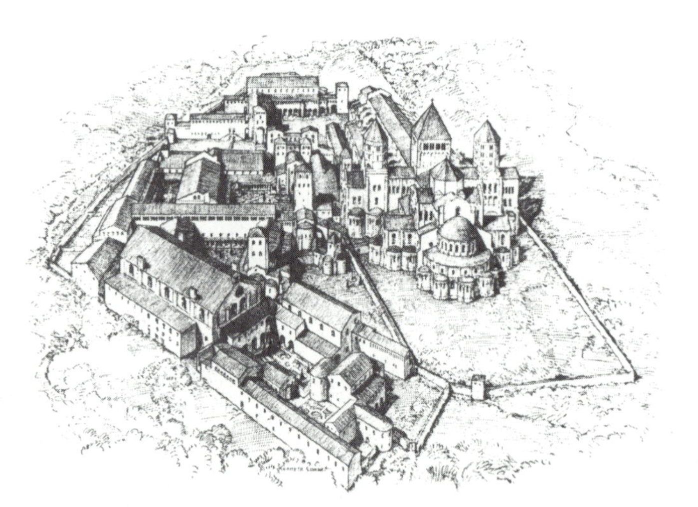

FIGURE 7.40 *Cluny III, 1088–1130.* (From Kenneth J. Conant, *Cluny: Les Églises et la maison du chef d'ordre.* [Cambridge, Mass.: The Medieval Academy of America, 1968])

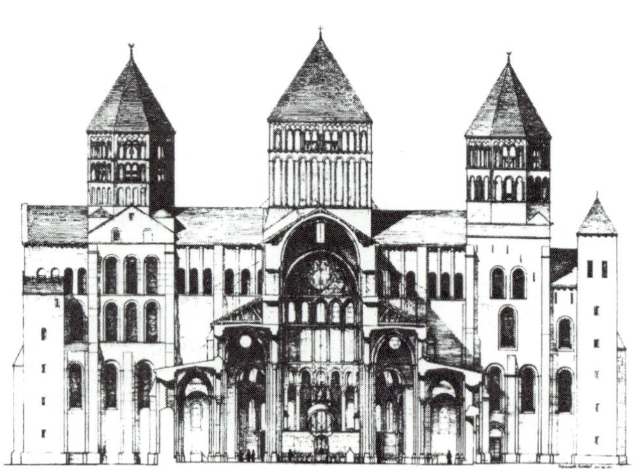

FIGURE 7.42 *Section through the nave of the church of Cluny III.* (From Kenneth J. Conant, *Cluny: Les Églises et la maison du chef d'ordre.* [Cambridge, Mass.: The Medieval Academy of America, 1968])

FIGURE 7.41 *Plan of Cluny III.* (From Kenneth J. Conant, *Cluny: Les Églises et la maison du chef d'ordre.* [Cambridge, Mass.: The Medieval Academy of America, 1968])

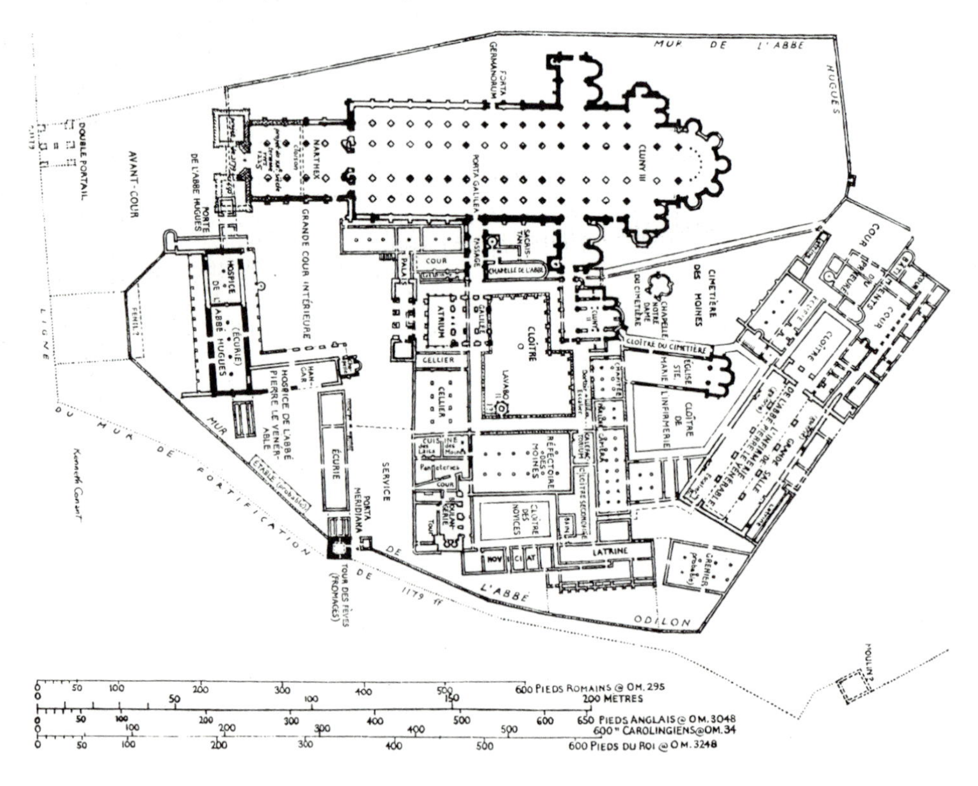

gun to accommodate the ever-increasing number of monks (Figure 7.40).

The church of Cluny III had the features of mature Romanesque architecture for it was appropriate to the grandeur of Cluny that its major church should be the largest and most splendid in Christendom. Based on the basilican plan, the church was enriched by a double set of transepts and further augmented by a series of radiating chapels around the apse and eastern walls of the transepts (Figure 7.41). The nave, 100 feet high and 496 feet long, was large to accommodate impressive processions and was flanked by two aisles on each side, the innermost pair of which continued around the choir as an ambulatory, linking the five radiating chapels of the east end (Figure 7.42). On the exterior, each of the plan elements was clearly expressed as an individual volume, but all were skillfully integrated into a coherent whole. Towers provided vertical emphasis: a pair at the western entrance, one over each arm of the major transept, the highest tower at the intersection of the major transept and nave, and a shorter tower over the crossing of the minor transept. Viewed from the east, the church appeared as a triangular mass, with roofs ascending from the chapels to the ambulatory, the apse semidome, the minor crossing tower, and finally the major crossing tower. Inside, the effect was even more wonderful, for the sanctuary at the east end was filled with light from the many windows in the chapels and clerestories. Images of how this may have appeared come largely from the research of Kenneth John Conant, since the actual church of Cluny III was systematically dismantled for its stone after the French Revolution. Only the south arm of the major transept remains (Figure 7.43).

FIGURE 7.43 *South transept from the church of Cluny III.* (Photo: French Government Tourist Office)

Considered from the standpoint of structure, Cluny III represented the great progress made in building art since the completion of St. Martin at Canigou. The paired aisles, which stepped down in height, buttressed the high vaults of the nave. The vault itself was not a continuous barrel vault as at Saint-Sernin, but a broken barrel vault, banded in each bay for visual articulation and structural reinforcement. Whether by accident or deduction, the monks who served as architects of Cluny III, the musician Gunzo and the mathematician Hézelon, found that a broken semicircular or pointed arch exerts less outward thrust than the Roman arch, and they exploited this discovery in the vaulting of nave and aisles. Even so, a portion of the nave vault collapsed in 1125, but it was repaired before the general dedication of the church on October 25, 1130.

FIGURE 7.44 *Interior of Sainte-Madeleine, Vézelay, 1120–1132.* (From R. Sturgis)

Light for the nave was provided directly by rather small clerestory windows located just under the vaulting, since the great loads sustained by the walls severely restricted the possibilities for larger openings.

The great vaulted spaces of the church created excellent acoustics for the exceptionally beautiful and elaborate services sung by the monks. The rich splendor of the heavenly kingdom was further reflected in Cluny's artistic embellishment, particularly sculpture, lavished on the building. Some of this sculpture survived postrevolutionary destruction, although in considerably damaged condition. To assess the artistic impact of Cluny, therefore, it is necessary to see the better-preserved work at the affiliates of Cluny, for where the religious influence of Cluny traveled, so did its policy of artistic patronage. At Sainte-Madeleine, Vézelay, the abbey was enlarged during a period of Cluniac reform, and the church nave preserves its stately Romanesque dignity (Figure 7.44). Polychromed semicircular arches divide the nave vault into bays, each of which is groin vaulted; the choir was rebuilt during the Gothic period. Splendid sculptural work on column capitals and the narthex portals remains. The capitals depict a range of subjects, from Old Testament

FIGURE 7.45 *Narthex tympanum from Sainte-Madeleine, Vézelay.* (Photo: Marburg)

FIGURE 7.46 *Tympanum from Saint-Lazare, Autun, 1120–1135.* (Photo: Marburg)

events to the lives of the saints and allegories illustrating teachings of the Church. The tympanum over the door from the narthex to the nave (dated 1120–32) represents the Descent of the Holy Spirit at Pentecost, in which Christ sends the Apostles to the corners of the earth to preach, teach, and heal (Figure 7.45). The sculptor here has bordered the central scene with signs of the zodiac, illustrations of the months of the year shown through agricultural labors, and the diverse peoples of the world, including Scythians with collapsible, elephant-sized ears, Ethiopians with pig snouts, and pygmies with ladders. All express the fact that Christ is present at all times, in all places, to all people.

There is a more austere tympanum at the Cluniac church of Saint-Lazare at Autun (Figure 7.46). Here the subject is the Last Judgment, replete with hideous demons and risen souls summoned to the final reckoning. An impassive and enormous figure of Christ occupies the center of the panel, with heaven on his right and the weighing of souls on his left, next to the miseries of hell. The sculptor Gislebertus signed his work on a ledge under Christ's feet. The interior of the church repeats many of the architectural features of Cluny III at a reduced scale (Figure 7.47); the beautifully carved capitals of the nave and choir present a range of biblical stories, including a Nativity cycle, as well as fanciful beasts and foliage.

Aquitaine and Provence

As one would expect from a period when communication was limited and political control dispersed, a number of regional variants of the Romanesque developed in the area of present-day France. All share the common heritage of Romanesque influences, but they differ according to the materials, culture, and artistic interests of the individual locales. The major portion of France south of the Loire comprised the area of Aquitaine, an important region that was successively independent, allied with

FIGURE 7.47 *Interior of Saint-Lazare, Autun.* (Photo: Marburg)

FIGURE 7.48 *Saint-Front, Périgueux, after 1120.* (Photo: J. Feuillie/© C.N.M.H.S./S.P.A.D.E.M.)

the King of France, and the territory of the King of England. Seat of a flourishing culture, its architecture was perhaps the most open to varied influences from other parts of Europe, especially from eastern Christendom. Aquitaine has a series of some seventy churches with domes, an atypical feature in western medieval architecture. That they reflect Byzantine influence is strongly implied by their use of pendentives, a characteristically eastern device.

The church of Saint-Front at Périgueux (Figure 7.48), built largely after 1120, provides an interesting parallel with St. Mark's in Venice. St. Mark's, itself modeled on the Greek cross plan of the now-vanished Church of the Holy Apostles in Constantinople, was rebuilt after a fire, with the work being completed about 1089. Nearly thirty years later, the existing church of Saint-Front at Périgueux was greatly enlarged into a Greek cross plan remarkably similar to St. Mark's. Five domes on pendentives

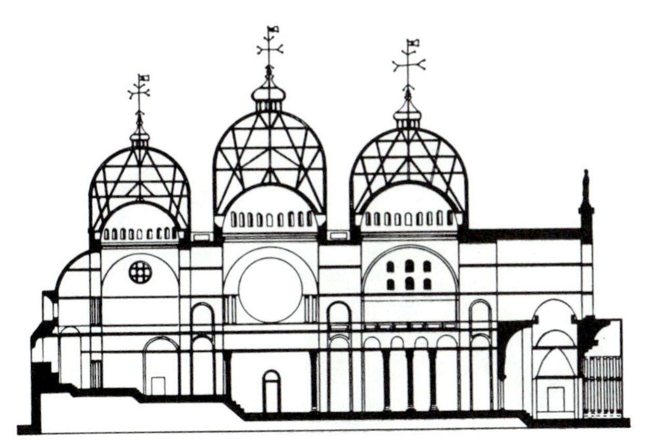

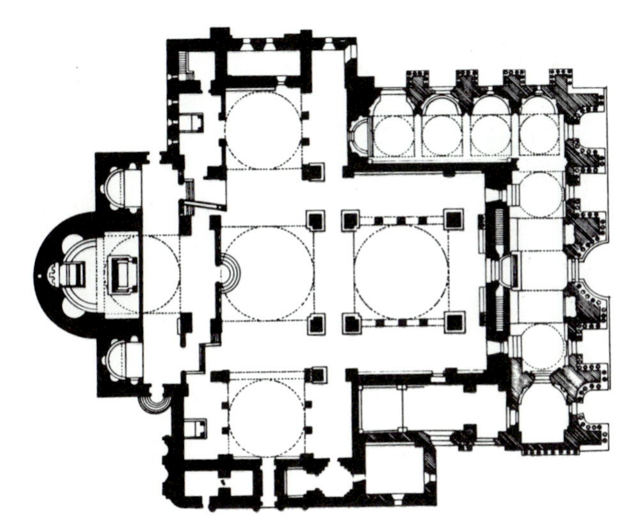

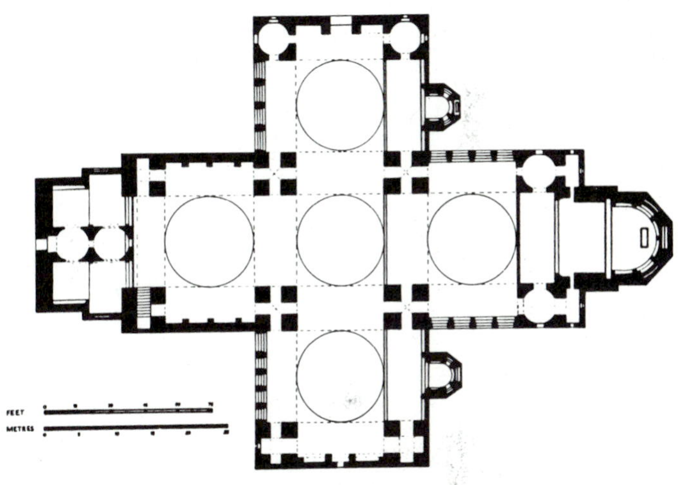

FIGURE 7.49 *Comparative sections and plans of St. Mark's, Venice, and Saint-Front, Périgueux.* (From W. Blaser)

FIGURE 7.50 *Interior of Saint-Front, Périgueux.* (Photo: J. Feuillie/© C.N.M.H.S./S.P.A.D.E.M.)

rise from massive pierced piers to cover the arms and crossing of the church (Figure 7.49). At Périgueux, the work lacks both the typical Byzantine mosaic decoration inside and the exterior profile of Byzantine domes (Figure 7.50). Instead the detailing is based on classical architecture, including closely spaced classical columns on the **lantern** turrets above the conical roofs over each dome.

FIGURE 7.51 *Cathedral Saint-Pierre, Angoulême, 1105–1128.* (Photo: J. Feuillie/© C.N.M.H.S./S.P.A.D.E.M.)

FIGURE 7.52 *Plan of Cathedral Saint-Pierre, Angoulême.* (From W. Blaser)

FIGURE 7.53 *Interior of Cathedral Saint-Pierre, Angoulême.* (Photo: J. Feuillie/© C.N.M.H.S./S.P.A.D.E.M.)

Périgueux is somewhat exceptional even among the unusual churches of Aquitaine. The other domed churches there, such as the Cathedral Saint-Pierre at Angoulême (1105–1128 and later) (Figures 7.51, 7.52), are aisleless basilicas with domes replacing the customary vaulting in the nave. The major structural loads in each bay were concentrated by pendentives to four piers set in the wall, allowing a reasonable area to be opened for windows, thereby providing direct illumination to the nave. The sequence of pointed arches framing each bay provides a stately processional space (Figure 7.53). On the west front is an inaccurately restored sculpture depicting a vision of the Second Coming of Christ.

Not all Romanesque churches in Aquitaine have domes, however. There are also fine examples of vaulted structures, including the abbey church of

Figure 7.54 *Saint-Savin-sur-Gartempe, 1060–1115.* (Photo: Marburg)

Figure 7.55 *Interior of Saint-Savin-sur-Gartempe.* (Photo: Marburg)

Saint-Savin-sur-Gartempe (Figures 7.54, 7.55), built in stages between 1060 and 1115. Massive cylindrical piers support a continuous barrel vault over the nave, which is braced by groin vaults in the aisles that rise nearly as high as the nave to counteract thrust where it is greatest, just above the springing of the vault arch. As at Angoulême, radiating chapels without an ambulatory form the east end, and a crossing tower provides vertical emphasis. On the interior, the uninterrupted nave vault, the narthex, and the crypt have been adorned with a notable series of frescoes, called the Bible of St. Savin, which form the finest existing example of Romanesque mural painting.

The region of Provence, centered around the Mediterranean close to Italy, remained the most faithful to the classical architecture of Rome. Provence had been a major Roman colony, and well-preserved Roman buildings still exist at Nîmes and other cities. Not surprisingly, therefore, Romanesque architecture there exhibits strong Roman influence in its composition, proportions, and details. The Cluniac priory church of Saint-Gilles-du-Gard (ca. 1140–1170) (Figure 7.56) has a triple-arched west façade based on the model of a Roman triumphal arch. Accurately proportioned Corinthian columns, some of which were actually recycled from Roman buildings, were incorporated in the work. Little remains of the original church, which was an important regional center of pilgrimage. The contemporary façade of the former cathedral of Saint-Trophîme at Arles (Figure 7.57) also recalls Roman construction in its dignified setting of sculpture in classical surroundings.

FIGURE 7.56 *Saint-Gilles-du-Gard, 1140–1170.* (Photo: Marburg)

FIGURE 7.57 *West portal of Saint-Trophîme, Arles, ca. 1170–1180.* (Photo: Marburg)

Cistercian Monasteries

The eleventh century witnessed the establishment of several new monastic groups, none of which would be more important architecturally than the Order of Cîteaux, known as the Cistercians. Like the Cluniacs the Cistercians originated in Burgundy, but in artistic and religious development they would be in many respects the antithesis of the Cluniacs. The Cistercians were founded in 1098 by a group of twenty-two monks from Molesme who desired a stricter observance of the Benedictine Rule, and their name came from that of their first monastery, Cîteaux, located in a wooded swamp donated by the Viscount of Beaune. The first years were difficult, but the new monastery gained an important convert in 1112 when Bernard, a young nobleman, joined the order. His religious zeal and organizational skill shaped the Cistercians into a uniform, ascetic, and highly regulated community. In 1115 Bernard founded the third daughter house at Clairvaux, where he was to be the guiding spiritual force for all Cistercian houses until his death in 1153.

In time the Cistercians rivaled the Cluniacs in influence, although their affiliated monasteries totaled only about half the number of Cluniac houses. The Cistercian Order required a great measure of conformity from its dependent monasteries, and this uniformity extended to architecture as well. As was appropriate to the austere life laid out for its monks, Cistercian abbeys were of the simplest possible construction consistent with durable masonry building. In sharp contrast to Cluniacs, the Cistercians did not allow luxurious features like towers, stained glass windows, or paved floors; did not use expensive materials; and discouraged sculptural ornament. Cistercian monasteries had straightforward, orderly plans based on a square module and devoid of the elaborate articulation of many Cluniac designs. Thus the Cistercians produced an international set of buildings with unmistakable common features.

All Cistercian houses were located near a reliable water supply and at least twenty miles from any existing settlement. In the early years the monks provided for all their own needs, supplying their vegetarian diet from garden plots adjacent to the monastery. As with many medieval monastic movements, success spoiled the Cistercians. They became wealthy and relaxed the rigors of their religious observances, becoming more like any other monastic group, and when religious institutions came under attack, Cistercian abbeys were particularly ravaged. While their original ideals were intact, however, they were a powerful religious and architectural presence, contributing much to the spread of learning, progressive agricultural practices, and sound building techniques across western Europe.

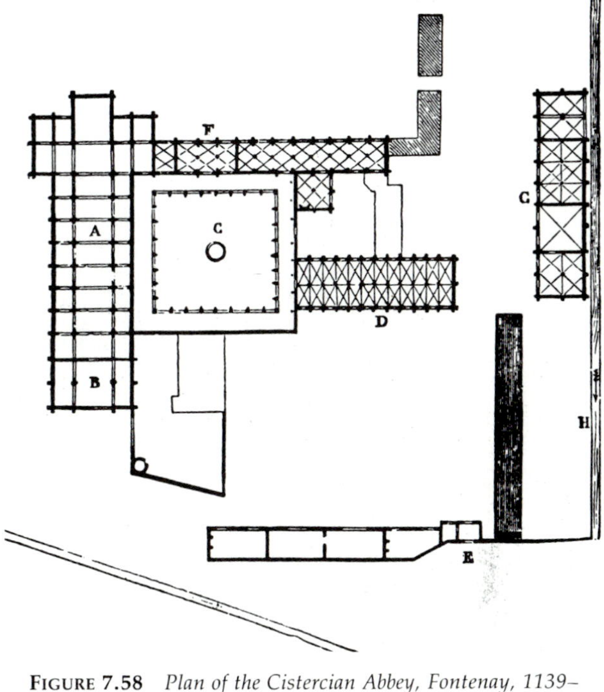

FIGURE 7.58 *Plan of the Cistercian Abbey, Fontenay, 1139–1147 and later.* (From E. Viollet-le-Duc)

The Abbey of Fontenay in Burgundy is today the best-preserved Cistercian monastery (Figure 7.58). Built from 1139 to 1147 (with some portions reconstructed in the thirteenth and sixteenth centuries), it is a splendid illustration of Bernard of Clairvaux's architectural ideals. The monastery is closely modeled on the layout of the Plan of St. Gall, having a modular unit established by the square bay of the church aisle. Two of these units determine the

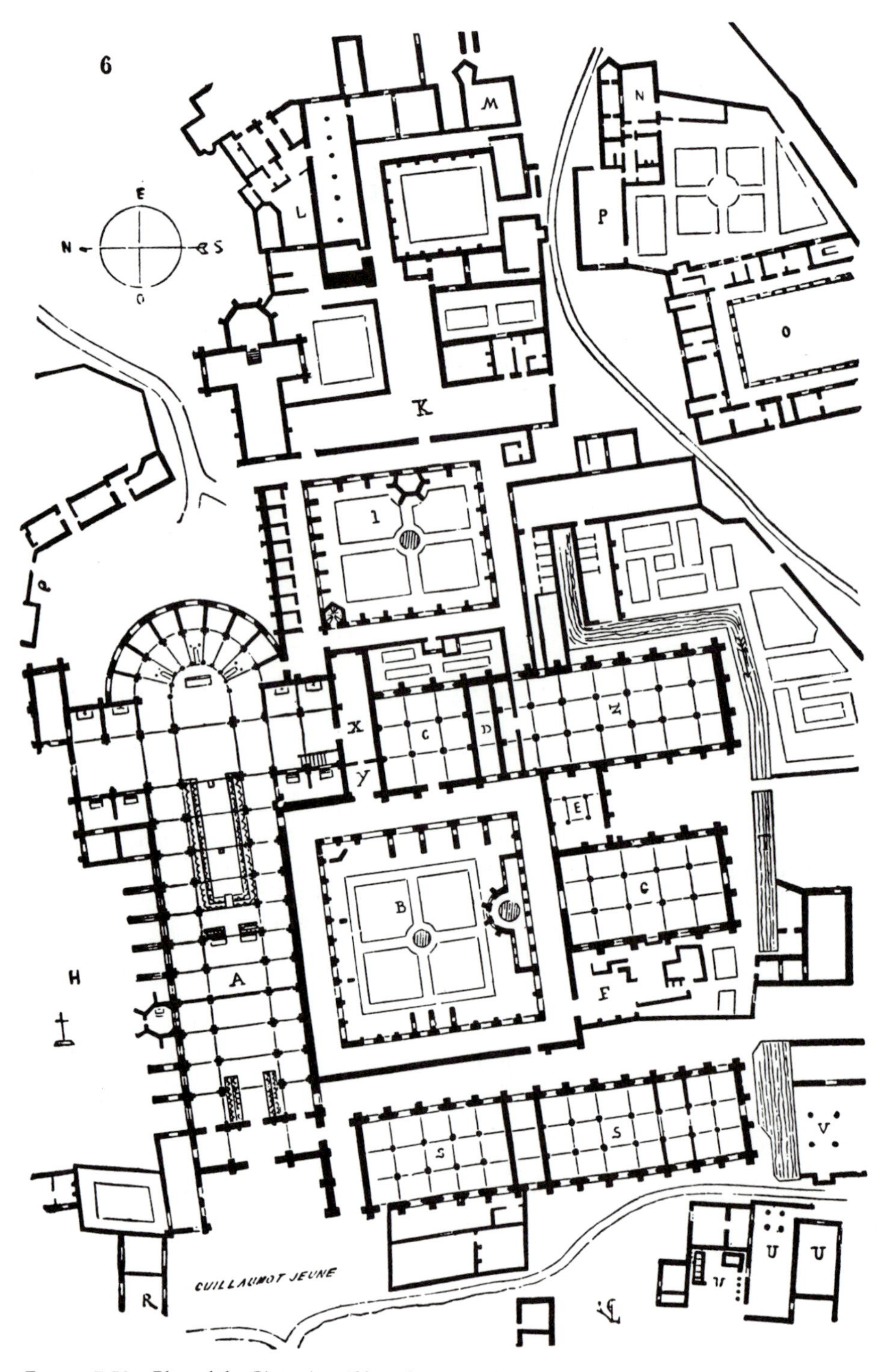

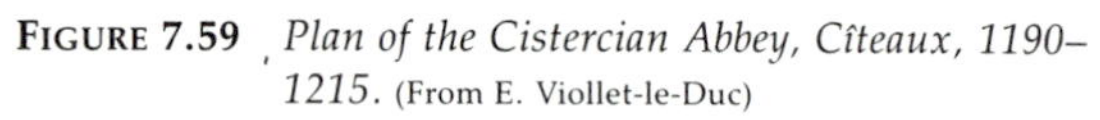

FIGURE 7.59 *Plan of the Cistercian Abbey, Cîteaux, 1190–1215.* (From E. Viollet-le-Duc)

width of the nave; four, the area of the crossing; and one for each of the four chapels on the east wall of the transept. The module continues as the standard unit for the cloister walk, and it is repeated in the chapter house, workroom, and forge building. (The nonmodular refectory is a sixteenth-century rebuilding.)

This same simplicity distinguishes the three-dimensional reality of the buildings. The nave, modest in height, is enclosed with broken banded barrel vaults, while the aisles have transverse broken barrel vaults over each bay, reminiscent of the nave vaults at Saint-Philibert at Tournus. Light for the church comes from windows in the aisles and at the east and west end walls, as there are no clerestories. The church floor is of compacted earth, with only the raised choir section being paved in stone. The utter plainness of the construction is enlivened by the harmonious proportions. The cloister walk, with its semicircular arcading, reflects sunlight softly and creates an appropriately human scale.

The Cistercians built well. Their standardized designs did much to spread sound building practices and the progressive Romanesque style preferred by Bernard across most of Europe. After Bernard's death, many Cistercian houses built more elaborate monasteries than that at Fontenay. Choirs in particular were enlarged, as in the plan of Cîteaux (Figure 7.59), where the original square-ended chapels were replaced with a radial layout, producing a design copied later at many daughter houses. Although minor regional variants are reflected in Cistercian work, monasteries as distant from one another as Fossanova in Italy, Le Thoronet in Provence, Poblet in Spain, Maulbronn in Germany, and Fountains in England all share the fundamentally straightforward and unadorned character of Cistercian architecture, the first international style of the medieval period.

STAVE CHURCHES AND NORMAN ARCHITECTURE

Scandinavia, the land of the Vikings, remained outside the Christian sphere until the middle of the eleventh century. From 793, when Norwegian pirates sacked Lindisfarne, organized raids were made almost annually on communities in France, England, Ireland, Germany, and Spain. The shallow-draft, swift Viking ships sailed up the navigable rivers along which medieval settlements clustered, and the burning, looting, and massacre visited on these communities added to the instability of the time. (The Vikings thus provided an incentive for the erection of more nearly fireproof buildings in stone.) In the tenth century, the raids gradually ceased, due in part to the emergence of strong national kingdoms in Denmark, Sweden, and Norway, and also to the conversion of these vigorous pagans to Christianity.

In Norway conversion was accomplished primarily through Anglo-Saxon missionaries who returned with Viking raiders from England. These missionaries brought knowledge of Anglo-Saxon church architecture with them, so the simple plans of parish churches in Britain, themselves based on Early Christian precedent, became the models for equally small Norwegian churches. The combination of these simple plans with native building traditions created a unique and distinctive architecture, the stave church.

The church at Urnes (Figure 7.60), the oldest extant stave church, dates from about 1130–1150, and its design illustrates the type. The staves are upright poles, similar in size to ordinary utility poles, that form the basic structure for the building. They are supported on four crossed horizontal sills forming a rectangular chassis. The chassis is raised off the ground by large flat stones at the intersections of the sill planks because excavated foundations would be subject to heaving as the ground froze and thawed. These corner stones also protect the timber structure by isolating it from ground moisture. Low exterior walls, made of vertical boarding anchored by rounded corner posts, rest on an outer chassis sill supported on the short cantilevered ends of the main chassis, while the upper wall, braced above head height, follows the vertical line of the stave frame up to the roof rafters. A crowning **cupola** visually completes the roof ridge, although it has no connection to the interior space. The major structural elements, the staves, are kept dry by shorter exterior boards that are renewed from time to time as required. The exterior wood of stave churches is further protected from decay by coatings of pine

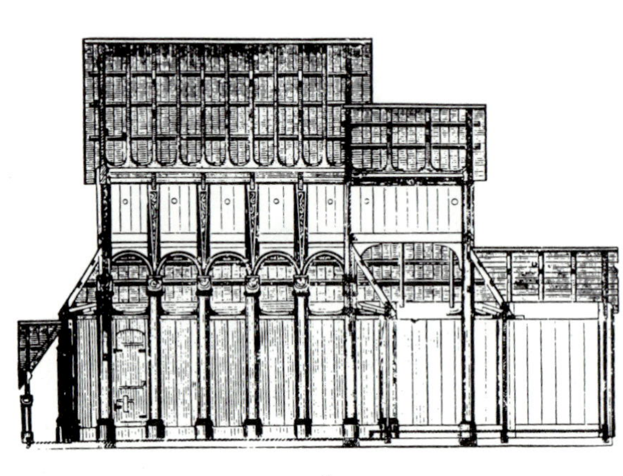

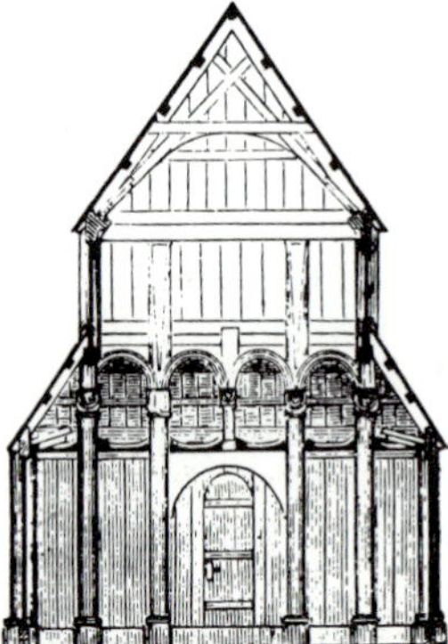

FIGURE 7.60 *Sections of the Stave Church, Urnes, 1130–1150.* (From L. Dietrichson)

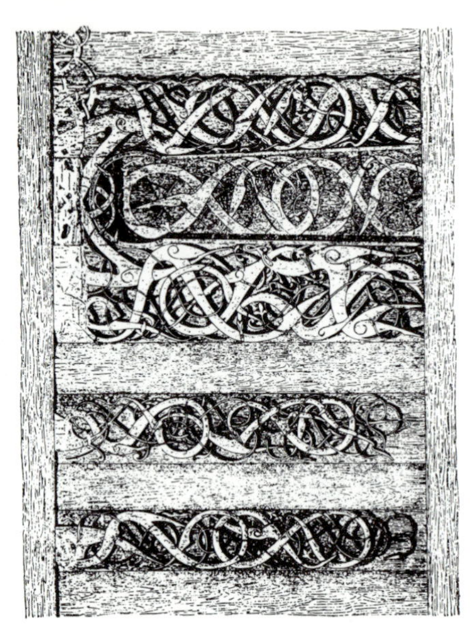

FIGURE 7.61 *Detail of north side carving on the stave church, Urnes.* (From L. Dietrichson)

pitch, which impart an almost-black color to the outside. The church is very dark inside, for the original design had no windows, depending instead for light and ventilation on small circular openings located high in the walls.

Urnes also possesses a remarkable carved portal, now located on the north wall of the church (Figure 7.61). Bands of boldly undercut figures, cut from single planks of wood, represent four-legged beasts and serpentlike animals intertwined in intricate patterns. The similarity of this work to Animal Style ornament is immediately apparent. What is less clear at first glance is why such carving should be found as ornament around a church doorway. Although no documents provide absolute proof, modern scholars believe that these figures represent a carryover from the pagan past, applied here to the purposes of the Christian faith. In Norse mythology the end of the world was to come when snakes and dragons, representing the forces of evil, were locked in mortal combat. Known as *Ragnarok,* this struggle was the pagan equivalent of the Christian Last Judgment theme, which was already widely established as a subject for sculptural reliefs on the doorways of churches in other parts of Europe. In Norway, as elsewhere, the early missionaries converting diverse peoples to Christianity found it convenient to adapt established traditions to the causes of the Church, and this seems to be the best explanation for these remarkable portals on stave churches.

Many Norwegian stave churches were probably constructed in the sparsely populated and isolated valley communities along the fjords. As late as the nineteenth century 322 such buildings could be documented through remains or textual references; today only 32 survive under careful protection. All have been restored. The church at Borgund (Figures 7.62–7.65) probably represents the most authentic mature stave church (ca. 1200), although its portal carvings are not the artistic equal of those at Urnes.

The Vikings also influenced architecture on the European mainland. In 911 they were granted territory in western France in exchange for cessation of their raids on settlements within the Frankish kingdom. The settled Vikings became known as Normans, their land as Normandy, and their ruler as the Duke of Normandy. Within the span of a century the Normans developed into capable builders

FIGURE 7.62 *Stave Church, Borgund, ca. 1200.* (Photo: Royal Norwegian Ministry of Foreign Affairs)

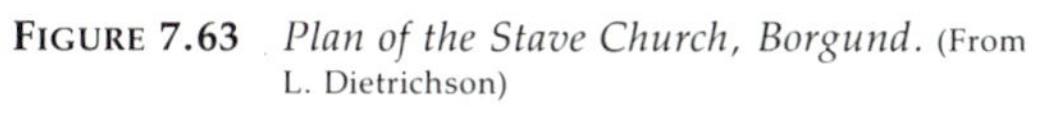

FIGURE 7.63 *Plan of the Stave Church, Borgund.* (From L. Dietrichson)

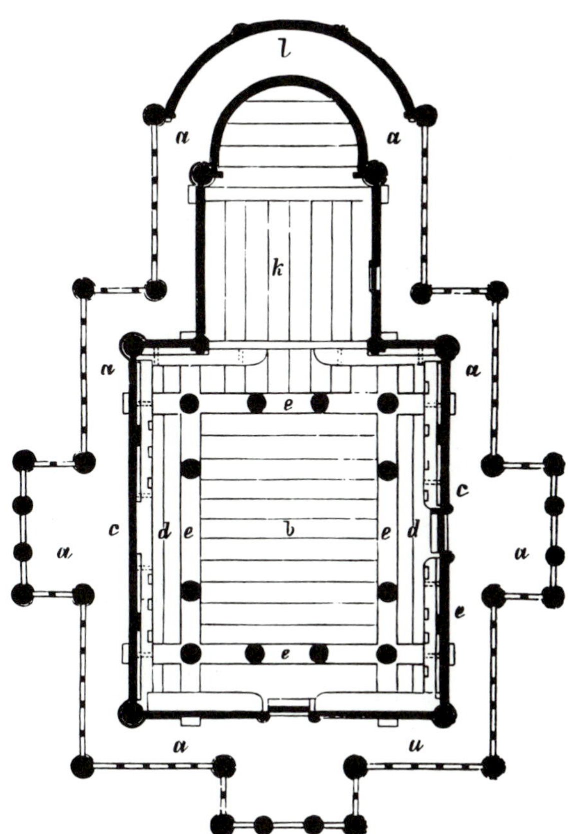

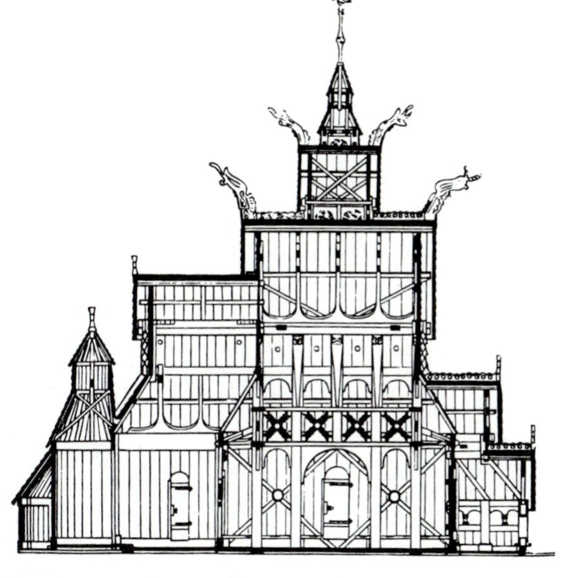

FIGURE 7.64 *Section of the Stave Church, Borgund.* (From L. Dietrichson)

FIGURE 7.65 *Perspective section of the Stave Church, Borgund.* (From L. Dietrichson)

Figure 7.66 *Nôtre-Dame, Jumièges. 1037–1066.* (Photo: Marburg)

in stone, and, like Charlemagne, they encouraged the construction of monasteries.

The power and boldness of Norman architecture can still be seen at the ruined abbey church of Nôtre-Dame at Jumièges (1037–1066) (Figures 7.66, 7.67). The church is large, with a long nave, single aisles with galleries, compact transepts, and an ambulatory without radiating chapels surrounding the apse. Twin towers, square in the lower stories and octagonal in the upper portions, stand on either side of the west entrance in a composition recalling Carolingian westwerks. The stonework is severe and restrained throughout with few sculptural embellishments, although some architectural details were probably painted. The major space of nave, transepts, and choir and the crossing tower lantern were roofed in wood; only the aisles had groin vaulting.

A generation later, work began on the abbey church of Saint-Étienne at Caen, also known as the Abbaye-aux-Hommes (1068–1120), founded by William, Duke of Normandy, to expiate his consanguineous marriage (Figures 7.68, 7.69). As at Jumièges, the original church had a long nave with double

Figure 7.67 *Interior of Nôtre-Dame, Jumièges.* (Photo: Marburg)

Figure 7.68 *Saint-Étienne, Caen, 1068–1120.* (Photo: Marburg) ▶

FIGURE 7.69 *Interior of Saint-Étienne, Caen.* (Photo: Marburg)

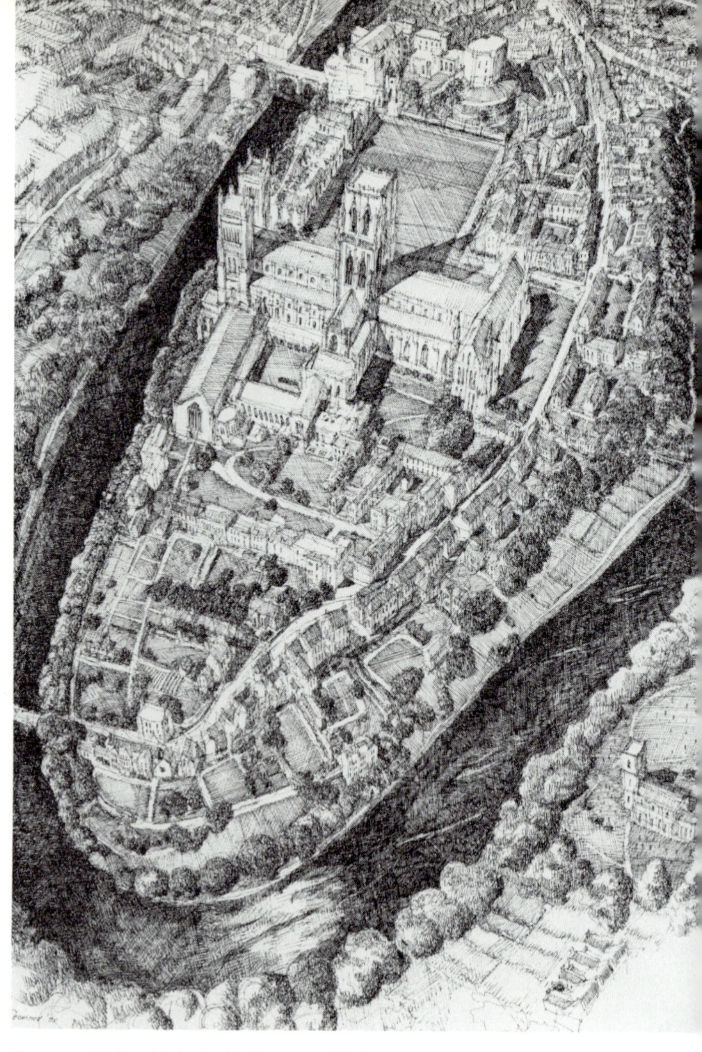

FIGURE 7.70 *Cathedral, Durham, 1093–1130.* (Delineator: J. Desmond)

western towers. Aisles flanked the wooden-roofed nave, and with groin vaults supported the galleries above. About 1115 the wooden roof was removed, and the upper stage of the nave wall was rebuilt to incorporate ribs of sexpartite vaulting constructed across the nave. These vaults, encompassing two bays of the nave for each unit, have major and minor supports in the alternate grouped and single wall ribs that continue the line of the vaulting rib down to the floor.

Duke William is remembered in history for more than his endowment of Saint-Étienne. In 1066 he led an army of Normans across the English Channel, defeated the assembled Anglo-Saxon forces at the Battle of Hastings, and extended Norman rule to England. Henceforth he was known as William the Conqueror, and his military triumph was to have lasting consequences for English history and architecture. Compared with contemporary Norman work, Britain's Anglo-Saxon buildings were small and poorly built. William reorganized the English church and began a major campaign of church building. He encouraged monasteries, and great cathedrals arose at Canterbury, Durham, Lincoln, Winchester, Gloucester, Norwich, Ely, and many other sites.

The cathedral at Durham (1093–1130) (Figure 7.70) was planned from the first to be completely vaulted. In the Norman tradition the cathedral is substantial. Two west front towers and a square crossing tower announce its presence on the hilltop above the river Wear. Its plan is simple and the massing is bold (Figure 7.71). The nave and choir are composed of double bays, built with semicircu-

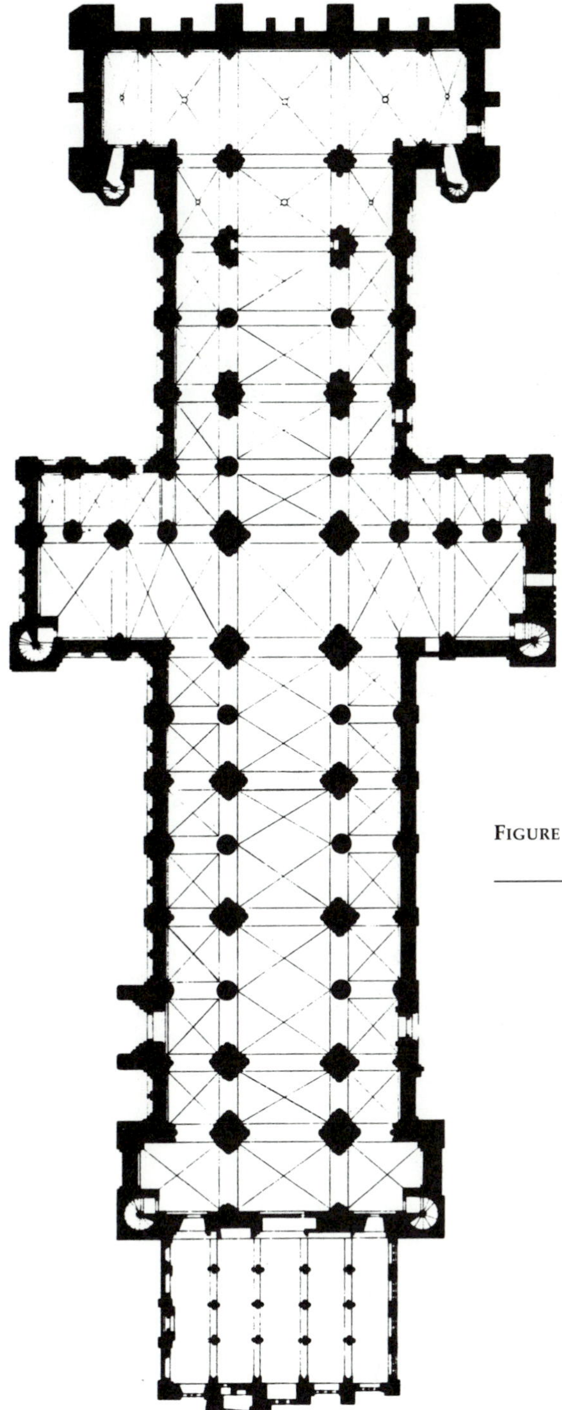

FIGURE 7.71 *Plan and section of the Cathedral, Durham.*
(From W. Blaser)

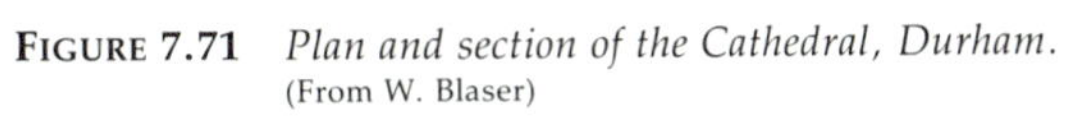

Figure 7.72 *Interior of the Cathedral, Durham.* (From T. Bonney)

Figure 7.73 *Galilee Chapel of the Cathedral, Durham, ca. 1175.* (From R. Sturgis)

lar-arched rib vaults supported by grouped piers alternating with distinctive cylindrical columns (Figure 7.72). Galleries over the aisles help counter the thrust of the high vaults but conclude sufficiently below the crown of the vaulting to allow clerestories to light the nave. The heavy quality of the construction is increased by the relative absence of figural ornament. Striking geometric designs of chevrons, diaper patterns, and fluting are incised on the cylindrical columns, almost like the abstractions of Viking interlace work, while the arch moldings in the **galilee** chapel (ca. 1175) (Figure 7.73) have dogtooth patterning. At Durham, the structural components of Gothic architecture — the rib vault, the buttress, and the pointed arch — are all present in embryonic form. The rib vaults of the interior span the nave, choir, and transepts; the quadrant vaults under the aisle roofs, which brace the ceiling vaults, perform the task of flying buttresses, although they are not exposed; and the pointed arch is suggested in the interlaced arcading of the aisle walls. A lightening of construction, the refinement of proportions, and some experimentation to determine the most effective combination of these elements in a working whole would produce a new architectural style. Within fifteen years after the completion of Durham, the Gothic style emerged at the abbey church of Saint-Denis.

8.

Gothic Architecture

Gothic is perhaps the only style in the history of architecture that can be considered an invention. Although the components that went into its creation were developed in various places during the Romanesque period, bringing these pieces together into a new style was a synthetic process that first occurred in the construction of the Abbey Church of St. Denis outside Paris. At its heart Gothic is a structural technique that made possible soaring heights and generous window areas. Unlike Romanesque building, in which a continuous mass of wall is necessary to sustain the load, Gothic building is a skeletal system that transfers roof loads down to the ground at specific points.

There are three structural elements of Gothic architecture:

1. The pointed arch, which is far more efficient structurally than the Romanesque semicircular arch. Pointed arches approximate a catenary curve, which represents the line of compressive force acting in any arch, and thus exert less outward thrust.
2. The rib vault, understood by structural engineers as thin shell construction with folded plates (Figure 8.1). Medieval builders discovered they could halve the material weight of groin vaults by using vaults with lighter webbing. As the dead load on the vaulting was created primarily by the weight of the stone, reducing this weight not only economized on material but also facilitated greater building heights.
3. The **flying buttress,** which was a development based on the integral wall buttress used in Romanesque construction. Since Gothic skeletal

Figure 8.1 *Rib vault and pointed arch.* (From E. Viollet-le-Duc)

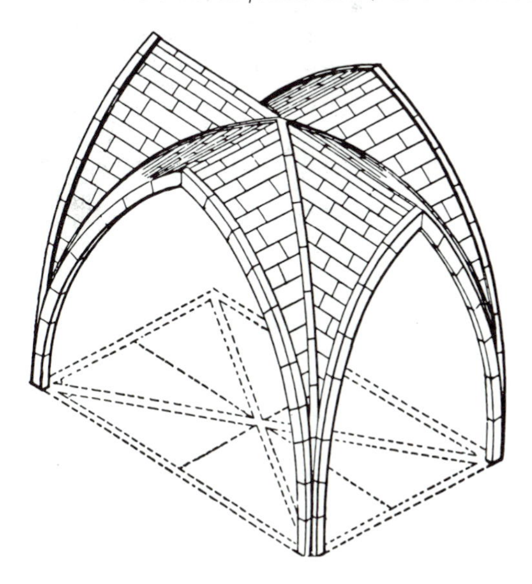

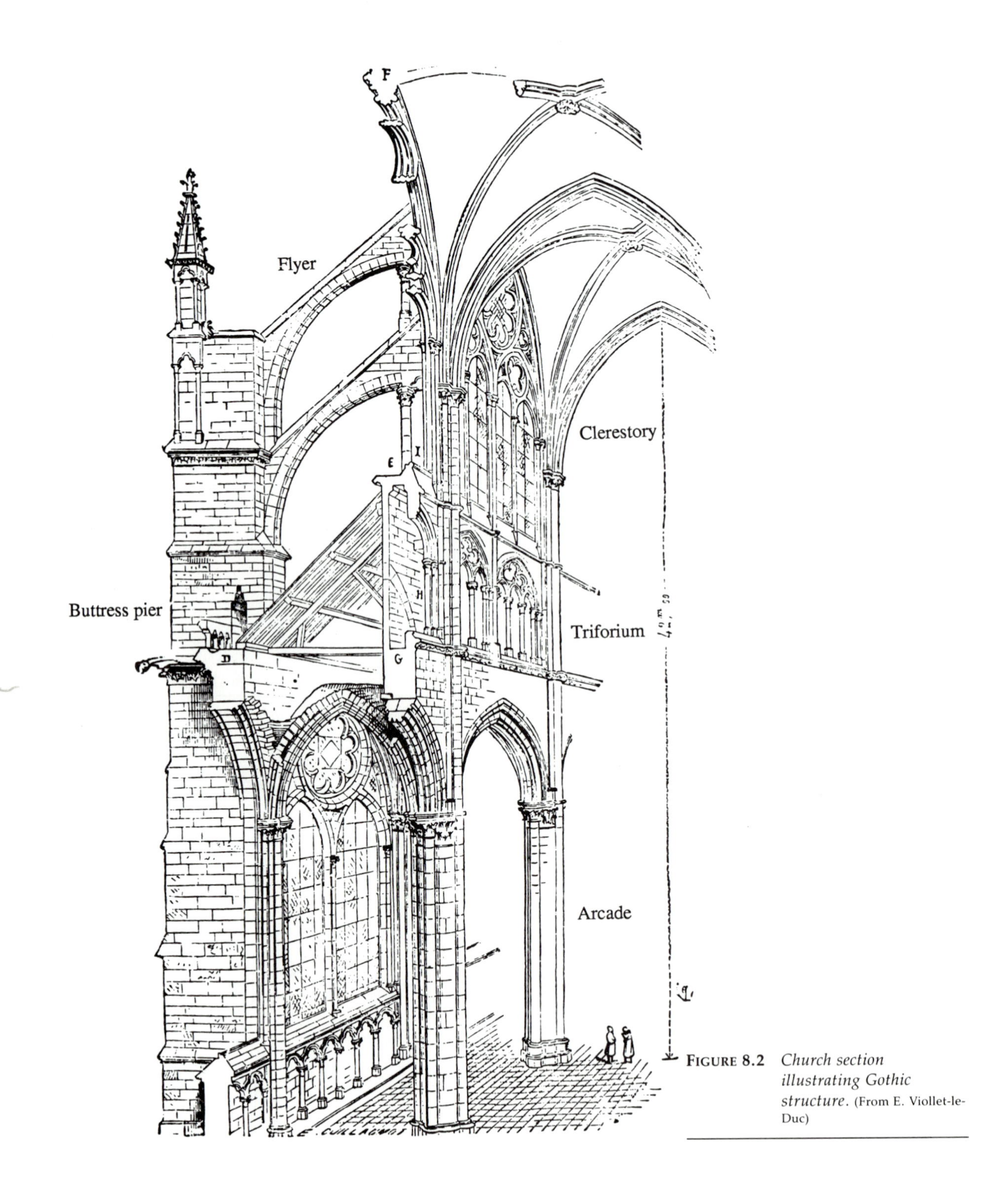

FIGURE 8.2 *Church section illustrating Gothic structure.* (From E. Viollet-le-Duc)

construction concentrates loads at piers, the need for reinforcement at these points is great. Gothic architects soon developed external buttressing, built at right angles to the wall and connected to it at strategic points by slender arches, which appear to "fly" or leap as they reach out to strengthen the upper sections of the skeleton frame (Figure 8.2).

Gothic architecture is more than a collection of technical tricks, however, for it embraces an integrated aesthetic system. The flexibility of the pointed arch allowed irregular areas to be vaulted while maintaining a common ceiling height. The ribs of the vaulting permitted continuity in line from the floor to the crown of the vaults overhead, and the reduced vaulting weight allowed the height of interior space to rise dramatically. Flying buttresses stabilized the thrust of the vaults invisibly when viewed from the interior, and the wall area between piers could be opened for large windows to provide much-desired natural light in the major spaces of the church. Indeed it was probably this search to increase light, for both metaphysical and practical reasons, that stimulated the technical innovations of the Gothic style.

EARLY GOTHIC

The Gothic style originated in northern France, in the region around Paris known as the Ile-de-France. This area had relatively little Romanesque building, so perhaps it was more open to developments from other places. It also was the home of one of the period's most energetic, informed, and innovative patrons of the arts, Abbot Suger. Suger came from humble origins. His parents had donated him to the Abbey of St. Denis when he was three years old, and he was raised in the monastery school to become a monk. Among his young companions in the school was the future King Louis VI of France. Suger's diplomatic and administrative skills were soon noticed, and he rose rapidly in the church hierarchy. In 1122, at the age of thirty-six, he was elected abbot of St. Denis.

St. Denis was the French royal monastery. It was the burial place of Denis, the first Bishop of Paris, who was martyred by the Romans in the third century and later became the patron saint of France. The kings of France were buried at the Abbey, located about six miles north of Paris, and the royal banner, the Oriflamme, was kept there between wars. For all its prestige, the Abbey was overcrowded and somewhat decayed when Suger became abbot. The existing building, consecrated in 775, was a Carolingian basilica that had received an enlarged eastern chapel in 832. Suger wanted to rebuild the church for the greater glory of God and France, but first he had to set the Abbey's financial affairs in order and respond to criticism from Bernard of Clairvaux by reforming the religious practices of its monks. While he worked toward these goals, Suger developed images of what he wished the new church to be. He studied the Biblical descriptions of the Temple of Solomon, a design dictated by God; he read the writings of St. Denis in which there was much discussion of the mystical and metaphysical properties of light, especially colored light; and he inquired of travelers from Constantinople for descriptions of the church of Hagia Sophia (see Figure 5.14), widely regarded as the most splendid in Christendom, which Suger was determined to exceed. (Modern scholarship has revealed that Suger was mistaken in his reading. What he thought was written by St. Denis was actually the work of a different author.)

By 1137 Suger was ready to build. To enlarge the church he built a new west front and narthex (Figure 8.3) forward of the existing structure, probably to the designs of a Norman architect who could translate Suger's ideas into reality. This work, consecrated in 1140, incorporated both the tripartite, twin-towered west façade of Norman churches and the tradition of sculptured portals developed in the south of France. The three doorways had carved tympana and jamb statues, while the articulation of windows, including a circular or rose window, went beyond the linear façade compositions of Normandy. On the interior, rib vaults in the narthex were sprung from grouped piers, thus exploiting the potential for continuity of line.

So enthusiastic was the reception of this new work that construction began almost at once on an enlargement of the east end (Figure 8.4). In less than four years (1144) the new choir was dedicated

FIGURE 8.3 *West front of the Abbey, St. Denis, 1137–1144.* (Lithograph of 1850)

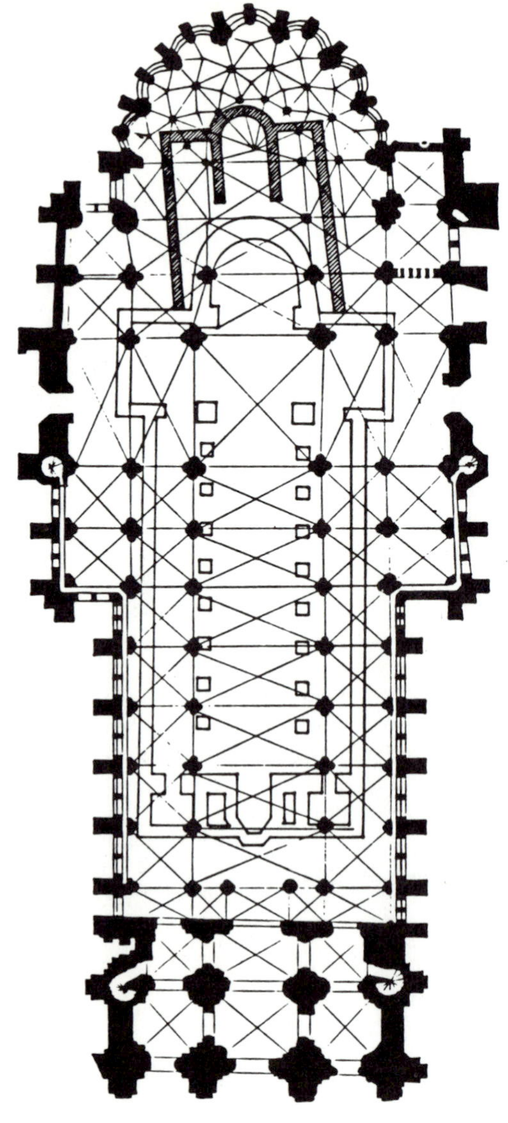

FIGURE 8.4 *Plan of the Abbey of St. Denis.* (Redrawn after S. Crosby)

in elaborate ceremonies involving distinguished churchmen and royalty. Suger's preoccupation with colored light is clearly manifested in the choir. Seven shallow radiating chapels, each with two large stained glass windows, open off the double ambulatory, itself an impressive processional space. The irregular bays of this complex plan are consistently covered by rib vaults rising to a uniform crown height, while slender buttresses, set in the angles between the chapels, reinforce the upper wall. The ensemble creates an airy, luminous, rich interior that glows like a jewel, precisely the effect desired by Suger: "a circular string of chapels, by virtue of which the whole church would shine with the wonderful and uninterrupted light of most sacred windows, pervading the interior beauty."

Planned next for construction was a nave to link the new narthex and choir, but Suger did not live to see the completion of his ambitious dream. Louis VII departed for the Second Crusade in 1147, leaving Suger as Regent of France, with neither time nor money for building, and Suger died shortly after Louis returned from the Holy Land in 1151. The present nave at St. Denis was completed a century later, when the upper portions of Suger's choir were

Figure 8.5 *Cathedral Notre-Dame, Laon, 1165–1205.*
(Photo: Marburg)

raised to match the height of the nave vaults attained with mature Gothic skills. Suger's west front has been sadly defaced over the years, so its present appearance, lacking one tower and much of the original sculpture, is but a shadow of the original.

The wondrous quality of light and space created by Suger's new choir at St. Denis was not lost on the church authorities and laypeople who visited the Abbey. Within a decade of its dedication, Gothic churches were under construction at several sites in the Ile-de-France, most often for cathedral churches in the growing towns. Unlike the predominantly rural Romanesque, Gothic came to be associated especially with urban settings and with the extension of the French kings' political influence. In regions where royal influence was weak and theological interest in the symbolic properties of light was not strong, such as the south of France, the mature Romanesque style continued to be used for at least a century after the Gothic was introduced, and few Gothic churches were ever built there.

Two of the early Gothic cathedrals in northern France are of particular interest. The Cathedral of Notre-Dame at Laon (Figures 8.5–8.8) was begun about 1165 to replace an older structure that had become too small for the needs of the prosperous town and the growing cathedral school. The choir and transepts were finished within twenty years,

FIGURE 8.7 *Interior of the Cathedral Notre-Dame, Laon.* (Photo: Marburg)

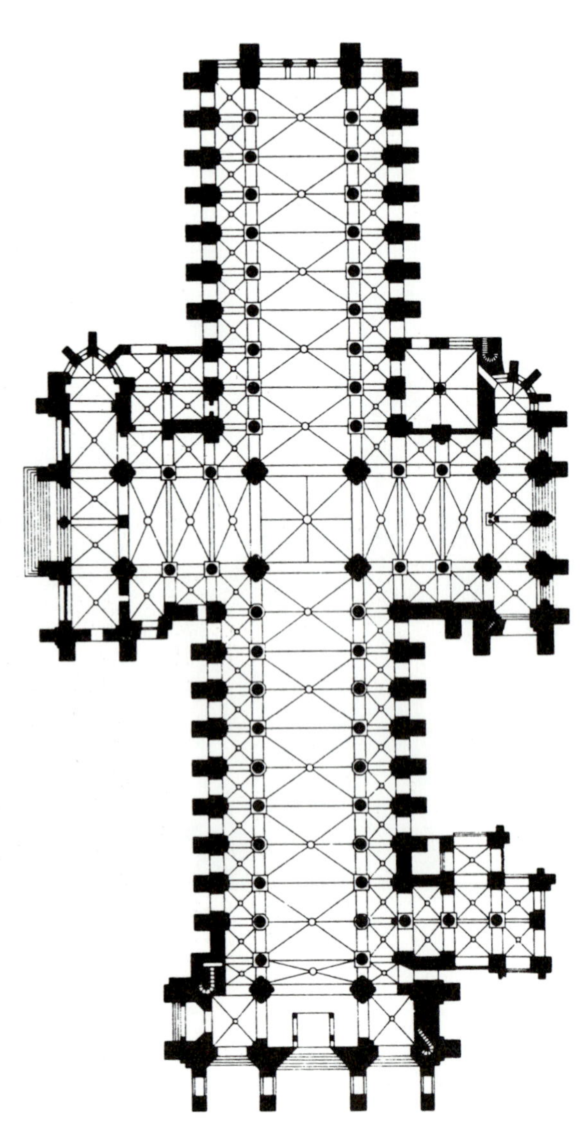

FIGURE 8.6 *Plan of the Cathedral Notre-Dame, Laon.* (From W. Blaser)

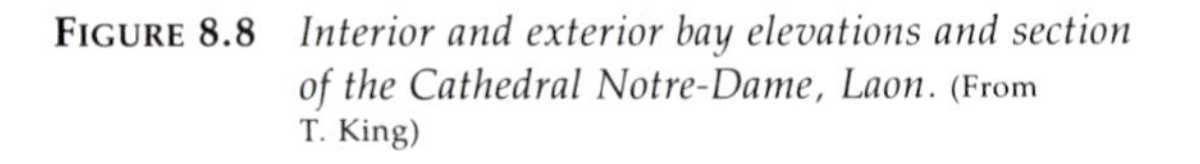

FIGURE 8.8 *Interior and exterior bay elevations and section of the Cathedral Notre-Dame, Laon.* (From T. King)

and the nave, west front, and crossing tower were completed by about 1205. The original semicircular Gothic choir was replaced early in the thirteenth century by the present square-ended east end to provide more space for services. Flying buttresses were added in the thirteenth century to modernize the appearance of the church, even though they are not required structurally because the galleries over the aisles stabilize the vaults.

At Laon one can see how cautiously architects and builders experimented with new Gothic techniques. Laon retained several elements from Romanesque churches, especially in its pre-1205 choir. The long nave, lantern crossing tower, galleries, semicircular choir, and alternating grouped piers and cylindrical columns in the nave could be found in Norman churches like Jumièges. It is the sexpartite rib vaults and above all the enlarged clerestory windows that mark the interior as Gothic. On the exterior, the three-dimensional, sculptural quality of the west front is distinctly innovative, for even the most ambitious of Cluniac churches was never conceived this boldly (Figure 8.9). The western towers begin on square plans and are transformed into octagons in the upper stages. Oxen carved from stone peer down from the towers' heights, silent reminders of the patient animals who hauled the construction stone up to the ridge on which the cathedral sits. Villard de Honnecourt, a medieval architect whose sketchbook has survived to modern times, drew the towers of Laon and noted, "I have traveled in many lands, but in no place have I seen such a tower as the one at Laon." Even with its later modifications, Laon stands as the purest example of the Early Gothic.

FIGURE 8.9 *West front elevation of the Cathedral Notre-Dame, Laon.* (From J. Guadet)

In 1163 the Bishop of Paris began construction on the new Cathedral of Notre-Dame (Figures 8.10, 8.11), clearing a site on the Ile de la Cité and laying substantial foundations for the church. Work began on the choir (1163–1182), progressing to the nave by 1178–1200. The flying buttress made its first appearance in the course of nave construction (around 1180), although the Paris cathedral retains the galleries over the aisles as does the cathedral at Laon. The west front was completed between 1200 and 1250. During that time, however, modifications were already being made in the fabric of the church. Notre-Dame is a tall church, 108 feet from the floor to the crown of its vaults, and the direct light admitted into the nave by the small original clerestories was insufficient for the space (Figure 8.12). To bring in more light, therefore, the clerestories all around the cathedral were enlarged in about 1225, flying buttresses were added to the choir to stabilize the great hemicycle, and the original nave buttresses were rebuilt (Figure 8.13). The transepts are

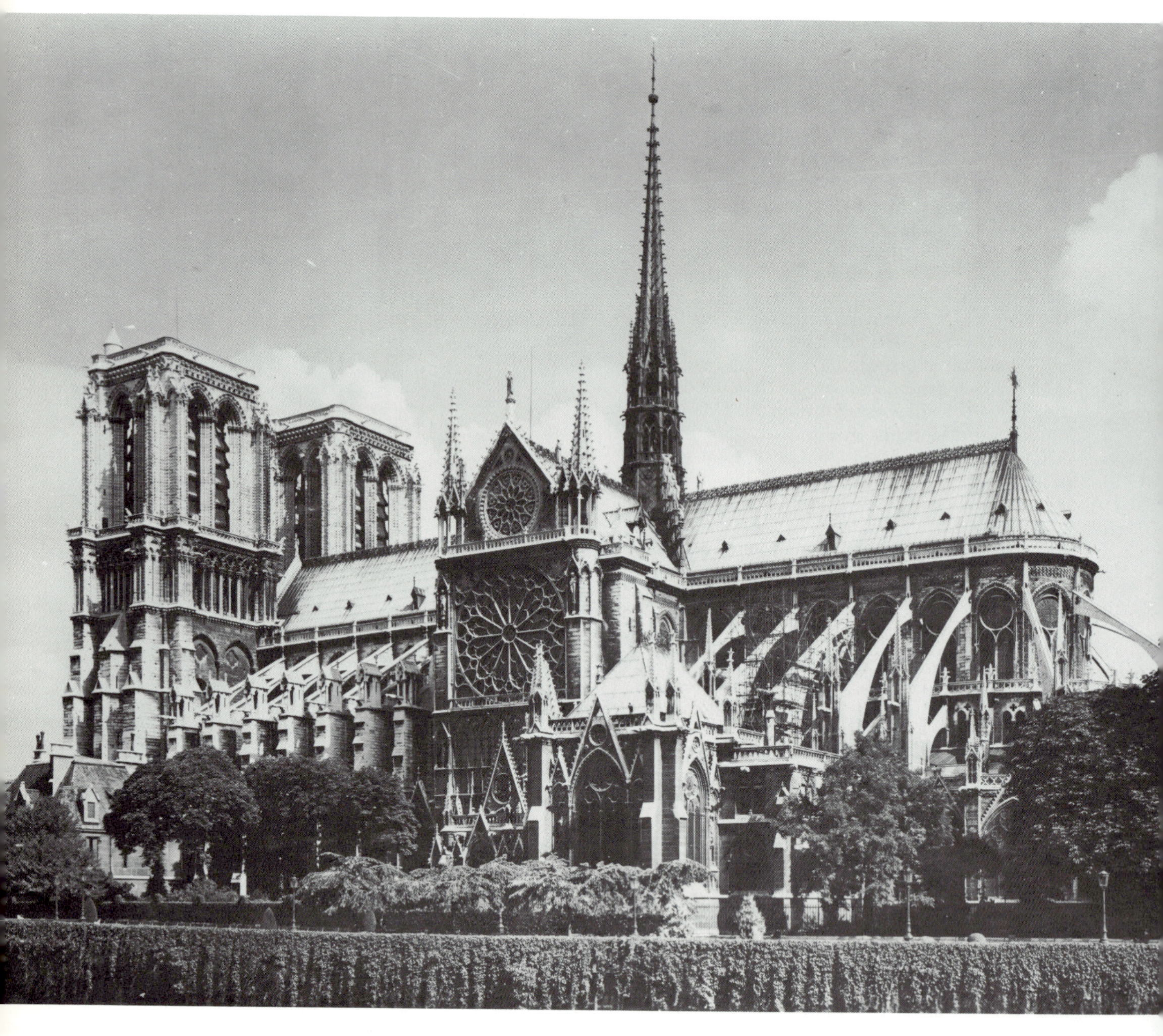

FIGURE 8.10 *Cathedral Notre-Dame, Paris, 1163–1250.*
(Photo: Marburg)

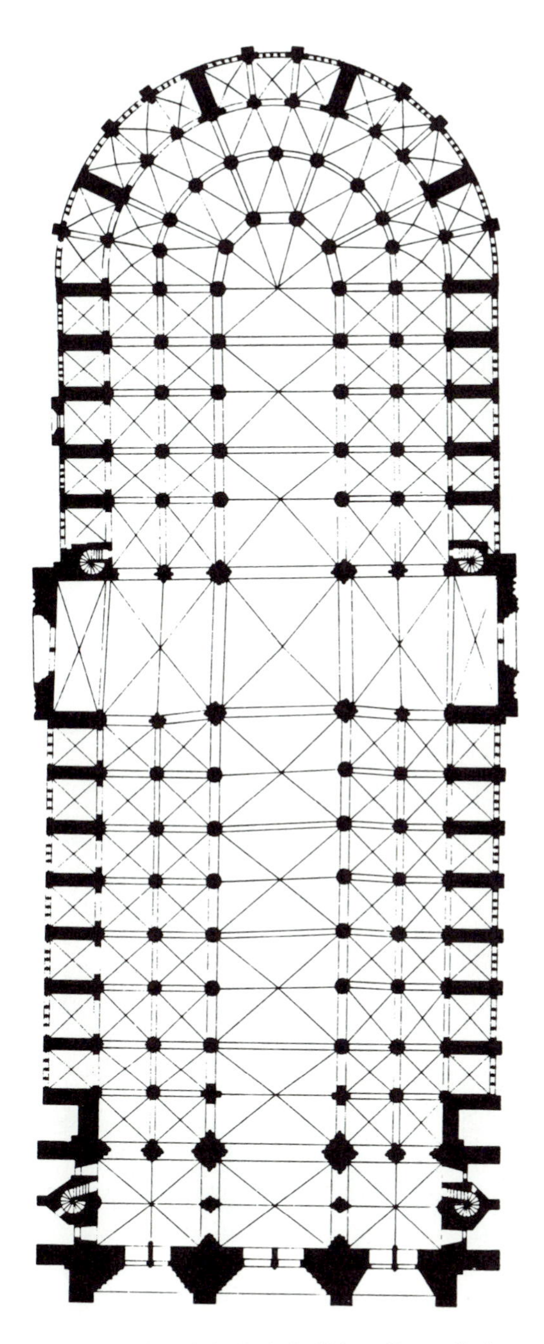

FIGURE 8.11 *Plan of the Cathedral Notre-Dame, Paris.* (From W. Blaser)

FIGURE 8.12 *Interior of the Cathedral Notre-Dame, Paris.* (Photo: Marburg)

another addition. The north transept was built from 1246 to 1257 to designs of Jean de Chelles, and the south transept was constructed in 1258–61 by Jean de Chelles and Pierre de Montreuil. In the course of the thirteenth century, chapels were inserted between all the buttresses around the choir and nave, further darkening the church interior. Finally, in the nineteenth century, Viollet-le-Duc restored the cathedral, rebuilding all the flying buttresses, restoring the bays at the crossing to their original design, and repairing the sculpture on the exterior.

With all these modifications, the Early Gothic qualities of Notre-Dame in Paris have not been so well preserved as at Laon. Nevertheless the cathedral is an important monument of the period. Its original plan was innovative and ambitious on a

FIGURE 8.13 *Section with interior and exterior wall elevations showing revised clerestory design of the Cathedral Notre-Dame, Paris.* (From E. Viollet-le-Duc)

large scale. A long church, completely surrounded by a double ambulatory, it was the first Gothic building to exceed the height (but not the length) of Cluny III. The slight misalignment of its choir and nave and the absence of transepts in the original design probably resulted from the close proximity of existing buildings, including the bishop's palace, which severely restricted the cathedral's site. (Several clearance projects have since removed all the medieval surroundings of the cathedral.)

The west front (Figure 8.14), a splendid study in proportions, has a solid, almost military quality, quite a contrast to the rather open character of Laon. At Paris it is the strength of the wall that commands attention. Triple portals, each slightly different in size and shape, are surmounted by a horizontal Gallery of Kings, representing twenty-eight kings of the Old Testament. A radiant rose window, flanked by paired lancet windows, forms a halo backdrop

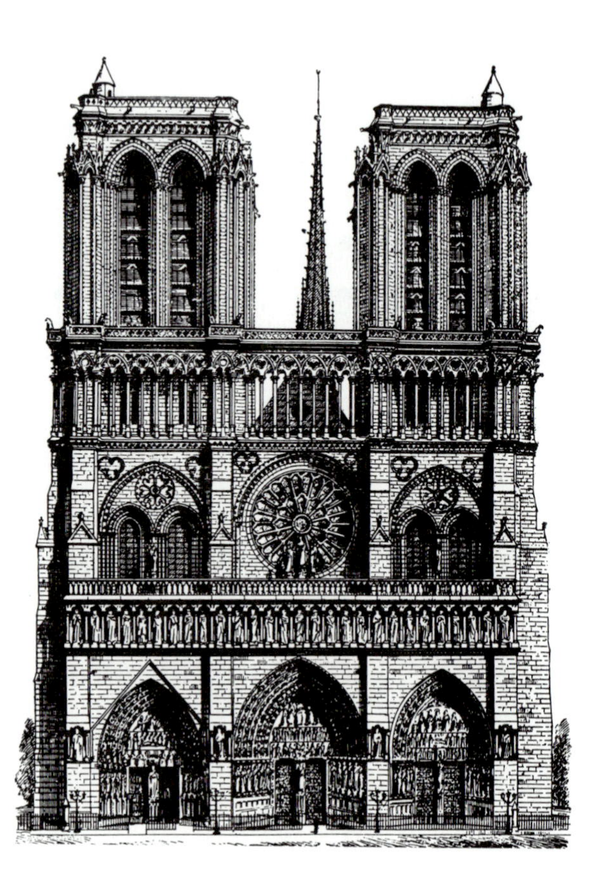

FIGURE 8.14 *West front elevation of the Cathedral Notre-Dame, Paris.* (From J. Guadet)

for a sculpture of the Virgin and Child with two angels. Below the twin towers, which are of different sizes, is a second arcaded horizontal gallery that lightens the upper wall while completing the basically square proportions of the lower façade. This elevation rewards close study. From a distance the basic disposition of seemingly symmetrical features within the overall 2:3 proportions is obvious, while the slight irregularities in individual elements become noticeable (and endearing) as one looks more closely. The sculptural programs of the three portals extend Christian teachings to the uneducated just as Romanesque work did. On climbing the stairs to the upper parapets, one gets an intimate view of the individually designed **crockets** projecting from the stones at the corners of the towers and of the fanciful sculpture (generally of the nineteenth century) perched high up on the wall.

HIGH GOTHIC

The development of flying buttresses during the construction of the Cathedral of Notre-Dame at Paris, integrated the three structural components of Gothic, and redundant features from the Romanesque could be deleted from subsequent Gothic building. The period of tentative exploration was over, and the mature or High Gothic that followed saw the erection of churches with increasingly refined artistic and structural features.

The first monument of the High Gothic was the Cathedral of Notre-Dame at Chartres (Figure 8.15), where flying buttresses were planned from the start so that the galleries over the aisles could be eliminated. This simplified the interior elevations to three divisions: the nave arcade, the **triforium** passage, and the clerestory windows (Figure 8.16).

FIGURE 8.15 *Cathedral Notre-Dame, Chartres, 1194–1230.* (Photo: Marburg)

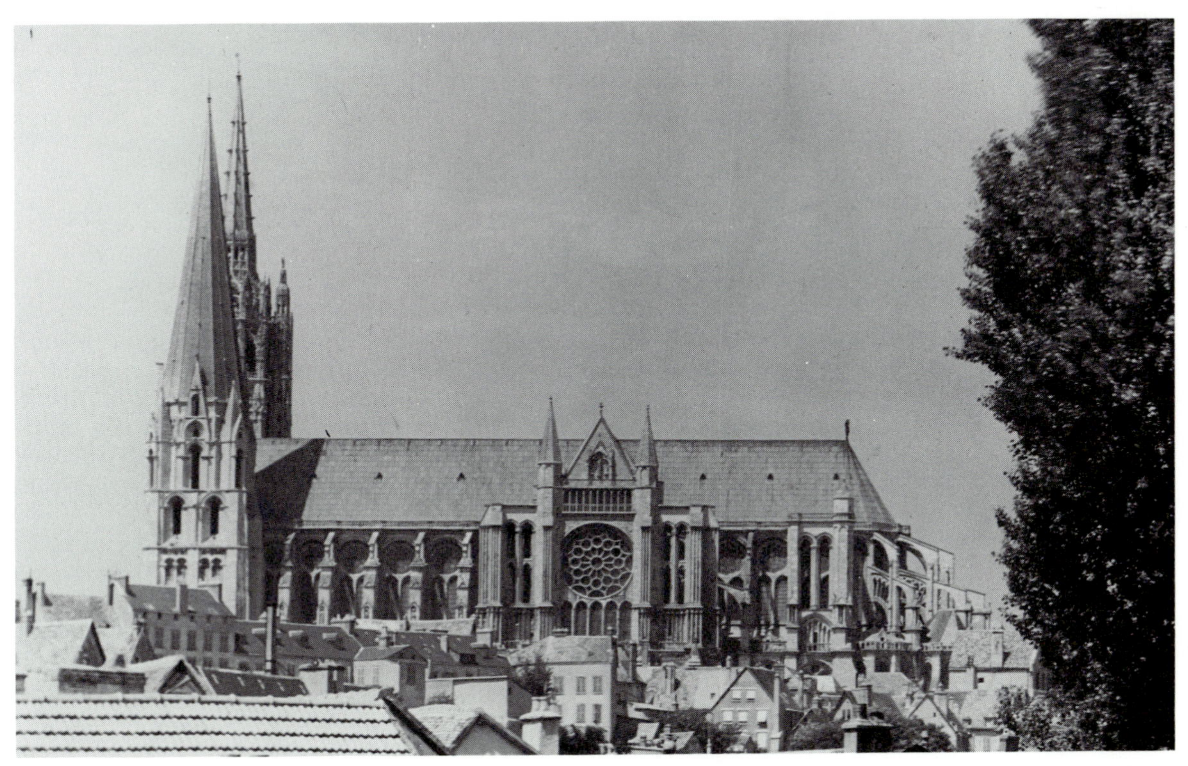

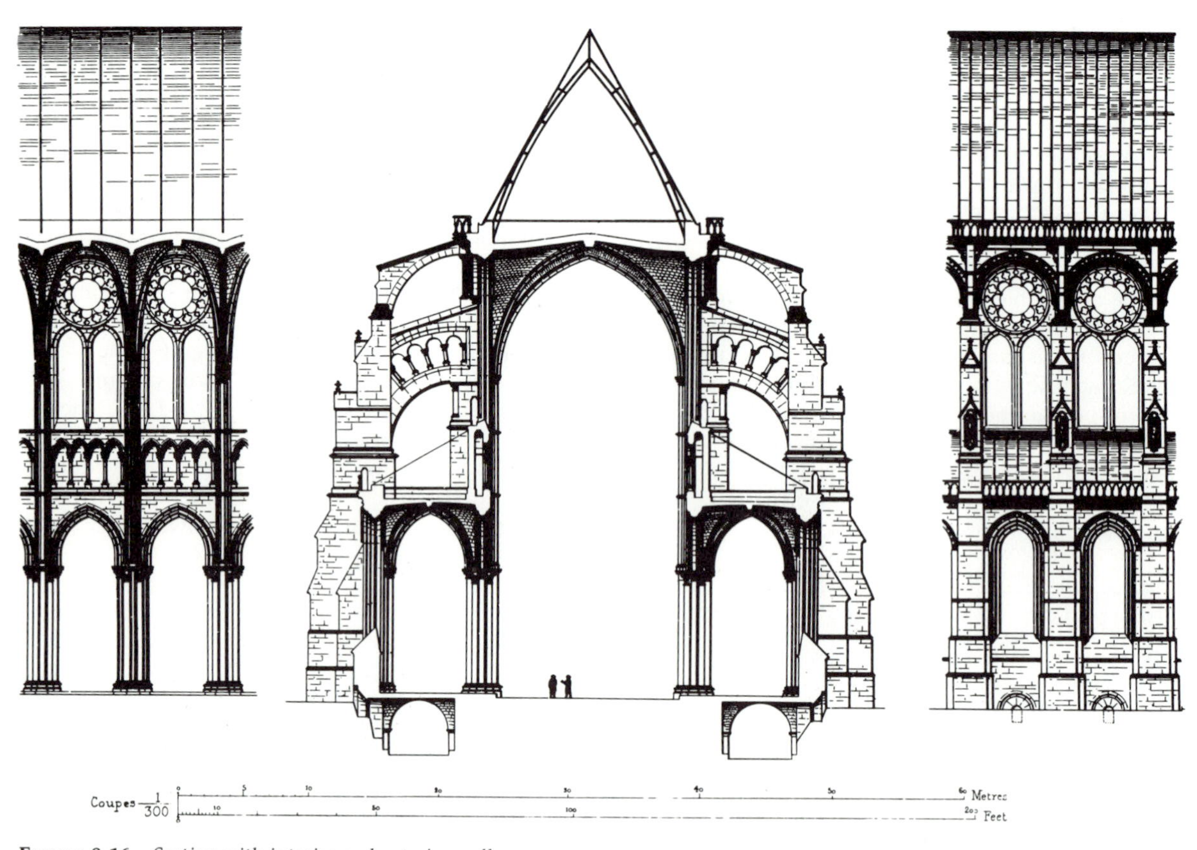

FIGURE 8.16 *Section with interior and exterior wall elevations from the Cathedral Notre-Dame, Chartres.* (From T. King)

In the process, the clerestory windows increased markedly in size, and vaulting shifted from sexpartite (over two bays) to quadripartite (over one bay).

Chartres Cathedral has an even more complicated chronology than the Cathedral of Paris. The site at Chartres had long been sacred to the Virgin Mary, and the cathedral treasure contained, among other valuable relics, a tunic believed to have been worn by Mary. Chartres became a center of pilgrimage, and from 1020 to 1037 a Romanesque basilica with three deep radiating chapels was constructed to replace an earlier church destroyed by fire. By the twelfth century, this church had itself been enlarged, and a fire in 1134 had damaged the westwerk. Work began that same year to build a new west front and narthex in much the same manner that Abbot Suger was to extend St. Denis. Sculptors from the workshops at St. Denis came to Chartres in 1145–1150 to carve the three portals of the new west façade, and the three lancet windows overhead were filled with stained glass depicting themes pioneered at Suger's church.

On the night of June 10, 1194, fire again struck the cathedral and town, destroying the wooden-roofed basilica and 80 percent of the city. Even though the new west front survived without major damage, the people of Chartres interpreted the fire as a sign of divine displeasure. Sensing the general feeling of hopelessness, the visiting Bishop of Pisa called a town meeting, during which the sacred

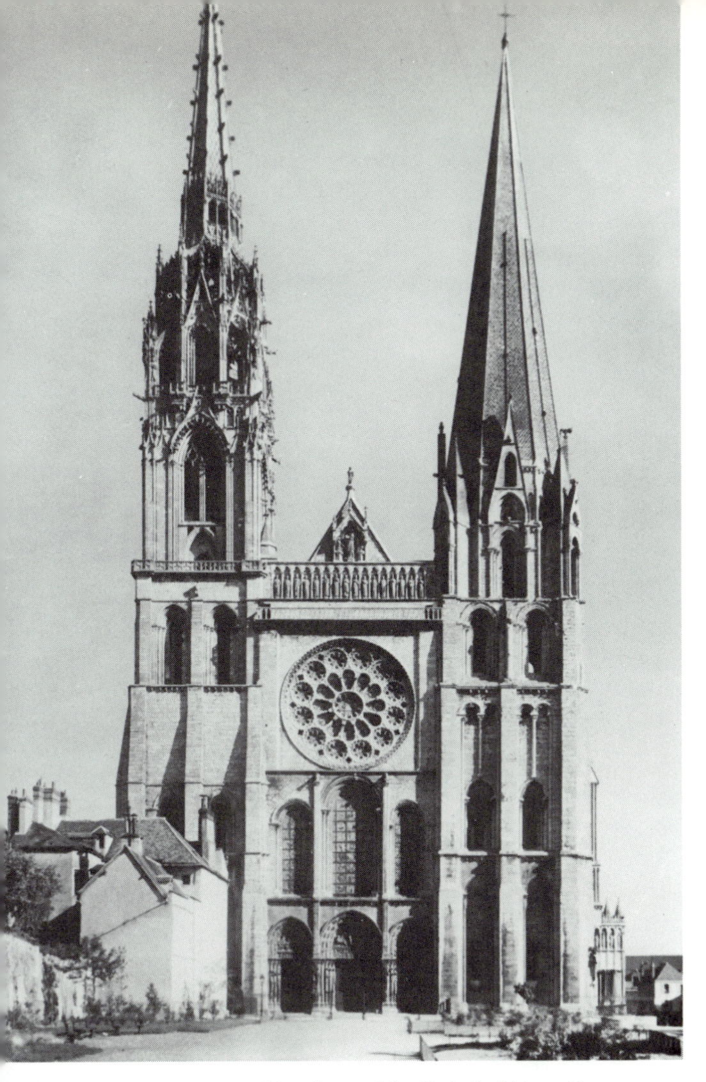

FIGURE 8.17 *West front of the Cathedral Notre-Dame, Chartres.* (Photo: Marburg)

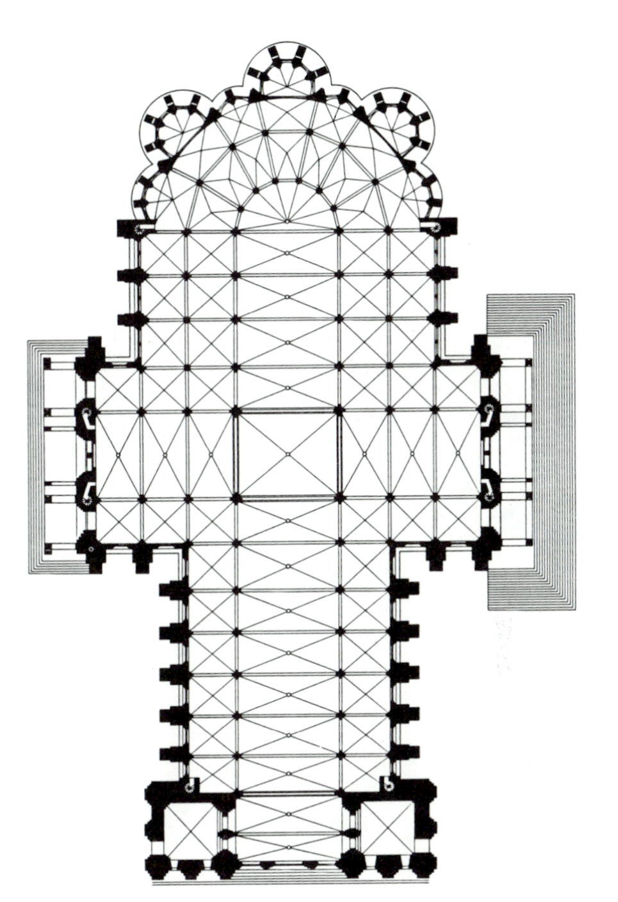

FIGURE 8.18 *Plan of the Cathedral Notre-Dame, Chartres.* (From W. Blaser)

tunic was carried out, unharmed, from the ruins of the crypt. The mood quickly changed from sorrow to jubilation as the townspeople decided the fire was a sign that Mary desired a larger church. Building funds were raised with remarkable speed and construction commenced. The Gothic cathedral at Chartres was built in the span of twenty-six years, from 1194 to 1220. The sculpted north and south transept porches were finished 1224–1250, and the north tower on the west front was completed in 1513, giving the cathedral a balanced asymmetry.

In rebuilding the cathedral, the master masons reused the foundations and crypt and incorporated the surviving west front (Figure 8.17). On the exterior one can still see the seam where the new work was joined to the old, a horizontal string course immediately below the western rose (which itself is slightly off center). The Romanesque apse was transformed into a Gothic choir by the insertion of four shallow chapels between the three existing deep chapels of the crypt, thus creating seven shallow chapels with a double ambulatory on the upper level (Figure 8.18). The builders also added a transept to the original Romanesque basilica plan and, after construction was underway, decided to include three sculpted portals on each transept arm, giving Chartres a total of nine entrances.

The completed cathedral glows inside with a wonderful luminosity (Figures 8.19, 8.20). Of all Gothic cathedrals Chartres alone has preserved

FIGURE 8.19 *Interior looking east of the Cathedral Notre-Dame, Chartres. Wartime photograph showing the interior without its stained glass.* (Photo: Marburg)

FIGURE 8.20 *Interior looking west of the Cathedral Notre-Dame, Chartres. Wartime photograph showing the interior without its stained glass.* (Photo: Marburg)

FIGURE 8.21 *Jamb sculpture from the west front [Royal Portal] of the Cathedral Notre-Dame, Chartres, ca. 1150.* (From J. Guadet)

FIGURE 8.22 *Jamb sculpture from the south porch of the Cathedral Notre-Dame, Chartres, ca. 1230–1250.* (From J. Guadet)

about two-thirds of its original stained glass, now carefully restored. Trade guilds and wealthy families of the town donated aisle and clerestory windows, while the royal family paid for the north transept sculpture, rose, and lancet windows, and the Count of Brittany and his family underwrote similar work on the south transept. The twelfth-century lancets of the west front, originally designed to open onto a chapel above the narthex, now illuminate the nave, and the change in viewing level makes their detail somewhat difficult to perceive. Suger's ideal of "pervading interior beauty" is nowhere more evident than at Chartres.

The west front doorways, known as the Royal Portals because the kings and queens of the Old Testament are shown in the jamb statues, provide a splendid image of what the abbey church of St. Denis must have looked like in 1150 (Figure 8.21). The influence of Suger's façade can be seen in the stately, although somewhat stylized and stiff, jamb figures, while the tympana subjects reflect the teachings of the School of Chartres, a prominent medieval university associated with the cathedral. The portals carved a century later on the north and south transepts provide a measurement of the progressive realism of Gothic sculpture (Figure 8.22).

FIGURE 8.23 *West front of the Cathedral St. Étienne, Bourges, 1195–1250.* (Photo: Marburg)

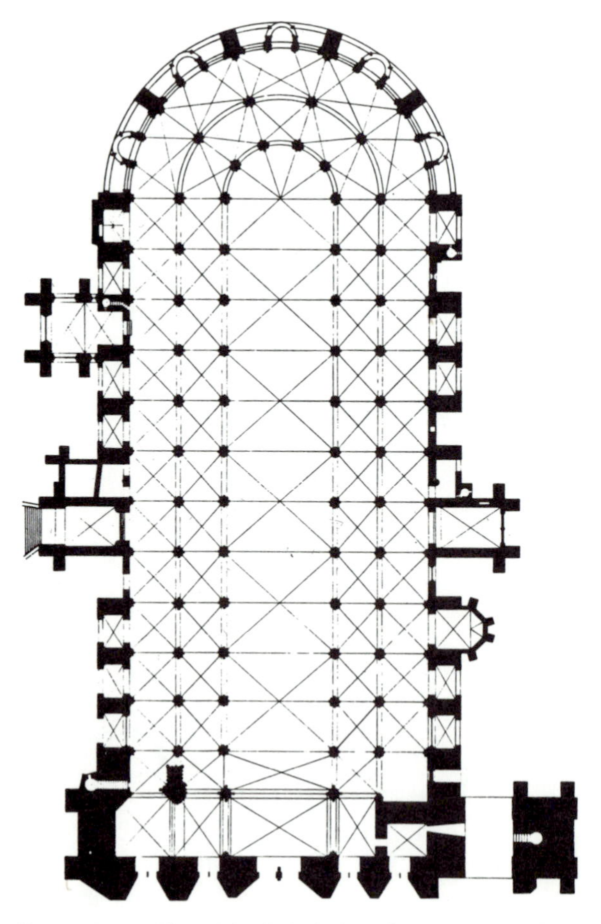

FIGURE 8.24 *Plan of the Cathedral St. Étienne, Bourges.* (From W. Blaser)

Some of the subjects shown are repeated from the Royal Portals, but their treatment is far more lifelike.

The Cathedral of St. Étienne at Bourges (1195–1250) illustrates a contrasting design approach to that of Chartres (Figure 8.23). In plan the building seems similar to the original transeptless plan of Notre-Dame in Paris. Double aisles flank the nave and continue in uninterrupted arcs around the choir (Figure 8.24). The five radiating chapels at the east end seem like afterthoughts, which they probably were, as their support depends on corbeled piers set between the crypt windows. A glance at the interior (Figure 8.25), however, indicates immediately that Bourges is no copy of Paris, but an original adaptation of High Gothic vocabulary. The paired aisles increase in height to help brace the high

FIGURE 8.25 *Interior of the Cathedral St. Étienne, Bourges.* (Photo: Marburg)

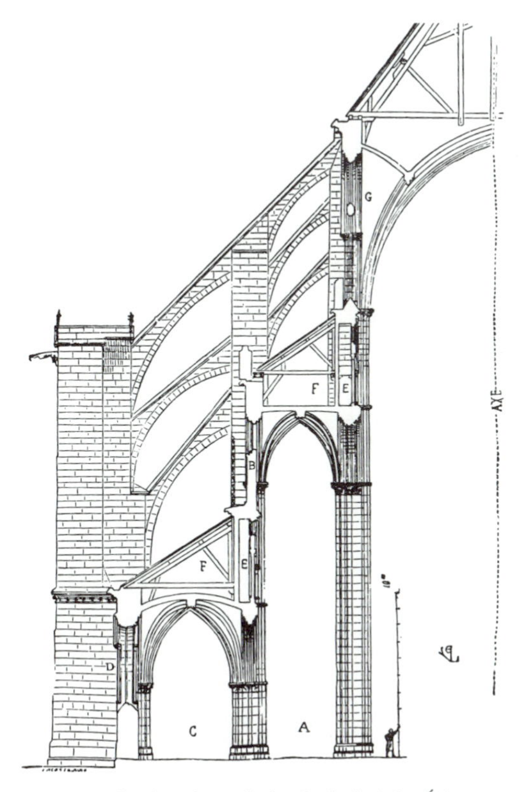

FIGURE 8.26 *Section through the Cathedral St. Étienne, Bourges.* (From E. Viollet-le-Duc)

FIGURE 8.27 *South side of the Cathedral St. Étienne, Bourges.* (Photo: Marburg)

vaults of the nave and choir, recalling the triangular cross section of Cluny III, with the addition here of flying buttresses (Figures 8.26–8.27). At Bourges, the sexpartite choir and nave vaults spring from alternating major and minor piers set on a square module plan; the spatial effect is one of breadth and expansiveness, but the layered aisle vaults and roofs preclude clerestory windows on the scale of Chartres. On the west front, the five major interior volumes are reflected in five portals.

Twentieth-century structural engineers, extolling the structural logic of Bourges, have wondered why the inherently less stable model of Chartres was adopted for the tallest cathedrals of the Gothic era. The answer may lie in the soaring, airy character possible with its single-aisle design; the medieval preference for high luminous spaces ruled out the most rational structural design, for the Gothic was not primarily an expression of technique, but an architectural embodiment of religious and cultural ideals. Cathedrals built on the model of Bourges are most numerous in northern Spain, where bright skies prevail. In France, however, the general design of Chartres was followed in the great cathedral series of Reims, Amiens, and Beauvais. Intent on dramatizing the sense of verticality and light, the builders of Chartres elevated its vaults 113 feet over a 53-foot-wide nave; at Reims, the vaults rose 122 feet over a 45-foot-wide nave; at Amiens, the vaulting was 139 feet high for the same width; and at Beauvais, the most daring venture of all, the choir vaults rose 158 feet and collapsed. Although they were rebuilt in a strengthened form, Beauvais was never completed, and only the choir and transept

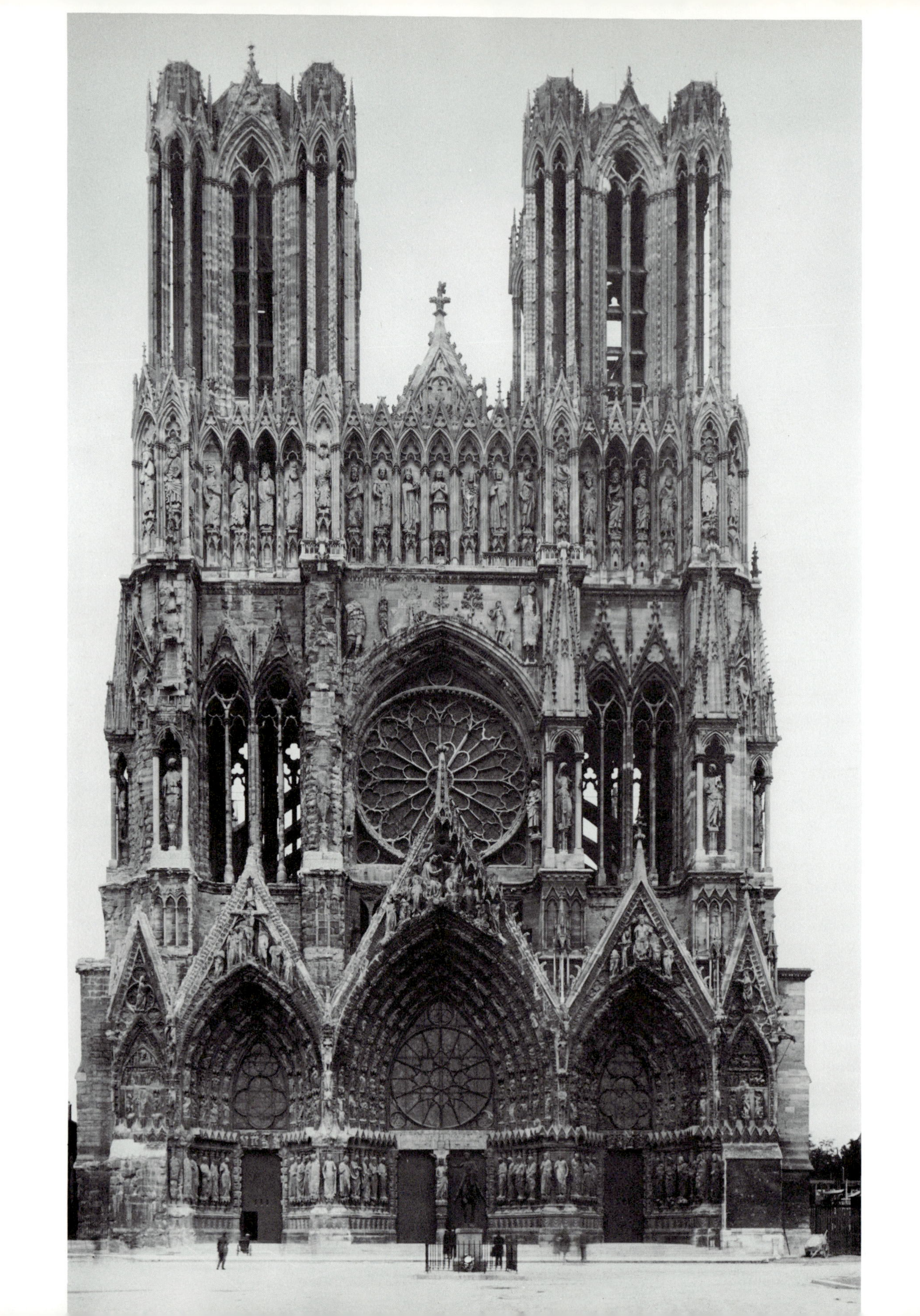

Figure 8.29 *Plan of the Cathedral, Reims.* (From W. Blaser)

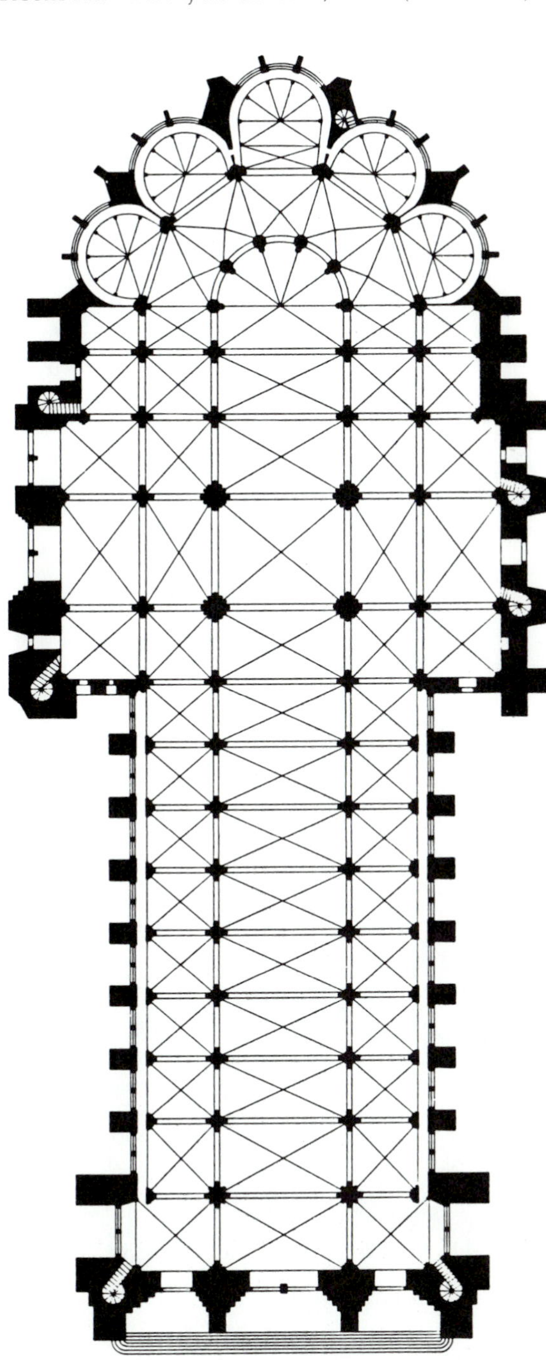

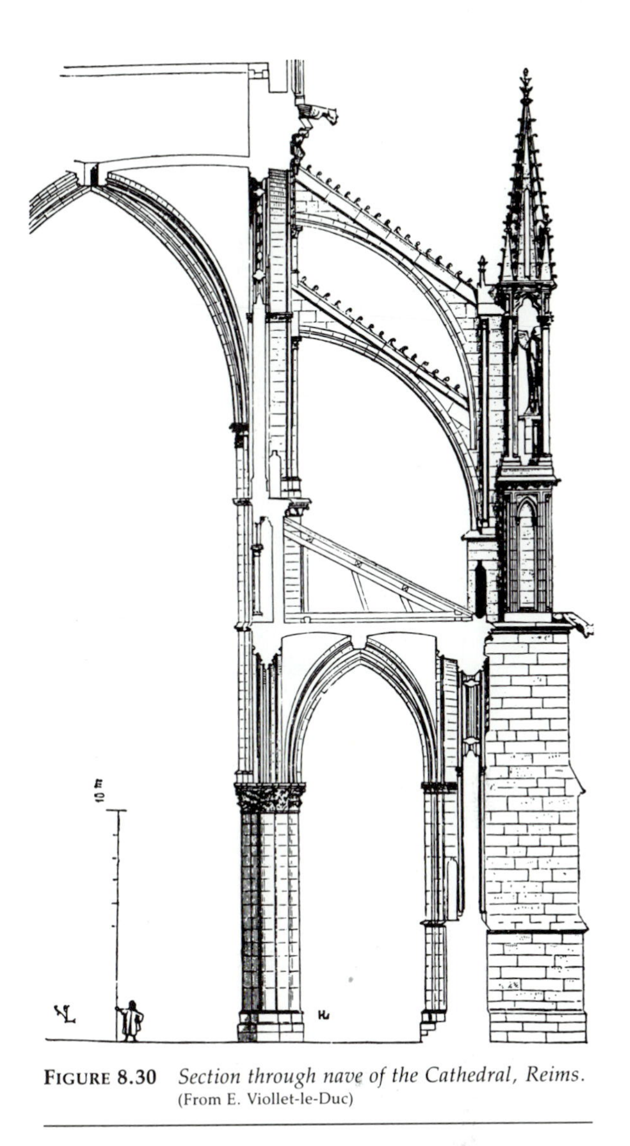

Figure 8.30 *Section through nave of the Cathedral, Reims.* (From E. Viollet-le-Duc)

stand today to indicate the grandeur of the intended Gothic building.

The Cathedral at Reims (Figure 8.28) was begun in 1211 after fire had destroyed the previous church the year before; by 1241 the choir was complete. Its nave and transept were probably finished by about 1290. In plan, five apsidal chapels, deeper than those at Chartres, radiate off a single ambulatory (Figure 8.29). The design is based on Chartres, with a greater sensation of height provided by adjusting the proportions of the nave and enlarging the clerestories to fill virtually all the wall plane between the piers (Figures 8.30, 8.31). Reims Cathedral's special glory is its west front sculpture, carefully restored after damage during the French

◀ **Figure 8.28** *West front of the Cathedral, Reims, 1211–1290.* (Photo: Marburg)

FIGURE 8.31 *Interior of the Cathedral, Reims.* (Photo: Marburg)

Revolution. The jamb figures of the Annunciation and the Visitation show remarkable attention to detail along with an increased understanding of the human body, now believably represented under flowing drapery. Even the angle from which these statues would be seen was considered: the figures have elongated necks to compensate for the foreshortening of perspective.

Amiens Cathedral (Figures 8.32–8.34) continues the development of High Gothic architecture, remaining the tallest completed French Gothic church. It was begun in 1220 and substantially finished by 1269, although later modifications were

FIGURE 8.32 *Cathedral, Amiens, 1220–1269.* (Photo: French Government Tourist Office)

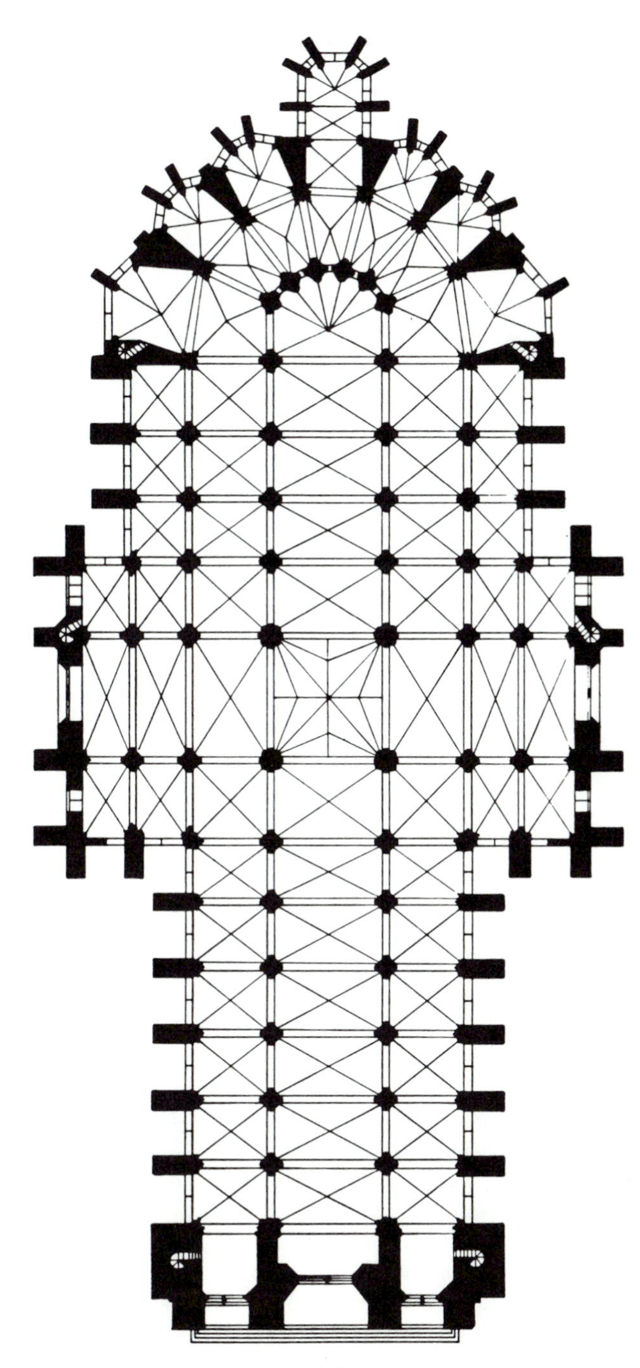

FIGURE 8.33 *Plan of the Cathedral, Amiens.* (From W. Blaser)

made. The scale has become truly gigantic. The portals dwarf the worshipper, and the feet of the jamb figures stand well over the visitor's head. Sculptural detail cannot be comprehended easily on the great tympana, and the rose window appears small in the immensity of the façade. Inside, the aisle vaults rise sixty feet (almost the same dimension as the entire nave of St. Sernin at Toulouse), while the emphasis on verticality has reduced the thickness of every

FIGURE 8.34 *Section through the Cathedral, Amiens.* (From E. Viollet-le-Duc)

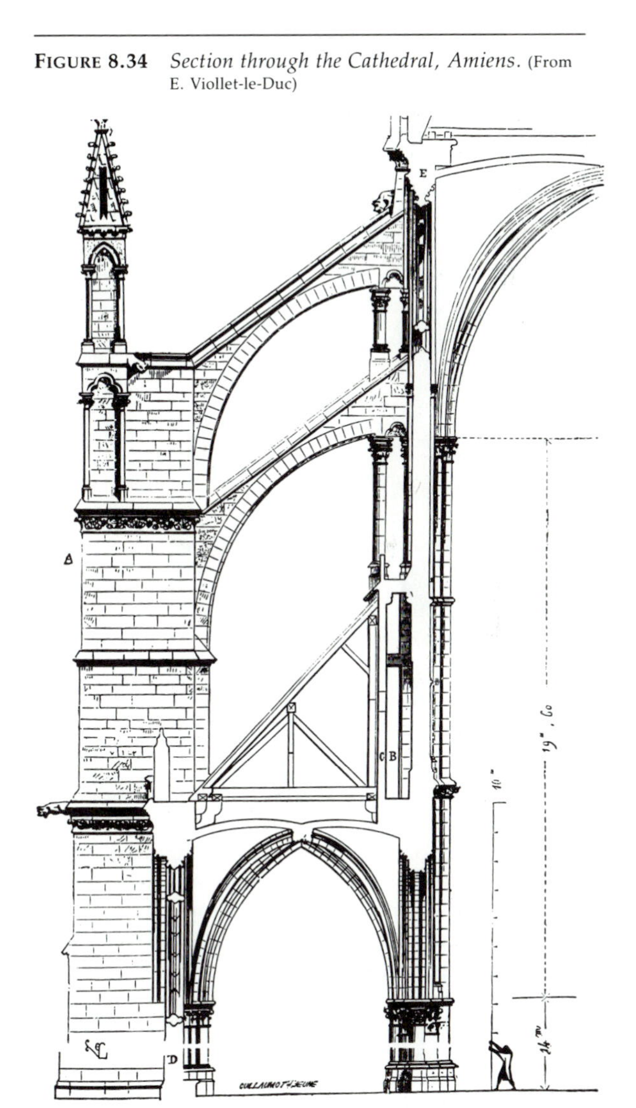

FIGURE 8.35 *Interior of the Cathedral, Amiens.* (Photo: French Government Tourist Office)

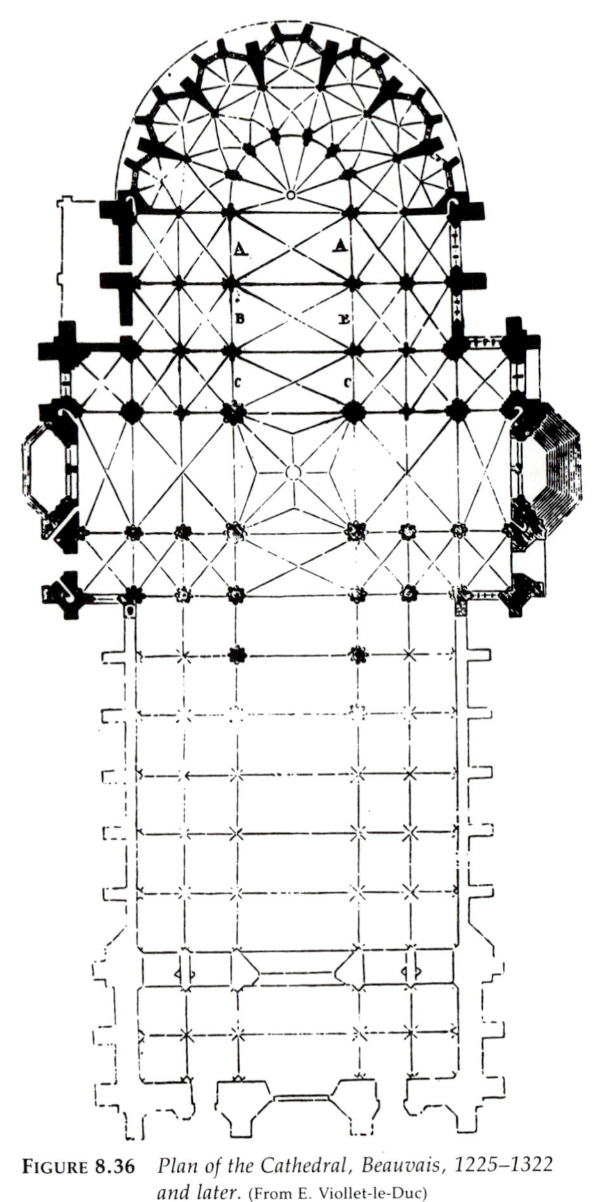

FIGURE 8.36 *Plan of the Cathedral, Beauvais, 1225–1322 and later.* (From E. Viollet-le-Duc)

possible structural member. The clear glass in most of the clerestory windows creates the sensation of being in an enormous, fragile cage (Figure 8.35).

At Beauvais, structural collapse and waning enthusiasm for large-scale building projects resulted in an incomplete cathedral (Figures 8.36, 8.37). Work on the choir began in 1225, but its high vaults fell in 1284, possibly due to inadequate bracing. Between 1284 and 1322 they were rebuilt and strengthened by the insertion of six new piers, which created sexpartite vaulting in place of the original quadripartite design and destroyed some of the original sense of openness in the choir elevation. Construction of the transept was started in 1500 and completed by 1550. A crossing tower of stone and wood 497 feet high was added from 1558 to 1569, but it gave evidence of instability and was removed in 1573. The nave at Beauvais is the surviving remnant of a ninth-century Carolingian basilica that would have been replaced had the original Gothic plan been completed. Because it was not, Beauvais Cathedral stands today as the alpha and omega of medieval architecture, illustrating in one building the constructional and artistic accomplishments of five centuries.

Modern structural analysis has identified the probable source of Beauvais's instability, a misaligned intermediate buttress pier that is forced to make a five-foot offset before reaching the ground as an outer column of the ambulatory. The extreme, unbraced slenderness of the buttresses also contributes to the difficulty. (A close look at the present-day exterior reveals that all the buttresses are now linked by iron tie-rods to forestall further problems.) Had the nave been constructed before the erection of the crossing tower, its eastern bays would probably have equalized the transfer of loads, which might have prevented the tower's demise. Not technical obstacles but financial shortages ultimately stopped work at Beauvais. The Church no longer commanded sufficient resources (about a quarter of the total wealth of all Europe) to sustain enormous building campaigns, and, although churches continued to be built or remodeled, the scale seen during the eleventh through thirteenth centuries would never be matched.

Even during the High Gothic era, not all churches were on the scale of cathedrals. In Paris King Louis IX had a small palace chapel built in 1243–1248 to house relics he had acquired from Constantinople, including the Crown of Thorns and a piece of the True Cross. The chapel, known as the Sainte-Chapelle (Figures 8.38, 8.39), has two levels, a ground-floor chapel for use by the household ser-

FIGURE 8.37 *Section through the Cathedral, Beauvais.* (From V. Leblond)

FIGURE 8.38 *Palais Royale with the Sainte-Chapelle, Paris, 1243–1248.* (From E. Viollet-le-Duc)

FIGURE 8.39 *Section through the Sainte-Chapelle, Paris.* (From E. Viollet-le-Duc)

FIGURE 8.40 *Interior of the Sainte-Chapelle, Paris.* (Photo: Marburg)

vants and an upper chapel, surrounded by stained glass lancet windows, for the use of the royal family. This upper chapel (Figure 8.40) is a jeweled reliquary space in which the walls have been diminished to slender piers set between the great expanses of glass containing illustrations of the entire Old and New Testaments. As a miniature statement of the dematerialization of masonry walls and the wondrous properties of colored light sought by Abbot Suger, the Sainte-Chapelle has no equal.

MASTER BUILDERS AND MEDIEVAL CONSTRUCTION

The scarcity of documentation related to the great medieval building campaigns limits our ability to make definitive statements about the nature of medieval architectural practice or construction procedures. Nevertheless historians have analyzed what materials are available — a few sketchbooks, isolated drawings, works accounts, monastic chronicles, and the evidence provided by the buildings themselves — to piece together an understanding of building in the medieval world.

A building designer in the Middle Ages was usually called a master builder, the title of architect not being used until rather late in the period. The master builder's training would have included the acquisition of language and mathematical skills in a grammar school run by the local priest or monastery, followed by apprenticeship in one of the building trades (carpentry or masonry) at about age thirteen. The apprentice would be taught all aspects of the craft, including theoretical matters and practical applications. After three to seven years thus spent under the direction of a master craftsman, the apprentice would be certified as a journeyman, a worker qualified to hire himself out for a daily wage. For several years, he would work on different building sites, traveling about and keeping a sketchbook while gaining practical experience. To advance to the level of master he would be required to present a masterpiece — either an actual building or a finely executed model — to the masters of his craft guild. They would evaluate his fitness to be recognized as a master who might then direct journeymen and teach apprentices. Only the most capable and experienced master craftsmen would be entrusted with the direction of an entire project and thus acquire the title of master builder.

A sketchbook kept by one medieval master active ca. 1230–1250 has survived. Known as the Notebook of Villard de Honnecourt, it contains a wide range of observations and drawings: geometry problems and their solutions (Figure 8.41); timber roof trusses (Figure 8.42); sculpture and carved ornament; nature sketches (Figure 8.43); church plans (Figure 8.44); sketches of Laon (Figure 8.45),

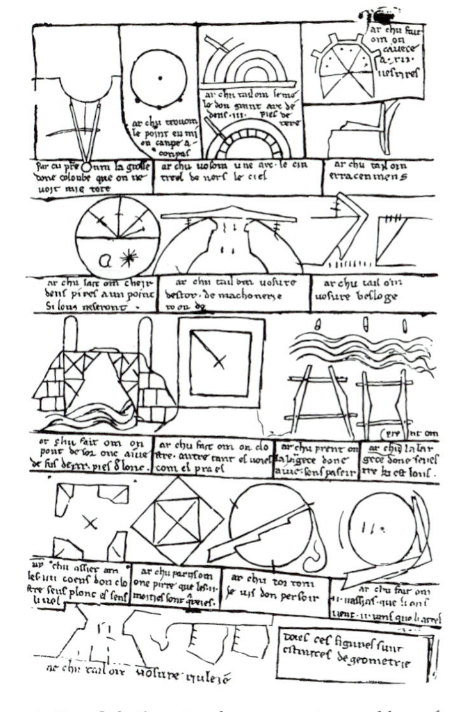

FIGURE 8.41 *Solutions to plane geometry problems from the Sketchbook of Villard de Honnecourt, ca. 1225.* (From R. Willis)

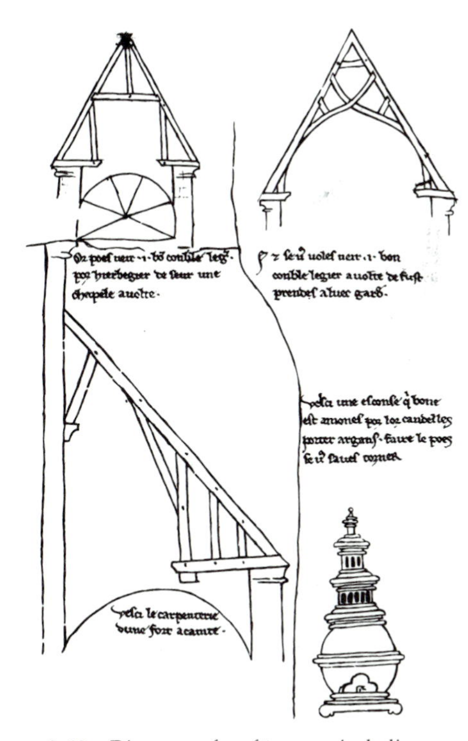

FIGURE 8.42 *Diagrams of roof trusses, including a hammerbeam roof from the Sketchbook of Villard de Honnecourt.* (From R. Willis)

FIGURE 8.43 *Geometric analysis of human and animal forms from the Sketchbook of Villard de Honnecourt.* (From R. Willis)

FIGURE 8.45 *Elevation of a tower from Laon Cathedral from the Sketchbook of Villard de Honnecourt.* (From R. Willis)

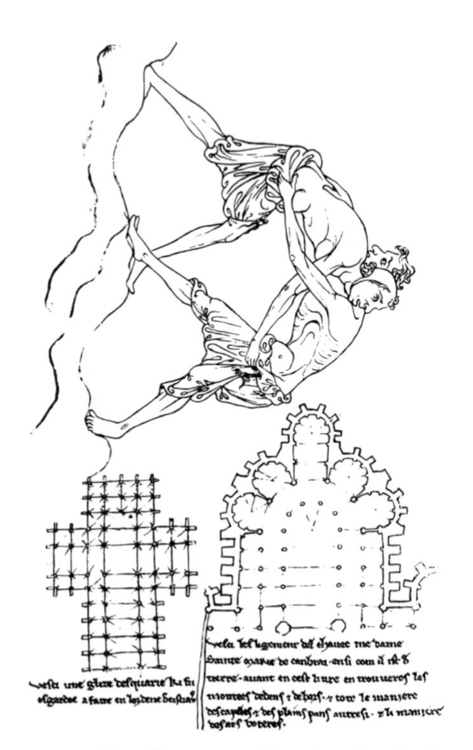

FIGURE 8.44 *Wrestling men, a Cistercian church plan, and plan of the choir of St. Mary at Cambria from the Sketchbook of Villard de Honnecourt.* (From R. Willis)

Chartres, and Reims cathedrals; machines and devices; and such esoteric information as how to tame a lion. Other than what is contained in his notebook, little is known of Villard or his works. He claims to have traveled from the Low Countries to Hungary and back, and historians surmise that he was employed by the Cistercians on various projects, none now extant (Figure 8.46). From an inscription on the opening pages of the book, it is obvious that Villard intended his notes to be used by others; he identifies geometry as the basis of drawing, claims to present advice on masonry and carpentry, and asks that readers remember him and pray for his soul.

Geometry was indeed the theoretical core of medieval architecture. Following Roman practice, the master established basic building dimensions by a module, and derived all other measurements through the manipulation of compass and straightedge. (The medieval world used cumbersome Roman numerals, precluding all but the simplest arithmetical calculations.) Masons' "secrets" were no more than plane geometry and the use of triangles, squares, pentagons, and other figures to generate proportional lines, most of which have irrational numbers by dimensional measurement.

Building a large or small church required money to pay skilled craftsmen. Masters and their workshops moved as construction funds were available, so it is sometimes possible to trace specific influences from project to project. (The idea that churches were built either by monks or by volunteer laymen is a misconception.) The overall size of the church and its major features would be determined by the master builder in consultation with church officials, and then professional quarrymen, masons, carpenters, sculptors, glaziers, and roofers would be employed to execute the work. Depending on the wealth of the client, a major cathedral could be built in as few as thirty years, or construction could drag on in discontinuous campaigns stretching over many centuries.

FIGURE 8.46 *Plans of two Cistercian church choirs from the Sketchbook of Villard de Honnecourt.* (From R. Willis)

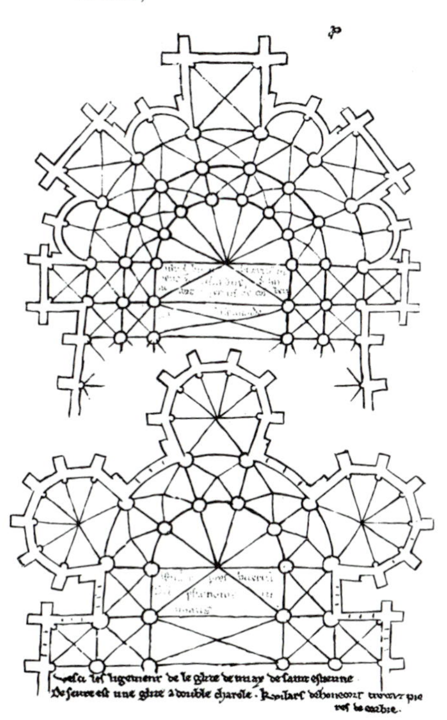

GOTHIC ARCHITECTURE IN ENGLAND

Although the Gothic style originated in France, it spread to other parts of Europe, particularly Germany and England, and became the predominant style of northern Europe until the fifteenth century. (The term *Gothic* was not applied to the style until the seventeenth century and was meant to be derogatory because the style lacked classical proportions.) The Germans followed French models fairly closely, as did the English at first. The English soon formed their own Gothic aesthetic, however, and within a century had created Gothic churches that varied considerably from those built in France. English Gothic cannot be seen, therefore, simply as French architecture transported across the Channel.

The nineteenth-century historians who first studied the medieval buildings of England categorized the work in four overlapping phases, which are still useful for describing the progressive development of English Gothic. The first was Norman, which derived directly from Romanesque work in Normandy and was built from 1066 to 1190. It is distinguished by semicircular arches, groin vaults, and massive construction generally. Norman work is followed by Early English, built from 1175 to 1265, which corresponds roughly to High Gothic work in France. Master masons from France brought the Gothic to England and obviously brought French design approaches with them. As a result, Early English Gothic looks French superficially, but on closer examination it has distinct differences from contemporary French works. Vaulting is straightforward, usually quadripartite, and windows are lancet-shaped.

More clearly English is the Gothic of the Decorated period, built from about 1250 until 1370. It features an elaboration of the ornament developed in the Early English period. Vaulting becomes enriched with extra ribs, called **tiercerons** and **liernes,** and window **tracery** is worked into trefoil or quatrefoil cusped shapes. The final phase, the Perpendicular, is the most distinctly English version of Gothic. Constructed from about 1330 until 1540, it is distinguished by window tracery in simple orthogonal patterns (hence the name perpendicular)

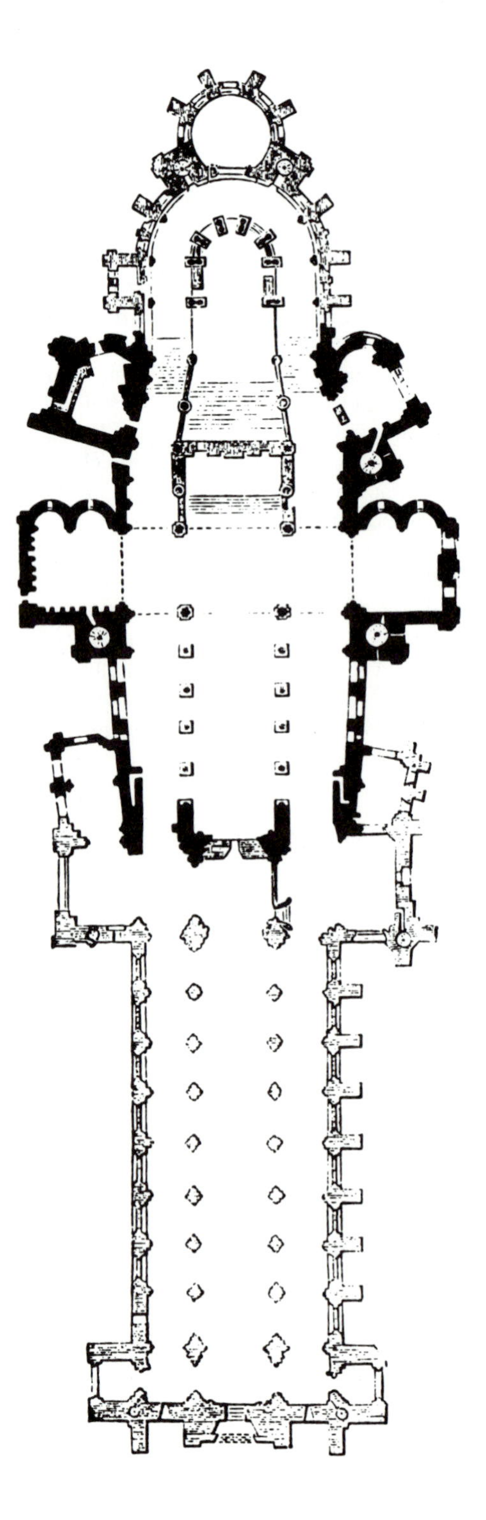

◀ FIGURE 8.47 *Plan of the Cathedral, Canterbury, 1175–1184 and later.* (From J. Fergusson)

and vaulting in elaborate conical fan shapes. Despite their visual magnificence, **fan vaults** represent no structural advance; in fact they are best suited to smaller churches where great heights and spans are not required. It is not possible to examine English cathedrals in a strict chronological order. Portions of all four medieval periods are represented in the fabric of almost every English cathedral. The discussions here will present the buildings as a whole, rather than the chronological periods.

The Gothic style first came to England at Canterbury Cathedral, where the Norman church, begun in 1070, was devastated by fire in 1174. Leading master masons of England and France were summoned to give their advice about rebuilding the ruined choir, and one William of Sens was selected to direct the work. He convinced the monks to demolish the remaining sections of the choir because the stone had been damaged beyond repair, but he confidently retained the fine Norman crypt and aisle walls (Figure 8.47). Between 1175 and 1184 the choir was rebuilt to a Gothic design based on the Cathedral of Sens (Figures 8.48, 8.49). During this time, William was severely injured in a fall from the scaffolding, and he returned to France in 1179, leaving his assistant, William the Englishman, to complete the work.

The choir at Canterbury was designed to house England's most popular shrine, that of Thomas à Becket, advisor to King Henry II and Archbishop of Canterbury, who was murdered in the cathedral in 1170 by four of Henry's knights. Pilgrims from all over Europe soon flocked to Canterbury to partake of the miracles performed at the tomb of St. Thomas, and the monks, enriched by the pilgrim traffic, needed suitable accommodation for the steady stream of visitors and their own services. As was the case in earlier pilgrimage churches, a satisfactory arrangement involved an aisle and ambulatory, which linked the site of Thomas's martyrdom with his shrine in the Trinity Chapel.

Canterbury's somewhat rambling plan can be explained by the reuse of the Norman crypt and the pilgrim traffic to Becket's shrine. The Norman basil-

FIGURE 8.48 *Interior of the Cathedral, Sens, 1145–1164.* (Photo: Marburg)

FIGURE 8.49 *Choir interior of the Cathedral, Canterbury.* (Delineator: K. Moffett)

ica had transepts with two chapels on each east wall and two apsidal chapels set at angles to the main axis rather than radiating from it; beyond these, William the Englishman built the Trinity Chapel and its single axial chapel, the Corona, which terminates the church on the east. A second, smaller transept was constructed to the west of the choir; and the wider, majestic nave was built early in the Perpendicular period, 1377–1405, possibly to the designs of Thomas of Hoo. The crowning element in the cathedral is the 235-foot-high crossing tower named Bell Harry after the bell hung there, which was erected in mature Perpendicular (1491 to 1498) to the designs of John Wastell. The fan vaults of the tower are forerunners of those Wastell would erect later at King's College Chapel in Cambridge.

Salisbury Cathedral (Figure 8.50) presents the rare example of an English Gothic cathedral built almost entirely in a homogeneous style, Early English. It was begun in 1220 (contemporaneously with Amiens) on an entirely new site, the town having been relocated near more reliable water sources. Construction of the majority of the church progressed with remarkable rapidity and was completed by 1258, leaving only the soaring crossing tower and spire to be built from 1334 to 1380. Salisbury incorporates features from monastic plans — the double transepts of Cluny III and the square east end of the Cistercians — in a long angular building that is distinctly English (Figure 8.51). On the interior quadripartite vaults rise from three-story nave elevations, yet the continuous vertical line exploited

Figure 8.50 *Cathedral, Salisbury, 1220–1258.* (From B. Taylor)

by the French has been replaced by a horizontal emphasis created by a string course under the triforium and another under the clerestory windows (Figure 8.52). Even the ribs of the vaults do not extend down the wall; they spring instead from wall corbels at the base of the clerestory. Surfaces are articulated by shafts and trim in black Purbeck marble, an English stone that is not marble but takes a highly polished finish. The exterior receives the same horizontal emphasis as the interior. The flying buttresses do not have a strong vertical character, and the walls are coursed in horizontal bands that extend across the west front. With all this horizontality, the 404-foot tower and spire provide the necessary vertical emphasis, and their great weight has noticeably deflected the piers at the crossing. The

Figure 8.51 *Plan of the Cathedral, Salisbury, 1220–1258.* (From W. Blaser) ▶

cloisters are fine examples of early Decorated tracery.

At Lincoln Cathedral, a more complicated building history has resulted in a splendid combination of English Gothic periods. The Norman church, damaged by an earthquake in 1185, survives today

Figure 8.52 *Interior of the Cathedral, Salisbury.* (Photo: Marburg)

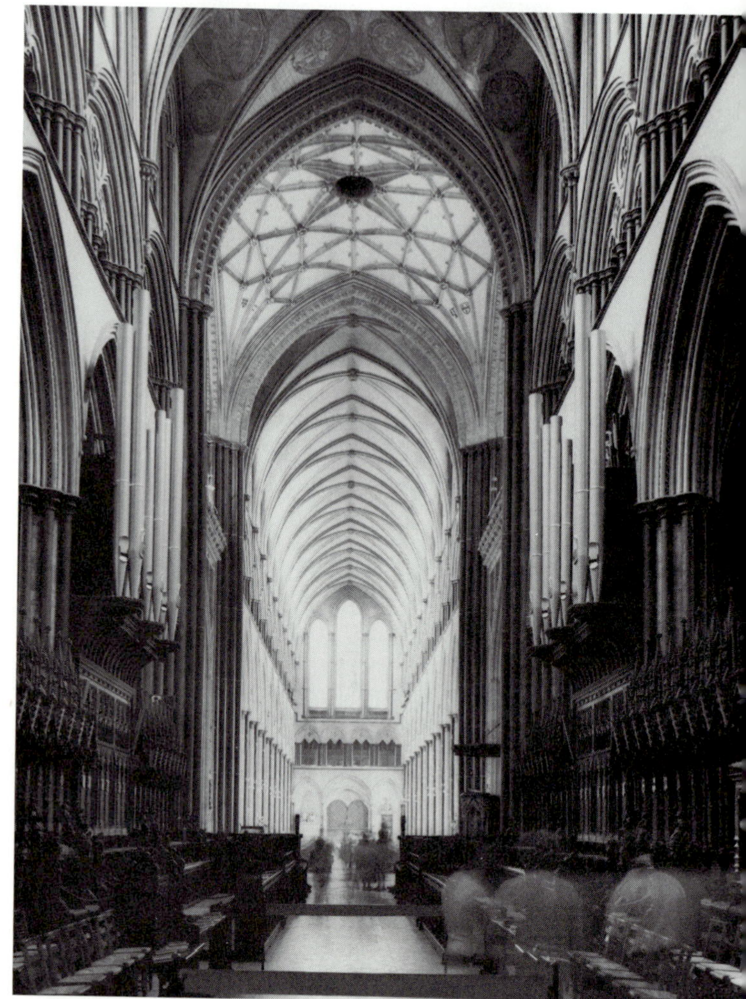

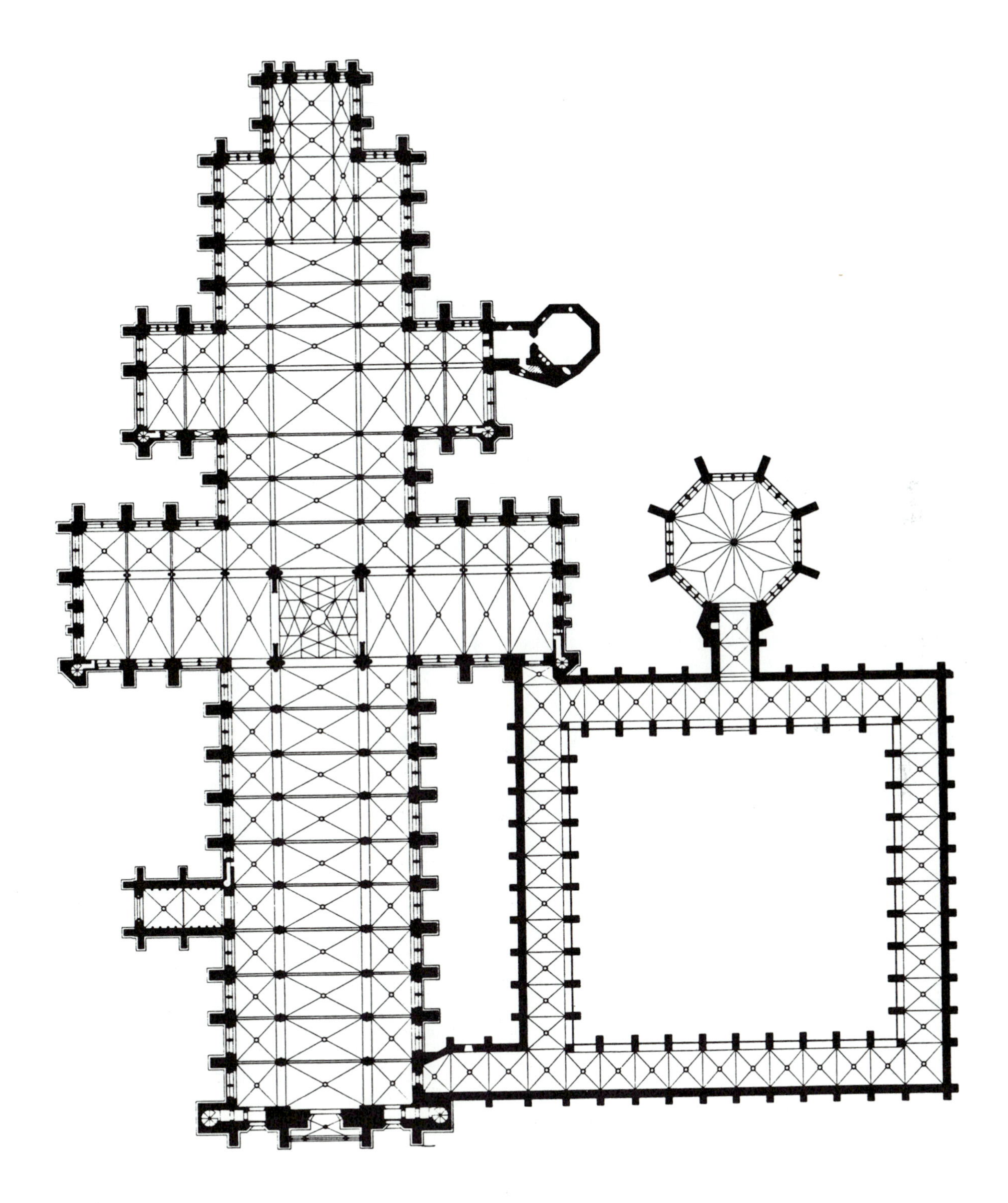

FIGURE 8.53 *Cathedral, Lincoln, 1192–1280.* (Photo: Marburg)

only in lower portions of the west front (Figure 8.53). Rebuilding work, started in 1192, continued harmoniously through 1280. Construction began with the choir and eastern transept, followed by the main western (major) transept, chapter house, nave, and west front upper portions. The retrochoir (meaning "behind the choir" and here known as the Angel Choir) was begun in 1256. Concluded by an enormous eastern window, it was finished in 1280.

Lincoln offers several interesting architectural features. Most obvious on the interior are the varied vaulting systems, including the tierceron rib vaults of the nave which link with an ornamented ridge rib (Figure 8.54). The "crazy" vaults of the choir represent an asymmetrical experiment that was never repeated elsewhere. Throughout the cathedral, but above all in the Angel Choir (Figure 8.55), there is a wealth of elaborate trim in the form of Purbeck mar-

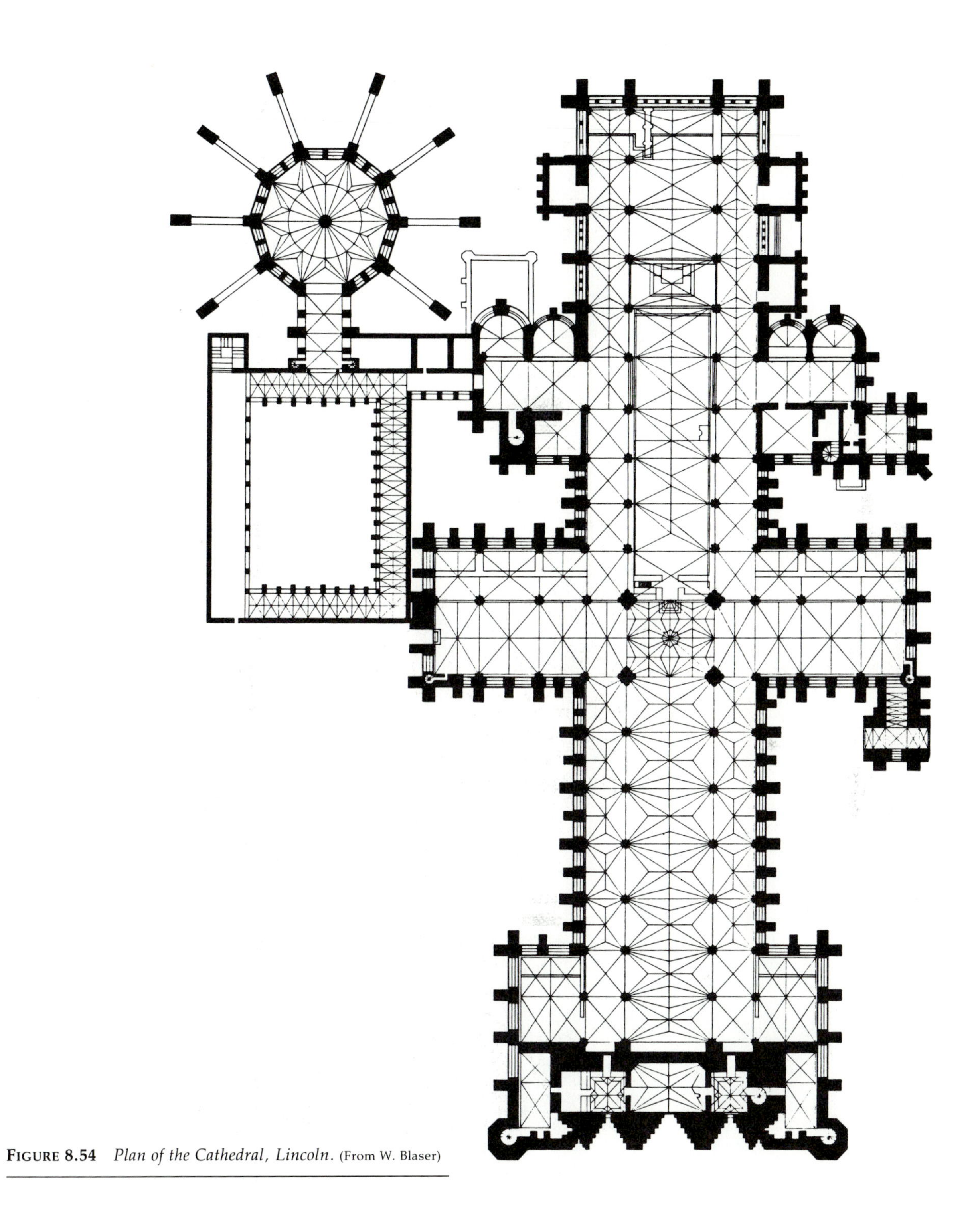

FIGURE 8.54 *Plan of the Cathedral, Lincoln.* (From W. Blaser)

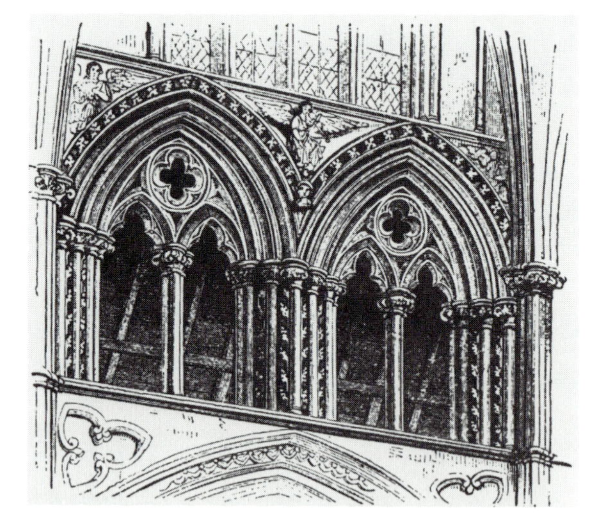

Figure 8.55 *Angel Choir detail from the Cathedral, Lincoln.* (From R. Sturgis)

ble shafts, stiff-leaf capitals, and the sculpted angels that give the retrochoir its name. The Angel Choir clerestories and east end window have tracery of the Decorated period. On the west front, a broad screen wall extends from the Norman work to increase the apparent width of the façade, obscuring the bases of the west front towers, which define the actual width of the church. Finally the ten-sided chapter house with its bold flying buttresses represents a departure from the usual octagonal form.

Figure 8.56 *Cathedral, Wells, 1186–1350.* (Photo: Marburg)

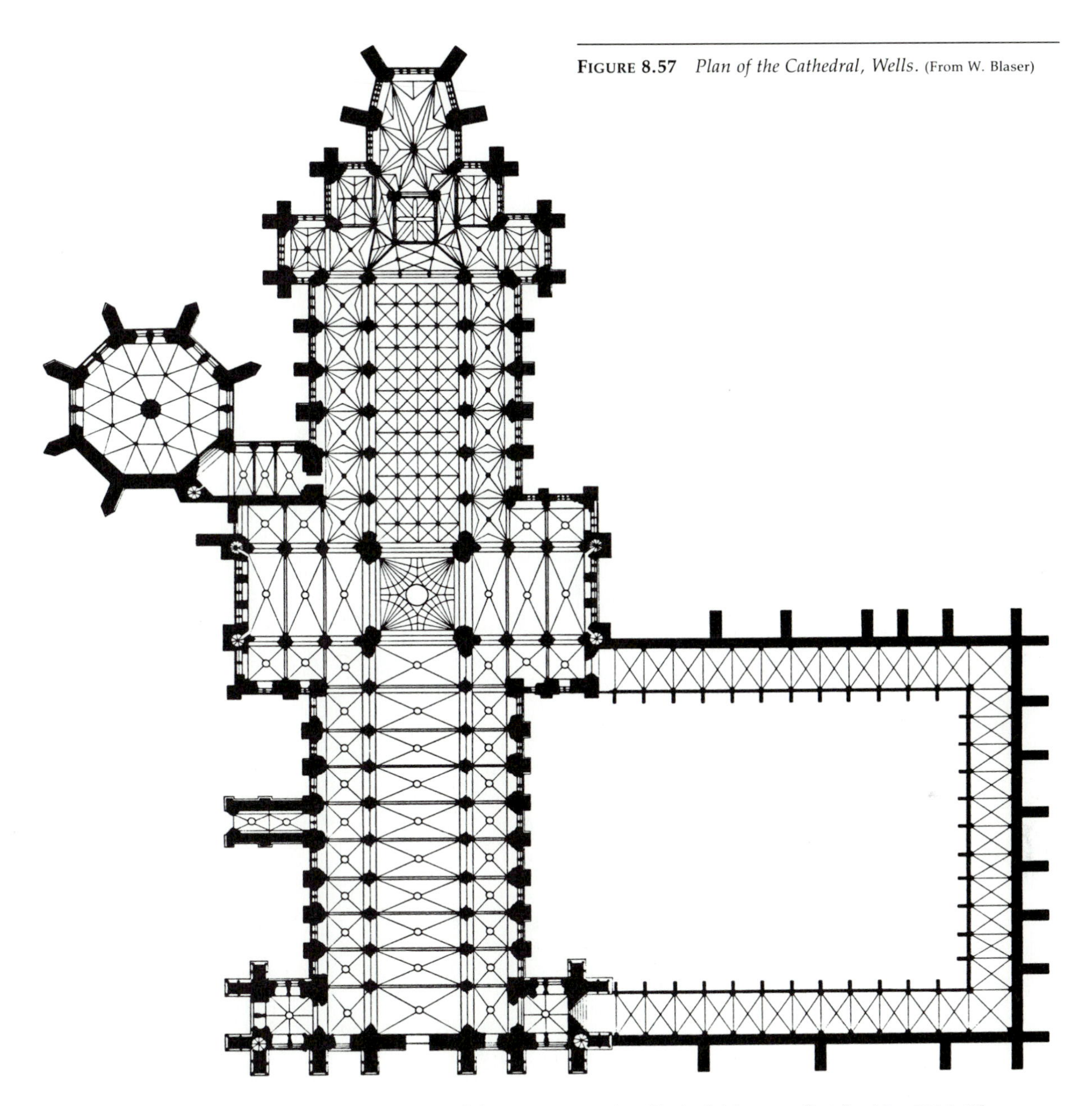

FIGURE 8.57 *Plan of the Cathedral, Wells.* (From W. Blaser)

Wells Cathedral (Figures 8.56, 8.57) is widely regarded as one of the finest of English cathedrals, and it is also among the first English Gothic buildings, dating from at least 1186 and possibly a decade earlier. Today the oldest portions are the transepts, the easternmost bays of the nave, and the north porch, all of which were finished by 1215. The nave and west front were constructed from 1215 until about 1240, and the choir, including the elongated octagonal Lady Chapel, and the chapter house were built from 1300 to 1350. During this period, the crossing tower was enlarged, placing excessive

◄ **FIGURE 8.58** *Interior of the Cathedral, Wells.* (Photo: Marburg)

loads on the piers below. To strengthen them, great scissor-shaped strainer arches were inserted on the west, north, and south sides of the crossing in 1338, breaking the continuity of line from nave to choir but forestalling the collapse of the tower (Figure 8.58).

Wells is a modestly scaled cathedral (the nave vaults are only sixty-seven feet high), but it is endowed with excellent sculptural detail in its capitals and most notably on the ambitious west front screen wall, 147 feet wide, which is covered with niches in which 340 statues depicting Bible stories and the apotheosis of the Church were formerly placed. Only half of these remain, some sadly mutilated. The octagonal chapter house, linked by a stairway to the cathedral, has a central column from which ribs radiate out to the side walls. (It is thought that the inspiration for fan vaulting came from the vaults of Decorated chapter houses.)

FIGURE 8.59 *Cathedral Chapterhouse, Southwell, 1290.* (Photo: Wodehouse)

FIGURE 8.60 *Details from the Cathedral Chapterhouse, Southwell.* (Photo: Marburg)

The chapter house at Southwell Minster and the arcaded vestibule that connects it to the largely Norman church contain some of the finest carving of the Decorated period (Figures 8.59, 8.60). Construction began about 1290, and plants from the countryside were used as models by the trio of sculptors who worked on the capitals and moldings. Leaves from trees (oak, maple, hawthorn, wild apple, and whitethorn), flowers (wild rose, potentilla, buttercup, and white bryony), and vines (ivy, hop, and grape) are carved in exquisite detail with deep undercutting so that the natural qualities of the foliage are accurately represented. Different stages of foliage growth are shown in different capitals, from opening buds to fully developed leaves. Southwell is a small English cathedral, and its chapter house, likewise small, is vaulted without a central column.

Ely Cathedral illustrates another aspect of medieval architecture in England, large-scale construction in timber. Norman work predominates in the nave, which is covered by a timber roof; on the west front, a late Norman project designed with transepts but never finished; and in the transepts east of the nave. Opening into the south aisle of the nave from the now-vanished cloister is the Prior's Doorway, one of the finest Norman-sculpted portals in England, in which Christ is represented most atypically without a beard. The original Norman choir

FIGURE 8.61 *Interior view showing the Cathedral lantern, Ely, 1322.* (From J. Fergusson)

was enlarged (1230–1250) by an eastern extension of six additional bays, based on the Early English nave of Lincoln.

The collapse of Ely's Norman crossing tower (built ca. 1100) in 1322 provoked the most extraordinary construction. The church foundations were insufficient to support a masonry reconstruction, so the tower was replaced by a lantern in wood, the design of which also increased the light and usable space at the crossing (Figures 8.61–8.63). The designer of this masterpiece of medieval engineering was William Hurley, the King's Carpenter; he used eight giant oak posts — 63 feet long, 40 inches thick, and 32 inches wide — for the vertical members of

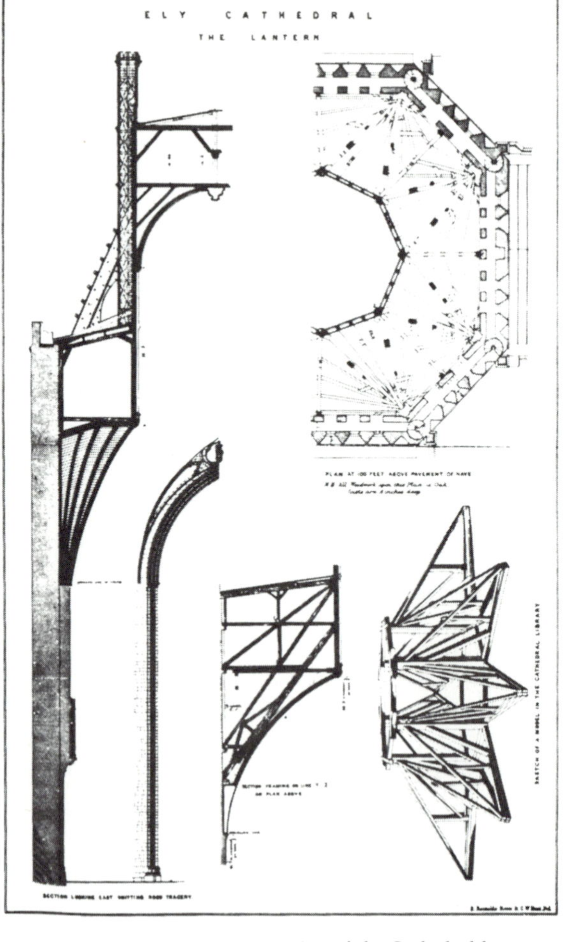

FIGURE 8.62 *Section and elevation of the Cathedral lantern, Ely.* (Delineators: R. R. Rowe and C. W. Hunt)

FIGURE 8.63 *Interior view into the Cathedral lantern, Ely.* (Photo: Marburg)

the octagonal tower, which has a diameter of 69 feet. These are supported on hammerbeams tied to the masonry crossing piers. The octagon itself is set at 22½ degrees to the axis of the nave, providing a spatial contrast at the crossing. Viewed from below, most of the vaulting of the octagon is wood made to look like stone; the actual structural members are visible only if one climbs into the lantern via the access stair.

English construction in timber, as represented at Ely, is remarkable. A number of late medieval hammerbeam roofs survive, the grandest being Westminster Hall in London (1394–1402) (Figures 8.64, 8.65). Hammerbeam construction is actually a series of successive short cantilevers that enable builders to roof a span wider than the length of available timbers. (Triangulated trusses, except for the king and queen post trusses, were unknown until the late Renaissance, and even then they had to be reinvented in the nineteenth century.) The craftsmanship behind the hammerbeam roofs, with their interlocking pegged joints, is a testimonial to the carpentry skills of medieval builders.

Two late Gothic buildings that are not cathedrals deserve mention for their exceptional fan vaults. At Westminster Abbey, the Chapel of Henry VII (1503–1519) (Figures 8.66, 8.67) was added to the eastern end of the existing church. Its fan vaults, embellished with hanging pendants, form a delicate and intricate pattern on the ceiling, complementing the

FIGURE 8.64 *Plan of Westminster Palace Hall, London, 1394–1402.* (From J. Fergusson)

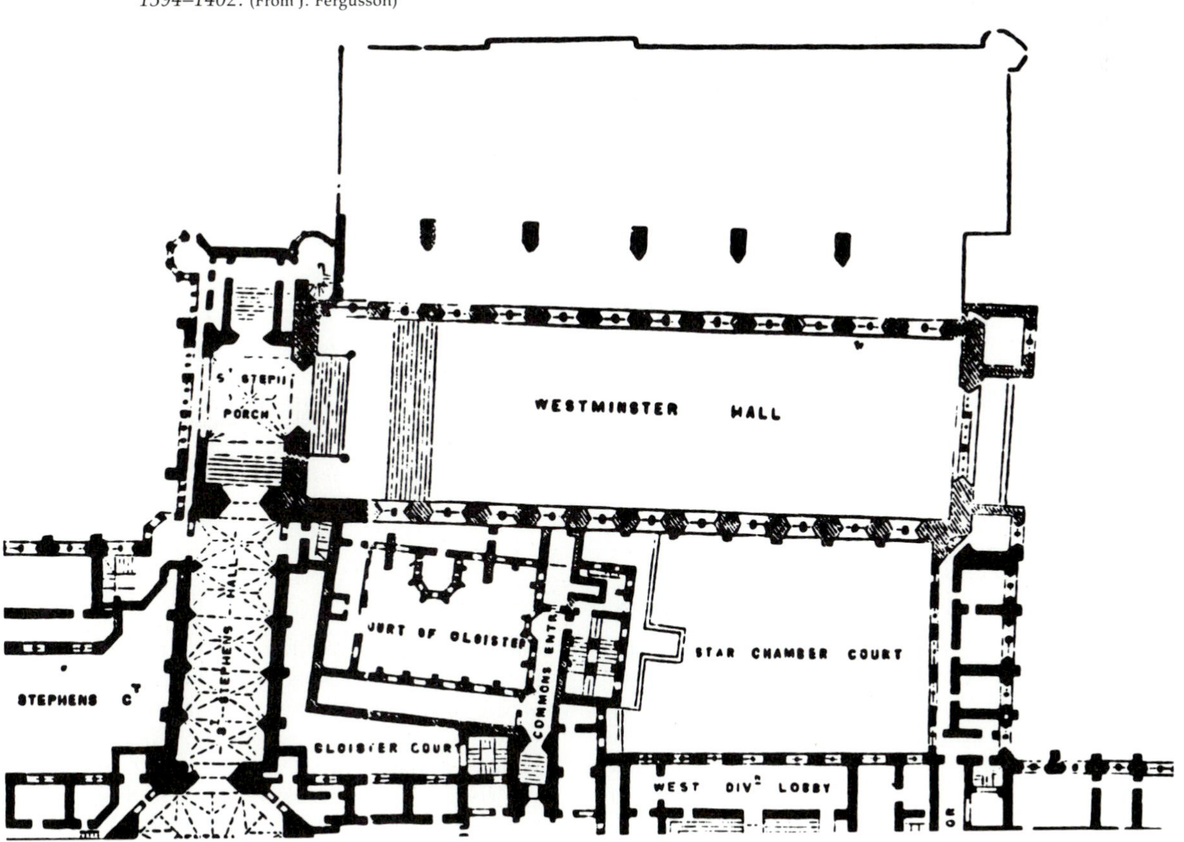

FIGURE 8.65 *Hammerbeam roof detail from Westminster Palace Hall, London, 1394–1402.* (From E. Viollet-le-Duc)

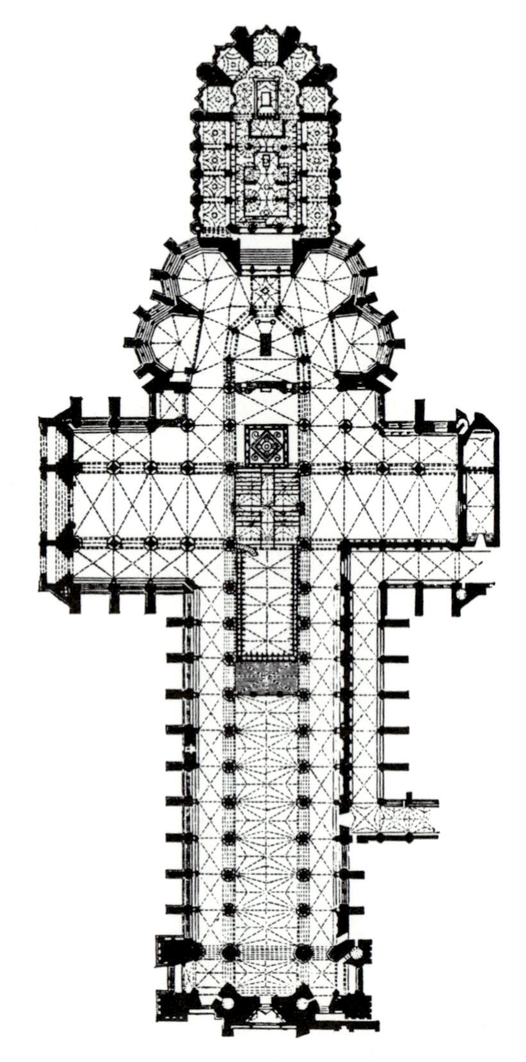

FIGURE 8.66 *Plan of Westminster Abbey, showing the Chapel of Henry VII, London, 1503–1519.* (From J. Fergusson)

airy openness of the walls. Larger in scale is the chapel at King's College, Cambridge (Figures 8.68–8.71), begun in 1446 with donations by Henry VII and completed by 1515 with contributions from his son, Henry VIII. Because this church was designed for use in an era when the sermon had become an important part of church services, it was built with a simpler plan and smaller area to reduce reverberation time so that speech could be understood. (Medieval monastic chant is enhanced by long reverberation times, but the spoken word is virtually incomprehensible in the same space. Use of medieval churches for modern-day church services is made possible by electronic systems that help cancel

FIGURE 8.67 *Interior of Henry VII Chapel, Westminster Abbey, London.* (From T. Bonney)

out reverberation.) King's College Chapel is basically rectangular in plan, with Perpendicular tracery in the large windows and majestic fan vaults overhead. The ornate organ loft atop the choir screen divides the space into two parts, one for townspeople and one for students. King's College Chapel is contemporary with the High Renaissance in Italy, and the woodwork of the choir screen contains classical detail in what is otherwise a late medieval building.

FIGURE 8.68 *King's College Chapel, Cambridge, 1446–1515.* (From J. Britton)

FIGURE 8.69 *West front of King's College Chapel, Cambridge.* (From J. Britton)

FIGURE 8.71 *Interior of King's College Chapel, Cambridge.* (Photo: Marburg)

FIGURE 8.70 *Plan of King's College Chapel, Cambridge.* (From W. Blaser)

SECULAR ARCHITECTURE AND CIVIC DESIGN

The discussion of Romanesque and Gothic architecture has directed attention to the design of religious buildings, primarily because the best design talents and greatest financial resources were commanded by the Church. Medieval buildings remaining for modern scholars to study are from 400 to 1100 years old now, and only the best-constructed architecture can be expected to last that long. In the Middle Ages, churches formed the main group of buildings erected with great care, so they comprise the bulk of medieval architectural history.

However, enough secular structures survive from the Gothic period to give a general idea of the buildings in which ordinary people lived. Rural houses of peasant families would have been simple indeed, providing minimal shelter for cooking and sleeping. These vernacular buildings used local materials, mostly wood and thatch, and simple construction techniques, and they were probably built by the families that inhabited them. Archaeological excavations have led to reconstruction studies of early medieval frame farmhouse-barns, which probably varied little over the course of later centuries.

Peter Brueghel the Elder depicts just such a house in the background of *The Birdnester,* painted in 1568, which indicates that these rural structures were even then common sights in the countryside.

Houses built in towns would be more compact, often including several floors to conserve available land. The structure would again be wood; the roof would be thatch, and the entire building would accordingly be very combustible. Devastating fires are frequent events in the chronicles of medieval cities. Larger towns eventually regulated building by insisting on masonry construction and tile or slate roofs to reduce the spread of fire. Nevertheless some wooden dwellings survive in England and on the Continent to illustrate **half-timber** construction (Figures 8.72, 8.73). These buildings have a heavy timber frame, exposed on the exterior, which is completed by nonstructural wattle and daub, plaster, brick, or other infill. Whether of masonry or timber, town houses would typically have a shop on the ground floor and the dwelling apartments on the floors above. The kitchen would be on the ground floor separated by a small light court from the rear of the shop to keep its odors and fire haz-

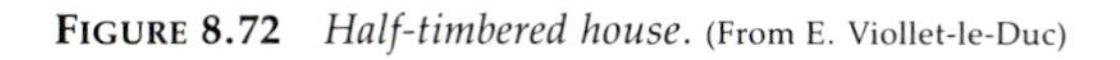

FIGURE 8.72 *Half-timbered house.* (From E. Viollet-le-Duc)

FIGURE 8.73 *Framing detail for a half-timbered house.* (From E. Viollet-le-Duc)

FIGURE 8.74 *Tower of London, 1067 and later.* (Photo: Marburg)

ards away from the main part of the house. Residents would carry water from the town well or the river and dispose of waste by throwing the slops and trash out into the street for the pigs.

More impressive were the fortified residences of the nobility, although they probably offered little more in the way of creature comforts than the homes of the townspeople. The essential quality of these residences (called variously castles or châteaux) was protection from military assault. Walls with battlements, reinforced by towers and heavily guarded gates, provided a secure enclosure, which could be supplemented by an encircling ditch (a moat, if filled with water). Inside the wall would be assorted small structures and the masonry **keep,** the second line of defense. A view of the Tower of London (Figures 8.74, 8.75) illustrates all these elements preserved in one historic site. The medi-

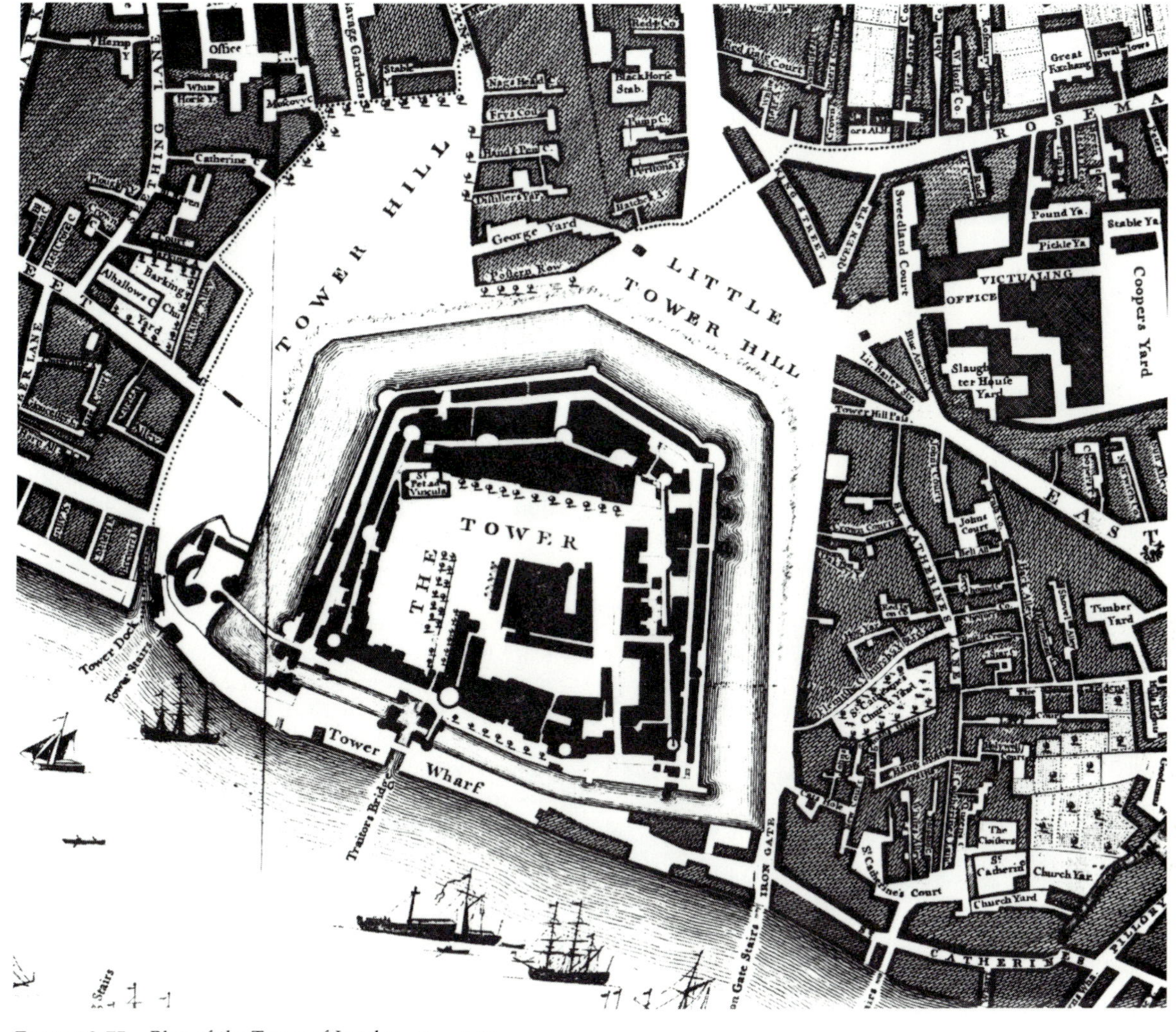

FIGURE 8.75 *Plan of the Tower of London.* (From J. Pine)

eval world was well supplied with similar castles (France alone had about 2000), but many are very much ruined today.

Every medieval town had to have a solidly constructed wall to protect its citizens from attack. The innumerable armed struggles that characterized the Middle Ages usually had the capture of towns as their objective, for the economic and strategic value of urban settlements was high. Fortunately for cities, medieval warfare was seldom a sustained event with large armies, and weapons before the introduction of gunpowder and metal cannonballs (ca. 1400) were rather primitive: battering rams, catapults, siege towers, and bows and arrows (Figure 8.76). A well-built city wall, punctuated by towers, provided defenders with a platform to return catapult and arrow fire and to dump stones or boiling oil down on persons trying to scale the wall.

FIGURE 8.76 *Illustration of medieval siege warfare.* (From E. Viollet-le-Duc)

The art of fortifying towns advanced considerably from the experience gained in the Crusades for the Islamic fortifications in the Holy Land were superior in design to contemporary work in western Europe. In particular the double set of walls built by the Crusaders at Krak des Chevaliers (Figure 8.77) in present-day Syria probably influenced the double walls of Carcassonne (Figures 8.78, 8.79), built from 1248 onward as the King of France strengthened the existing fortifications. It was his intention to make Carcassonne impregnable as part of a southern strategy to bring the area under royal control. To prevent overcrowding within the hilltop fortifications, he developed a new town in the valley below. Its regular grid plan contrasts sharply with the irregular layouts of medieval towns that grew without regulation or advance planning. We shall never know how successful the double wall fortifications were because no one tried to attack the town after the work was complete. Carcassonne's strategic importance waned with the medieval period, but when there was a proposal to pull the crumbling walls down in the nineteenth century, preservationists intervened and restored the battlements and tower roofs to the condition seen today.

Some graceful, nonmilitary civic structures were built during the Gothic period, particularly in Italy. As towns gained independence from the local lord or bishop and became wealthy through the revival of commerce, they sought to express their self-governing status and civic pride by erecting splendid structures for governmental functions. The Campo at Siena was designed as a great bowl-shaped piazza to focus attention on the Palazzo Pubblico or town hall (begun 1298) (Figure 8.80), distinguished by its tall, slender bell tower. In Florence the Palazzo Vecchio (Figures 8.81, 8.82) served a similar civic function. The military character suggested by its battlements belies the nondefense use

FIGURE 8.77 *Krak des Chevaliers, Syria, ca. 1200.* (From G. Rey)

FIGURE 8.78 *Carcassonne, 1248 and later.* (Photo: Marburg)

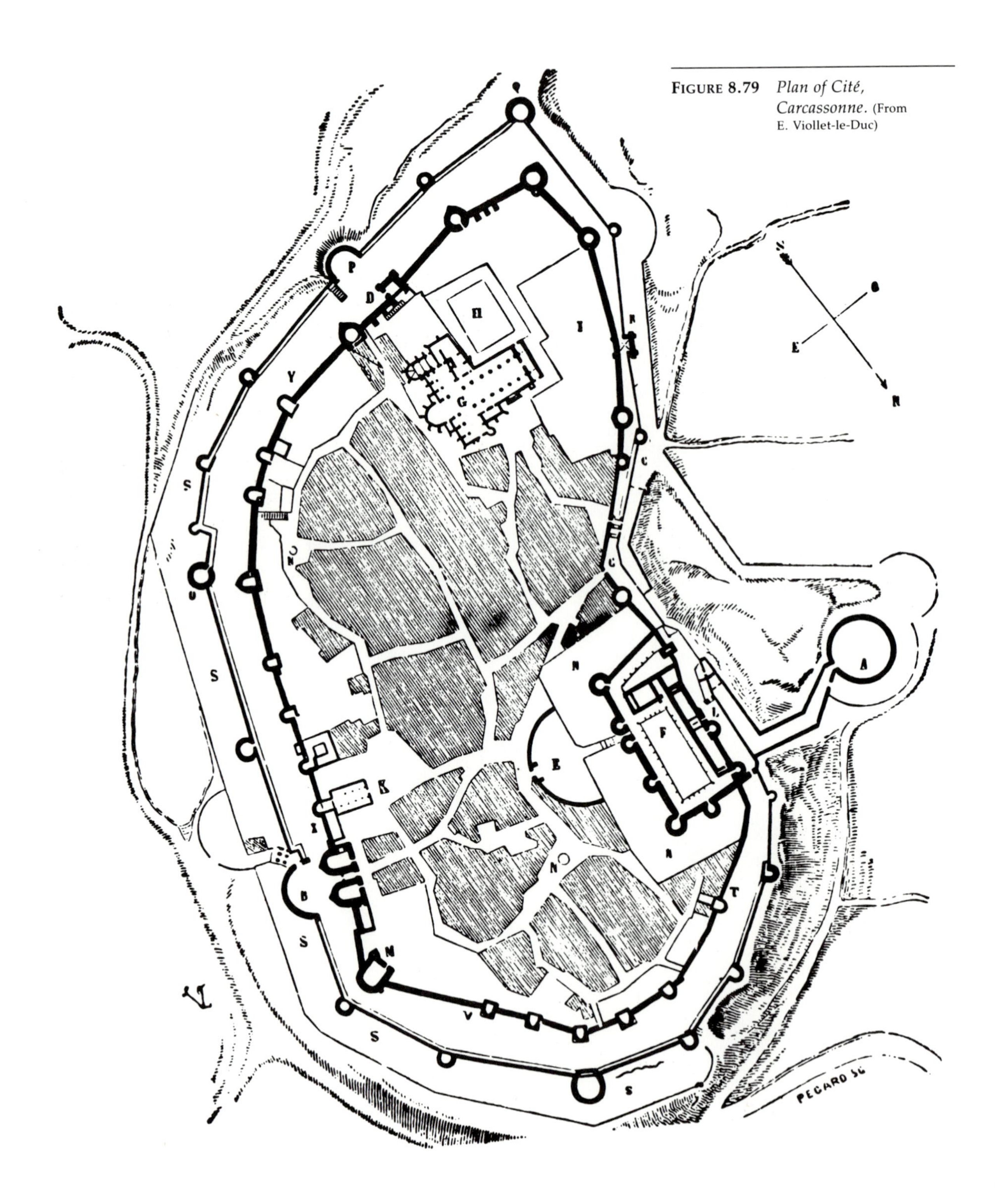

Figure 8.79 *Plan of Cité, Carcassonne.* (From E. Viollet-le-Duc)

FIGURE 8.80 *Palazzo Pubblico, Siena, 1298.* (Photo: Special Collections, University of Tennessee)

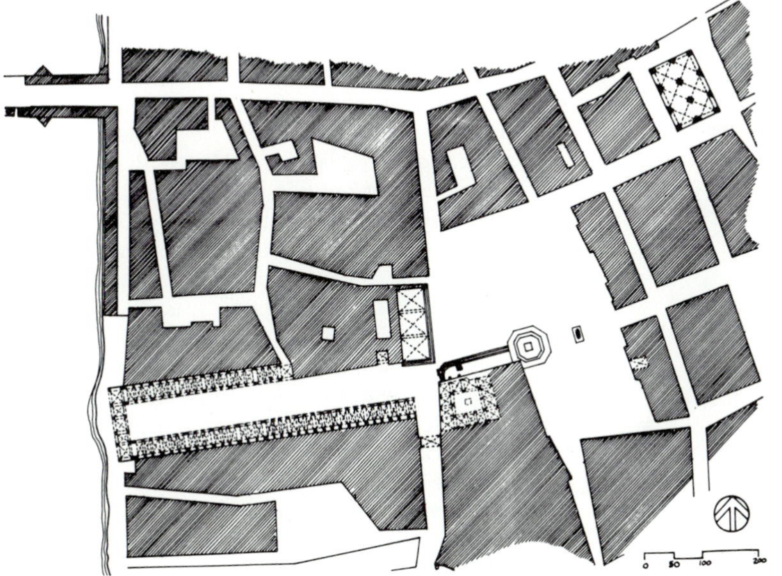

FIGURE 8.81 *Plan of the Piazza della Signoria and Uffizi, showing the Palazzo Vecchio, Florence, 1298–1314.* (Delineator: Gary Best)

Figure 8.82 *Palazzo Vecchio, Florence.* (Photo: Instituto Italiano di Cultura)

Figure 8.83 *Doge's Palace, Venice, 1309–1424.* (Photo: School of Architecture, University of Tennessee)

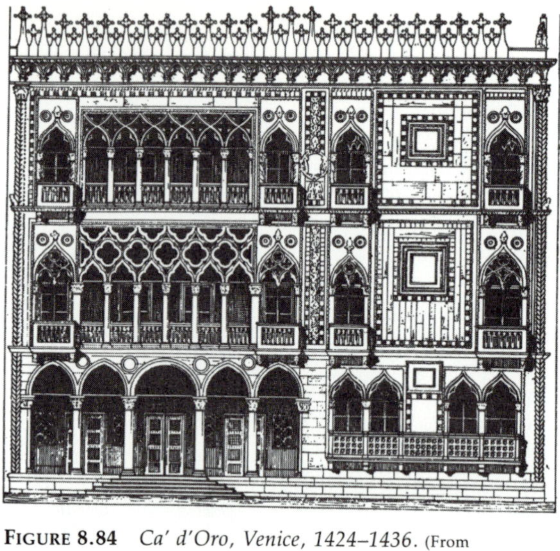

Figure 8.84 *Ca' d'Oro, Venice, 1424–1436.* (From J. Fergusson)

of the building, although Florentine politics could be quite stormy.

The Venetians developed a characteristic variant of Gothic, mingling the northern European features with exotic influences from the East. The result is an airy, decorative architecture animated by the shimmering light reflected by the city's canals. The Palace of the Doge (Figure 8.83) is perhaps the most famous example of Venetian Gothic. A blocky structure with an open courtyard, it has a solid exterior wall resting on two stories of open arcades. Pink and white diaper patterns enliven and lighten the visual impact of solid wall, so that it does not appear to overload the delicate filigree of the arcades below. The Ca' d'Oro (Figure 8.84) illustrates Venetian Gothic applied to the traditional merchant's house, with its central section of large arcaded windows that open onto the *grand salon,* the major living space that extends the full depth of the house.

As is obvious from this presentation, the Gothic was strongly identified with northern Europe and never gained any real significance in Italy. By the fifteenth century a new artistic movement, based on the ideals of classical antiquity, was developing in the urban centers of northern Italy. In the following centuries this new style, the Renaissance, would spread to the rest of Europe. In isolated communities, however, medieval building traditions continued with little change until the nineteenth century. Dubbed the Gothic Survival, they merged with the Gothic Revival, originated by reform-minded Victorians as a second flowering of medieval art and architecture.

9.

Renaissance Architecture

The preceding chapter contained little about buildings in Italy because the Gothic never became an important building style there. Even the Romanesque, which in French hands developed substantially from classical and other sources, remained in Italy more a continuation of building traditions emerging from Early Christian and Byzantine influences. A similar affinity with Byzantium is seen in medieval Italian art, where the iconographic conventions of mosaic work were carried into paintings. Sacred figures have timeless, distantly focused expressions, stiff frontal poses, and deeply colored robes, all set against a background of gold leaf. By the late medieval period, artists in both northern and southern Europe showed increased interest in less-stylized representation. While French Gothic sculptors were making considerable strides toward natural portrayals of forms, Italian artists were experimenting with accurate depiction of depth on a two-dimensional surface.

THE EARLY RENAISSANCE

The late medieval period in Italy was marked by a revival of urban life. Small, virtually autonomous city-states developed out of the feudal system, unfettered by the overriding control of a monarch. Whereas both France and England were essentially royal nations by the end of the Middle Ages, Italy remained an assemblage of fractious city-states and fiefdoms until unification in 1870. Trade flourished, encouraged by Italy's position between Byzantium and western Europe and enhanced by the adventurous merchants who imported luxury goods and organized the textile industries. Civic life in the major city-states came to be dominated by families whose wealth came not from inherited landholdings but from the profits of mercantile activity.

Nowhere was this truer than in Florence, the city regarded as the birthplace of the new artistic movement called the Renaissance. The patrons of this new art were the rich merchants and leading trade guilds rather than the nobility or the Church, the traditional patrons of medieval art. Florentine wool merchants and bankers were active across western Europe, and their agents began to buy and commission works of art in a manner previously restricted to princes or bishops. The eighty bankers of Florence lent money (at interest) to the kings of Europe and kept accurate records of their financial affairs through double entry bookkeeping, another Florentine invention. By the fifteenth century the wealthy bankers and leading guilds dominated Florence politically and economically. The city's political strength was a result of commercial daring and strong municipal pride, with its government based on a renewed understanding of Roman law rather than authoritarian feudalism.

The ambitious merchants of Florence did more than just make money, however. To a greater extent than had ever been the case in the medieval period, these men were actively interested in life in this world, not solely in the life hereafter. This does not mean they were irreligious, but they no longer interpreted the world exclusively through Church teachings as medieval men had done. For the first time literature was written originally in the language of everyday speech rather than being translated from Latin, the language of the Church. People avidly collected and studied the art and literature of ancient Greece and Rome. Leading bankers, such as the Medici, might find recreation in the composition of poetry or performance of music, and they welcomed distinguished artists, scholars, and writers into their homes, not as servants or entertainers, but as honored guests. It was a time of cultural excitement and discovery, and the creative talents of a group of young artists developed into a new artistic style, grounded in admiration for the antique, yet tempered by the search for new approaches to contemporary challenges.

Filippo Brunelleschi

The son of a notary, Filippo Brunelleschi (1377–1446) was admitted to the Silk Guild in 1398 as a goldsmith. Only three years later he entered the competition for a new set of bronze doors for the Baptistry of Florence Cathedral. His main competitor, who won the competition, was Lorenzo Ghiberti. After losing the commission Brunelleschi set off for Rome with his sculptor friend, Donatello, and it is quite possible that Brunelleschi's subsequent career as an architect owed much to the extended visit he paid to the Eternal City.

During his stay in Rome, Brunelleschi's observant eye and well-trained hand combined to discover the principles of mathematically accurate linear perspective, making possible the exact representation of a three-dimensional object on a two-dimensional surface. Various artists in Italy and elsewhere had struggled to achieve depth in their paintings, but their solutions fell short of the precision achieved by Brunelleschi. In making accurate drawings of what he saw when he viewed the repetitive elements of Roman arches (as in the aqueducts), Brunelleschi realized that parallel horizontal lines converge at a point on the horizon and that the rhythm of vertical motifs diminishes proportionally into the distance. Further studies in the geometric rules governing this phenomenon led to the formulation of what we know as one- and two-point perspective, still the most realistic drawing technique used in design. The development of this representation system was to have lasting consequences in art, architecture, and civic design during the Renaissance and later periods. And it was this achievement that probably brought Brunelleschi to the attention of Leon Battista Alberti, whose book, *On Painting*, was dedicated to one painter, one architect, and three sculptors who typified for Alberti the emerging Renaissance in Florence.

An early application of linear perspective came in Masaccio's fresco painting, *The Trinity* (1427–1428) at S. Maria Novella (Figure 9.1), which depicts God the Father standing on a large sarcophagus supporting the crucified Christ. Below stand Mary and St. John with two kneeling donors. The holy figures are framed by modified Ionic columns supporting an arch that creates a coffered, barrel-vaulted chapel, mathematically projected according to the rules of perspective. This portion is commonly attributed to Brunelleschi. Kneeling in front of the painting, the viewer is impressed by an intense sense of three-dimensional space beyond the wall of the church.

By 1407 Brunelleschi was again living in Florence. In that year the directors of the cathedral works were consulting distinguished engineers and architects from France, Spain, England, and Germany for advice on the cathedral's dome. The cathedral, properly known as S. Maria del Fiore, was begun in 1292 to designs of Arnolfo di Cambio. It was intended from the first to have a dome exceeding the splendor of that on the Cathedral of Pisa. The Cathedral in Florence was Italian Gothic in style rather than the Romanesque of Pisa, but local sensibilities did not permit the use of flying buttresses because of their association with German architecture and, by extension, with the Holy Roman Em-

FIGURE 9.1 *Masaccio:* The Trinity, *S. Maria Novella, Florence, 1427–1428.* (Photo: Alinari)

FIGURE 9.2 *Brunelleschi: Cathedral dome, Florence, 1420 and later.* (Photo: School of Architecture, University of Tennessee)

peror, who had political ambitions in Italy. The original dome was enlarged in the course of construction as various masters after Arnolfo di Cambio supervised the vaulting of the nave and construction of the walls that would support the dome. Work proceeded to the level of the octagonal drum, from which a dome spanning nearly 150 feet on the diagonal was to spring, without anyone having a firm idea how to achieve this span. The outward thrust of such a dome, untied by interior iron rods and unbraced by flying buttresses, would push the walls over, and the scale of centering required to support the masonry while construction was in progress vastly exceeded anything attempted in the medieval period.

This was the situation that Brunelleschi inherited. Like other well-traveled men, he had seen the Pantheon in Rome and marveled at its 142-foot hemispherical dome, but without Roman concrete technology, he could not replicate that dome in Florence. Instead Brunelleschi proposed to solve the problem by using a ribbed structure (Figures 9.2, 9.3). Brunelleschi had been involved with building projects related to the cathedral since 1404. The tribunes, exedras, and drum of the dome were all under construction from 1400 to 1418, and he

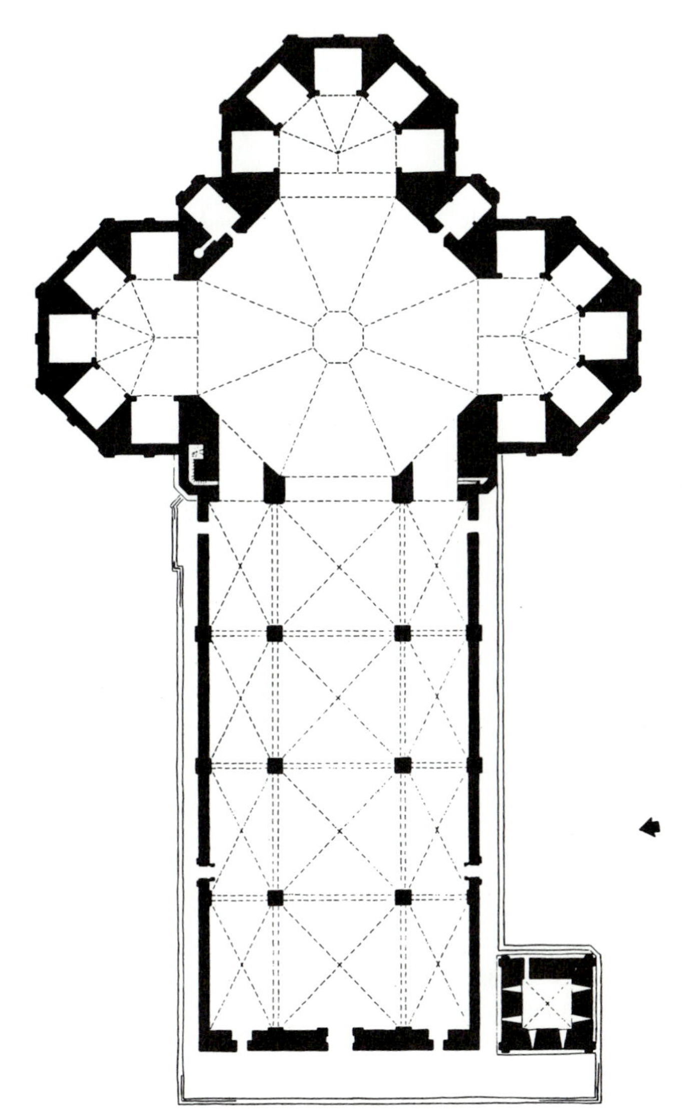

Figure 9.3 *Brunelleschi: Plan of the Cathedral, Florence.* (From W. Blaser)

must have contributed to their design. His proposal and novel construction procedure for the dome itself were demonstrated between 1418–1420 when a one-twelfth scale model was constructed in masonry beside the cathedral. The success of this model led to his being awarded the commission for the actual work in 1420, even though he had no completed buildings to his credit at this time. Ghiberti was appointed coarchitect, perhaps to temper Brunelleschi's inexperience, for his proficiency in sculpture was, to Renaissance thinking, proof of competency in all the arts. As construction proceeded, however, it became obvious that Brunelleschi alone was capable of directing the work, and Ghiberti was eventually eased out of his architectural responsibilities.

Construction on the octagonal vault that would comprise the Gothic-profile dome began atop the fourteen-foot-thick support walls of the drum. Brunelleschi's design called for a 105-foot-high double-shelled dome (Figures 9.4, 9.5). Building inner and outer domes reduced the weight (and thus the outward thrust) without sacrificing stiffness, because arch ties placed periodically at an angle from the horizontal united its inner and outer surfaces. At first the dome's sides rose at a steep angle, so that work was able to extend upward for fifty-eight feet without the need for support from underneath. Brunelleschi had observed diagonal bonding patterns in the ruins of Roman brickwork, and he adapted this to construction on the dome so that each horizontal ring layer locked into the preceding

Figure 9.4 *Brunelleschi: Section through Cathedral dome, Florence.* (From J. Guadet)

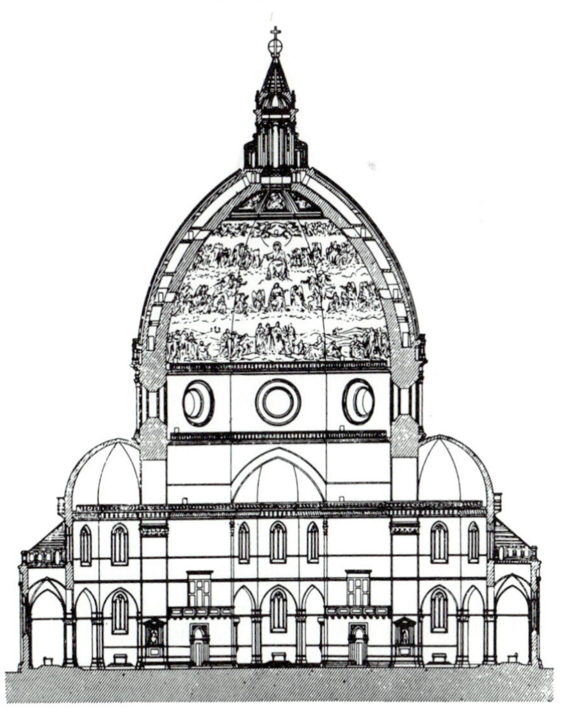

FIGURE 9.5 *Brunelleschi: Perspective half section of the cathedral dome, Florence.* (From A. Choisy)

course, and at the same time supported the next ring above it.

Sandstone ribs at each of the eight corners of the octagon unite the inner and outer shells and form the dominant external structure of the dome. At the lowest portion of the dome, they have a cross-section of eleven by seven feet, and they taper upward to an apex ring underneath the cupola (a small tower capping the dome). Between each of these main ribs is a pair of intermediate ribs, making a total of twenty-four vertical ribs. The inner and outer shells of the dome are held apart by five horizontal arch rings of limestone, which are connected by metal clamps. Brunelleschi had observed such imbedded metal fastenings in the ruins of Roman construction, and he used them here to reinforce the masonry. Near the base of the dome are twenty-four chestnut timbers, each one foot square and twenty-three feet long, banded together with straps and bolts into a continuous wooden tension ring that resists the outward thrust of the dome. By modern structural analysis this ring alone is insufficient to restrain the accumulated load, but the combination of structural devices designed by Brunelleschi was effective.

No less interesting than the dome itself are the various machines that Brunelleschi designed to facilitate construction. Many practical problems had to be resolved on a job of this magnitude, and Brunelleschi proved adept at inventing the necessary mechanisms. A hoist with a worm gear and safety brake was required to lift the large blocks of stone up to the working platform. Brunelleschi designed one with an oak gear that wore out quickly, so the gear was replaced by one cast in bronze by Ghiberti from a mold made by Donatello. The rope required to raise the stones had a diameter of 2½ inches, and 600 feet of it weighed half a ton. Brunelleschi found rope-makers in Pisa who could manufacture the required length, and he devised block and tackle pulleys that allowed the lifting of stones weighing up to nineteen tons. Brunelleschi also used efficient management procedures to expedite the work. For example, a canteen provided lunch for crews on the scaffold so that there was no time lost in ascending and descending from the high platform for midday meals.

Work on the cathedral dome continued through Brunelleschi's lifetime; the cupola was completed after his death. During this time Brunelleschi was able to build in Florence several smaller projects where the ideals of Roman architecture could be expressed more directly than in the cathedral dome. In these commissions, with less troublesome technical problems, Brunelleschi expressed his empathy with ancient Rome in both form and detail. The earliest of these, the Ospedale degli Innocenti (Foundling Hospital) (Figure 9.6), is often considered the first building of the Renaissance. Designed in 1419 and built from 1421 to 1444, it continues the link with classical tradition that had been maintained in Florence through such Romanesque buildings as S. Miniato al Monte and the Baptistry. (In Brunelleschi's time, these were erroneously considered to be late Roman structures worthy of emulation.) The Ospedale (in modern terms an orphanage) has a continuous arcade, carried on Corinthian columns across its main façade and around an internal courtyard, that is comparable to the ground-floor arcading in marble veneer that adorns both S. Miniato

FIGURE 9.6 *Brunelleschi: Ospedale degli Innocenti, Florence, 1419–1444.* (Photo: Marburg)

and the Baptistry; these Romanesque elements were ultimately based on Roman architecture. At the Ospedale the arcading is three-dimensional, creating a loggia with domed vaults in each bay. Semicircular arches span the width of the loggia, from the freestanding columns with abacus, to corbeled brackets on the opposite wall.

A similar columnar arcade is found in the aisles of the Latin cross church of S. Lorenzo (Figures 9.7, 9.8), begun in 1421. Here Brunelleschi defined each bay with arches that spring from columns of the nave arcade to pilasters set between side aisle chapels. This achieves a more balanced effect than the wall corbel at the Ospedale, yet Brunelleschi found an even more satisfactory resolution in his design for the church of S. Spirito (Figures 9.9, 9.10), begun as late as 1445, where half columns attached to the wall replace the pilasters used at S. Lorenzo. This may seem an undue emphasis on an admittedly minor architectural aspect, but such attention to coherent detail contributes substantially to continuity of the design, from its overall conception to the particulars of its interior.

In both these church commissions Brunelleschi sought to accommodate the practical requirements

FIGURE 9.7 *Brunelleschi: Plan of S. Lorenzo, Florence, begun 1421.* (From W. Blaser)

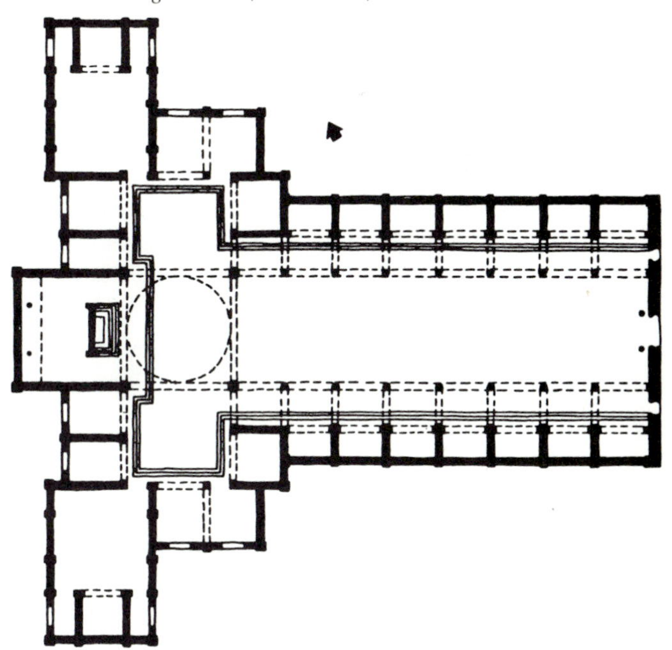

FIGURE 9.8 *Brunelleschi: Interior of S. Lorenzo, Florence.* (Photo: Alinari)

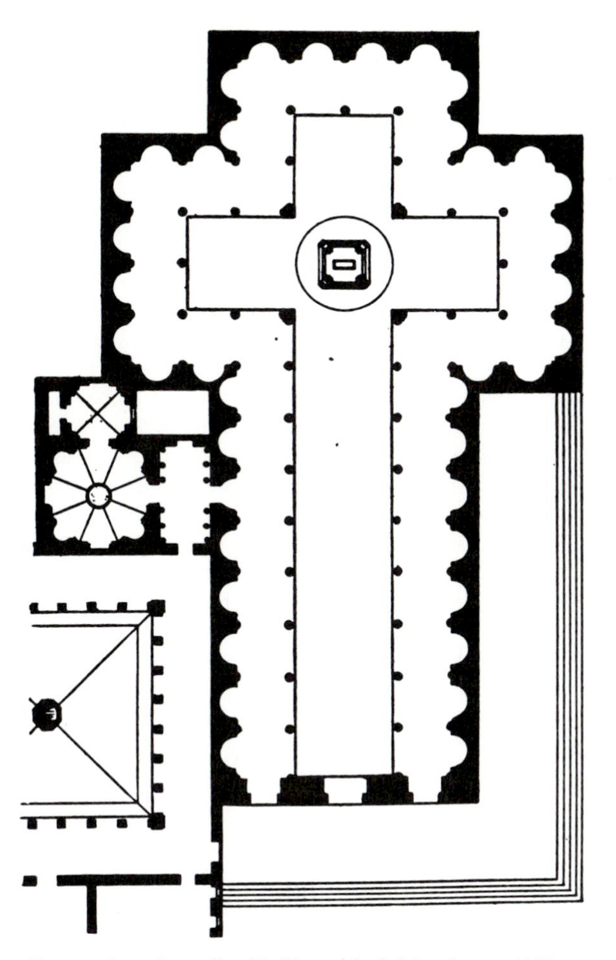

FIGURE 9.9 *Brunelleschi: Plan of S. Spirito, begun 1445.* (From R. Sturgis)

FIGURE 9.10 *Brunelleschi: Interior of S. Spirito.* (Photo: Alinari)

of his clients within the context of the simple geometries he admired in Roman buildings. At both S. Spirito and S. Lorenzo, the square bay of the aisle defines a module that is repeated throughout the church. Four modules form a double bay of the nave, and this larger square is repeated four times down the nave and then once for each transept, the crossing, and the choir. Taken as a cube the large square becomes a volume that defines half the height of the nave, extending the simple proportions of 1:2 into the vertical dimension. Roman elements, such as the semicircular arch, Corinthian columns, and coffering, impart a classical character to the interiors of both churches.

Renaissance architects, including Brunelleschi, continued the interest in geometry that had so strongly affected medieval architecture. Rather than using the complex transformations of medieval master masons, Renaissance architects favored simple figures — the square and the circle — and correspondingly straightforward numerical ratios, such as 1:2, 1:3, and so forth. Renaissance architects made drawings of the human figure inscribed within the basic outline of the circle and square, demonstrating that these proportions reflected divine ratios. Of these drawings, the most famous is the Vitruvian Man (Figure 9.11) in the Notebooks of Leonardo da Vinci, which, like the other drawings, illustrates the precedent established by Vitruvius in the third book of *De architectura*:

> For if a man be placed flat on his back, with his hands and feet extended, and a pair of compasses centered at his navel, the fingers and toes of his two hands and feet will touch the circumference of a circle described therefrom. And, just as the human body yields a circular outline, so too a square figure may be found from it. For if we measure the distance from the soles of the feet to the top of the head, and then apply that measure to the outstretched arms, the breadth will be found to be the same as the height, as in the case of plane surfaces which are perfectly square.

Brunelleschi made prominent use of simple numerical ratios in three of the smaller commissions he designed. For the church of S. Lorenzo, Brunelleschi erected the Old Sacristy (1421–1428) in a corner of the north transept (Figure 9.12). The floor, walls, and pendentives are essentially contained in a cube, surmounted by a hemispherical dome with an oculus. Pilasters, an entablature, and arches of grey *pietra serena* (a local stone much favored for architectural detail), are set against the white stucco of the walls, giving a linear definition to the interior. Slightly larger than the Old Sacristy is the Pazzi Chapel (1430–1433), erected off the major cloister at the monastery of S. Croce (Figure 9.13). The chapel's exterior features a portico of six Corinthian columns supporting a series of square panels instead of the expected pediment. These panels are the external expression of the portico's barrel vault, which covers the porch. Axial entrance to the chapel across the cloister court is indicated by the wider intercolumniation at the center, supporting an imitation Roman triumphal arch. A small dome on pendentives occupies the intersection of the portico vault and the entrance arch. Inside the chapel is a rectangle in plan, with a square altar recess off the long east side opposite the entrance (Figure 9.14). A hemispheri-

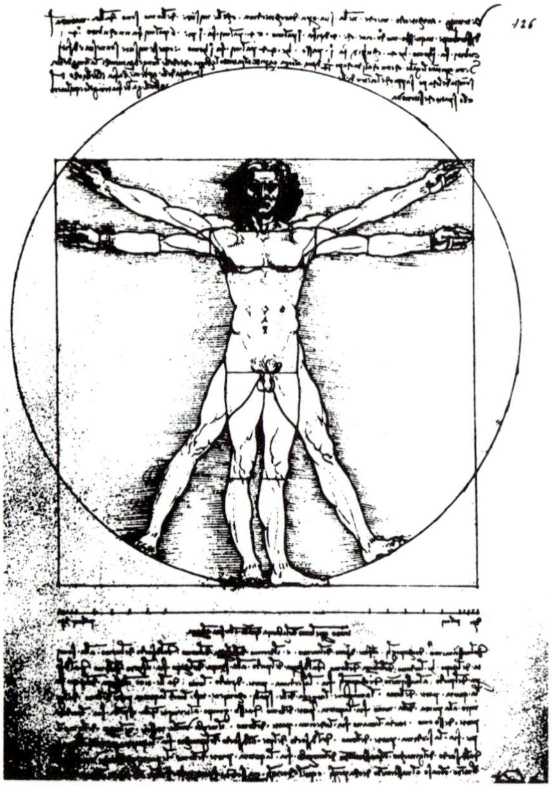

FIGURE 9.11 *Leonardo da Vinci: Vitruvian Man.* (Courtesy: Academy Library, Venice)

FIGURE 9.12 *Brunelleschi: Interior of the Old Sacristy, S. Lorenzo, Florence, 1421–1428.* (Photo: Alinari)

FIGURE 9.13 *Brunelleschi: Exterior of the Pazzi Chapel, S. Croce, Florence, 1430–1433.* (Photo: Alinari)

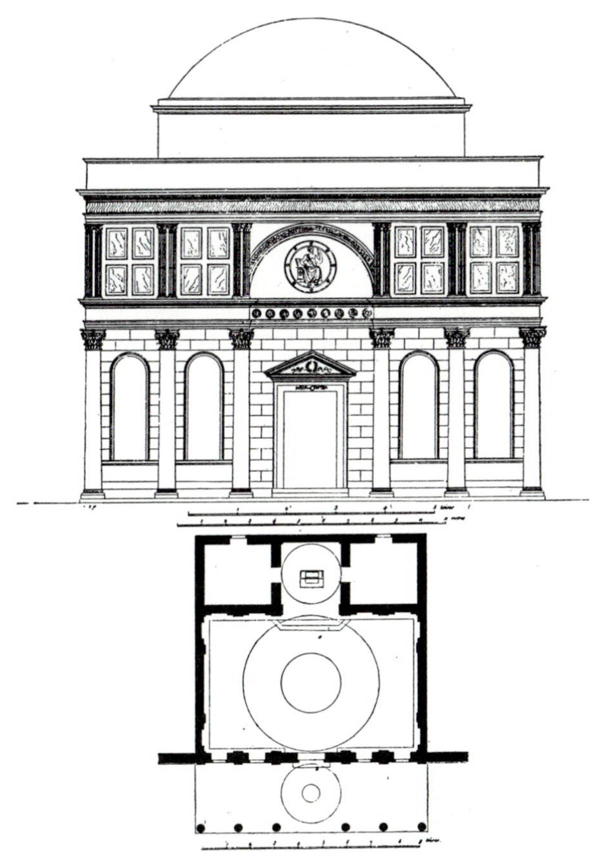

FIGURE 9.14 *Brunelleschi: Elevation and plan of the Pazzi Chapel, S. Croce, Florence.* (From A. Grandjean de Montigny and A. Famin)

cal dome over the inscribed square at the center of the major space is complemented by the smaller dome over the altar, while barrel vaults cover the end bays of the major space. Even though the plan is not identical to the Old Sacristy, the treatment of the interior articulation is quite similar.

Brunelleschi's design for S. Maria degli Angeli (1434–1437) was the first centrally planned structure of the Renaissance. Its plan is Roman, with a domed octagonal central space flanked by eight chapels. Piers composed of clustered pilasters provided support for the dome, and the overall spatial effect suggests that the chapels were carved from the solid exterior wall. Had the dome been constructed, its

Michelozzo di Bartolomeo (1396–1472), a student of Brunelleschi, worked not only in Florence but also in other cities of northern Italy. Although not as original a designer as Brunelleschi, Michelozzo was a capable architect and was awarded several commissions by the Medici. Most noteworthy of these was the Palazzo Medici (Figures 9.15, 9.16) in Florence, begun in 1444 after an earlier design by Brunelleschi was rejected as being too ostentatious. The client, Cosimo de' Medici, did not want a grandiose palace that would arouse feelings of envy among other important families in the city. Miche-

FIGURE 9.15 *Michelozzo: Palazzo Medici, Florence, 1444.* (Photo: School of Architecture, University of Tennessee)

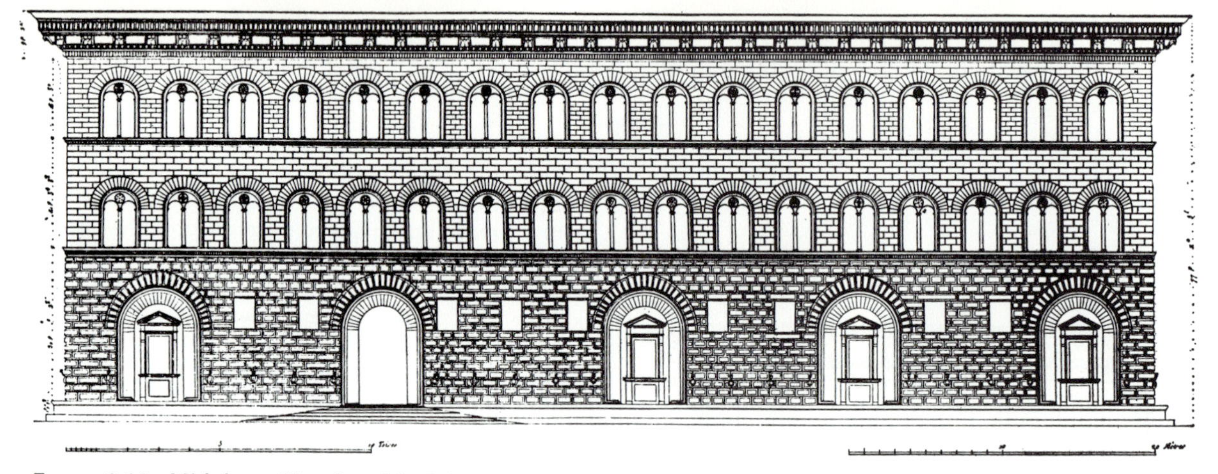

FIGURE 9.16 *Michelozzo: Elevation of the Palazzo Medici, Florence. Drawing includes later extension of the palace.* (From A. Grandjean de Montigny and A. Famin)

lozzo's design for the Medici Palace reflects the architecture of traditional Florentine domestic buildings. In plan the building is square with a central courtyard to serve as a circulation core for the perimeter rooms, which open one to another without a corridor connection (Figure 9.17). (Such an arrangement of rooms is termed *en suite.*) The street elevation features a three-tiered façade, consisting of rock-faced **rusticated** stone at the street level, smooth rusticated masonry with deeply raked joints at the second level, and smooth **ashlar** at the third level below a ten-foot-high crowning cornice of egg-and-dart molding. The cornice projects out eight feet from the building, supported by acanthus leaf **modillions** (brackets), and it combines with the string courses between floor levels to create a strong horizontal emphasis, even though the façade is eighty-three feet high.

FIGURE 9.17 *Michelozzo: Plan of the Palazzo Medici, Florence. Plan includes later addition.* (From A. Grandjean de Montigny and A. Famin)

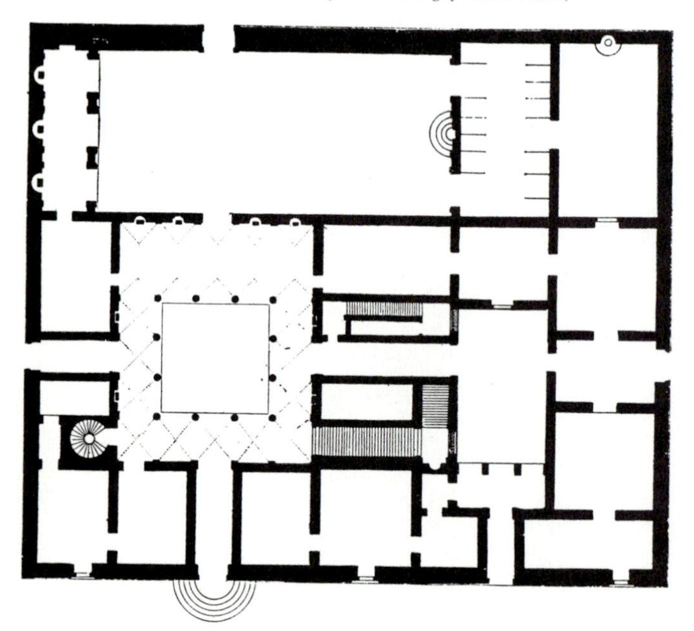

The ground floor originally had three open arches along the street, the central one giving access to the courtyard and rooms serving the Medici banking business. From the courtyard a staircase led to the major family rooms on the second floor or **piano nobile.** Deep shadows in the courtyard provide a cool and quiet core for the house, and the upper-level galleries, which provide access to individual, high-ceiling rooms, promote ventilation for the comfort of the inhabitants. Typical Romanesque windows with circular heads are used throughout. Romanesque arcading, as used by Brunelleschi at the Foundling Hospital, surrounds the courtyard. Turning the internal corner of this space created design problems where two arches intersect at right angles and are supported on a single column (Figure 9.18). Windows in the piano nobile, which are centered over the arches below, thus come together closely at the corner, breaking the rhythm of the courtyard façades. The solution built here, where a single column carries the load, also creates a visual sense of weakness where one would desire a sense of strength.

FIGURE 9.18 *Michelozzo: Interior court of the Palazzo Medici, Florence.* (Photo: Wodehouse)

Cosimo's grandson Lorenzo, known as *Il Magnifico,* patronized artists who followed the traditions of Brunelleschi as his grandfather had done. Guiliano da Sangallo (1445–1516) was commissioned in 1480–1485 to design a villa for the Medici at Poggio a Caiano, five miles from Florence (Figures 9.19, 9.20). Here a two-story, barrel-vaulted central hall links the four independent corner apartments. This segregates the various families within the Medici household, with the central room being used for grand gatherings. The entrance porch, barrel-vaulted along its length, with columns, entablature, and pediment, shows the Renaissance architects' increasing facility in the use of classical elements.

FIGURE 9.19 *Sangallo: Villa Medici, Poggio a Caiano, 1480–1485.* (Photo: Special Collections Library, University of Tennessee)

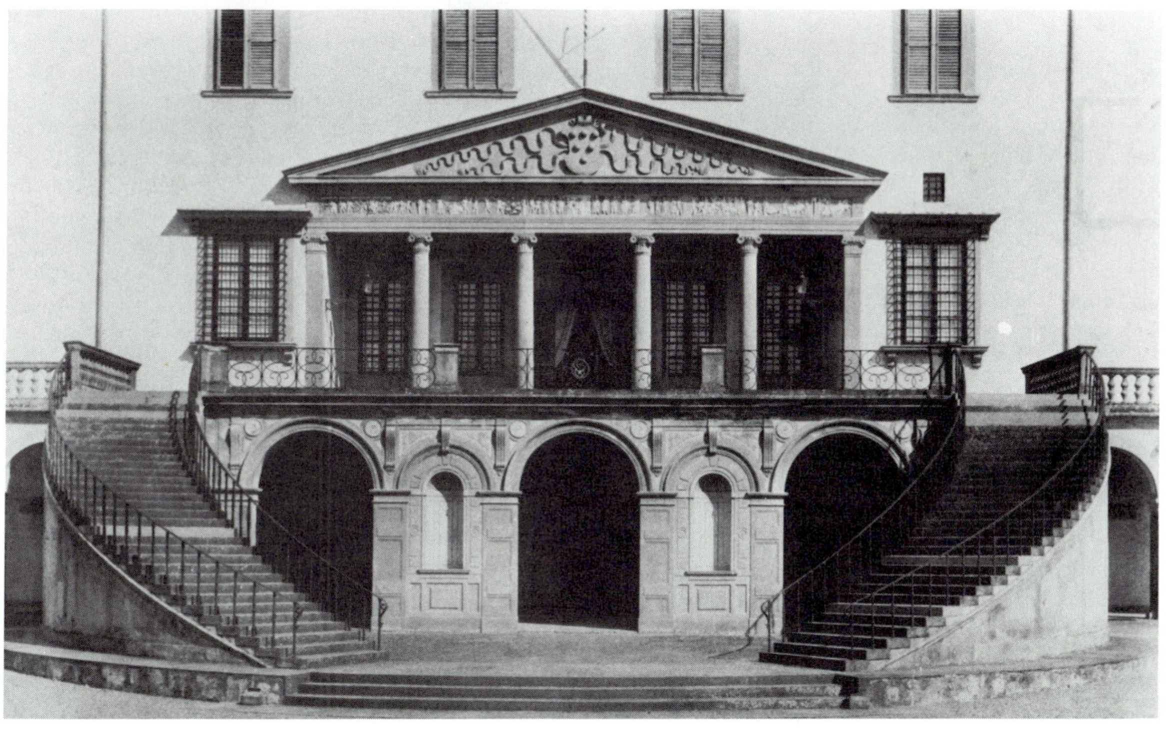

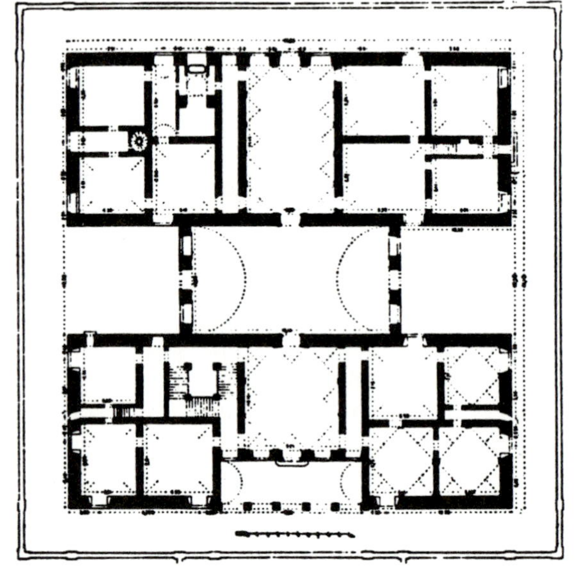

FIGURE 9.20 *Sangallo: Plan of the Villa Medici, Poggio a Caiano.* (From C. Stegmann and H. Geymuller)

Although the porch at Poggio a Caiano presents a similar design problem to the one faced by Brunelleschi a half-century earlier in the entrance porch to the Pazzi Chapel, Sangallo's design demonstrates a more mature understanding of Roman architecture.

Leone Battista Alberti

Compared to the talented and practical Brunelleschi, Leone Battista Alberti (1404–1472), was a classical theorist who approached architecture as a way to express his philosophy of design. Alberti, an accomplished scholar from an exiled Florentine family, became one of the most influential thinkers of his time. His education at the universities of Padua and Bologna included studies in mathematics, music, Greek, Latin, philosophy, and Roman law.

On completing his studies, Alberti entered the Papal Chancery in Rome as secretary to the chancellor. During this time, he began his first treatise, *Della Pittura* (On Painting). Living in Rome provided him many opportunities to meet artists visiting the monuments of antiquity, while his travels gave him the chance to observe the works of artists in many cities in northern Italy. Alberti searched the writings of Plato, Aristotle, Plutarch, and Pliny the Elder for references to the arts, and he carefully studied the collections of antique sculpture that were being assembled by patrons of the arts. His writings thus reveal a mixture of scholarly research and informed observations, some of which came from works by the artists to whom he dedicated his book. For example, he realized that gold leaf reflected light so that it was not a true representation of gold when it was applied to the surface of a painting. Alberti therefore recommended that a mixture of pigments be used to simulate gold objects in paintings. Similar visual studies led him to conclude that black and white do not exist in nature and that all colors appear to fade in relation to their distance from the observer. Such insights did not come from the writings of ancient authors. Alberti's study of ancient sculpture suggested an anatomical approach to the depiction of the human form. "Begin with the bones, then add the muscles and then cover the body with flesh in such a way as to leave the position of the muscles visible," he wrote. If draperies were to be added, he stated that they should be shown as if wafted by a light breeze, accurately revealing the underlying figure.

The manuscript of *Della Pittura,* finished in 1435, was dedicated to five young artists of Florence. Alberti's choice of these men reflected the high esteem he had for their works, for of all the artists he had met or whose works he had observed, these five came closest to creating a personal style that reflected the art of ancient Rome. We now regard these five artists — the sculptor Lorenzo Ghiberti (1378–1455), the architect Filippo Brunelleschi, the painter Masaccio (1401–1428), and the sculptors Donatello (1386–1466) and Luca della Robbia (1399–1482) — as the founders of the Renaissance.

Alberti's interest in architecture was probably first aroused when he came across an already well known manuscript, *De architectura libri decem* (Ten Books on Architecture) by Marcus Vitruvius Pollio, a Roman architect active about 30 B.C. Of all the Roman treatises on architecture, of which there must have been many, that of Vitruvius is one of the few to have survived until the fifteenth century by virtue of its inclusion in medieval monastic libraries. Vitruvius was not a skillful writer, and his text is often ambiguous. Nevertheless, as an authentic book from Roman times, his treatise was greatly respected by Renaissance architects.

In response to the obscurities in Vitruvius's text and in order to discuss principles of Roman buildings designed after the time of Vitruvius, Alberti began writing his own treatise, modeled on the antique text and, like it, organized into ten books (chapters). For example, Vitruvius's description of the knowledge an architect should possess states:

> Let him be educated, skillful with the pencil, know much history, have followed the philosophers with attention, understand music, have some knowledge of medicine, know the opinions of the jurists, and be acquainted with astronomy and the theory of the heavens.

The comparable passage by Alberti elaborates on the original text and probably describes Alberti himself:

> [He was] assiduous in science, and skilled in dealing with arms, horse, and musical instruments; as well as the pursuit of letters and the fine arts, he was devoted to the knowledge of the most strange and difficult things. His genius was so versatile that you might almost judge all the fine arts to be his. He played ball, hurled the javelin, ran, leapt, wrestled, and above all delighted in the steep ascent of mountains. He could leap over the shoulders of men and had almost no equal among those hurling the lance. . . . He was considered an expert among the leading musicians.

Alberti worked on his book from 1435 until his death, completing a first version by 1452, which was circulated in manuscript form and printed posthumously in Florence in 1485. As the first architectural treatise of the Renaissance, it is important for cataloging the features and proportions of the orders of antiquity and establishing a theory of harmonious proportions to be observed in buildings. Alberti adapted proportional systems expounded by Vitruvius because, as a typical Renaissance architect, he believed that they should encompass plan, elevations, and sections of a building. For example, church plans could be centralized, such as a circle, hexagon, octagon, decagon, or dodecagon, or based on a square, such as square-and-half, square-and-a-third, or double square. Whatever the plan selected, the three-dimensional realization was to be derived from it. To assume its proper symbolic role in the cityscape, the church should be centrally located, isolated from other structures so that its volume could be seen from all sides, and raised above ground level by a plinth or base.

Although Alberti was concerned with the theoretical and aesthetic implications of proportional systems, he was equally attentive to the practical aspects of architecture and city planning. Vitruvius had written of public health considerations in the siting of towns, and Alberti extended this analysis to include such factors as the purity of the water supply and the allocation of land use within the town. His suggested arrangements respond to both convenience and hygiene. He recommended that facilities for noxious trades, such as dye works and slaughterhouses, be positioned away from residential districts and studied the location of recreation facilities and the dimensioning of streets and open spaces with respect to heights of buildings. He proposed individual house plans with consideration for the needs and ordinary uses of the inhabitants. As kitchens are noisy, they should be away from quiet parts of the house and yet near enough to the dining room. Bedrooms should face east toward the rising sun, and the master's room should be near the library and office, whereas the bedroom of the mistress of the house should be near the children's quarters and the linen closets. Old people should have rooms without drafts, and guests should have rooms near the entrance to enable them and their friends to enter and leave without disturbing the whole household. A country house could be more elaborate in design than a town house, where restrained ornamentation could add to the unity of the streetscape. He even described the quality of basic building materials in a manner not too different from the style of modern specifications. Sand should be clean and free of impurities; lime should be well slaked; and timber should be straight, well seasoned, and free of knots and checks.

Some of this advice is reflected in Alberti's design for the façade of the Palazzo Rucellai, Florence (1446–1451), where the classical proportions of the orders of architecture have been applied with sensitivity to demarcate the different floors of the palace (Figure 9.21). Alberti had particular admiration for classical precedents to be found in the city of Rome. To organize the façade of this Florentine palace, he used the orders as superimposed on the Colosseum, interpreted as flat pilasters rather than as attached columns; and since the height of pilasters is directly related to their width, he raised the order

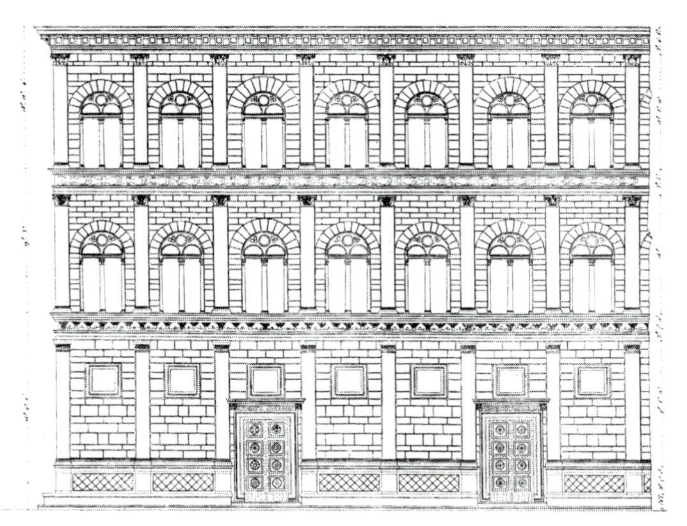

FIGURE 9.21 *Alberti: Palazzo Rucellai, Florence, 1446–1451.* (From A. Grandjean de Montigny and A. Famin)

FIGURE 9.22 *Alberti: S. Francesco, Rimini, begun 1450.* (Photo: Alinari)

FIGURE 9.23 *Alberti: S. Maria Novella, Florence, 1456–1470.* (Photo: School of Architecture, University of Tennessee)

of the ground floor (based loosely on the Tuscan) on a high plinth. This plinth is scored into diamond shapes in imitation of Roman *opus reticulatum*, where the work is used as an internal formwork for concrete walls. Here, however, it serves only as a surface texture derived from antique precedent. Alberti used a rather elaborate Corinthian order at the second-floor level and a simplified Corinthian order overhung by a generous cornice on the third story.

Alberti's four other major commissions were for ecclesiastical structures. Sigismondo Pandolfo Malatesta was his client for the modernization of the thirteenth-century church of S. Francesco at Rimini (Figure 9.22), begun in 1450 but never completed. A medal cast in 1450 by Matteo de' Pasti, Alberti's assistant on the site, illustrates the projected Tempio (an addition to S. Francesco where Malatesta entombed the remains of Gemistus Pletho, an authority on Plato and apostle of Renaissance paganism) with a triumphal arch front and a hemispherical dome over the east end. Of the triple arches on the west front, the widest central one distinguished the entrance, while side arches with blank panels were planned to have niches for the sarcophagi of Sigismund and his mistress, Isotta. Left unfinished at Malatesta's death in 1466, the Tempio's main façade lacks its concluding upper story, but enough remains to show Alberti's desire to create a classical composition on a basilican form by using scroll brackets to hide the lower roof levels and adding an upper-level arch over the doorway to complete the façade. Alberti's renovations of the side walls of the church encase the original medieval building like a screen, and here the deep arch recesses frame sarcophagi intended for Renaissance artists, writers, and philosophers.

The task of adapting classical details to the façade of a basilica was a compositional problem for Renaissance architects. Alberti's façade for S. Maria Novella, Florence (ca. 1456–1470) is the first completed design for a church façade of the Renaissance, but in some respects it is an extension of eleventh-century Florentine tradition executed with geometric panels of white and green marbles (Figure 9.23). Alberti was obliged to preserve some aspects of the Gothic façade, particularly the pointed arches of the ground level and the circular window above the central entrance. Rudolf Wittkower's analysis of the façade emphasizes the predominance in the composition of the square as a unifying element (Figure 9.24). As at the Tempio, Alberti attempted here to unify the façade by linking lower aisle roofs to the pedimented higher nave with flanking scrolls, a solution on which he would improve in projects in Mantua, where he designed two churches that today are essentially incomplete. S. Andrea (1472–1494) has an entrance portico based on a Roman triumphal arch, a treatment that was originally intended for entrances into the east

FIGURE 9.24 *Alberti: Façade proportions of S. Maria Novella, Florence.* (From P. Laspeyres with superimposed grid)

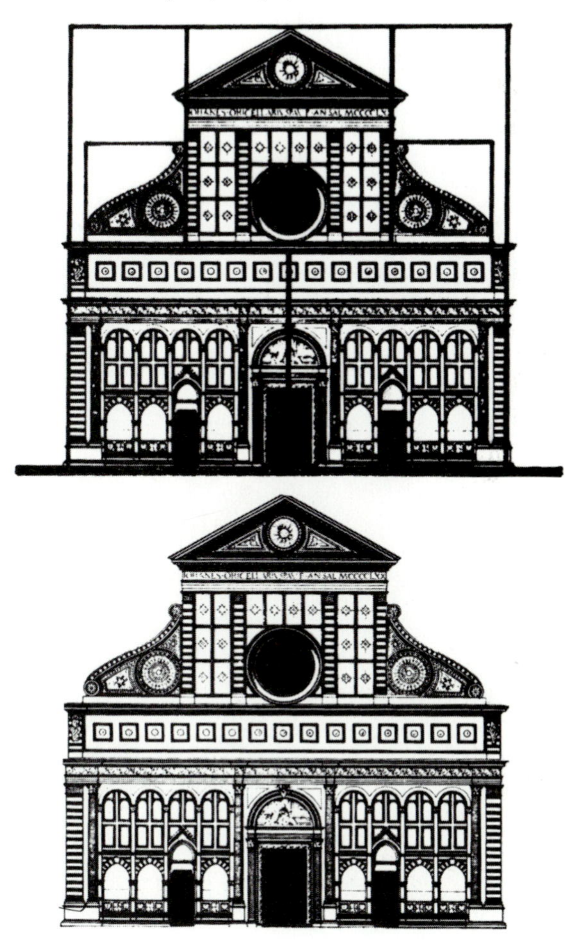

OROLOGERIA

◀ FIGURE 9.25 *Alberti: S. Andrea, Mantua, 1472–1494.* (Photo: Alinari)

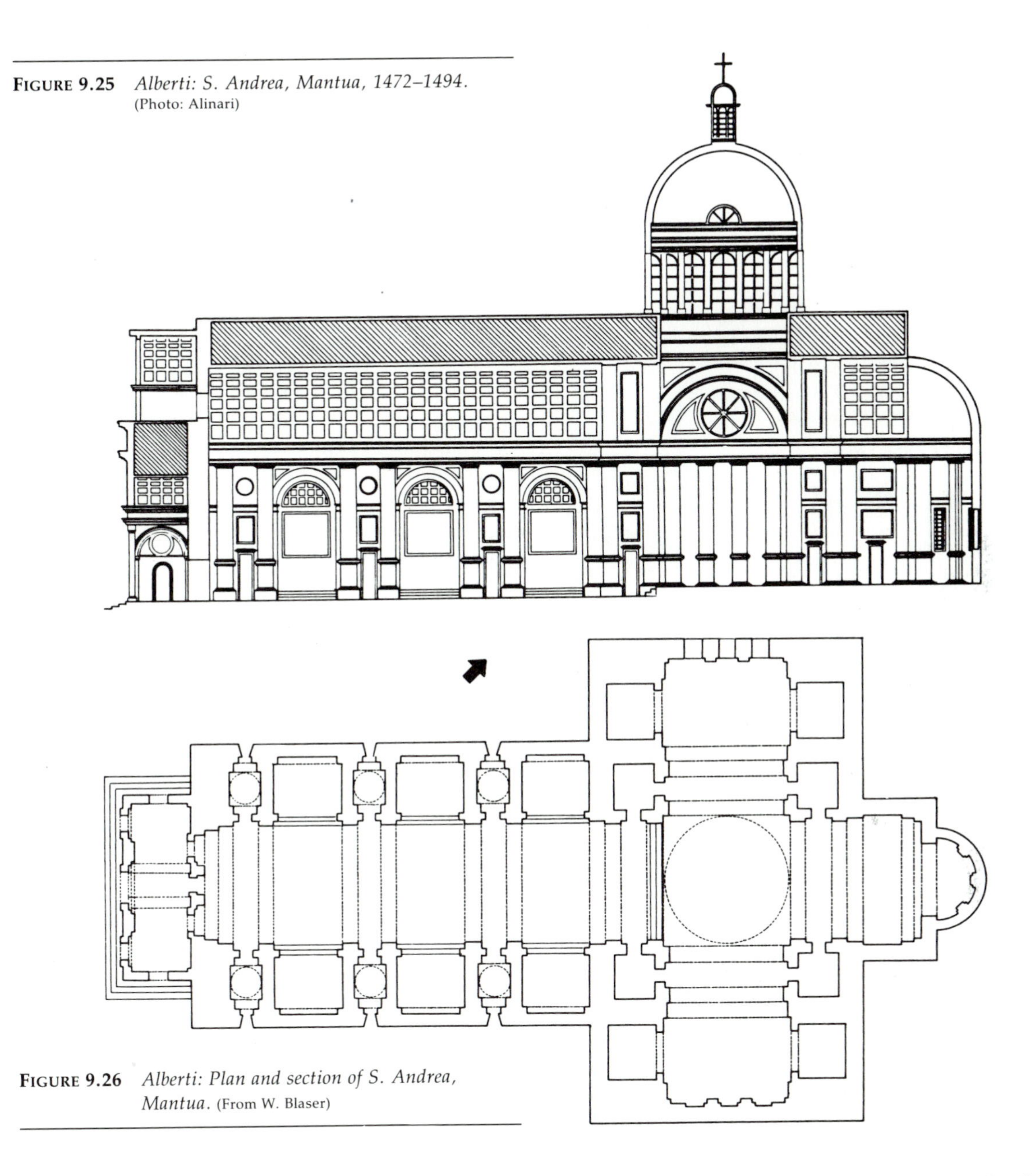

FIGURE 9.26 *Alberti: Plan and section of S. Andrea, Mantua.* (From W. Blaser)

and west transepts as well (Figures 9.25, 9.26). The major order of Corinthian pilasters on pedestals, which supports the entablature and pediment of the external portico and the subsidiary order of pilasters, is continued internally as a rhythmic series of elements framing three chapels on either side of the nave. Alberti's innovative use of the triumphal arch on a bold scale for the façade is matched by his unification of exterior and interior through the repetition of the A-B-A rhythm.

FIGURE 9.27 *Alberti: S. Sebastiano, Mantua, 1459.* (Photo: Alinari)

S. Sebastiano (1459) was designed as a Greek cross plan with a hexastyle pilastered temple front, the second and fifth pilasters having been omitted (Figure 9.27). There is a clear possibility that Alberti intended to build steps the full width of the portico, as in the temples of antiquity. The central interior space is spanned by a groin vault, not a dome as one might expect; the stubby arms of the Greek cross are barrel-vaulted. In its present incomplete state, the church does not clearly reflect its designer's intentions. Alberti's goal of a centrally planned temple was also represented in Perugino's fresco, *Giving of the Keys to St. Peter* (1481–1482), Raphael's *The Marriage of the Virgin* (1504), and the *cassone* panels (the sides of a wooden chest) of Luciano Laurana in the Palazzo Ducale in Urbino. Each of these art works depicts the Albertian ideal of the temple of God in the center of a geometrically planned city.

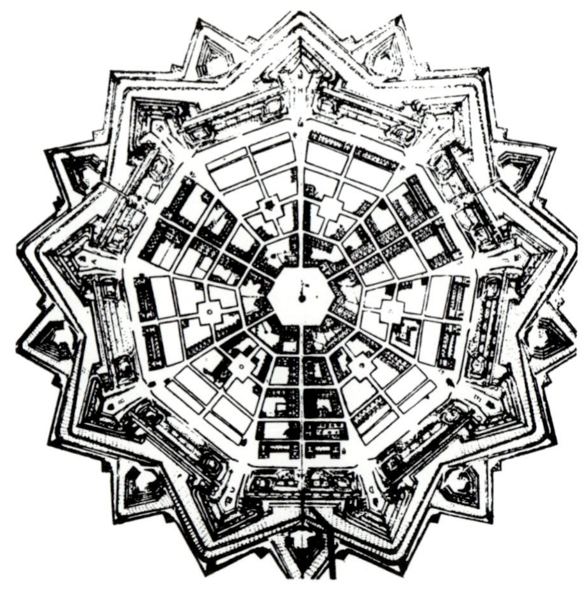

FIGURE 9.28 *Palmanova, 1593.* (Delineator: Cacogliatti)

Alberti's design for S. Sebastiano, as well as his theoretical writings, emphasized the ideal city form, in which a centrally planned church is set in a broad piazza in the middle of the town. The horizontal cornice lines of the buildings lining the approach streets converge as lines of perspective at the focal point, the church. This ideal was less often realized by architects than by painters, who were not restrained by the physical dimensions of actual cities. Renaissance placement of the church contrasts with medieval practice, where the church commonly formed part of the piazza's edge, if there was an open space at all. Ideal city schemes drawn by various Renaissance architects often extended the centralized concept to include radial streets and a polygonal town wall with arrowhead-shaped bastions at the vertices. Such fortifications are also a departure from the towers and turrets of medieval city walls. Changes in military technology, most notably the introduction of metal cannonballs and gunpowder after 1400, rendered high city walls vulnerable, for a well-placed shot could shatter the masonry. Renaissance town walls were thus low and earth-sheltered, to absorb the impact of cannonballs, and complex outerworks of ditches and moats set in the cleared area beyond the wall impeded an attacking army's advance. Cannons pivoted on the bastions could direct their fire over a range of more than 180 degrees, even shooting parallel to the town walls if necessary.

Few existing cities could transform themselves totally into this Renaissance ideal of civic design, but many modified their fortifications, and the concept of an ideal town center influenced urban designs. One actual town, Palmanova, built late in the sixteenth century, followed the pattern well (Figure 9.28). It was constructed on the mainland north of Venice to protect that city from an anticipated invasion by the Turks, an attack that never came. (The Turks besieged Vienna instead and were defeated there.) Because Palmanova was primarily a military outpost, it had the commander's office in its central space rather than the church, which was placed at the side of the piazza.

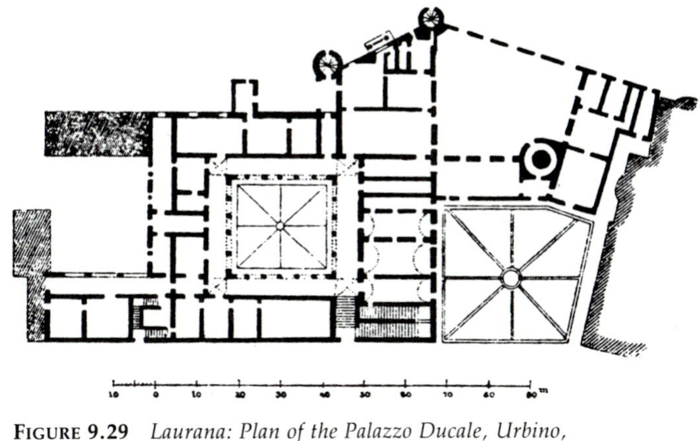

FIGURE 9.29 *Laurana: Plan of the Palazzo Ducale, Urbino, 1465–1472.* (From J. Burkhardt)

THE SPREAD OF THE RENAISSANCE

As the Renaissance expanded beyond Florence, it developed different qualities. Not far from the domain of Sigismondo Malatesta at Rimini is Urbino, situated in hilly terrain about twenty miles from the east coast of Italy. Here the humanist and *condottiere* Federigo da Montefeltro held court, governing an area of about 3600 square miles that included about 400 villages. Federigo was a loyal commander who served the dukes of Naples and Milan and three Popes and raised an army for Florence in 1448. His military accomplishments were balanced by his patronage of liberal learning. Humanists resided at his court, and thirty or forty scribes were employed to hand-copy ancient manuscripts.

Francesco di Giorgio was Federigo's engineer, and the Dalmatian-born Luciano Laurana was his architect for the Palazzo Ducale in Urbino (1465–1472) (Figure 9.29). The palace is centered around a **cortile** but is slightly more rambling in plan than a typical Florentine merchant's residence. Rooms are large, light, and airy, with high, billowing, sail-like vaulted ceilings, all constructed in masonry for fire resistance. The design is mature and articulate, as can be seen in the corner of the cortile where the colonnades end on half columns abutting pilastered piers (Figure 9.30). These give strength to the corner while preserving the rhythm of the windows on upper floors, two qualities lacking in the analogous situation at Michelozzo's Medici Palace. An inscription on the entablature above the colonnade praises Federigo. The walls of his small study are covered with exquisite variegated wood intarsia (inlay) executed

FIGURE 9.30 *Laurana: Palazzo Ducale, Urbino.* (Photo: Alinari)

by Baccio Pontelli to designs made by Botticelli. Cupboards with doors ajar exhibit their contents. A spinet, a squirrel, and a basket of fruit on the ledge of a colonnaded opening are all rendered in different colored woods on the two-dimensional surface. Even the distant landscape is shown beyond the simulated open window. Such a unified extension of space beyond the actual walls of a room anticipates sixteenth-century design.

Architecturally Venice was like Ravenna in being linked to the trading patterns of Constantinople and thus tending to cling to medieval and Byzantine traditions after Renaissance ideas had reached other Italian cities. Although Venice ultimately contained a considerable amount of Renaissance architecture, the early style developed as a variant relying on local traditions, climate, and disposition. Mauro Codussi (ca. 1440–1504) represents a progressive element in Venetian architecture, and his Palazzo Vendramini-Calergi (1500–1510) has pilasters, columns, and cornices of the Corinthian order, framing large round-headed windows that are also decorated with classical detailing (Figure 9.31). These large windows catch the breezes across the lagoon, thereby replacing the courtyard that figured so prominently in the domestic architecture of the Italian mainland. Martino Lombardo employed perspective in low-relief panels (by Tullio Lombardo) at

FIGURE 9.31 *Codussi: Palazzo Vendramini-Calergi, Venice, 1500–1510.* (Photo: Special Collections Library, University of Tennessee)

the ground level of the Scuola di S. Marco (1487–1490) (Figure 9.32). The scenes are lions (the animal identified with St. Mark) peering out from an implied barrel-vaulted space behind the plane of the façade.

For almost thirty years before being sacked in 1499 by the forces of Louis XII of France, Milan was a focal point of the Renaissance, attracting both Leonardo da Vinci (1452–1519) and Donato Bramante (1444–1514) in the early 1480s. Renaissance influence had come early to Milan when Francesco Sforza gave Cosimo de' Medici a palace for a branch of the Medici bank, vital to Florentine trade links with the north. Michelozzo's alterations to the two-story palace, which became the Banco Mediceo in the 1460s (Figure 9.33), paid homage to the applied brick and terra-cotta decorative traditions of Milan. The bank's central entrance is quite elaborate, almost akin to the flamboyance of northern Gothic, with cusped and pointed arches set between roundels. Antonio Averlino, called *Il Filarete* (ca. 1400–1469), a Florentine architect and sculptor, used a similar combination of elements on the Ospedale Maggiore (Figure 9.34) in Milan, dated about 1460–1465. Filarete visited his hometown to analyze Brunelleschi's design for the Ospedale degli Innocenti, and patterned the continuous arcade of his Ospedale Maggiore after the earlier design. Other elements remain Gothic, such as the pointed and flamboyantly decorative windows set between columns at ground level and in rectangular frames on the upper levels. Filarete's plan for the hospital consisted of two cruciform wards with central observation points, which, with a continuous rectangular perimeter of accommodations, created eight courtyards, and an additional major courtyard projected to contain a centrally planned chapel. Filarete became interested in centralized Renaissance geometry, writing a *Trattato d'architectura* (Treatise on Architecture) in 1461–1464, one copy of which was dedicated to Piero de' Medici, son of Cosimo and father of Lorenzo, and another to Francesco Sforza, his patron from 1451 to 1465. To flatter his patron Filarete projected an imaginary ideal city named Sforzinda.

More typical of Milanese architecture than the combination of Gothic and Renaissance features in buildings by Michelozzo and Filarete is the Certosa

FIGURE 9.32 *Lombardo Brothers: Scuola di S. Marco, Venice, 1487–1490.* (From J. Guadet)

FIGURE 9.33 *Michelozzo: Banco Mediceo, Milan, 1460s.* (From C. Gurlitt)

FIGURE 9.34 *Filarete: Ospedale Maggiore, Milan, 1460–1465.* (From J. Guadet)

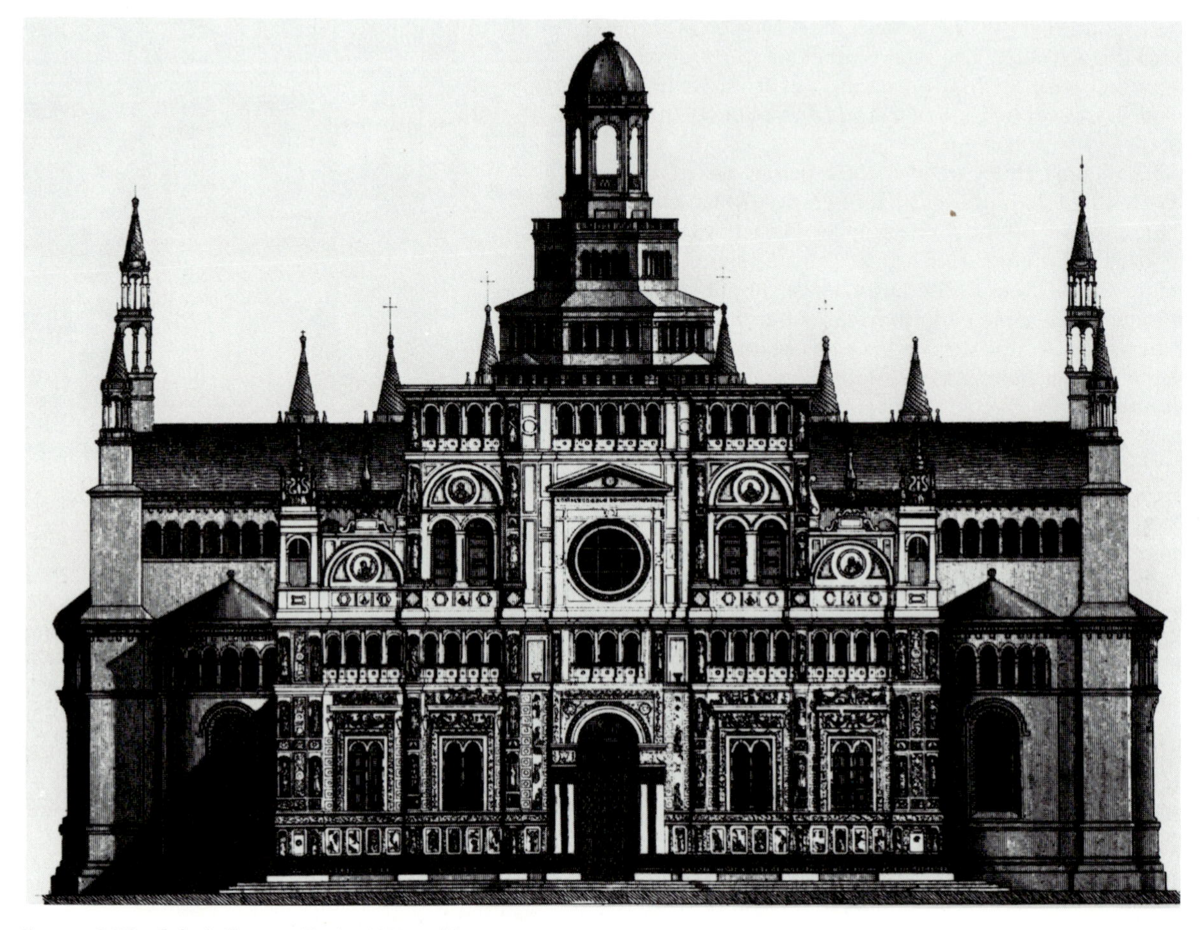

FIGURE 9.35 *Solari: Certosa, Pavia, 1459 and later.* (From J. Heck)

(Figure 9.35), a Carthusian monastery located just outside Milan at Pavia. Begun in 1396, the brick and terra-cotta church was finished in 1497. Completion of the marble exterior to designs of Guiniforte Solari (1429–1481) was the climax of building operations begun in 1473, although the façade design dates back to about 1459. It incorporates both Gothic and Renaissance elements in a profusion unsurpassed anywhere. Niches, medallions, arcades, columns, cornices, and buttressing compete within an allover pattern of surface relief on this ornate design.

Milan Cathedral dates from approximately the same period. It was begun in 1385, and the choir and transepts were completed by 1450. The nave and aisles have a scholastic, almost Renaissance geometry established by the proportion system used in the design made by Gabriel Stornaloco and others in 1391. Pythagorean and equilateral triangles are employed on a vertical and horizontal grid having a module of fourteen braccia (approximately twenty-eight feet), so that vaulting between the inner and outer aisles on either side of the nave springs from capitals fifty-six feet above floor level. Between the inner aisles and nave, the vaults spring at eighty feet, and across the nave the vaulting has its apex at 152 feet. Milan Cathedral thus reflects profuse late Gothic detailing and proto-Renaissance proportional simplicity.

Renaissance influence devoid of Gothic associations reached Milan in 1481–1482 when Donato Bramante, a student of Laurana at Urbino, arrived at about the same time as Leonardo da Vinci. During 1481 Leonardo had written to Lodovico Sforza, advertising himself as a military engineer seeking employment. His letter discussed siege bridges, the removal of water from moats, cannon to "throw out stones similar to a tempest," secret tunnels, tanks, dart throwers, and numerous field pieces. The letter ended by stating that in times of peace he was also competent in architecture, sculpture, and painting. Furthermore, Leonardo wanted to start work on a bronze equestrian statue of Lodovico's father, Francesco Sforza.

Leonardo prepared sketchbooks illustrating his inventions, observations, experiments, and discoveries to document his potential to prospective clients. Pages from these sketchbooks, which have been widely dispersed over the centuries, include anatomical drawings; studies of geological formations, air currents, and water movements; proposals for architecture and city planning; and a host of drawings, sketches, and studies related to his paintings and sculptures. Other drawings illustrate his inventiveness in such diverse devices as canal locks; underwater craft; parachutes; helicopters; wing attachments for flying; and tanks, guns, cannon, and other instruments of war. Leonardo's experiments and research brought him close to understanding blood circulation in the human body, to verifying that the earth was more than 5000 years old, and to proposals for magnifying glasses to observe the moon, all discoveries that would later be made independently by other men. In his sketchbooks Leonardo noted various designs for centrally planned churches (Figure 9.36), and S. Maria della Consolazione at Todi (begun in 1508) (Figures 9.37, 9.38) is so similar to some of Leonardo's sketches

FIGURE 9.36 *Leonardo da Vinci: Sketches for centralized churches.* (Photo: Bulloz/Institute de France)

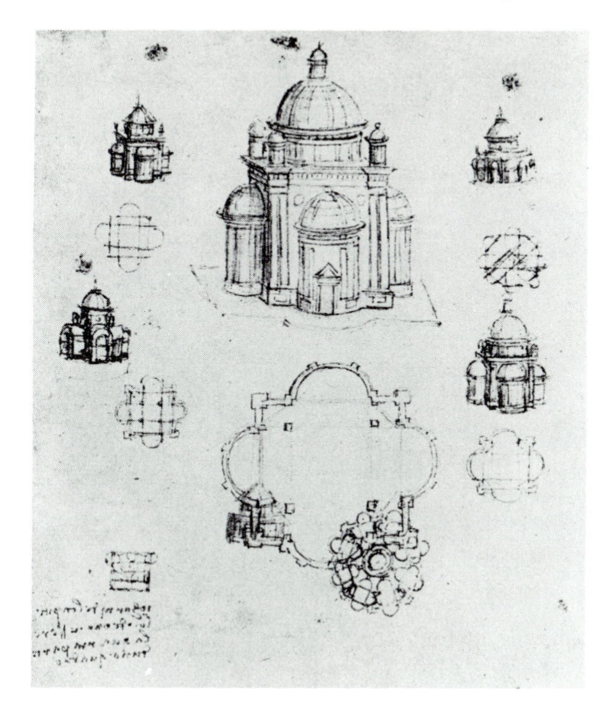

FIGURE 9.37 *Caprarola: S. Maria della Consolazione, Todi, 1508.* (Photo: Alinari)

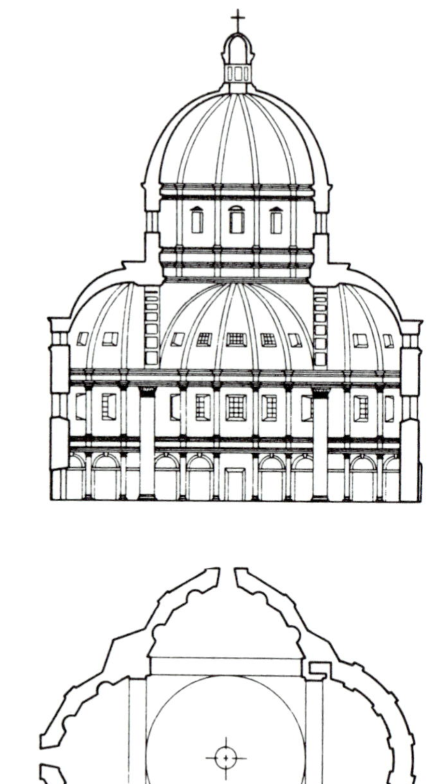

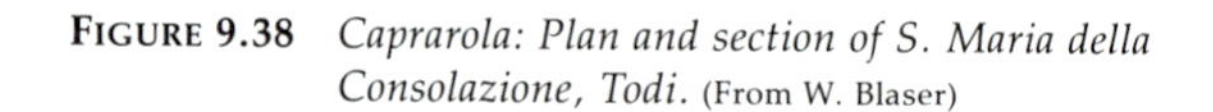

FIGURE 9.38 *Caprarola: Plan and section of S. Maria della Consolazione, Todi.* (From W. Blaser)

that its master mason, Cola da Caprarola, must have known of their existence, perhaps through Bramante's works. The church at Todi is square in plan, with semicircular apses on all four sides. Its plan is clearly articulated in its volumetric expression. The square generates a cube, while the apses are expressed as half-cylinders terminated by half-domes. Above the major interior space rises a dome set on a drum and pendentives.

At the Sforza court Leonardo designed costumes and masques for the marriage and entertainment of Ludovico and his wife Beatrice d'Este; he proposed a two-level city with pedestrian and vehicular separation; and, when the 1485 plague in Milan killed 5000 people, he suggested building ten satellite towns, each of 30,000 people, to reduce the likelihood of subsequent outbreaks. Between 1487 and 1490 he and Bramante worked on designs for the

FIGURE 9.39 *Bramante: S. Maria delle Grazie, Milan, 1492–1497.* (Photo: Alinari)

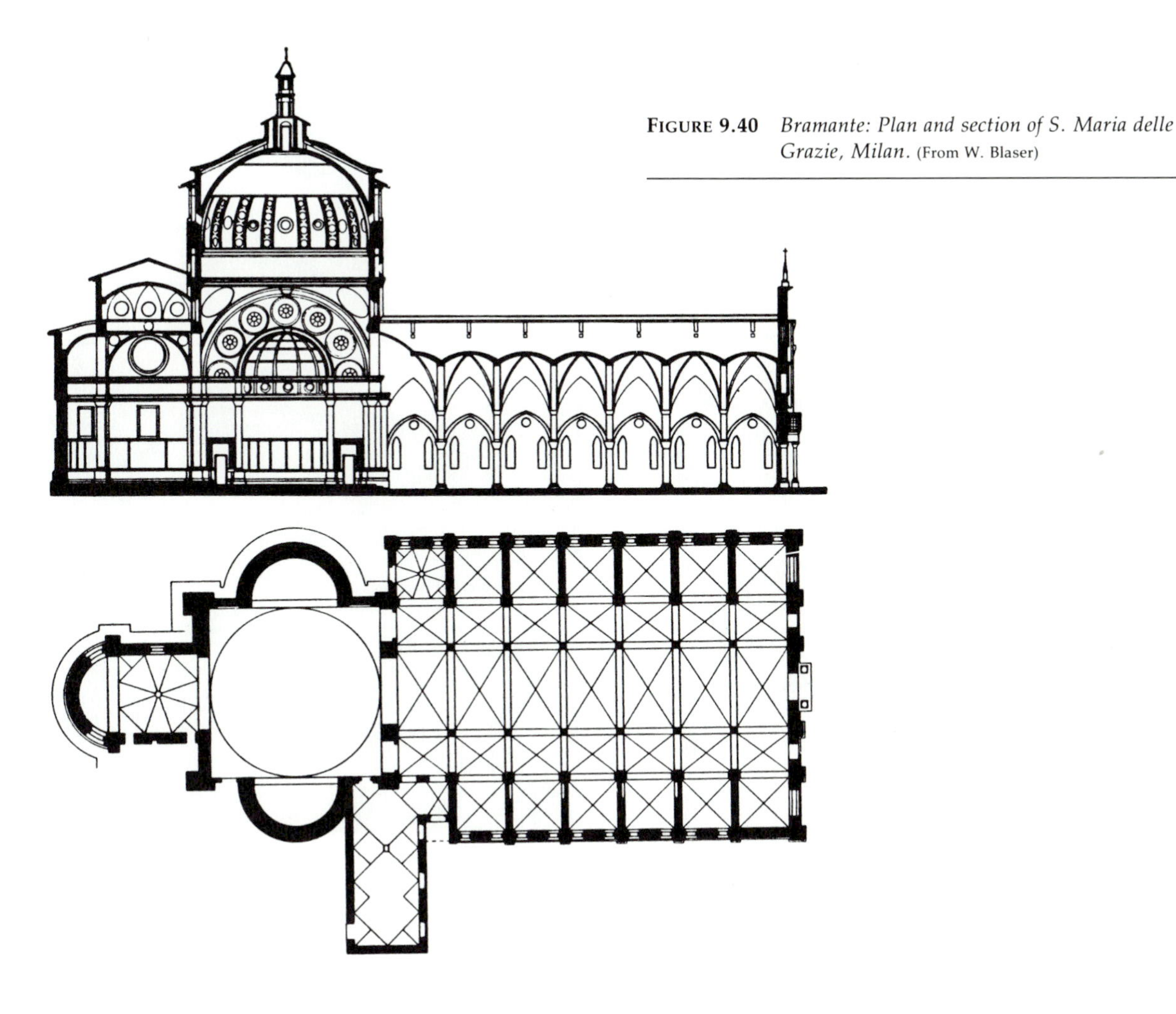

Figure 9.40 *Bramante: Plan and section of S. Maria delle Grazie, Milan.* (From W. Blaser)

central crossing of Milan Cathedral, but these were never built. The 1499 attack on Milan by French forces brought down the Sforza family, and Leonardo briefly sought employment as a military engineer to Cesare Borgia. Leonardo later returned to Milan to work for the French military governor, Charles d'Amboise, eventually becoming a painter and engineer for Louis XII. In 1516 he moved to France under the patronage of Francis I and lived in comfort near Amboise until his death in 1519.

From 1482 to 1499 in Milan Leonardo was a close associate of Donato Bramante, and he undoubtedly influenced two of the younger architect's commissions that emphasized concepts of central planning. The first project was an addition to the wide Milanese church of S. Maria delle Grazie (Figures 9.39, 9.40), a medieval building consisting of a nave, aisles, and chapels. Between 1492 and 1497 Bramante added the centralized crossing, capped by a dome sixty-five feet in diameter, and completed on either side by transept apses and a choir with apse. Although in harmony with the spirit of Leonardo's sketches of centrally planned churches and consistent with Renaissance detail on the interior, Bramante's design is *retarditaire,* its overly decorative exterior details falling into the Milanese tradition of brick and terra-cotta applique. The church's major interior feature, the hemispherical dome, is not even expressed on the exterior.

A far more original design is Bramante's earlier church, S. Maria presso S. Satiro (1482–1492), a rebuilding that included part of the old ninth-century

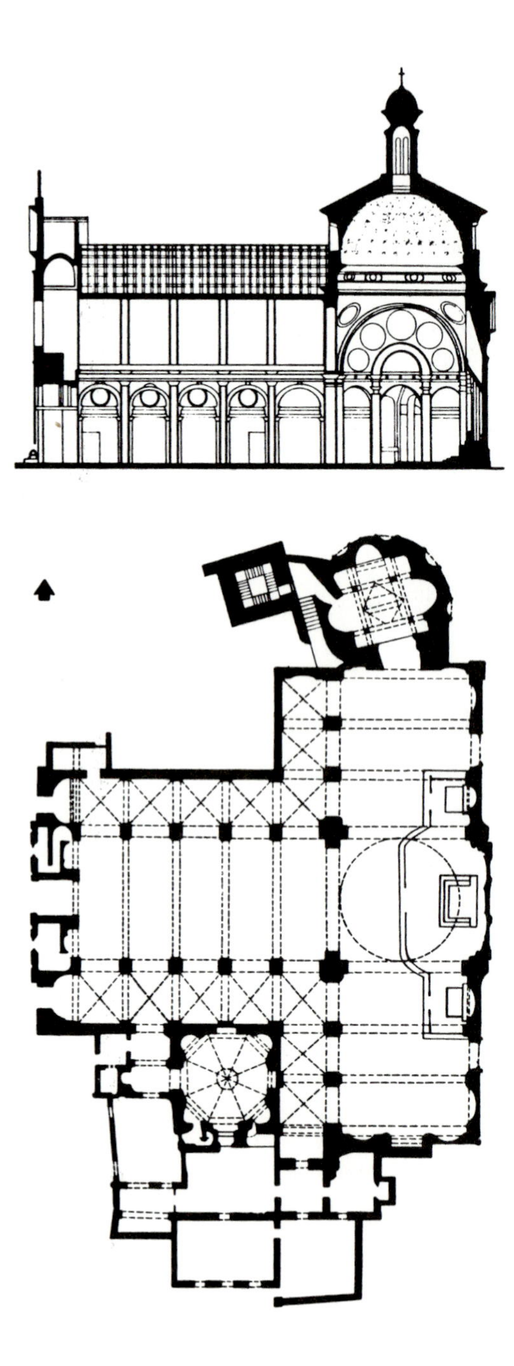

FIGURE 9.41 *Bramante: Plan of S. Maria presso S. Satiro, Milan, 1482–1492.* (From W. Blaser)

FIGURE 9.42 *Bramante: Interior of S. Maria presso S. Satiro, Milan.* (Photo: Wodehouse)

church and campanile of San Satiro (Figure 9.41). Bramante's design for the interior included a barrel-vaulted nave and transepts that intersect at a central crossing with a coffered dome on pendentives concluded by an oculus. An existing street restricted the site east of the crossing, and it prevented Bramante from adding a choir to complete the intended centrally planned space. Although the wall behind the altar is almost flush with the east wall of the transepts, Bramante created there a low relief that, when viewed on axis, has the convincing appearance of a barrel-vaulted choir (Figure 9.42). Using the illusionistic potential of one-point perspective, he simulated the space he wished to build in actuality, thereby creating what must be the ultimate use of linear perspective in fifteenth-century architecture.

THE HIGH RENAISSANCE IN ROME

Bramante's two churches in Milan were the beginnings of an evolutionary process that culminated in his designs for a new Basilica of St. Peter in Rome. After the sack of Milan in 1499, Bramante, then fifty-five, moved to Rome, where he was commissioned by Ferdinand and Isabella of Spain to design a chapel over the site where St. Peter was martyred. This commission imposed on him the task of designing a large monument or a small building to be placed in the center of the cloister at S. Pietro in Montorio. Bramante's solution, the Tempietto (begun 1502), consists of a cylinder surmounted by a drum and hemispherical dome, surrounded on the exterior by sixteen Tuscan columns (Figure 9.43). Tuscan pilasters on pedestals support a frieze on the interior. This carefully articulated, centrally planned temple fits into a tradition established in the writings of Vitruvius and extended by the theories of Alberti and Filarete and the sketches of Leonardo, that is, a circular temple standing at the center of a city. The Tempietto has the sculptural, three-dimensional quality established by Brunelleschi in S. Maria degli Angeli. It could have been inspired by the Temple of Vesta in Rome (see Figure 4.14), which dates to the third century B.C., but Roman circular temples were never concluded by a drum and dome. The harmonious integration of parts within the whole is remarkable; even the balustrade creates a pause in the ascending rhythm of elements. Bramante intended to rebuild the square cloister that defines the Tempietto's site in a concentric circular form to reinforce the idea of centrality, but his proposal remained unbuilt.

The Tempietto was a foretaste of Bramante's projected rebuilding of St. Peter's (1505), where his client was Pope Julius II. At the same time Michelangelo was also working for the pope, having been commissioned to design Julius's tomb. It was to measure twenty-three by thirty-five feet in plan; to have three tiers embellished with forty over-life-size sculptures; and to conclude with a portrait of Julius at the summit, symbolizing the apotheosis of the Holy Church. Such a huge monument would not fit readily into the old and crumbling fourth-century St. Peter's. Both Julius and Bramante first considered a centrally planned addition for the tomb at the western end of the existing church, similar to Bramante's addition to the church of S. Maria delle Grazie in Milan. Eventually, however, they decided to replace the old building entirely.

FIGURE 9.43 *Bramante: Tempietto S. Pietro in Montorio, Rome, begun 1502.* (From P. Letarouilly)

This was not the first Renaissance attempt to modify or add to St. Peter's. Pope Nicholas V had instructed Alberti to report on the condition of the building. Not surprisingly Alberti found the walls out of plumb and the 1100-year-old fabric in such a dilapidated state that he considered repairs inadvisable. Nicholas accepted this recommendation and in 1451 appointed Bernardo Rossellino to design an apse as the first stage of an anticipated new St. Peter's. The deaths of Nicholas in 1455 and of Rossel-

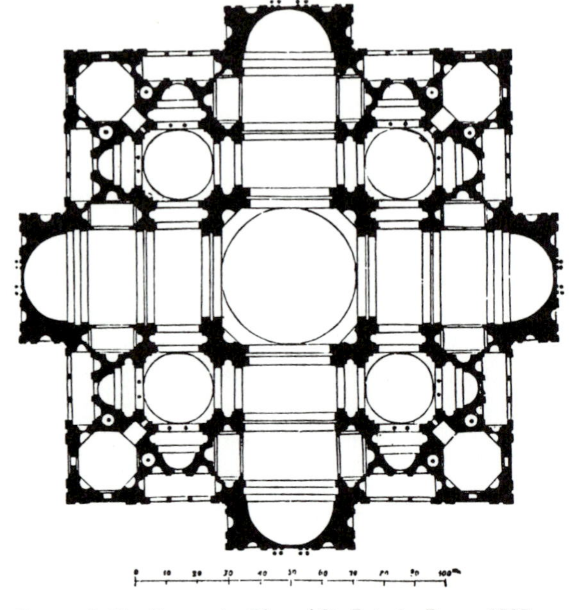

FIGURE 9.44 *Bramante: Plan of St. Peter's, Rome, 1505.* (From J. Burkhardt)

FIGURE 9.45 *Bramante: Cloister of S. Maria della Pace, Rome, 1504.* (From P. Letarouilly)

lino in 1464 terminated this project, even though Rossellino's choir was eventually built.

After this tentative beginning the rebuilding of St. Peter's languished through another fifty years of inaction. Once Julius II decided that a completely new church was the only suitable accommodation for the tomb he envisioned for himself, Bramante created an appropriately bold, Greek cross design in 1505 (Figure 9.44). A medal cast in 1506 depicts the scheme Bramante conceived, which represented a building of the scale of the Baths of Diocletian capped by a dome comparable to that of the Pantheon. This juxtaposition was carefully considered by Bramante. A drawing of the church in his notebooks showed it surrounded by gardens and a colonnade, while on the reverse was his drawing of the baths. Rather than continuing patterns of antiquity, Bramante was thus attempting to outdo Roman builders by proposing a domed structure more ambitious than any ancient edifice. The structural concept of a dome and drum supported on pendentives and semicircular arches actually had more in common with Byzantine works (themselves a development from Roman models) than with Roman constructions. Bramante's audacious design exceeded his structural understanding, however, for the piers shown on the plans would undoubtedly have been inadequate for the great loads imposed by the dome.

The cornerstone of this vast project was laid on April 18, 1506, as a labor force of 2500 began the foundations for the crossing piers. Bramante died in 1514, when the central piers were scarcely above ground level, and ultimately these were considerably enlarged to support Michelangelo's design for the dome. By the time the church was completed nearly 150 years later, almost every major architect of the sixteenth and seventeenth centuries had been engaged on the work at one time or another. The rebuilding of St. Peter's thus embraces work of several periods, from the High Renaissance to the Baroque.

High Renaissance buildings were generally more Roman and three-dimensional in spatial concept than the less massive Early Renaissance buildings. Architects such as Bramante had reconciled the theoretical postulates of Vitruvius, Alberti, and Leonardo with a thorough understanding of actual Roman practice and had achieved the confidence to design buildings suitable to the requirements of that age, while at the same time maintaining the spirit of antiquity. They handled matters of proportion, the manipulation of space, and correct detailing skillfully and subtly so that in the span of less than a century the explorations of Brunelleschi had matured into the calm, self-assured style of the High Renaissance.

While Bramante's projects in Milan link him with the end of the Early Renaissance, his later works in Rome place him firmly in the forefront of the High Renaissance. In addition to the Tempietto and his project for St. Peter's, Bramante designed the clois-

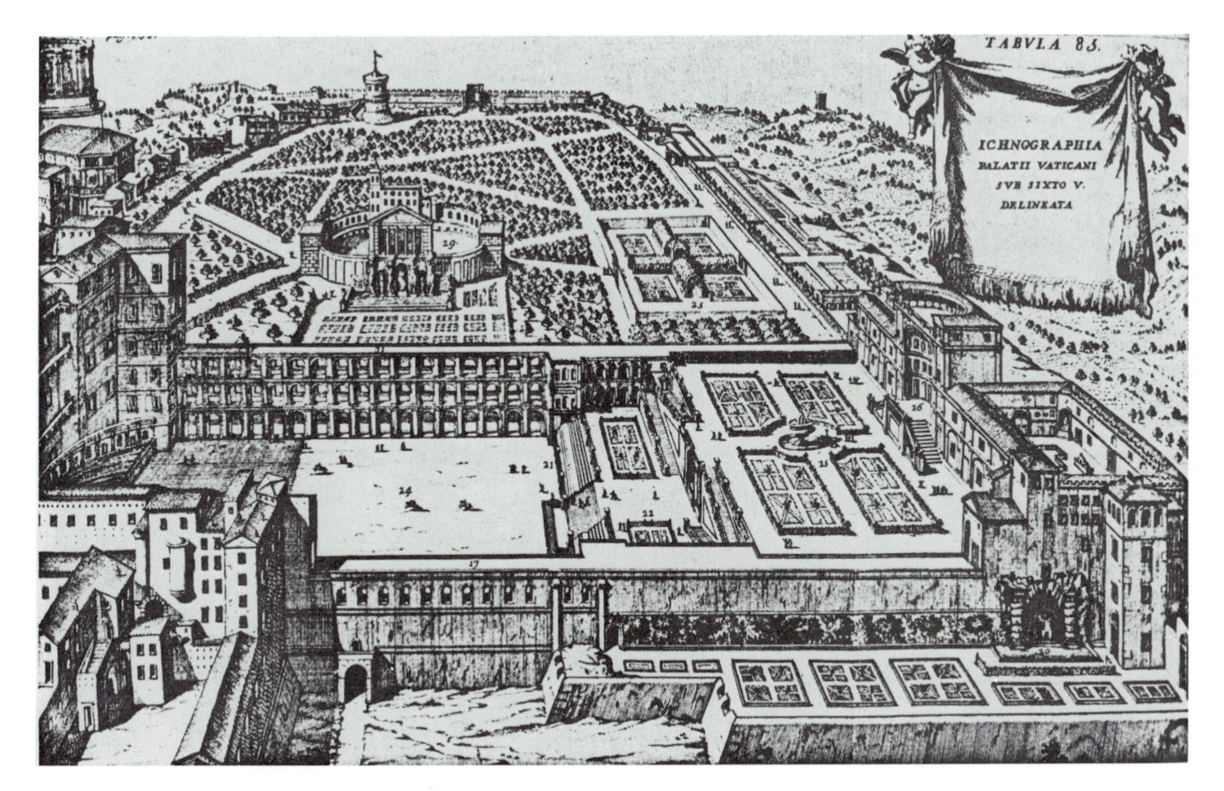

FIGURE 9.46 *Bramante: Belvedere Courtyard, Vatican, begun 1505.* (16th century engraving)

ter for S. Maria della Pace (1504), involving the kind of stacked arches and columns found on the Colosseum (Figure 9.45). The cloisters consist of piers and arches, with attached Ionic pilasters at ground level and columns alternating with piers supporting an architrave above. Bramante's design for the Belvedere Courtyard (Figure 9.46) of the Vatican Palace, a vast space measuring 950 by 225 feet, was a reinterpretation of antiquity and a continuation of themes from Imperial Roman villas. The courtyard was divided into three levels, with linking stairs providing a surround successively one, two, and three stories high. The Belvedere Courtyard was thus an early example of a Renaissance terraced garden layout with a theater at the lowest level (Figure 9.47). An exedra in the center of the upper courtyard has circular steps leading from it, flanked by a single story wall of arches between pairs of pilasters as a repetitive triumphal arch motif. All this work has been altered and modified in later periods, most notably by Sixtus V's library, which cuts across the original courtyard, eradicating the terracing and creating instead three smaller courts.

FIGURE 9.47 *Bramante: Section across the Belvedere Courtyard, Vatican.* (From J. Burkhardt)

FIGURE 9.48 *Bramante: House of Raphael, Rome, ca. 1512.* (Engraving by Lafreri)

Bramante also built a house for himself in Rome ca. 1512 (Figure 9.48). Like many urban dwellings it had shops at the street level, treated here as the rusticated base for pairs of engaged Doric columns articulating the piano nobile above. This design was a distinct innovation in palace façades because it gave a three-dimensional quality to the building, especially when compared with the flat modeling of the orders on Early Renaissance buildings such as the Rucellai Palace. Bramante's house, no longer extant, was purchased by the artist Raphael (1483–1520) after he had been summoned to Rome to decorate the papal apartments, and it became commonly known as the House of Raphael.

Raphael founded his architectural style on the Roman themes of Bramante, as can still be seen at the Villa Madama (so called because it became the dowry of Margaret of Parma, daughter of Charles V), begun in 1517 for Guilio Cardinal de' Medici, later Pope Clement VII (Figures 9.49, 9.50). The villa was to become a characteristic building type for Renaissance architects. In contrast to the urban dwelling or palace, the villa was a country retreat, ostensibly inspired by the Roman estate-farm, but in fact having few features of a practical dwelling house, such as kitchens or bedrooms. The essential architectural attribute was a **loggia** or open elevated porch, from which one could view the carefully designed gardens of the villa and perhaps enjoy a distant vista. The wealthy owner of a villa would come there to escape the city's summer heat, to rest and relax, and to stroll about and talk with friends. At the Villa Madama, the building was set into the hill on a south-facing slope of Monte Mario, beyond the

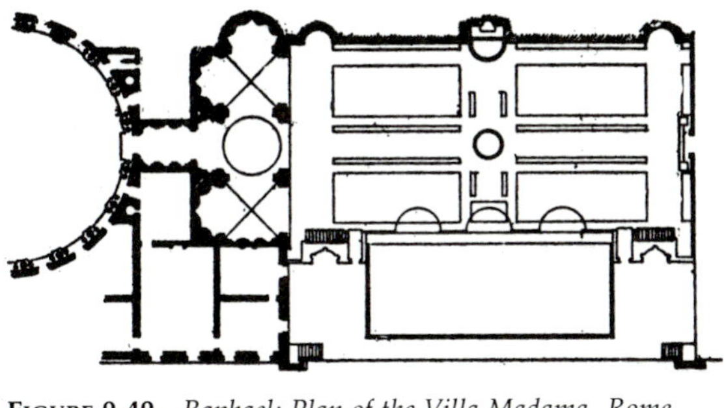

FIGURE 9.49 *Raphael: Plan of the Villa Madama, Rome, begun ca. 1516.* (From G. Gromort)

FIGURE 9.51 *Raphael: Interior of the Villa Madama, Rome, begun ca. 1516.* (Photo: Special Collections Library, University of Tennessee)

walls of Rome with a view over the city and the Tiber. The hill, terraced into a number of levels, had formal gardens with fountains spouting and pouring water from one level to another. Had its buildings been finished, the villa would have had a circular courtyard with a design based on an inverted Colosseum, off which loggias and other rooms would have radiated. Only half the work was completed, however. Its major space consists of a loggia, inspired in part by the three groin-vaulted bays of the Basilica of Constantine, except that the middle space here is covered by a dome on pendentives (Figure 9.51). Pavements were set in mosaic, and walls and ceilings were covered with frescoed festoons containing mythological, religious, and Medicean symbolism. Most of the paintings were completed after Raphael's death by his two major assistants, Giovanni da Udine, who rediscovered the lost technique of Roman stucco, and Giulio Romano (1499?–1546), of the Late Renaissance.

FIGURE 9.50 *Raphael: Section through the Villa Madama and adjoining gardens, Rome.* (From J. Burkhardt)

THE LATE RENAISSANCE

The era of the Late Renaissance was not a stylistic period of concerted effort toward a definite goal — as emulating antiquity was for the Early or High Renaissance — but a period of personal artistic expression. Whereas the High Renaissance was disciplined and resolute and in the realm of architecture attempted to produce integrated harmonious buildings, Late Renaissance architecture, sometimes termed Mannerism, tended toward disharmony, discord, imbalance, tension, distortion, and unresolved conflicts. The greatest exponents of the period were Michelangelo Buonarroti (1475–1564), Giorgio Vasari (1511–1574), Giulio Romano, and Andrea Palladio (1508–1580).

During the Renaissance the individual artist emerged as a distinct personality and was increasingly identified with his productions. But in the Late Renaissance architects developed a flair for exaggerated artistic statements loosely based on the traditions of antiquity. They began to exploit the void as a feature in buildings and civic designs, as can be seen in Giorgio Vasari's design for the Uffizi (Figure 9.52), begun in 1560 in Florence. The building, an office annex for the Palazzo Vecchio, consists of a long, narrow courtyard flanked on the two long sides by multifloor wings that have been given minimal horizontal articulation. One end of the courtyard terminates at the Arno River with a **Serliana** (a series of three openings, the center one wider and arched), and the opposite open end dis-

FIGURE 9.53 *Romano: Palazzo del Tè, Mantua, 1525–1534.* (Photo: Alinari)

charges into Piazza della Signoria, with the tower of the Palazzo Vecchio viewed off-center (see Figure 8.81). Both ends of the courtyard essentially dissolve into empty space. The focal point so admired by Renaissance designers had given way to nothingness.

Unlike many artists of the High Renaissance, Giulio Romano was actually born in Rome, so he understood antiquity from personal, intimate experience rather than from the study of classical precedent for stylistic reasons. It is therefore not surprising that, as one of the creators of Mannerism, Romano chose to represent the ruined condition of ancient monuments as his contribution to sixteenth-century architecture. This can be seen in one of his early paintings, *The Stoning of St. Stephen* (1523), in which Roman ruins in the background provide the setting.

Giulio's architectural works feature the willful and amusing misuse of classical elements. In his own house at Mantua (1544), he built a Pantheon Salon, with Julius Caesar, his namesake, carved over the fireplace. His most important building is the Palazzo del Tè (1525–1534), designed for Federigo II Gonzaga as a honeymoon villa on an island at the edge of Mantua (Figure 9.53). The Gonzaga were horse breeders, supplying steeds to the courts of Europe, and they were also extensively involved in political intrigue and military alliances. The palace was originally conceived as an enormous stable complex. It consists of a large square courtyard, enclosed on all four sides by a series of rooms en suite, with entrances centered on the north and east sides (Figure 9.54). A loggia on the west side leads into a garden, at the end of which is a semicircular colonnade. The garden is laid out in geometric flower beds, and a moat used for staging miniature naval battles is adjacent to the villa, which is linked to the garden by a bridge. The loggia is barrel-vaulted and supported on alternate paired and single columns, while the north entrance has rusticated columns, deliberately made to appear unfinished. These columns support lintels with keystones, above which is an octagonally coffered ceiling as in the Basilica of Constantine. In the courtyard heavy Doric columns support a light architrave with dropped triglyphs (Figure 9.55). Together with the unframed niches and windows, pediments lacking a bottom cornice, and heavy rustication, these features create a sense of ambiguity and tension.

The illusion of imbalance and the perverse use of classicism continues on the interior. The wall and ceiling surfaces of the rooms around the courtyard are filled with frescoes by Giulio Romano and his assistants, with additional enrichment provided by inlaid doors and mantels of oriental jasper, gold, and marble. Cracked brick lintels painted on the wall surfaces above doors create an uncomfortable psychological effect as one passes beneath. Above the cracked lintels in the Sala dei Giganti is painted a scene of great destruction, with the weight of collapsing columns crushing the limbs and bodies of

◄ **FIGURE 9.52** *Vasari: Uffizi, Florence, begun 1560.* (Photo: Alinari)

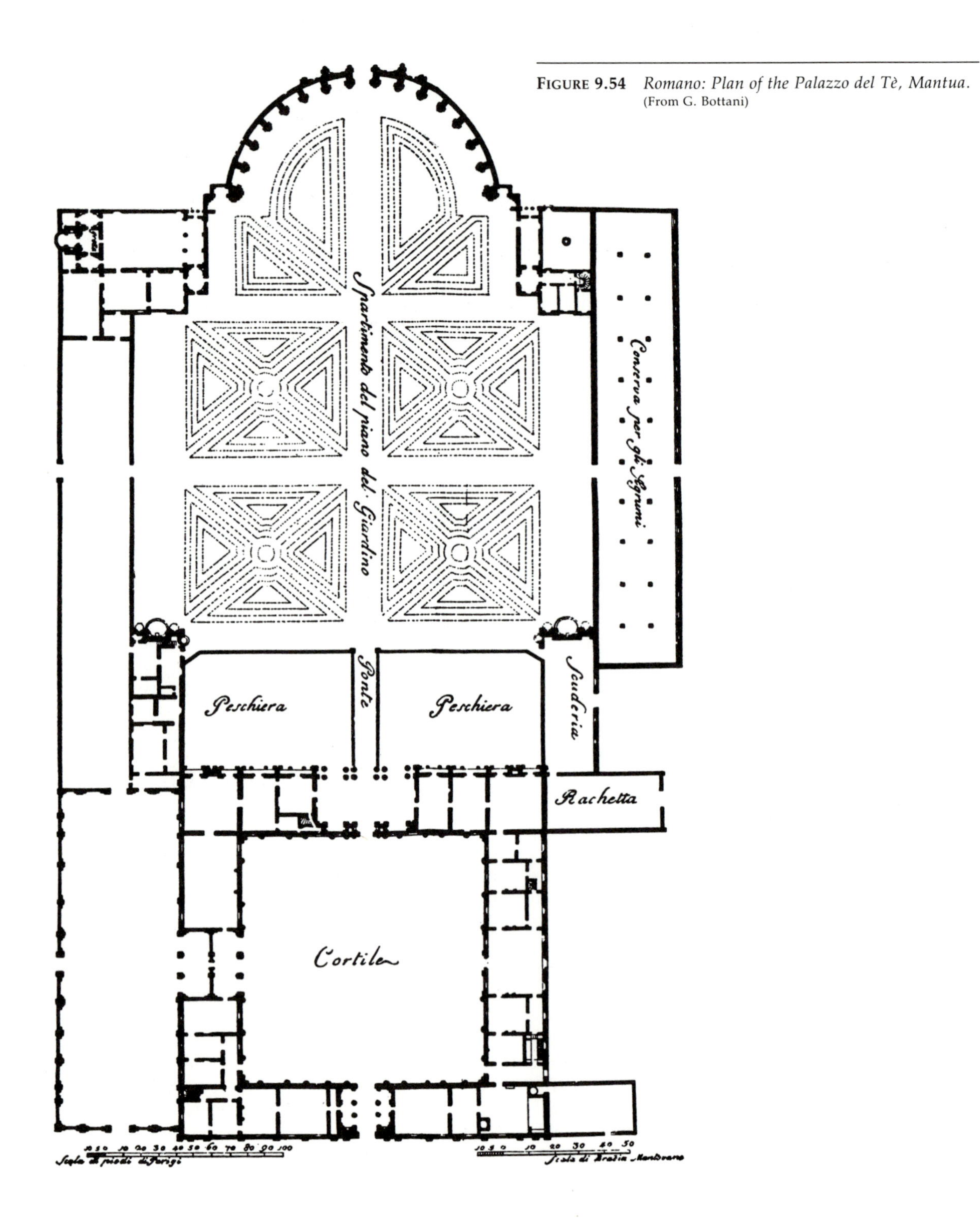

FIGURE 9.54 *Romano: Plan of the Palazzo del Tè, Mantua.* (From G. Bottani)

Figure 9.55 *Romano: Courtyard of the Palazzo del Tè, Mantua.* (Photo: Alinari)

giant figures, one going cross-eyed as his head becomes trapped between two falling boulders. Walls merge into the billowing clouds painted on the ceiling, the center of which carries a representation of a colonnaded drum supporting a hemispherical dome. Horses painted in the Sala dei Cavalli stand on cornices more than half the height of this large chamber, and behind them are landscapes seen through painted window surrounds between the pilasters and architectural detailing. On the outside the four-square building consists of variations on a theme of the Serliana. The Palazzo del Tè was never entirely finished, yet it remains a masterpiece of the Late Renaissance, designed by a sophisticated architect as a play on the conventions of classical architecture. Only those who share Romano's understanding of Roman architecture can fully appreciate his accomplishment.

Michelangelo

Michelangelo Buonarroti, widely regarded as one of the most creative geniuses in Western art, made important contributions to the fields of sculpture, painting, and architecture during the course of his long and productive life. The second son of a minor governmental official in Florence, he was apprenticed at the age of thirteen to the painter Domenico del Ghirlandaio, despite his father's reluctance to have his son become an artist. His training in sculpture began a year or so later when Michelangelo was invited to join the workshop sponsored by Lorenzo de' Medici as part of the Medici effort to revive the sculptural arts of antiquity. Until the death of Lorenzo in 1492, Michelangelo lived in the Palazzo Medici as a member of the household, gaining an humanist education from the eminent scholars, writers, and poets who gathered there under Lorenzo's patronage.

Under Pope Leo X, younger son of Lorenzo de' Medici and successor to Pope Julius II, Michelangelo embarked on his first of three architectural commissions for the monastery of S. Lorenzo, Florence, in 1515. His design for the façade of the basilican church was a screen consisting of two equally developed stories divided by an attic, forming a backdrop for relief panels and sculptures set in niches. Nothing had come of this design by the time Leo died in 1521, and the church exists today without a façade, but Michelangelo's proposals established a second tradition in façade architecture, providing an alternative to Alberti's S. Maria Novella type.

Before the façade design was abandoned the Medici asked Michelangelo to design a funerary chapel adjacent to the south transept for the burial of Lorenzo the Magnificent and four of the lesser

Medici, including Lorenzo, Duke of Urbino (grandson of Lorenzo the Magnificent), and Giuliano, Duke of Nemours (brother of Lorenzo the Magnificent and father of Pope Clement VII). This New Sacristy or Medici Chapel (Figure 9.56), was to complement Brunelleschi's Old Sacristy off the north transept (see Figure 9.7). Michelangelo paid homage to the older master by employing a similar form (a hemispherical dome on pendentives over the cubical main space) and using some of the same materials (white stucco walls trimmed with warm gray *pietra serena*). The tombs themselves are marble. The number of statues and Michelangelo's placement of them underwent a series of changes; his sketches show that he considered a central mausoleum, but he finally placed two sarcophagi on either side of the chapel. Each supports symbolic but unfinished sculptures of the Times of Day, with seated figures of the dukes Lorenzo and Giuliano placed above in niches set into the thickness of the wall. The large symbolic figures of Day and Night (on Guiliano's tomb) and Dawn and Dusk (on Lorenzo's) recline precariously on the top surface of the sarcophagi, their very weight seeming to cause them to slide off the curved lids. The ghoulish mask on Night emphasizes nightmares and bad dreams. These sculptures are in the lowest of three levels within the chapel, where a profusion of architectural elements — heavy blank tabernacles above the doors, tapering blank windows, and even pilasters without capitals — vie with one another. Above are the lunettes, punctuated with tapering windows; and surmounting all is the coffered dome with oculus, capped by a cupola.

Pope Leo X's illegitimate cousin, elected to the papacy as Clement VII, wished to house the Medici library for scholars to use within the cloister of S. Lorenzo, the family parish church, perhaps to emphasize that the Medici were no longer mere merchants but members of intellectual and ecc-

FIGURE 9.56 *Michelangelo: Interior of the Medici Chapel, S. Lorenzo, Florence, begun 1520.* (Photo: Special Collections Library, University of Tennessee)

FIGURE 9.57 *Michelangelo: Laurentian Library, S. Lorenzo, Florence, begun 1524.* (From J. Burkhardt)

siastical society. Michelangelo began work on the Laurentian Library in 1524. It was built above existing monastic quarters on the east range of the cloister, with an entrance from the upper level of the cloisters. Michelangelo wanted to use a skylight over the vestibule, but the pope believed that a skylight would ultimately leak, so clerestory windows were incorporated into the west wall overlooking the cloister instead. The vestibule (Figure 9.57) is thus an ungainly space, almost half again as tall as it is wide. Blank tapering windows, framed in *pietra serena,* surround the interior of the vestibule; these are separated by paired columns set into the wall to support the roof beams. The seeming illogicality of recessing columns into a wall is evocative of Mannerism, yet their position is actually necessitated by the existing walls of the building below the library. Walls between columns are in effect skins stretched between the vertical supports. Michelangelo has emphasized the apparent instability of the whole by having the columns appear to be supported on consoles, so that weight seems to be carried on rather weak elements, and one is not sure visually whether columns or walls support the roof. In the center of this awkwardly proportioned space, with its exaggerated vertical emphasis, sits a huge staircase leading up to the reading room. Michelangelo's original sketches for the library showed the stair as divided flights placed against the wall. By 1558–1559, when the present stair was designed, his proposal had grown into a highly sculptural stair that pours from the upper level like molten lava and compresses the limited floor space of the vestibule. As it descends, the stair divides into three flights, the outer ones having no handrails. On the central flight, the convex treads vary in width, making the whole arrangement somewhat impractical. By contrast the library's reading room is serene, quiet, and restful, entirely appropriate for reading and study. In the manner of monastic libraries, it is a long room lit by evenly spaced windows set between pilasters in the side walls. Reading desks, arranged perpendicular to the side walls, were thus amply illuminated by natural light.

In 1534, with both the Medici Chapel and the Laurentian Library still incomplete, Michelangelo left Florence for Rome, where he remained until his death in 1564. One of his first architectural commissions in Rome came from the local government authority, which decided to reestablish the grandeur of Rome by developing the Campidoglio, which was the ancient seat of government on the Capitol or Capitoline Hill, occupied since the twelfth century by a communal palace. Shortly thereafter Pope Paul III transferred the great equestrian bronze of Marcus Aurelius specifically for use as the centerpiece on the Capitoline Hill. Thus Michelangelo was required to provide a setting for the statue and to bring order to an irregular hilltop already encumbered with two crumbling medieval buildings set at an acute angle to one another. Despite these conditions, it was a Renaissance architect's ideal commission, for it offered the opportunity to build a monumental civic plaza for a major city, and Michelangelo produced a brilliant response to the situation. A trapezoidal square was planned to regularize the difficult geometry established by the ex-

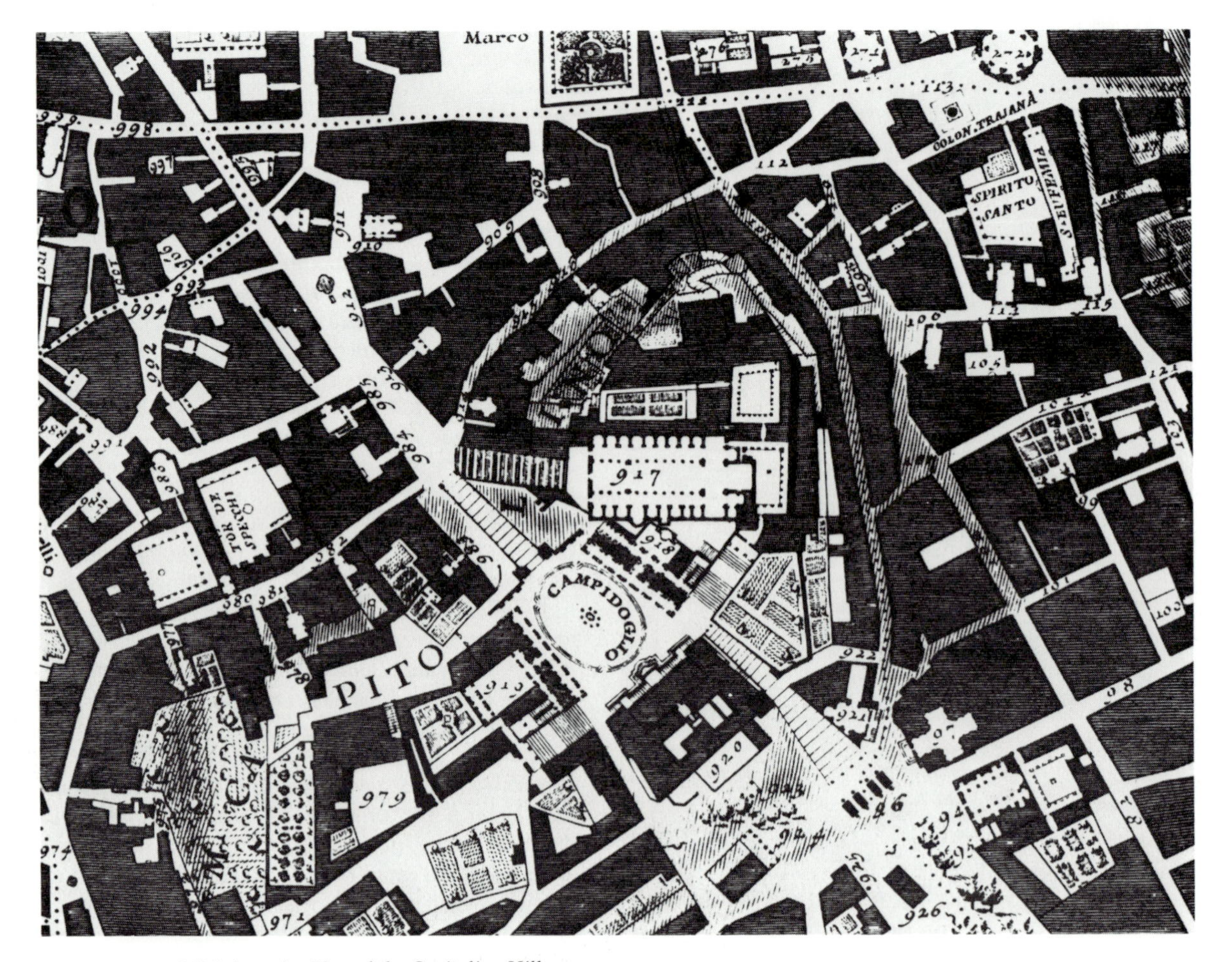

FIGURE 9.58 *Michelangelo: Plan of the Capitoline Hill, Rome, begun 1537.* (From G. Nolli)

isting buildings, and an oval paving pattern was inserted to focus on the equestrian statue in the center (Figure 9.58). Precedent for this general disposition of elements can be found in Rossellino's plan for the cathedral square at Pienza (1456–1464), although the scale and coherence of Michelangelo's design is much greater.

Axiality and symmetry govern all parts of the Capitoline Hill work. Michelangelo gave the medieval Palace of the Senators (Figure 9.59), remodeled ca. 1547 and later, a central campanile, a renovated façade, and a grand divided external staircase. He designed a new façade for the colonnaded Palace of the Conservators with giant order Corinthian pilasters extending over two stories and projected an identical structure, the Palazzo Nuovo (now the Capitoline Museum) for the opposite side of the square. On the narrow side of the trapezoidal piazza, Michelangelo extended the central axis with a magnificent ramp-stair to link the hilltop with the city below. Work on the Capitoline Hill was incomplete when Michelangelo died, but his designs were carefully followed in subsequent centuries, down to the installation of the pavement pattern in 1928.

Figure 9.59 *Michelangelo: Capitoline Hill, Rome.* (Photo: School of Architecture, University of Tennessee)

In 1546 Pope Paul III employed Michelangelo to continue the Palazzo Farnese (Figure 9.60), the pope's family residence, begun in 1517 by Antonio da Sangallo the Younger. Sangallo had raised the structure one story above ground level, and Michelangelo added the two upper stories. His work included the pedimented windows set on thin string courses attached to the flat wall plane; the central doorway overshadowed by a **cartouche** squeezed into position on the piano nobile; the window with a balcony above the entrance door; the large crowning cornice composed of numerous

Figure 9.60 *Michelangelo: Palazzo Farnese, Rome, 1546.* (Photo: School of Architecture, University of Tennessee)

small elements from a mixture of the orders; and the central courtyard, a perfect cube, based on the stacked orders of the Colosseum. As an expression of the social position and wealth of the newly rich Farnese family, the palace commands the piazza on which it fronts, lending an impassive dignity to the square.

Pope Paul III had been in office five years before the Vatican had adequate funds to resume the building of St. Peter's, begun in 1506 by Bramante. Plans had been submitted by Raphael, Giuliano da Sangallo, and Baldassare Peruzzi, but the sack of Rome in 1527 had emptied the Vatican coffers and prevented much actual construction. Antonio da Sangallo the Younger, a nephew of Giuliano, spent the equivalent cost of building a small church in making a model to illustrate the conglomerations and underscaled classical orders he proposed for the north and south transept ambulatories. Even though these admitted poor indirect light into the great central space, the southern transept was completed according to his proposals in 1546, the year in which Sangallo died. Michelangelo's appointment as architect-in-charge provoked Vasari to write that Paul III was indeed fortunate that God had ordained that Michelangelo should have lived during his pontificate: "How great are thy merits elevated by his art." Michelangelo, who considered himself primarily a sculptor, agreed to the assignment as a pious act for the glorification of God, and he accepted no more than a minimum living wage for his architectural work on St. Peter's. He quickly saw the faults of Sangallo's unimaginative scheme and razed the exterior walls of the transept ambulatories, in part because they encroached on the Vatican Palace and would have necessitated the destruction of several buildings had they been completed around the church. They would also have provided dark internal passageways in which vagrants could hide and attack pilgrims. Michelangelo made a small clay model of the church, from which a wooden model was constructed; the design restored Bramante's initial conception of a Greek cross plan, but in a reduced and simplified version (Figure 9.61). Michelangelo corresponded with his nephew in Florence for dimensions of Brunelleschi's dome on the cathedral there, a design he admired and wished to emulate. "I am going to make its sister bigger, yes, but not more beautiful," he wrote.

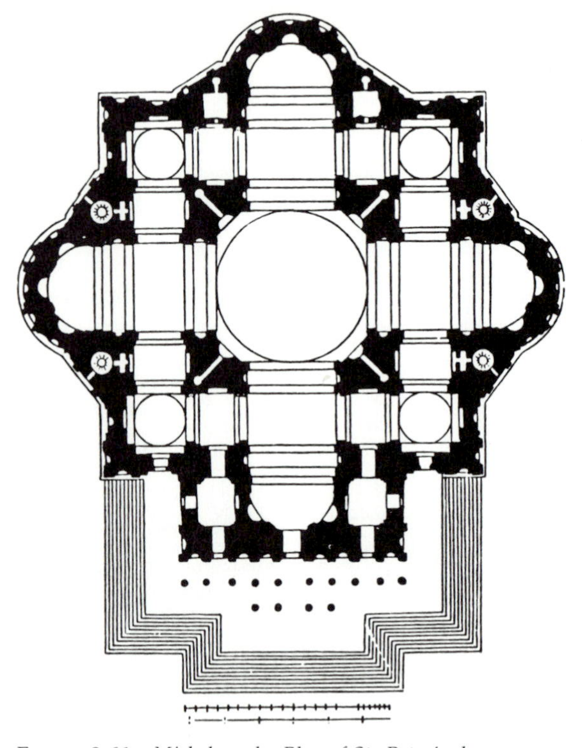

FIGURE 9.61 *Michelangelo: Plan of St. Peter's, begun 1546.* (From C. Ricci)

Although construction on the dome of St. Peter's was not begun in his lifetime, Michelangelo endowed its design with internal and external unity. Brunelleschi's dome for Florence Cathedral has a tall Gothic profile, which Michelangelo modified to a hemispherical form (Figure 9.62). He also increased the number of stone ribs expressed on the outside of the dome from eight to sixteen to eliminate the faceted octagonal massing of the Florence cathedral. Had the dome been constructed as planned by Michelangelo, the outward thrust of the ribs would have been enormous, and it is doubtful whether a masonry drum could have withstood the accumulated forces. Giacomo della Porta, who constructed the dome after Michelangelo's death, employed a slightly taller profile for engineering reasons, with the lantern cupola thrusting the weight of the dome down the ribs to pairs of columns in the drum. These columns, attached visually to the drum by a broken entablature, act as buttresses that transpose the loads downward to arches and the four great piers of the central crossing. Even so, ten tension chains were subsequently incorporated into the brickwork of this double-shelled dome (which is only five feet smaller in diameter than the Pantheon dome). The triangulated

FIGURE 9.62 *Michelangelo: St. Peter's.* (Photo: School of Architecture, University of Tennessee)

Figure 9.63 *Michelangelo: Porta Pia, Rome, begun 1561.* (Photo: Alinari)

massing of the whole project rises to a height of 452 feet, enough to have strong visual presence had Michelangelo's façade been built on the major entrance. Eventually, however, St. Peter's was finished early in the seventeenth century with a nave and entrance façade designed by Carlo Maderno.

In his later designs Michelangelo anticipated the Baroque in several ways, particularly in his design of the Porta Pia (Figure 9.63), a city gate built at the end of the Via Pia. This was not a defensive gateway within a fortified city wall; it was a decorated scenic backdrop terminating a vista. Stone architectural elements are isolated against a brick backdrop wall and the volute predominates, whether as part of a broken pediment or draped over crenellations. The whole emphasis of the design is focused on the central passageway demarcating the edge of the city; the concatenation of architectural details recalls Renaissance stage set designs for the theater. Begun in 1561, the Porta Pia was almost complete, unlike so many other of Michelangelo's architectural commissions, at the time of his death.

Andrea Palladio

Andrea Palladio is widely considered to be the most influential architect in western history, having an impact on architecture in every century since his death. Born Andrea di Pietro della Gondola in 1508, he was trained as a stonemason. When he was about thirty, he was employed on a building site where his talents attracted the attention of the humanist Count Giangiorgio Trissino. Trissino became his mentor, renaming him Palladio after the Pallas Athena, goddess of wisdom, and providing him with a humanist education through association with Trissino's academy. This, with several study trips to Rome, gave Palladio an education in architecture. In particular, by measuring the buildings of ancient Rome, Palladio gained accurate information on classical proportions, which he later used in designing his own buildings.

His first public commission was a new exterior for the medieval market and council hall, or Basilica, at Vicenza, to which Palladio added a two-story

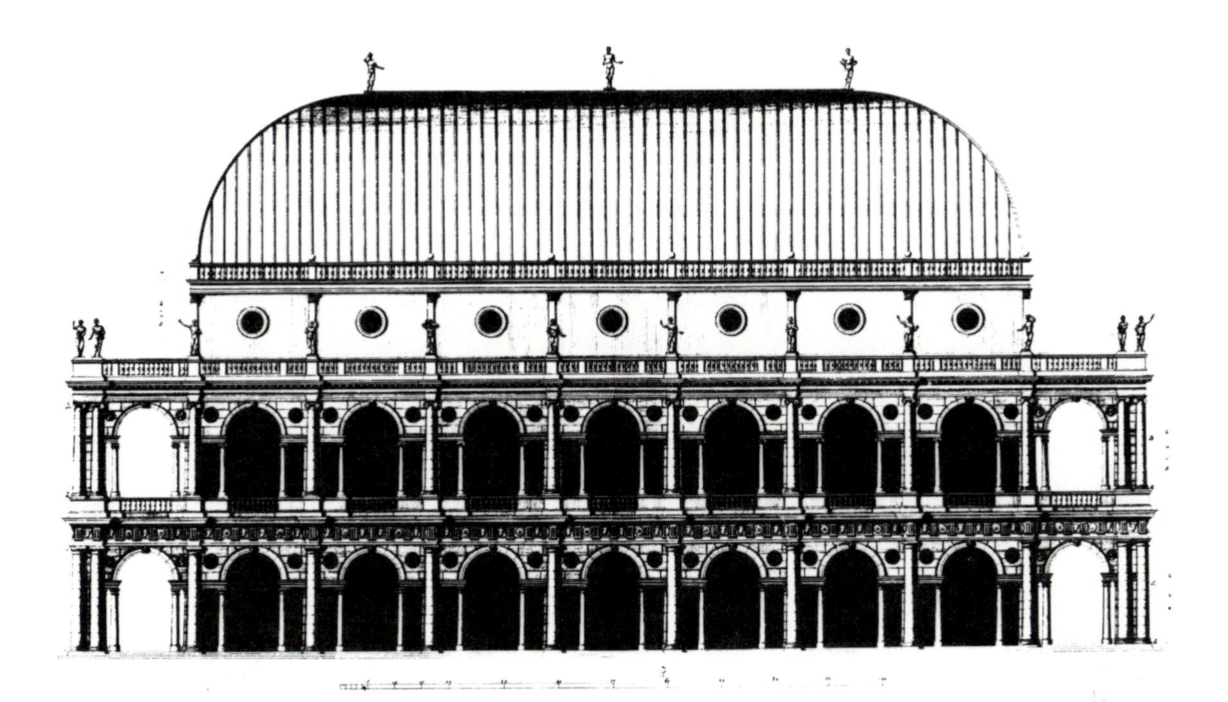

FIGURE 9.64 *Palladio: Basilica, Vicenza, 1549.* (Engraving by Scamozzi)

FIGURE 9.65 *Sansovino: Library of St. Mark's, Venice, begun 1537.* (From J. Guadet) ▶

arcade of the Doric and Ionic orders (Figure 9.64). He submitted proposals for the project in 1546 at the request of civic authorities, who accepted them with modifications in 1549. Construction was based on Roman brick groin-vaulting techniques, but the dominant element of the design is the repeated unit of three openings, the central one arched, supported on pairs of small columns, set off with a larger half column between each bay. The end bays were smaller to give the appearance of strength to the corner, which had double columns. Although Bramante was the first architect to use an arch flanked by square-headed openings, the unit is sometimes known as a **Palladian motif,** or a Serliana because it was first illustrated in Sebastiano Serlio's *Tutte le opere d'architettura et prospettiva* (commonly known as The Five Books of Architecture), parts of which were published as early as 1537. In using the Serliana here, Palladio was undoubtedly more directly influenced by Jacopo Sansovino's Library of St. Mark (1537–1553) in nearby Venice (Figure 9.65).

FIGURE 9.66 *Palladio: Palazzo Chiericati, Vicenza, 1550–1552.* (Photo: School of Architecture, University of Tennessee)

FIGURE 9.67 *Palladio: Plan and elevation of the Palazzo Chiericati, Vicenza.* (From A. Palladio)

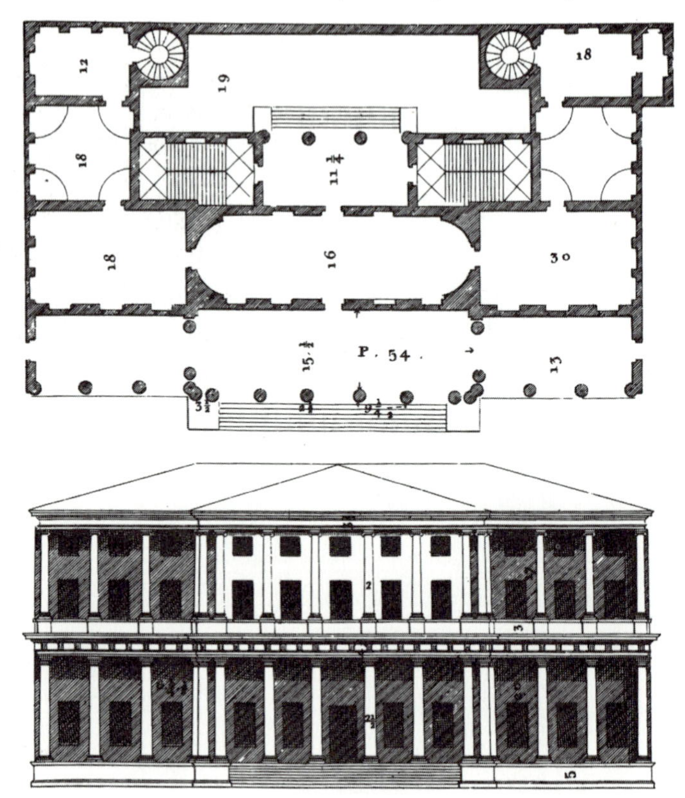

The Palazzo Chiericati in Vicenza (1550–1552) was erected on a very shallow site with a long frontage onto a public open space (Figures 9.66, 9.67). Palladio treated the building like a Roman palace, two stories high, fronting onto a forum, with a ground-level Roman Doric colonnade intended to link with other colonnades (never built) on buildings around the remaining sides of the square. Like those of many Palladian houses the palace's façade is divided into three parts, the central section being a pavilion (a projecting bay) accentuated by clustered columns that create an impression of strength. The second floor is composed in the Ionic order, with loggias flanking the main salon. By thus projecting the salon over the public colonnade below, additional space was gained for the largest room in the house. The palace is open and airy. Because of the restricted site the long axis of its entrance hall and the majority of its rooms parallel the street frontage, rather than being perpendicular to it.

Palladio's villa designs were the major architectural work that gained him such a wide following among later architects. Unlike most Renaissance villas, his country estates were generally working farms owned by the younger sons of Venetian nobles. Their lands were located on the mainland north of Venice, the Veneto, and their agricultural products were essential to feed the inhabitants of the city. Although isolated from sophisticated Venetian society, these gentleman farmers maintained an elegant and cultured life in appropriately grand houses. Two of Palladio's early clients were Daniele Barbaro, a scholarly author and editor of a published version of Vitruvius, and his brother Marcantonio. Palladio designed the Villa Barbaro at Maser for them (1557–1558) (Figures 9.68, 9.69). As with all his villas, the scheme is symmetrical, the central living block balanced by end pavilions connected by flanking arcades. The building is sited on a slight rise, so although it is connected to the ground, it affords a view out into the landscape. Practical requirements have not been neglected. The arcade's openings provide space for farm equipment and animals, while dovecotes are set underneath the arches.

Inside the dwelling, the rooms are gracefully proportioned, well lit, and ingeniously ornamented with perspective frescoes by Paolo Veronese (ca.

FIGURE 9.68 *Palladio: Villa Barbaro, Maser, 1557–1558.*
(Photo: Alinari)

1528–1588). Through the magic of pigment, walls merge into barrel-vaulted ceilings. In one room balustraded balconies appear to support spiraled columns, behind which are painted openings from which emerge the mistress of the house with a page boy, her servant, lap dog, and a parrot. Shadow projections help increase the sense of depth in a series of rooms where actual architraves and pedimented doorways may be confused with those painted on flat wall surfaces. Huntsmen and children appear in open doorways, and sculptures stand in niches flanked by columns, all created by the painter's brush. Landscapes lead the eye beyond columns and pilasters in the dining room to imaginary vistas inspired by scenes from antiquity.

With the Villa Barbaro, Palladio made a contribution to residential design that continues in architecture of our own time: the application of the temple front (columns and pediment) to a house, used earlier by Sangallo on the Medici villa at Pog-

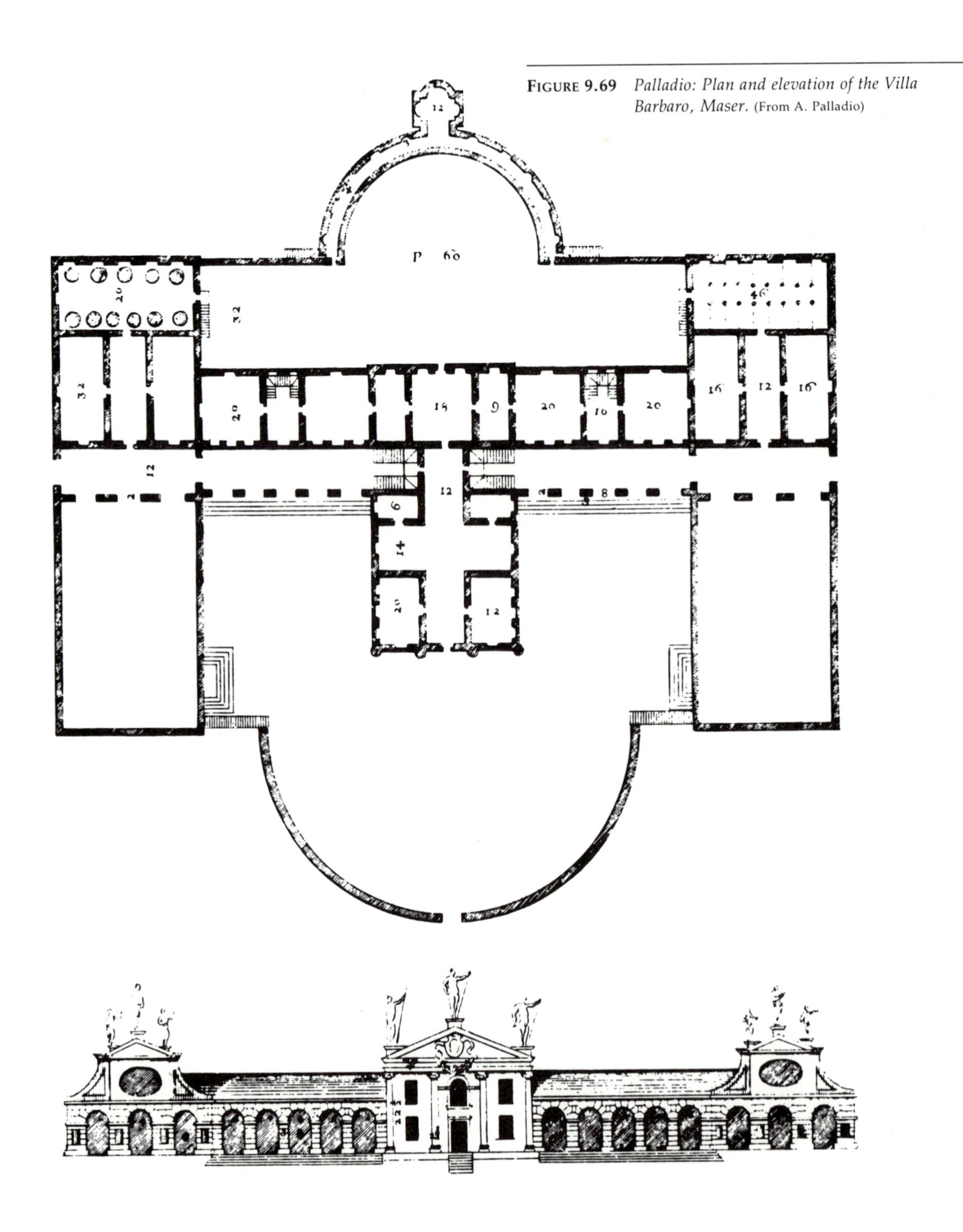

FIGURE 9.69 *Palladio: Plan and elevation of the Villa Barbaro, Maser.* (From A. Palladio)

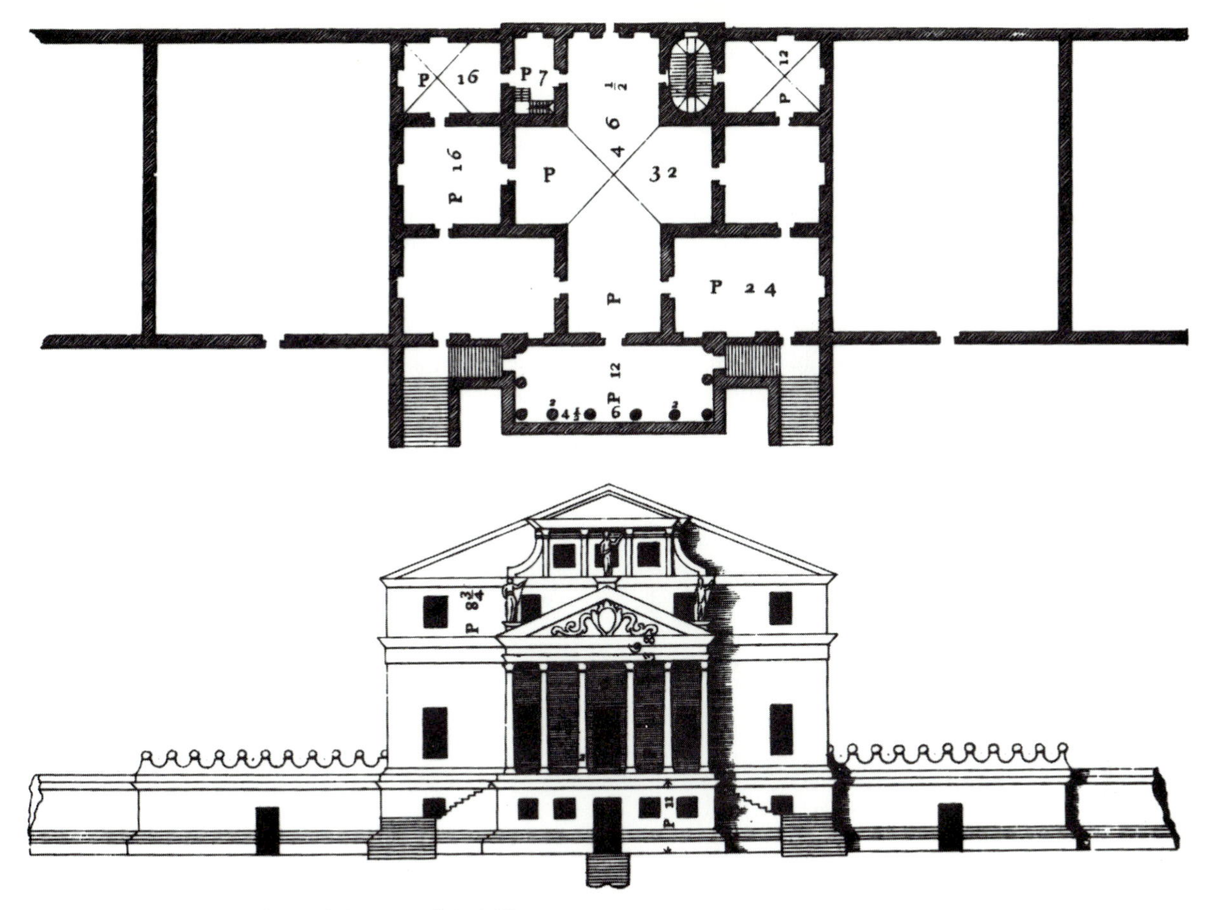

FIGURE 9.70 *Palladio: Plan and elevation of the Villa Foscari, Malcontenta.* (From A. Palladio)

gio a Caiano (see Figure 9.19). Palladio's was a new use for the motif, even though he had no intention of being innovative. He had read in Vitruvius that the designs of Greek temples were based on their designs for houses, an observation that may refer to the similarity of the megaron and the cella of a temple. Having no knowledge of the megaron, Palladio interpreted Vitruvius' remark to mean that Greek houses looked like Greek temples, which he knew to have columns and a pediment. In using these on the façade of a house, therefore, Palladio believed he was conforming with Greek precedent, when in fact he was breaking new ground.

The Villa Foscari at Malcontenta (1559–1560), located on the Brenta Canal outside Venice, was designed on a single axis, with the intention that side courts would mask the end elevations, but these courts were not built (Figures 9.70, 9.71). Dog-leg stairs lead to a portico on axis at piano nobile level and the entrance from the portico opens into a

FIGURE 9.71 *Palladio: Villa Foscari, Malcontenta, 1559–1560.* (Photo: Alinari)

vaulted cruciform space extending the full depth of the building. One of the barrel vaults in the arms of the cross is expressed on the garden side. There is a consistent proportion system throughout the house, all rooms having ratios of 1:1, 2:3, 1:2, or 3:4. In plan the building's measurements of length to width conform to the Golden Section ratio of 8:5, while the height is 5.

By far the most famous residence by Palladio is the Villa Almerico-Capra, known as Villa Rotonda, outside Vicenza (1566–1570) (Figures 9.72, 9.73). The client for this villa was a retired churchman, who used the house for elaborate entertainments. The practical farming accommodations found at other Palladian villas are thus absent here, and the building takes full advantage of its hilltop site overlooking the countryside. It is square in plan, with a central two-story domed space over the circular room on the middle. As Palladio describes it, "there are loggias made on all four fronts" so that "it enjoys from every part most beautiful views, some of which are limited, some extended, and others which terminate with the horizon." Internally the central domed space radiates out to the four porticoes and to the magnificently proportioned rooms in the corners. It is a simple yet powerful scheme, a design that would often be copied later.

Palladio himself started with the Villa Rotonda

Figure 9.72 *Palladio: Villa Almerico-Capra [La Rotonda], Vicenza, 1556–1557.* (Photo: Alinari)

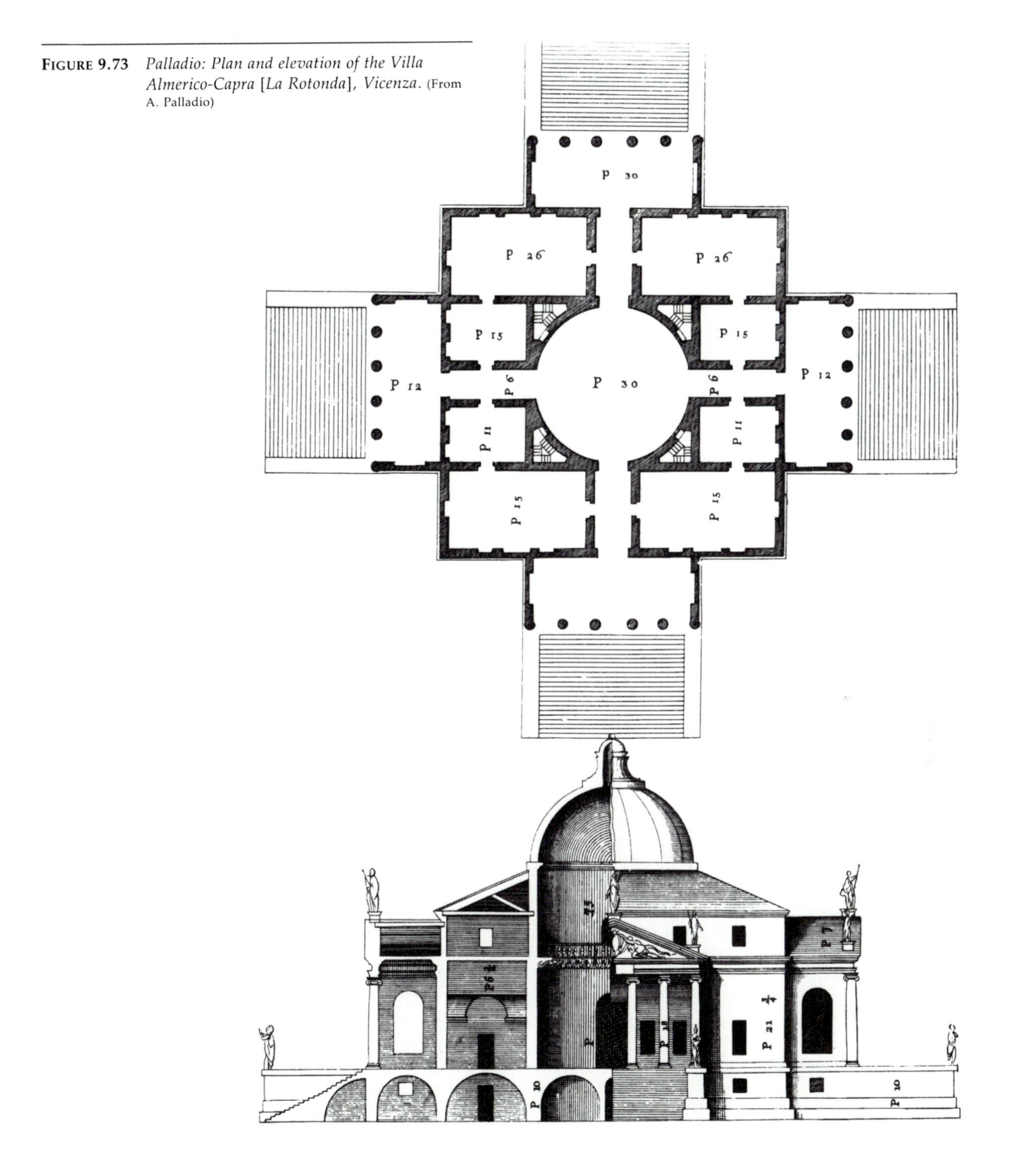

FIGURE 9.73 *Palladio: Plan and elevation of the Villa Almerico-Capra [La Rotonda], Vicenza.* (From A. Palladio)

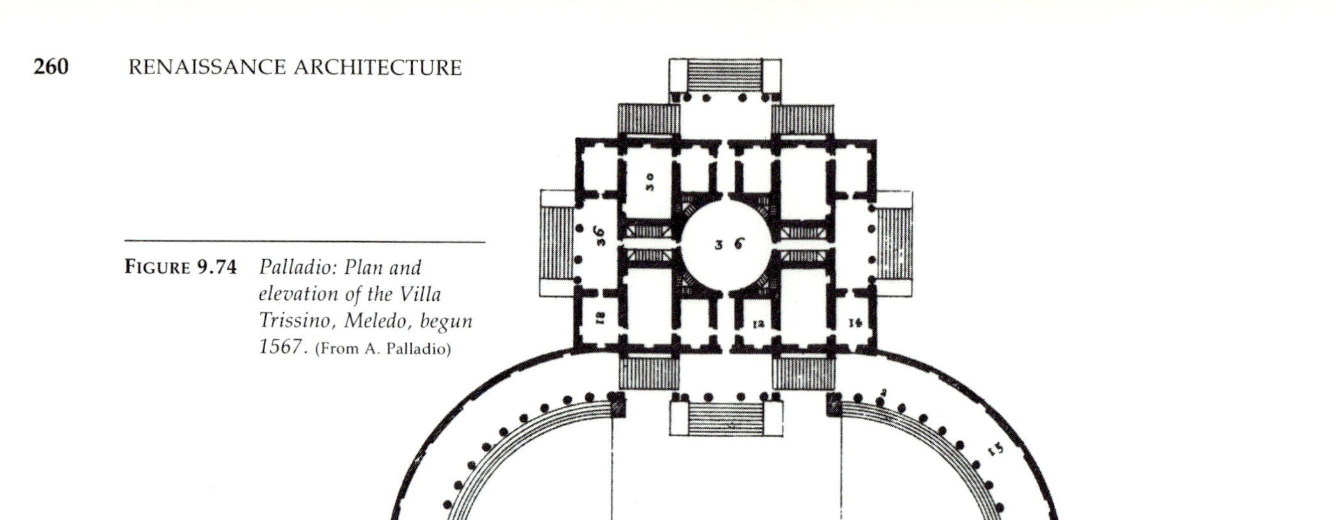

Figure 9.74 *Palladio: Plan and elevation of the Villa Trissino, Meledo, begun 1567.* (From A. Palladio)

plan in his project for the Villa Trissino at Meledo (Figure 9.74), an ambitious scheme of which only a tiny end fragment was ever built. To the basic cube of the house, he added quarter-circle colonnades to either side of one porticoed entrance, widening out to define a rectangular forecourt. Comments made by the architect about the villa indicate that the ground floor was to be given over to domestic services, while the dependencies sheltered farm activities — hay lofts, stables, granaries, and housing for farm families — thus integrating gracious living quarters for the owner with the agricultural requirements of a great estate. It was an imaginative recreation of a Roman villa, reinterpreted in the light of sixteenth-century life.

Palladio's most significant church was S. Giorgio Maggiore in Venice (Figure 9.75), which has a façade design derived from his earlier S. Francesco della Vigne in Venice. Both churches offered a new solution to the Renaissance problem of satisfactorily elevating the façade of a basilica. Palladio superim-

Figure 9.75 *Palladio: Elevation of S. Giorgio Maggiore, Venice, 1565.* (From R. Sturgis)

posed two temple fronts: a tall one, consisting of four Corinthian columns on pedestals that support a pediment at the end of the nave; and a wide pediment, with smaller Corinthian pilasters, that matches the sloping aisle roofs. The idea of using double pediments on one façade was legitimized by the Pantheon, where pedimental cornices on the drum act as a second temple front. (Vitruvius had also discussed a double arrangement of gables.) At S. Giorgio, the Corinthian columns and pilasters on the front carry through to the interior arcading between nave and aisles, providing an Albertian unity to this ecclesiastical building. Palladio looked to the Roman thermae for precedent in handling the interior. Barrel vaults are illuminated by the semicircular clerestory windows found in the Baths of Diocletian, and the whole is painted white to reflect light and emphasize the church's volumetric clarity.

One of Palladio's last works was the Teatro Olimpico in Vicenza (1579–80), inspired by Roman theaters with proscenium like the Theater of Marcellus, but roofed here with a ceiling painted to depict the open sky. Steeply-banked rows of seats are arranged in a semicircle facing the stage, where the original stage set designed by Scamozzi remains as the scenery for all productions. The set shows an urban piazza, from which three streets extend back into the distance, their apparent length exaggerated by perspective and a sloped floor plane (Figures 9.76, 9.77). When the actors leave the stage, they appear to recede along the street, even though their height does not diminish according to the perspective of the set.

Palladio expressed many of his ideals in his *I Quattro libri dell' architettura* (The Four Books on Architecture), published in Venice in 1570 (Figure

FIGURE 9.76 *Palladio: Proscenium of the Teatro Olimpico, Vicenza, 1579–1580.* (Photo: Instituto Italiana di Cultura)

FIGURE 9.77 *Palladio: Section through the Teatro Olimpico, Vicenza.* (From Scamozzi)

9.78). Topics covered there include the orders of architecture, domestic architecture, public buildings, town planning, and temples, "without which no civilization is possible." Although he could measure and illustrate actual Roman temples, theaters, bridges, triumphal arches, and baths, Palladio had to speculate about the design of Roman houses, and he therefore included illustrations of his own buildings to demonstrate antique ideals. Numerals printed in the plans give the dimensions of ceiling heights, so his proportioning system can be exactly scaled. Whether knowingly or not, he thus assured a wide dissemination of his designs, for printed editions of his book enabled many architects who never traveled to the Veneto to know the villas and palaces of Palladio. In these, as in all his architectural designs, he was concerned with practical convenience as an essential component of good design; firmness, commodity, and delight were to him the basic tenets of all architecture.

The continuing influence of Palladio on western architecture is in no small measure due to the logical planning, careful proportions, and conceptual clarity that characterize his designs. Indeed the principles Palladio advocated have been found applicable to a variety of circumstances. His writings and buildings both demonstrate the achievements of this stonemason turned architect who declared, "Vitruvius is my master, Rome is my mistress, and architecture is my life."

FIGURE 9.78 *Palladio: Frontispiece to the first English edition of* I Quattro libri dell' architettura *(1738) by Isaac Ware*

Garden Design

The history of landscape architecture is in some respects more difficult to reconstruct accurately than the history of architecture; without continual maintenance and replanting, the living materials that constitute the designer's work decay more rapidly or vanish more completely than most buildings do. We know that sacred enclosures and sanctuary precincts of Egypt, Mesopotamia, the Aegean, and Rome were landscaped, although the appearance of these gardens is known now only from reliefs, descriptions, or other representations. Better preserved are many Islamic works, such as the Alhambra, where the garden embodied the idea of Paradise. The medieval gardens illustrated in manuscripts and described in literature tended to be

FIGURE 9.79 *Ligorio: Gardens of the Villa d'Este, Tivoli, ca. 1565–1572.* (From J. Guadet)

functional, laid out in orderly beds and contained within a wall or hedge. Many of these were purposeful plantings for culinary or medicinal herbs.

In the Renaissance the garden as an extension of architecture became important once again, with designs that originated as free adaptations of antique landscapes. Roman terraced gardens, for example, influenced both Bramante's design for the Belvedere Courtyard (see Figure 9.47) and Raphael's designs for the Villa Madama (see Figure 9.50). At the Villa Madama, geometric perimeters of miniature box hedges encircled colorful planting beds, and the taller backdrop of trees defined the limits of the garden. During the Renaissance, however, landscape architecture was raised to the level of a major art, a stage setting for the splendor of the aristocracy and princes of the church. Pope Julius III, who commissioned the Villa Giulia just outside Rome, made use of its loggias and courts for theatrical performances and leisurely promenading. Late Renaissance gardens were elaborate, using water, sculpture, and foliage in an architectural manner. A number of these also provided a foretaste of Baroque urban planning, so they deserve attention here.

The first major Mannerist garden was built at the Villa d'Este in Tivoli (Figure 9.79) outside Rome, to the designs of Pirro Ligorio (ca. 1510–1583). His

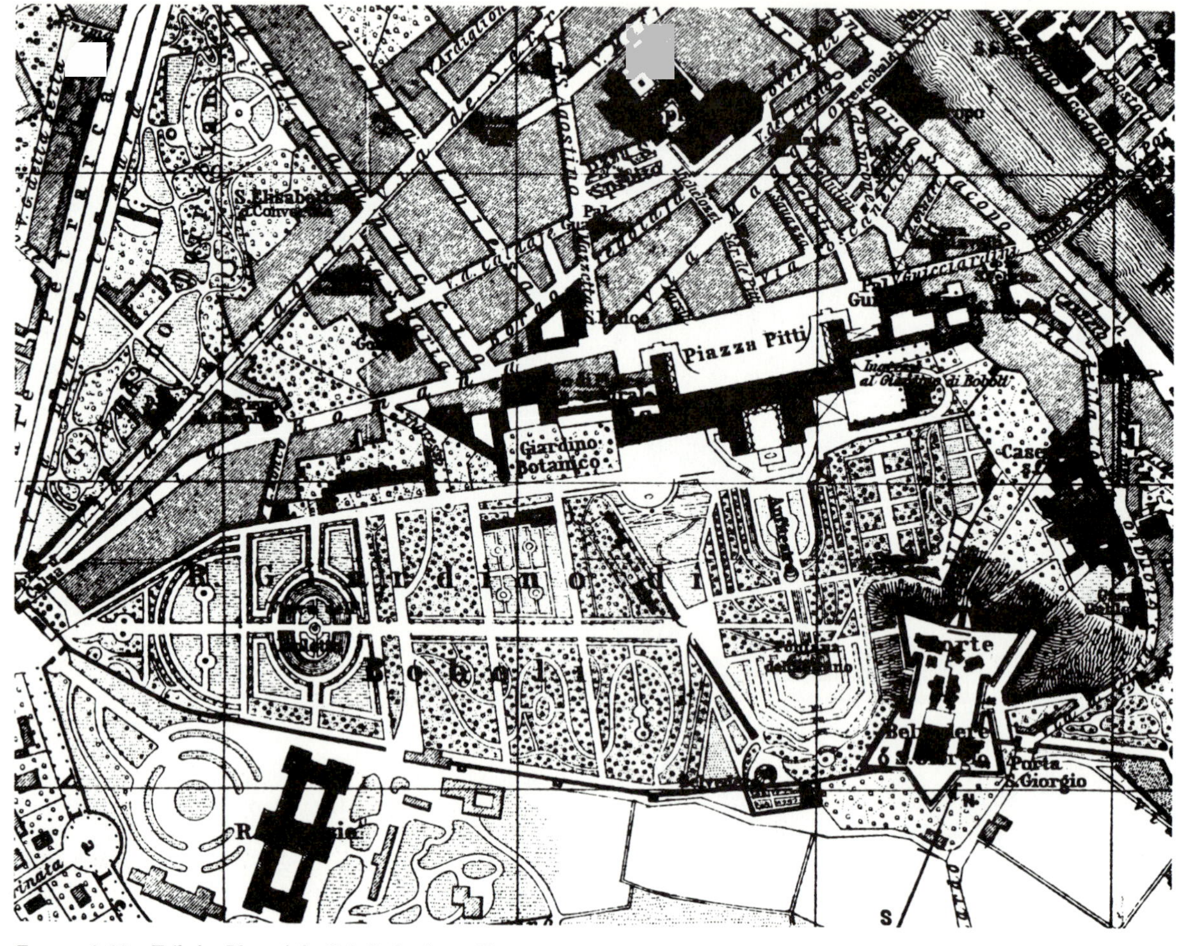

FIGURE 9.80 *Tribolo: Plan of the Boboli Gardens, Florence, begun 1549.* (From Baedeker)

client, Ippolito II Cardinal d'Este, had a site that included both a north-facing slope and a large reliable water supply at the top. Ligorio manipulated these two features into a remarkable ensemble of paths and plantings animated by the endless play of water in quiet pools, gurgling streams, great fountains, gentle sprays, multiple cascades, and dripping grottoes. His work may have been inspired by the extensive ruins of Hadrian's Villa (see Figure 4.36) just outside of Tivoli, where Roman architects had tried to evoke the architecture that Hadrian had seen in his lifetime of extensive travels. By the sixteenth century, little of the original landscape at Hadrian's Villa could have been extant, although the general disposition of buildings and major water features was (and still is) discernible. The layout at the Villa d'Este is far from an antique reconstruction, however. Its plan is virtually symmetrical around a central axis that descends the hillside. A stroll through its shady walks on a hot summer's afternoon rewards the visitor with the many sounds of moving water; sights of numerous ingenious sculptures, a labyrinth, and a miniature model of ancient Rome; and music from a water-powered organ. Even in its rather overgrown present condition, the gardens of the Villa d'Este are full of delight.

Contemporary with the gardens of the Villa d'Este were the Boboli Gardens (Figure 9.80), another major Mannerist work located in Florence behind the Palazzo Pitti. When the Medici acquired the property in 1549, they enlarged the building by adding substantial front wings enclosing the forecourt and extensive new construction at the back of the original palace. The rear extension was organized around three sides of a rectangular courtyard, the fourth side of which was attached with a semi-

FIGURE 9.81 *Tribolo: Amphitheater of the Boboli Gardens, Florence.* (Photo: School of Architecture, University of Tennessee)

circular stairway up to the Boboli Gardens beyond (Figure 9.81). Work on the gardens, to the landscape designs of Niccolò Tribolo, began even before work on the palace. The garden layout was governed by a strong central axis rising up the hillside from the rear courtyard. In sequence it traverses a large horseshoe-shaped amphitheater, rises up a ramp to a pool adorned with a fountain of Neptune, and finally arrives at the highest terrace, which features a statue of Abundance set in a background of foliage to terminate the vista. Over the next 150 years, others extended this ambitious design down the slope to the northwest almost parallel to the long façade of the palace, developing around a secondary axis that cuts arbitrarily across the original axis centering on the courtyard. The second axis is in turn intersected by crossaxes that divide the garden into trapezoidal sections laid out in centralized geometric patterns. Tall cypress trees line the axial route, which ends at an oval island set in the middle of an artificial pond. A central fountain there provides the focal point for the vista, and a semicircular hedge closes off the far end of the enclosure. The various landscape architects who worked on the Boboli Gardens brought a high degree of order to the natural world by using plant materials, mostly evergreens, to create the foliated equivalent of a Renaissance street within a geometric town plan. The major and minor axes control the vista and focus the visitor's eye on a dominant element, placed as a monument to mark important points within the design. All this work provided an elaborate setting for parties, spectacles, and concerts staged by the Medici, but the Boboli Gardens also incorporated ideas that appeared shortly thereafter on a much larger scale in the city of Rome.

THE RENAISSANCE IN FRANCE

The extension of artistic developments from the Italian Renaissance to France was hastened in part by French military interventions in the peninsula. In 1494 the armies of Charles VIII invaded Italy in pursuit of claims to the Kingdom of Naples; in 1498 Louis XII attacked Milan, toppling the Sforza (and precipitating Bramante's departure for Rome); and Francis I campaigned in Italy until 1525, when his defeat at Pavia brought a halt to French pretensions in the region of Milan. Although these military excursions ultimately resulted in no permanent expansion of French territory, the reverse flow of Italian artistic ideas was to have lasting consequences for architecture in France. By the end of the fifteenth century, France was changing from a feudal society into a strong centralized state headed by the king. Unlike urban-centered Italy, where merchant princes eclipsed the landed nobility and commissioned works from the great Renaissance artists, the court was the dominant force in French society, and the king led the way in supporting design in the Italian style. As Milan was the center of French contacts in Italy, the early Renaissance buildings there, including the Ospedale Maggiore of Filarete and the nearby Certosa at Pavia, were the best known and most generally admired buildings, perhaps because their combination of highly ornamented surfaces and classical details was not far removed from the late Gothic style with which the French were most familiar. From the last years of the fifteenth century, the French transported Italian art back to France, invited Italian artists and architects north to undertake commissions, and sent French artists to Italy to train in Renaissance workshops.

The cultural center of France in the early sixteenth century was not in Paris, but in the valley of the Loire, where the king and his nobles maintained elaborate chateaux (castles) for leisure, entertaining, and attending to the pleasures of the hunt. Among these chateaux are found some of the earliest architectural manifestations of the Renaissance style. Blois in particular illustrates the transition from medieval to Renaissance through the successive stages in its construction. The chateau was begun in the thirteenth century with the construction of a large medieval hall and associated rooms. Between 1498 and 1504, Louis XII added an east wing, incorporating an entrance gate to what would ultimately be a large courtyard. The construction, in red brick with light-colored stone trim at corners, doorways, and window surrounds, reflects the continuity of medieval traditions. Above the entrance way there is an equestrian statue of Louis set into a large niche with double-cusped pointed arches and other Gothic detailing in stone. Windows align vertically one above the other, culminating in elaborate Gothic **dormers** in the steeply-pitched roof; these dormers read as a series of vertical elements, even though string courses and the cornice established horizontal lines. Between 1515 and 1524 Francis I embarked on extensive building operations at Blois, adding a north wing to the medieval hall to form the north side of the court, with the opposite side facing over the town (Figure 9.82). Francis demolished an old tower and upon its foundations built the famous open spi-

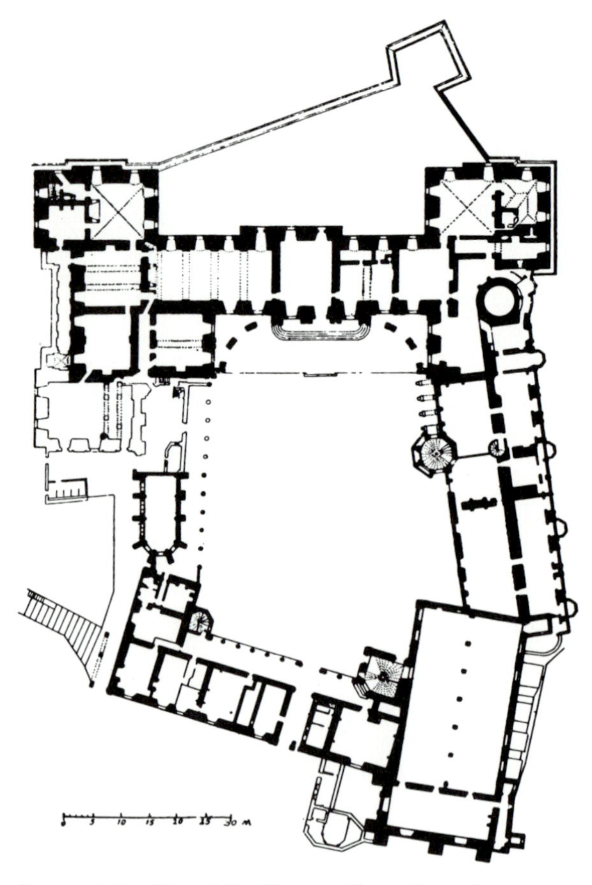

FIGURE 9.82 *Plan of the Chateau, Blois, 1515–1524.* (From J. Guadet)

FIGURE 9.83 *Staircase of the Francis I Wing, Chateau, Blois, 1515–1524.* (From J. Guadet)

raling stair (Figure 9.83). It features decorative carving of wreaths, porcupines, and salamanders, emblems of the royal family. Windows on the courtyard façade are regularly arranged, although again their vertical emphasis clashes with horizontal elements. All rooms are en suite; corridor access was to be a later innovation. On the town façade, the Francis I wing is like a cliff face, with two loggias and an open third story with free-standing columns (Figure 9.84), modeled on papal palaces at the Vatican and at Pienza. Its mixture of classical columns and details also includes Gothic **gargoyles.**

In contrast to this town-based chateau, the Chateau of Chambord (1519–1547) was built in the countryside in the style of a fortified castle within a

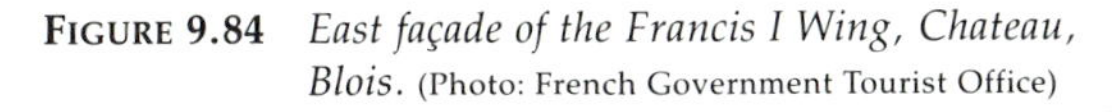

FIGURE 9.84 *East façade of the Francis I Wing, Chateau, Blois.* (Photo: French Government Tourist Office)

FIGURE 9.85 *Cortona: Chateau, Chambord, 1519–1547.* (Photo: French Government Tourist Office)

bailey, thus neatly overlaying Renaissance symmetry and detailing on a fundamentally medieval building type (Figures 9.85, 9.86). Its Italian architect, Domenico da Cortona, designed simple cylindrical shapes, which were to have been surrounded by open loggias, but these were not built since shade from intense sunlight was not as necessary in France as in Italy. The "keep" of the castle has a suite of rooms in each corner, divided by a cruciform circulation pattern like the one in the Medici villa at Poggio and a double staircase undoubtedly influenced by a sketch of Leonardo's (Figure 9.87). Persons ascending one stair of the double helix staircase can do so without seeing persons descending on the other. A great lantern above the staircase is one of a whole cluster of cones, chimneys, and dormers on the roof, presenting an almost medieval profile against the sky. Surrounding this abundance of vertical roof features is a terrace from which the ladies of the court could view the progress of the hunt in the wooded countryside beyond the chateau. The contrast between the ordered clarity of the walls and the wild exuberance of the rooftops reflects the partial assimilation of Renaissance design into a firmly established medieval building tradition.

Not all the Loire chateaux were built for the King. Chenonceau (Figures 9.88, 9.89) is an example of a chateau constructed by a wealthy courtier, Thomas Bohier, a financier. Begun in 1515 Chenonceau has a regularity of plan — all the major rooms open off a central corridor — and a straight-run stair that indicate Renaissance influence in the

FIGURE 9.86 *Cortona: Plan of Chateau, Chambord.* (From J. Guadet)

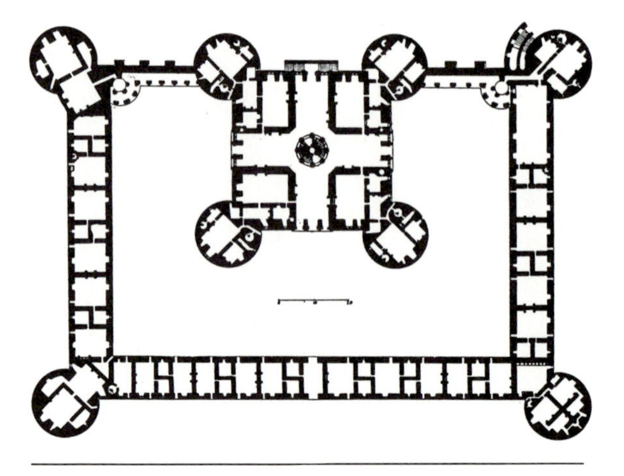

FIGURE 9.88 *Chateau, Chenonceau, begun 1515.* (Photo: Marburg) ▶

FIGURE 9.87 *Cortona: Staircase of Chateau, Chambord.* (From J. Guadet)

FIGURE 9.89 *Plan of Chateau, Chenonceau.* (From Du Cerceau)

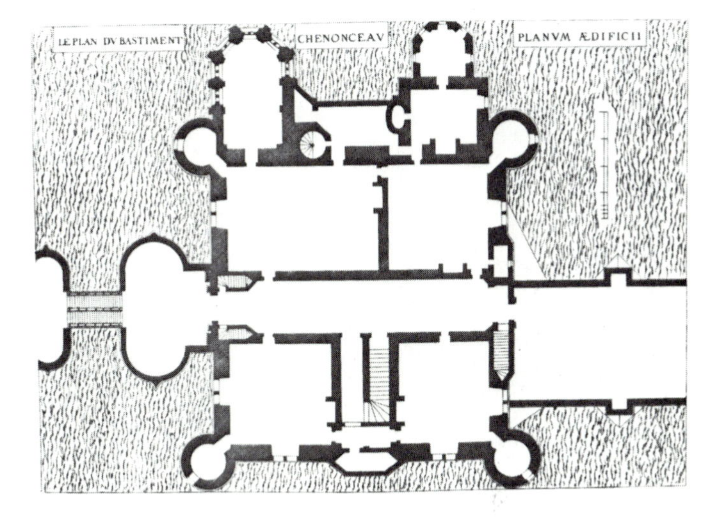

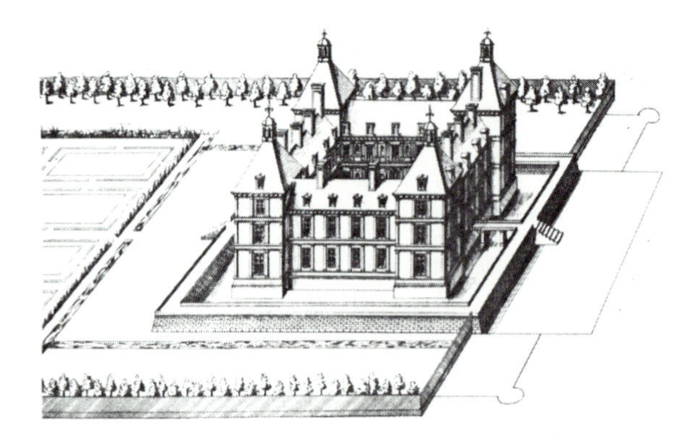

FIGURE 9.90 *Serlio: Chateau, Ancy-le-Franc, begun 1546.* (From Du Cerceau)

design, even as its moat, turreted corners, and chapel with rib vaults, pointed arches, and buttresses reflect medieval practice.

A second phase of Renaissance development in France began around 1540 with the arrival of Sebastiano Serlio (1475–1554), an Italian architect who came north at the invitation of the king, and the return of Philibert de l'Orme (ca. 1510–1570), a Frenchman who trained in Rome and settled in Paris to practice as an architect and engineer. Both these men brought knowledge of High Renaissance work in Rome, especially the work of Bramante, and their writings did much to explain Renaissance design principles and improve building practices in France. Little of Serlio's architecture survives, aside from the exteriors of the chateau Ancy-le-Franc (Figure 9.90), a square plan building with an open courtyard in the center. The design, with its corner pavilions, Doric pilasters, and rustication is almost entirely north Italian in derivation, but the high-pitched roof is typically French. Of greater importance were Serlio's writings on architecture, published in several installments from 1537 to 1551 and accumulated in 1584 as *Tutte l'opere d'architettura et prospettiva* (known as the Five Books of Architecture). The first architectural treatises not composed in Latin, these books contained woodcut illustrations, and the text addressed the ordinary builder more than the architectural scholar. Book One explained geometry; Book Two covered the construction of perspective drawings; and Book Three illustrated antique Roman buildings and the High Renaissance works of Bramante and Raphael. Book Four outlined the five orders of architecture (Doric, Ionic, Corinthian, Tuscan, and Composite), illustrated arched rusticated door and window surrounds appropriate for each order, and included notes on construction materials. Book Five contained centralized church designs. Three further volumes completed the opus; these contained many of Serlio's own designs.

Philibert de l'Orme's writings were also practical in nature. His first volume, published in 1561, was *Nouvelles inventions pour bien bastir et à petits frais;* it considered the construction of vaults and roofs from an engineering standpoint. His major work, *Architecture,* was published in 1567. While it draws some content from the earlier treatises by Vitruvius and Alberti, the writing relies extensively on de l'Orme's personal experiences in building to offer architects reasoned guidance grounded in both theory and practice. Of the many buildings on which de l'Orme worked, only a few remain. One of the most celebrated is the addition he made to the chateau at Chenonceau, a bridge over the river Cher composed of five arches of varying span (see Figure 9.88). (The building atop the bridge was built later by others.)

After 1526, when the French capital became fixed in Paris, Francis I decided to update the medieval Louvre Palace, beginning with the removal of the cylindrical keep in the center of the square courtyard. Some years later, Francis decided to rebuild one wing of the enclosed court, possibly extending the design around all four sides of the palace. Serlio proposed a design incorporating a series of courtyards, but the commission for rebuilding the Louvre wing went instead to the French architect Pierre Lescot (ca. 1500–1578). Lescot's design (Figure 9.91) dates from 1546, and while it is more correct in its use of the classical orders than most French buildings of the same period, his design would never be confused with Italian work. Lescot's façade emphasizes verticality rather than the horizontal line characteristic of the Italian Renaissance, even though it has cornice lines between floors. The courtyard façade is three stories high including the attic and is composed of Corinthian and Composite half columns and pilasters, with elongated windows and pavilions at the extremities and in the center. The architecture is complemented by sculpture executed by Jean Goujon, one of the most talented artists of the period. It is possible that Lescot's façade was derived from Serlio's courtyard plan for the Louvre, although it seems that both miscalculated the interior implications of the courtyard's proportions. The height of the building in relation to the width of the courtyard was such that, had the three additional façades been built to form the intended courtyard, the palace rooms would have received little direct sunlight. As events progressed, however, a later designer, Jacques Lemercier (1585–1654), enlarged the courtyard in 1624 to 400 feet square, more than four times the size proposed by either Serlio or Lescot.

For the last four decades of the sixteenth century, France was tormented by civil strife, the so-called Wars of Religion, which had economic and social causes as well as religious ones. Order was not restored until the ascendency in 1594 of King Henry IV, whose policies brought an end to domestic and foreign turmoil. In the relative tranquility of his reign, France implemented Italian ideas of town planning that were to have an impact on later architecture in both Britain and colonial America. In an effort to unify the aristocracy and rebuild Paris, which was still largely medieval, Henry IV sanctioned the construction of a number of residential squares, bounded by row houses with uniform façades. The Place Royale, now the Place des Vosges (Figures 9.92, 9.93), was the first of these urban squares used exclusively for residential purposes; it was laid out from 1605 to 1612. In addition to lending the enterprise his title, Henry supported the project by constructing two pavilions, one in the center of each of the north and south sides of the square. Thirty-eight plots surrounding the 460-foot-square court were then leased on condition that the row houses constructed there would conform to the overall design scheme: each house was four bays wide and three stories high (not including the dormered attic story), built of brick with stone trim, and roofed with slate. The royal pavilions featured more elaborate details and higher rooflines, although they shared the continuous ground-level arcade that linked the buildings, a detail derived from Renaissance squares in Italy, such as the Piazza SS. Annunziata in Florence, on which Brunelleschi's Foundling Hospital fronts. Originally the central open space of the Place Royale was unplanted; its sand surface was used for festivals and tournaments. An equestrian statue of the king later served as the focal monument in the center. The houses proved to be too small for the aristocrats whom Henry wished to attract to Paris, however, so the first residents of the Place Royale were actually minor nobility and wealthy Parisian merchants instead.

FIGURE 9.91 *Lescot and Lemercier: Louvre (with later additions), Paris, begun 1546; extended 1624.* (Photo: French Government Tourist Office)

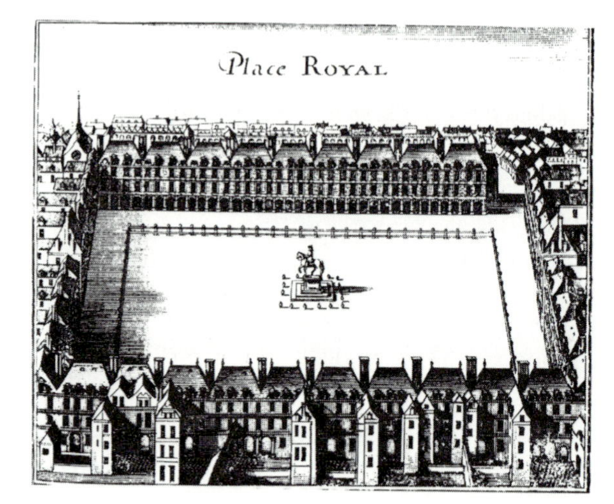

FIGURE 9.92 *Place Royale (Place des Vosges), Paris, 1605–1612.* (From M. Merian)

FIGURE 9.93 *Place Royale (Place des Vosges), Paris.* (Photo: J. Feuillie/C.N.M.H.S./S.P.A.D.E.M.)

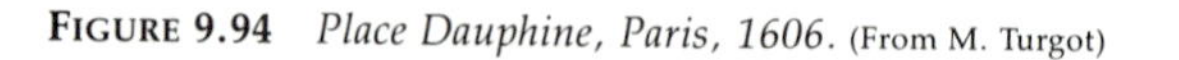

FIGURE 9.94 *Place Dauphine, Paris, 1606.* (From M. Turgot)

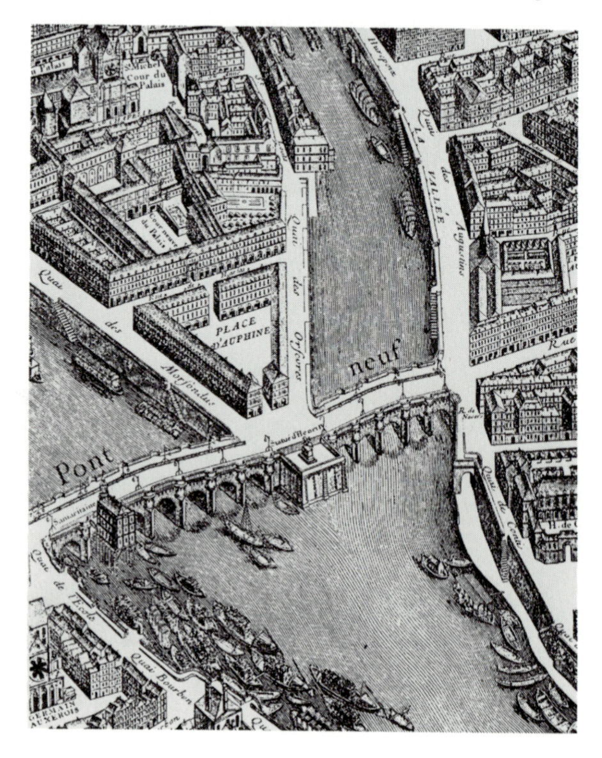

Henry also encouraged a reclamation scheme at the west end of the Ile de la Cité, where in 1578 his father, Henry III, had begun construction of the Pont Neuf to link the business center of the city on the north bank to the university on the south. In conformance with medieval practice, houses were to line the bridge, and triumphal arches were to be set at each end. Henry IV ruled out both these encumbrances to prevent unnecessary blockage of traffic. Instead a trapezoidal point of land at the end of the island was developed in 1606 for another residential square, the Place Dauphine (Figure 9.94). One entered the Place Dauphine from the center of the bridge, and the entrance axis was further distinguished by an equestrian statue of Henry, commissioned from Giovanni da Bologna by Marie de' Medici in 1604 and erected in 1614 after the king's assassination. As at the Place Royale, the houses lining the square had uniform façades; merchants lived upstairs and their shops extended along the ground level, making the Place Dauphine a commercial area.

Henry's queen, Marie de' Medici, became regent after the assassination of her husband, and in 1615, she commissioned the Luxembourg Palace (Figure 9.95, 9.96) from Salomon de Brosse (1571–1626). The building is symmetrically arranged around a central

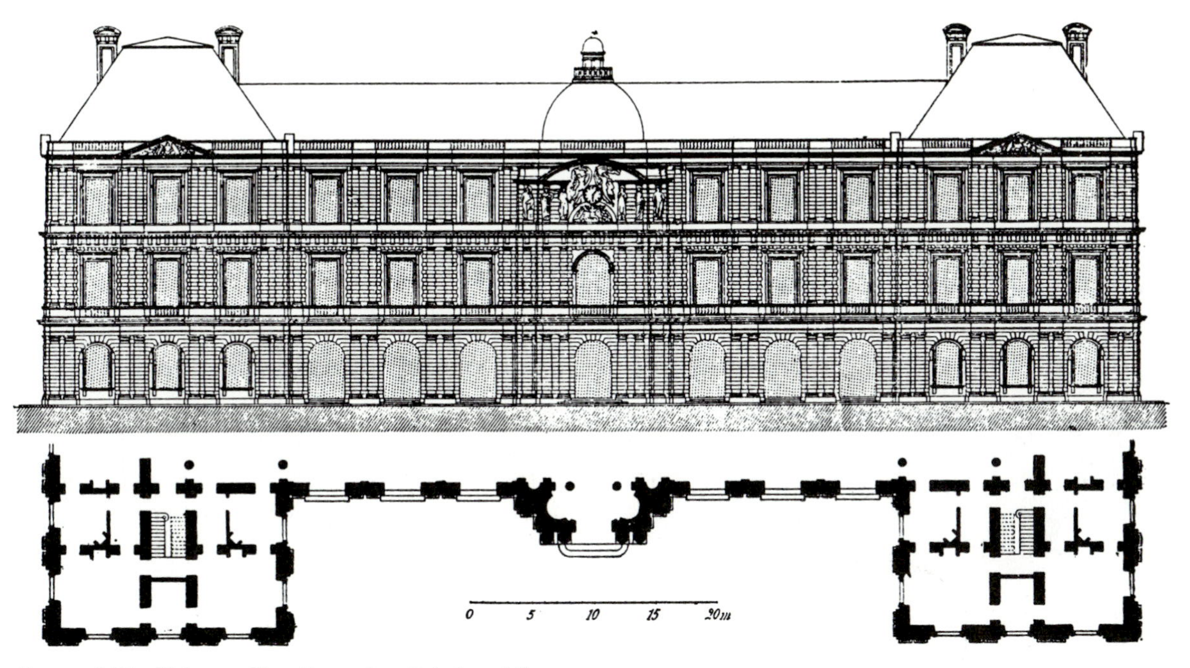

FIGURE 9.95 *de Brosse: Elevation and partial plan of the Luxembourg Palace, Paris, begun 1516.* (From J. Guadet)

FIGURE 9.96 *de Brosse: Plan of the Luxembourg Palace, Paris, begun 1516.* (From C. Gurlitt)

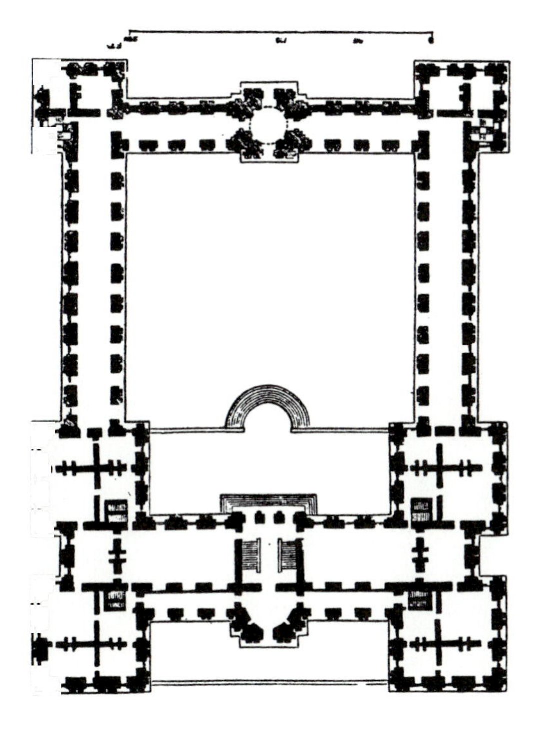

axis; the three-story main block or *corps-de-logis*, is a linear building that connects four corner pavilions, each containing an interconnected suite of rooms (*appartements*). (The similarity of these arrangements to those in the chateau of Chambord should be noted; the *appartements* became the basic unit for domestic architecture in French town residences or *hôtels*. The French *hôtel* generally contained several *appartements* connected to common reception rooms and salons.) Extending perpendicular to the *corps-de-logis* are two long, single-story galleries that terminate with a screen wall and central entrance pavilion enclosing a court. The ensemble has clear massing with each element in the composition articulated distinctly, yet the whole building is united by a common use of lightly rusticated masonry and steeply pitched roofs.

THE RENAISSANCE IN ENGLAND

As was the case in France, Gothic architecture continued to be the predominant building style in England long after the Renaissance had originated and matured in Italy. Perpendicular Gothic, a particularly English variant, enjoyed favor well into the sixteenth century. The earliest expression of the Renaissance in Britain was in sculpture and the decorative arts. Henry VIII employed Pietro Torrigiani (1472–1528) from 1511 to 1518 on a number of royal

FIGURE 9.97 *Torrigiani: Tomb for Henry VII, Westminster Abbey, London, 1511–1518.* (From *American Architect and Building News*)

commissions, the most important of which was a tomb for Henry's parents, Henry VII and his queen (Figure 9.97), placed in the late Gothic chapel of Westminster Abbey (see Figure 8.67). Cardinal Wolsey employed Italian sculptors, including Giovanni da Maiano, to make ten glazed terra-cotta roundels containing busts of Roman emperors. These roundels, which followed antique models and were thoroughly Renaissance in spirit, were ultimately incorporated into the gateways of the Cardinal's medieval castellated palace at Hampton Court (Figure 9.98), begun in 1515. After the Cardinal's fall from royal favor, Henry VIII confiscated the palace and enlarged Hampton Court to more than twice its original size. He added courts, galleries, a chapel, and a hall, but the building remained more medieval than Renaissance; the hall even had a hammerbeam roof built from 1531 to 1536.

Another essentially Gothic building of this same era is King's College Chapel, Cambridge (see Figure 8.71), begun in 1446 and completed in 1515. Inside, however, the wooden choir screen is a piece of early Renaissance design. It was erected in 1533–1535 as a gift from Henry VIII, to separate collegians from townspeople and to support the organ. The artist is unknown, but his work represents the first truly Renaissance design in Britain, exhibiting a wide range of classical details with only a few pendants suggesting Gothic influence.

Henry broke with the Church of Rome in 1534, and numerous Italian artists of the Roman Catholic faith left Britain soon thereafter. The full flowering of the Renaissance in Britain was thus delayed until the beginning of the seventeenth century. This does not mean that Italian ideals ceased to influence Britain but that the direct inspiration from Italian artists resident in Britain stopped, while a more indirect wave continued to come from Italy via the Low Countries. The treatises of Scamozzi, Vignola, and Serlio were translated into English from the Dutch, not directly from the Italian, and numerous Dutch architectural books were exported to England because trade between the two countries was strong. The interlaced strapwork decoration of Flemish and Dutch architects, such as Hans Vredman de Vries, found its way into the works of the English architects Robert Smythson (1536–1614) and John Thorpe (ca. 1563–1655).

Renaissance influence from Italy continued to come into Britain via Flanders during the reign of Queen Elizabeth I. Her own architectural commissions were insignificant, but her courtiers and governmental officials built on a lavish scale for the queen and her traveling entourage. Wollaton Hall (1580–1588) is an example of a great house built dur-

FIGURE 9.98 *West gatehouse, Hampton Court Palace, London, begun 1520.* (Photo: Wodehouse)

FIGURE 9.99 *Smythson: Wollaton Hall, Nottingham, 1580–1588.* (From J. Britton)

ing the Elizabethan era (Figures 9.99, 9.100). Designed by Robert Smythson for the Sheriff of Nottingham, the house relies on numerous sources. The great hall with ancillary accommodations in the center of the scheme is medieval; the symmetrical square plan with corner pavilions is taken from Serlio; and a long gallery for the lodging of courtiers comes from France. Although built in masonry, the huge expanse of windows across the façade is comparable to the fenestration found in timber construction. Renaissance pilasters and cornices punctuate the elevation, while the parapets are inspired by de Vries, and the upper clerestory levels of the great hall (Figure 9.101) protrude above the roofline as a great medieval keep with pepper pot corner turrets. Another great Elizabethan mansion, in all probability designed by Smythson, is Hardwick Hall in Derbyshire (1590–1597) (Figure 9.102). It shares many of Wollaton's characteristics in plan and elevation, but of greater importance here is the symmetrical arrangement of the main hall and its contiguous exterior colonnades, which reflect contemporary Italian design. Like all these grand and pretentious late-sixteenth-century country residences, Hardwick helped advertise the wealth and social standing of its owner, the eccentric Elizabeth of Shrewsbury, known as Bess of Hardwick. Her initials, E.S., are displayed in the house's decorative crowning balustrade.

John Thorpe's houses, if in fact they are by him,

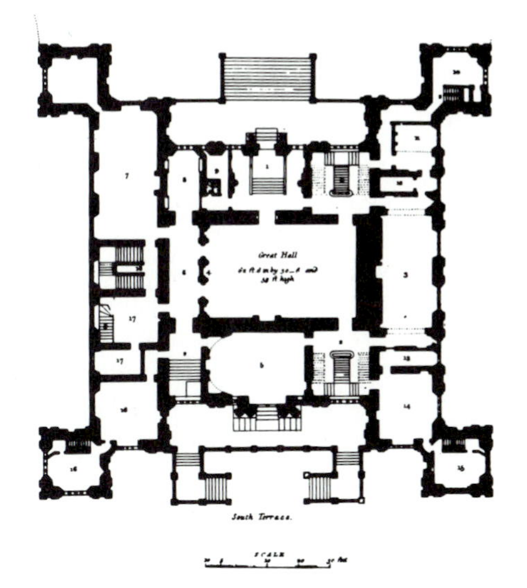

FIGURE 9.100 *Smythson: Plan of Wollaton Hall, Nottingham.* (From J. Britton)

FIGURE 9.101 *Smythson: Great hall of Wollaton Hall, Nottingham.* (From J. Britton)

are more French in style than Smythson's. Kirby Hall in Northamptonshire (1570–1575) has ranges of rooms around a central symmetrical courtyard. The designer uses classical orders freely, but at such a variety of scales and in such improbable positions (as where roofs butt into gables) that the whole seems primitive and immature. The axis of the courtyard centers on a two-story triumphal arch capped by an elaborate gable, perhaps inspired by the earlier central pavilion of Lescot's courtyard façade of the Louvre in Paris. This same motif also dominates the design for William Cecil at Burghley House (1577–1587), also situated in Northamptonshire.

It is amazing how backward looking this second phase of the English Renaissance appears to be compared to what was projected under Henry VIII or what was to come during the reign of Elizabeth's successor, James VI of Scotland, who became James I of England. Inigo Jones, an architect usually considered to be the father of English architecture, emerged during the reign of James I. Jones was born in 1573, seven years before the death of Palladio, and his first building, the Queen's House at Greenwich, introduced Palladian ideals to England. With the architecture of Inigo Jones, English achievements equalled those of late sixteenth-century Italy.

Unlike earlier English architects Jones acquired his knowledge of Italian architecture firsthand. He was in Italy as early as 1601. Two years later he traveled to Denmark, and he made a second trip to Italy during 1613–1614 in the entourage of the Earl of Arundel. In his baggage Jones carried a copy of Palladio's *Four Books of Architecture*, which he annotated generously. He met Scamozzi and visited Vicenza, where Palladio's works profoundly influenced him. On his return his works for the English court consisted at first of stage sets, in which he could experiment with Renaissance forms, although he eventually had the opportunity to build lasting architectural spaces.

FIGURE 9.102 *Smythson: Hardwick Hall, Derbyshire, 1590–1597.* (Photo: Wodehouse)

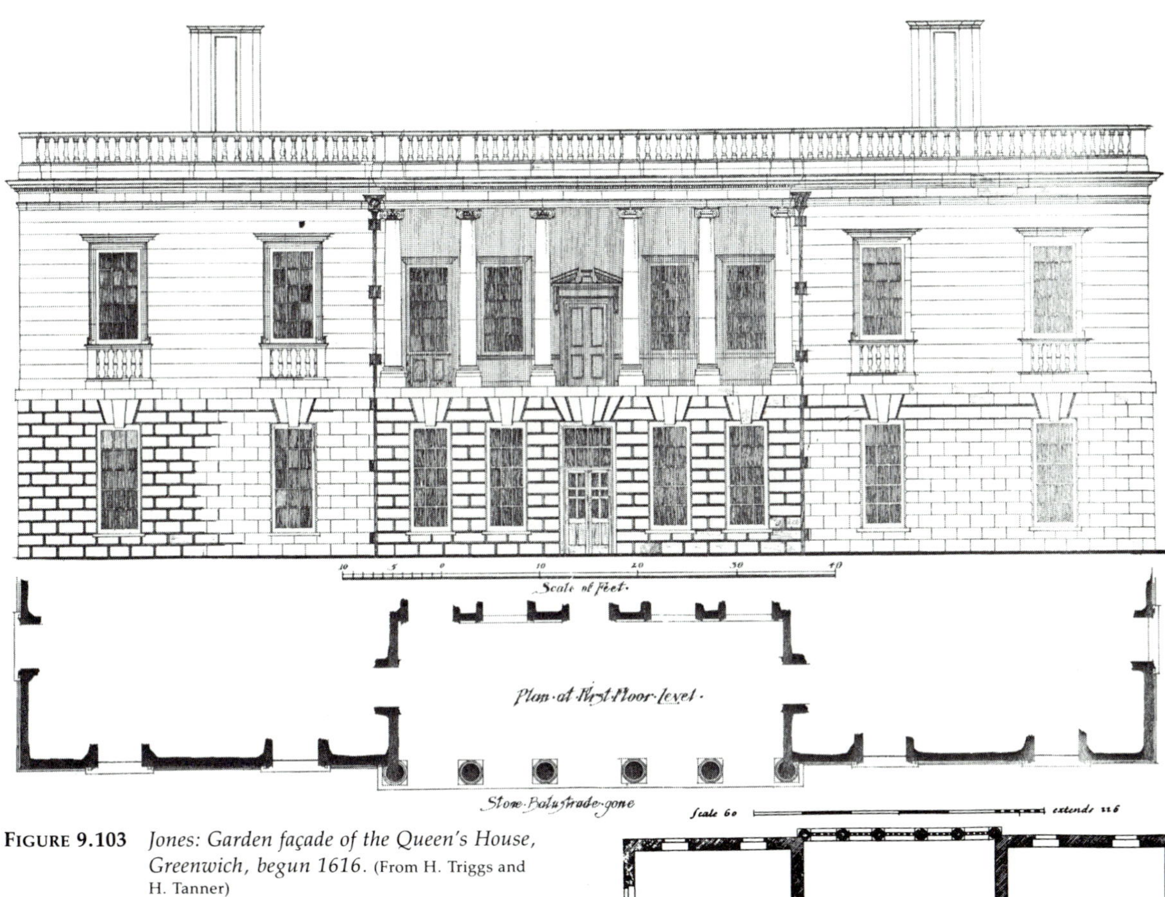

FIGURE 9.103 *Jones: Garden façade of the Queen's House, Greenwich, begun 1616.* (From H. Triggs and H. Tanner)

The Queen's House (Figures 9.103, 9.104), begun in 1616 but still being extended in 1661, was situated astride the road from Deptford to Woolwich, which divided the house into two halves. A bridge spanned the road at the second-floor level and acted as a porte-cochère (a covered drive-through for vehicles) to the entrance in the center of the building. From the rather modest doorway, one is led directly into a room with the proportions of a cube. Access to the second floor is gained by a circular stair without a newel, a daring structural accomplishment in its day. A **balcony** across the cube room connects second floor rooms, including the Queen's bedroom, with the bridge. The garden façade of the house is based on Palladio's Palazzo Chiericati (see Figure 9.67) at Vicenza; but whereas the Palladian building has a two-story colonnade interrupted in the center of the second floor with a ballroom, the garden front of the Queen's House is a fenestrated

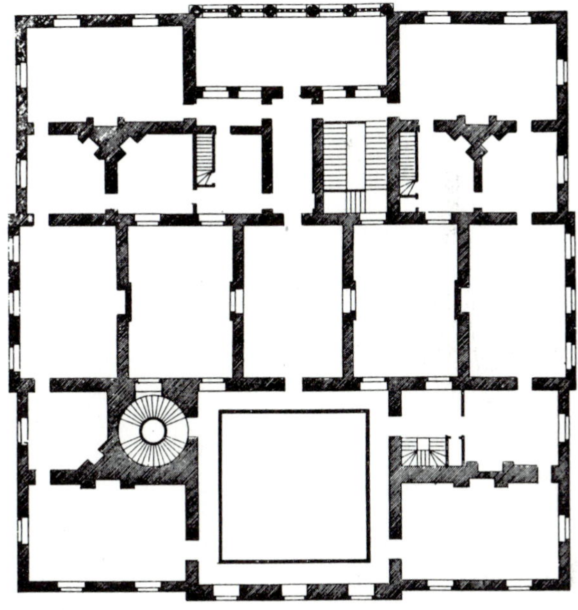

FIGURE 9.104 *Jones: Upper level plan of the Queen's House, Greenwich.* (From H. Muthesius)

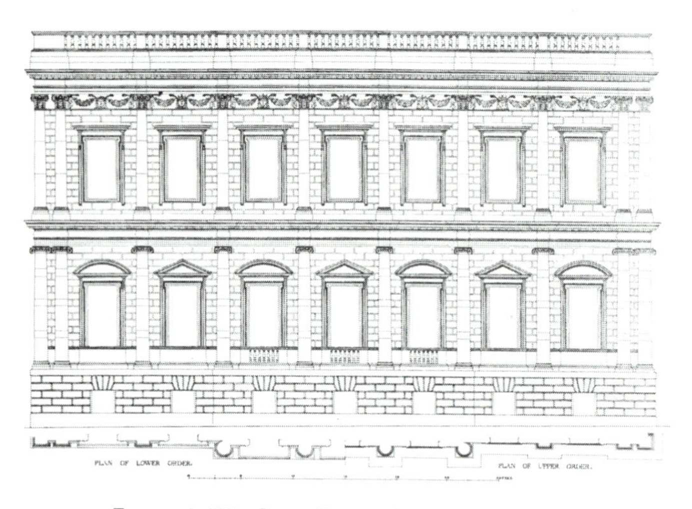

FIGURE 9.105 *Jones: Banqueting House, London, 1619–1622.* (From H. Triggs and H. Tanner)

wall with a central recessed loggia well-protected from the cool winds of Greenwich. Solid and void have been reversed in the exteriors of the two buildings.

Jones's most famous structure, the Banqueting House (1619–1622) at Whitehall in London (Figure 9.105), was built to replace an earlier structure that had burned. Its design was an anglicized version of a Vitruvian basilica as interpreted by Palladio. The main interior space consists of a double cube room with continuous balcony, expressed on the exterior as a two-story structure with a pedimented pavilion on its long main elevation. This was ultimately modified into a simpler elevation, articulated in thirds according to the example of Palladio and omitting the pediment. Half-columns on the central pavilion provide a contrast in depth with the flat pilasters on either side. Windows have alternate segmental and triangular pediments along the main level to distinguish the piano nobile from the rusticated masonry of the base, where flat lintels are used. The roofline of this building is masked by a balustrade.

FIGURE 9.106 *Jones: Project for Whitehall Palace, London, 1638.* (From H. Muthesius)

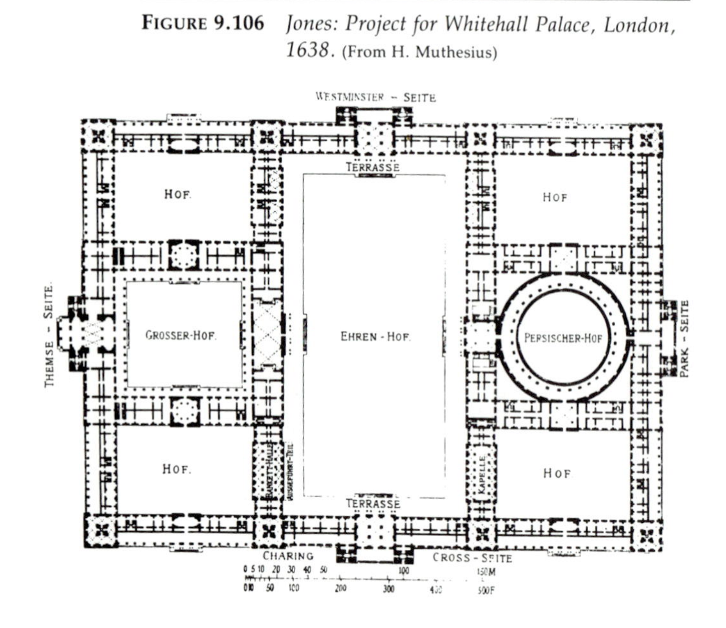

When Jones proposed a new design for the whole of Whitehall Palace in 1638, the Banqueting House would have been incorporated into half of one side of the central court (Figure 9.106). The enormous palace would have created many courts replacing an area of rambling medieval structures. Although Jones's palace design was never built, the Banquetting House stood tall and monumental in its surroundings of earlier domestic-scaled medieval buildings, and its basic features were adapted in subsequent centuries for the ranks of overscale governmental buildings that form its present-day context.

On a site approximately halfway between the Banqueting House and the City of London to the east, the fourth Earl of Bedford employed Jones in 1630 to design his speculative development of the garden area of Bedford House, known as Covent Garden (Figure 9.107). Jones collaborated with Isaac de Caux in this work, the first of the English residential town squares based on the designs for Henry IV's Place Royale in Paris. As in its French predecessor, the houses facing Covent Garden had continuous ground-level arcades, masking entrances to the individual houses but providing a covered passageway around two sides of the square. Five streets entered the square, which had Bedford House to its south and a church based on an Etruscan temple to the west. Although rebuilt after a fire in 1795, the church of St. Paul's Covent Garden (1631–1635) still resembles Jones's original

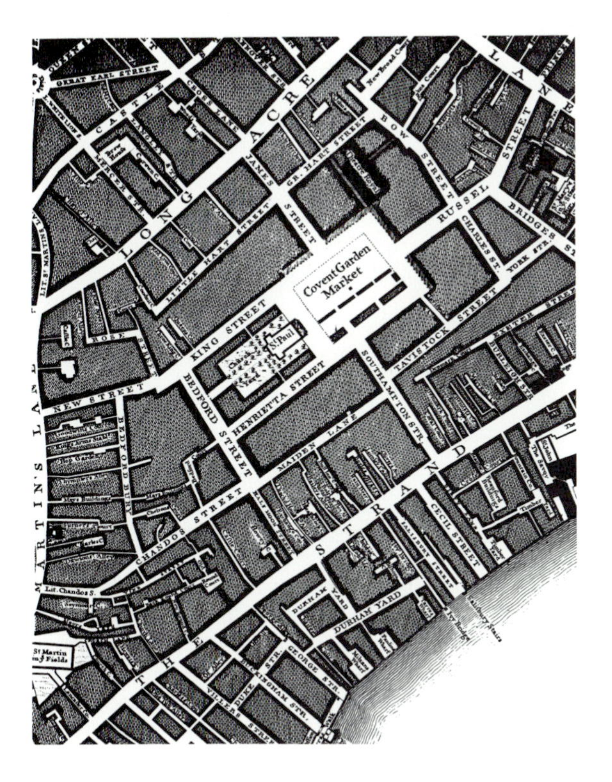

FIGURE 9.107 *Jones: Covent Garden, London, 1630.* (From J. Pine)

design, a simple box with portico, false door and altar at the east end, and the actual entrance at the west (Figure 9.108). The open space of the square soon became the site of a flourishing market, a use that continues to this day in permanent cast-iron halls constructed during the nineteenth century.

St. Paul's Cathedral in London was in poor repair at the beginning of the seventeenth century, and Jones was commissioned to restore it. He added a Corinthian portico to the west front, incorporating large scrolls to mask the aisle roofs, but the whole church was badly damaged in the fire of 1666, and both church and portico were demolished to make way for the later design of Christopher Wren, whose works belong to the seventeenth century and will be considered with other Baroque designers in Chapter Ten.

FIGURE 9.108 *Jones: St. Paul's, Covent Garden, London, 1631–1635.* (From H. Triggs and H. Tanner)

10.

Baroque Architecture

Just as the bankers and merchants of Florence supported Early Renaissance artists and architects, the Catholic Church was the primary patron of art and architecture around Rome in both the seventeenth and eighteenth centuries, and the works it commissioned gave rise to a new style, the Baroque.

By the end of the Renaissance, the Church had great temporal power, but its moral foundations had grown shaky as the institution became increasingly corrupt. The rank of cardinal was sold openly; high and low Church officials maintained mistresses and sought sinecures for their sons (euphemistically called nephews); and donations of the pious were spent on projects wholly lacking in spiritual purpose. The popes lived grandly, treating the Church's treasuries as their personal funds. To finance both sacred and secular projects, the Church instituted questionable fund-raising practices, such as the sale of pardons and indulgences to save the payer or his relative from a stipulated number of days in Purgatory. As could be expected, the corruption of the Church eventually brought about calls for religious reform, some as early as the thirteenth century. The most effective came from the monk Martin Luther of the monastery at Wittenberg, Germany. In 1517 he nailed his ninety-five theses to the door of All Saints Church, in the opening salvo of what would become known as the Protestant Reformation, which proclaimed justification by faith alone. Until this time the Church had always overcome challenges from deviants within its ranks, usually by declaring them heretics and destroying them by force. This time, however, the discontent was too widespread for inquisitional methods to work, although they were tried.

The Church's more reasoned response was the Catholic Counter-Reformation, a program that involved both reform within the Church itself and a sustained campaign to win people back to the beliefs of Catholicism. All the arts were deployed in this public relations effort, and the artistic style that developed to restate traditional Catholic teachings became known as the Baroque. Based on an elaboration of classical forms, already made highly individual by artists and architects in the earlier sixteenth century, the Baroque was a didactic, theatrical, and highly emotional style. Critics have faulted its exaggerated gestures, excessive ornamentation, and unconcealed emotionalism. Seen in the context of its time, however, when such appeals were as genuinely felt as the harrowing Romanesque depictions of hell were in the twelfth century, the Baroque should be viewed as an artistic period that aimed to involve people directly with religious ideals. Baroque architecture is characterized by spatial complexity and the drama of light from undisclosed sources. This was achieved through the dynamic

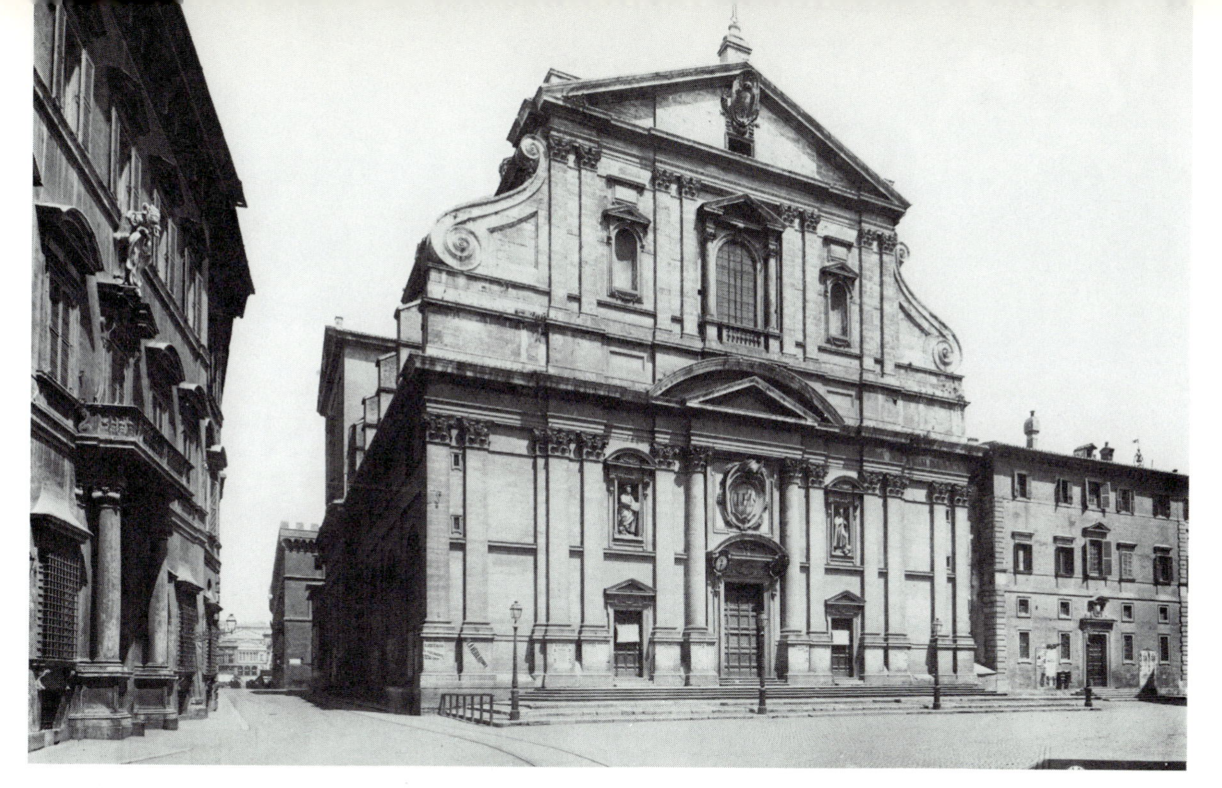

Figure 10.1 *Vignola and della Porta: Il Gesù, Rome, 1568–1576.* (Photo: Alinari)

play of concave against convex curves; a preference for axial and centralized spaces that found particular expression in the ellipse or oval, at once axial and centralized; and the imaginative integration of painting, sculpture, and architecture to create illusions and dissolve physical boundaries.

Among the new institutions of the reformed Catholic Church was the militant Order of the Society of Jesus, established by St. Ignatius Loyola in 1534 and commonly known as the Jesuits. Serving as missionaries and educators, particularly in remote areas, the Jesuits reached China by 1550 and accompanied Spanish conquistadores to the Americas. Their headquarters were in Rome, however, and it is fitting that one of the earliest Baroque architectural designs, Il Gesù (Figures 10.1, 10.2), was their principal church, begun in 1568 to plans by Giacomo Vignola and completed in 1576 by Giacomo della Porta, who designed the façade and dome.

Il Gesù resembled Alberti's S. Andrea at Mantua in plan, having chapels flanking the nave in place of aisles. Il Gesù differs from Alberti's design in that the transepts are shallow and do not project beyond the line of the side walls, and the nave is much broader. The Gesù design was also forward looking

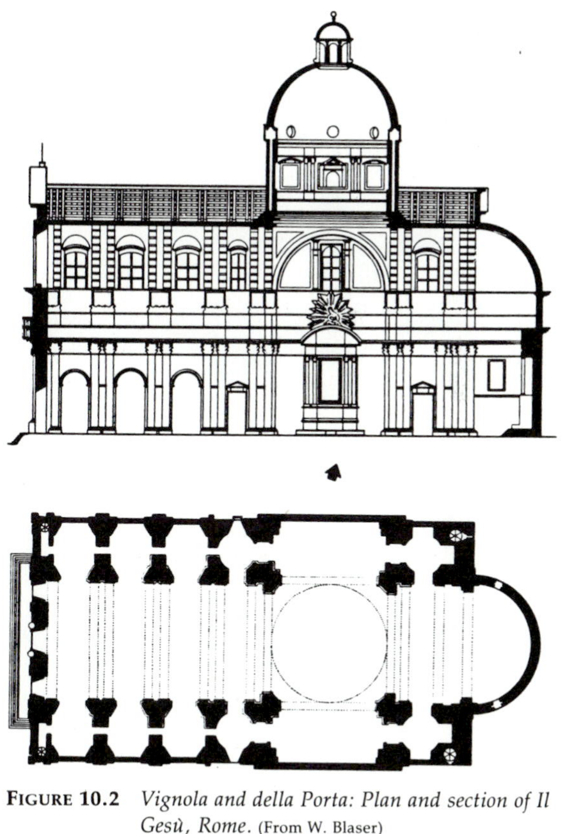

Figure 10.2 *Vignola and della Porta: Plan and section of Il Gesù, Rome.* (From W. Blaser)

FIGURE 10.3 *Maderno: S. Susanna, Rome, 1597.* (Photo: Alinari)

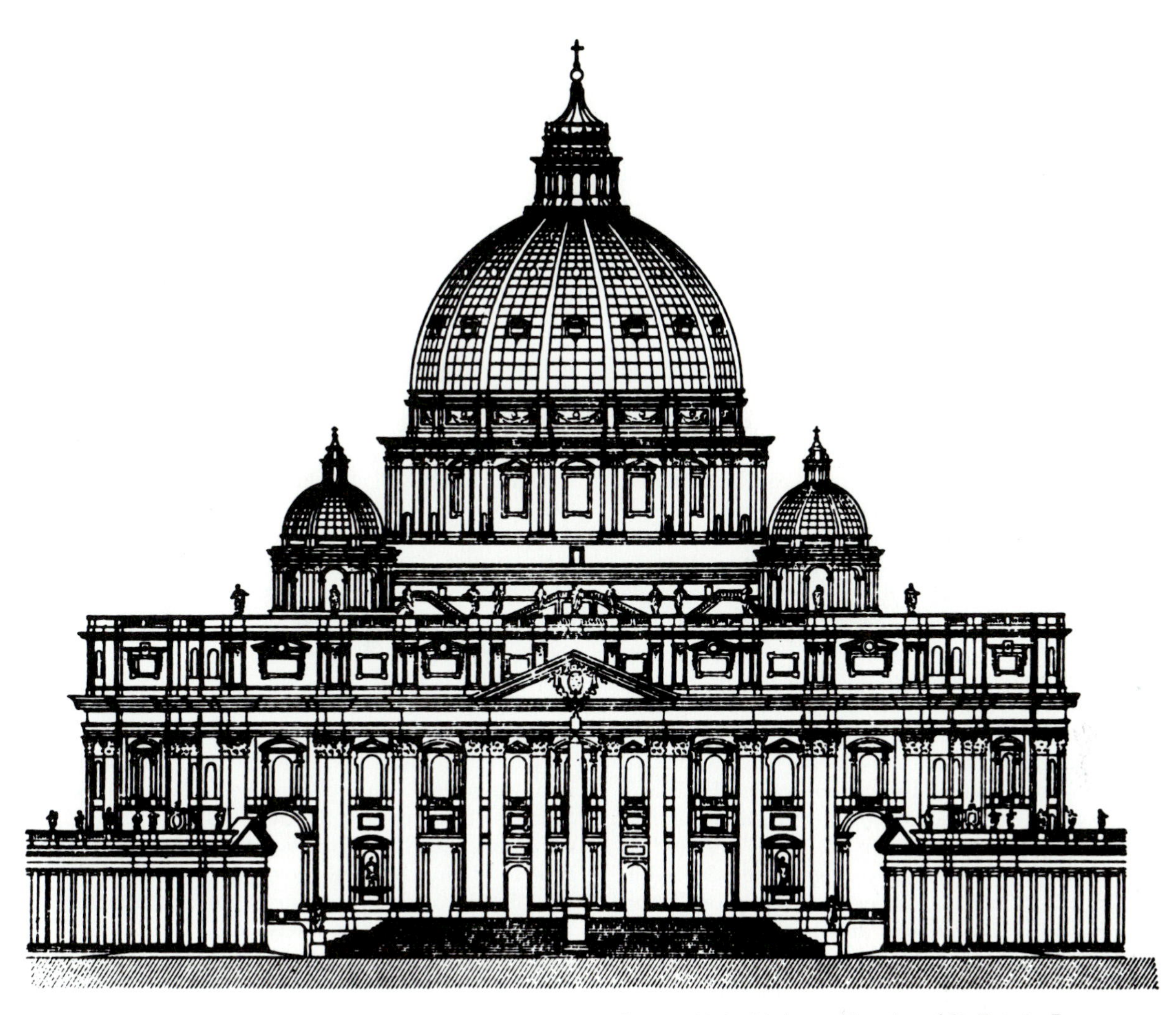

FIGURE 10.4 *Maderno: Elevation of St. Peter's, Rome, 1606–1612.* (From J. Guadet)

in its strong axial emphasis and in the buildup of elements on its west front. The composition of this façade derives from Alberti's S. Maria Novella in Florence, with classical orders replacing the geometry based on squares. Pairs of pilasters step out on forward projecting planes until, on either side of the entrance, engaged columns support a triangular pediment, which in turn is framed by a segmental pediment supported by flanking pilasters. The original interior design was absolutely pristine; the interior seen in the church today reflects a decorative campaign that began in the late seventeenth century. Looking up at the nave ceiling, one is never sure where the architecture stops and the sculpture begins, or where the sculpture terminates and the fresco of the *Adoration of the Name of Jesus* (painted between 1675 and 1679 by Giovanni Battista Gaulli) begins. Clouds, draperies, and human bodies float in space, and one's view extends up into heaven.

The façade of Il Gesù became the model for many Jesuit churches built in Rome and elsewhere. As Jesuit missionaries traveled and constructed new churches, their designs retained features from the mother church in Rome, where all Jesuits received their training. Within Rome itself one church that expands on the theme of Il Gesù is Carlo Maderno's early Baroque church of S. Susanna (1596–1603), where the façade design progresses from pilaster to half column to paired engaged columns (Figure 10.3). S. Susanna in turn became the basis for the monumental façade of St. Peter's (Figure 10.4), designed by Maderno in 1606.

SIXTUS V AND THE PLANNING OF ROME

Within a decade of the completion of Il Gesù, early Baroque influences could be seen in the modifications made to the urban pattern of Rome. Pope Sixtus V instigated these modifications (1585–1590), and the design he set guided the city's development for the next hundred years or more.

Sixtus V was not the first pope to be concerned about the neglected physical character of Rome. His work can be seen as a vigorous elaboration and extension of initiatives begun in the 1450s by Pope Nicholas V (1448–1455), the first Renaissance pope to gain full control over the city following the 200-year period when the pope resided in Avignon. Nicholas had undertaken fundamental repairs to ancient structures, such as the city walls, bridges, aqueducts, and roads on which Romans still relied, and he also had certain monuments modified to suit current use, such as the conversion of Hadrian's Mausoleum into the Castel Sant'Angelo, a fortress for the papal court. Pope Sixtus IV (1471–1484) had restored old churches and commissioned the building of others and had attempted to improve circulation within the chaotic and densely populated medieval quarter by straightening the streets that led to the Ponte Sant'Angelo, the bridge over the Tiber that connected the bulk of Rome with St. Peter's. Julius II (1503–1513), continued Sixtus IV's projects, as discussed earlier in conjunction with Julius's patronage of Bramante and Michelangelo. In addition to those notable works around the Vatican and St. Peter's, Julius directed his energies to civic improvements, including the creation of three straight streets radiating like spokes from the Porta del Popolo, the northern city gate, and the cutting of two roughly parallel straight avenues on either side of the Tiber downstream from the Ponte Sant'Angelo. One of Julius's successors, Paul III (1534–1550), commissioned Michelangelo's redesign of the Capitoline Hill. Pius IV laid out a straight avenue, the Via Pia (1561–1562), for which Michelangelo designed the Porta Pia (see Figure 9.63) to be the terminating portal.

FIGURE 10.5 *Fontana: Sixtus V plan for Rome, showing the new street cut toward S. Maria Maggiore, 1585–1590.* (From J. Heck)

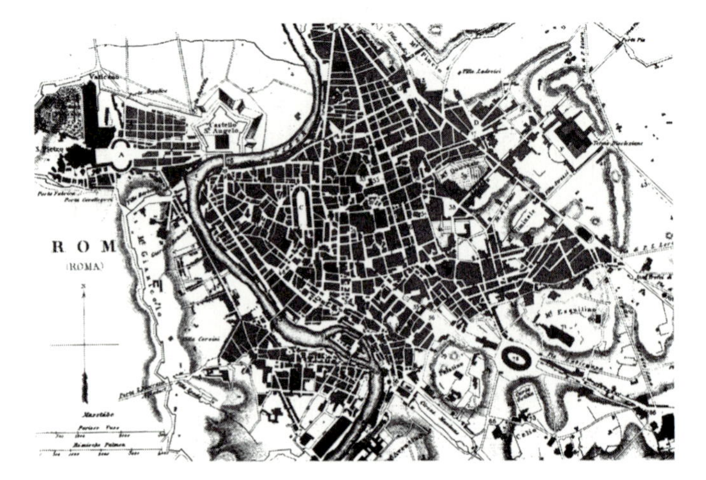

These interventions in Rome were accelerated and intensified during the five years and four months of the reign of Sixtus V. Public works were undertaken, including the building of twenty-seven new fountains and the provision of reliable water supplies through the repair of ancient aqueducts and the construction of a new one, even as law and order were brought into the city's government. The wool and silk industries were revived, further increasing employment opportunities. Had Sixtus lived another year, the Colosseum might have been refurbished into a wool-spinning establishment!

The people who most benefited from the changes wrought by Sixtus were visitors and pilgrims coming to see the major Christian shrines in Rome. Realizing that these religious visitors were important to the city, Sixtus planned to link the seven Early Christian basilicas of Rome with direct processional routes, punctuated by vertical elements and fountains to mark major points along the way (Figure 10.5). This was a much larger realization of ideas first developed in sixteenth-century gardens, such as the Boboli Gardens in Florence. Given the irregular topography of the city, this was no easy task, for a plan on paper of straight roads could not always be superimposed successfully on the terrain. The reworking of the city proposed by Sixtus was so convincing, however, that nearly all architects, planners, and civic authorities who have continued the work in the following centuries have done so in accordance with his scheme.

Sixtus began with the construction of a new street, the Strada Felice, which extended from Santa Maria Maggiore to Santa Croce in Gerusalemme in one direction and in the other direction to Trinità dei Monti on the Esquiline Hill. The initial intention was to continue this street on to the Porta del Popolo, the major city gate for visitors arriving from the north, but the intervening hills prevented this idea from being realized. As a related project, therefore, the Piazza del Popolo was redesigned to provide an appropriate entranceway for visitors. After passing through the gate, visitors came into a space that focused on a central obelisk. Radiating from this center were three existing streets, which provided direct access to major districts of the city. From the Piazza del Popolo, the left radial street was the via del Babuino, which led to a fountain at the base of the Esquiline Hill on which the church of SS. Trinità dei Monti sits. Sixtus dedicated the church in 1585, and a connector linking the church and the fountain below was built over a century later.

The most important Christian monument in Rome was the Basilica of St. Peter, located across the Tiber from the older parts of the city. During Sixtus's reign, work was again resumed on the construction of the dome after twenty-five years of relative inaction following the death of Michelangelo. Sixtus also turned his attention to the route linking St. Peter's to the rest of Rome. Pilgrims crossed the Tiber on the Ponte Sant'Angelo, at the end of which was the massive Castel Sant'Angelo. The route to St. Peter's continued to the west, but the direct link projected by Sixtus did not become a reality until the 1930s, when Mussolini pushed through the Via della Concilazione to provide a majestic axial approach to the great church. From a distance one can clearly see the dome of St. Peter's rising above the nave and wide façade, although Michelangelo's dome, designed for a naveless church, gradually recedes from view as one comes closer to the actual building.

Centered in the Piazza of St. Peter's is Sixtus's contribution to the shaping of the space in the front of the basilica, the eighty-three-foot tall Vatican Obelisk, which was moved there in 1586. Technical direction for this monumental feat of engineering was provided by Domenico Fontana, who later wrote a book describing and illustrating the entire process (Figure 10.6). The Vatican Obelisk was the largest intact specimen of the dozen Egyptian obelisks moved to Rome during the Empire. How the ancient Romans had maneuvered these is unknown, but the presence of several broken ones indicates that their methods were not always successful. Fontana's task was to lower the obelisk (which weighed 681,221 pounds) from its position

FIGURE 10.6 *Fontana: Various schemes for moving the Vatican Obelisk, 1586.* (From D. Fontana)

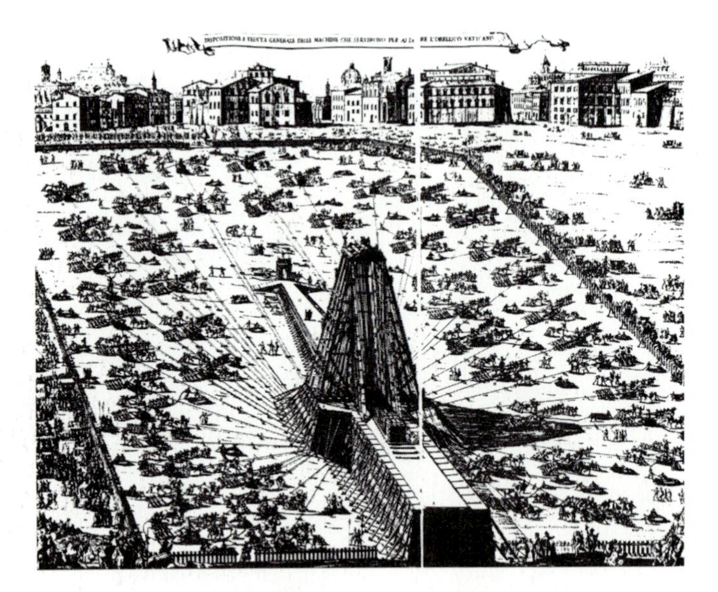

FIGURE 10.7 *Fontana: Erection of the Vatican Obelisk in St. Peter's Square, 1586.* (From D. Fontana)

in the former Circus of Nero and move it about 260 yards to its new location in the Piazza of St. Peter's, all without damaging the monolith or its carvings. His solution to the problem involved encasing the obelisk in a protective timber framework, transferring it to a horizontal position by means of ropes and pulleys (controlled by the coordinated action of men and horses working thirty-eight windlasses), and then moving it over rollers to the new site. An elevation drop of approximately thirty feet between the old and new sites facilitated the horizontal transport. Once in the Piazza, the obelisk was moved down an inclined plane, and reerected using the same hoists and capstans employed to lower it. The entire operation was carefully planned and supervised by Fontana, who was empowered by the pope to appropriate men, materials, and horses as necessary for the completion of the work. As the obelisk was raised in front of St. Peter's on 29 April 1586, the entire College of Cardinals along with the citizenry of Rome turned out to watch the spectacle (Figure 10.7). Barricades kept the curious at a safe distance, and absolute silence was enforced during the critical lifting stages so that the workmen could hear and respond correctly to Fontana's signals, given by a trumpet and a bell.

Following his successful removal of the Vatican Obelisk, Fontana was commissioned to relocate three smaller obelisks in Rome. The obelisks standing today in the Piazza del Popolo, at S. Giovanni Laterano, and at S. Maria Maggiore were all positioned by Fontana. The pyramidal points of these great shafts are prominent beacons indicating the important monuments in the city. Sixtus V's work in Rome was doubtless a major influence on the twentieth-century city planner Edmund Bacon, who was responsible for major redevelopment work in Philadelphia in the 1950s and 1960s. Bacon's use of axial avenues to link major areas of the city and high-rise buildings (instead of obelisks) to mark different areas shows the continuing impact of Baroque city planning in Rome.

THE COMPLETION OF ST. PETER'S

Gianlorenzo Bernini

After the death of Sixtus V, work continued at St. Peter's, and this project, so long in construction at the direction of architects whose abilities, styles, and philosophies varied considerably, was at last brought to completion during the Baroque period. The dome was finished in 1612 under the direction of Giacomo della Porta and Domenico Fontana, and the nave addition, not envisioned by Michelangelo was designed by Carlo Maderno, who also designed the main façade (Figure 10.8). The nave shifts ever-so-slightly to align with the Vatican Obelisk, which Fontana had mistakenly set off-center; Maderno considered it easier to turn the nave imperceptibly than to move the Egyptian needle. Pope Urban VIII consecrated the church in 1626.

Urban VIII's artist was Gianlorenzo Bernini (1598–1680), one of the outstanding creative talents of western history, a man who might easily be compared with Michelangelo. Both were recognized as prodigies at an early age; both had long and productive lives; and both were immensely inventive sculptors who also did important work in architecture and city planning. Bernini was the son of a sculptor, and his artistic education was directed in

FIGURE 10.8a *Plan of the completed St. Peter's, Rome.* (From W. Blaser)

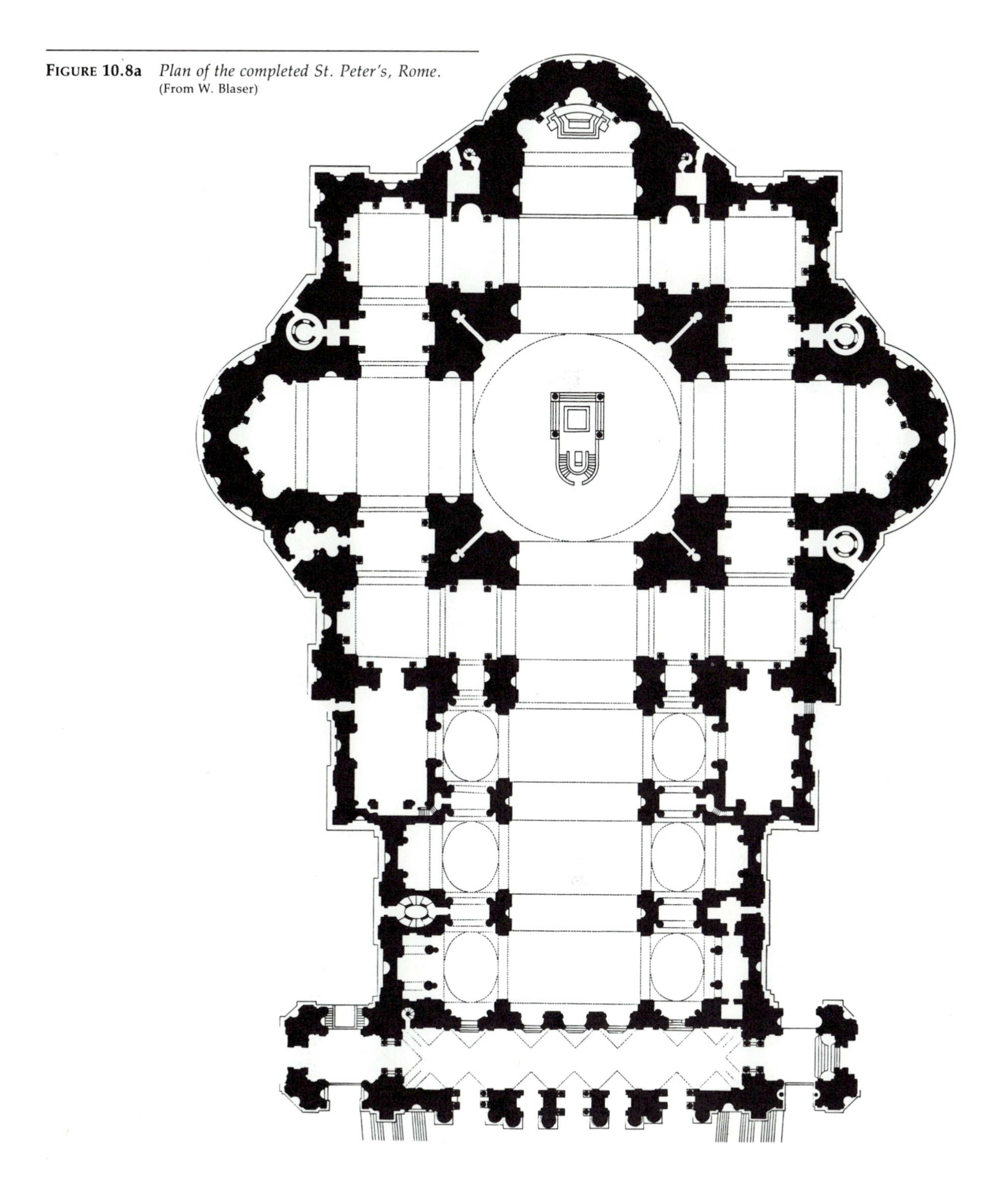

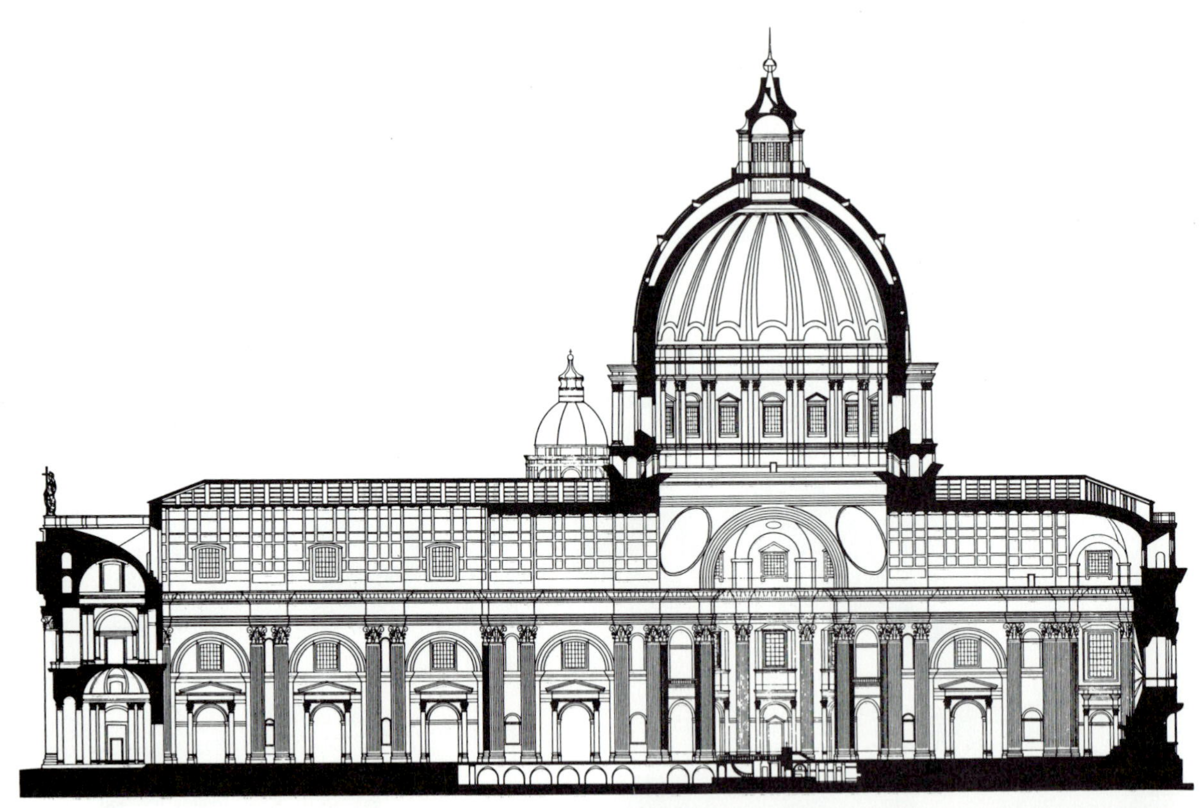

Figure 10.8b *Section of the completed St. Peter's, Rome.* (From W. Blaser)

part by Maffeo Cardinal Barberini, a noted patron of the arts even before he was elected Urban VIII. The invigorated building programs of the Catholic Church in the seventeenth century were responsible for the development of the Baroque style, and for over fifty years, Baroque work in Rome was dominated by Bernini.

Nowhere is his presence felt more strongly than at St. Peter's, where he served as official architect from 1629 until his death. Much of the present interior's character is the result of Bernini's genius. Either directly or through workshops under his supervision, Bernini was responsible for the flooring in the nave and narthex, for the decoration of the nave piers, and for the design of four sculptural groupings for altars and tombs. His designs for the crossing and main apse of the church, however, are the most substantial contributions he made to the interior. To reduce the scale of the vast space under Michelangelo's dome, Bernini designed the bronze

Figure 10.9 *Bernini: Baldacchino, St. Peter's, Rome, 1624–1633.* (From R. Sturgis)

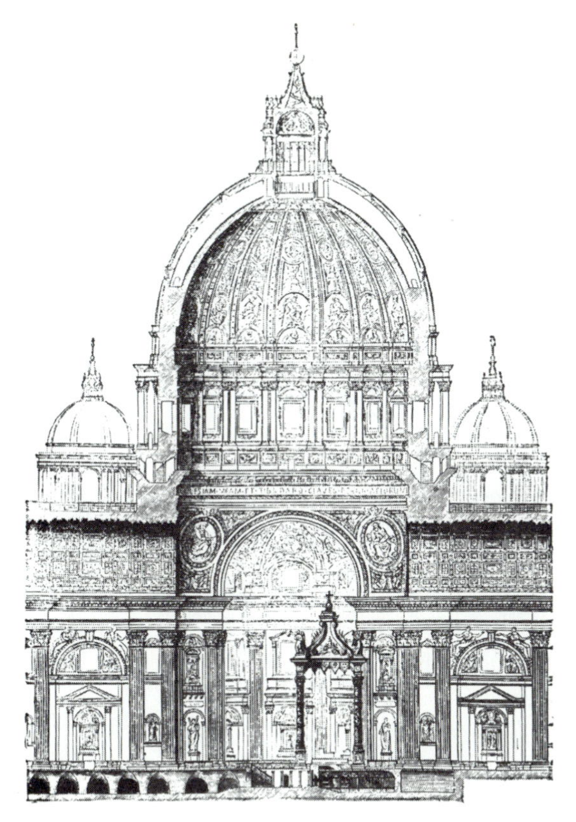

FIGURE 10.10 *Bernini: Section through the dome and Baldacchino, St. Peter's, Rome.* (From J. Fergusson)

Baldacchino (1624–1633), a symbolically protective canopy over the high altar above the tomb of St. Peter. To match the scale of the rotunda, the Baldacchino is nearly ninety feet high; its twisted columns are not a Baroque invention, but a greatly enlarged version of marble columns from the Constantinian basilica, some of which are preserved as part of the reliquaries at the second floor level of the crossing piers. It was believed that the original twisted columns were brought by Constantine from the Temple of Solomon in Jerusalem, so their continued use here links St. Peter's with the Holy Land. Material for the Baldacchino was obtained by melting down the Roman bronze roof trusses of the Pantheon's portico, a reuse of historic material sanctioned by the pope over popular opposition; there was even enough metal left over to cast eighty cannon for defense of the city. In the enormous space of the basilica, the Baldacchino distinctly marks the spiritual center of the church, which would otherwise appear insignificant. So large is the interior that the Baldacchino's height, equivalent to a nine-story building, is not overpowering from a distance.

In the angles of the crossing piers Bernini's design placed four dramatic statues of saints associated with the Passion of Christ, all more than twice life-size. Of these Bernini himself carved the St. Longinus (1629–1638), the Roman centurion who pierced Christ's side at the Crucifixion; Longinus is shown at the very moment he realizes Christ's divinity. Beyond the Baldacchino and framed on axis by its columns is Bernini's culminating work in the basilica, the Cathedra Petri, or Chair of Peter (1657–1666), an elaborate reliquary in bronze constructed around the reputed wooden seat of the first apostle (Figure 10.11). Lightly supported by four figures representing Doctors of the Church (those men who established the doctrine of the faith), the chair floats

FIGURE 10.11 *Bernini: Cathedra Petri, St. Peter's, Rome, 1657–1666.* (From J. Guadet)

ALEXANDER·VII·PONT·MAX

above the visitor's head against a glorious backdrop, where golden rays emanate from a brightly illuminated stained-glass center on which floats the dove of the Holy Spirit. The church of St. Peter's, as with some other Early Christian buildings, is not aligned with its apse to the east but rather to the west, so the rays of the afternoon sun pass through the window and merge with the golden radiance of the sculpture surrounding the chair. By incorporating a window behind the work to provide brilliance for the ensemble, Bernini's design admirably illustrates the theatricality of the Baroque.

In addition to these major features Bernini designed the Scala Regia (1663–1670), leading from the main audience hall in the Vatican to the north colonnade of the piazza and the north end of the church's narthex, as a replacement for the old irregular stair (Figure 10.12). Bernini's design turns to full advantage the difficult context into which the work had to be set; he designed a staircase tapering in width and height from bottom to top, thus accentuating the effect of perspective from the bottom of the stairs. A landing halfway up creates a pause in the ascent; lit by an undisclosed source, it becomes a dramatic element in the design (Figure 10.13). As the Scala Regia is almost perpendicular to the narthex, Bernini made an equestrian statue of Constantine for the side wall at the bottom of the stairs to terminate the axial vista at the end of the narthex. The emperor is depicted at the moment of his conversion on the battlefield; a huge drapery blown by the wind provides a dynamic directional backdrop to the statue.

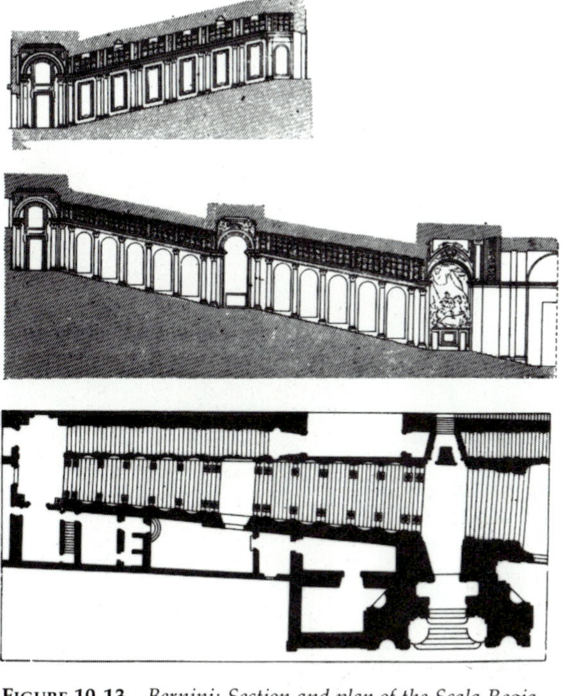

FIGURE 10.13 *Bernini: Section and plan of the Scala Regia, Vatican.* (From J. Guadet)

As the greatest church in western Christendom, St. Peter's required an appropriate approach and exterior setting, and Bernini was also commissioned to undertake this work. In 1637 he proposed that two bell towers be constructed at the ends of the narthex in order to counter the horizontal emphasis of Maderno's façade. Only the southernmost tower had been partially built when soil subsidence and subsequent cracking of the building necessitated removal of the campanile in 1645, almost ending Bernini's architectural appointment in disgrace. In 1657, however, Bernini designed the Piazza of St. Peter's, one of the most famous urban spaces in the world (Figures 10.14, 10.15). Composed of two parts, the Piazza has an oval section, the *piazza obliqua,* which focuses on the Vatican Obelisk, followed by a trapezoidal section, the *piazza retta,* directly in front of the church entrance. Both sections work together to provide a symbolic embrace for Christians who come to visit the tomb of St. Peter. The *piazza retta* attempts in two ways to ameliorate the proportions of the façade by increasing the apparent height of the church. Its trapezoidal shape, which is perceived as a rectangle, "squeezes" the façade to emphasize verticality, and its side walls diminish in height as they extend toward the church, thereby providing a smaller unit to which the engaged Corinthian columns of the façade are compared. Although the converging sides of the *piazza retta* may suggest influence from Michelangelo's Piazza del Campidoglio, the form was probably generated by the oblique placement of the Vatican Palace relative to the narthex of the church.

The *piazza obliqua* is more characteristically Ba-

◄ **FIGURE 10.12** *Bernini: Scala Regia, Vatican, 1663–1670.* (Photo: Alinari)

FIGURE 10.14 *Bernini: Piazza of St. Peter's Rome, begun 1657.* (Photo: Special Collections Library, University of Tennessee)

roque, with curving arms that do not form a true oval but are actually two semicircles connected to a square. Two symmetrically placed fountains and the obelisk establish a cross axis to the approach to St. Peter's, thus introducing an element of tension in the design. The piazza's sides are formed by free-standing Tuscan colonnades, thirty-nine feet high and four columns deep, arranged in radial lines to provide a constantly shifting pattern of light and shadow as one moves around the edge. The colonnades generate a sense of enclosure without confinement; space is defined without being cut off from the fabric of the city. Over 250,000 people can gather in the Piazza of St. Peter's to be blessed from the Benediction Loggia above the central entrance to the church or from a window in the papal apartments, at the right of the Piazza. Through its dignified and all-encompassing design, the Piazza S. Pietro extends the Church's welcome beyond the boundaries of the Basilica itself.

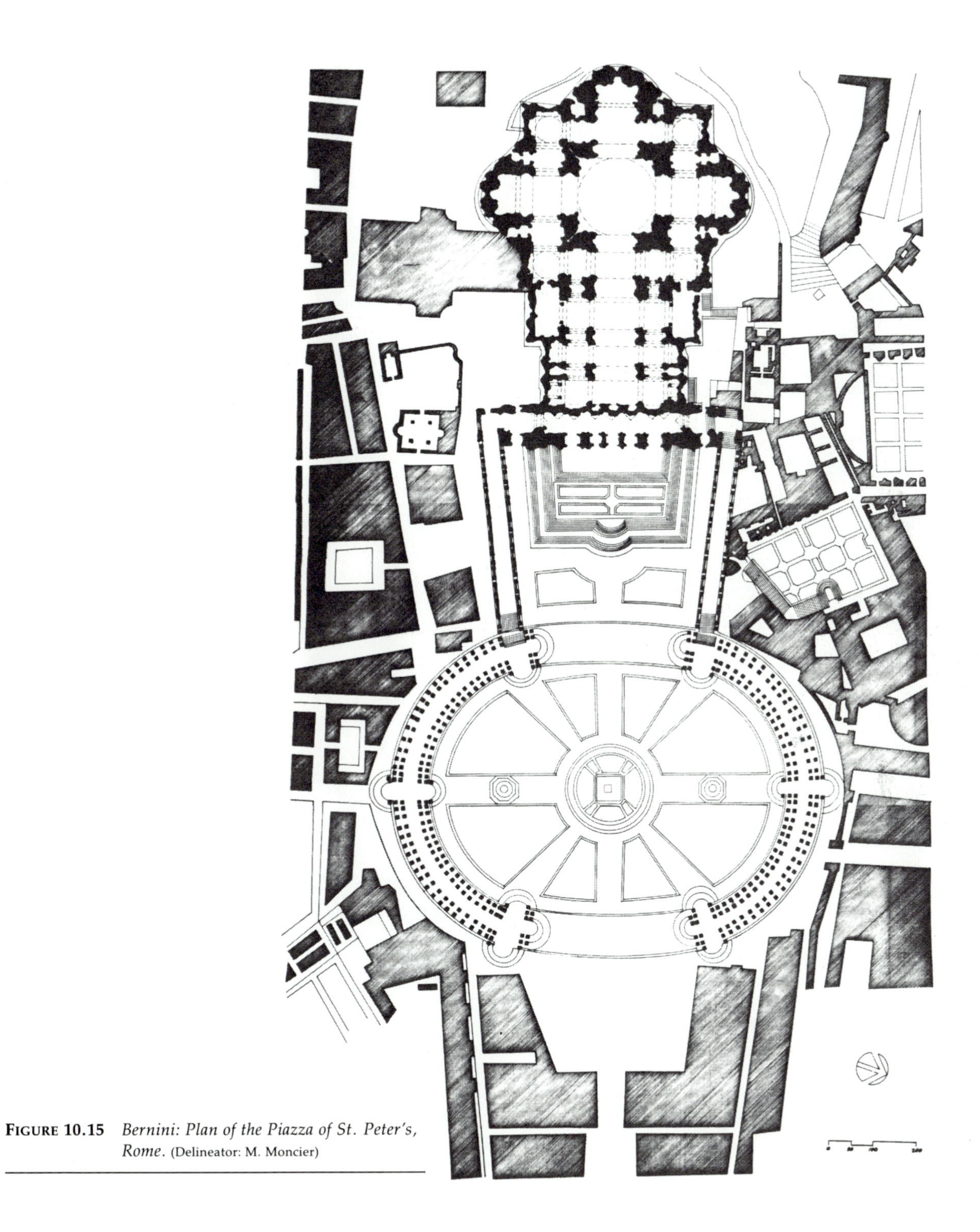

FIGURE 10.15 *Bernini: Plan of the Piazza of St. Peter's, Rome.* (Delineator: M. Moncier)

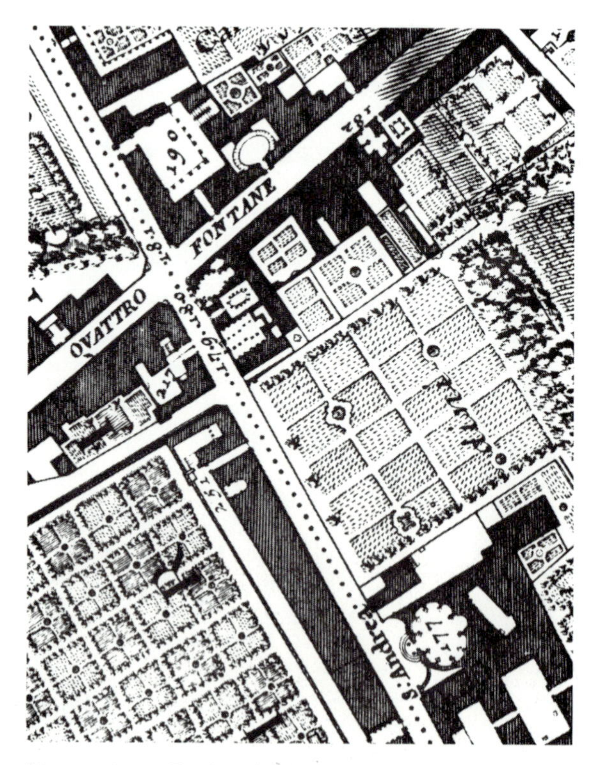

FIGURE 10.16 *Portion of Nolli's* Map of Rome *showing location of S. Carlo alle Quattro Fontane and S. Andrea al Quirinale.* (From G. Nolli)

Francesco Borromini

While the completion of the interiors of the Basilica and construction of the Piazza of St. Peter's were to occupy a substantial part of Bernini's time, these were not by any means the only projects undertaken by this enormously gifted and energetic artist. Nor did he accomplish the work on St. Peter's singlehandedly. He had assistants, some of whom became prominent designers in their own right. This was the case with Francesco Borromini (1599–1667), who began as a stonecutter in Carlo Maderno's shop and rose quickly to become a master mason and Bernini's collaborator on the Baldacchino. After a time these two men of great talents and strong personalities clashed, and before 1630 Borromini had emerged as an independent architect, the rival of Bernini. Of Borromini's many commissions around Rome, two are of particular interest as demonstrations of his strikingly original approach to design.

Projects for the church of S. Carlo alle Quattro Fontane (Figure 10.16) involved Borromini on and off from 1634 until his death. He began with renovations to the monk's living quarters, including a new refectory and cloister (1634–1638), a courtyard in which curves replaced the customary corners. In 1638 he designed the splendid church (Figure 10.17) at the corner of the Strada Felice and the via Pia (today known as the Via Quattro Fontane), one of Sixtus V's grand routes linking districts of the city. He

FIGURE 10.17 *Borromini: S. Carlo alle Quattro Fontane, Rome, begun 1634.* (Photo: Alinari)

embellished the intersection with four fountains (hence the descriptive Quattro Fontane appended to the name of the church) set diagonally across each corner. The church plan consists of an undulating oval set with the main altar on the long axis from the entrance (Figure 10.18). The curvaceous side walls swell outward on the short axis to form shallow side chapels in a counterpoint evoking the spirit of a Trinitarian cross, appropriate here since the church was for the Trinitarian Order. Pendentives above the entablature reduce the free plan to an oval drum supporting an oval dome, elaborately coffered into octagons, hexagons, and Trinitarian crosses, diminishing to an oval oculus (Figure 10.19). The exterior front, constructed in 1665–1667, mirrors the internal play of concave and convex, swinging in and out over its three-bay width, the two stories of which are tied together by an intermediate curving entablature. The crowning balustrade is broken by a large oval medallion. With consummate skill Borromini incorporated the mitered corner with the fountain into the façade design, so that all parts project the dynamism of the Baroque.

At S. Ivo alle Sapienza (Figure 10.20) Borromini created an archetypal masterpiece of the Baroque.

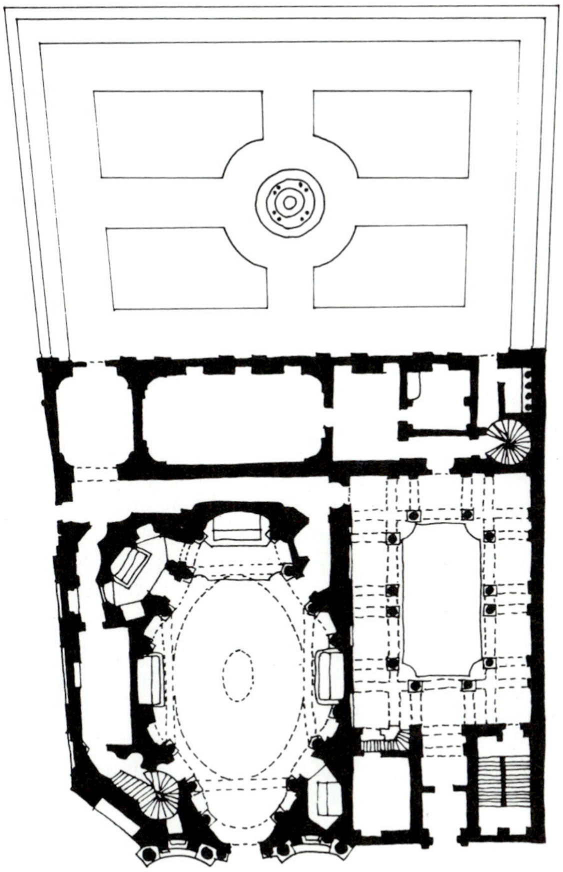

Figure 10.18 *Borromini: Plan of S. Carlo alle Quattro Fontane, Rome.* (Redrawn after H. Stierlin)

Figure 10.19 *Borromini: Interior of dome from S. Carlo alle Quattro Fontane, Rome.* (Photo: Alinari)

FIGURE 10.20 *Borromini: S. Ivo alle Sapienza, Rome, begun 1642.* (From F. Borromini)

FIGURE 10.21 *Borromini: Plan of S. Ivo alle Sapienza, Rome.* (From F. Borromini)

The building consists of a chapel inserted into the curved end of an existing two-story courtyard at the Archiginnasio (a college popularly known as La Sapienza and now part of the University of Rome). Leo X donated the site, but the chapel was not begun until 1642 under the patronage of Urban VIII. Urban's coat of arms incorporates bees of the Barberini family, and Urban was affectionately known as "King of Bees." It is not therefore surprising that Borromini, who had waited ten years for the commission, flattered his patron by incorporating the shape of a flying bee into the form of the plan, which is geometrized as a hexagon (Figure 10.21). The internal entablature between the lower level of the church and the dome does not separate the two areas. Rather, the concave-convex rhythms of the plan rise in planes through the entablature into the ribs of the dome (Figure 10.22). The external lantern tower spirals upward in a form that admits multiple associations: that of the papal tiara, which contains bands of a triple crown, here merged into the continuous spiral, symbolizing the pope's authority in priestly, royal, and imperial affairs; that of a conch shell, one species of which was generally known as the *corona papale* because of its resemblance to the papal tiara; and that of Divine Wisdom, which complemented the symbolism of an upwardly rising spiral. In fact, the iconography of the whole chapel expresses the idea that "all wisdom is from the Lord

FIGURE 10.22 *Borromini: Perspective half section through S. Ivo alle Sapienza, Rome.* (From F. Borromini)

FIGURE 10.23 *Bernini: S. Andrea al Quirinale, Rome, 1658–1670.* (Photo: Alinari)

God" and that "fear of the Lord is the beginning of wisdom." (Ecclesiasticus 1:1)

Just down the via Pia from S. Carlo is Bernini's oval plan church of S. Andrea al Quirinale (1658–1670), designed as a quiet retreat for Jesuit novices (Figures 10.23, 10.24). It affords an interesting contrast to S. Carlo. The shape of the interior is clearly expressed in the curving exterior wall, while an over-scaled Corinthian portico introduces a countercurve. The entrance and altar are opposite one another across the short axis of the space. To maintain emphasis on the altar and establish the short axis as the dominant one, Bernini placed pilasters on the cross axis to bring the visitor's attention back to the important focus, where a sculpted figure of St. Andrew rises through a break in the curving pediment and ascends into the heavenly zone of the dome to the open sky painted in the cupola over the oculus. Whereas Borromini's S. Carlo emphasized the dynamic interplay of concave and convex in geometric variation, movement in Bernini's S. Andrea is concentrated in one direction, upward. This movement in design emphasizes an ephemeral lightness. Painting, sculpture, and architecture are blended together effectively to advance this one idea.

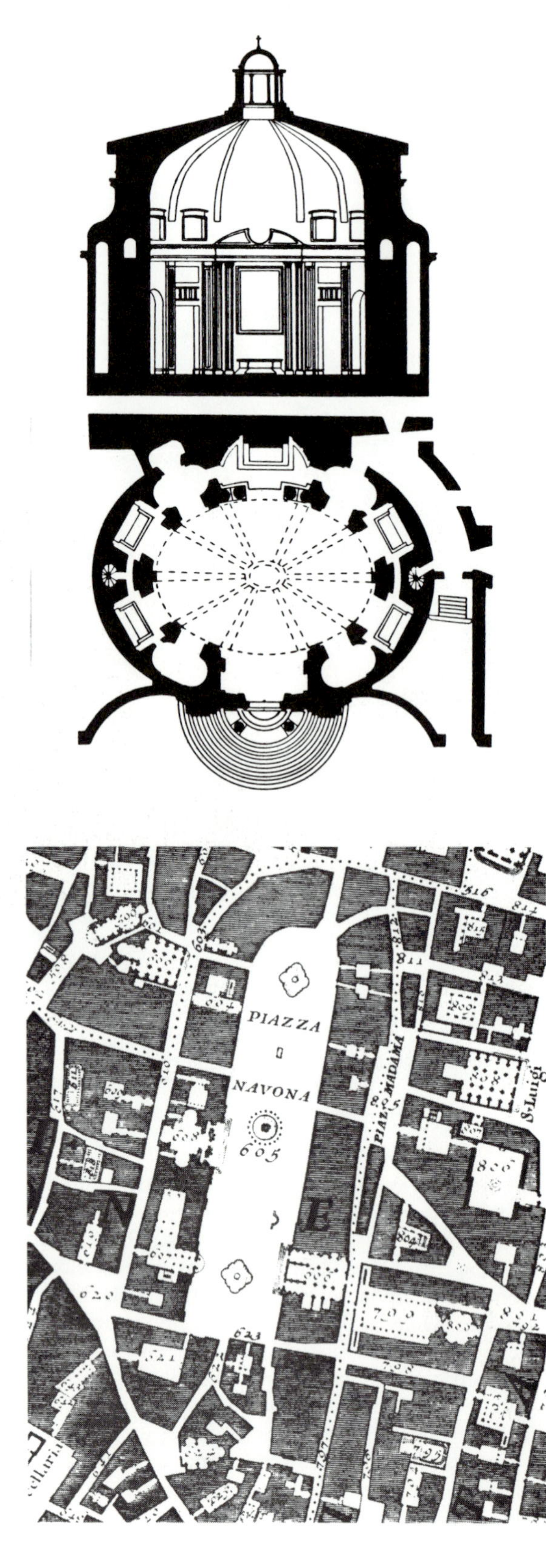

FIGURE 10.24 *Bernini: Plan of S. Andrea al Quirinale, Rome.* (From W. Blaser)

URBAN SPACES IN BAROQUE ROME

With a few notable exceptions, urban design is generally a shared undertaking, evolving over several lifetimes. The bold strokes of Sixtus V's plan for Rome created opportunities for later architects to complete his grand scheme with designs for churches, fountains, and piazzas that enrich civic life. For example, Fontana's placement of the Vatican Obelisk did not necessarily predict Bernini's design for the Piazza, but its position in front of St. Peter's identified the area as one of major importance within the city and contributed to the specific spatial conception realized in 1657. The collaboration of talented designers in Rome on various urban projects has endowed the city with many handsome public squares; three particularly fine Baroque ones will be discussed here.

Bernini and Borromini jointly created the urban design of the Piazza Navona, an unusually proportioned space (177 by 906 feet) that was once the Stadium of Domitian (Figure 10.25). In the medieval period houses were built on the ruins of the stands, while the open center was used for informal games and a market. Pope Innocent X's palace faced the square, and on his election in 1644 he undertook the refurbishing of the piazza and its church, S. Agnese in Agone (Figures 10.26, 10.27). The church comission was first given to Girolamo and Carlo Rainaldi, but their designs displeased Innocent, and in 1653, with the foundations already in place, Borromini assumed control of the building. He retained their Greek cross plan but pulled back the flight of steps protruding into the all-too-narrow square and provided a new concave façade, above which rose a high drum, elongated dome, and slender cupola.

FIGURE 10.25 *Piazza Navona, Rome, begun 1644. S. Agnese in Agone is #608; S. Maria della Pace is #599; and S. Ivo alle Sapienza is #800.* (From G. Nolli)

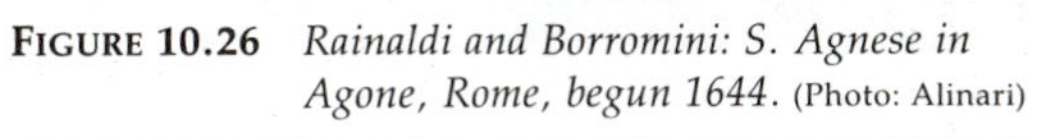

FIGURE 10.26 *Rainaldi and Borromini: S. Agnese in Agone, Rome, begun 1644.* (Photo: Alinari)

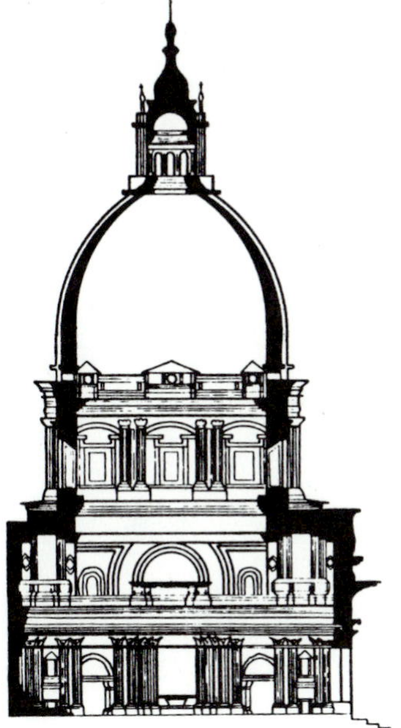

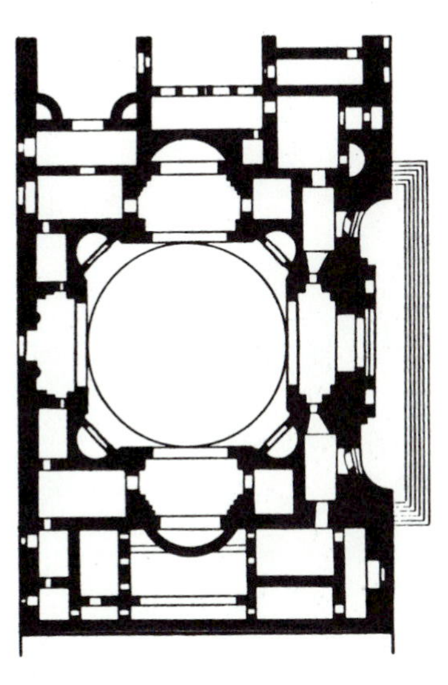

FIGURE 10.27 *Rainaldi and Borromini: Section and plan of S. Agnese in Agone, Rome.* (From W. Blaser)

After 1657 Carlo Rainaldi completed the work, adding the twin towers positioned on either side of the curved façade. In its massing S. Agnese represents the silhouette that St. Peter's might have had without the nave addition.

Bernini, temporarily out of favor for political reasons and the failure of the towers at St. Peter's, was not considered a possible architect for S. Agnese, yet his proposal for the central fountain in the Piazza Navona so pleased Innocent that he disregarded personal animosities and awarded Bernini the fountain commission. The Fountain of the Four Rivers (1648–1651), located in the center of the piazza but off the main axis of S. Agnese so as not to compete with it, has symbolic figures set amid splashing water to represent the major rivers of the continents to which Catholicism had spread. The Ganges figure holds an oar because of that river's

FIGURE 10.28 *Cortona: Façade and Piazza of S. Maria della Pace, Rome, 1656–1658.* (Photo: Wodehouse)

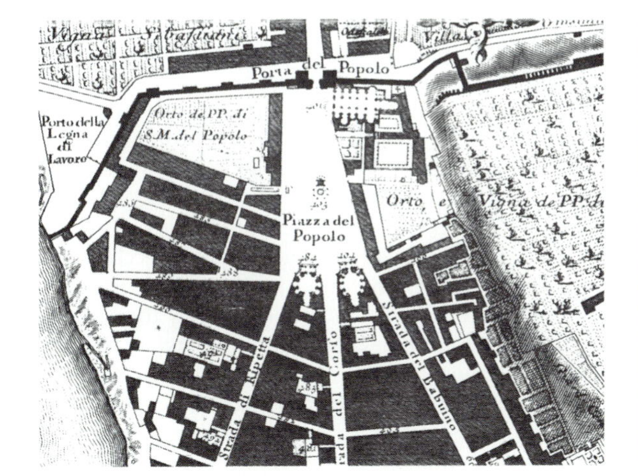

FIGURE 10.29 *Plan of the Piazza del Popolo, Rome.* (From G. Nolli)

FIGURE 10.30 *View of the Piazza del Popolo, Rome.* (Engraving by Piranesi)

great navigable length; the Danube looks toward emblems of Innocent X; the Nile's face is obscured because its origin was then unknown; and the Rio della Plata figure is a creative interpretation of a native South American, bald, bearded, and surrounded by coins to reflect the wealth of the New World. The figures support a central obelisk, crowned with a representation of the dove of the Pamphili family to symbolize the triumph of Christianity over paganism, and, by extension, Catholicism over Protestantism. Thus in Baroque hands, even so secular an item as a public fountain becomes an allegory for the Roman Catholic church. At either end of the Piazza are additional fountains; all three provide visual delight while refreshing the air with cooling moisture.

Just behind the Piazza Navona is one of Rome's smallest squares, in front of the church of S. Maria della Pace (façade designed 1656–1658) (Figure 10.28), which is entirely the work of Pietro da Cortona (1596–1669). The church dates to the fifteenth century; Cortona gave it a new concave façade, whose plasticity is restrained by flanking Corinthian pilasters supporting a pediment. That pediment frames yet another pediment with a curved top cornice and a dropped lower one. Cortona improved access to the church by demolishing parts of surrounding buildings to create a tiny piazza. A semicircular portico with paired Tuscan columns protrudes from the church into the square, and the portico's curve is answered by countercurving wing walls beside the church. The concave-convex interplay is subtle but effective in this diminutive Baroque stage setting.

The next Baroque square to be considered is the Piazza del Popolo (Figure 10.29). Fontana's placement of an obelisk there at the point where its three radial streets converge gave the space a monumental focus. In the mid-seventeenth century Roman planners wanted to further regularize this important gateway to Rome by placing identical domed churches on the trapezoidal sites between the three radial streets. This posed a geometric dilemma, however, for the sites were of unequal width. Carlo Rainaldi, assisted by Bernini, solved the problem by giving one church, S. Maria dei Miracoli (1675–1679), a circular plan, and the other, S. Maria in Montesanto (1662–1675), an oval plan to accommodate its narrower site. Viewed from the obelisk the churches look identical because of their domes and porticoed façades, and their profiles strengthen the dignity of the piazza (Figure 10.30). In 1816–1820, the curved sides were added to the piazza in imitation of Bernini's plan for the Piazza San Pietro.

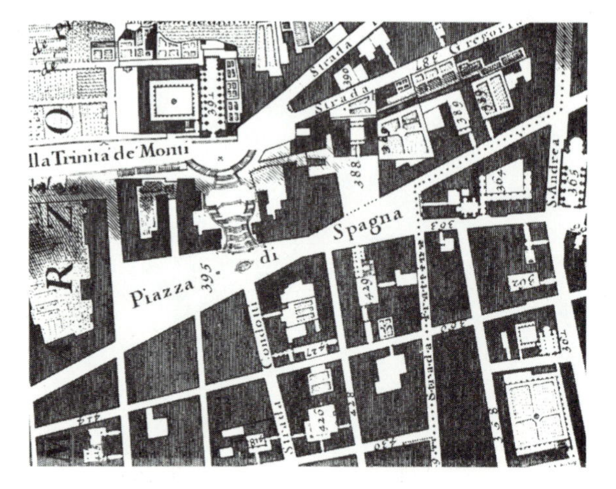

FIGURE 10.31 *Sanctis and Specchi: Plan of the Spanish Steps, Rome, 1723–1726.* (From G. Nolli)

FIGURE 10.32 *Sanctis and Specchi: View of the Spanish Steps, Rome.* (From J. Guadet)

Halfway down the via del Babuino from the Piazza del Popolo is the point where the route to S. Maria Maggiore envisioned by Sixtus V sidesteps to connect with the via Sistina at the top of the Pincio Hill. Topographic difficulties here required the route to make a steep ascent, which was imaginatively resolved by the Spanish Steps (1723–1726), built by Francesco de Sanctis following designs made a decade earlier by Alessandro Specchi (Figures 10.31, 10.32). The project was underwritten by a wealthy Frenchman on land owned by the French church of SS. Trinità dei Monte; the steps were so named because the Spanish Embassy was nearby. From the fountain at its base, gentle curves and countercurves form a dramatic cascading stair that narrows and then divides before reaching an intermediate platform, beyond which the stairs again unite, only to split once more into opposing curves that ultimately ascend to the platform in front of SS. Trinità dei Monti, at the foot of the Strada Felice. It is a popular and effective stage setting inviting promenaders to be both actors and audience, and the design brings enjoyment to the mundane task of climbing or descending by encouraging the pedestrian to linger and look. In the frantic pace of Rome, the Spanish Steps are much appreciated.

THE SPREAD OF BAROQUE ARCHITECTURE

Borromini's work, especially his design for S. Ivo alla Sapienza, became the starting point for the architecture of Guarino Guarini (1624–1683), a designer whose buildings in Turin represent the northern extension of Baroque Rome. Guarini was a member of the Theatine Order, and he served an eight-year novitiate in Rome from 1639–1647. His early work in Turin for the Theatines does not survive; political difficulties led to his expulsion from the city in 1655, and he was to spend the following decade in various places, including France and Spain. On his return to Turin in 1666, he worked on two central plan churches, which remain today as his major buildings.

The Chapel of the Holy Shroud, or Cappella della SS. Sindone (Figures 10.33, 10.34), was added to the east end of the Cathedral of Turin to house

FIGURE 10.33 *Guarini: Section through the Cappella della SS. Sindone, Cathedral, Turin, begun 1667.* (From G. Guarini)

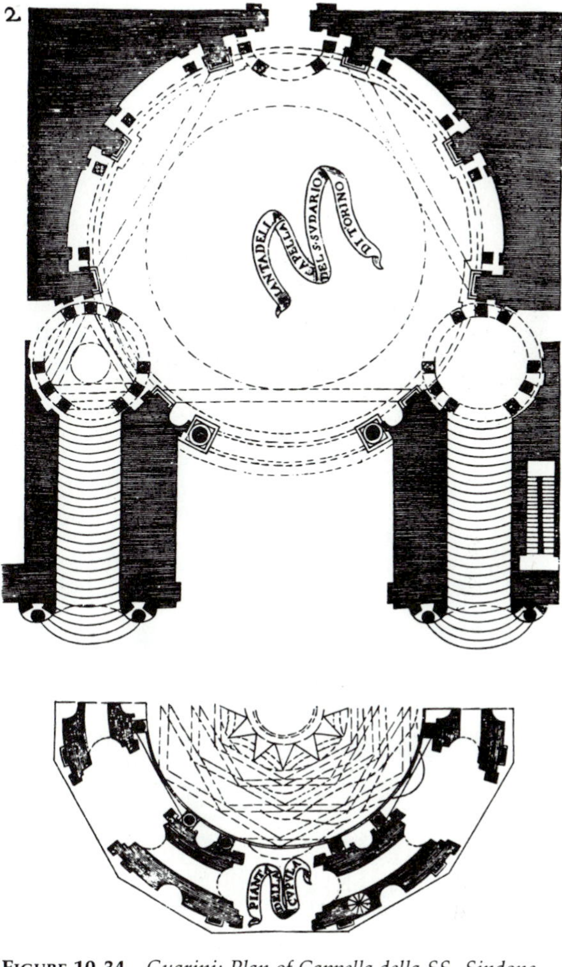

FIGURE 10.34 *Guarini: Plan of Cappella della SS. Sindone, Cathedral, Turin.* (From G. Guarini)

the important relic of the Holy Shroud. Guarini received the commission in 1667, after another architect had begun construction on a circular plan, which Guarini was obliged to retain. By inscribing an equilateral triangle in the circle and redesigning the access stairs and landing vestibules, Guarini brought dynamism to an unimaginative scheme. The domed chapel pulsates with the countercurves introduced by the vestibules and the axial niche, and three pendentives reduce the circular chapel to the smaller circle for the dome, which is not really a dome but an ascending hexagonal network of arches diminishing to an interlaced arch oculus topped by a spiraling lantern. Light filters into the upper zone through small windows set within the arch network and pours in from six large windows at the base of the dome.

For his own order Guarini designed S. Lorenzo (1668–1680), based on an octagon defined by convex Serliana surfaces bulging into the main space, all set

FIGURE 10.35 *Guarini: Section of S. Lorenzo, Turin, 1668–1680.* (From G. Guarini)

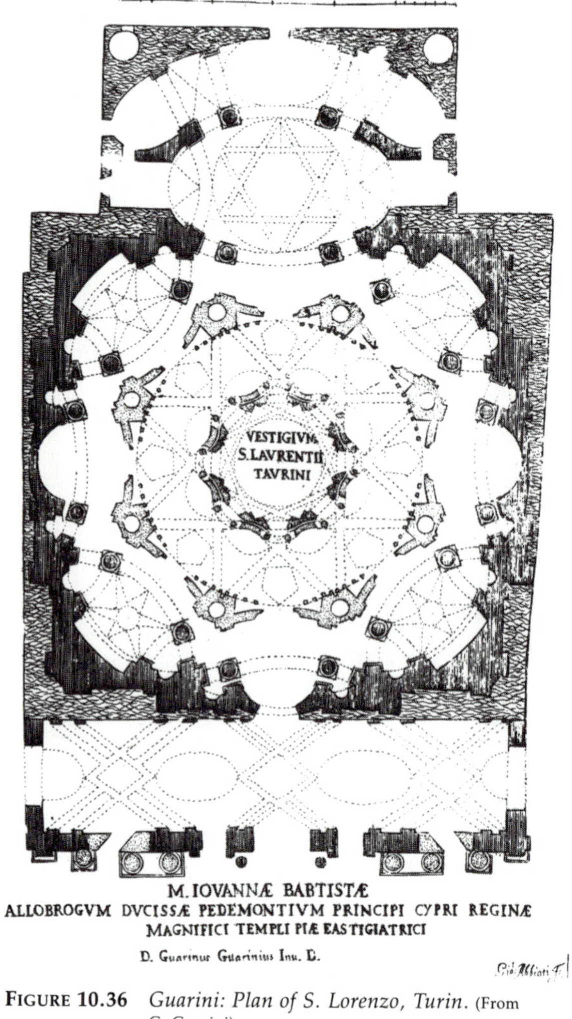

FIGURE 10.36 *Guarini: Plan of S. Lorenzo, Turin.* (From G. Guarini)

within a square and completed by an elliptical choir (Figures 10.35–10.37). The geometric complexity here is astonishing. Squares, octagons, a Greek cross, and circles are involved along with ovals. Again the dome is not so much a solid vault as a ribbed structure with eight interlacing arches, illuminated by oval, pentagonal, and circular openings set between the ribs. Over the choir is a lower, six-pointed ribbed star vault, which, like the main vault, is reminiscent of Islamic ribbed domes at the Great Mosque of Córdoba, which was known to Guarini from his travels. S. Lorenzo's dome, drum, and cupola mirror the play of concave and convex seen on the interior. Further examples of ribbed domes on unbuilt projects appear in Guarini's *Architettura civile,* published posthumously in 1737.

FIGURE 10.37 *Guarini: Interior of S. Lorenzo, Turin.* (Photo: Alinari) ▶

FIGURE 10.38 *Vittone: Dome of the Chapel of the Visitation, Vallinoto, 1738–1739.* (Photo: Wodehouse)

Guarini's greatest successor was Bernardo Vittone (1702–1770), who edited Guarini's treatise for publication. Vittone's early works share Guarini's exuberance, while those of his later years displayed classical tendencies, returning more closely to the architectural principles of Rome. In the Chapel of the Visitation at Vallinotto (1738–1739), superimposed equilateral triangles inscribed in its dome (Figure 10.38) recall Guarini's S. Lorenzo, and the plan harks back to Borromini's S. Ivo. On both the interior and exterior, the chapel is a fusion of the circle and the triangle, with ellipses worked in as chapels (Figure 10.39). Throughout there is a con-

FIGURE 10.39 *Vittone: Chapel of the Visitation, Vallinoto, 1738–1739.* (Photo: Wodehouse)

FIGURE 10.40 *Vittone: Parish Church, Grignasco, 1752–1767.* (Photo: Wodehouse)

FIGURE 10.41 *Vittone: Interior of dome of the Parish Church, Grignasco.* (Photo: Wodehouse)

sistent effort to deny the solidity of the wall and to dissolve physical boundaries of the space. Arches support free-standing pendentives that function as screens behind which light enters from unseen windows. On the ceiling, painted legions of angels circle around the central lantern, where another painting depicts the Holy Trinity.

The chapel at Vallinotto may be contrasted with one of Vittone's late works, the parish church at Grignasco (1752–1767), where both interior and exterior are organized with classical elements: columns, piers, entablatures, and pediments (Figures 10.40, 10.41). The plan is based on a hexagon extended with a square apse terminating in a semicircle. While Baroque love of curves is not extinguished completely — the exterior walls gyrate as convex planes, and the clerestory windows assume irregular oval shapes — the more flamboyant elements of the late Baroque have been considerably subdued.

Palaces were also built as the Baroque spread into northern Italy and northeast into central Europe. The independent princes who governed this territory aspired to splendid residences, and Baroque architects brought drama and exuberance to their commissions. In Turin the extended front added to the Palazzo Madama (Figures 10.42, 10.43) in 1718–1721 by Filippo Juvarra (1678–1736) makes a major feature of a functional necessity, the stair. In Renaissance palazzi, stairs were generally sandwiched between rooms leading off the central courtyards; at the Palazzo Madama, the grand staircase occupies the entire width and length of the extension. It begins at the central entrance, leads up to half-landings at the far extremities, reverses to the center, and turns ninety degrees into a bridge element entering the palace. The exterior reflects influences from seventeenth-century France.

Juvarra later designed the royal hunting lodge at Stupinigi (1729–1731) outside Turin (Figure 10.44).

FIGURE 10.42 *Juvarra: Palazzo Madama, Turin, 1718–1721.* (Photo: Instituto Italiano di Cultura)

Its symmetrical plan is organized around a large hexagonal entrance court and focuses on a central domed rotunda, off which short wings project diagonally. Rectangular service courts flank the entrance to the hexagon, and secondary wings extend off its vertices and terminate in pavilions. It is an unorthodox scheme, complemented by formal landscaping tailored in geometric plantings. Interiors echo the dynamism characteristic of late Baroque churches. Spaces interpenetrate, cornices curve free from the enclosing walls, and stucco ornaments adorn walls and ceilings. Perspective and the artful application of shade and shadow combine to bring

FIGURE 10.43 *Juvarra: Interior view of the stair hall of Palazzo Madama, Turin.* (Photo: Wodehouse)

FIGURE 10.44 *Juvarra: Royal Hunting Lodge, Stupinigi, 1729–1731.* (Photo: Alinari)

FIGURE 10.45 *Juvarra: Interior of the Royal Hunting Lodge, Stupinigi.* (Photo: Alinari)

drama to the great rotunda hall (Figure 10.45), where a surprising amount of detail, including fluting on pilasters, scrolls on brackets, and upper niche statuary, is created with paint, not surface relief.

The Baroque in Central Europe

While Vittone and Juvarra were active in and around Turin, the artistic ideals of Baroque Italy were being spread north and eastward through Switzerland, Austria, southern Germany, and Bo-

FIGURE 10.46 *Fischer von Erlach: Karlskirche, Vienna, 1716–1725.* (From Fischer von Erlach)

hemia. There Italian influences merged with local tastes and surviving craft guild traditions to create a version of the Baroque distinct to central Europe. As in Italy, the driving force was the Catholic Counter-Reformation, yet the style received support not only from Church officials but also from princes and monarchs, who hoped to project a progressive image, and from the common people, for whom it reflected deeply held religious beliefs. In many respects Baroque churches in central Europe continued medieval themes. Architecture, sculpture, and painting advanced a single idea, the evocation of a heavenly realm. Number symbolism is prominent, as are the images of saints serving as intercessors between earth and heaven. Twin-towered west fronts are commonly found capped by bulbous domes rather than Gothic spires. The impression of lofty volume that is conveyed in Gothic by soaring vaults, is created in the Baroque by much lower plaster vaults on which paint and stucco have been expertly applied to create the illusion of an open sky filled with heavenly hosts. Baroque churches are bright and airy; the windows are glazed with clear glass, and daylight is directed onto white interior surfaces embellished with gold and pastel hues.

The Baroque monuments of Italy were important sources for central Europe. Il Gesù in Rome was particularly influential because its design led to the development of the wall pillars *(Wandpfeiler)* that characterize many central European Baroque churches. At Il Gesù the side aisles of a traditional basilican plan were transformed into a series of chapels, separated one from another by buttress sections turned inward. North of the Alps, these internal buttresses became wall pillars, which Baroque architects exploited for structural stability and the shaping of internal space. Although the churches may retain side aisles, some even with galleries overhead, the wall pillars were used as screening elements to establish the concept of centrality within what were generally longitudinal plans. The interaction of axial and centralized plans, already seen in the oval designs of Borromini and Bernini, is thus continued in the Baroque of central Europe.

The life and work of Johann Bernhard Fischer von Erlach (1656–1723) represent one of the ways in which Italian ideas were transferred to central Europe. Fischer came from an Austrian family of masons, and he was sent to Rome for training in the studio of Bernini. During the sixteen years he spent in Rome he became familiar with both ancient and contemporary works there, and these influences, combined with knowledge from travels across Europe, were later reflected in his own designs and in the illustrated *Entwurf einer historichen Architektur* (History of Architecture) he published in 1721. Fischer von Erlach's architectural fortunes were tied to those of the Hapsburgs. He joined the imperial court at Vienna as architectural tutor to Joseph I in 1689, was raised to the nobility in 1696, and served as chief inspector of court buildings from 1705 until his death. During his lifetime Austria experienced a surge of nationalistic pride after decisively repelling the Turkish attack on Vienna in 1683. Seeking to create an impressive international city that would rival Rome or Versailles, Viennese princes built Baroque palaces and raised new churches.

Fischer von Erlach's major contribution to Vienna was the Karlskirche (1716–1725), a building that reflects his view that every work should be unique (Figure 10.46). By borrowing from a wide range of historical sources Fischer created a highly original design that referenced major buildings of the past. The church was dedicated to St. Charles Borromeo, the Emperor's patron saint, and was built in fulfillment of a vow Charles VI made in 1713 during the plague. Its broad façade is dominated by a dome on drum rising above a pedimented portico, flanked by paired columns in a manner recalling the front of S. Agnese in Agone, where the central dome is flanked by twin campaniles. Elements from historical buildings incorporated here include the columned portico from Roman temples such as the Pantheon; Trajan's column (doubled and adorned with scenes from the life of St. Charles Borromeo rather than reliefs of the Dacian Wars) from imperial Rome; the drum and dome from papal Rome; and an overall composition suggesting the dome and minarets of Hagia Sophia in Constantinople. The interior is impressive for its elongated oval nave (Figures 10.47, 10.48), the ceiling of which is embellished with illusionistic perspective frescoes depicting St. Charles Borromeo appealing to the Virgin Mary as intercessor for relief from the plague. Fischer had seen the ceiling frescoes being installed at Il Gesù during his residence in Rome, and he used these, rather than coffering or ribs as Bernini or Borromini would have done, to complete the dome's interior.

The rather severe and classical approach of Fischer von Erlach contrasts with the work of his contemporary, the Tyrolese architect Jacob Prandtauer (1660–1726), who was trained in Munich as a mason and practiced as an architect-sculptor in the master builder tradition. The works of Borromini and Guarini are reflected in his designs, but he was also influenced by Fischer von Erlach. A member of a religious brotherhood, Prandtauer was closely involved with his designs while they were in construction, and he is known primarily for monastic projects, including rebuilding the great abbey of Melk (1702–1714), set dramatically atop a rocky ridge rising 200 feet above the Danube. The monastery's buildings are set in a greatly elongated U shape, with the church placed in the interior space and its compressed cloister interrupting one long range of rooms on the U. From the river below and the small courtyard that precedes the west front, the twin towers of the main façade dominate, while the drum and dome over the crossing are best seen from the major courtyard at the east end of the church. This is a wall pillar church with galleries over the oval chapels ranged in place of aisles; a longitudinal emphasis was unavoidable because of site

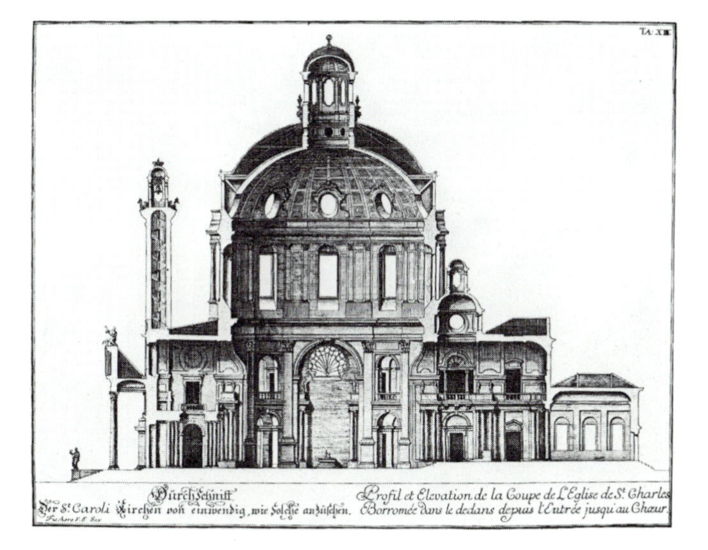

FIGURE 10.47 *Fischer von Erlach: Section through the Karlskirche, Vienna, 1716–1725.* (From Fischer von Erlach)

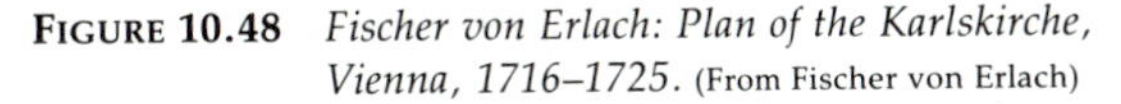

FIGURE 10.48 *Fischer von Erlach: Plan of the Karlskirche, Vienna, 1716–1725.* (From Fischer von Erlach)

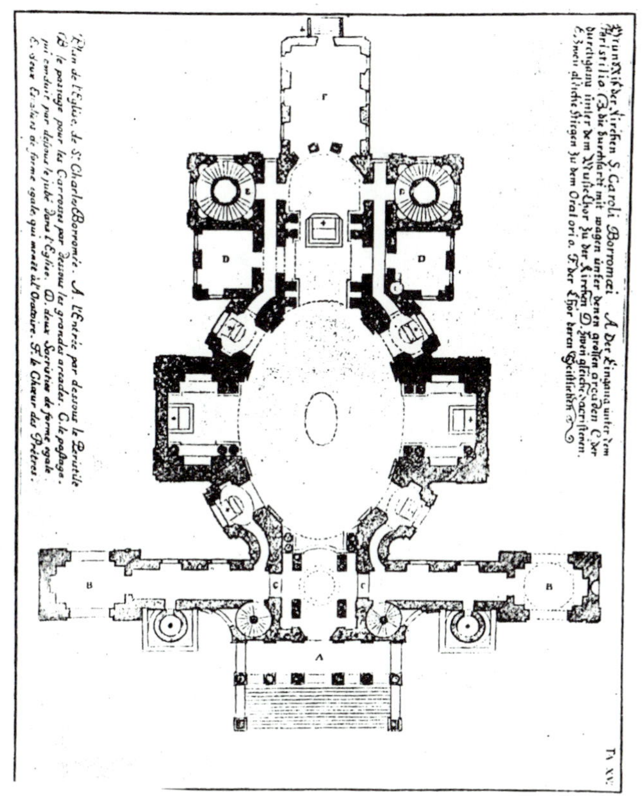

strengstens untersagt.

FIGURE 10.50 *Caspar Moosbrugger: Abbey, Einsiedeln, 1719–1735.* (19th century steel engraving)

FIGURE 10.51 *Caspar Moosbrugger: Plan of the Abbey Church, Einsiedeln, 1719–1735.* (Redrawn after Stierlin)

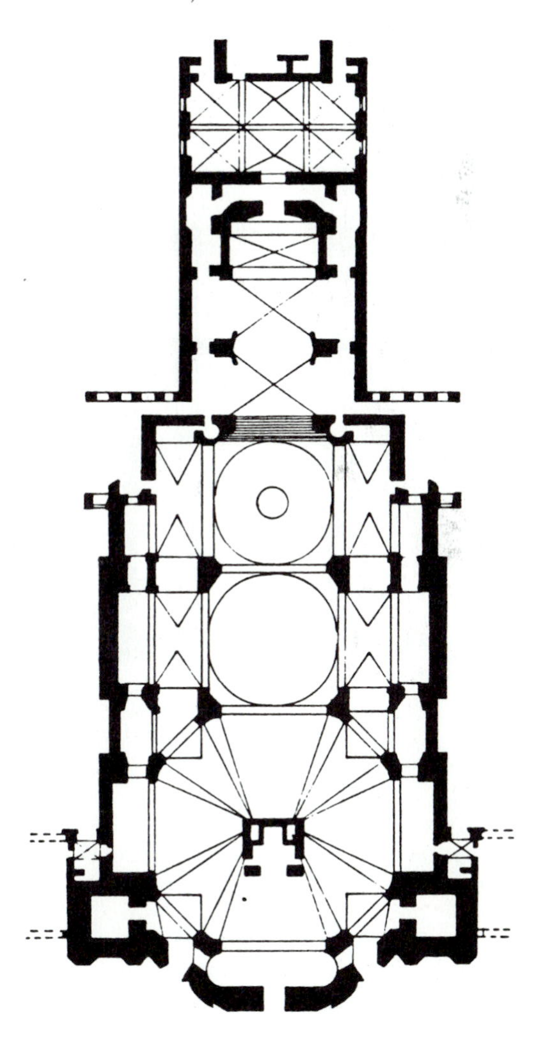

restrictions, and Prandtauer has emphasized vertically through fluted pilasters and a dome on pendentives that soars above the clouds and swirling drapery of figures in the ceiling frescoes (Figure 10.49). The undulating cornice of the nave supports recessed arches around clerestory windows, causing the whole ceiling to appear as a floating world. The painted illusion of heavenly figures spilling from the vaults above provides a dramatic link between earthly matters and the spiritual world.

In Switzerland, Bavaria, and Bohemia, Baroque design was generally the province of families of architects, sculptors, and painters, in which fathers, sons, uncles, and nephews collaborated on building projects. For example, five Dientzenhofer brothers — Georg, Christoph, Leonhard, Johann, and Wolfgang — were active in Bohemia and southern Germany just before and after 1700, where they combined the free-swinging curves found in the works of Borromini and Guarini with Slavic and Gothic motifs; Christoph's son, Kilian Ignaz, also became an established designer. These families of master builders should not be thought of as rustics; a number of them were trained in major centers such as Turin, Vienna, and Prague, and they knew both the built and the unbuilt designs of leading Italian architects, even though they practiced architecture as guild members.

The collaboration of two sets of brothers can be seen in the abbey church of Einsiedeln (1719–1735), where the design is credited to a lay brother of the monastery, Caspar Moosbrugger (1656–1723), and was finished after his death by his brother Johann Moosbrugger and others. Einsiedeln is still a major center of religious activity in Switzerland, and the monastery has an appropriately grand façade fronting a sloping plaza at the end of the town (Figure 10.50). In the center of the composition is the church, its great bowed front with twin towers projecting from the straight line of the flanking monastic buildings (Figure 10.51). This curved element directly reflects the major element of the interior, the shrine constructed on the site of the cell of St. Meinrad, who is venerated here. A great octagon completed by a dome centers on the shrine, which thus occupies the first and largest bay of the nave. Wall pillars pierced by aisles and galleries help define this space and form the transition to the

◀ FIGURE 10.49 *Jakob Prandtauer: Interior of the Abbey Church, Melk, 1702–1714.* (Photo: Austrian Tourist Office)

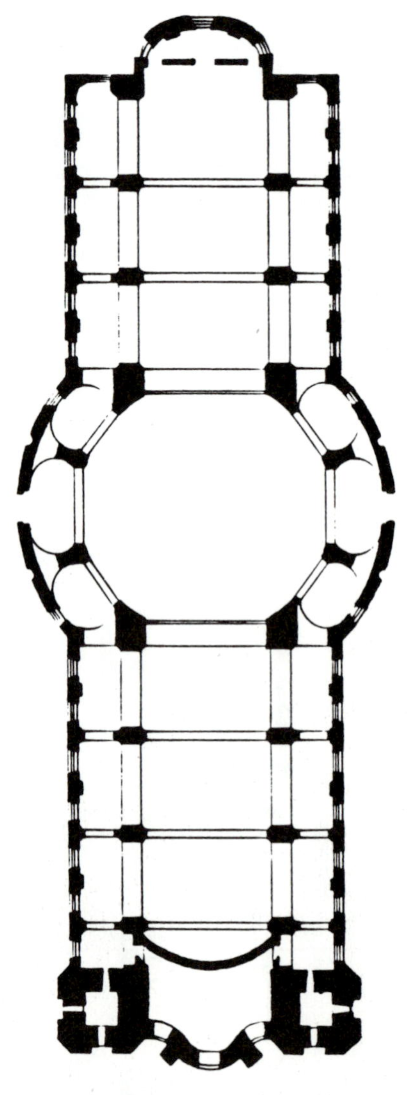

FIGURE 10.52 *Peter Thumb: Plan of the Abbey Church, St. Gallen, 1755–1768.* (Redrawn after Stierlin)

smaller, circular domed bays of the nave. The Asam brothers, painter Cosmas Damian (1686–1739) and sculptor Egid Quirin (1692–1750), were responsible for the wonderfully coordinated fresco and stucco work that graces the interior. The narrower choir, built to designs of Egid Quirin, is completed by an enormous altar and embellished with floating stucco figures that complement the ceiling frescoes above. The Asams tended to create pictorial rather than architectural space. With paint and stucco they transformed what appear to be rather commonplace plans and sections into an extraordinary confection of light, color, and illusionistic space. The nave ceilings combine paint and plaster to create a joyous expression of the Nativity, with angels perched on high cornices and putti floating down to earth bearing the good news.

The influence of Einsiedeln's plan may be seen at the abbey church in St. Gallen (1755–1768), where a rotunda space has been inserted into a longitudinal basilica, thus accommodating the needs of pilgrims in the nave while reserving the choir for monastic use (Figure 10.52). St. Gallen is the same monastery for which the Carolingian Plan of St. Gall was drawn. Although there is evidence that the church of the Carolingian scheme was built, later rebuildings in the Gothic obscure the older foundations. The present Baroque church, however, retains the double-ended apse of the original basilica. Its design is credited to Peter Thumb (1681–1766), with the towered east façade being the work of Johann Michael Beer (Figure 10.53). St. Gallen is a wall pillar church with a central rotunda expressed on the exterior as a bow in the middle of the side elevations. There are no transepts, and the west front remains unfinished. Save for the east façade the exterior of St. Gallen is rather plain, with tall windows set evenly spaced. Even the interior fresco and stucco work by Christian Weinzinger is less dynamic than the exuberance of Einsiedeln. St. Gallen is the last great Baroque church built in central Europe and one of the last in all of Europe. The style, nourished by Italian inventiveness and responding to the emotional piety of prince and peasant, was losing its vitality in an era becoming more interested in rationalism and classical restraint.

Not all central European Baroque buildings were churches. As in Italy and France, the nobility desired to display themselves in great places, and the theatricality of the Baroque was well-suited to provide the appropriate setting. Of these princely residences, the grandest was the Würzburg Residenz (Figure 10.54), begun in 1720 for the prince-bishops of the Schönborn family. Its architect was Johann Balthasar Neumann (1687–1753), generally

FIGURE 10.53 *Johann Michael Beer: East façade of the Abbey Church, St. Gallen, 1755–1768.* (Photo: Wodehouse)

regarded as the greatest master of the German Baroque. Neumann was trained in mathematics, engineering, and architecture. He served the Schönborns as an artilleryman, civil engineer, and military engineer before being encouraged to devote his designing talents and engineering dexterity to the creation of elegant spaces. The enormous Residenz was symmetrically disposed around a deep entrance court, with four interior courts pro-

FIGURE 10.54 *Neumann: Würzburg Residenz, begun 1720.* (Photo: German Information Center)

viding light and air to the side wings. Neumann's plans for the palace were scrutinized by leading architects in Paris and Vienna before construction began and as the work proceeded; this and changes in the office of prince-bishops resulted in a twenty-three-year construction period, with an additional five years required to complete the interior decorations. Neumann's masterpiece within this complex was the sequence of major reception rooms, beginning with the low vestibule, made large enough that a coach could turn around in the column-free space, extending through the majestic Stair Hall to the White and Imperial halls on the second floor.

It is the lofty Stair Hall that most clearly exhibits the architect's technical skill (Figure 10.55). At nearly 100 by 60 feet, the hall is the largest single room in the palace, and it is roofed by a stone vault without internal supports. The centrally placed stair rises in a single flight to a landing, where it reverses direction and divides before extending to the upper floor. A balcony placed around the staircase allows onlookers a view to the processional space. The ceiling is enriched with the world's largest fresco (executed by Giovanni Battista Tiepolo), celebrating the Sun God Apollo and the prince-bishop as patrons of the arts. Representations of the seasons, the zodiac, Europe, Asia, Africa, and America are assembled at the perimeter, gazing into the clouds opening in the heavens or staring down at those ascending the stair. Among the figures on the parapet are Tiepolo, the stucco artist Antonio Bossi, and Neumann himself, seated with his dog among artillery pieces and taking a well-earned rest. Statues on the balustrades and stucco cartouches, swags, and putti above the door and window surrounds harmonize with the allegorical host overhead. Further delights of stucco and fresco await in the subtle shades of the White Hall, which serves as a foil for the Imperial Hall, the most important room in the palace. Its oval-like form is actually a rectangle with mitered corners rising to a high oval-vaulted ceiling filled with Tiepolo's allegorical frescoes alluding to historical scenes of the Holy Roman Empire peopled with contemporary members of the Würzburg court.

Neumann was also a designer of churches, the most celebrated of which was the pilgrimage church of Vierzehnheiligen, outside Bamberg (Figure 10.56). Designed in 1744 and built on the foundations already laid by another architect, Vierzehnheiligen commemorates the hilltop on which a shepherd boy in 1445 had an apparition of the fourteen Helpers in Need, for whom the church was named. A previous chapel on the site had become inadequate, and jurisdictional conflicts between the

FIGURE 10.56 *Neumann: Vierzehnheiligen, Bamberg, begun 1744.* (Photo: German Information Center)

◀ **FIGURE 10.55** *Neumann: Stair Hall of the Würzburg Residenz.* (Photo: German Information Center)

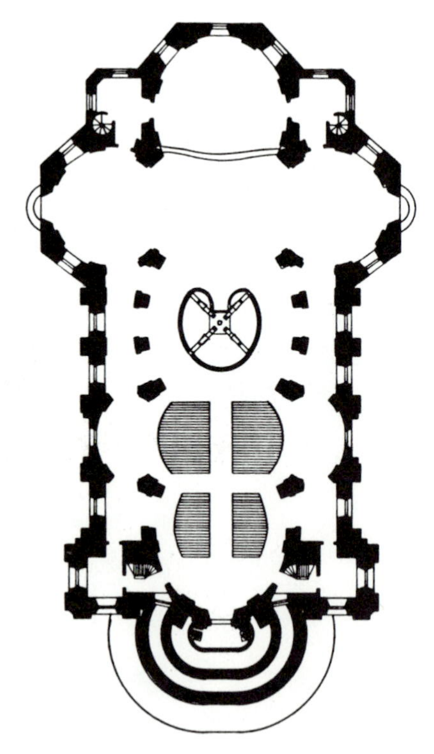

FIGURE 10.57 *Neumann: Plan of Vierzehnheiligen, Bamberg.* (From W. Blaser)

prince-bishop of Bamberg and the Cistercian abbot whose monastery was financing the work led to confusion over Neumann's appointment as architect. Vierzehnheiligen is remarkable for the way its basically basilican ground plan is transformed into a symphony of Baroque circles and ovals (Figure 10.57). The freestanding altar of the fourteen saints occupies a central position in the nave, while the transepts become circles and the apse is defined as an oval. Neumann manipulated the interior space by arranging the aisle piers freely, both to support the oval vaults overhead and to form screens obscuring direct vision of windows in the side wall, thus combining the drama of light from unseen sources with swirling, curving forms. He used delicate pastel colors, accented with gold, on marble piers and ceiling frescoes to emphasize the airy volumes of the interior. The warm sandstone exterior is grand but restrained, and the twin towers of its entrance front respond to the axis established by the Baroque abbey of Banz on a hill across the valley.

This discussion of major Baroque monuments should not obscure the fact that Baroque became an almost vernacular style for churches in the countryside of southern Germany, Switzerland, Austria, Czechoslovakia, and Poland, much as medieval styles characterize the French and English landscape. Existing churches were remodeled and new ones were built in the Baroque style; their distinctive reverse-curve domed towers still dot the rural districts. The Baroque even had an impact in Russia, where St. Petersburg was laid out early in the eighteenth century by French and Italian architects.

The Baroque in France

The ideas of the Italian Baroque were transferred, although not without modifications, to France. By the mid-seventeenth century, as Louis XIV was coming into his majority, Renaissance-inspired classicism was sufficiently well established in France to mute the most elaborate excesses of Roman Baroque, so the Baroque in France was always tempered by classical restraint. French official patronage of the period was more than ever centered around the royal court, and the propaganda of the Catholic Counter-Reformation was not an important issue. The official court style glorified the monarch, and the primary function of the state-run artistic establishment was to provide splendid settings, furnishings, and objects for the display of royal power. In pursuit of this objective, French architects built impressively elaborate works on a scale seldom seen, and the manners, costumes, and style of the French court became the model for other European capitals.

Several building projects are examples of this process. In Paris the rebuilding of the Louvre, begun over a century earlier with the interior court wing by Lescot, was still not complete. First Lemercier and then Louis Le Vau (1612–1670) had worked on the interior elevations of the square court. During the 1660s a number of architects, including four Italians, were invited to submit designs for the east façade. Bernini, the leading European

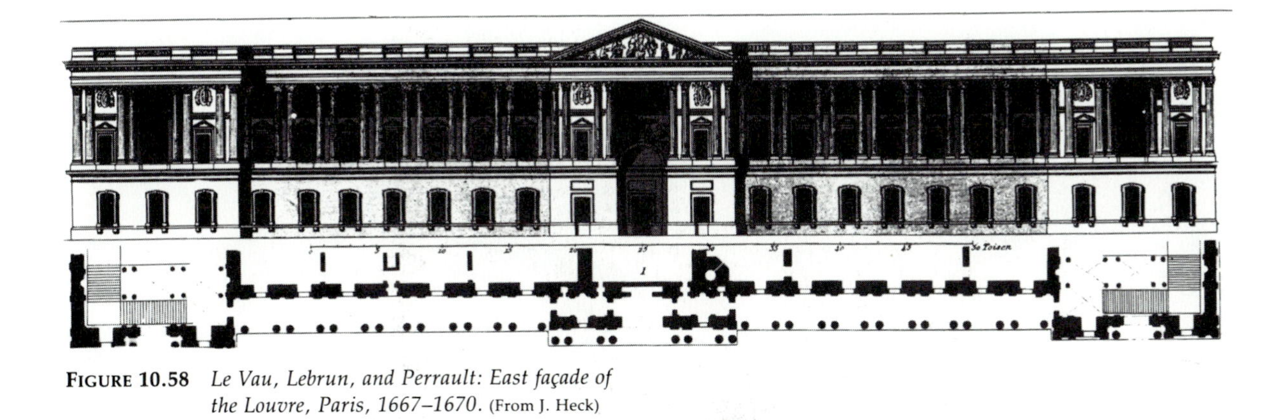

FIGURE 10.58 *Le Vau, Lebrun, and Perrault: East façade of the Louvre, Paris, 1667–1670.* (From J. Heck)

architect, sent a design proposing a central oval pavilion terminated by end pavilions, the whole composed of giant engaged columns and colonnades better suited to the bright sun of Italy than to the overcast skies of northern Europe. After hearing French objections to the scheme, Bernini sent a second proposal, this time with a concave plan, but the king and his ministers were still not satisfied. At the insistence of Louis XIV, Bernini came to Paris for six months in 1665 to consult directly on the Louvre design, in spite of opposition from French architects who hoped to receive the commission themselves. While in Paris Bernini prepared a third proposal, not just for the east wing but for the entire palace. In this plan the original square court was completely encased by open loggias with blocky staircases protruding into the corners. The exterior façades were no longer curved but articulated by giant engaged columns on the central pavilion and pilasters on the end pavilions; the ground floor was treated as a rusticated base for the giant orders above.

Perhaps because Bernini failed to reflect French tastes in his designs, Louis decided not to build any of these projects for the Louvre. Instead he gave the commission to a trio consisting of the architect Le Vau, the painter Charles Lebrun (1619–1690), and a doctor of medicine, Claude Perrault (1613–1688). The design was largely that of Perrault, an amateur in architectural design who nevertheless possessed a technical background from his training in medicine. He later edited a French edition of Vitruvius. Together these three men were responsible for the present-day east façade (1667–1670), composed of a colonnade of paired Corinthian columns with central and end pavilions set atop a rusticated ground story (Figure 10.58). This use of paired columns links the work to Baroque precedent, although the design is far more restrained than contemporary architecture in Italy. In contrast to earlier French Renaissance works the roof of the Louvre is hidden by a balustraded parapet, reinforcing the horizontal emphasis of the whole elevation.

The designers of country estates enthusiastically adopted the Baroque style. Sixteenth-century chateaux had set a standard of elaborate design that continued into the next century, with increasingly splendid effects culminating in the lavish palace and garden designs of Vaux-le-Vicomte and Versailles. On August 17, 1661, Nicolas Fouquet, the Attorney General and Superintendent of Finances for Louis XIV, invited the King and Queen and 6000 other guests to festivities at his recently completed estate, Vaux-le-Vicomte (1657–1661) (Figures 10.59–10.61). The chateau, designed by Le Vau, stood on 170 acres of land and had a majestic view over the grounds, landscaped by André Le Nôtre (1613–1700) to include formal gardens, fountains, and sculptures extending to the background forest. The chateau itself was a freestanding block with pavilions at each corner containing *appartements* for Fouquet on one end and the king on the other. The axial

FIGURE 10.59 *Le Vau, Lebrun, and Le Nôtre: Chateau, Vaux-le-Vicomte, 1657–1661.* (Photo: French Government Tourist Office)

entrance approach led across a moat to a paved terrace, through triple-arched entrance doors into the vestibule. In the center was a projecting oval salon, entered on its short axis through triple arches corresponding to the triple-arched openings on the opposite wall, through which the gardens beyond could be seen. Lebrun had organized the stucco

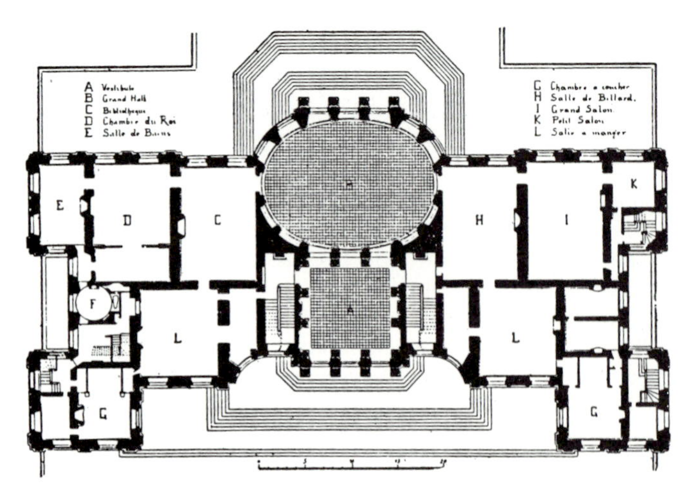

FIGURE 10.60 *Le Vau, Lebrun, and Le Nôtre: Plan of the Chateau, Vaux-le-Vicomte.* (From: J. Guadet)

FIGURE 10.61 *Le Vau, Lebrun, and Le Nôtre: Entrance façade of the Chateau, Vaux-le-Vicomte.* (Photo: Marburg)

work, gilding, painting, and tapestries of the interior to provide a magnificent setting for living.

The chateau and festivities were entirely too grand to suit Louis XIV, who became jealous of the splendor in which his minister was living. Within three weeks of the opening of his chateau, Fouquet was charged with mismanagement of royal funds and embezzlement, his property was confiscated, and he was thrown into prison, where he died in 1680. Louis bought all the interior furnishings for a token sum and trundled them off to his own chateau at Versailles. He also commanded the designers of Vaux-le-Vicomte — the architect Le Vau, the decorator Lebrun, and the landscape architect Le Nôtre — to come and work at Versailles.

In 1624 Louix XIII had built a hunting lodge on swampy land at Versailles, some twenty miles southwest of Paris. When the future Louis XIV was a child, he spent relatively happy times in the twenty-room chateau there, and on becoming monarch he decided to enlarge the building. In 1661 Le Vau added two service wings, and in 1669 Louis de-

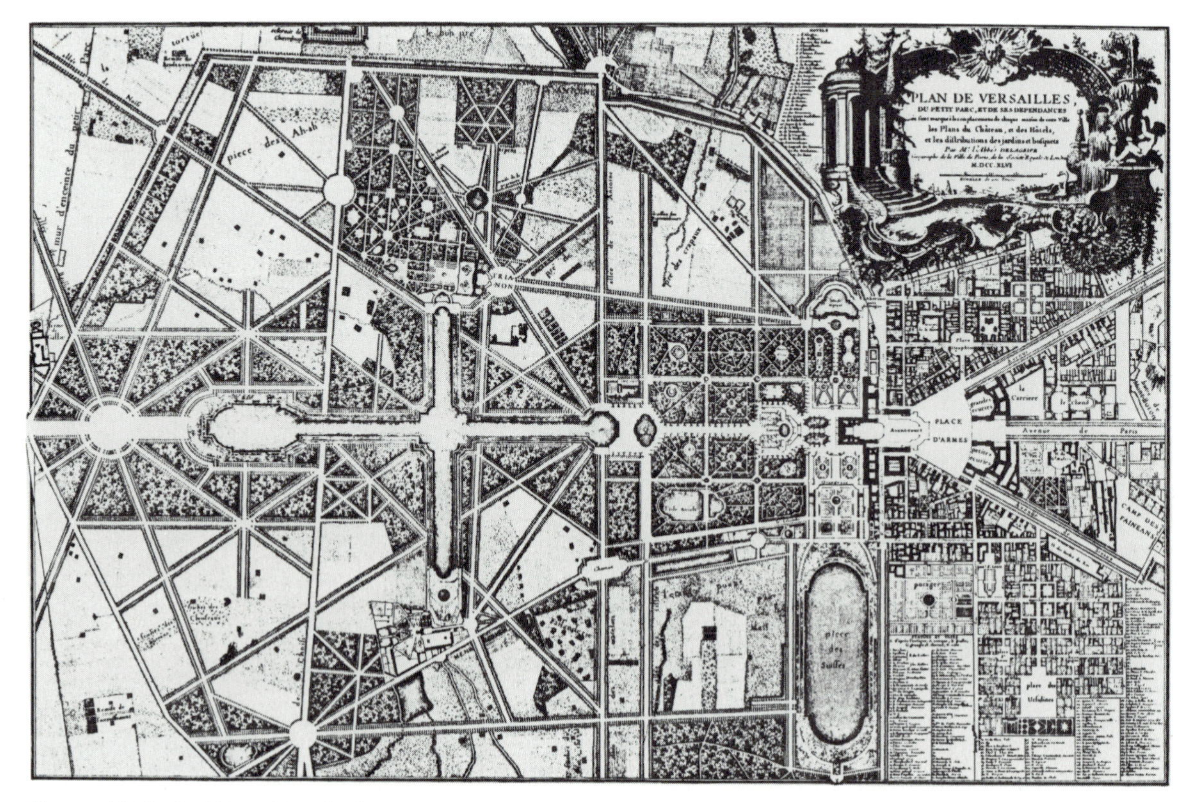

FIGURE 10.62 *Le Nôtre: Plan of palace and gardens, Versailles, begun 1661.* (18th century engraving)

cided to enlarge the whole complex by building around the original chateau, keeping the entrance court but adding new work on the garden façade. Louis XIV was sentimental about the original lodge and allowed none of it to be removed during the enlargement of the palace buildings. Le Vau thus built around it, adding wings and partially enclosing the central block in a symmetrical design.

From the first Louis intended Versailles to be the permanent residence for the royal court, discarding medieval Paris as unfit to be the setting for the Sun King. A site less suitable for major construction than Versailles would have been difficult to find. The marshy ground was fine for game, but it was incapable of supporting elaborate plant life, and there was no adequate water supply readily available to run fountains. Under the direction of Le Nôtre, the army drained 37,000 acres of land and diverted an entire river thirty miles away to supply water for the fountains, which eventually numbered 1400. Vast gardens were laid out, with axial vistas, terraces, sculpture, formal flower beds, fountains, water basins, and paths integrated into a grand plan that focused on the King's bedroom in the center of the palace (Figure 10.62).

In 1678, when the entire court took up residence at Versailles, the palace was again enlarged, this time under the direction of Jules-Hardouin Mansart (1646–1708), the work continuing until his death thirty years later. At one time in 1685, 36,000 men and 6,000 horses were involved in construction of the buildings and grounds. A town of about 20,000 people grew up adjacent to the palace to house the aristocracy, their soldiers, servants, and minor cour-

FIGURE 10.63 *Le Vau, Le Nôtre, and Mansart: Palace, Versailles.* (Photo: French Government Tourist Office)

tiers. Like the gardens, the town was organized around radiating boulevards (called "crow's feet") extending from the center of the palace. Mansart extended the palace symmetrically on both the north and south ends, continuing the elevations established by Le Vau but destroying in the process the subtle effects of advancing and receding planes that characterized Le Vau's work; Mansart's wings have linear façades that continue without interruption (Figure 10.63). Mansart also added the Galerie des Glaces (Hall of Mirrors) and two adjacent salons of war and peace to the central block (Figures 10.64–10.66). Le Vau's Staircase of the Ambassadors (begun 1671) divided to lead to both salons, so that any ambassador would know of Louis's intent long before it was announced to him in the appropriate setting. A large circular panel in the Salon of War depicted Louis as Mars in triumph over his enemies. The king's own suite of rooms included salons depicting monarchs of antiquity with the attributes of the gods representing the seven planets: Mercury and wisdom; Venus and love; Mars and war. His throne room was the Salon of Apollo. The only vertical feature at Versailles is the chapel added by Mansart in 1698–1710, a building of Gothic proportions and structure with classical details. Its gallery was linked to the King's apartments, while the court was relegated to the lower level.

All the interior design at Versailles was under the direction of Lebrun, and the triumvirate of Le Nôtre, Le Vau, and Lebrun, which had so successfully coordinated the scenic backdrop for fêtes at Vaux-le-Vicomte, achieved a far more grandiose effect at Versailles. Lebrun's decorations, furniture,

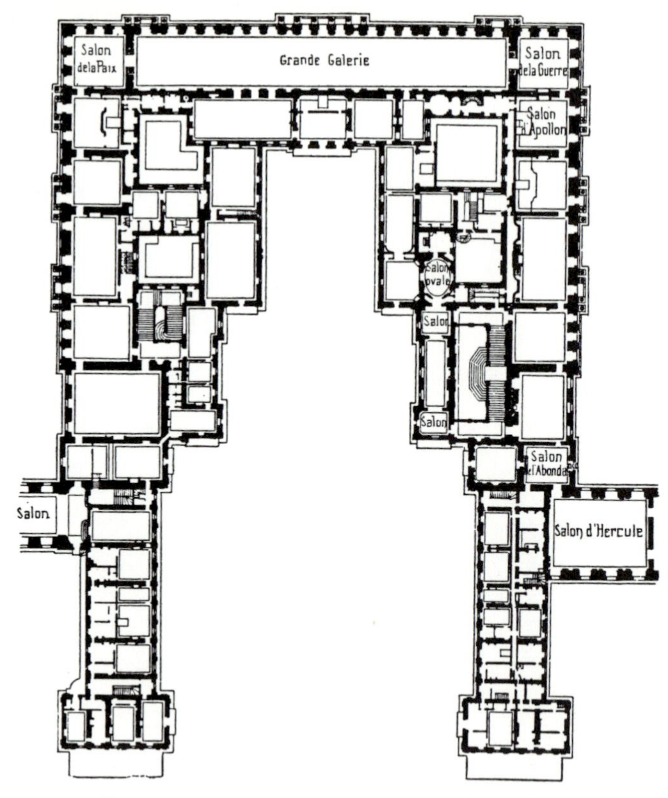

FIGURE 10.64 *Le Vau and Mansart: Plan of the central portion of the Palace, Versailles.* (From J. Guadet)

FIGURE 10.66 *Mansart: Interior of the Gallerie des Glaces in the Palace, Versailles, begun 1678.* (From C. Gurlitt)

FIGURE 10.65 *Le Vau: Garden façade of the Palace, Versailles.* (From C. Gurlitt)

FIGURE 10.67 *Mansart: Saint-Louis-des-Invalides, Paris, 1670–1708.* (Photo: Marburg)

tapestries, reliefs, and paintings were as elaborate as anything to be found in Baroque palaces of the period. Versailles has much of the grandeur but little of the dynamism of seventeenth-century architecture in Italy.

Baroque architecture in France does not consist solely of palatial residences in the formal landscape; there were numerous private and religious commissions as well. Of the ecclesiastical works in Paris, Jules-Hardouin Mansart's church of St.-Louis-des-Invalides (Figures 10.67, 10.68), added to the hospital for disabled soldiers, deserves mention. Although the interior of Les Invalides was still incomplete at Mansart's death in 1708, it was essentially finished by 1691.

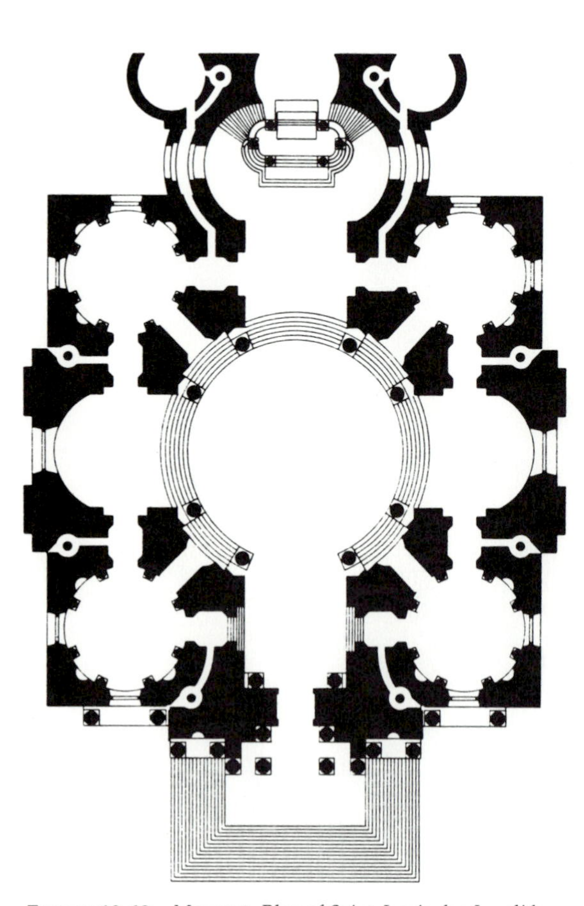

FIGURE 10.68 *Mansart: Plan of Saint-Louis-des-Invalides, Paris.* (From W. Blaser)

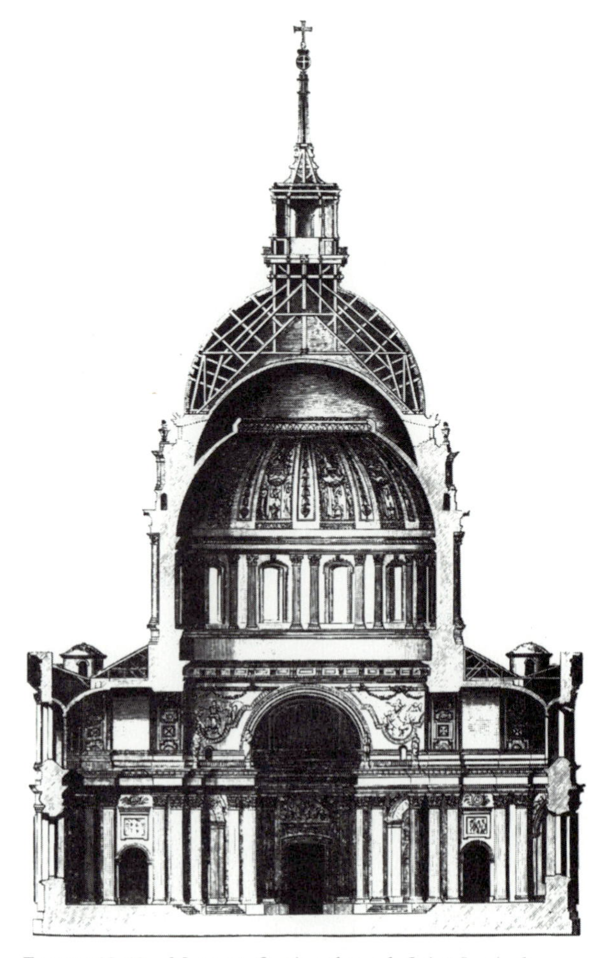

FIGURE 10.69 *Mansart: Section through Saint-Louis-des-Invalides, Paris.* (From J. Guadet)

Its plan is based on Bramante's design for St. Peter's, and the drum and dome are derived from Michelangelo's design for the same church, even though Mansart gave them a strong vertical accent. The dome of Les Invalides is buttressed by pairs of Ionic columns protruding from the fenestrated surface of the drum. The dignity of the exterior is achieved by a system of two structural domes (Figure 10.69) with wider separation between the two surfaces than is found at St. Peter's. The innermost masonry dome relates to the scale of the interior space; the second masonry dome supports the external timber-framed dome, covered with lead sheets, which is scaled to the building's exterior silhouette, mass, and composition.

The Baroque in England

Christopher Wren. Mansart's design for Les Invalides was to have a direct impact on the most outstanding architect of the English Baroque, Christopher Wren (1632–1723). Wren came to national prominence as a result of the great fire of September 2, 1666, which destroyed 373 of the 448 acres comprising the walled area of the City of London, including 13,200 houses, forty-four city companies, eighty-seven churches, the Royal Exchange, the Custom House, and St. Paul's Cathedral. Numerous prominent men made plans for rebuilding the burnt area. Wren produced a plan on September 11

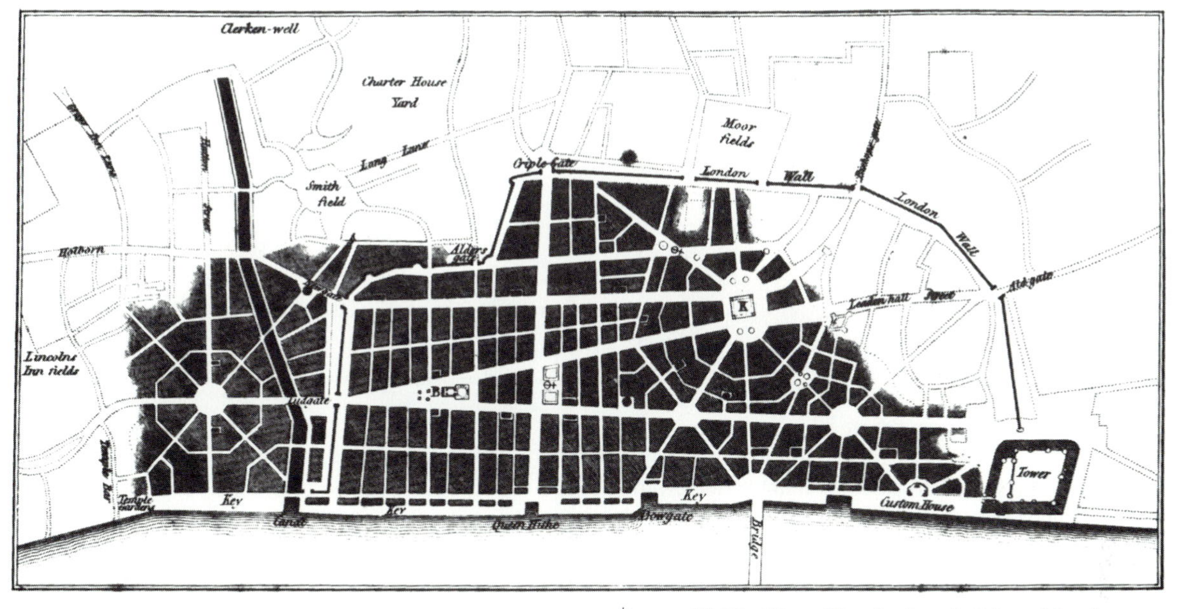

FIGURE 10.70 *Wren: Plan for the rebuilding of London, 1666.* (From J. Elmes)

(Figure 10.70); John Evelyn on September 13; and Robert Hooke, Curator of Experiments at the Royal Society, on September 19. Wren's plan is fundamentally a grid scheme superimposed with axial routes connecting commercial, religious, and governmental centers within the city. Precedent for this plan organization can be found in the Baroque designs for Rome and Versailles. None of the plans submitted for the rebuilding of London were used in the actual work. Merchants wanted to reestablish their homes and businesses as rapidly as possible, in the same location within the city, without waiting for idealistic planning to be approved and implemented.

Christopher Wren has been acclaimed as Britain's greatest architect. Trained as a mathematician, Wren was also well-connected with the church, his father having been Dean of Windsor. In 1661 Wren became Professor of Astronomy at Oxford University. While there he designed the Sheldonian Theater (1662–1663) for an alumnus, Archbishop Sheldon, basing it on the semicircular plan of the Theater of Marcellus in Rome (see Figures 4.25, 4.26). Huge wooden roof trusses above the theater space support a canvas ceiling, which has been painted to resemble the open sky, complete with simulated ropes to hold the shading device taut. The entrance front is a pedimented pavilion with a raking cornice carried down to the perimeter walls (Figure 10.71). Arcades, half columns, pilasters, oval dormers, and a cupola complete the design. It was based on a plate in Serlio's *Architettura,* as was the pilastered and pedimented design of the street façade of Pembroke College Chapel, Cambridge (1663–1665), designed for his uncle, Matthew Wren,

FIGURE 10.71 *Wren: Sheldonian Theater, Oxford, 1662–1663.* (From D. Logan)

the Bishop of Ely. The chapel's ceiling is elaborate, and its woodwork was richly carved by the master, Grindling Gibbons.

Wren was in Paris from July 1665 through March 1666, probably to escape the plague that was sweeping Britain at the time. There he met Bernini and wrote, "I would have given my skin for . . . a few minute's view" of Bernini's design for the Louvre.

After the fire of 1666 Wren was one of the six commissioners who prepared the Act for Rebuilding the City of London (1667), specifying, among other things, the use of brick walls and slate roofs to reduce the spread of any future fires. Fifty-one (just over half) of the burned parish churches of the city were rebuilt to designs done by Wren from 1670 to 1686, although much of the detailing was probably left to the master carpenter or master mason in charge of each particular church because Wren was preoccupied with his major lifework, the rebuilding of St. Paul's Cathedral. The towers and spires of his churches created a distinctive silhouette on the skyline, rising above the lower brick buildings and contrasting with the domed profile being developed in the design of St. Paul's. Wren's parish church designs vary considerably as he had to accommodate varying site conditions; he sometimes provided a reinterpretation of the earlier church destroyed in the great fire, so not all the designs are classically derived. Several of the steeples are particularly well remembered. The spire of St. Mary-le-Bow rises on a circular plan above a square-plan tower, while St. Bride's, Fleet Street, has four diminishing octagons of arched openings in its upper stories. In contrast, the steeple of St. Dunstan-in-the-East is simplified Gothic that reflects the previous church.

FIGURE 10.72 *Wren: Plan of St. Stephen Walbrook, London, 1672–1687.* (From J. Elmes)

FIGURE 10.73 *Wren: Section through St. Stephen Walbrook, London.* (From J. Elmes)

FIGURE 10.74 *Wren: Interior of St. Stephen Walbrook, London.* (Photo: Marburg)

One church, St. Stephen Walbrook (1672–1687), served as an experimental model for his dome design for St. Paul's Cathedral. Except for its dome and rather medieval tower capped by a Renaissance crown, the exterior of St. Stephen Walbrook is insignificant, but the interior is a centrally planned space developed with a stubby nave and a coffered Pantheonlike dome (Figures 10.72–10.74). The dome rests on eight arches supported by an octagonal arrangement of Corinthian columns on high pedestals. Since the dome was a wooden construction, the supports could be slender and refined, and in this respect they were not a foretaste of the structural problems involved in the triple-shelled masonry dome of St. Paul's.

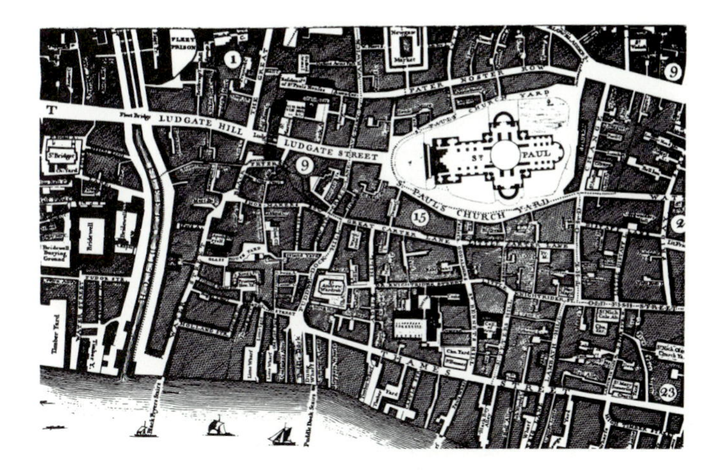

FIGURE 10.76 *Wren: Site plan of the St. Paul's Cathedral area, London.* (From J. Pine)

FIGURE 10.75 *Wren: "The Great Model" plan for St. Paul's Cathedral, London, 1673.* (From C. Gurlitt)

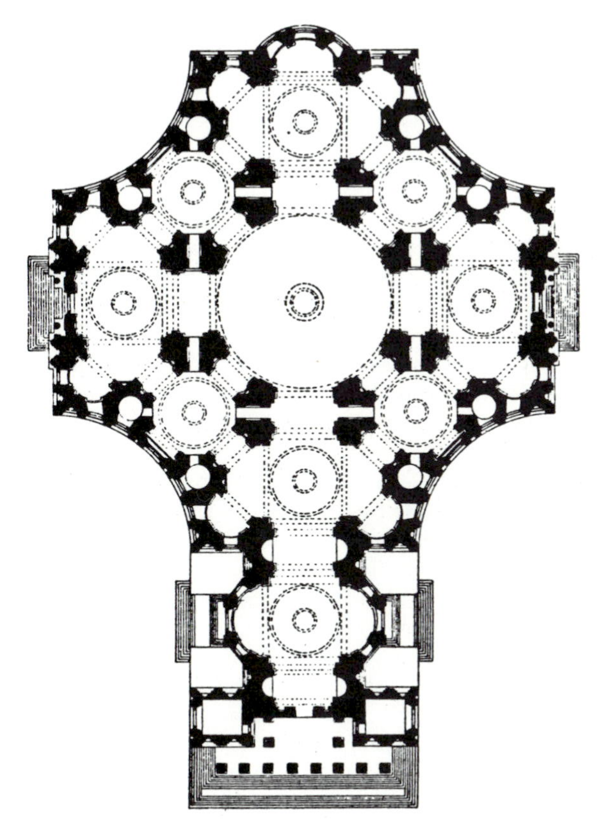

Wren's design for St. Paul's Cathedral went through a number of changes. The Great Model (Figure 10.75), dating from 1673, consisted of a major dome on eight piers ringed with secondary domes forming a continuous ambulatory similar to Bramante's 1506 design for St. Peter's, but this design was too strongly linked with Roman Catholicism to be accepted by the cathedral's dean and chapter. A Latin cross plan, essentially similar to the destroyed Gothic building, was requested, and that was what Wren provided in the Royal Warrant Design of 1675. Even the silhouette of this design was Gothic, consisting as it did of a minuscule drum and dome capped by a six-tiered cupola. Construction began on the Warrant Design, which Wren modified slowly over the thirty-year building period. The design completed in 1709 was refined and academic, incorporating elements from a wide variety of sources (Figures 10.76–10.78). In plan the cathedral is a basilica, a form that Wren admired in Vitruvius's Basilica at Fano. Most of Wren's nave and aisle churches were based on the Roman basilica. At St. Paul's the basilican structure is comprised of saucer domes in the nave and aisles, with buttresses above the aisle roofs. To hide these buttresses and impart a classical character to the exterior, Wren raised the aisle walls to create screens articulated in a manner similar to Inigo Jones's Banquetting

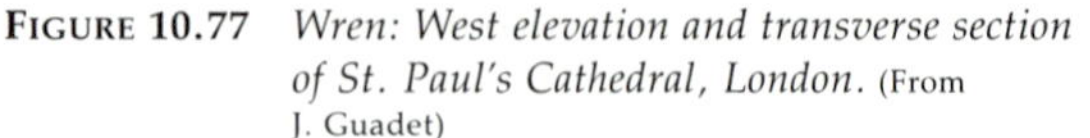

FIGURE 10.77 *Wren: West elevation and transverse section of St. Paul's Cathedral, London.* (From J. Guadet)

House (see Figure 9.105), while the north and south transept porticos were a restatement of Cortona's façade of Santa Maria della Pace (see Figure 10.28) in Rome. The west front is based on Perrault's façade for the Louvre (see Figure 10.58), with towers based on S. Agnese in Piazza Navona (see Figure 10.26). The dome, not begun until 1697, was greatly changed from that of the Warrant Design of 1675, synthesizing in the intervening years Michelangelo's buttressing system for St. Peter's in Rome with Bramante's original design for the drum of 1506. Such a large dome required substantial supporting piers, necessitating the infill of the sides of the four diagonal arches of the central crossing to create segmental rather than hemispherical arches. The external massing of the dome had to be tall and dignified to dominate the London skyline, but this would have created an excessively vertical internal space. Wren thus resorted to the triple-domed idea of Mansart's Church of the Invalides (see Figure 10.68). The innermost dome was of masonry. Above this, a brick cone supports both the cupola and the wooden superstructure of the lead-covered exterior dome. Despite Wren's academic background as a mathematician, there is no evidence that he used his knowledge to calculate structural designs.

The richness of St. Paul's relies equally on the architecture and the internal decoration, which includes work by master woodcarver Grindling Gibbons (1648–1721) and master ironmonger Jean Tijou (1689–1711). Gibbons was born in Rotterdam and discovered there by the diarist Sir John Evelyn. He carved numerous Wren interiors, including the Trinity College Library at Cambridge and St. James Picadilly in London, but he excelled himself in the choir stalls and organ case of St. Paul's. Tijou, a French Huguenot, was introduced and patronized by William and Mary. He worked mainly at Hampton Court and St. Paul's, where rosettes and embossed leaves distinguish his elaborate creations in wrought iron.

FIGURE 10.78 *Wren: Plan and longitudinal section of St. Paul's Cathedral, London, begun 1675.* (From W. Blaser)

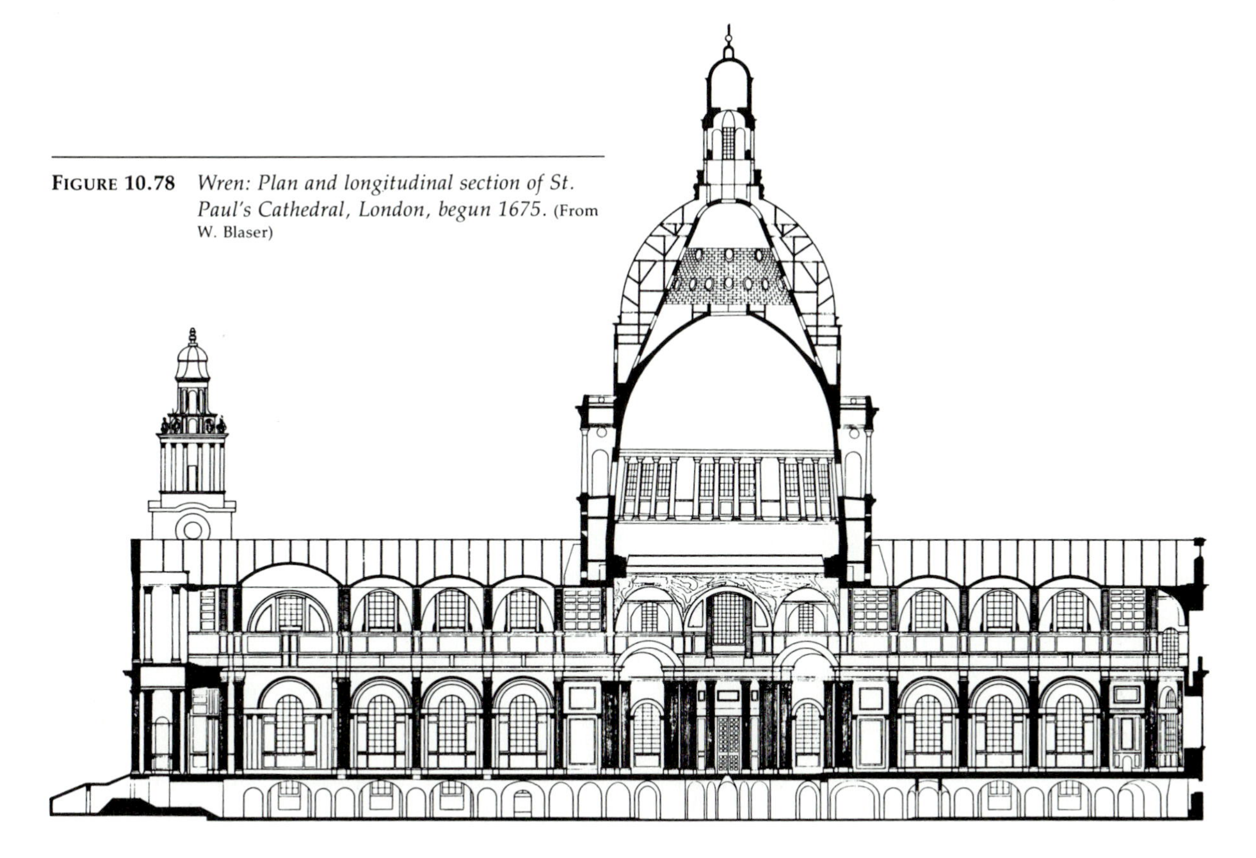

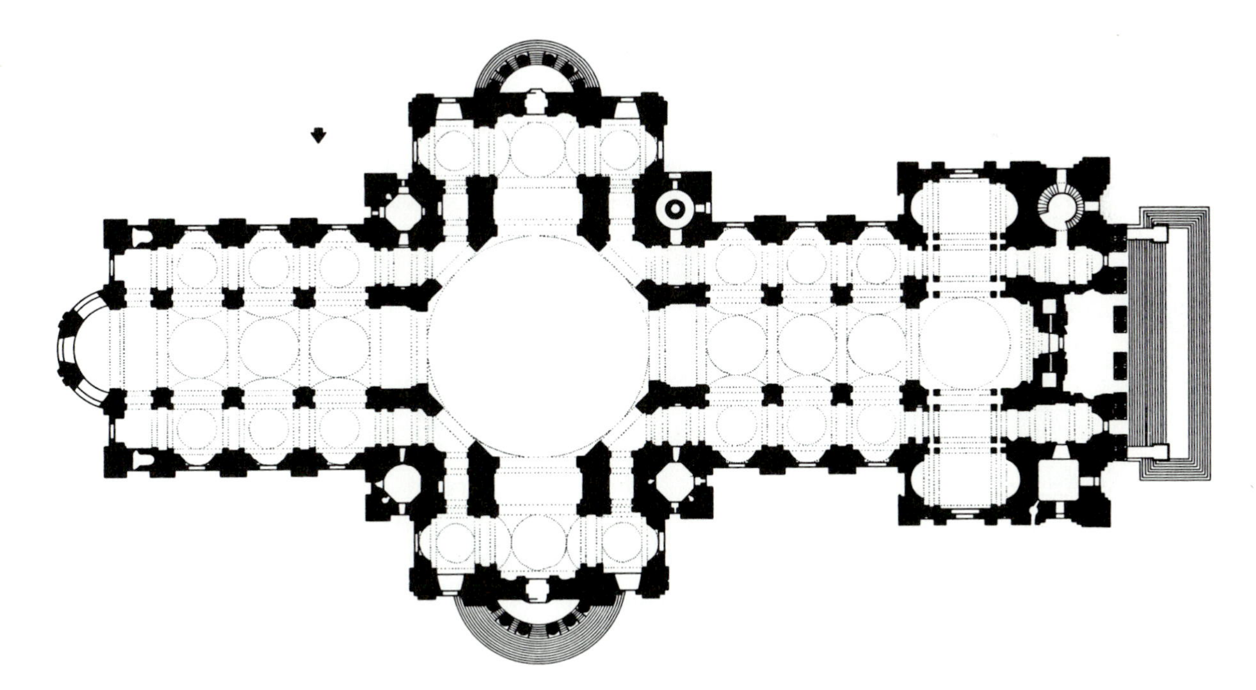

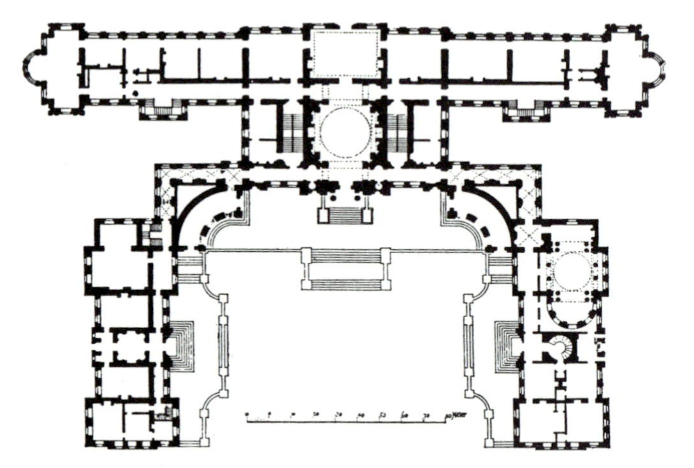

FIGURE 10.79 *Vanbrugh: Plan of Castle Howard, Yorkshire, begun 1701.* (From C. Gurlitt)

Hawksmoor, Vanbrugh, and Gibbs. While working on St. Paul's Wren employed a domestic clerk who eventually became his assistant. This man was Nicholas Hawksmoor (1661–1736), who added to St. Paul's the west front towers that emphasize massing, in contrast to the linear façades and accurate detailing of Wren's design. Hawksmoor also collaborated with an equally famous contemporary, Sir John Vanbrugh (1664–1726), a gentleman-soldier and colorful character who at one time was imprisoned by the French on suspicion of spying in Calais. Returning to England he was a successful comic playwright until 1669 when the Earl of Carlisle asked him to design a palace in Yorkshire called Castle Howard (Figure 10.79). Work on this elaborate and extensive complex began in 1701, with the assistance of Hawksmoor, who contributed architectural know-how to Vanbrugh's theatrical daring. The design is symmetrical, centered on a domed great hall from which the principal apartments extend laterally. Flanking curved colonnades maintain strict axiality while connecting the main block with subsidiary courts for kitchens and stables.

The most famed house of the Vanbrugh-Hawksmoor partnership was Blenheim Palace (Figures 10.80, 10.81), built by a grateful England for the Duke and Duchess of Marlborough in commemoration of the duke's success at the battle of Blenheim in 1704. A large and pompous building following

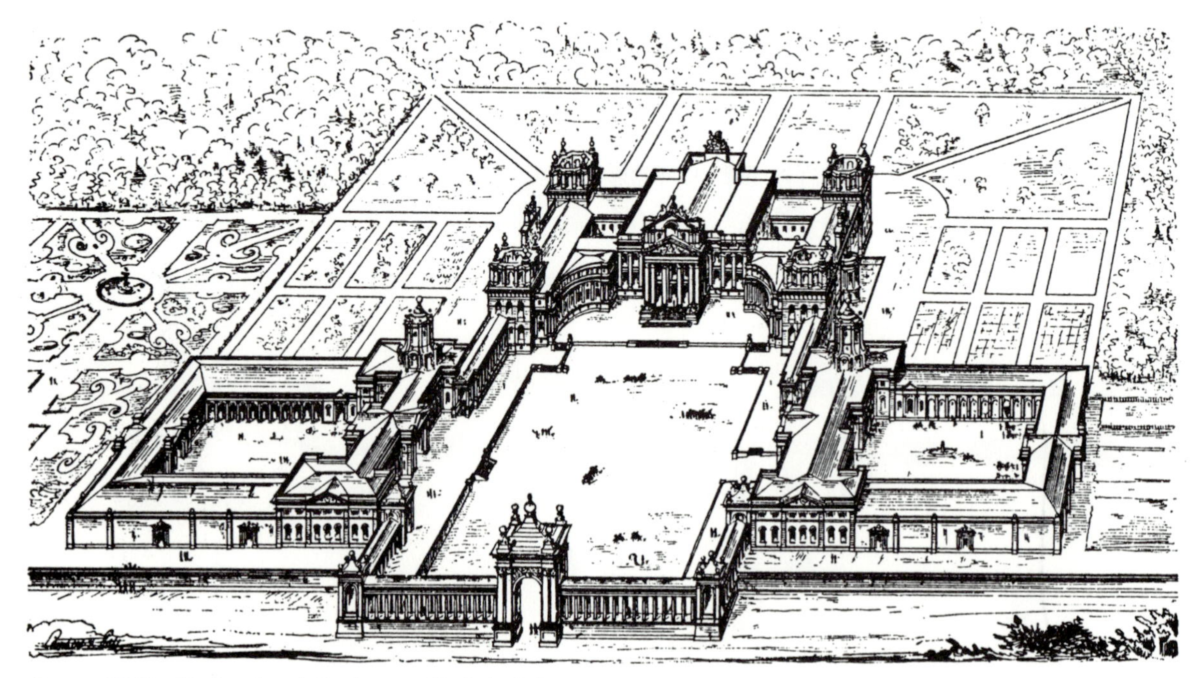

FIGURE 10.80 *Vanbrugh and Hawksmoor: Blenheim Palace, Woodstock, 1705.* (From C. Gurlitt)

the themes established at Castle Howard, Blenheim is representative of this period of grandiose design and is one of the most monumental pieces of domestic architecture of any period in Britain. The exterior is dominated by giant Corinthian columns and massive corner pavilions enlarged by extensive façades. Entrance is through the north portico leading on axis from the great court into the hall and salon. Symmetrically disposed on either side of this central group are smaller rooms arranged around two internal courts; on the west front is a long gallery. Colonnades link the main block to the kitchen and stable courts, which balance each other on either side of the great court. Sarah, the Duchess of Marlborough, objected to its impracticality as a home, because kitchen and dining room are a quarter-mile apart. Alexander Pope, the poet, observed, "'Tis very fine, But where d'ye sleep, or where d'ye dine?"

Vanbrugh designed about ten grand country houses, whereas Hawksmoor's major architectural works were the six churches he built in London, two of which were paid for under the Act for Building Fifty New Churches of 1711, for which he was appointed commissioner. Most of his basilical planning is derived from Wren, but the exuberance is all Hawksmoor's. At Christ Church, Spitalfields, London (1723–29), Hawksmoor's interest in the late Roman temples at Baalbek is reflected in his overscaled and unusually detailed design. Here the nave is lighted from clerestories above elliptical barrel vaults running parallel to the nave. Below these vaults, the nave arcade is composed of cylindrical columns with complete entablatures surmounting each one. The nave itself is not vaulted but covered with a flat coffered ceiling, and the whole of the interior is bold. On the exterior, the porch is composed of a large Serliana, above which the tower rises, buttressed at front and back by screen walls containing windows arranged in another Serliana composition (Figure 10.82). The style of Vanbrugh and Hawksmoor is very personal and individual, forming a rich extension of the more academic work of Wren and thus remaining a part of the English tradition.

James Gibbs (1682–1754), another follower of Wren, came perhaps nearest to achieving the Baroque style in England since he had studied in

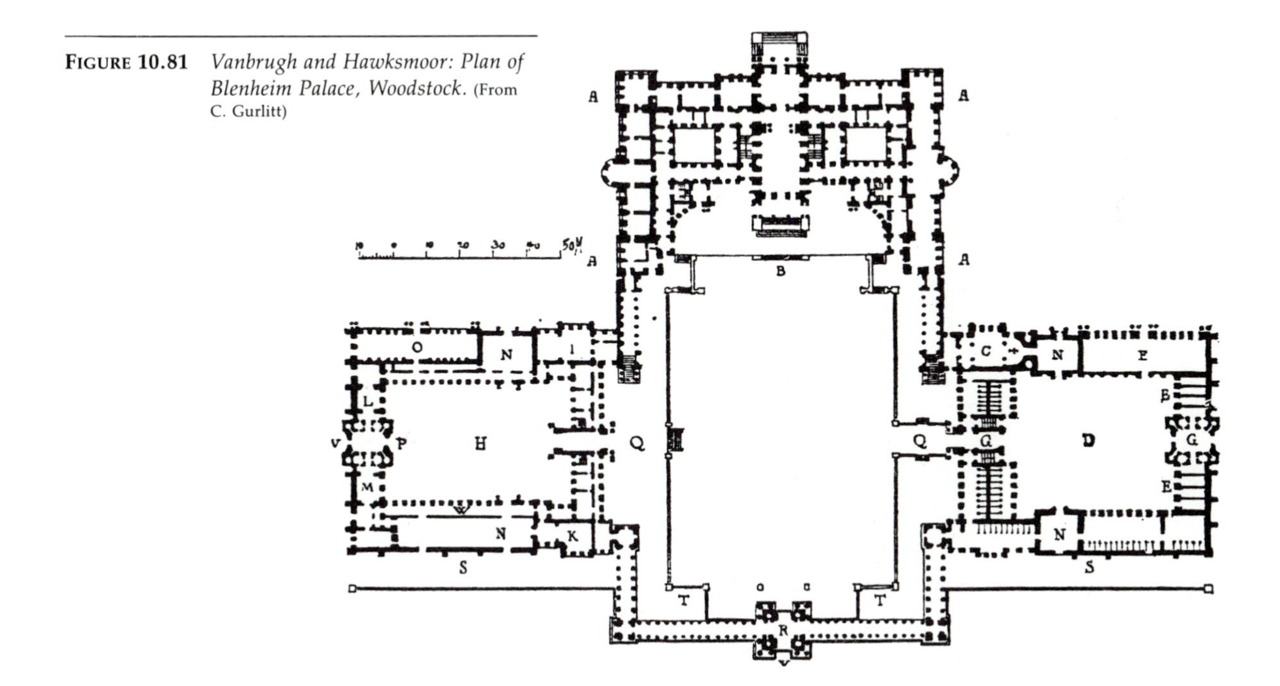

FIGURE 10.81 *Vanbrugh and Hawksmoor: Plan of Blenheim Palace, Woodstock.* (From C. Gurlitt)

Rome under Bernini's principal follower, Carlo Fontana, from 1703 to 1709. He, too, was a commissioner of the New Churches Act, for which he designed St. Mary-le-Strand in London (1714–1717) (Figure 10.83). The entrance façade of St. Mary's was based on the transept elevation of St. Paul's and was thus ultimately derived from S. Maria della Pace. The sides of St. Mary's, however, have an ebullient plastic rhythm of tabernacled windows, segmental and triangular pediments, and modeling comparable to the late Roman Baroque work.

Gibbs's St. Martin-in-the-Fields, London (1721–1726) is an essay in the Corinthian order, employing giant columns and pilasters both inside and out (Figures 10.84–10.86). A Wren-derived tower and steeple are on the main axis, with the entrance to the church beneath its main structure protected by a dominating Corinthian portico. This church set a precedent for religious buildings, most notably in the American colonies both before and after the Revolution, mainly through Gibbs's *A Book of Architecture,* published in 1729 to illustrate his numerous designs. Joseph Brown's Baptist Church at Providence, Rhode Island (1774–1775), is based on St. Martin's, as are St. Michael's in Charleston, South Carolina (begun 1752, possibly by Peter Harrison), and several churches in Vermont and Connecticut by Lavius Fillmore.

Gibbs is an architect whose works form a bridge between the most elaborate English Baroque and more restrained designs based on the serenity of Andrea Palladio. The designs in his publications illustrate both inspirations. By the middle of the eighteenth century, the return to purer interpretations of classical antiquity emerged as Neo-Classicism, an important movement to which Gibbs gave an impetus.

FIGURE 10.82 *Hawksmoor: Christ Church Spitalfields, London, 1723–1729.* (Photo: Marburg)

FIGURE 10.83 *Gibbs: St. Mary-le-Strand, London, 1714–1717.* (From J. Gibbs)

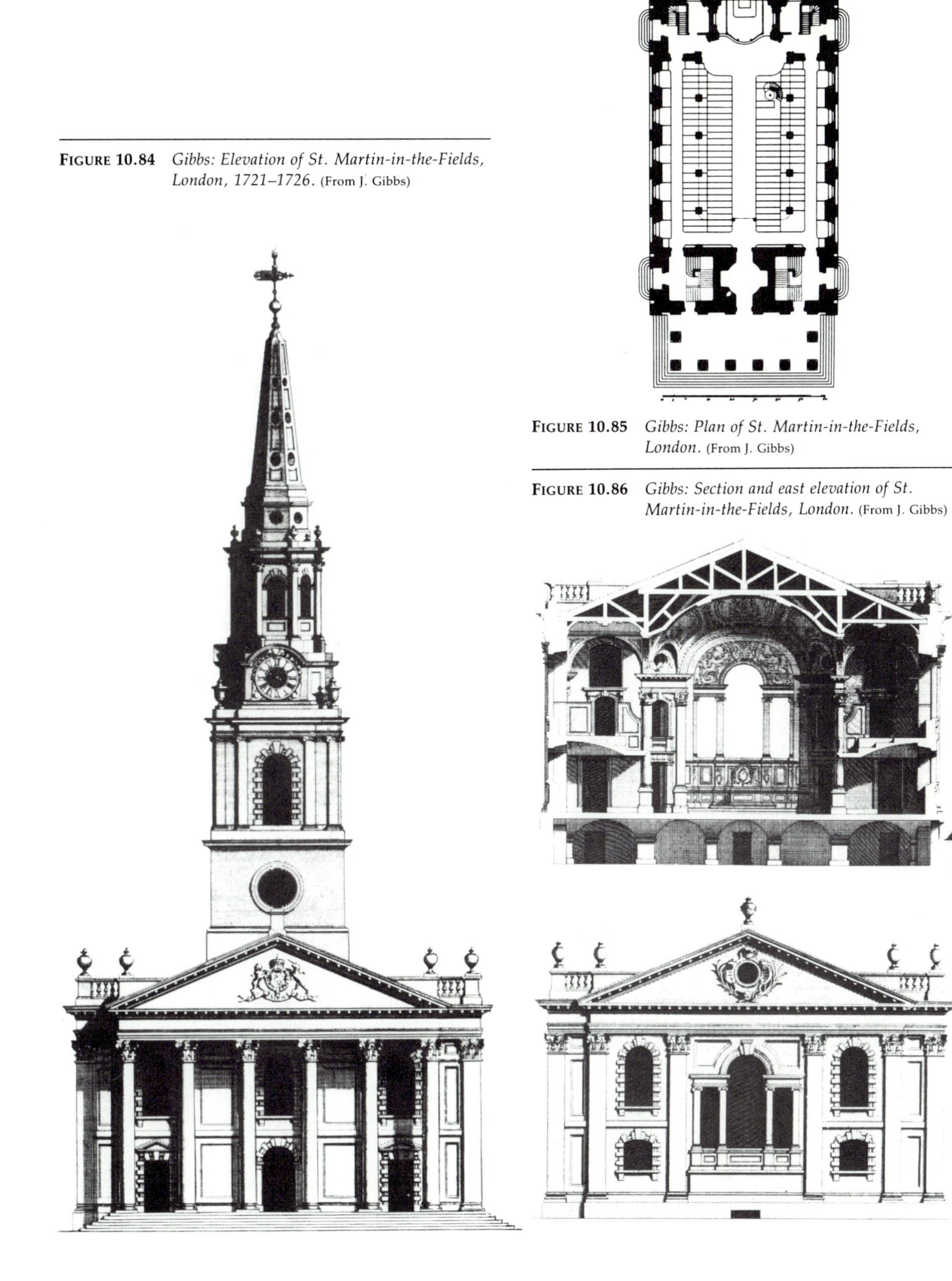

FIGURE 10.84 *Gibbs: Elevation of St. Martin-in-the-Fields, London, 1721–1726.* (From J. Gibbs)

FIGURE 10.85 *Gibbs: Plan of St. Martin-in-the-Fields, London.* (From J. Gibbs)

FIGURE 10.86 *Gibbs: Section and east elevation of St. Martin-in-the-Fields, London.* (From J. Gibbs)

11.

The Eighteenth Century

Architectural developments during the eighteenth century encompassed several seemingly divergent elements. In central Europe, for example, late Baroque and Rococo work predominated, particularly in major commissions for the nobility or the Catholic Church. Vierzehnheiligen, the Würzburg Residenz, Blenheim Palace, and the later stages of construction at Versailles are all of the eighteenth century. But the period also saw the emergence of other architectural approaches; some were a reaction to the decorative exuberance of the Baroque and others were a result of curiosity about other times, places, and cultures.

Historically the eighteenth century was part of the Age of Enlightenment, an era in which scientists and mathematicians laid the foundation for modern achievements in their fields; philosophers proposed rational forms of government that were put into practice by the American and French revolutions; archaeologists and explorers probed the past and distant civilizations for an understanding of other cultures; and practical tinkerers invented devices and machines that were to transform industry, commerce, and transportation. Just as the effects of eighteenth-century changes in technology, economics, and society continue to be felt in the twentieth century, the changes in architecture during this period were of signal importance in shaping the direction of modern design. Three developments in particular can be considered the roots of twentieth-century architecture: Neo-Classicism, Romanticism, and industrial technology. All emerged in the eighteenth century and continued during the nineteenth, and their influence is still evident today. Both Neo-Classicism and Romanticism stem in part from the English revival of Palladio, and it is there that an account of eighteenth-century innovations must begin.

THE PALLADIANS

Even as construction was being completed on the grandiose Blenheim Palace, some English architects were turning away from the style of Wren, Vanbrugh, and Hawksmoor in favor of the simpler approaches to architecture that they found in the works of Palladio. The leaders of this Palladian movement included Colen Campbell (1676?–1729), a Scottish architect and editor of the influential book, *Vitruvius Britannicus,* which appeared in three volumes from 1715 to 1725; Richard Boyle, third Earl of Burlington (1694–1753), a wealthy nobleman who practiced as an architect in addition to fulfilling government duties; and William Kent (1685–1748), an Englishman who originally trained in Rome as a painter and branched into architecture and landscape architecture under the patronage of Lord Burlington. Central to Palladian thought was a great respect for Vitruvius, enthusiasm for the buildings of Palladio, and admiration for the works of Inigo Jones, who first brought Roman ideals into British architecture. All three men were Whigs and staunch supporters of the house of Hanover, which had replaced the Stuart line on the English throne. Both the first volumes of *Vitruvius Britannicus* and Leoni's English translation of Palladio's *I quattro libri dell'architettura* were dedicated to King George I.

Colen Campbell may well have been responsible for converting Lord Burlington to the cause of Palladio. His illustrations of classical English buildings, including country houses influenced by Inigo Jones and his own designs in *Vitruvius Britannicus,* brought Campbell to the attention of Lord Burlington, who commissioned him to undertake renovations to Burlington House in London (now modified and enlarged into the Royal Academy). At Mereworth Castle (1723) in Kent, Campbell designed a near-replica of the Villa Rotonda at a slightly larger scale (Figure 11.1). Four Ionic porticos are attached to a simple cube, crowned with a pyramidal roof and dome. Mereworth contains several practical and ingenious devices, such as the incorporation of fireplace flues in ribs of the dome, with the cupola used as the chimney exit.

Like many aristocrats of the period Lord Burlington went on the Grand Tour of Europe from 1714–1715, but during 1719 he returned to Italy specifically to study the buildings of Palladio. There he met William Kent, whose work so impressed him that they returned together and began a lifetime of friendly collaboration. With Kent's assistance in landscape design and interior detailing, Lord Burlington designed his own variation of the Villa Rotonda at Chiswick House (1725–1729) outside London (Figures 11.2, 11.3). Chiswick is a smaller version of the Palladian original, enlivened by a certain amount of creative borrowing from various sources. It has only one portico instead of four, and its octagonal drum and dome perhaps owe more to Scamozzi than to Palladio. Obelisks placed at the edge of the roof contain the chimney flues in an antique disguise (precedent for this treatment had been observed on villas in the neighborhood of Vicenza), while the garden elevation is distinguished by three windows of original design, composed of Palladian motifs recessed in relieving arches. The interior spaces follow Palladian proportions and in-

FIGURE 11.1 *Campbell: Section through Mereworth Castle, 1723.* (From R. Blomfield)

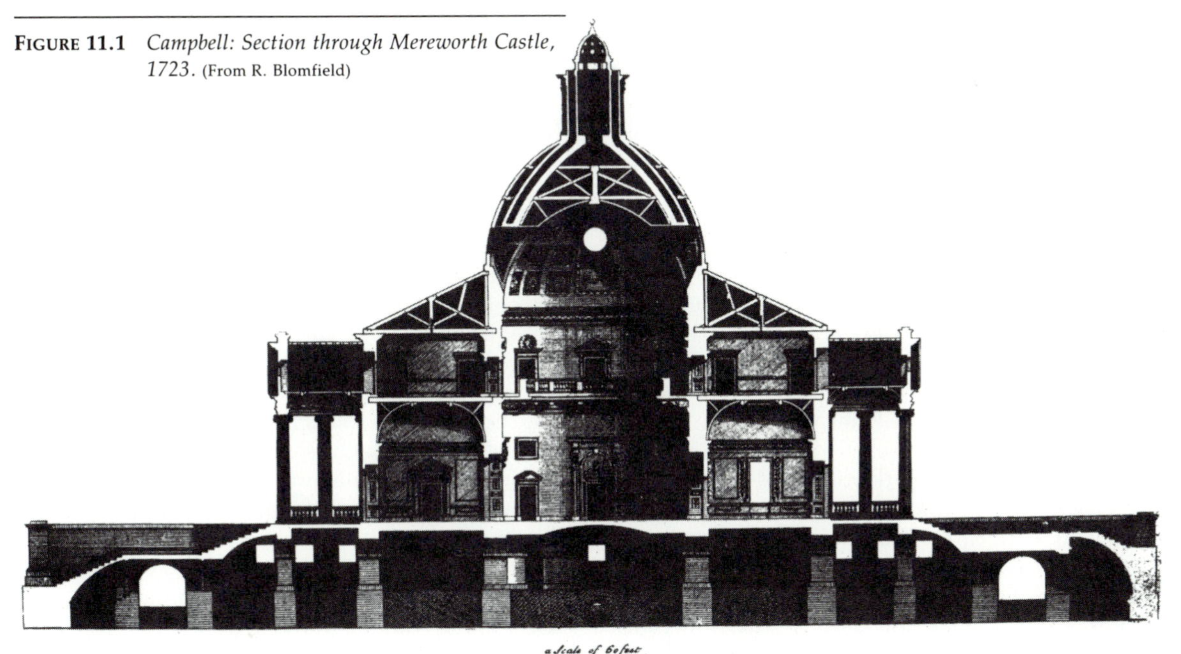

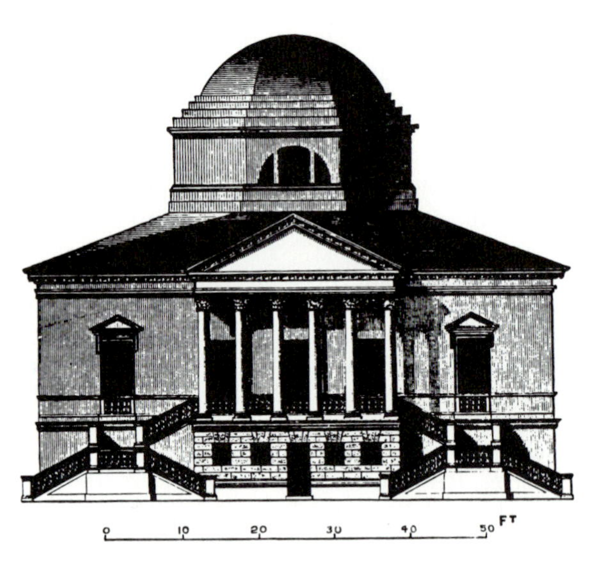

FIGURE 11.2 *Lord Burlington: Elevation of Chiswick House, 1725–1729.* (From J. Fergusson)

FIGURE 11.3 *Lord Burlington: Plan of Chiswick House.* (From J. Fergusson)

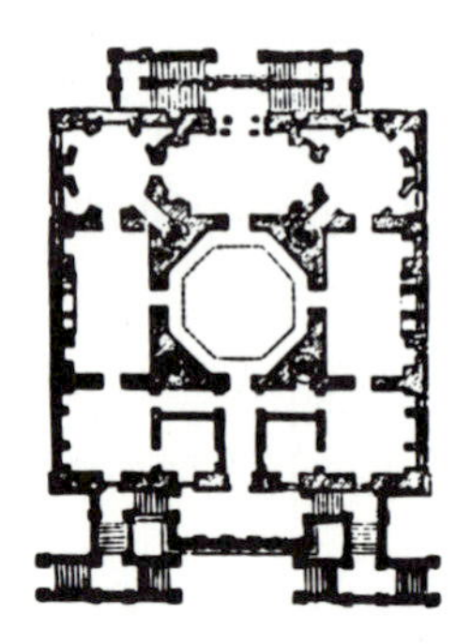

corporate elements from designs by Inigo Jones in their details. Lord Burlington used Chiswick to house his architectural library and to provide space for entertainments; he actually lived in an existing house that was attached to the new villa at one corner.

In addition to his work with Lord Burlington at Chiswick, Kent edited a two-volume collection published in 1727 as the *Designs of Inigo Jones.* After about 1730 Kent began to practice architecture on his own, designing Holkham Hall in Norfolk in 1734 (Figure 11.4). It is a grand country seat in the tradition of Vanbrugh and thus much larger than the villas of Palladio. Pavilions, pediments, Palladian windows, and a simplicity in the composition of elements recapture the spirit of the sixteenth-century master in what could be termed a cluster of five Italian residences, consisting of a central reception mass and four wings containing the kitchen, a chapel, a music gallery, and private rooms with associated accommodations.

Kent's landscape creations, including the grounds of Holkham Hall, are probably more important than his architectural contributions. He is regarded as one of the founders of the English landscape garden tradition, in which the landscape architect improved on and encouraged natural qualities of the park. Instead of the rigid geometric plantings favored by the French, English garden designers cultivated a certain irregular wildness. They built dams on streams to form serpentine lakes following the contours of the land, grouped trees in clusters, and provided limited views of the country seat as one approached the house along a winding carriageway. Carefully planned views from the house extended beyond the clumps of trees into the landscape where cows grazed. A ditch with a fence or hedge at its bottom prevented the cows from encroaching upon the lawns in the immediate vicinity of the house; discovery of this concealed barrier was a surprise, causing one to laugh or exclaim, ahah!, thus providing the name ha-ha for this landscape device. To the Palladians, who saw "natural" qualities in the architecture of Palladio and Jones, there was nothing contradictory in having a completely symmetrical classical house set in a landscape with naturalistic elements that reflected a painter's version of the Roman countryside.

Lancelot Brown (1716–1783) was the leader of this picturesque attitude toward landscape architecture. When asked his opinion on any piece of ground, he would say that it had capabilities, and thus he became known as Capability Brown. He practiced as an architect in the Palladian tradition, but in that field he was a minor figure compared to Kent, for whom he worked as a gardener at Stowe from 1740. He also relandscaped Blenheim Palace beginning in 1758, providing the driveway that encircles the serpentine lake as one approaches the palace from the kitchen side, with glimpses of the building at various vantage points along the way (Figures 11.5, 11.6).

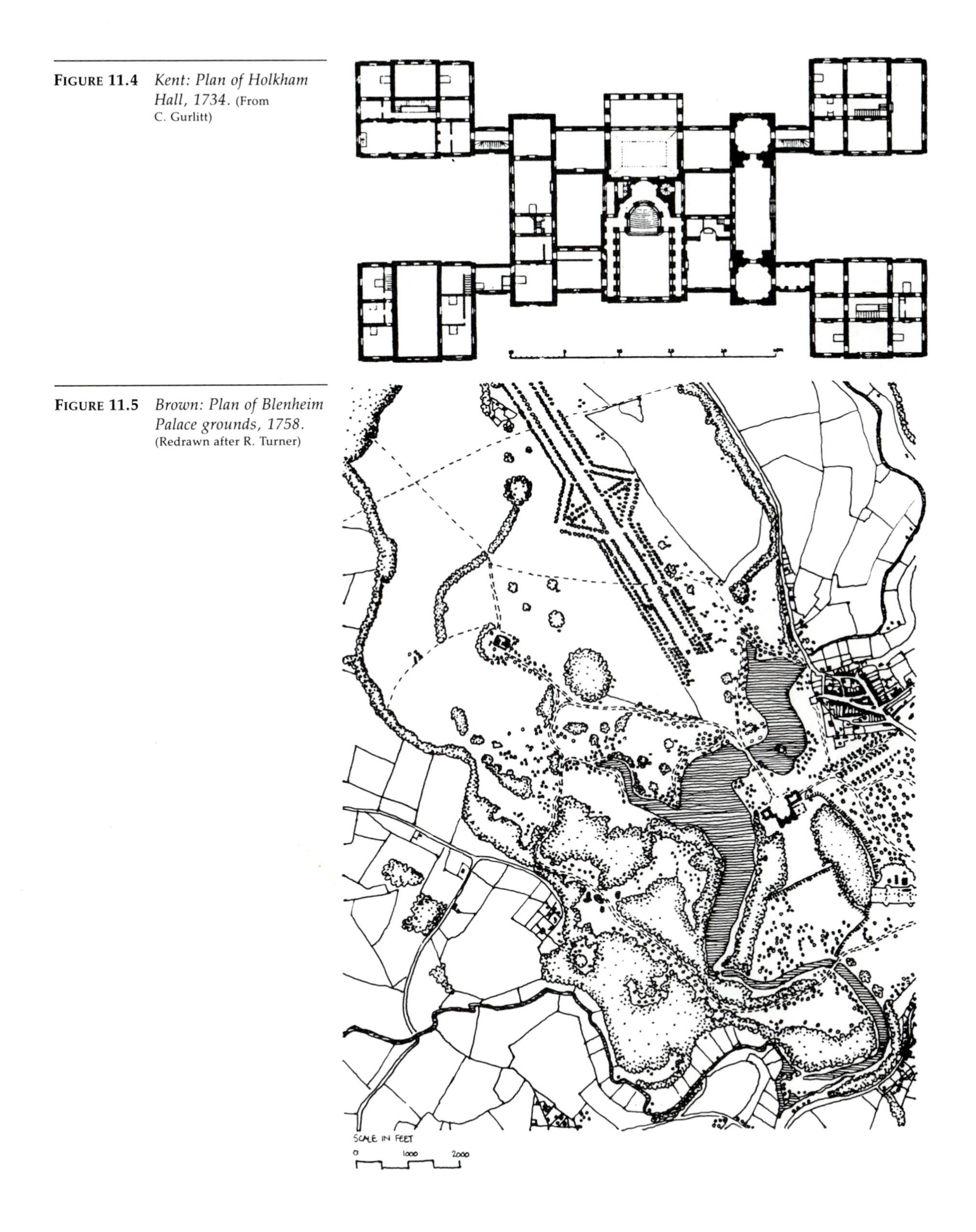

FIGURE 11.4 *Kent: Plan of Holkham Hall, 1734.* (From C. Gurlitt)

FIGURE 11.5 *Brown: Plan of Blenheim Palace grounds, 1758.* (Redrawn after R. Turner)

Figure 11.6 *Brown: Blenheim Palace grounds.* (Photo: Wodehouse)

Brown was one of a number of followers of the Palladians; others who were inspired by them developed in a slightly different manner. Such an architect was Robert Adam (1728–1792), a Scotsman of international significance in all aspects of design. At the age of twenty-six he met and accompanied Charles-Louis Clérisseau to Nîmes. Together they traveled to Split, Yugoslavia, where they made measured drawings, which Adam published in 1764 as *Ruins of the Palace of the Emperor Diocletian at Spalato, in Dalmatia.* Adam was just as interested in Vitruvius as the Palladians, but during a trip to Italy (lasting from 1754 to 1758) he became aware that the greatest archaeological interest was focused on the religious architecture of antiquity, not on the houses. Adam devoted his attention to what little was known of residential design and interior detailing, in part because he realized that his architectural practice, like that of his father and brothers, would rely on clients who required homes, not temples, based on the classical styles. His practice did develop into one in which he remodeled the interiors of existing country seats. In Adam's designs, decoration and furniture became linear and refined, delicate and colorful. He also contributed to the townscape of Edinburgh, where the north side of Charlotte Square was completed to his designs in 1793. Architecturally, his most interesting and successful development (although disastrous financially) was the Adelphi scheme (1768–1772) fronting on the River Thames in London (Figure 11.7). (It was partially demolished in the 1930s, but a few pieces remain.) The Adelphi consisted of houses facing four streets, two parallel and two perpendicular to the river. The houses were of brick with stone and terra-cotta trim. As in any palatial façade, the eleven houses facing the river had central and end pavilions without incorporating the giant pilasters or columns of an earlier age. Instead Adam introduced decorative panels of Greek **acroteria** design. The interior decoration was similar, with Greek vine decorations on wall panels complementing the thin, flat geometric designs of the ceilings.

NEO-CLASSICISM

The Palladians in England were among the first to undertake a thorough study and revival of architecture from the past. By the middle of the eighteenth century the artistic elite of Europe had developed a renewed interest in the buildings of antiquity. This

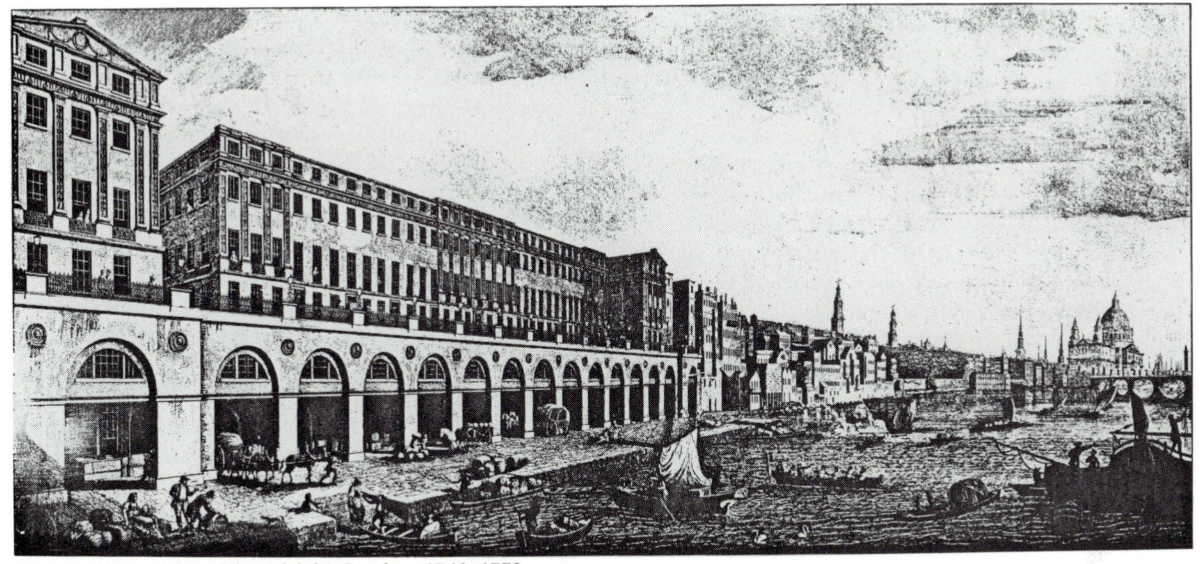

FIGURE 11.7 *Adam: The Adelphi, London, 1768–1772.* (From R. and J. Adam)

had happened before. Carolingian architects had looked to Roman, Early Christian, and Byzantine buildings for inspiration, and the architects of the Italian Renaissance had made extensive studies of the ruins of Rome and the writings of Vitruvius for guidance in matters of proportion and design. This eighteenth-century interest in antiquity, however, differed from previous "returns to Rome" in both its scope and its impact on design, and historians have termed the movement Neo-Classicism. Artists and architects of the Neo-Classical Period gained an accurate understanding of actual buildings and art works from the past, and historians began comprehensive studies of ancient civilizations. Popular curiosity about remote places and exotic cultures encouraged travel and the acquisition of artifacts and curios.

During the eighteenth century, publications of measured drawings from ancient settlements greatly expanded architectural historical information. Remains of the Greek colonial town of Paestum and the Roman cities of Herculaneum and Pompeii were discovered in the course of road construction in the Kingdom of Naples. Excavations, begun at Herculaneum in 1735 and at Pompeii in 1748, freed the buildings from the volcanic ash and mud that had buried both during an eruption of Mount Vesuvius in 79 A.D. For the first time scholars and architects had accurate examples of Imperial Roman architecture and decoration. Thomas Major published *The Ruins of Paestum* in 1768, contributing measured examples of archaic Greek temples to the growing knowledge of Greek architecture; in 1762 James Stuart and Nicholas Revett began publishing their four volumes on the *Antiquities of Athens*, a series completed by others in 1816. Roman settlements around the Mediterranean were also investigated. Robert Wood's *Ruins of Palmyra* (1753) and *Ruins of Baalbec* (1757) documented these important sites in the Middle East, and Robert Adam recorded his work at Split (on the Adriatic coast of present-day Yugoslavia) in his *Ruins of the Palace of the Emperor Diocletian at Spalato* (1764). The Frenchman Charles-Louis Clérisseau published the *Antiquities of Nîmes* in 1778.

This interest in antiquity was not confined to the classical civilizations of Greece and Rome. Napoleon's military expedition to Egypt in 1798 included a large group of archaeologists and engineers whose reports, notably the *Voyage dans la basse et la haute Égypte pendant les campagnes du Général Bonaparte* (1807) and the twenty-volume *Descriptions de l'Égypte* (1809–1822) by Baron Dominique Vivant Denon, encouraged popular enthusiasm for things Egyptian. Public interest in non-Western civilizations had already been sparked by trading contacts and Jesuit translations of the writings of Confucius and the *Koran;* soon architectural knowledge was enhanced by Sir William Chambers's *Design of Chinese Buildings* (1757) and Thomas Daniell's *The Antiquities of India* (1800). Historical information documented through drawings of ancient buildings provided designers with a great repertoire of artistic styles than ever before, and eighteenth-century publications made possible the freedom in design that ultimately endowed twentieth-century architects with the choice of personal expression.

The leading exponent of Neo-Classicism in Italy was Giovanni Battista Piranesi (1720–1778), a man known not so much for his architectural designs as for his engravings of architectural subjects, which number over 3000. The ruins of Rome were the most common subjects depicted; Piranesi even made a large-scale map of ancient Rome, including with the actual buildings imaginary projects composed of complex geometric shapes. For the subsequent history of architecture, however, the most influential set of Piranesi engravings were the *Carceri* (Prisons), a series of fourteen plates made in 1745 illustrating visions of vast spaces teeming with unidentified toilers whose workings are illuminated by obscured light sources (Figure 11.8). The scale is gigantic, of the magnitude of the great Roman baths, while the spatial organization is far more complex. Arches, vaults, and staircases rise in the gloom and are revealed by shafts of light that owe more to Baroque than to Roman designs. Because they were inexpensive, produced in large quantities, and easily transported, Piranesi's engravings were widely distributed across Europe in his own time, and they continue to impress architects and artists of our day.

FIGURE 11.8 *Piranesi: Carceri, 1745.* (Engraving by Piranesi)

In France the Neo-Classic movement developed somewhat differently. There, architects were interested in the primary geometric solids of the cube, sphere, and pyramid as the logical basis for architectural expression. (This approach parallels that of the contemporary French philosophers, who were exploring rationality as a basis for human affairs.) While there is some similarity to early Renaissance interest in the circle, square, and triangle, the Neo-Classic designers of France went beyond previous geometric investigations to propose entire buildings dominated by simple solid geometries.

The leading French Neo-Classicists were Étienne-Louis Boullée (1728–1799) and Claude-Nicholas Ledoux (1736–1806), both of whom designed far more on paper than they actually built. (The upheavals of the French Revolution severely restricted opportunities for construction.) Boullée's projects give prominence to primary geometric forms, including domes, pyramids, and cones. His design of a cenotaph for Sir Isaac Newton, the discoverer of the laws of physics, was a hollow sphere 500 feet in diameter, the top half of which represented the dome of heaven, perforated with holes to give the impression of stars and the moon on the interior (Figure 11.9). Suspended inside the sphere was to be a giant lamp representing the

FIGURE 11.9 *Boullée: Cenotaph for Sir Isaac Newton.* (Photo: Bibliothèque Nationale)

FIGURE 11.10 *Boullée: Library project.* (Photo: Bibliothèque Nationale)

sun. Boullée's concept of the design is explained in a tribute to Newton contained in his *Treatise on Architecture*: "Sublime mind! Vast and profound genius! Divine Being! Newton! Accept the homage of my weak talents. . . . I conceive the idea of surrounding thee with thy discovery, and thus, somehow, surrounding thee with thyself." Another project of Boullée, this one for a library, also incorporates simple geometric forms (Figure 11.10). The library was essentially a cylinder placed on its side, with the bottom half stepped in terraced bookstacks down to a level floor. Books could thus be lowered from level to level by attendants, obviating the need for hazardous step ladders.

The projects of Ledoux are similarly influenced by primary forms. His designs for the city of Chaux (1775–1779) show his ideas for an ideal town to accommodate a salt works (Figure 11.11). In plan the community was organized in a great ellipse of worker's houses, with the buildings for the salt works placed across the lesser diameter. Outside the ellipse were gardens, recreational facilities, and various communal buildings. Through its integration of planned open space with residential and industrial development, the design of Chaux anticipates the Garden City movement of the late nineteenth century, which was similarly concerned with providing a healthy environment for the city dwellers. In architectural terms the linkage of man and nature at Chaux was expressed in basic geometries. The cemetery building was a sphere, symbolizing the eternal cosmos; and the wheelwright's house was identified by large circles incorporated on its façade. His design for the Inspector's House at the source of the Loue River illustrates Ledoux's continuing fascination with houses built over water (Figure 11.12). Here, the house is shaped like a large cylindrical pipe set horizontally on a podium, with the stream flowing through the lower half of the cylinder and the rooms of the building arranged in buttresslike rectangular blocks along its tunnel sides. None of these highly symbolic projects was actually constructed, although portions of the plan of Chaux were built at Arc-en-Senans. Ledoux's executed designs there use simplified versions of the classic orders realized in heavily rusticated masonry. He also built a series of tollgates for the city of Paris, at least one of which, the Barrière de la Villette (1784–1789), still stands. This tollgate is composed of a cylinder rising out of a lower square block, which is articulated by projecting Doric-derived porticoes on three of its four sides. The massing and the masonry are handled to convey a sense of ponderousness.

FIGURE 11.11 *Ledoux: Chaux, 1775–1779.* (From C. N. Ledoux)

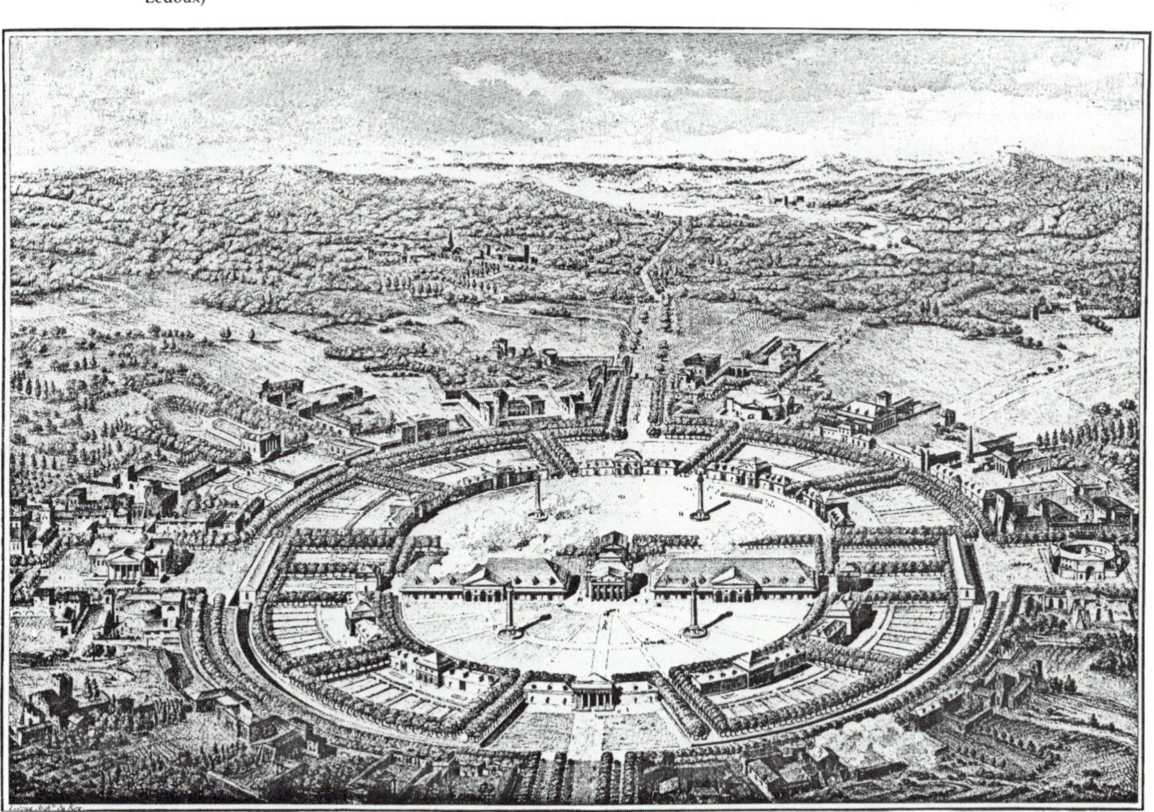

FIGURE 11.12 *Ledoux: Inspector's House at the source of the Loue.* (From C. N. Ledoux)

THE ROMANTIC MOVEMENT

Even as Neo-Classical architects and antiquarians were reassessing the past through archaeological work and scholarly inquiry, a parallel and often overlapping orientation to art and architecture was developing. Its beginnings can be seen in the English landscape movement that accompanied the Palladians. Developed further and applied to architecture and art, it has been termed Romanticism. In some respects Romanticism was a reaction to the order and regularity inherent in Neo-Classicism; in other cases it was an expression of deeply held religious and moral convictions. Romanticism delighted in the asymmetrical and the irregular for their highly picturesque qualities. Contradictory as this may seem at first to the ideals of Neo-Classicism, Romanticism was actually a complementary movement, and a number of established Neo-Classicists did Romantic works as well. For example, Piranesi's engravings, which were manifestations of Neo-Classicism, also influenced Romanticism; although the inspiration for his designs goes back to Rome, the ruggedness, wildness, and fragmentation of the ruins embodies Romantic ideals. The works of William Kent also exhibit both classical and romantic tendencies.

Romanticism in England started through a playful use of medieval-inspired structures as focal points in the layout of gardens. At Hagley Park, Worcestershire, Sanderson Miller built a sham ruin in the Gothic style in 1747, and other landscape designers soon copied the idea. Horace Walpole had his house at Strawberry Hill near London done in a medieval manner by a committee of architects and literary friends. Work on Strawberry Hill began in 1749, and the structure soon emerged as an eclectic assortment of Gothic details. The Holbein Room had a chimneypiece adapted from the tomb of Archbishop Wareham at Westminster Abbey; the long gallery (Figure 11.13) featured pendant vaulting based on that in the Henry VII Chapel at Westminster Abbey (see Figure 8.67); and the Round Room had ceiling plaster work inspired by the rose win-

FIGURE 11.13 *Walpole: Long gallery, Strawberry Hill, Twickenham, 1748 and after.* (Photo: Marburg) ►

FIGURE 11.14 *Mique: Hameau at Versailles*. (Photo: French Government Tourist Office)

dow of old St. Paul's Cathedral. The Rococo chandeliers and purple wallpapers used throughout contributed to a sense of playfulness in this passionate, picturesque toy. This early phase of Romanticism in England is often termed Gothick (the misspelling is deliberate) to reflect the rather lighthearted character of the work. More serious evocations of medieval designs were to come in the nineteenth century with the Gothic Revival.

Designers in other places adopted a picturesque approach to architecture as a way of retreating to what were perceived to be simpler, more rustic times. At Versailles, the epitome of formality and pomp, Marie-Antoinette commissioned Richard Mique (1728–1794) to design the Hameau or Hamlet (Figure 11.14), based on the folk architecture of her native Austria. Here she and her ladies-in-waiting could escape from the splendors of the court and, in peasant costume, spend an afternoon playing at being simple milkmaids. Mique used a variety of materials, textures, and colors in the hamlet buildings, which were irregularly clustered around an artificial lake, creating a romantic composition. The Hameau anticipates nineteenth-century architects' employment of vernacular architecture to evoke national character or style.

INDUSTRIAL TECHNOLOGY

Industrial technology advanced in the eighteenth century as inventive men sought more efficient means of accomplishing various tasks that were necessary to society: the spinning of yarn, the weaving and finishing of cloth, the mining of metallic ores, and so on. Machine work replaced the handwork of men and women, and engines powered by steam supplanted the motive power of men and horses. The changes these new inventions brought to society were many and far-reaching, including an increase in population, the rise of a new working class, the substantial growth of factory towns, some redistribution of wealth, and generally improved living conditions for people.

Increased production of material goods included new and improved methods for making building materials, while scientific advances increased understanding of the how and why of structures. Structural calculations were first applied to a new design in the building of the Panthéon in Paris (1755–1792), and by the middle of the next century it was possible to calculate in advance of construction the behavior of most structural materials under load, freeing engineers and architects from complete reliance on what had worked in the past. Another invention, that of descriptive geometry, enabled designers to depict in drawings the true shapes of complex three-dimensional objects, so that architects could completely describe a building in drawings rather than remain daily at the job site to direct progress of the work. A related system for representing land contours made accurate site work possible.

One result of these developments was the increasing separation of architecture and engineering. Since the middle ages the architect — described by Vitruvius as a man skilled in the design of everything from cities to buildings, mechanical devices, astronomical instruments, and machines of war — had been gradually released from responsibility for mechanical contraptions and defense, which passed to the newly recognized fields of mechanical and military engineering. Now a growing body of scientific data on materials provided the basis for civil engineering, which was taught at schools organized apart from architectural academies. Civil engineers were charged with the increasing amount of utilitarian construction — roads, bridges, mines, factories, warehouses, lighthouses, and canals — while architects were employed on buildings where appearance was symbolically important. Thus it was the engineer who first experimented with the building materials made possible by industrial technology, and it was in utilitarian structures that they were first used.

Of all the construction materials improved during the Industrial Revolution none was more important than iron. People had been smelting iron from ore since the prehistoric Iron Age, but the quantity of metal produced was small and its quality was highly variable. The use of the material in buildings was therefore limited to occasional ornamental work, fasteners, and hardware. Improved means of producing iron were sought by refiners, including Abraham Darby, whose furnaces at Coalbrookdale, Shropshire, can be traced back to 1696. In an attempt to advance his work, Darby imported Dutch ironworkers in 1704 and soon succeeded in smelting cast iron for commercial use. Cast iron has a relatively high (3.5%) carbon content and is brittle, though very strong in compression. By 1713 Darby had pioneered a method for producing cast iron by using coal instead of expensive charcoal in the furnace. The structural properties of his cast iron made it a suitable material for columns, where its 80,000 to 120,000 psi compressive strength could be exploited. When used as a beam, cast iron is comparatively weak, having a tensile strength between 15,000 and 30,000 psi. If refined iron with a low carbon content (0.4%) is hammered into shape instead of cast, it is known as wrought iron, a material with 70,000 to 80,000 psi compressive strength and up to 60,000 psi tensile strength. Its superior tensile properties made wrought iron much better than cast iron for beams.

Builders soon found applications for these two types of iron. Darby's furnaces produced wrought iron railroad tracks as early as 1750, and supplied cast iron for the world's first all-metal bridge at Coalbrookdale in 1779 (Figure 11.15). Abraham Darby III, grandson of the pioneer industrialist, collaborated with the architect Thomas Pritchard to design a bridge of five parallel semicircular arches to span one hundred feet over the River Severn, a wa-

FIGURE 11.15 *Abraham Darby and Thomas Pritchard: Coalbrookdale Bridge, 1779.* (From G. Rondelet)

FIGURE 11.16 *Strutt: Section and plan of West Mill, Belper, 1793–1795.* (From *Transactions of the Newcomen Society*, Volume 30)

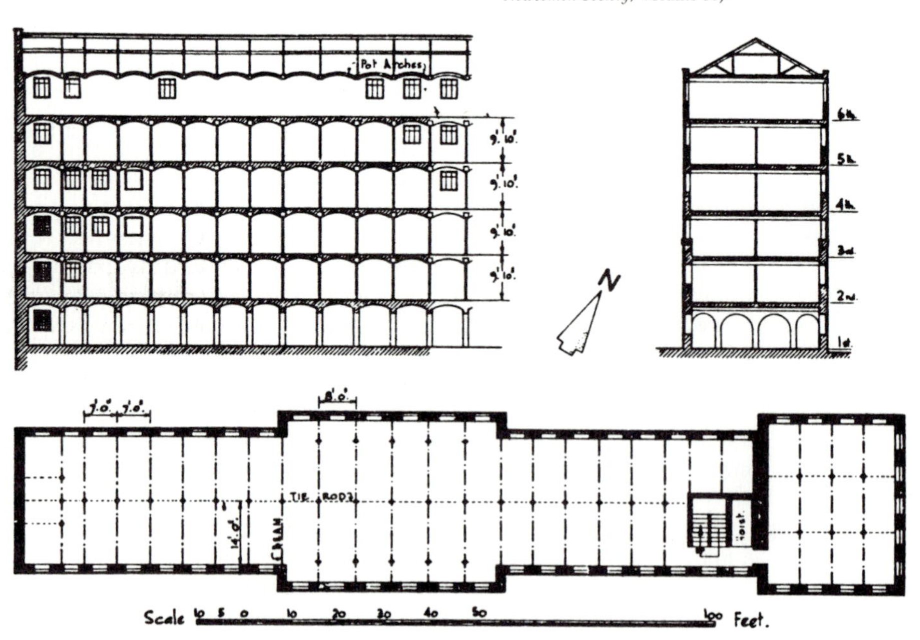

tercourse prone to intense flooding that would wash out intermediate piers. The bridge cost six thousand pounds, a large sum but only about one-third the price of an equivalent masonry span. Its design was conservative and over-engineered, with the members sized as if they were made of wood, but it represents the first essay in metal construction for bridges.

The incombustible properties of iron, together with its strength, were exploited in the construction of "fireproof" multistory textile mills. As early as 1792 William Strutt designed and built a six-story calico mill at Derby with cast-iron columns; his West Mill at Belper of the following year is similar (Figure 11.16). The dust-laden air of textile mills, combined with coagulated oil and lint on the floors under the machinery and illumination from open flames, created ideal conditions for mill fires in which equipment, raw materials, and workers' lives were lost. To protect the basic structure, improve sanitation and ventilation, and reduce the opportunities for fire, Strutt and others designed mills with external walls of masonry, cast-iron internal columns, and protected wood beams. An early version of "fireproof" construction had the large wooden floor beams socketed into cast-iron shoes attached to the cast-iron columns. Segmental brick arches spanned the beams, supporting level floors made of sand, screed, and clay tiles, with wrought-iron rods used to tie the structure together. Undersides of the wooden members were coated with plaster; with sand on top and plaster below, the wood was protected from fire. Later improvements to this system substituted wrought-iron rails (forerunners of rolled I-beam sections) (Figure 11.17) for the wooden beams; a surviving example of such a structure is the former Benyon, Benyon, and Bage Flax Mill at Shrewsbury (1796). Eventually the segmental brick arches were discarded in favor of other materials, but even with these changes, the metal frame structure of today remains essentially the same as that built by Strutt in 1792.

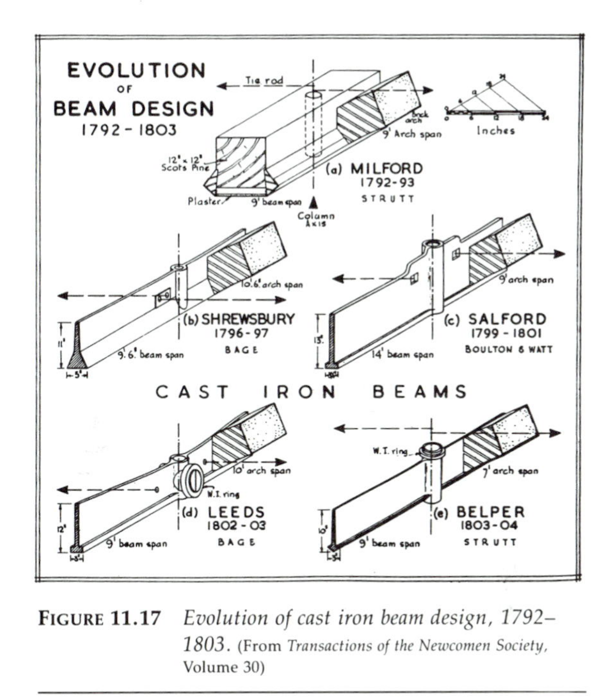

FIGURE 11.17 *Evolution of cast iron beam design, 1792–1803.* (From *Transactions of the Newcomen Society,* Volume 30)

Bridge designs, rather than building designs, generally exploited the structural properties of cast and wrought iron most eloquently, and it is there that the new materials achieved their purest expression. For example, Darby's Coalbrookdale bridge was soon surpassed by Thomas Telford (1757–1834), who built an iron bridge three miles upstream at Buildwas in 1795–1798. Telford's bridge was a segmental arch spanning 130 feet with a rise of 27 feet; he used less than half the iron required to construct the Coalbrookdale Bridge while achieving a longer span. Engineers in the nineteenth century continued to reduce material-to-load ratios and experiment with systems, such as tensile structures, that were impossible in masonry or timber, and we will pick up those developments in the next chapter.

12.

NINETEENTH-CENTURY DEVELOPMENTS

Architecture in the nineteenth century was perhaps more varied than ever before. The freedoms introduced by Neo-Classicism and Romanticism encouraged revivals of historical styles, such as Gothic, Greek, Islamic, Egyptian, Byzantine, and Early Christian, along with inventive new creations, such as the Chinoiserie, Japonais, Moorish, and Hindoo styles. As illustrations of this, consider any number of English and American buildings designed after 1750. In England nabobs (colonial officials from India returning to retire in Britain with their fortunes) built pleasure palaces designed in the styles of India, such as Sezincote (Figure 12.1) in Gloucestershire, designed in 1805 by Samuel Pepys Cockerell (1754–1827) for his brother Charles. In the same spirit, between 1818 and 1821, John Nash built the Royal Pavilion at Brighton for the Prince Regent. Sir William Chambers built a Chinese pagoda, a Roman arch, and classical temples at Kew Gardens in 1757–1763.

FIGURE 12.1 *Cockerell: Sezincote, 1805.* (From J. Britton)

The Egyptian style was proposed for buildings related to medicine, which was considered to have originated in the Nile Valley, or death, since the great monuments of Egypt were associated with the pharaohs and their journey in the afterlife, or wherever suggestions of massiveness or eternity were desired, as in factories, prisons (Figure 12.2), suspension bridges, and libraries. In the United States, Benjamin Henry Latrobe (1764–1820) proposed an Egyptian-style Library of Congress, and Henry Austin built Egyptian cemetery gates at New Haven in 1837. Thomas S. Steward selected the Egyptian style for the Medical College of Virginia in Richmond (1854), as did William Strickland (1788–1854) for the First Presbyterian Church in Nashville (1848). (This church has a later but equally remarkable Egyptian interior, including a perspective hypostyle hall painted on the wall between lotus columns.) Examples of Islamic influence can also be found in the now-vanished Moresque Building in Lafayette Square, New Orleans, by William and James Freret (Figure 12.3).

FIGURE 12.2 *Haviland: City Prison (The Tombs), New York, 1838.* (From E. Gillon)

Progress in materials science enabled architects and engineers to tackle construction problems in fundamentally new ways, contributing further to the diversity observable in nineteenth-century projects. Buildings in Britain and the United States now termed Victorian often have little in common with one another save that they were built during the exceptionally long reign (1837–1901) of Queen Victoria. Amid the stylistic revivals and engineering accomplishments came trends in design that were to have a major impact on twentieth-century architecture. This chapter is addressed to those developments.

NEO-CLASSICISM

Nineteenth-century Neo-Classicism in Germany is most closely identified with the work of Karl Friedrich Schinkel (1781–1841), who shared some of the formal concerns of Boullée and Ledoux but had a much stronger reliance on elements of Greek architecture. His most famous structure is the Altes Museum (Old Museum) in Berlin, built in 1823–1828 (Figure 12.4). Here the continuous Ionic colonnade across the façade reinforces the orthogonal simplicity of the exterior and gains dignity by being raised on a podium. In plan the long rectangular galleries are disposed symmetrically around a central colonnaded rotunda domed like the Pantheon, an arrangement that would be common for museum designs well into the twentieth century (Figure 12.5, 12.6).

The leading exponent of Neo-Classicism in England at that time was Sir John Soane (1753–1837), a highly individual architect whose work also has Ro-

FIGURE 12.3 *Freret: Moresque Building, New Orleans, 1859–1865.* (Courtesy New Orleans Public Library)

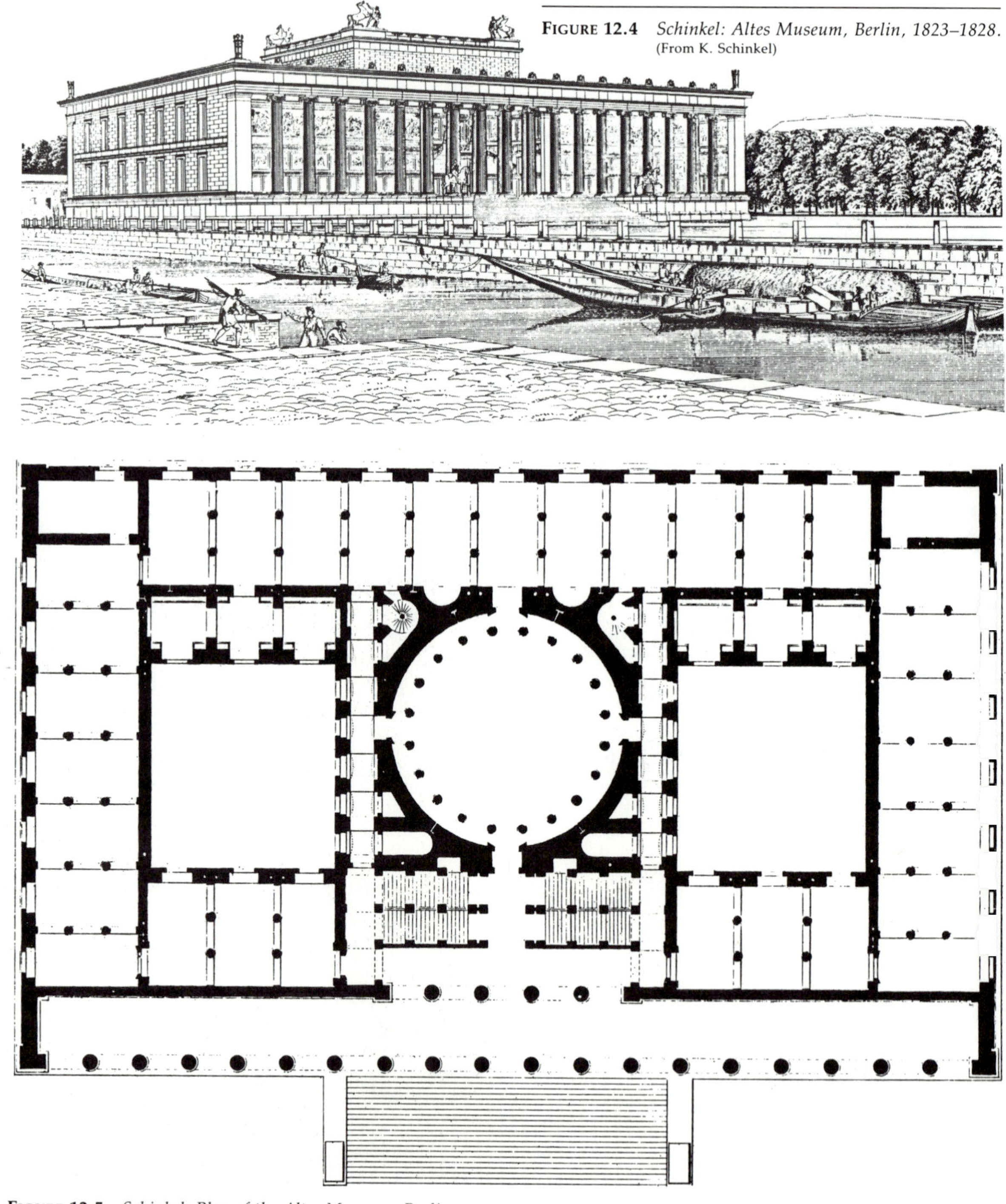

Figure 12.4 *Schinkel: Altes Museum, Berlin, 1823–1828.* (From K. Schinkel)

Figure 12.5 *Schinkel: Plan of the Altes Museum, Berlin.* (From K. Schinkel)

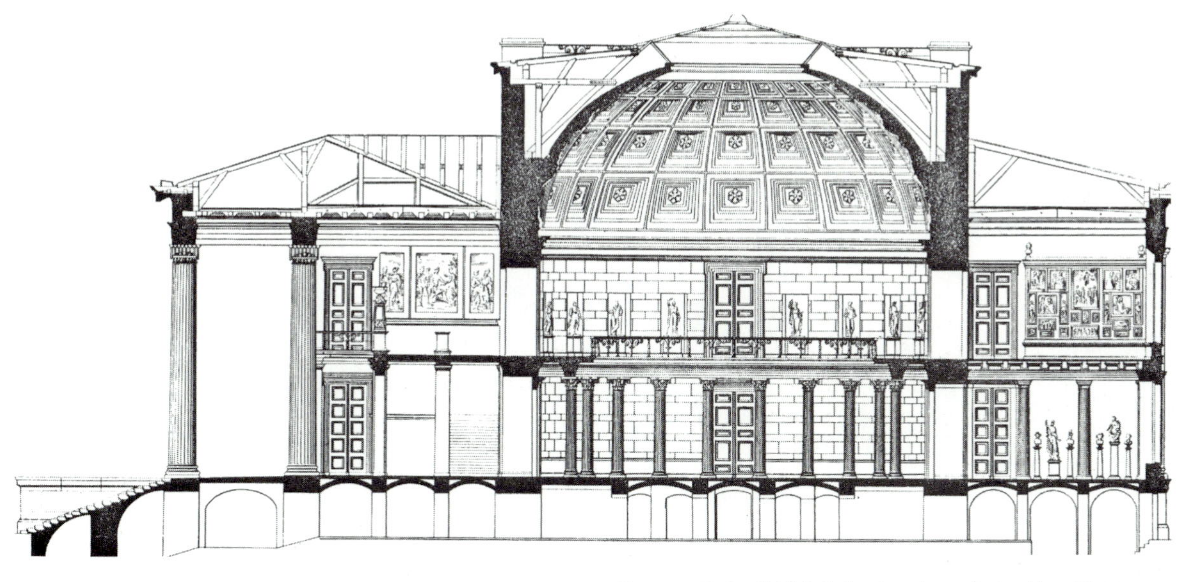

Figure 12.6 *Schinkel: Section through the Altes Museum, Berlin.* (From K. Schinkel)

mantic qualities. His buildings for the Bank of England (1788 and later; now destroyed except for its perimeter wall) used daylighting in imaginative ways, since bank security required an absolutely blank exterior wall (Figure 12.7). Soane met the challenge with clerestories and skylights that, when coupled with the pure forms of the rotundas and vaulted spaces of the interior of the Stock Office, seem inspired by Piranesi engravings. (Soane may in fact have met Piranesi in Italy.) The bank's interiors featured linear simplicity. Decoration was etched into the stone rather than sculpted out of it, while detailing was greatly simplified and minimal. Soane's own London house (now a museum) at 13 Lincoln's Inn Fields contains a diverse array of spaces and levels, lit by clerestories and top lights, articulated by layered wall planes, and reflected by both flat and convex mirrors (Figure 12.8). Such an idiosyncratic design does not fit easily into any one architectural movement, although one can detect traces of Neo-Classicism in the form of the saucer-

Figure 12.7 *Soane: Rotunda of the Bank of England, London, 1788 and after. Drawing by J. M. Gandy.* (Photo: Sir John Soane's Museum)

FIGURE 12.8 *Soane: The Colonnade, 13 Lincoln's Inn Fields, London, 1812–1837. Drawing by J. M. Gandy.* (Photo: Sir John Soane's Museum)

FIGURE 12.9 *Soane: Breakfast room, 13 Lincoln's Inn Fields, London.* (Photo: Sir John Soane's Museum)

FIGURE 12.10 *Latrobe: U.S. Capitol, Washington, after 1803. Tobacco and corncob capitals.* (From G. Brown)

domed breakfast room (Figure 12.9), where the brilliantly handled daylighting goes beyond the architecture of its time.

Soane's contemporary in the United States was Benjamin Henry Latrobe (1764–1820), who was born in England and educated there and in Europe before emigrating to America to become its first professional architect. In 1803 his friend Thomas Jefferson commissioned Latrobe to work on the U.S. Capitol, which had been begun by Dr. William Thornton and continued haphazardly by Stephen Hallet and James Hoban. Latrobe completed both the north and south wings, introducing in the work his own designs for the American orders of architecture, tobacco leaf capitals in the rotunda of the Senate chamber and corncob capitals in the north basement vestibule (Figure 12.10). Capitals based on those of the archaic Greek temples at Paestum were used in the Supreme Court chamber.

In Philadelphia Latrobe designed the Bank of Pennsylvania (1799), combining there an essentially Greek exterior (an Ionic colonnade supporting a projecting pediment) with a rather Roman interior (a masonry-vaulted dome with oculus over the monumental banking space). Late in his life Latrobe was commissioned to design the Roman Catholic Cathedral in Baltimore (Figures 12.11, 12.12). For this project he supplied two alternative designs for the same plan, one based on Gothic precedent and one of a more Roman character. The latter version was selected by the client, resulting in a building of remarkable simplicity, with a dome sixty-five feet in diameter at the crossing.

Latrobe's interest in Grecian architecture was to flourish after his death as the Greek Revival, a style in which one of his pupils, William Strickland, worked extensively. Like Latrobe Strickland was an engineer involved with the construction of canals, railroads, and harbor works for most of his professional life. His most notable architectural works include the Second Bank of the United States, built in Philadelphia from 1819 to 1824 to a design by Latrobe that was modified by Strickland (Figure 12.13). The building is Grecian in inspiration, as is his later Philadelphia Exchange (1834), which is based on the circular Choragic Monument of Lysicrates (see Figure 3.32). That Greek monument ap-

FIGURE 12.11 *Latrobe: Roman Catholic Cathedral, Baltimore, 1805–1818.* (Photo: H.A.B.S.)

FIGURE 12.12 *Latrobe: Interior of the Roman Catholic Cathedral, Baltimore.* (Photo: H.A.B.S.)

FIGURE 12.13 *Strickland: Second Bank of the United States, Philadelphia, 1819–1824.* (From E. Gillon)

FIGURE 12.14 *Strickland: Tennessee State Capitol, Nashville, 1845–1859.* (Photo: H.A.B.S.)

pears again on Strickland's last building, the Tennessee State Capitol in Nashville (1845–1859), reinterpreted as a cupola on the roof (Figures 12.14, 12.15). All of Strickland's works show a consistent freedom and originality in interpreting the architectural forms of ancient Greece for contemporary use, conveying in the process an appropriate sense of dignity and grandeur.

The only other American architect who was as versatile and talented as Latrobe was the Roman-Revivalist Thomas Jefferson (1743–1826), who also served as the country's third president. A graduate of William and Mary College, Jefferson trained to be a lawyer, yet he made contributions in many fields. In addition to other things, he was a statesman, philosopher, scientist, educator, economist, inventor, and architect — in short, a personification of the

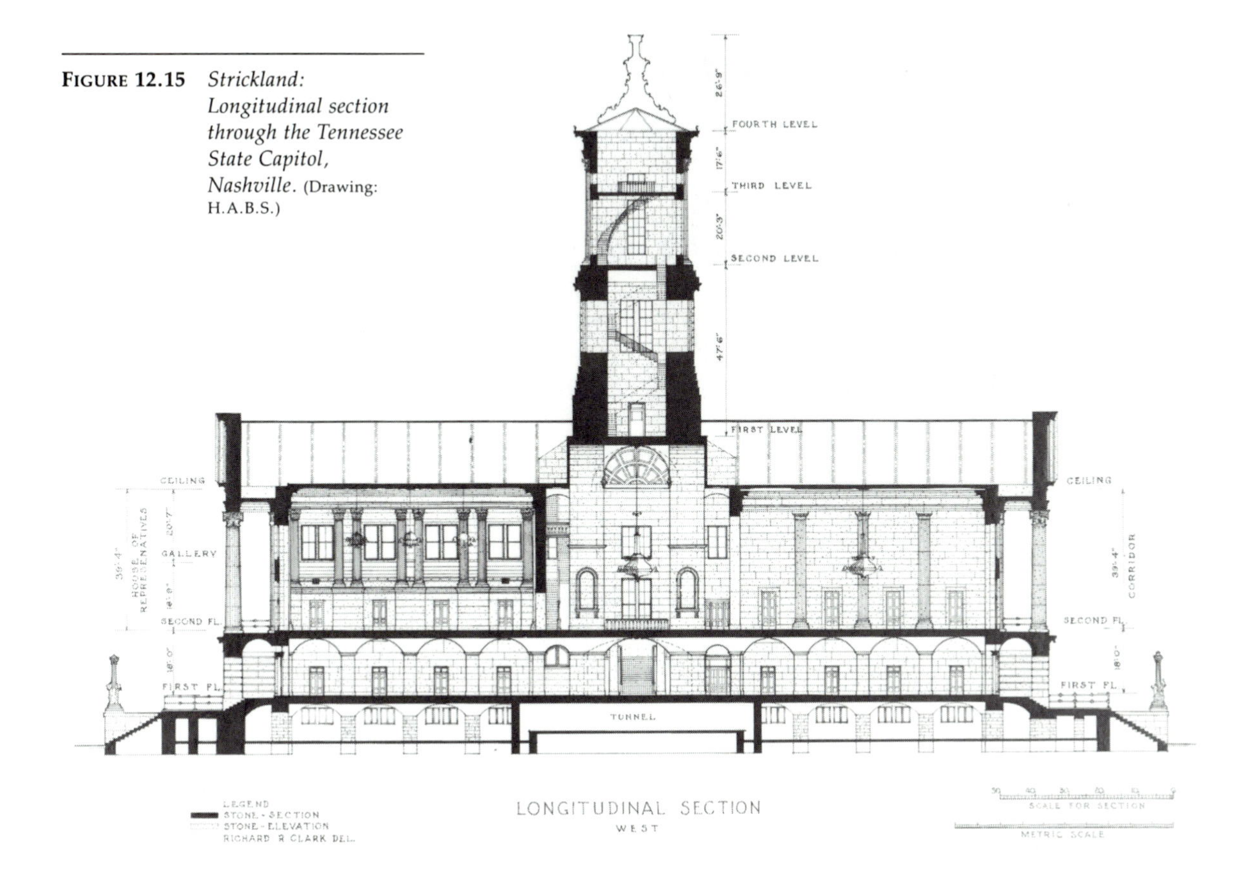

FIGURE 12.15 *Strickland: Longitudinal section through the Tennessee State Capitol, Nashville.* (Drawing: H.A.B.S.)

Renaissance ideal of an educated man. While serving as minister to France in 1785 Jefferson was asked to propose a design for the State Capitol of Virginia (Figure 12.16). The model he prepared was based on the Maison Carrée in Nîmes (see Figure 4.15), a building he knew then only through the architectural treatise of Colen Campbell. Jefferson converted the relatively small Roman temple into a two-story legislative building with a circular domed assembly room that is not expressed on the exterior. The Corinthian order of the Maison Carrée was changed to the Ionic for Richmond because Jefferson feared American stonecarvers would lack the skill to handle the more complex Corinthian capitals.

FIGURE 12.16 *Jefferson: Virginia State Capitol, Richmond.* (From E. Gillon)

Over a longer period of time Jefferson revised his designs for his own home, Monticello (Figure 12.17), which was begun in 1770. His early sketches

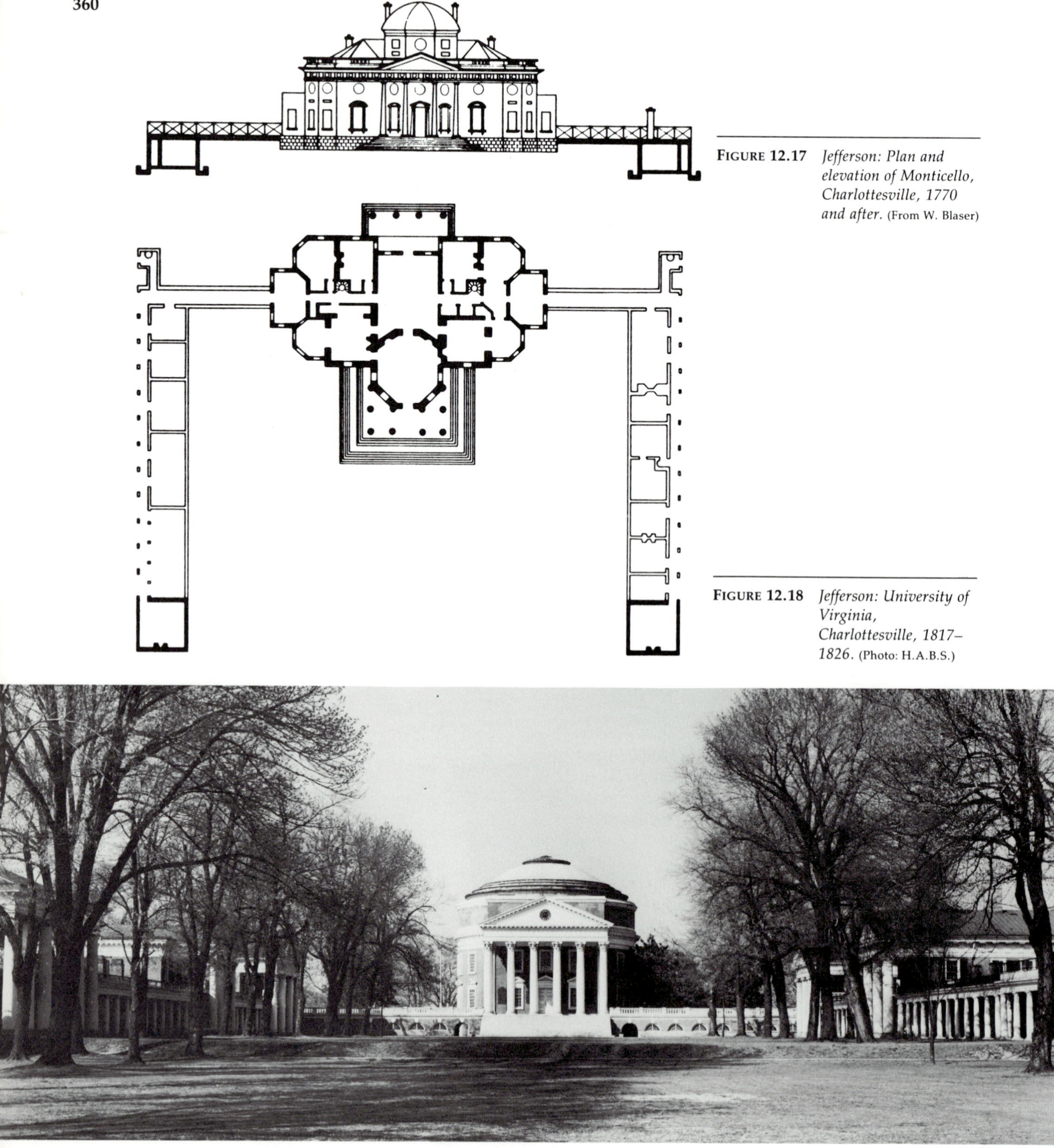

FIGURE 12.17 *Jefferson: Plan and elevation of Monticello, Charlottesville, 1770 and after.* (From W. Blaser)

FIGURE 12.18 *Jefferson: University of Virginia, Charlottesville, 1817–1826.* (Photo: H.A.B.S.)

indicate the strong influence of Palladio's architecture on his thinking, but the final realization also shows the overriding effect of Jefferson's own fertile mind. The central block of the house is crowned by an octagonal dome and connected to the landscape by two wings that extend to enclose the front lawn. Service functions — kitchens, storage, the icehouse, stables, and so on — were deftly placed in these wings below the grade of the lawn, so they remained close at hand yet out of sight. A promenade atop their roofs allows access to the end pavilions, the Honeymoon Cottage and Jefferson's law office. Details inside the house testify to the inventiveness of the owner. A clock in the entrance hall operates all week on a mechanism driven by cannonball weights. Wind direction can be found from a weather vane atop the cupola that can be read from indoors. Double doors to the public rooms open together if only one is pushed because of an interlocked mechanism beneath the floor. Jefferson's bed separates his study and sleeping quarters so that the narrowing of space between the two rooms gives greater velocity to summer breezes passing through the house.

In his later years Jefferson turned his architectural talents to the design of the campus of the University of Virginia at Charlottesville (1817–1826), an institution that he had done much to establish and for which he served as rector after its opening in 1825 (Figure 12.18). His early plan for the campus consisted of a three-sided square of student rooms, linked by colonnades and punctuated by larger pavilions for lecture halls and faculty residences. The architecture of each pavilion was derived from a different classical prototype, so that students would be made aware of the best of architecture from antiquity. Jefferson called it an "academical village," and he solicited comments on the plan through correspondence with William Thornton and Latrobe. Thornton contributed a suggested design for a pavilion, and Latrobe contributed two. Latrobe also recommended that the plan should have a dominant focal element, an idea Jefferson had originally rejected because of his opposition to centrality in government. The compositional improvement of a focus became obvious, however, and Jefferson designed a library based on the Pantheon (at half scale) to serve as the head of the scheme (Figures

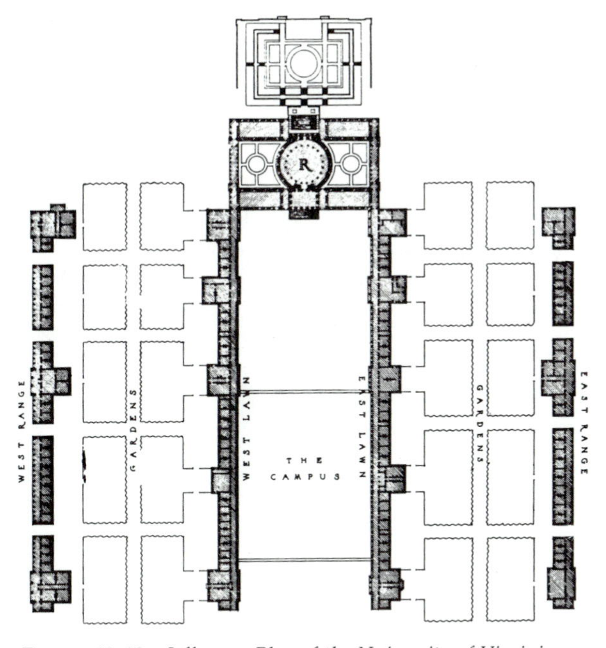

FIGURE 12.19 *Jefferson: Plan of the University of Virginia, Charlottesville.* (From McKim, Mead and White)

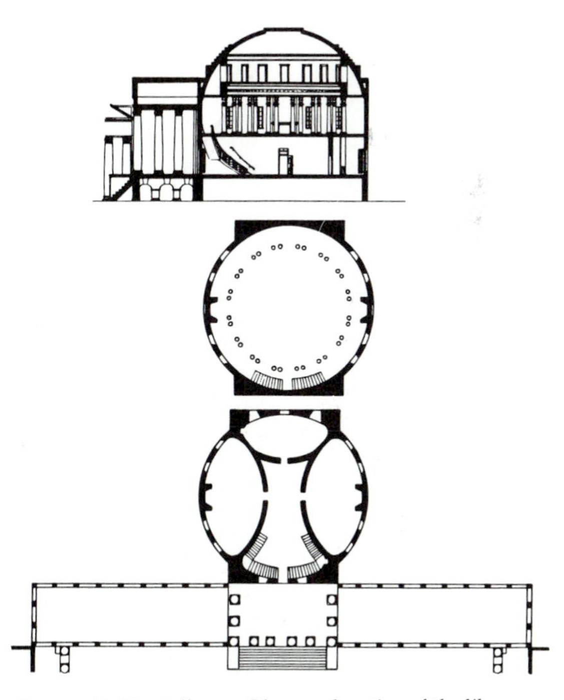

FIGURE 12.20 *Jefferson: Plans and section of the library, University of Virginia, Charlottesville.* (From W. Blaser)

Figure 12.21 *Jefferson: Pavilion X, University of Virginia, Charlottesville.* (Photo: H.A.B.S.)

Figure 12.22 *Jefferson: Pavilion VII, University of Virginia, Charlottesville.* (Photo: H.A.B.S.)

12.19, 12.20). All the buildings surrounding the lawn are carefully maintained today, serving for the most part their original intended functions (Figures 12.21–12.23).

THE GOTHIC REVIVAL

The Romantic Movement acquired a more serious tone with the emergence of the Gothic Revival. In England the leading Gothic Revivalist was Augustus Welby Northmore Pugin (1812–1852), a convert to Catholicism who regarded Gothic as an embodiment of moral and religious values from the past that he felt were all but absent in his own time. Unlike the Gothick designers, Pugin was well-versed in the design of actual medieval buildings, having worked with his father as a draftsman in preparing a four-volume study of Gothic ornament. It was another book by Pugin that brought him into the public eye, however. In 1836 he published *Contrasts, or, A Parallel between the Noble Edifices of the Fourteenth and Fifteenth Centuries, and Similar Buildings of the Present Day; Shewing the Present Day Decay of Taste,* a brief volume whose title sums up the author's message. Pugin compared medieval and modern conditions with drawings (Figure 12.24). The "Catholic Town in 1440" had fifteen church spires and a guildhall tower marking its skyline, while "The Same Town in 1840" had factory smokestacks as the dominant element in an industrial townscape. Protestant chapels of a vaguely Classical form had replaced Catholic churches, and many spires had had their tops lopped off.

Pugin's comparison of public charity was even more damning (Figure 12.25). The medieval "residence of the poor" was shown as a monastery where the almoner received the needy with kindness; fed them a hearty diet of beef, mutton, ale, cider, milk, porridge, bread, and cheese; robed them in clean garments; preached a sermon to enforce discipline; and provided them with a decent Christian burial. By contrast the "modern poor house" was a prisonlike walled building with a tem-

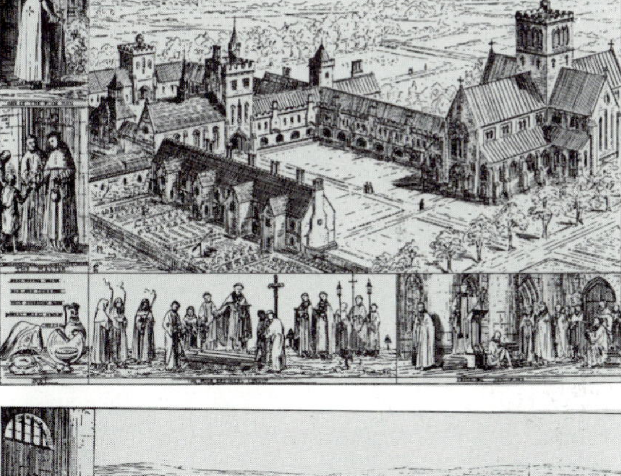

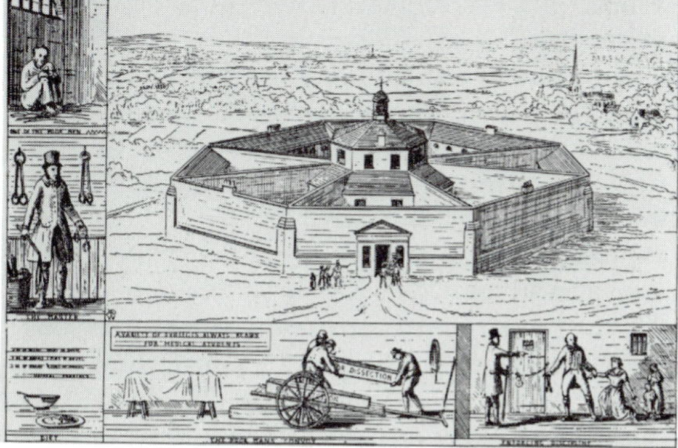

FIGURE 12.25 *Pugin: Ancient and Modern Poor Houses Compared, from* Contrasts, *1836.* (From A. Pugin) ▶

◀ **FIGURE 12.23** *Jefferson: Colonnade, University of Virginia, Charlottesville.* (Photo: H.A.B.S.)

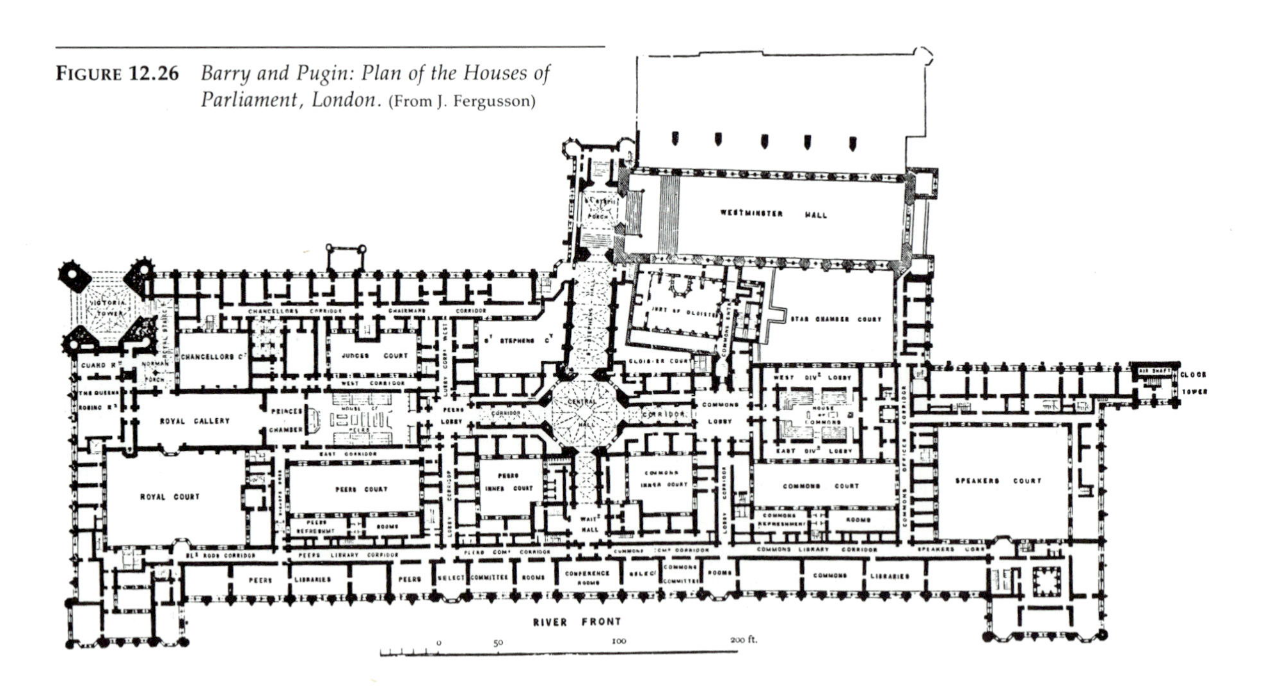

FIGURE 12.26 *Barry and Pugin: Plan of the Houses of Parliament, London.* (From J. Fergusson)

ple-front portico. The poor here were kept shackled in cells; fed a diet of small amounts of oatmeal, potatoes, gruel, and bread; cruelly beaten to enforce discipline; and loaded in a box labeled "for dissection" after death! Pugin was of course overstating the virtues of medieval institutions while detailing all the evils of his own time, but to him the medieval town was a total visual and religious environment, while the industrial town, with its vested interests and greedy capitalists, was a detestable degradation of human existence.

In 1841 Pugin published *The True Principles of Pointed or Christian Architecture,* in which he enumerated his ideals: "First, that there should be no features about a building which are not necessary for convenience, construction, and propriety, and second, that all ornament should consist of the enrichment of the essential construction of the building." He regarded Gothic as the "only correct expression of the faith, wants, and climate" of England and advocated its use for all buildings, including such modern secular uses as railroad stations.

While writing treatises and giving lectures Pugin was also busy as a designer. He collaborated with Sir Charles Barry on the competition-winning design for rebuilding the Houses of Parliament, which had been destroyed by fire in 1834. The overall conception of the building was Barry's (Figure 12.26), while the prolific and correct detail, inside and out, was Pugin's substantial contribution (Figure 12.27). On his own Pugin was responsible for the design of at least two dozen churches, chapels, and cathedrals. For himself he designed a house and chapel at Ramsgate, Kent (1846–1851) (Figure 12.28). The design of the chapel, dedicated to St. Augustine, was based on fourteenth-century parish churches of Kent, and its construction of knapped flint with narrow inset bands of freestone used materials common to the area. The inside of the chapel was finished in ashlar masonry carved under Pugin's supervision. After its completion Pugin donated St. Augustine's to the local Catholic diocese. His nearby house, constructed of coarse brick dressed with stone, had a **crenellated** tower, gables, dormers, and bay windows; but the important innovative feature was the revival of the medieval great hall as both a horizontal and a vertical circulation space, a feature that would continue in domestic architecture through the end of the century and even appear in the designs of H.H. Richardson and Frank Lloyd Wright. Pugin's work firmly established the Gothic style as a suitable one for the construction of

Figure 12.27 *Barry and Pugin: Monarch's throne in the House of Lords, Houses of Parliament, London.* (From *The Illustrated London News*)

buildings, especially churches. He died at the age of forty having completed a relatively small number of buildings, but his influence extended to other architects who would be far more prolific, such as Gilbert Scott in England and Richard Upjohn in the United States.

Richard Upjohn (1802–1878) was the first American architect to follow Pugin's principles, although Upjohn was Episcopalian rather than Catholic and built only Episcopal churches out of the sincere belief that it was the only acceptable denomination. His first major commission was for Trinity Church in New York City (1839–1846), designed for a growing and wealthy congregation. Upjohn used Decorated Gothic for the church, which featured an extended chancel, raised altar, and ceiling vaults constructed of plaster rather than stone (Figure 12.29).

On a smaller scale was the design for Christ Church in Raleigh, North Carolina (Figure 12.30), which was begun in 1848 and finished in 1854 (ex-

Figure 12.28 *Pugin: St. Augustine, Ramsgate, 1846–1851.* (From B. Ferrey)

FIGURE 12.29 *Upjohn: Trinity Church, New York, 1839–1846.* (From *Harper's Weekly*)

FIGURE 12.30 *Upjohn: Christ Church, Raleigh, 1848–1861.* (Drawing: H.A.B.S.)

cept for the tower, which was completed in 1859–1861) at a cost of $18,000. The building is in stone, with tall, narrow lancet windows evocative of Early English Gothic. Its spire reflects the medieval traditions of English districts where building stone is plentiful. On the inside the church is monumental on the small scale suitable to the needs of a modest congregation. The priest of Christ Church wrote to Upjohn in 1847, "I am heartily rejoiced we have got this far and I hope the erection of our church will be the means of introducing a new style of church architecture in the South."

Upjohn was genuinely concerned for small parishes, and he tried to design at least one church a year for rural parishes without charging a professional fee. In his eagerness to be of service to small parishes, Upjohn devised a copybook illustrating plans, elevations, details, cost figures, and quantities of materials necessary to build a small wooden Episcopal church for congregations numbering 125 to 150 persons. Everything was provided so that "any intelligent mechanic will be able to carry out the design." *Upjohn's Rural Architecture,* published in 1852, provided detailed drawings and specifications for erecting a $900 chapel and a $3000 church with tower and spire (Figure 12.31), all designed in wood with "carpenter Gothic" details, plus a $4000 school and a $2500 parsonage. The book cost only five dollars and placed good architectural design well within the means of any congregation.

The leading proponent of the Gothic Revival in France was Eugène-Emanuel Viollet-le-Duc (1814–1879), an architect who shared Pugin's energy and intensity for medieval works. The moral and religious tones that so strongly colored Pugin's writings were not shared by Viollet-le-Duc, who was more interested in the rational basis of medieval structure. He saw the rib vault, pointed arch, and flying buttress as analogous to nineteenth-century iron framing, and he hoped for a modern architecture based on engineering accomplishments with the integrity of form and detail found in medieval works (Figure 12.32). His theoretical writings — especially the two volumes of *Entretiens sur l'Architecture* (Lectures on Architecture), published between 1863 and 1872 — stress the importance of rationality in design, a concept that was to be restated in the twentieth century.

Much of Viollet-le-Duc's time was spent opposing the French architectural establishment's denial of all medieval styles. The only government-sponsored school for architects, the École des Beaux-

FIGURE 12.31 *Upjohn: Wooden church from* Upjohn's Rural Architecture, *1852.* (From R. Upjohn)

Arts, was firmly committed to Classicism, and various efforts by Viollet-le-Duc and others to have its courses include the study of Romanesque and Gothic buildings met with little success. However, the extended controversy identified Viollet-le-Duc as an architect knowledgeable about medieval architecture, and from 1840 onward he was involved in scores of restoration projects for the major historical monuments of France, including the Cathedral Notre-Dame and the Sainte-Chapelle in Paris; the Abbey Church of St. Denis; St. Sernin at Toulouse; Ste. Madeleine at Vézelay; the ramparts of Carcassonne; and the cathedrals of Reims, Amiens, and Beauvais. Out of this rich experience in dealing first-hand with medieval projects came the ten-volume *Dictionnaire raisonné de l'architecture française du XIe au XVIe Siecle* (Encyclopedia of French Architecture from the Eleventh to the Sixteenth Centuries) (1858–1865), which remains an important scholarly study for medievalists. Twentieth-century architectural preservationists shudder at his philosophy of restoration: "to restore a building is not only to preserve it, to repair it, or to rebuild, but to bring it back to a state of completion such as may never have existed at any given moment," which is quite the opposite of current attitudes toward this sort of work. Nevertheless one must acknowledge that many of the buildings on which Viollet-le-Duc performed restorations might not have survived into the twentieth century without his intervention. For better or worse, his work marks the beginning of scholarly attempts at historic preservation. The architectural projects he designed as original undertakings are not particularly distinguished.

FIGURE 12.32 *Viollet-le-Duc: Iron-framed assembly hall from* Entretiens, *1863–1872.* (From E. Viollet-le-Duc)

THE ÉCOLE DES BEAUX-ARTS

Victorian architects in the United States and England engaged in a series of revival styles — Greek, Gothic, Italian, Tudor, Romanesque, and variants — and waged a continuing argument over the merits of Gothic versus Classic architecture as an appropriate model for present-day design. But in France there was less debate because the architectural establishment, the Academy of Beaux-Arts (created in 1803 as the successor to the Royal Academy of Architecture) had largely decided the issue in favor of the Classic style. The academy held a virtual monopoly on all official architecture in France, and it also controlled the only architectural school in the country (and for a time, the only one in Europe), the École des Beaux-Arts (1819–1968). Because the École was for so long the leader in architectural education, attracting American students from 1846 onward, its approaches to education and design deserve mention, for they have left an indelible mark on European and American architecture.

The École des Beaux-Arts was organized to provide training for students who had usually completed secondary studies and passed a competitive entrance examination. Instruction was based on lectures in theoretical and practical subjects, such as history, structures, construction, and professional practice, but the focus of students' efforts was directed to the *atelier* (studio), where all levels of pupils worked on design projects under the direction of a designated *patron* (studio master). The professor of theory wrote design projects for all levels, and students developed solutions in their separate *ateliers* and returned the finished drawings to the École for evaluation by a closed jury, which made awards for first, second, and honorable mentions. Students advanced through the school by passing the requisite lecture courses and accumulating a sufficient number of awards for design projects. The course could take as little as three years to complete, but a typical stay was six or seven years. The École awarded no degrees, but it held an annual competition to select the best advanced project, which was awarded the Grand Prix de Rome. This entitled the winner to a free four-year stay at the French Academy in Rome, followed by guaranteed lifetime employment as an official government architect.

Classical architecture provided the exclusive basis for design at the École des Beaux-Arts. Students began with a study of the orders of architecture and their application to façades, then moved on to simple buildings studied in plan and elevation. Advanced students had to design ever larger and more complex buildings with monumental and imposing architectural conceptions. Throughout all the work of students at the École, certain themes remain constant: the clear ordering of spaces in pian, the careful study of proportions, and the composition of all elements around axes of symmetry. Their beautiful ink-wash and watercolor renderings are masterpieces of architectural drawing.

This elaborate system of instruction was unmatched in Europe or the United States, where apprenticeship in the office of a practicing architect was the norm for architectural education during most of the nineteenth century. Some technical universities in Germany offered architectural studies as part of engineering programs, but American land-grant colleges were to lead the world in placing architecture in the university curriculum. M.I.T. established a School of Architecture in 1861, and fifteen other universities did so before the end of the century. Their curricula were all based on that of the École des Beaux-Arts. Architectural graduates of American universities seeking additional polish would attend the École in Paris, although they were not eligible for the Grand Prix competition, and American universities sought to hire Frenchmen from the École to direct their studies in architectural design. As a result of this cultural exchange, and the economic prosperity and westward expansion that came to the United States after the Civil War, the United States has far more Beaux-Arts-influenced architecture than France.

The first American to attend the École des Beaux-Arts was Richard Morris Hunt (1827–1895), who entered in 1846 after living in Paris since 1832, when his family had moved there after the death of his father. Returning to New York, Hunt established a practice that prospered greatly until his death. Newly rich industrial magnates wanted houses that imitated the ancestral mansions of European nobility, and of all American architects, Hunt was best able to provide the designs desired. His work for the Vanderbilt family — a town house on Fifth Av-

FIGURE 12.33 *Hunt: The Breakers, Newport.* (Photo: H.A.B.S.)

enue; a "cottage" called The Breakers at Newport, Rhode Island (Figure 12.33); and Biltmore, a hunting lodge at Asheville, North Carolina (Figure 12.34) — are well known, but he also designed the base for the Statue of Liberty (1880) and the central portion of the Fifth Avenue façade of the Metropolitan Museum of Art in New York (1895).

Perhaps Hunt's greatest impact on American architecture came through his involvement with the 1893 World's Columbian Exposition in Chicago. A committee of the country's most important archi-

FIGURE 12.34 *Hunt: Biltmore, Asheville, 1890–1895.* (Photo: Moffett)

FIGURE 12.35 *World's Columbian Exposition, Chicago, 1893.* (From *Scientific American*)

FIGURE 12.36 *Hunt: Administration Building, World's Columbian Exposition, Chicago.* (From *Scientific American*)

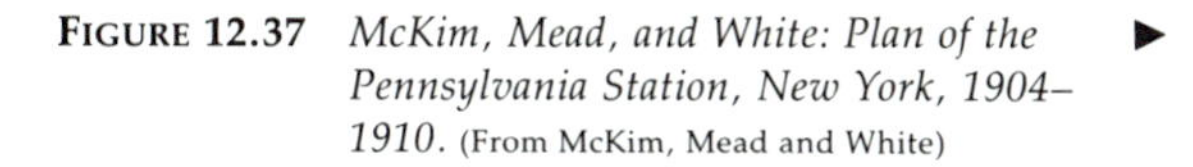

FIGURE 12.37 *McKim, Mead, and White: Plan of the Pennsylvania Station, New York, 1904–1910.* (From McKim, Mead and White) ▶

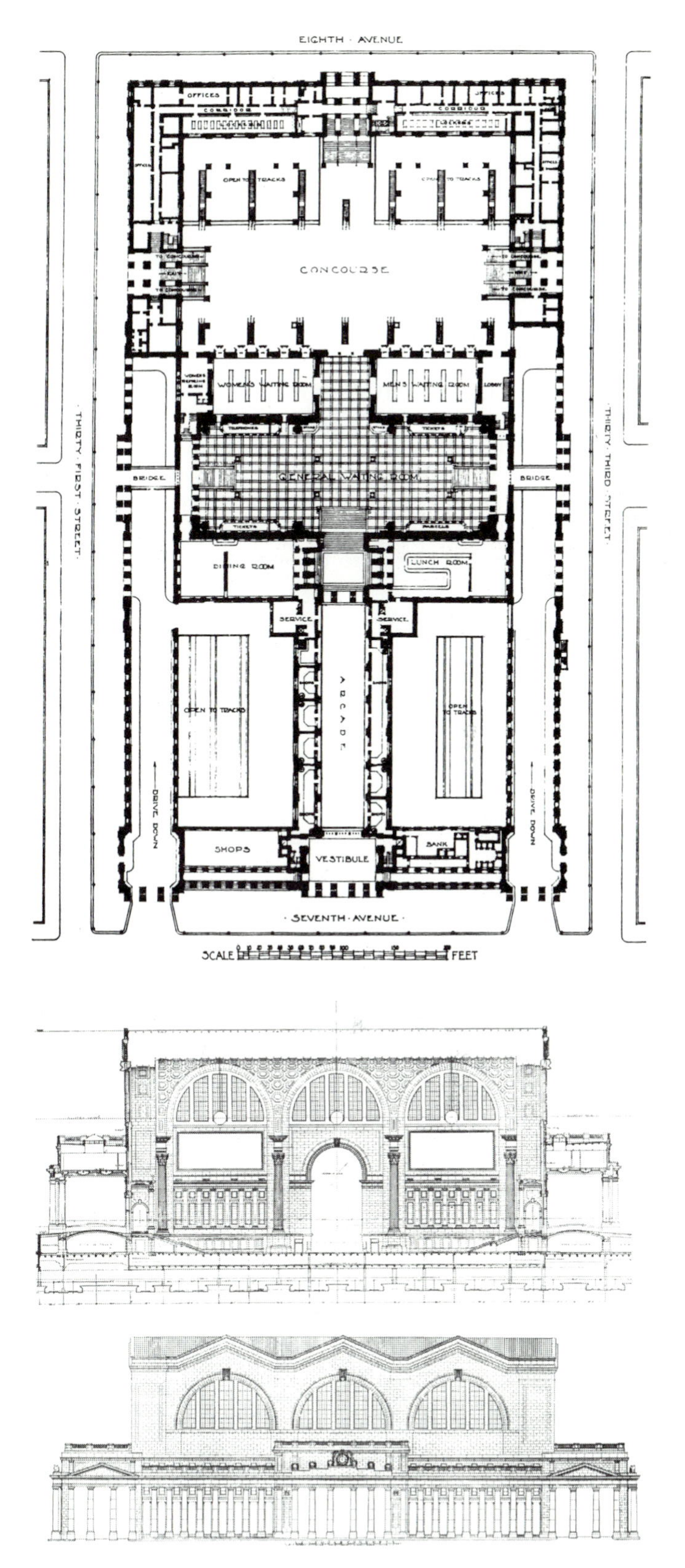

tects was formed under the leadership of Daniel H. Burnham to design the temporary buildings for the fair, and Hunt used his influence as the profession's leading practitioner to direct the entire plan along Beaux-Arts principles of design. The principal buildings, each assigned to a different firm, were disposed around a large Court of Honor, with the domed Administration Building (Figure 12.35) by Hunt at its head and an open peristyle by Charles B. Atwood terminating the vista out to Lake Michigan (Figure 12.36). To ensure unity around the Court of Honor, it was agreed that all designs would be based on the precedent of the Italian Renaissance; use a common material, stucco (plaster), painted white; and maintain a uniform sixty-foot cornice line. The effect was startling. Visitors named it the White City and went away greatly impressed by the dramatic spectacle. The 1893 Exposition did much to advance the ornate and monumental Beaux-Arts style as the appropriate one for important American buildings and civic designs. Train stations, art museums, city halls, post offices, and churches were built across the country in emulation of the White City. Many of these involve significant feats of engineering, such as McKim, Mead, and White's design for Pennsylvania Station (1904–1910) in New York City (Figures 12.37, 12.38), although classical cladding concealed much of the innovative steel work.

In their enthusiasm for Beaux-Arts architecture, fair visitors completely overlooked the truly innovative buildings in Chicago, the metal-framed tall buildings of downtown. Louis Sullivan, an architect who participated freely in the design of the fair, later remarked that it set the cause of American architecture back by fifty years. His observation is a pessimistic one, for the construction of great Beaux-Arts buildings was finally terminated by the economic hardships of the Great Depression; and the

FIGURE 12.38 *McKim, Mead, and White: Section and elevation of the Pennsylvania Station, New York.* (From McKim, Mead and White) ▶

fair did no damage to the architects, including Sullivan, who formed the American avant-garde of the late nineteenth century.

PROGRESS IN IRON AND STEEL FABRICATION

Eighteenth-century industrial production of cast and wrought iron so increased its availability as a construction material that iron replaced wood in the frame of any building where heavy loads or the danger of fire were of concern. Cast iron was favored for columns, while the superior tensile qualities of wrought iron made it the recommended material for beams. In the nineteenth century, iron began to be used instead of wood in the fabrication of truss bridges that were built for roads and railroads required to cross rivers or valleys. A rigid framework composed of shorter members, the truss can be used to span great distances. The Romans certainly used wooden trusses for bridge construction, but during the medieval period the important aspect of truss triangulation for rigidity was largely forgotten, and most medieval builders used the **king post** or **queen post truss,** which required the bottom chord to be as long as the span. Palladio clearly illustrates statically determinate trusses in his *Four Books on Architecture,* but he seems never to have used them (Figure 12.39). The seventeenth- and eighteenth-century revivals of Palladio did not include interest in his truss designs, leaving the truss to be reinvented by builders in the nineteenth century.

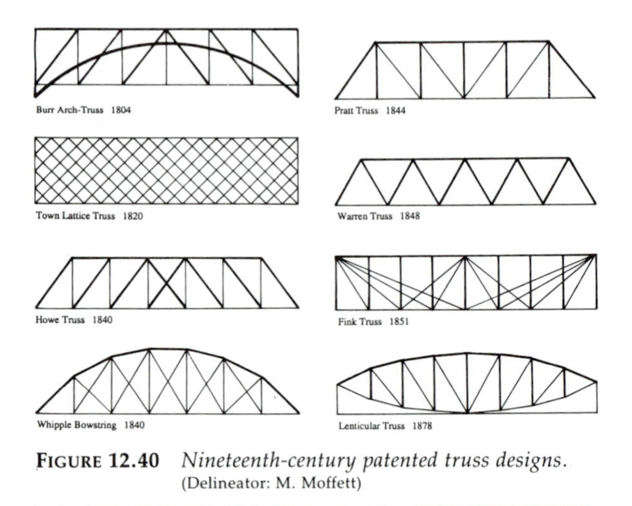

FIGURE 12.40 *Nineteenth-century patented truss designs.* (Delineator: M. Moffett)

FIGURE 12.39 *Palladio: Truss designs.* (From A. Palladio)

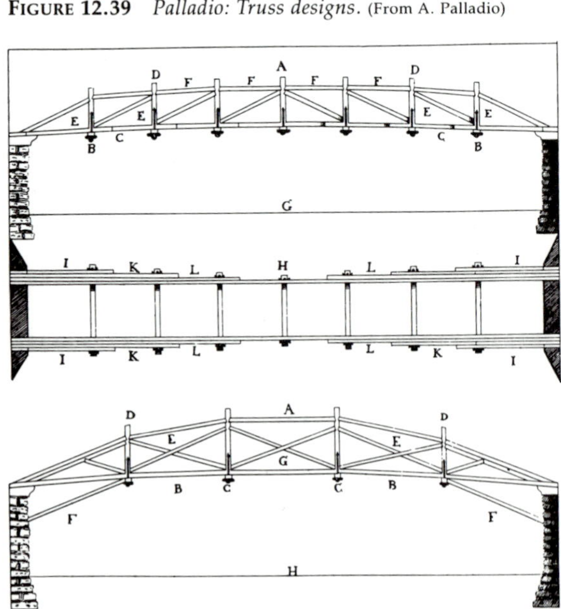

Faced with many streams to cross and surrounded by an abundance of timber, American builders soon appreciated the principle of the truss for bridge construction (Figure 12.40). Theodore Burr patented his arch-truss in 1817, and Ithiel Town grew rich off his patent obtained in 1820 for a lattice truss. Other truss patents soon followed, Long (1830), Howe (1840), Pratt (1844), Whipple (1847), Warren (1848), and Fink (1854) being among the most important. The first iron truss bridge in the United States, the Frankfort Bridge on the Erie Canal, was built in 1840, and the first steel truss bridge was constructed in 1878–1879 over the Missouri River for the Chicago and Alton Railroad. The railroads used metal truss bridges extensively after the Civil War because they offered stability under the moving load of a heavy train, where a suspension bridge was too lively.

FIGURE 12.41 *Stephenson: Britannia Bridge, Menai Straits, 1845–1850.* (From *Illustrated London News*)

Bridge builders met the challenge posed by navigable bodies of water by designing long-span designs with high clearances. Robert Stephenson (1803–1859) designed the Britannia Bridge (1845–1850) across the Menai Straits in Wales as two parallel box tubes, each a hollow rectangular beam of riveted wrought iron plates spanning 1511 feet between three pylons and the shore abutments (Figures 12.41, 12.42). The bridge was constructed by

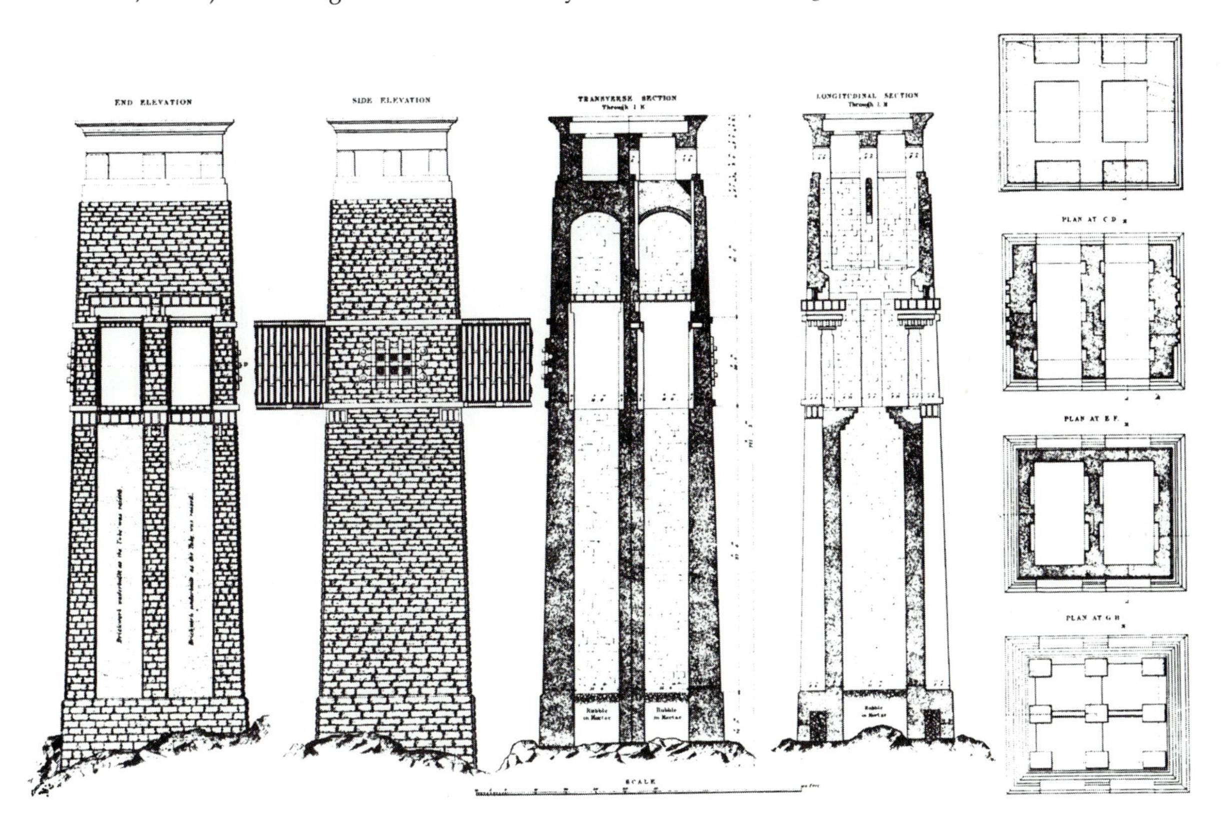

FIGURE 12.42 *Stephenson: Pier design of the Britannia Bridge, Menai Straits.* (From E. Clark)

erecting the stone piers, floating the completed tubular sections, each 463 feet long, on pontoons, and hoisting the tubes up with giant hydraulic jacks. Once all sections were in place, railroad tracks were laid inside the tubes, and one open sea ferry crossing in the route to Ireland was eliminated.

Stephenson was prepared to reinforce the Britannia Bridge with suspension cables (hence the higher tops of the pylons), but this proved unnecessary. The principle of suspension bridge construction had been known for centuries; vines, hides, or ropes had long been twisted together and strung across chasms in China, India, and Peru. Modern suspension bridges, using chains of iron links or eyebars, were built shortly after 1800, with early work being done by James Findley in Philadelphia, who obtained a patent on his system in 1801. English engineers, including Thomas Telford, learned of Findley's work through illustrations in Thomas Pope's *Treatise on Bridge Architecture* (1811) and soon applied it to their own projects. Telford's bridge over the Menai Straits (1819–1826) was supported by sixteen eyebar chains of wrought iron, anchored to cast-iron frames embedded in rock abutments and suspended from masonry towers 153 feet high (Figure 12.43). At 579 feet this was the longest suspension span in the world at the time of its completion. The American designer Charles Ellet was the first to see the advantages of using flexible wire cable in place of chains for suspension structures, although the greatest nineteenth-century engineers for cable suspension bridges would be John Augustus Roebling and his son, Washington Augustus Roebling, designers and builders of the Brooklyn Bridge (1869–1883).

In seeking to expand the market for iron and improve the desirable qualities of the material, nineteenth-century ironmongers experimented with new methods for manufacturing steel, which is an alloy of low-carbon iron and trace amounts of other metals. Small quantities of steel had been manufactured in India as early as 1500 B.C., and

FIGURE 12.43 *Telford: Menai Bridge, 1819–1826.* (Photo: Marburg)

Celtic peoples in Austria, Spain, and Britain had made and worked the material at sites where iron ore containing manganese occurred in natural deposits. Blacksmiths, knifesmiths, and sword makers could work the extracted iron and make steel, which was greatly respected for its ability to hold a superior cutting edge. Industrialization of this handcraft process involved reducing the carbon content of the molten iron and using less charcoal in the furnace for that fuel was becoming scarce and expensive.

An American ironmonger, William Kelly (1811–1888), was the first to develop a converter that burned off excess carbon with a blast of air. He constructed seven converters at his works in Eddyville, Kentucky. When he was ready to apply for a patent on his pneumatic process in 1856, however, he found that the Englishman Henry Bessemer (1813–1898) had just been granted one for the same idea. Although Kelly's prior claim to the process was subsequently demonstrated, he reaped neither the recognition nor the financial rewards that should have been his. Bessemer became known as the inventor of the converter that made reliable quantities of steel efficiently and affordably. From 1875 onward steel began to replace both cast and wrought iron in construction because its compressive and tensile strengths exceeded those of iron and it was cheaper to produce than wrought iron.

Steel was first used for railroad track and in engineering works. The first steel bridge built in the United States was the Eads Bridge (1869–1874) over the Mississippi at St. Louis (Figure 12.44). Its designer, Captain James B. Eads (1820–1887), had been a riverboat captain and salvage operator on the Mississippi, and despite his complete lack of engineering training he was able to gain the confidence of local businessmen who backed the construction of the bridge. Assisted by capable engineers and mathematicians who provided the technical abilities he lacked, Eads understood the behavior of the Mississippi and insisted that the bridge foundations extend to bedrock, which lay under fourteen feet of

FIGURE 12.44 *Eads: Eads Bridge, St. Louis, shown under construction with scaffolding in place, 1869–1874.* (From C. Woodward)

water and eighty-one feet of sand. The bridge required four stone piers to support three segmental arched steel spans of 502, 520, and 502 feet; the arches were fabricated of eighteen-inch diameter cast steel tubes, interconnected by triangulated bracing to form an integrated unit. Construction was accomplished by sinking pneumatic caissons for pier foundations and then cantilevering the arch sections out from each pier until the arch could be closed. (Using centering to support the arch in construction would have interfered with navigation on the river.)

Steel was also employed for the major suspension bridge of the nineteenth century, the Brooklyn Bridge, connecting Manhattan and Brooklyn over the East River with a 1600-foot clear span (Figure 12.45). The bridge was designed by John Augustus Roebling (1806–1869) and constructed under the supervision of his son, Washington Augustus Roebling (1837–1926). They sank two gigantic caisson foundations for the bridge towers, and spun galvanized steel wire for the two main cables that supported the roadway (Figure 12.46). Each cable contains over 5000 strands of wire, compacted and wrapped with a continuous spiral of softer steel. Diagonal stays radiating from the towers provide wind bracing and are probably strong enough to carry the bridge's loads by themselves should the main cables break, while a stiffened deck checks any tendency the bridge may have to develop destructive vibrations under wind loads.

FIGURE 12.45 *Roebling: Brooklyn Bridge, 1869–1883.* (From *Harper's Weekly*)

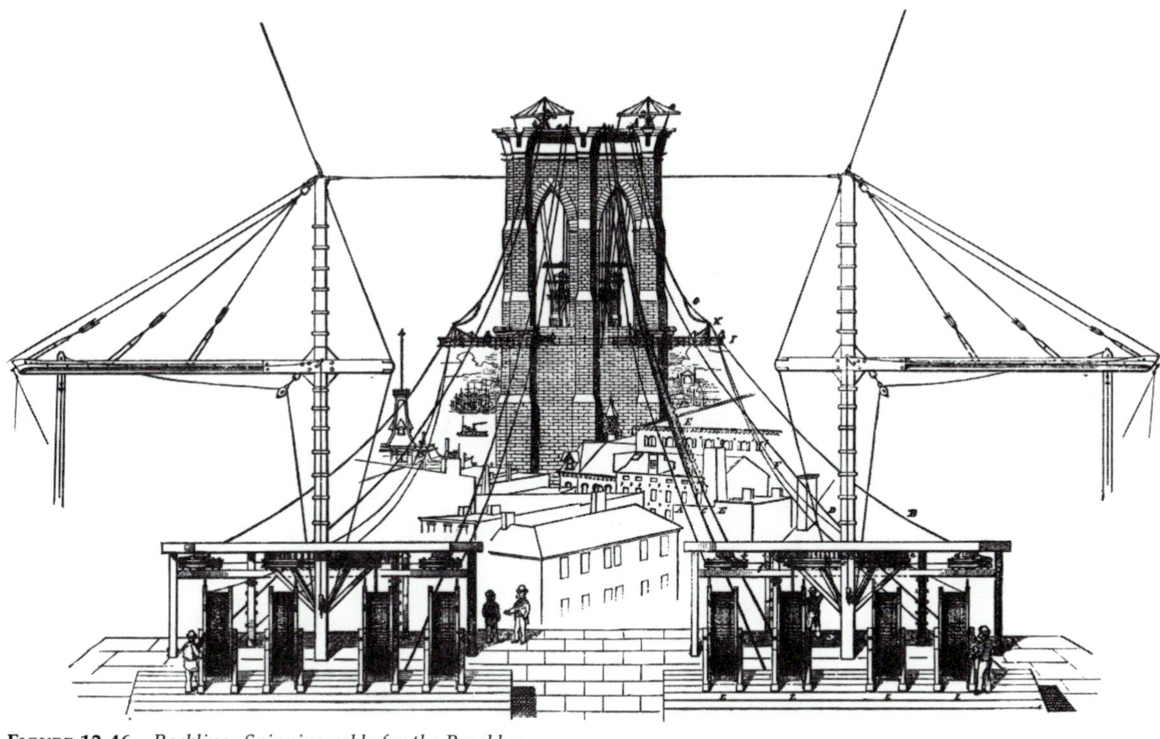

FIGURE 12.46 *Roebling: Spinning cable for the Brooklyn Bridge.* (From *Scientific American*)

ARCHITECTURAL APPLICATIONS OF IRON AND STEEL CONSTRUCTION

Iron and steel were not required for architecture since prevailing Neo-Classic and Romantic attitudes looked back to past ages when architecture had always been load-bearing masonry construction. Everything that architects (and their clients) admired and felt comfortable with could be constructed by using traditional materials and methods. Thus architects were slow to exploit the possibilities of iron and steel, which were first used in buildings that architects did not design, such as textile mills, warehouses, and greenhouses.

Iron was most elegantly employed in landscape gardening. Victorian England, prosperous from the wealth of her empire, had a fascination with the tropical plants that were brought back from India, Africa, and the Far East. Keeping these specimens alive in the cool, overcast climate of Britain required housing them in structures that could reproduce the humid heat of their native countries, so builders and gardeners set about erecting greenhouses large enough to contain palms or banana trees. Unfettered by ancient precedent the builders turned to lightweight iron framing systems with glass infill panes. The Palm House at Kew Gardens, London (1845–1847) by Decimus Burton and Richard Turner (Figure 12.47), is an example of this work, as is the Conservatory at Chatsworth House (1836–1840) by Burton and Joseph Paxton (Figure 12.48). The strength of the building at Chatsworth derived from its glass and iron skin, which was arranged in alternate ridges and furrow-like folds.

Joseph Paxton (1801–1865) was a landscape gardener by training, acquiring through experience his skill at building with glass and iron for greenhouses. He revolutionized architecture with the unsolicited design he submitted for a building in Hyde Park, London, to house the first modern world's fair in 1851. The building committee for the London Ex-

FIGURE 12.47 *Burton and Turner: Palm House, Kew Gardens, 1845–1847.* (From *Illustrated London News*)

FIGURE 12.48 *Burton and Paxton: Conservatory, Chatsworth House, 1836–1840.* (From *The Civil Engineer and Architects Journal*)

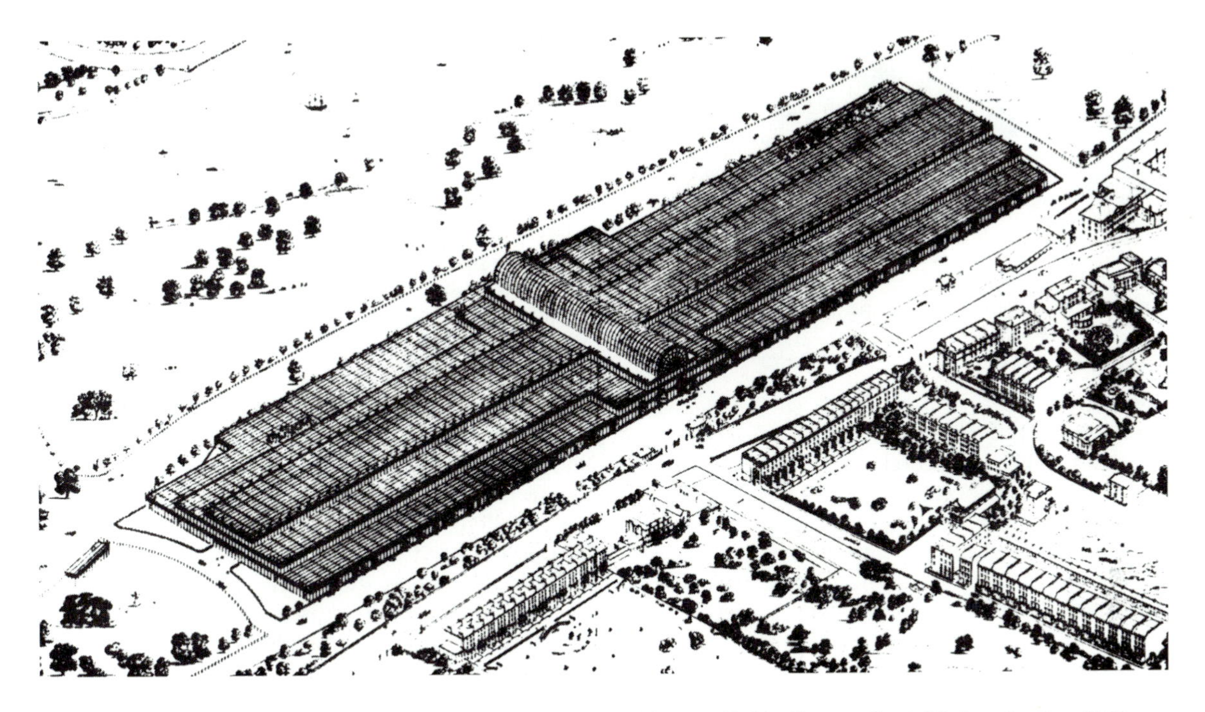

FIGURE 12.49 *Paxton: Crystal Palace, London, 1851.* (Lithograph, Ackerman and Co., 1851)

hibition had received 245 designs of all sorts for the structure, none of which was entirely suitable, so the committee had made its own design, a great domed structure with a brick drum and adjacent walls. Even this could probably not be built on time and for the £300,000 of the allocated budget, which made Paxton's tardy submission in July of 1850 all the more attractive (Figure 12.49). His design proposed an 1851-foot-long structure of glass and iron at an estimated price of £150,000; and through negotiations with the manufacturers who would supply the materials, Paxton could guarantee completion on time. His scheme was accepted. In constructing the building, the contractors Fox and Henderson made one of the first large-scale demonstrations of prefabrication. The repetitive iron and glass sections required a limited number of individual components, so that supplying factories could easily mass-produce the tremendous quantity of material required for the eighteen-acre building: 3800 tons of cast iron, 700 tons of wrought iron, twenty-four miles of rainwater guttering, 900,000 square feet of glass, and 600,000 cubic feet of wood (Figures 12.50, 12.51). To the extent possible mate-

FIGURE 12.50 *Paxton: Transept of the Crystal Palace, London.* (*The Crystal Palace Exhibition Illustrated Catalog*)

FIGURE 12.51 *Paxton: Interior of the Crystal Palace, London.* (*The Crystal Palace Exhibition Illustrated Catalog*)

rials arrived on the site assembled into subsections, and final assembly proceeded at an unprecedented rate. Once the exhibition opened, the building was visited by about one quarter of the population of England and universally acclaimed for its vast, airy space. Journalists dubbed it the Crystal Palace, a name it has retained. The construction success and public praise for the Crystal Palace had much to do with the increasing acceptance of a larger amount of glass and iron in buildings designed by architects. After the exhibition ended, the building was dismantled and reerected in a park at Sydenham, outside London, where it remained until destroyed by fire in 1936.

Just a few years after the Crystal Palace was completed, iron framing was used for another building, which had no impact on architectural developments but is nonetheless interesting for its remarkably advanced appearance. The building is the Boat Store of the Naval Dockyard at Sheerness, England, built in 1858 by Colonel G. T. Greene (Figures 12.52, 12.53). It responds to the utilitarian demands of the program and site in a straightforward rather elegant way. Iron roof trusses on fifteen-foot centers define the interior of the building, which measures 210 feet long by 135 feet deep by 56 feet high. Riveted connections are used throughout, and the exterior of the building reflects the interior structure. In the 1950s the building was "discovered" by the architectural historian Eric de Maré, who assumed it to be a work of the 1930s until he checked the original

FIGURE 12.52 *Greene: Boat Store, Sheerness, 1858.* (Photo: Courtesy The Medway Ports Authority)

FIGURE 12.53 *Greene: Interior of the Boat Store, Sheerness.* (Photo: Courtesy The Medway Ports Authority)

FIGURE 12.56 *Baltard: Interior of Les Halles, Paris.* (Photo: Marburg) ▶

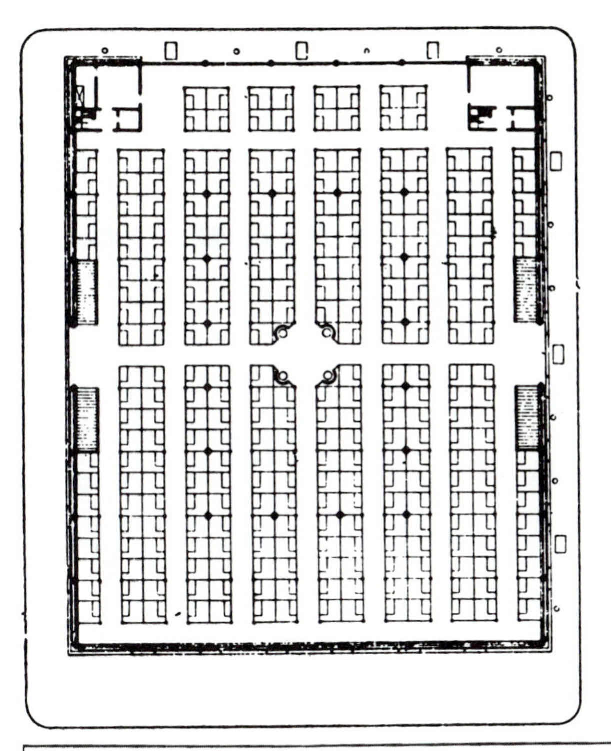

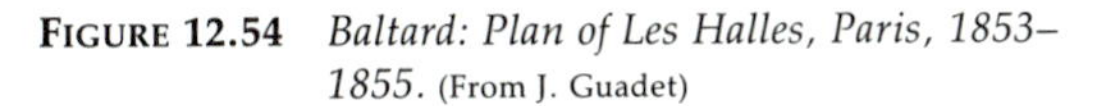

FIGURE 12.54 *Baltard: Plan of Les Halles, Paris, 1853–1855.* (From J. Guadet)

drawings. Its "modern" appearance is remarkable, but it could not possibly have had any impact on the twentieth century.

Designers in France soon took up the techniques of glass and iron construction as well. Victor Baltard (1805–1874) was a rather undistinguished architect who produced one notable building, Les Halles (the Market Halls) in Paris (1853–1855). This great complex of glass-roofed, iron-framed pavilions (Figures 12.54–12.56) housed the city's wholesale fresh fruit,

FIGURE 12.55 *Baltard: Section through Les Halles, Paris.* (From J. Guadet)

FIGURE 12.57 *Labrouste: Elevation of the Bibliothèque Ste-Geneviève, Paris, 1842–1850.* (From J. Guadet)

FIGURE 12.58 *Labrouste: Section through the Bibliothèque Ste-Geneviève, Paris.* (From J. Guadet)

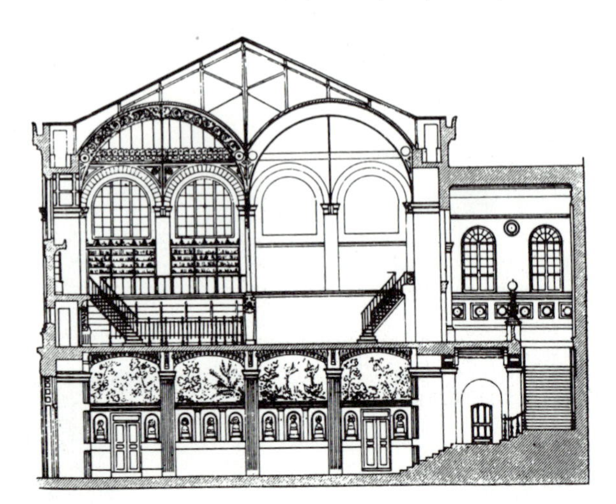

vegetable, and meat markets until the mid-1960s, when it was torn down after a replacement facility with better transportation connections was constructed on the outskirts of Paris.

Henri Labrouste (1801–1875) made a finer architectural use of cast iron in the Bibliothèque Ste-Geneviève (1850) in Paris (Figures 12.57–12.59). On the exterior the building presents a correct Neo-Classic façade recalling Italian Renaissance palace designs; but on the interior at the second floor level one finds an unprecedented great reading room, extending the length and width of the building, covered by light semicircular cast-iron arches. Sixteen slender cast-iron columns, of a proportion to be found only in Pompeiian wall paintings, divide the long space into two barrel-vaulted halves. The ceiling vaults, consisting of interlaced wires covered

FIGURE 12.59 *Labrouste: Plan of the Bibliothèque Ste-Geneviève, Paris.* (From J. Guadet)

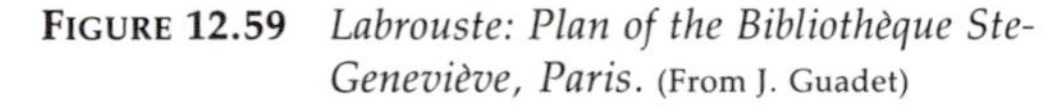

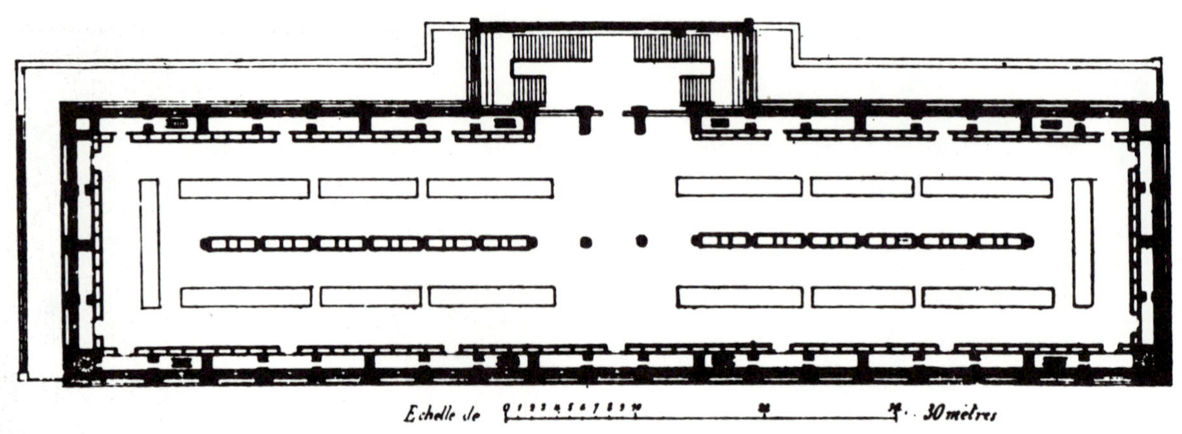

FIGURE 12.60 *Labrouste: Interior of the Bibliothèque Ste-Geneviève, Paris.* (Photo: Marburg)

with plaster, rest on the delicately scrolled cast-iron arches (Figure 12.60).

In 1854 Labrouste was named architect of the Bibliothèque Nationale (the French National Library), an institution with a rapidly growing collection of volumes and inadequate quarters in several converted town palaces. Labrouste worked on the buildings for the library for the next twenty-one years, designing around existing structures to provide a central reading room (Figure 12.61) and a separate book stack, the first to be provided in a library (Figure 12.62). As in the Bibliothèque Ste-Geneviève, Labrouste used masonry for the Neo-Classic exterior walls and iron for the interior. The most spectacular use of iron is in the reading room, where nine domes, each nearly thirty-five feet in diameter, rest on a grid of sixteen slender iron columns. Illumination for the space comes from clerestories and oculus windows in each dome. Equally important, but less celebrated, is the iron framing of the book stacks. Here there are six floors of shelving and aisle space, top lit by skylights and light wells. The grillwork of the floors and the columns supporting the shelf units form a structural framework independent of the enclosing masonry walls.

The most famous French designer using iron in

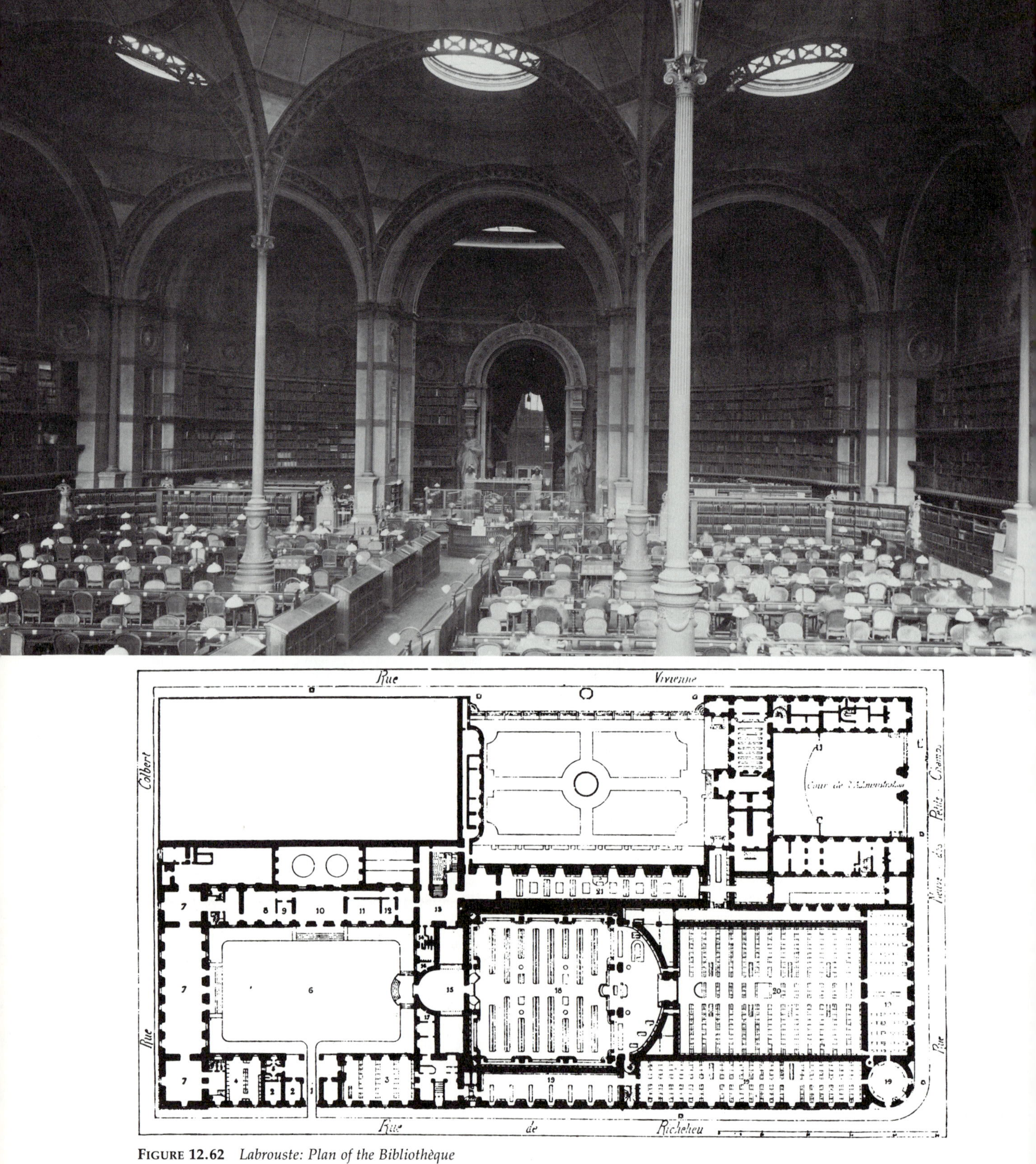

FIGURE 12.62 *Labrouste: Plan of the Bibliothèque Nationale, Paris.* (From J. Guadet)

◀ **FIGURE 12.61** *Labrouste: Reading room interior of the Bibliothèque Nationale, Paris, 1858–1868.* (Photo: Marburg)

the second half of the nineteenth century was Gustave Eiffel (1832–1923). This engineer gained fame for his graceful bridge designs, such as the Garabit Viaduct over the Truyère (1880–1884) in southern France (Figure 12.63), and then used his experience with iron construction to build the world's tallest tower, the 1010-foot-high Eiffel Tower, erected for the Paris International Exposition of 1889 (Figure 12.64). Not until the completion of the Chrysler Building in New York was Eiffel's tower exceeded in height, and it remains the largest iron construction in the world, for steel was rapidly becoming the preferred material for metal framing. Eiffel's tower design was derided by the artistic elite of France before and during construction, but Parisians of all classes were thrilled by the magnificent views from its top, and they soon adjusted to its gigantic size on the skyline. The opening of the tower in 1889 also gave the first large-scale demonstration of the passenger safety elevator, a model by the American Elisha Graves Otis being installed as original equipment in the Tower.

FIGURE 12.63 *Eiffel: Garabit Viaduct, 1880–1884.* (Photo: Marburg)

FIGURE 12.64 *Eiffel: Eiffel Tower, Paris, 1889.* (Photo: Marburg)

FIGURE 12.65 *Eiffel, Bartholdi, and Hunt: Statue of Liberty, New York, 1883–1886.* (From *Scientific American*)

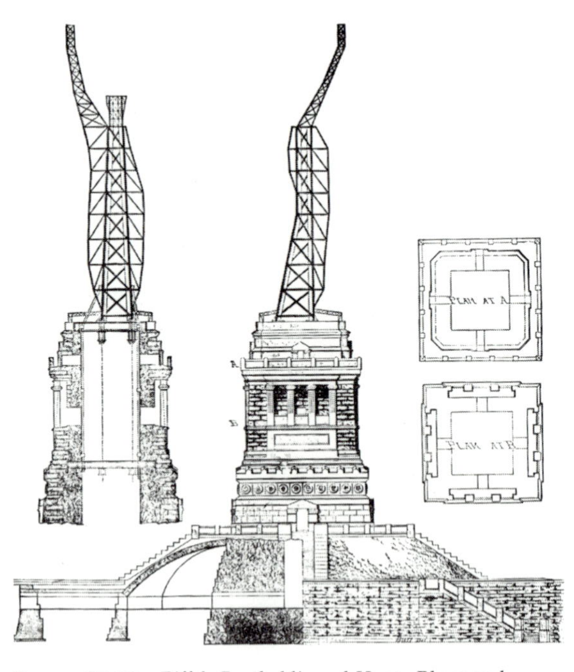

FIGURE 12.66 *Eiffel, Bartholdi, and Hunt: Plans and section of the Statue of Liberty, New York.* (From *Scientific American*)

In New York harbor stands another engineering work of Eiffel, the internal skeleton for the 151-foot-tall Statue of Liberty (1883–1886) (Figures 12.65, 12.66). Miss Liberty's copper skin is supported on iron straps attached to a steel framework that Eiffel designed to withstand the considerable wind loads of the harbor. At the time of its construction the Statue of Liberty had the most advanced diagonally braced frame to be found in any building in the United States. Its incorporation of steel members for the major load-bearing posts marked only the second time steel had been used for nonbridge construction in the United States. The first all-iron frame French building, the Menier Chocolate Factory at Noisel-sur-Marne (1871–1872) by Jules Saulnier, gave artistic expression to the diagonals of its bracing (Figure 12.67). The iron used effectively made the building's exterior into a lattice truss, and the architect embellished the diamond shapes on the façade with diagonal brickwork and decorative crosses at the intersections.

American builders were to become the primary innovators in metal frame construction for buildings. From about 1865 onward architects in New York and then Chicago developed an original building type, the skyscraper, on a scale and level of sophistication that was unmatched by European designers. Tall buildings were a response to rising urban real estate values and the desire of businesses to remain close to established centers. A whole range of technical improvements — including mass-produced structural components, the safety elevator, and fireproofing techniques — made them feasible, and their structure was most logically executed in steel frame, braced to withstand lateral wind loads.

Pre-Civil War building technology included the first structural uses of iron for buildings in the cast-iron fronts and building frames that were mass-produced by men like James Bogardus (1800–1874) and Daniel Badger in New York and shipped as far as steamships traveled (Figure 12.68). Cast iron was fa-

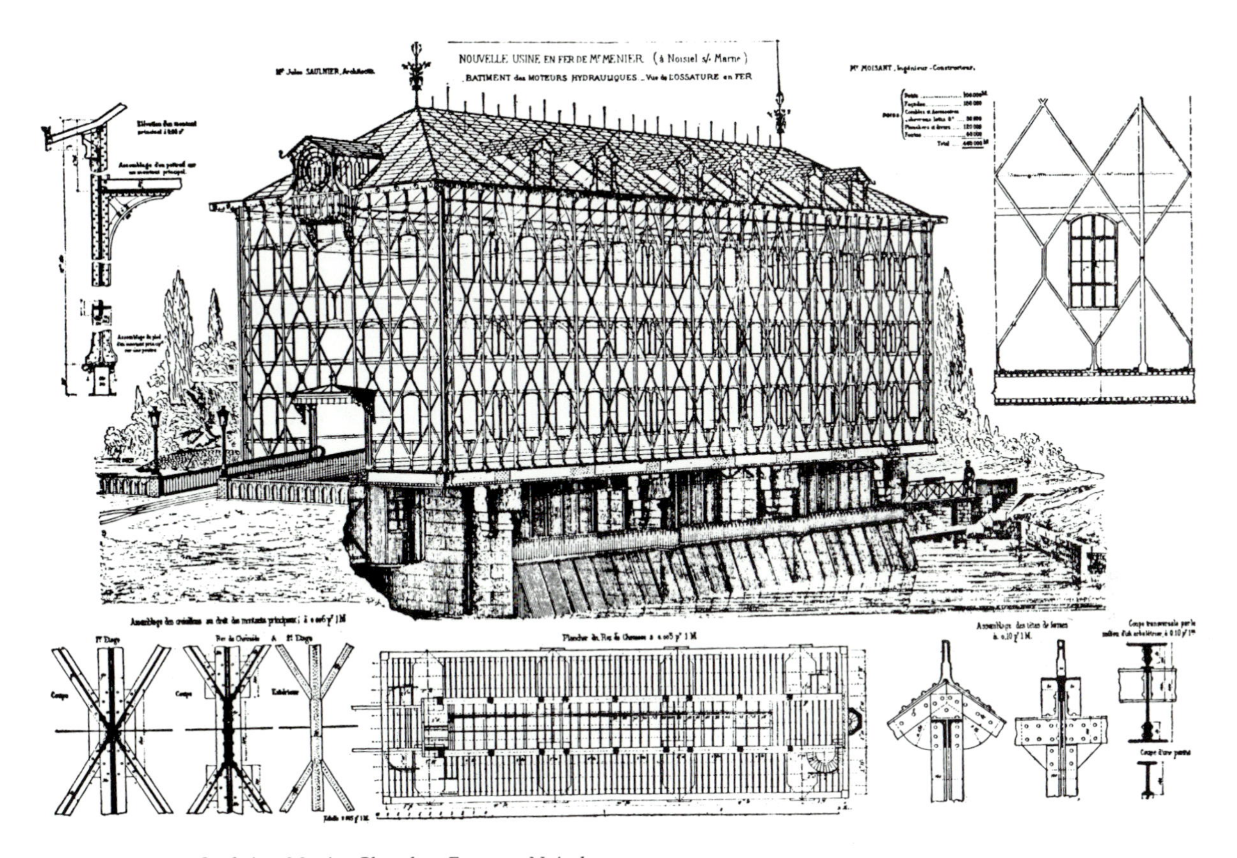

FIGURE 12.67 *Saulnier: Menier Chocolate Factory, Noisel-sur-Marne, 1871–1872.* (From R. Sturgis)

vored for its strength, fire resistance, and plastic qualities. The classical detail desired for commercial structures could be economically cast from molds and repeated for as many bays and stories as desired, and the finished façade could be painted to resemble stone or any other material. The simplicity of construction appealed to many businessmen, who built increasing numbers of cast-iron structures from 1849 onward. Whole districts of them, such as SoHo in New York City, appeared when extensive fires destroyed the previous timber-framed buildings.

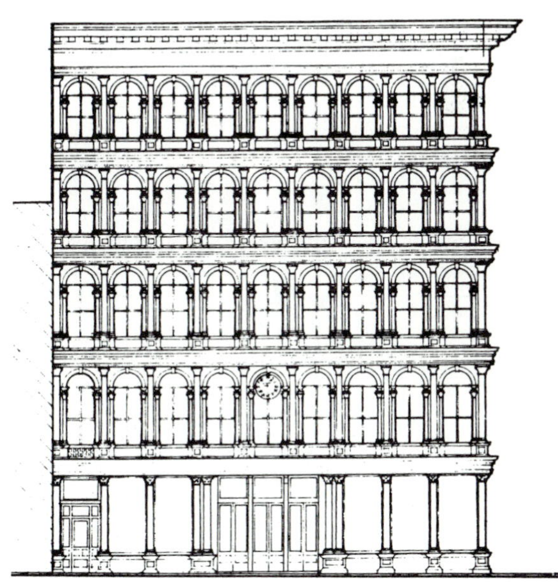

FIGURE 12.68 *Gaynor and Badger: Haughwout Store, New York, 1856.* (Drawing: H.A.B.S.)

In most instances cast-iron buildings lacked the wind bracing essential to high-rise construction, so they cannot be considered the first skyscrapers. However, James Bogardus introduced the European iron I-beam, now universally employed for steel framing, and his concept of an all-iron building must have encouraged others to think more seriously about the alternatives to masonry bearing wall construction. In the process of rebuilding the business district of Chicago, largely destroyed by fire in 1871, a number of inventive men perfected metal frame construction for high-rise buildings and thus created the skyscraper. William LeBaron Jenney (1832–1907), the engineer for the Home Life Insurance Building (1884–1885), is generally credited with the early development of the skyscraper, although the Home Insurance Building is not entirely metal-framed for the first floor contains sections of masonry bearing wall (Figure 12.69). Above the ground floor the masonry exterior was supported on shelf angle supports attached to the frame, and

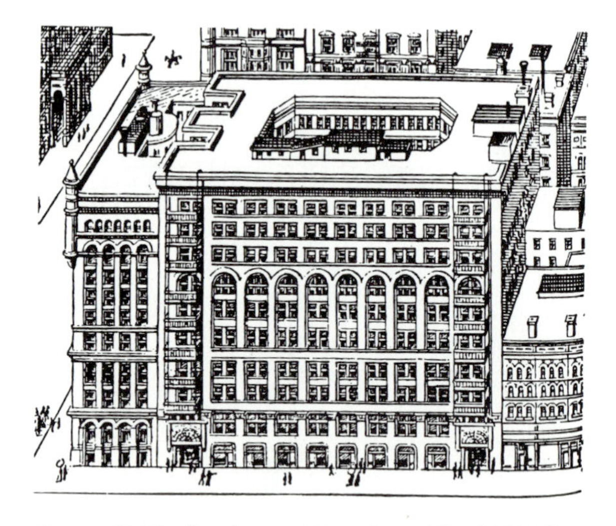

FIGURE 12.70 *Burnham and Root: Second Rand McNally Building, Chicago, 1889–1990.* (From Rand McNally)

FIGURE 12.71 *Burnham and Root: Monadnock Building, Chicago, 1890–1891.* (Photo: H.A.B.S.)

FIGURE 12.69 *Jenney: Home Life Insurance Building, Chicago, 1884–1885.* (From A. Andreas)

steel rather than iron was employed for the structure above the sixth-floor level. The second Rand McNally Building (1889–1890) by Daniel H. Burnham (1846–1912) and John Welborn Root (1850–1891) had all the elements of the modern skyscraper, including a completely steel frame designed by the structural engineering firm of Wade and Purdy, even though its external appearance looked backward rather than forward (FIgure 12.70). Even where masonry bearing walls were retained, as in Burnham and Root's Monadnock Building (1890–1891), an internal iron frame provided lateral bracing through riveted girder-column connections (Figure 12.71).

The buildings of Chicago from 1875 to 1925 are collectively termed the Chicago School, indicating the sharing of design attitudes and construction technologies. Innovative as the structures of these buildings are, they do not necessarily express their metal frames on their exteriors; most are clad in masonry, which gives the appearance of being the structural material. Their façades are derived from classical precedent, which presents very few buildings where the vertical dimension exceeds the horizontal measurement, and nothing in the past even approximated the scale of multifloor construction. Designers solved the problem in a variety of ways. The decorative terra-cotta cladding on the Reliance Building (1894–1895) repeats the same exterior elevation from the third floor to the attic story, expressing in the process the slenderness of its metal-frame columns and the depth of the beams supporting the floors (Figure 12.72). Other Chicago School buildings were composed by grouping floors in three or four horizontal layers, which could then conform to the proportional systems of columns and entablatures and the whole idea of streetscape established by Renaissance architects.

FIGURE 12.72 *Burnham and Company: Reliance Building, Chicago, 1894–1895.* (Photo: H.A.B.S.)

THE ARTS AND CRAFTS MOVEMENT

The rapid pace of industrialization in nineteenth-century England created a new social order based on investment in mechanized and trading enterprises. Factory towns, surrounded by long rows of dreary housing for workers, grew in the Midlands where water power and coal were readily available.

FIGURE 12.73 *Webb: Red House, Bexleyheath, 1859–1860.* (Photo: Marburg)

Factory-made goods from soap to steel were widely distributed and generally raised the material standard of living. Yet the picture was not entirely a rosy one. We have already seen how the unrestrained capitalist system affected men such as Pugin, who was dismayed by the decline of the moral and spiritual values that he associated with medieval times. Other men were becoming concerned about the decline of artistic standards in the goods manufactured because trained designers were not involved in designing wares for industrial production.

These two issues — concern for social values and for the artistic quality of manufactured products — were at the heart of the Arts and Crafts Movement, which flourished from about 1850 to 1900 in Britain and later (1876–1916) in the United States. Originating in Victorian England its ideas spread to Europe and finally found a "modern" resolution in postwar Weimar Germany. John Ruskin (1819–1900), a follower of Pugin and a prolific critic of art and society, may be regarded as the founder of Arts and Crafts ideals. In Ruskin's view the industrial revolution was a grievous error exerting a corrupting influence on society. Ruskin avoided technological progress whenever possible, insisting, for example, on coach transport rather than traveling on the railways, and vigorously advocating a return to handcraftsmanship, where the work produced reflected the shape of the tool and the passage of the worker's hand. Like Pugin before him, Ruskin associated high moral values with certain historical styles, especially Early English Gothic and the Italian Gothic in Venice, where he believed truth and beauty in building were to be found. Ruskin had only contempt for persons who hoped to teach industrial design to students:

> The tap-root of all this mischief is in the endeavor to produce some ability in the student to make money by designing for manufacture. No student who makes this his primary object will be able to design at all; and the very words "School of Design" involve the profoundest of art fallacies. Drawing may be taught by tutors, but design only by Heaven; and to every scholar who thinks to sell his inspiration, Heaven refuses his help.

His speeches and writings had tremendous influence on a younger generation of sensitive men, whose collective actions put many of Ruskin's ideals into practice. The leader of this activist group was William Morris (1834–1896), an Oxford divinity student turned poet who abandoned theology and studied both architecture and painting after encountering Ruskin's teachings. After his marriage Morris could find no house that met his standards

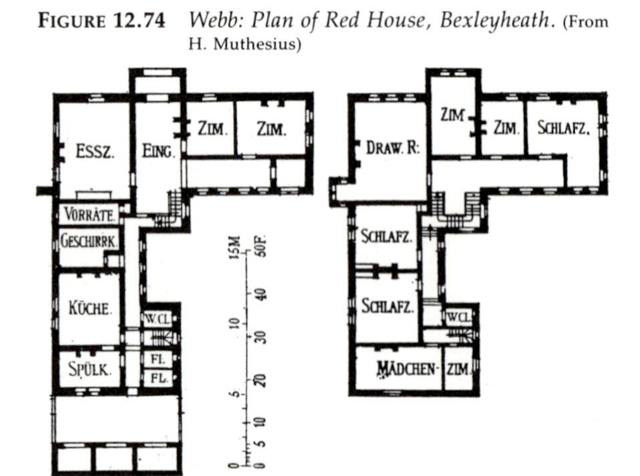

FIGURE 12.74 *Webb: Plan of Red House, Bexleyheath.* (From H. Muthesius)

for design, so he commissioned his friend, Philip Webb (1831–1915), to design what became known as the Red House at Bexleyheath (1859–1860), a red-brick structure that harkened back to medieval domestic vernacular forms (Figures 12.73, 12.74). Its straightforward approach to structure and its undisguised use of materials surprised contemporary visitors, as did its elaborate use of decorative detail on the interior. Partly as a result of collaborating with his artist friends in the work on Red House, Morris founded the firm of Morris, Marshall, Faulkner and Company in 1862, consisting of workshops where artist-craftsmen created wallpaper, textiles, stained glass, utensils, furniture, and carpets using handcraft techniques. Morris's firm reflected his philosophy of dignity and joy found through honest craftsmanship. It was intended to be an alternative to the factory system, where mass-produced elements were assembled by workers who had become little more than cogs in the machine and had no interest in, control over, or love for the goods produced. Morris believed that well-designed, handcrafted products in homes of ordinary working class people would raise them above the level of disinterested bread-winning employment. (His concern for the welfare of the working class led to his enthusiastic and active espousal of Socialism.) Unfortunately the limited output of Morris's workshops was insufficient to meet such a market, and the price on his well-made objects tended to be higher than comparable factory-made goods, so his vision of supplying quality furnishings to ordinary people was never realized. The establishment of his firm, however, marks the first attempt to address the inferior quality of manufactured goods and the dehumanizing aspects of industrial production, a problem that would remain for others to solve. The writings of John Ruskin and the firm of William Morris inspired Elbert Hubbard to create his Roycrofters Workshops in East Aurora, New York; Hubbard's work was much admired by the young Frank Lloyd Wright.

Of the English architects influenced by the Arts and Crafts movement, the most notable was Charles Francis Annesley Voysey (1857–1941), whose early commissions included wallpaper designs that owe much to Morris. He seldom used wallpaper in the houses he designed, however, preferring instead the purity of white plaster walls or unfinished oak paneling. Voysey houses, such as The Orchard in Chorleywood (1899) or Greyfriars near Guildford, Surrey (1896), are informal and reminiscent of the medieval vernacular. They feature wide, overhanging eaves; steeply pitched roofs; broad and bold chimneys; leaded casement windows; and either white-washed masonry or stone walls. The interiors feature natural finish materials, such as slate flooring and untreated oak paneling; Arts and Crafts furniture (some of it designed by Voysey himself); and the evidence of handcrafting in both ornamental and functional fittings, including carpets, pottery, clocks, candlesticks, hinges, and latches. Voysey created a simple scheme in his design for Broadleys (1898), a vacation house on Lake Windermere for A. Currer Briggs (Figures 12.75–12.78). Three bowfront windows extend through the two stories of the house, interrupting the roofline, to provide views over the lake to the west. The house is constructed of local stone, laid two feet thick in the walls, and is capped by a slate roof with a series of iron brackets supporting the overhanging eaves. The overall composition is asymmetrical yet dignified. With this design and others he made for residential commissions from 1890 to 1905, Voysey helped set the style for much suburban housing built in England and the United States before 1930.

The spirit of Arts and Crafts design was carried to Germany by Herman Muthesius, a representative of the Prussian Board of Trade attached to the German Embassy in London from 1896 to 1903. Germany was experiencing the same absence of good design in industrial products that had earlier been noted in Britain, and Muthesius was assigned the task of reporting on the state of English architecture and design, then very highly regarded on the continent. The result was a three-volume report, *Das Englische Haus* (The English House), which documented all aspects of late Arts and Crafts work, from architecture to plumbing fixtures. On his return to Germany in 1903 Muthesius was appointed head of the Prussian Board of Trade, where he was responsible for selecting notable designers to teach in the Prussian schools of arts and crafts. The impetus for the formation of the Bauhaus can be traced to the work of these men, including Peter Behrens, Hans Poelzig, and Bruno Paul, although discussion of that development must wait for a later chapter.

Figure 12.75 *Voysey: Broadleys, Lake Windemere, 1898.* (Photo: Marburg)

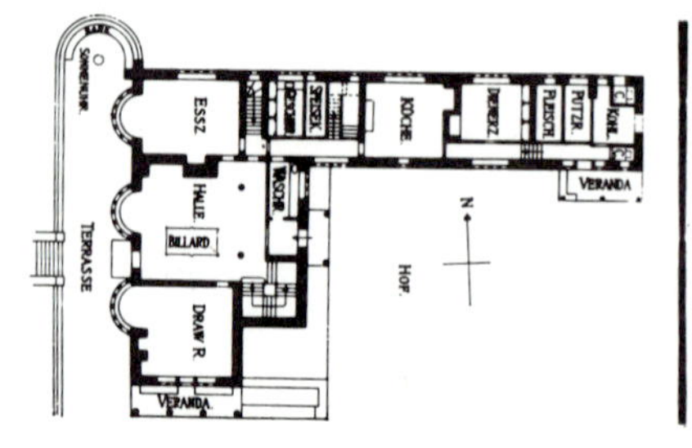

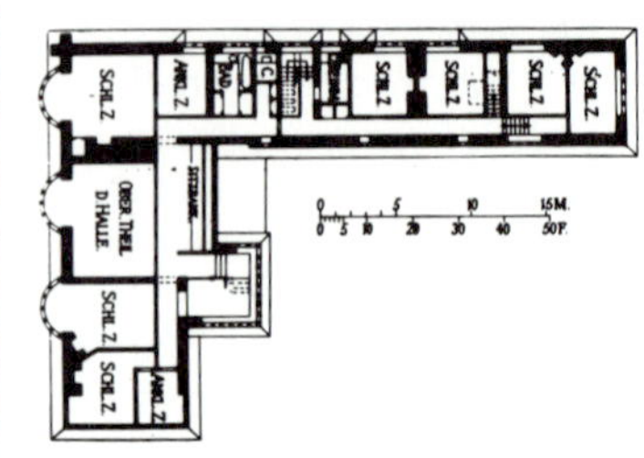

Figure 12.76 *Voysey: Plan of Broadleys, Lake Windemere.* (From H. Muthesius)

Figure 12.77 *Voysey: Terrace view of Broadleys, Lake Windemere.* (Photo: Marburg)

Figure 12.78 *Voysey: Interior view of Broadleys, Lake Windemere.* (Photo: Marburg)

ART NOUVEAU

A new decorative style arose during the era known as "La Belle Epoch" (about 1880 to 1905). Nurtured by a variety of sources, including the Arts and Crafts movement, the Gothic Revival, the Celtic Revival, late Baroque and Rococo, and the arts of China and Japan, it was a widely practiced style that was given different names. It was known as Art Nouveau in France, England, and the Low Countries; "Stile Liberty" or "Stile Floreale" in Italy; "Jugendstil" in Germany; and "Secession" in Austria. Whatever its name, the new style abandoned late-Victorian "battle of the styles" design by attempting a complete break with the past. The linear, tenuous lines found in late Baroque and Rococo work were developed into free-flowing designs based loosely on plant and animal forms. In fact a parallel can be drawn with Celtic art or the Animal Style of the early middle ages, although Art Nouveau curves have a freedom to change width and direction that exceeds medieval practice.

One finds the earliest emergence of Art Nouveau in England, although the fullest expression of the style was to come elsewhere. The design by Arthur Heygate Mackmurdo (1851–1942) for the title page of *Wren's City Churches* (1883) is commonly cited as the first Art Nouveau piece (Figure 12.79). Wallpapers and carpets designed by William Morris at about the same time share this linearity, as do the illustrations and decorative flourishes included in the Kelmscott Press editions published by Morris after 1890 (Figure 12.80). Other illustrators, especially Aubrey Beardsley, did woodcuts that exhibit the swirling, sensuous curving line; Beardsley's work often has demonic overtones in its representations of women. James MacNeill Whistler (1834–1903), an American painter with strong English ties, created the Peacock Room for Frederick Leyland's mansion, a design marked both by Japanese delicacy and by Art Nouveau peacocks representing the designer and his client feuding over the fee! (The Peacock Room is now installed at the Freer Gallery in Washington, D.C.)

The decorative rather than structural qualities of the design predominate in Art Nouveau work. Architects who worked in the style tended to turn structural necessity into organically derived curves,

FIGURE 12.79 *Mackmurdo: Title page of* Wren's City Churches, *1883.* (From A. Mackmurdo)

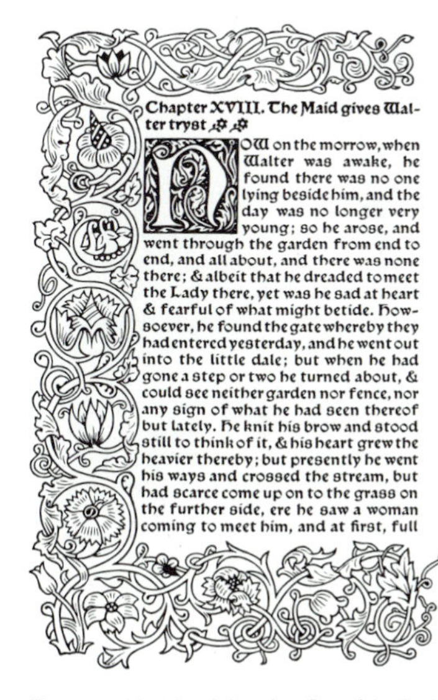

Chapter XVIII. The Maid gives Walter tryst

NOW on the morrow, when Walter was awake, he found there was no one lying beside him, and the day was no longer very young; so he arose, and went through the garden from end to end, and all about, and there was none there; & albeit that he dreaded to meet the Lady there, yet was he sad at heart & fearful of what might betide. Howsoever, he found the gate whereby they had entered yesterday, and he went out into the little dale; but when he had gone a step or two he turned about, & could see neither garden nor fence, nor any sign of what he had seen thereof but lately. He knit his brow and stood still to think of it, & his heart grew the heavier thereby; but presently he went his ways and crossed the stream, but had scarce come up on to the grass on the further side, ere he saw a woman coming to meet him, and at first, full as he was of the tide of yesterday and the wondrous garden, deemed that it would be the Lady; but the woman stayed her feet, and, stooping, laid a hand on her right ankle, & he saw that it was the Maid. He drew anigh to her, and saw that she was nought so sad of countenance as the last time she had met him, but flushed of cheek & bright-eyed. As he came up to her she made a step or two to meet him, holding out her two hands, and then refrained her, & said smiling: Ah, friend, belike this shall be the last time that I shall say to thee, touch me not, nay, not so much as my hand, or if it were but the hem of my raiment. The joy grew up in his heart, and he gazed on her fondly, and said: Why, what then hath befallen of late? O friend, she began, this hath befallen. But as he looked on her, the smile died from her face, & she became deadly pale to the very lips; she looked askance to her left side, whereas ran the stream; and Walter followed her eyes, and deemed for one instant that he saw the misshapen yellow visage of

The Maid cometh again

135

FIGURE 12.80 *Morris: Graphic design for the Kelmscott Press.* (From W. Morris)

Figure 12.81 *Horta: Tassel House, Brussels, 1892–1893.* (Photo: Institut Belge d'Information et de Documentation)

Figure 12.82 *Horta: Hall of the Van Eetvelde House, Brussels, 1897.* (Photo: Institut Belge d'Information et de Documentation) ▶

a development based on the rationalizing theories of Viollet-le-Duc. This can be seen in the early designs of Victor Horta (1861–1947), the Belgian architect for the Tassel House, Brussels, built in 1892–1893 (Figure 12.81). Swirling tendril designs are incorporated not only in the structure (the staircase, balustrades, and balcony railings) but also in surface patterning on floors, walls, and ceilings. The interior of the Van Eetvelde House (1897) in Brussels exhibits these same qualities (Figure 12.82). Horta's later Maison du Peuple (1896–1899) exploited its structural relationship to plant forms, particularly in the upper floor auditorium, where undulating iron ceiling trusses merged with upright supports in the manner of a branch attaching to a tree. Even the balcony was sculpted into a curvilinear form, its delicate supports terminating as protective railings. The expressive linearity of iron construction was masterfully handled in this, the first iron- and glass-façade building in Belgium.

Hector Guimard (1867–1942) was the French architect most celebrated for Art Nouveau designs. The most famous of his works were made fom 1899 to 1904 for entrances to the Paris Métro, the subway system (Figure 12.83). Essentially these are canopies over staircases descending from the sidewalk, and Guimard provided several designs that employ wrought-iron swirls and curves, some of which support glass roofs. The unity of these little projects is remarkable for all the elements are deftly integrated in the plantlike form. Light standards are terminated by bud-shaped electric bulbs, while patterns derived from vegetable leaves are used as infill on the railings. Guimard's other architectural projects reflect his ability to blend the decorative with the functional, as can be seen at the Castel Béranger (1894–1898), an apartment building in Paris, where latent medievalism is nicely balanced by free-flowing asymmetrical decoration in iron and ceramic to form a unified whole (Figure 12.84).

In Spain Art Nouveau reached its most highly idiosyncratic expression in the work of Antonio y Cornet Gaudí (1852–1926), a Catalan who began as

FIGURE 12.83 *Guimard: Métro entrance, Paris, 1899–1904.* (Photo: © Arch. Phot. Paris/S.P.A.D.E.M.)

FIGURE 12.84 *Guimard: Entrance to the Castel Béranger, Paris, 1898.* (Photo: B. Acloque/© C.N.M.H.S./S.P.A.D.E.M.)

FIGURE 12.85 *Gaudí: View into the incomplete interior of Sagrada Familia, Barcelona, 1884 and after.* (Photo: Moffett)

a Gothic Revival architect. Because of his medieval style he was asked in 1884 to take charge of construction of Sagrada Familia (the Expiatory Temple of the Holy Family) in Barcelona, begun two years earlier by another Gothic Revivalist and incomplete to this day (Figure 12.85). In the course of work on Sagrada Familia, Gaudí moved away from Gothic Revival into an intensely personal style that was used for apartment buildings, houses, and landscape design as well as ecclesiastical works. The flowing three-dimensional curvaceous forms, floral decoration, and plastic-flowing plans found in Gaudí's works link him more closely with Art Nouveau than any other stylistic movement, despite the fact that his work basically resists categorization. Sagrada Familia, for example, retains Gothic structural overtones, yet has such a heavy, towering, sculptural presence, enriched with lovingly crafted details, that it is clearly not Gothic. The Façade of the Nativity is an array of grotto-eroded elements flowing together, with four great spires towering above (Figure 12.86).

FIGURE 12.86 *Gaudí: Façade of the Nativity, south transept of Sagrada Familia, Barcelona.* (Photo: Moffett) ►

BUSREIZEN

◀ **FIGURE 12.87** *Gaudí: Casa Milá, Barcelona, 1905–1907.* (Photo: Moffett)

Gaudí's design for Casa Milá (1905–1907), an apartment house in Barcelona (Figure 12.87), has an undulating plasticity in its façade and plan that is made possible by its expressive exterior load-bearing wall. There are no bearing walls inside, giving the designer freedom to sculpt individual, nonorthogonal spaces, no two alike. His designs for Parc Güell (1900–1914) sited on a hillside west of Barcelona, allowed an extensive merging of naturalistic forms into walkways, stairways, and seating (Figure 12.88). Vaulting leans at oblique angles in a grotto walkway (Figure 12.89); stairs flow downward like lava; and benches, conforming precisely to the irregular curves of the seated human form, wind sinusoidally along the upper level plaza edge. Ceramic tile finishes and details contribute durable wearing surfaces and an appropriate touch of whimsy. The informal, amorphous, and rambling park is a skillfully inventive total design.

Gaudí's highly individualistic interpretations of Art Nouveau have a Scottish parallel in Charles Rennie Mackintosh (1868–1928), a gifted designer whose architectural career was brief. Mackintosh and a small circle of friends worked primarily in Glasgow, developing a unique style that is marginally related to Art Nouveau in using curves derived from natural forms. Other influences are detectable in Mackintosh's work as well, including the massive forms of Scottish baronial architecture and the delicate interlacing decoration of Celtic Art. His architecture tends to have bold massing deftly composed, with light and airy interiors accented by subtle attenuated curves or linear patterns that are usually symmetrical. Like other Art-Nouveau architects, Mackintosh was greatly concerned with small details such as furniture, light fixtures, and window hardware.

The Glasgow School of Art (1897–1909) was Mackintosh's first and largest commission (Figures 12.90, 12.91). Located on the north side of a sloping site, the building presents three elevations to the perimeter streets. The main entrance façade on Renfrew Street is a tight monolithic mass bounded by

FIGURE 12.89 *Gaudí: Colonnade in Parc Güell, Barcelona.* (Photo: Moffett)

◀ **FIGURE 12.88** *Gaudí: Entrance to Parc Güell, Barcelona, 1900–1914.* (Photo: Marburg)

FIGURE 12.90 *Mackintosh: School of Art, Glasgow, 1897–1909.* (Photo: Ralph Burnett)

LIBRARY

CORRIDOR

CORRIDOR

ELEMENTARY ORNAMENT

ADVANCED ORNAMENT

DESIGN ROOM

GROUND FLOOR PLAN

FIGURE 12.91 *Mackintosh: Plan of the School of Art, Glasgow.* (From *Academic Architecture*)

FIGURE 12.92 *Mackintosh: Scott Street façade of the School of Art, Glasgow.* (Photo: Ralph Burnett)

FIGURE 12.93 *Mackintosh: Library interior of the School of Art, Glasgow.* (Photo: Ralph Burnett)

two rows of large, north-facing studio windows, while the later west façade along Scott Street rises austerely as the hill drops, in the manner of medieval fortifications (Figure 12.92). This elevation, comprising the library, is a bold design broken by the three twenty-five-foot-high windows along the upper section of wall. The library interior is the most celebrated space (Figure 12.93). Mackintosh designed the furniture and light fixtures to harmonize with the dominant pattern of horizontals and verticals in the windows and mezzanine balcony. A more fluid linearity is found in other spaces, and the southern rear attic level has simple arched openings that remind one of Romanesque work.

FIGURE 12.94 *Mackintosh: Hill House, Helensburgh, 1902–1904.* (Photo: Stewart Guthrie/National Trust for Scotland)

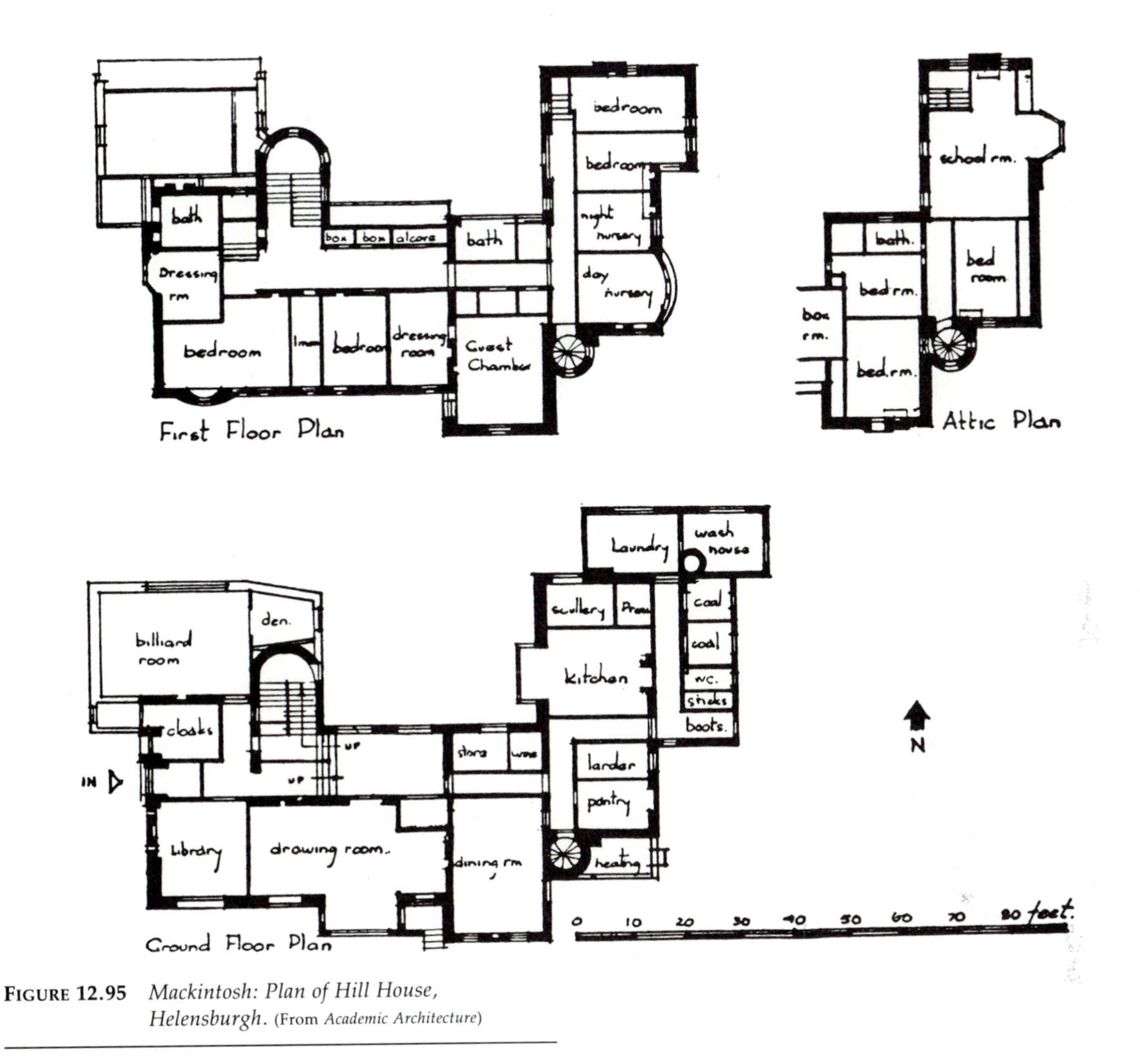

FIGURE 12.95 *Mackintosh: Plan of Hill House, Helensburgh.* (From *Academic Architecture*)

Other Mackintosh commissions include Windyhill (1900–1901), located outside Glasgow at Kilmacolm; Hill House (1902–1904) at Helensburgh; and the Scotland Street School (1904–1906) in Glasgow. Hill House (Figure 12.94), designed for a Glasgow publisher, stands like a castle on rising ground, reflecting the influence of the Scottish vernacular in its turrets, expressive chimneys, and dominant roof. The monolothic character of the exterior is achieved by pebble dash stucco. Its plan (Figure 12.95) is logically compartmentalized into functional areas: the library and cloakroom near the entrance, for easy conduct of business, followed by the reception rooms and a servant's wing at the end. Upstairs are the bedrooms, with the nursery and servant's bedrooms over the service wing. All interiors are handcrafted in the Arts and Crafts tradition, with custom-designed carpets, light fixtures, stencil decorations, and furniture (Figure 12.96). Dark woodwork contrasts with pastel colors on floor and wall surfaces. A barrel-vaulted ceiling in the bedroom becomes a canopy over the bed (Figure 12.97).

FIGURE 12.96 *Mackintosh: Entrance hall interior from Hill House, Helensburgh.* (Photo: Stewart Guthrie/ National Trust for Scotland)

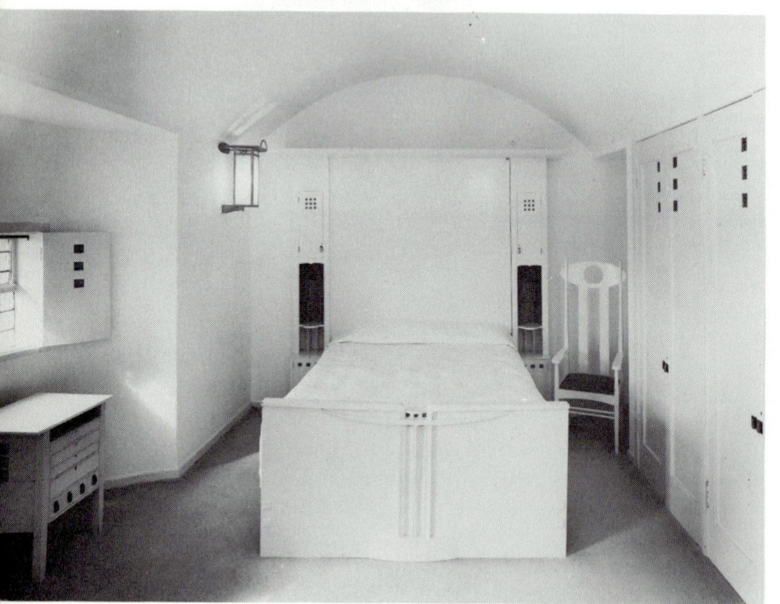

FIGURE 12.97 *Mackintosh: Master bedroom from Hill House, Helensburgh.* (Photo: Stewart Guthrie/ National Trust for Scotland)

Art Nouveau designers in various parts of Europe were aware of one another's work through publications. Mackintosh's entry in the 1901 German competition for a House of an Art Lover brought him second prize, and his project drawings became known through inclusion in a publication edited in Darmstadt. Darmstadt had become a center of Jugendstil in 1899, when Ernst Ludwig, Grand Duke of Hesse, established an artists' colony in the suburb of Mathildenhöhe, attracting artists from Munich and Vienna. While the colony's life as an art center was brief, the houses built in the Mathildenhöhe district remain a preserve of Jugendstil architecture. Major buildings in Jugendstil included a house for Ernst Ludwig designed by Joseph Maria Olbrich (1867–1908), who came from the Viennese Secessionists, and an elaborate and expensive residence built for his family by the young German

Figure 12.98 *Wagner: Postal Savings Bank, Vienna, 1904–1912.* (Photo: Austrian Press and Information Service, New York)

painter, Peter Behrens (1899). (Behrens quickly outgrew Jugendstil and went on to figure prominently in the development of modern architecture in Germany.) On the whole, Jugendstil is a late manifestation of Art Nouveau, and its architectural representation tends to be more linear and less free than comparable work in Belgium or France.

Art Nouveau in Austria was known as the Viennese Secession, an association primarily of artists formed in 1898. The oldest member of the group, although not one of its founders, was Otto Wagner (1841–1918), a Neo-Classical architect who was promoted to professor of architecture at the Vienna Academy of Fine Arts in 1894. Upon his appointment to academic life Wagner seems to have undergone a philosophical shift away from archaeological architecture to a more rational, modern expression suited to current-day requirements. The Viennese Secession was formed by some of his most outstanding students, and Wagner joined them in espousing Art Nouveau ornament.

Wagner's most notable designs in this mode were thirty-six stations for the Vienna subway system, the Stadtbahn (1894–1901). While not as exuberant as Guimard's work for the Paris Métro, Wagner's designs do employ characteristic stylized ornament in cast and wrought iron. After 1900 Wagner's enthusiasm for Art Nouveau waned, and he abandoned the style completely for his masterpiece, the Postal Savings Bank (1904–1906 and 1910–1912) in Vienna (Figures 12.98–12.100). The form of the interior banking hall is restrained and severe, almost Neo-Classical in the spirit of Schinkel. Its curving glass roof conveys a sense of lightness, and the plain wall surfaces are remarkable for a designer so recently designing Art Nouveau ornament. Wagner

FIGURE 12.99 *Wagner: Interior of the Postal Savings Bank, Vienna.* (Photo: Austrian Press and Information Service, New York)

FIGURE 12.100 *Wagner: Interior detail of the Postal Savings Bank, Vienna.* (Photo: Austrian Press and Information Service, New York)

used aluminum, then a relatively new material, to cover the internal structural members of the banking hall and on the exterior in bolts holding the thin marble facings to the wall. Like the interior, the exterior veneer is quite restrained, with only the minimum of stylized ornament on the upper wall.

Wagner's talented pupil, Josef Maria Olbrich, became the leading architect of the Viennese Secession, influenced in part by the work of Mackintosh. Like Mackintosh Olbrich found an essentially orthogonal basis for his architectural forms, embellishing them with the controlled vegetation of Art Nouveau. His first major commission was from the Secessionists themselves, a small building for meetings and exhibitions of art work. The Secession Hall (1898–1899) was essentially a cubical mass, crowned by a pierced openwork metal dome (Figure 12.101). Along the exterior walls between high windows Olbrich set low-relief ornament based on plants and flowers. In comparison with French or Belgian work Olbrich's designs seem rather heavy and symmetrical, the curving or flowing qualities definitely in control. Publication of this building brought widespread acclaim to its architect, and the Grand Duke of Hesse, Ernst Ludwig, invited Olbrich to join his artists' colony at Darmstadt.

From 1899 until his death from leukemia in 1908 Olbrich worked at Darmstadt, erecting numerous houses, studio buildings, entrance gates, and a Wedding Tower or Hochzeitsturm (1907–1908) to commemorate the Duke's marriage (Figure 12.102). The tower is a symbolic structure, rising above the colony with an arched and panelled gable that recalls the shape of organ pipes. It is built of brick and trimmed with contrasting stone around doors and windows. These windows are all the more unusual for wrapping around the corner of the tower, seeming to defy the mass required there for strength at the junction of the walls. The feature was to reappear on buildings by others in the 1920s and 1930s.

The third architect of the Viennese Secession, Adolf Loos (1870–1933), matured in a totally different manner from either Wagner or Olbrich. After completing his architectural education, he worked

FIGURE 12.101 *Olbrich: Secession Hall, Vienna, 1898–1899.* (Photo: Austrian Press and Information Service, New York)

and traveled in the United States from 1893–1896, where he saw the work of the Chicago School and encountered the writings of Louis Sullivan. The Chicago School's concept of eliminating ornament evidently impressed the young Loos, for when he returned to Europe to settle in Vienna, he soon began to speak against the inclusion of ornament on buildings. This was a difficult position to maintain when he joined the Viennese Secession, for Art Nouveau has nothing if not a highly refined sense of ornament. Some historians have theorized that Loos's turning against the prevailing Viennese school was his response to losing the commission to decorate and furnish the Secession council chamber. For whatever reasons, Loos never incorporated much applied ornament in his buildings, although one can detect a certain amount of stripped classicism in some works.

Loos' architectural designs were not nearly as influential as his theoretical writings, the most famous published in 1908 under the title *Ornament and Crime.* Here he took Sullivan's suggestion to abandon ornament in architecture a step further, proposing that the tendency to decorate surfaces was a sign of primitive culture or infancy. In advanced societies or in adults the urge to ornamental design was a sign of dependency or criminality.

> Children are amoral, and so — by our standards — are Papuans. If a Papuan slaughters an enemy and

FIGURE 12.102 *Olbrich: Hochzeitsturm, Darmstadt, 1907–1908.* (Photo: Marburg)

FIGURE 12.103 *Loos: Goldman and Salatsch Store, Vienna, 1910.* (Photo: Austrian Press and Information Service, New York)

> eats him, that doesn't make him a criminal. But if a modern man kills someone and eats him, he must be either a criminal or degenerate. The Papuans tattoo themselves, decorate their boats, their oars, everything they can get their hands on. But a modern man who tattoos himself is either a criminal or a degenerate. Why, there are prisons where eighty percent of the convicts are tattooed, and tattooed men who are not in prison are either latent criminals or degenerate aristocrats. When a tattooed man dies at liberty, it simply means that he hasn't had time to commit his crime. . . . I have therefore evolved the following maxim, and pronounce it to the world: the evolution of culture marches with the elimination of ornament from useful objects.

This was a strong polemic indeed, and after its original publication in the German art periodical *Der Sturm* (The Storm), it was translated into French and published in *Les Cahiers d'aujourd'hui* (The Notebooks of Today) in 1913. Loos became the darling of avant-garde artists in Paris, and he moved there in the early 1920s.

By extolling the virtues of architecture without ornament, Loos was addressing an issue that had been of general concern to designers in various places around the turn of the century. His writings led to admiration of the simple vernacular forms of undecorated peasant architecture and the rather plain, functional constructions of engineers, both types of buildings previously considered to have no particular aesthetic merits. In the logic of Loos to build without ornament was to build in a style appropriate to a mechanized age.

Loos's architectural designs remain fairly faithful to the position stated in *Ornament and Crime.* The Steiner House (1910) in Vienna, for example, is an unadorned white cubical mass, as is his later house for the Dada artist Tristan Tzara in Paris (1926). His Goldman and Salatsch Store on the Michaelerplatz (1910) in Vienna is less shocking than the houses. There is some relief from severe planes in the cornice line, the suggestions of a Doric colonnade along the ground floor, and the window boxes, which were demanded by the Archduke Ferdinand, whose palace faced Loos's building (Figure 12.103). In fact the building seems to owe something to Sullivan's compositional rules for tall buildings, and there is also a debt to the formal simplicity of Schinkel. In 1923 Loos submitted a late design for the Chicago Tribune Building competition that may be interpreted as either a joke or a serious comment on American architecture, particularly Stanford White's overscaled designs based on the Doric column. Loos's scheme was one enormous Doric column on a multistory base, with windows arranged in vertical rows corresponding to the fluting. In boldness it matched his writings on ornament.

In all Art Nouveau work, custom-designed detail was an integral element of building, necessary for the complete realization of the architect's conception. It was expensive in terms of both design and fabrication time, and it limited the appeal of the style for architectural purposes. Clients had to be both wealthy and indulgent to afford the cost and endure the designer's ultraindividualistic flights of fancy. This ultimately caused the decline of Art Nouveau for major projects like buildings. The style persisted longer in the decorative arts like jewelry and book design, where the investment required was much less. Architecture moved on from Art Nouveau to the stylistic and nonstylistic developments of the early twentieth century.

HENRY HOBSON RICHARDSON AND LOUIS SULLIVAN

A recurring theme in American architectural history is the search for a proper "American" style for building. Jefferson advocated the use of Roman architecture because it symbolized the greatness of the Roman Republic, which he saw as a worthy model for the new republic of the United States. Proponents of the Greek Revival cited similar desirable symbolic linkages with the democratic government of ancient Athens, while Gothic Revivalists drew parallels between Christian values of medieval times and the present day. Two American architects of the nineteenth century contributed to the search for a truly American expression in architecture, not by reviving past styles, but by evolving a fresh approach from the materials and building problems presented by life in the United States. Their accomplishments have had a lasting effect on the course of design.

The first of these designers, Henry Hobson Richardson (1838–1886), was the second American after Richard Morris Hunt to attend the École des Beaux-Arts. Born to a wealthy Louisiana family, Richardson completed the course at the Lawrence Scientific School of Harvard University before enrolling at the École in 1860. The onset of the Civil War cut off his financial support from home, forcing him out of school and into the office of Theodore Labrouste (brother of Henri), where he worked until 1865, when he returned to New York. After a few years there he moved his office to Boston and gained national acclaim for his competition-winning design for Trinity Church (1872–1877) in Copley Square, Boston.

Trinity Church (Figure 12.104) was to become the most celebrated building of its age; a national poll of architects made in 1885 identified it as the best building in the United States. What was it that designers (and the general public) admired so much about this church? In many respects the design is a pastiche, very much in the tradition of nineteenth-century eclecticism. The plan (Figure 12.105) is based on a stubby Latin cross basilica, and the polychrome stone work and general massing come from French Romanesque churches of Auvergne; the triple-arched portal is derived from St. Gilles-du-Gard in Provence; and the great crossing tower reflects the tower of the Old Cathedral in Salamanca, Spain. Despite these borrowings, an abundance of original thinking gives Trinity Church its distinctive character. Richardson conceived of the building as a colored church, both inside and out, and he carried out the design with a flair for scale and texture. Ashlar stonework in warm grey con-

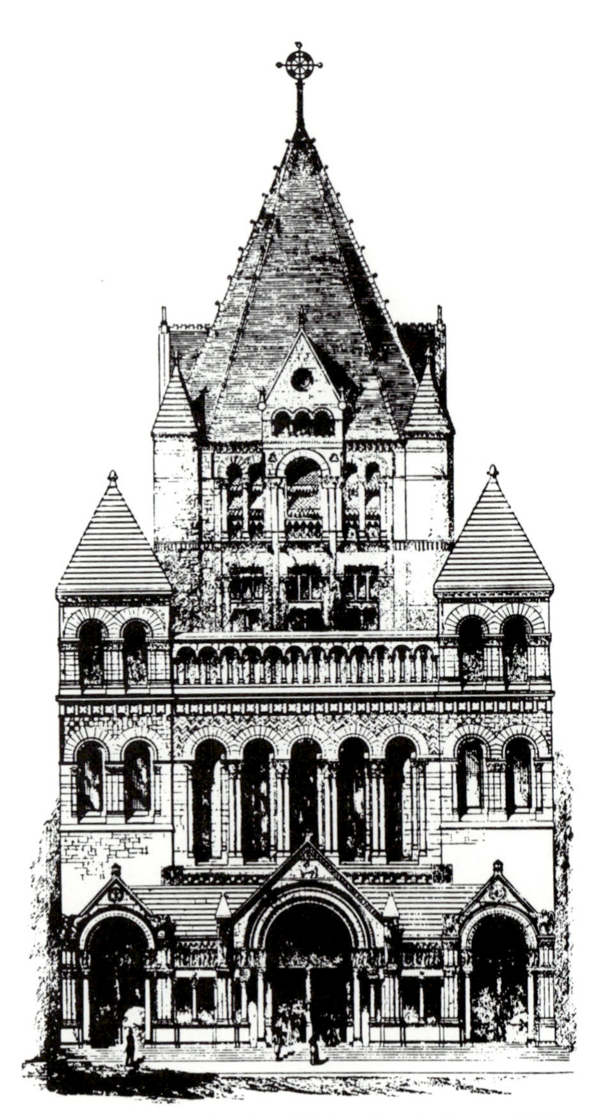

FIGURE 12.104 *Richardson: Trinity Church, Boston, 1872–1877.* (From M. van Rensselaer)

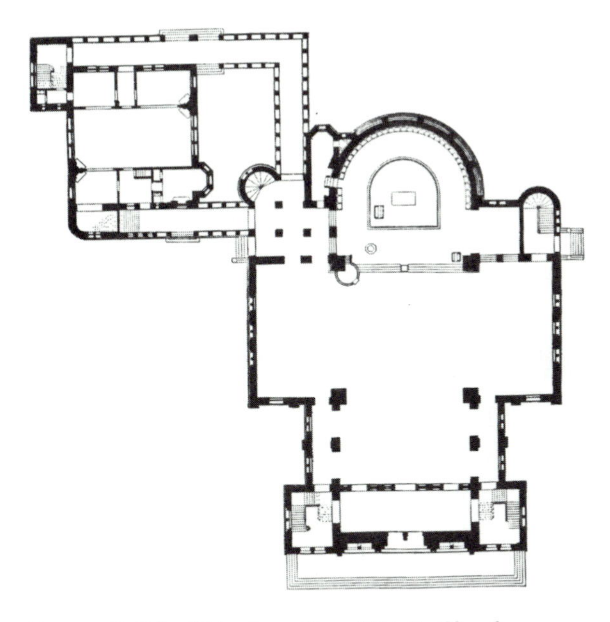

FIGURE 12.105 *Richardson: Plan of Trinity Church, Boston.* (From M. van Rensselaer)

FIGURE 12.106 *Richardson: Tower of the Brattle Square Church, Boston, 1870.* (From M. van Rensselaer)

trasts with the red-brown sandstone trim; slate roofs on the parish house set off the red clay tiles prominent on the tower roof. Murals painted by John LaFarge and his pupil Augustus Saint-Gaudens enriched the plaster walls inside; and William Morris and Edward Burne-Jones made the stained glass windows, a collaboration of artists that was entirely within the Arts and Crafts tradition. The success of Trinity Church assured the prosperity of Richardson's career, while atoning for the less satisfactory design of the earlier Brattle Square Church (1870) (Figure 12.106), which proved on completion to have faulty acoustics in the nave.

The design of Trinity Church also established what was to become Richardson's characteristic architectural style, an interpretation of the Romanesque. His use of the past was far from a slavish imitation, however, so his work is designated Richardsonian to indicate that this was not merely a revival. His adoption of Romanesque was in fact the

FIGURE 12.107 *Richardson: Marshall Field Wholesale Store, Chicago, 1885–1887.* (From M. van Rensselaer)

starting point in his search for an appropriate American building tradition, for he had not been instructed in any medieval modes at the École des Beaux-Arts. Richardson was a romantic who was inspired by the abundant stone of New England, and he worked to evolve a style worthy of its rugged massiveness and load-bearing capacities. (Technical advances in glass and metal construction had little impact on his work.) A chronicle of his major commissions illustrates the progressive development of his thinking about the expression of masonry. In 1878 he designed Sever Hall for his alma mater, Harvard University. Sever Hall is a classroom building, executed in brick to harmonize with existing structures in the Harvard Yard, but the expression Richardson has given to the material, built into a low arch at the entrance and modeled into bowfronts that resemble turrets, conveys a feeling of solidity, quite a contrast to the rather delicate Georgian buildings that are its neighbors. Two years later Richardson designed an almost symmetrical stone structure for the Law School (Austin Hall) as a free and romantic reinterpretation of Romanesque forms.

In 1885 Richardson designed two projects in Chicago, the Glessner House for a wealthy industrialist and the Marshall Field Wholesale Store (Figure 12.107). The store, now demolished, was a revela-

FIGURE 12.108 *Richardson: Glessner House, Chicago, 1885.* (From M. van Rensselaer)

FIGURE 12.109 *Richardson: Plan of Glessner House, Chicago.* (From M. van Rensselaer)

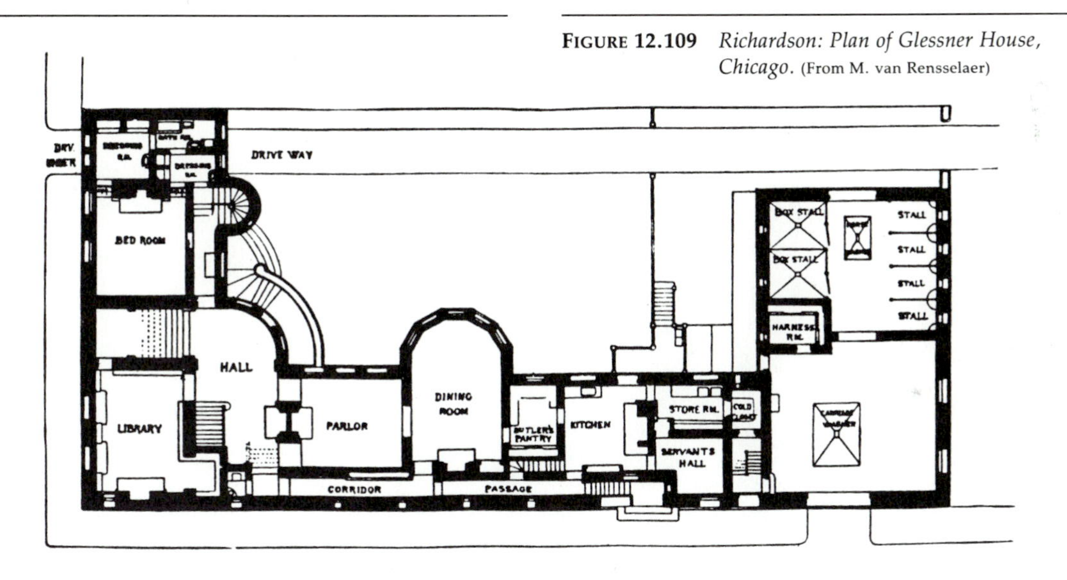

tion for architects in the city, providing a dignified and simple treatment for the six-story block. Richardson cast aside the florid ornamentation and historical trappings of earlier works, leaving the unadorned rusticated masonry and the great arched openings to convey power and monumentality. It has been proposed that Richardson's model for the great broad arches of the central stage of the Field Store may have been the Roman aqueduct at Segovia, Spain, a construction illustrated in Richardson's collection of photographs. Whatever the inspiration, Richardson succeeded in creating a design as bold and monumental as the Roman engravings of Piranesi. Behind the articulated stone bearing walls of the Field Store was an internal structural skeleton of iron. The Glessner House (Figures 12.108, 12.109) is similarly restrained and austere on the exterior, opening on an interior courtyard sheltered from street noise and dirt by the building's L-shaped plan. Another late work, the Gate Lodge (1886) for the Ames Estate in North Easton, Massachusetts, shows the almost radical directions Richardson was pursuing in his last years (Figure 12.110). Boulders are set into the masonry walls of the Lodge and ex-

FIGURE 12.110 *Richardson: Ames Gate Lodge, North Easton, 1886.* (From M. van Rensselaer)

tend into the interior as well. A massive red tile roof caps the structure, alligator-eye dormers breaking through its taut skin. Had Richardson lived beyond his forty-eight years, he would doubtless have been an even more powerful force in determining the shape of twentieth-century American architecture. As it is, his masonry works spawned a great number of Romanesque churches, town halls, libraries, and railroad stations, in addition to influencing the directions taken by Chicago School architects in designing tall buildings.

In residential commissions Richardson did much to create what became known as the Shingle Style. Built of wooden frame, these houses were given an enveloping cover of wooden shingles on both the wall and roof planes, providing a feeling of both volume and simplicity. His design for the Watts Sherman House (1874) in Newport, Rhode Island, has rusticated stone on the ground floor walls and shingles on the upper floor walls and roof, stretched like a membrane over the dormers and bay windows that articulate the façade (Figure 12.111). Great overhanging eaves on the steeply pitched roof and substantial chimneys present an irregular, picturesque profile to the sky. A later design for the Stoughton House (Figure 12.112) in Cambridge, Massachusetts (1882–1883) shows how far Richardson had gone toward simplifying the rather complex forms of the Sherman House. Here the shingle skin covers a bold composition of geometric solids arranged in an L-shaped plan. Although the design owes something to the forms of early colonial houses in New England, it transcends any one period or style, being as devoid of applied ornament as the slightly later Marshall Field Wholesale Store. The interior of the Stoughton House featured a two-story living hall, a feature originated in Pugin's design for his own house at Ramsgate.

Richardson's scheme for the Marshall Field Wholesale Store was particularly influential on the work of Louis Henri Sullivan (1856–1924), a Chicago architect who has already been mentioned as a participant in the design of the World's Columbian Exposition of 1893, where Sullivan was responsible for the design of the Transportation Building. At the time the Marshall Field Store was being completed, Sullivan (in practice with Dankmar Adler) was designing the Chicago Auditorium Building (1886–1890) (Figure 12.113), and he simplified the detail of his design after seeing Richardson's masterpiece, giving greater emphasis to the arches above entrance doors and arches for wall articulation.

FIGURE 12.112 *Richardson: Stoughton House, Cambridge, 1882–1883.* (Photo: H.A.B.S.)

◀ **FIGURE 12.111** *Richardson: Watts Sherman House, Newport, 1874.* (Photo: H.A.B.S.)

FIGURE 12.113 *Adler and Sullivan: Auditorium Building, Chicago, 1886–1890.* (Photo: H.A.B.S.)

Sullivan was as original an architect as Richardson, and his work applied traces of Neo-Classicism and Romanticism to the rapidly emerging building technologies of Chicago. Born in Boston, young Louis spent much of his childhood on his grandfather's farm north of the city, where he gained firsthand acquaintance with the natural plant forms that would later be incorporated in his architectural ornament. Determined to become an architect Sullivan spent a year in the newly created architectural program at M.I.T. and then worked briefly in the offices of Frank Furness in Philadelphia and William LeBaron Jenney in Chicago. He went to Paris in 1874 to study at the École des Beaux-Arts, where he found the teaching uninspired. After a year there, he traveled in Italy before returning to Chicago and joining the office of Dankmar Adler and Company in 1879. Adler's engineering expertise complemented Sullivan's artistic inclinations, and in 1881 the firm name became Adler and Sullivan.

Adler's demonstrated understanding of acoustics gained the firm the commission to design the Chicago Auditorium Building, one of the most complex multiuse buildings constructed in the country at that time. Its name derives from the huge 4,237-seat concert hall located in the center, but the building also contained a ten-story hotel and a seventeen-story office tower, with additional offices at the rear (Figure 12.114). Erecting all this on the muddy subsoil of Chicago challenged the engineering tal-

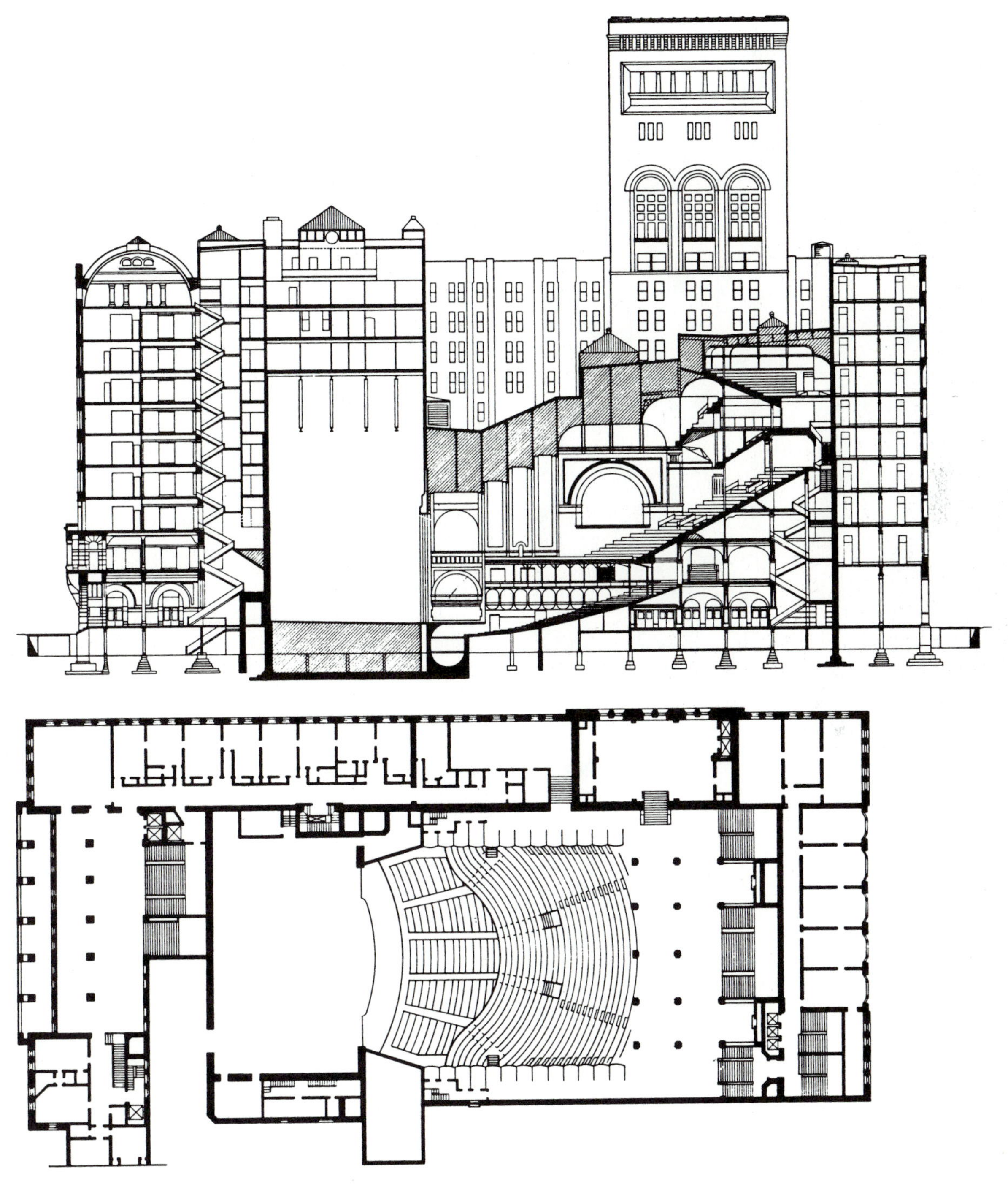

FIGURE 12.114 *Adler and Sullivan: Plan and section of the Auditorium Building, Chicago.* (From W. Blaser)

FIGURE 12.115 *Adler and Sullivan: Wainwright Building, St. Louis, 1890.* (Photo: H.A.B.S.)

ents of Adler, who also made sure that sight lines and acoustics were excellent for every seat in the auditorium. Sullivan's task was to give architectural harmony to the diverse elements of the building, and in the process he was influenced, as we have said, by the Marshall Field Wholesale Store.

Romantic that he was, Sullivan turned to Classical precedent for inspiration when he tackled the problem of artistic expression appropriate to a tall building. In 1890 a commission from a St. Louis brewer, Ellis Wainwright, gave Adler and Sullivan their first opportunity to design a skyscraper, and Sullivan's treatment of the exterior became the exemplar for much of later high-rise construction (Figures 12.115, 12.116). Rather than a layering of horizontal elements, the Wainwright Building had a base (the ground and first floor), a shaft (the rental office floors), and a capital (the top mechanical floor), just like any classical column. Sullivan in fact made this analogy to justify his design. Translated into an office building, this meant expression was given to the ground floor (where easy access could be made off the street into banks, shops, or the like) and mezzanine or second floor; rental space was concentrated on the third through top floors, where repetitive windows illuminated floor areas that could be subdivided to suit the requirements of various tenants; and a major cornice, often the height of one or more floors because it housed the mechanical units, water tanks, and elevator machinery, completed the building. Sullivan liked nothing better than to discover a general principle that was always applicable: "a rule so broad as to admit no exceptions." His most famous dictum was "form follows function," a statement not original with him. Sullivan's buildings, however, are generally poor examples of this principle in operation. The Wainwright Building, for example, has a steel frame with riveted columns behind its red granite, brick, and terra-cotta exterior cladding. The form of the exterior only partially reflects the structural function of the steelwork for every second vertical pier is a dummy, covering no steel but necessary for flexible internal planning arrangements and for the visual effect Sullivan desired. The elaborate flowing frieze adorns nothing more important than the mechanical floor.

It is better to think of Sullivan's work not in terms of "form follows function" but in terms of his original contributions to design. In addition to finding an unashamedly vertical expression for tall buildings, Sullivan evolved a characteristic ornamental style derived from natural plant forms. In fact his work can be considered part of Art Nouveau, al-

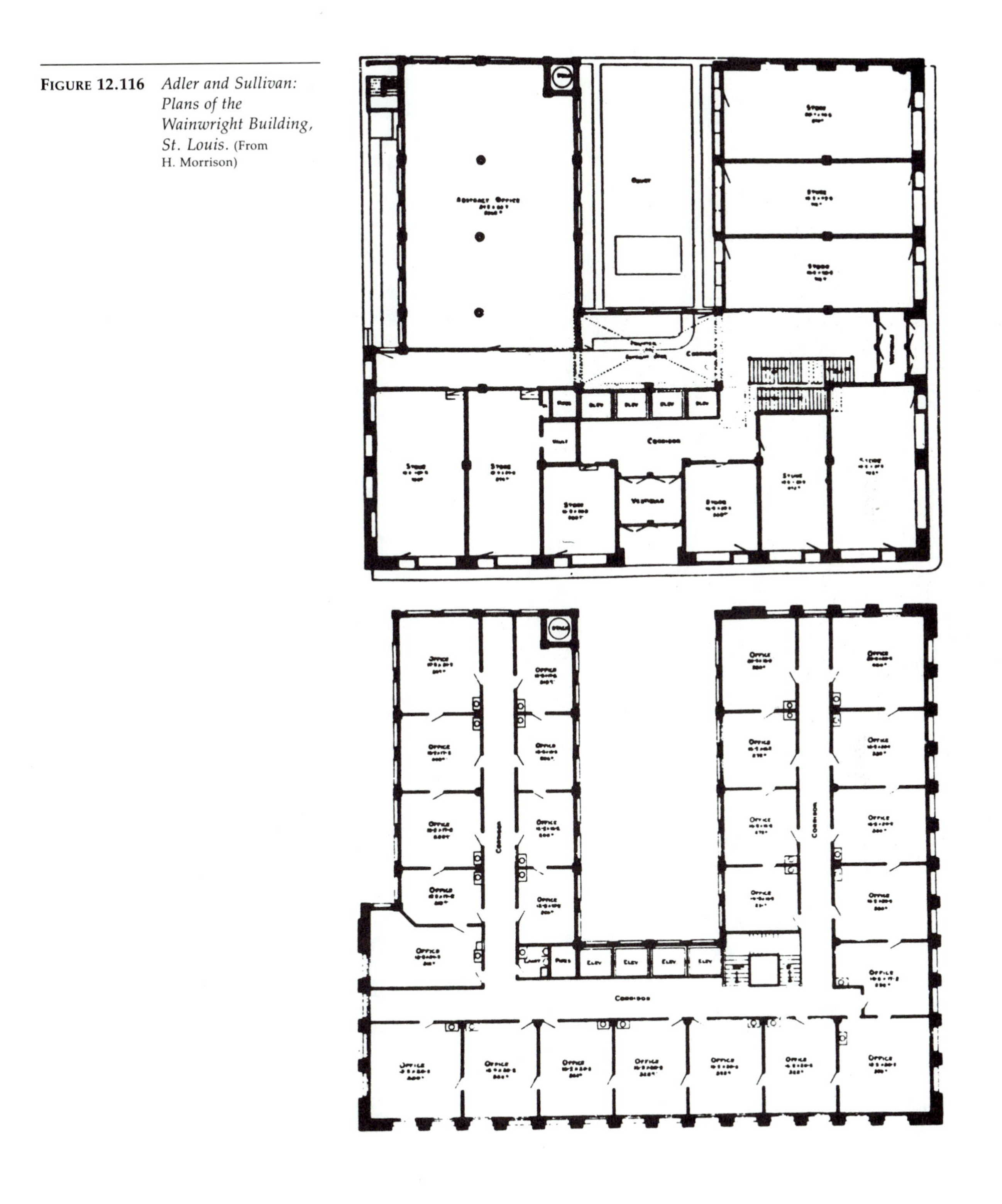

FIGURE 12.116 *Adler and Sullivan: Plans of the Wainwright Building, St. Louis.* (From H. Morrison)

though he seems neither to have been influenced by, nor to have had influence on, contemporary developments in Europe. Ornament for Sullivan was an integral part of the building's design, and his swirling circular patterns were generally designed for ease of production from a master mold or cast in terra-cotta, iron, or plaster. The Wainwright Building had ornate terra-cotta spandrels under each window and repetitive patterns on the frieze and roof **fascia.** He used essentially the same formula in the design of the Guaranty Building (1894) in Buffalo, New York (Figure 12.117).

With allowance for changing architectural fashions, Sullivan's conception of the skyscraper's composition remains valid today. In place of the brick and terra-cotta infill panels that Sullivan used, twentieth-century high-rise construction makes extensive use of glass **curtain walls,** where the lightweight frames holding the glass are brought forward of the structural columns, a technique first used by W. J. Polk in the Halladie Building (1918) in San Francisco (Figure 12.118). Under New York's zoning code of 1916, skyscraper façades were required to be tiered back from the street in relation to their height, giving the characteristic stepped profile of landmarks like the Chrysler Building and the Empire State Building. More recent codes have permitted unbroken vertical façades if a portion of the site is given over to a pedestrian plaza. This has resulted in elegant public open space at the base of the Seagram Building in New York, for example, but also in many lifeless plazas at other midtown towers. The proper massing, density, and location of high-rise buildings remains a very controversial subject for architects, urban planners, and the general public.

Sullivan used a more florid and three-dimensional ornament for the main entrance of the Carson Pirie Scott Department Store (1899–1904) in Chicago, a building that represents the maturity of Sullivan's design ideas for tall buildings (Figure 12.119). Here the large windows are set in wide bays, articulated by white terra-cotta cladding on the steel columns and spandrel panels. The overall effect of the building is more horizontal than vertical. Display windows on the ground floor are terminated by cast-iron ornamental panels that can be readily viewed from the street level. The ornament

FIGURE 12.118 *Polk: Halladie Building, San Francisco, 1918.* (Photo: Wodehouse)

becomes far more exuberant around the heads of the doorways, thereby giving emphasis to the entrance, which is further defined by its location at a slightly projecting radiused corner. Upper-level windows have slender ornamental frames. The

◀ **FIGURE 12.117** *Adler and Sullivan: Guaranty Building, Buffalo, 1894.* (Photo: H.A.B.S.)

FIGURE 12.119 *Sullivan: Carson Pirie Scott Department Store, Chicago, 1899–1904.* (Photo: H.A.B.S.)

FIGURE 12.120 *Sullivan: National Farmer's Bank, Owatonna, 1907–1908.* (Photo: © Edward S. Cunningham)

building thus provides visual rewards from several vantage points. From a distance, its austere white frame reads as a cleanly subdivided rectangular grid resting on a dark base; from a medium distance, the articulated entrance can be easily distinguished; and from a close view, one can appreciate the abundant detail around windows and doorways. With the Carson Pirie Scott Store, Sullivan achieved an integration of uninterrupted line and decorative detail that has seldom been equaled by later architects.

At the apogee of his creative powers, Sullivan's architectural practice declined precipitously. Carson Pirie Scott was to be his last major commission. He and Adler had dissolved their partnership in 1895, and neither prospered separately. Within a year Adler proposed rejoining forces, but Sullivan turned him down. Sullivan's misanthropy and growing alcoholism estranged him from his family, his wife, his professional colleagues, and most prospective clients. Between 1907 and 1924 he had only thirteen minor commissions, the most impressive of which was the National Farmer's Bank (1907–1908) in Owatonna, Minnesota (Figures 12.120, 12.121). A simple rectangular solid with one enormous semi-

FIGURE 12.122 *Sullivan: Foliated ornament design.* (From L. Sullivan)

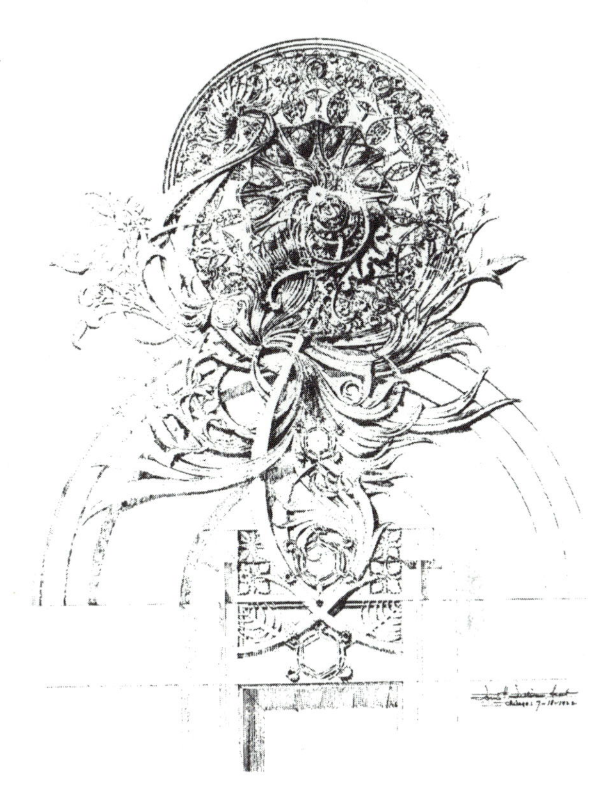

circular arch on each street front, the bank could be taken for a Neo-Classic composition if one disregarded the large inset ornament in terra-cotta, cast iron, and glass mosaic. The bank's form expresses security and dignity, desirable attributes for a financial institution, and it led to commissions for several other bank designs in scattered small midwestern towns. During this period Sullivan turned to writing, producing the articles that were later collected and published as *Kindergarten Chats,* his autobiography, and plates for *A System of Architectural Ornament* (Figure 12.112). The pessimistic observations contained in these works reflect his bitterness toward the world, which had by then virtually forgotten him. The important contributions he made to architecture and the influence he had on the young Frank Lloyd Wright, however, assure Sullivan's place in architectural history.

FIGURE 12.121 *Sullivan: Interior of the National Farmer's Bank, Owatonna.* (Photo: Courtesy Norwest Bank, Owatonna)

13.

Twentieth-Century Modern

Architecture of the twentieth century has been dominated by three major practitioners, sometimes termed the masters of modern architecture. They are Frank Lloyd Wright, Le Corbusier, and Ludwig Mies van der Rohe. Walter Gropius is often added to the group, although his most significant contributions were made in the field of architectural education. None of these architects evolved in a vacuum; all were influenced by earlier architects, the use of new materials of construction, and other artistic movements. For example, it would be difficult to conceive of Wright without the influence of Richardson, Sullivan, and the Arts and Crafts Movement. In turn, Wright had a profound influence on architects in Europe, mainly because of the 1910 publication of his early works by Ernst Wasmuth in Berlin. Through the Wasmuth portfolio, Wright's work influenced the Dutch de Stijl Movement, which had an effect on Gropius and the Bauhaus. Both Mies and Le Corbusier admitted their indebtedness to Wright, and in many respects, they emulated his designs. In addition to his borrowings from Wright, Mies looks back to Schinkel through the eyes of his master, Peter Behrens, while Le Corbusier is tied into developments in concrete construction of August Perret and the ideas of city planning espoused by Tony Garnier. Twentieth-century design is thus an intricate web of artistic influences, talented individual designers, and varied building opportunities.

FRANK LLOYD WRIGHT

Brief though it was, Louis Sullivan's architectural career profoundly influenced Frank Lloyd Wright (1867–1959). Wright was born in Wisconsin, the son of a domineering Welsh mother and an itinerant preacher-musician father, and he grew up in a variety of locations until his mother moved back near her family's holdings in Wisconsin when Wright was eleven. There he worked on his uncle's farm and attended school sporadically, all the while involving himself in drawing, crafts, painting, and printing. Wright's mother had decided before his birth that her son would become an architect, so she encouraged his interest in artistic and spatial investigations. After his parents divorced in 1885, Wright dropped out of high school and worked as an office boy for a professor of civil engineering at the University of Wisconsin. He later entered the university's evening school as a special student, taking one semester of descriptive geometry and French, a class he dropped. At the age of nineteen, he went to Chicago and found employment in the architectural office of Joseph Lyman Silsbee, a friend of his

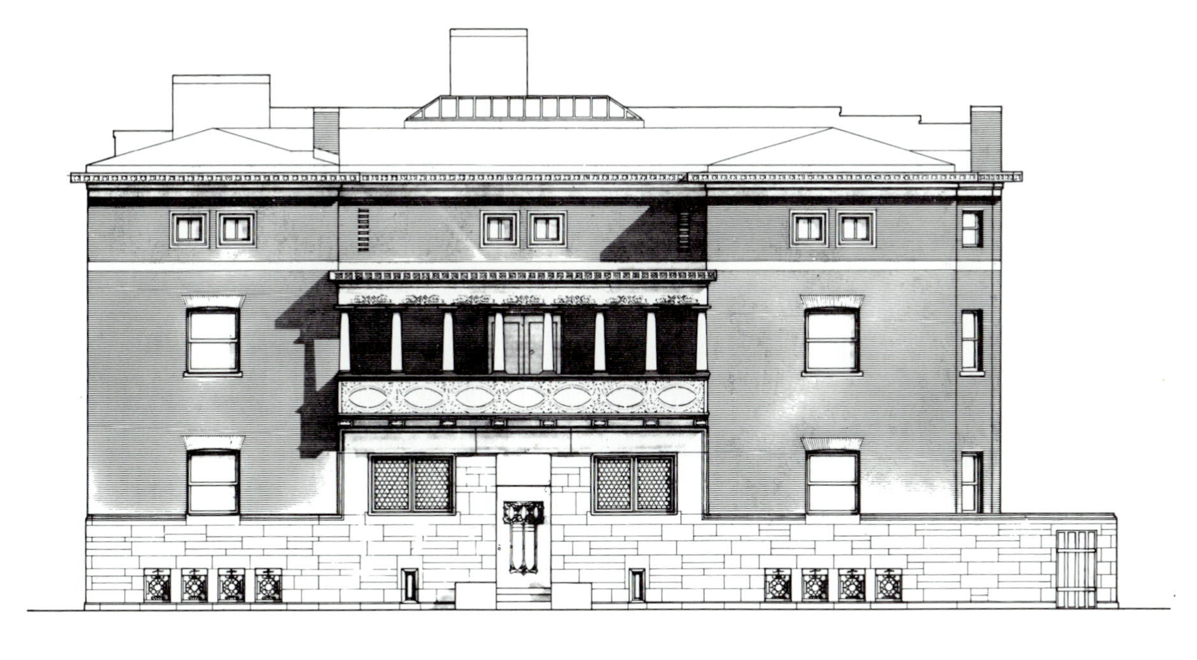

Figure 13.1 *Adler and Sullivan: Elevation of the Charnley House, Chicago, 1891.* (Courtesy, S.O.M. Foundation)

uncle's. Wright's ambition, however, was to work for Adler and Sullivan, and he practiced drawing Sullivanesque ornament so he could make a favorable impression at the job interview.

In 1888 he landed a job there, demonstrating his graphic skill to Sullivan's satisfaction and gaining a five-year contract as draftsman. With an advance on his salary Wright began construction on his own house (1889) in the Chicago suburb of Oak Park. The house began as a modest two-story building, with a Serliana in the shingle-covered gable end turned to the street. Over the years, as Wright's family grew to include six children and his mother, the house was greatly enlarged and reworked. In the office of Adler and Sullivan Wright was sometimes given a free hand with residential commissions, such as that for the James Charnley House (1891), a two-story structure on a narrow city lot in Chicago (Figures 13.1–13.3). Wright's symmetrical design has a central doorway with carved Sullivanesque ornament below a second-level loggia with Doric columns.

Wright began designing other houses outside of office time, a practice Sullivan denounced as a violation of Wright's contract with Adler and Sullivan when he discovered what was going on. Wright was fired and established his own practice, which would be based in a studio built onto his Oak Park house. His early years of independent practice were characterized by explorations of many styles of domestic architecture — Colonial, Tudor, Georgian, Shingle Style, and Queen Anne — although Wright later edited his work to reveal only those designs that contributed to the development of the Prairie House. Among these is his first independent commission, a house for William H. Winslow (1893) in River Forest, Illinois (Figures 13.4, 13.5). Like the Charnley House, the Winslow House is symmetrical with Sullivanesque ornament. Like the later Prairie houses, the Winslow house is organized around a central fireplace and dominated by a sense of horizontality. The hipped roof overhangs the second floor at the level of the window heads, and the apparent height of the ground floor extends to the

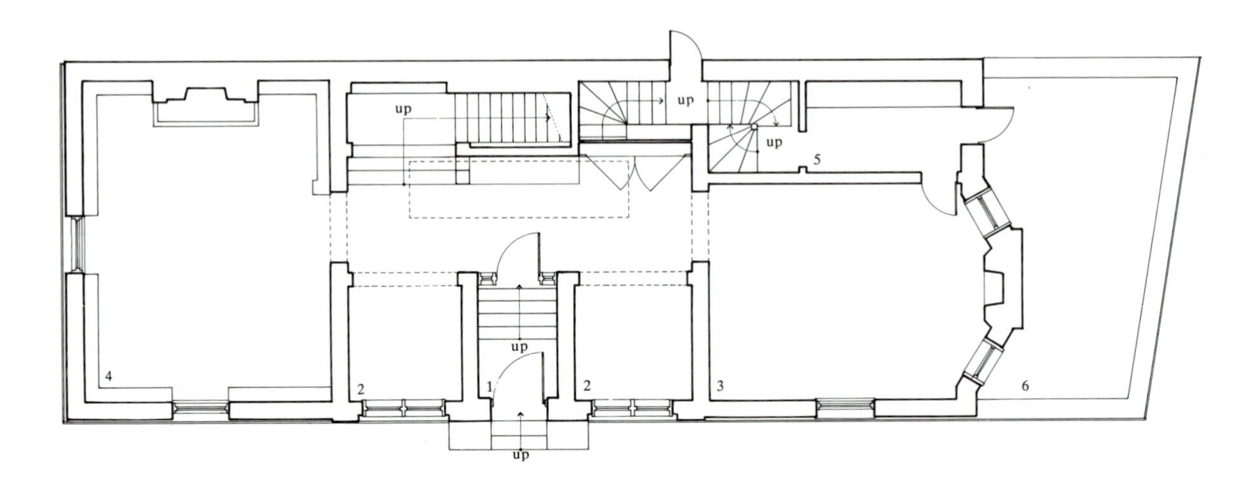

First Floor Plan

1. Entry Vestibule
2. Alcove
3. Dining Room
4. Living Room
5. Butler's Pantry
6. Service Court

north 0 2 4 8 16'

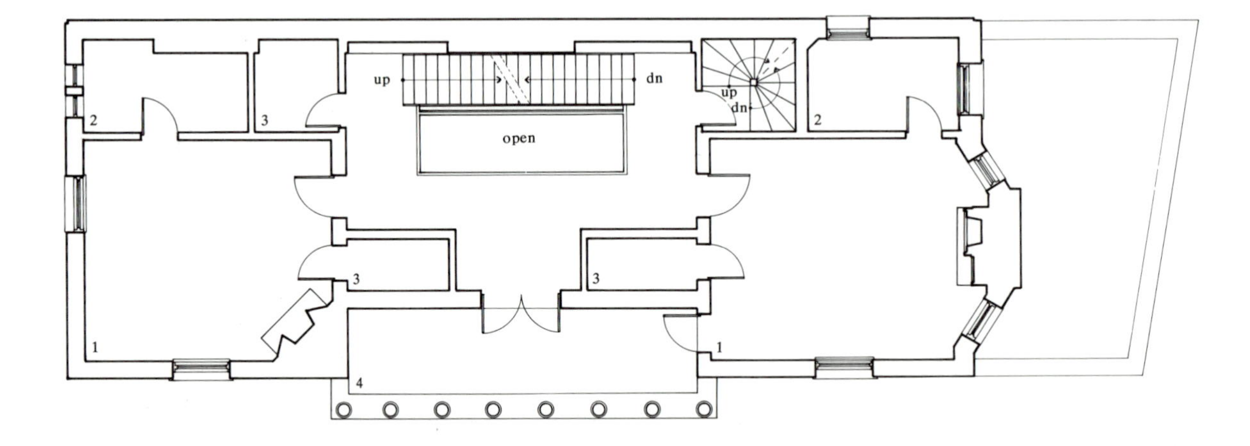

Second Floor Plan

1. Bedroom
2. Bathroom
3. Storage
4. Outdoor Porch

north 0 2 4 8 16'

FIGURE 13.2 *Adler and Sullivan: First and second floor plans of the Charnley House, Chicago.* (Courtesy, S.O.M. Foundation)

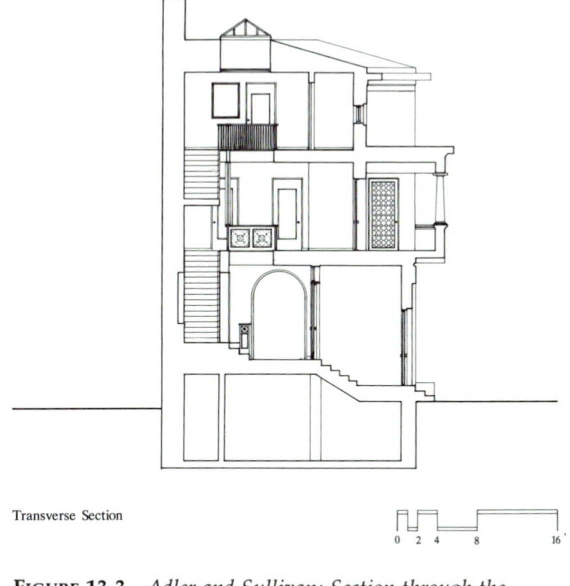

FIGURE 13.3 *Adler and Sullivan: Section through the Charnley House, Chicago.* (Courtesy, S.O.M. Foundation)

second-floor windowsills, effectively reducing the perceived volume of the upper level and creating the impression that the building hugs the ground. Even the chimney mass has been broadened to emphasize the horizontal aspect rather than the vertical.

With the design of the Ward Willits House (1901) in Highland Park, Illinois, Wright abandoned the compact composition of the Winslow House for a cruciform plan (a commonly used plan in many houses of the period 1900–1910) of four arms extending out into the landscape from the central chimney mass (Figure 13.6). Again the horizontal line dominated the exterior, accentuated by the overhanging eaves of the roofline and the extension of the transverse axis of the house to form a porte-cochere (a covered drive-through for vehicles) at one end and a covered porch at the other. The exterior stucco was banded by continuous horizontal strips of dark wood marking the first-floor level and the windowsill line. By lowering the eaves to the level of the window heads and diminishing the chimney's height, Wright again minimized the vertical component of this two-story house.

Wright developed the Prairie House out of his search for an appropriate regional expression for American homes, especially in the midwest. Taking his cue from the gently rolling land of the prairie, he designed houses that sat close to the ground and seemed to be tied organically to the landscape. The

FIGURE 13.4 *Wright: Winslow House, River Forest, 1893.* (From F. L. Wright)

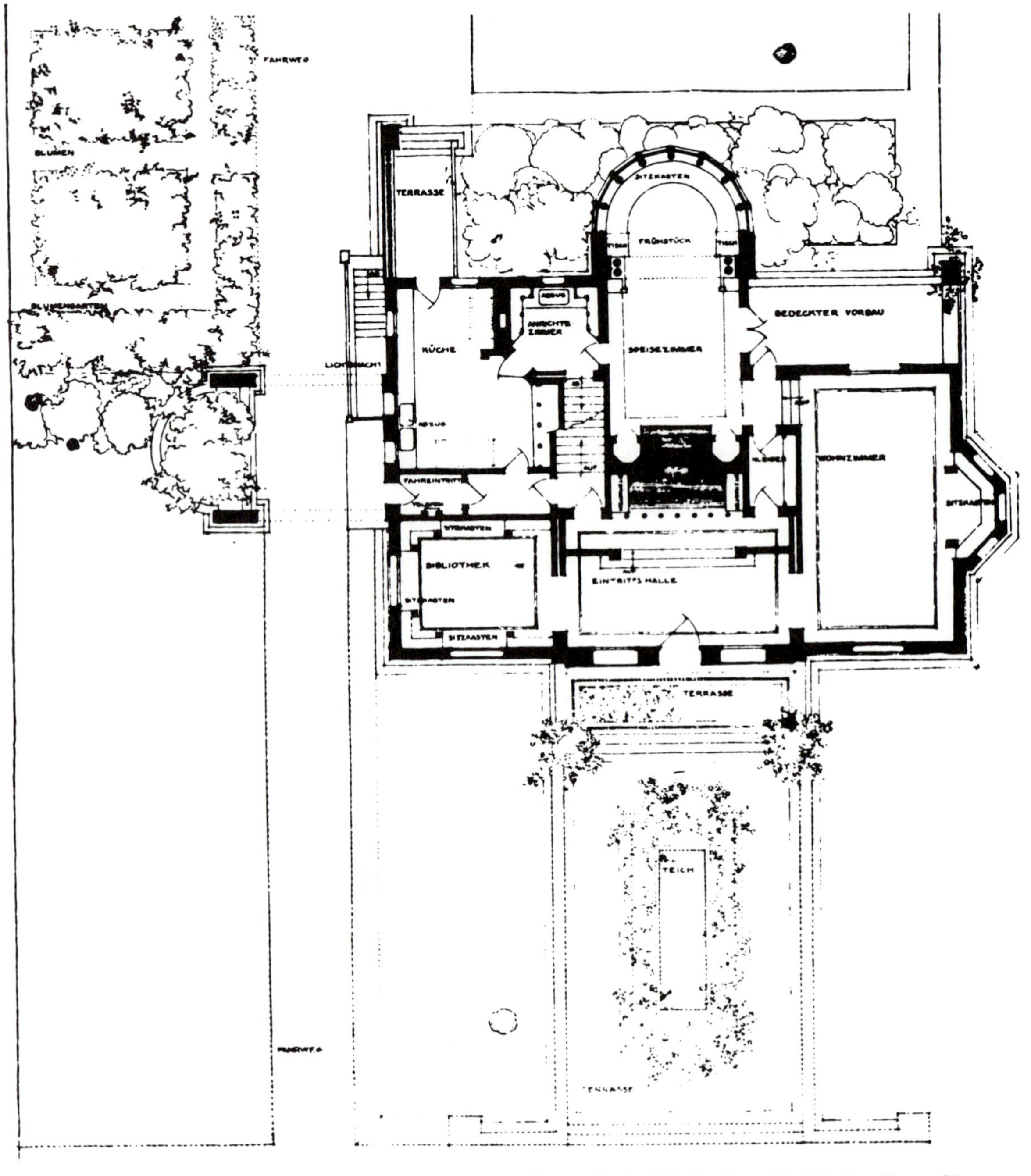

FIGURE 13.5 *Wright: Plan of the Winslow House, River Forest.* (From F. L. Wright)

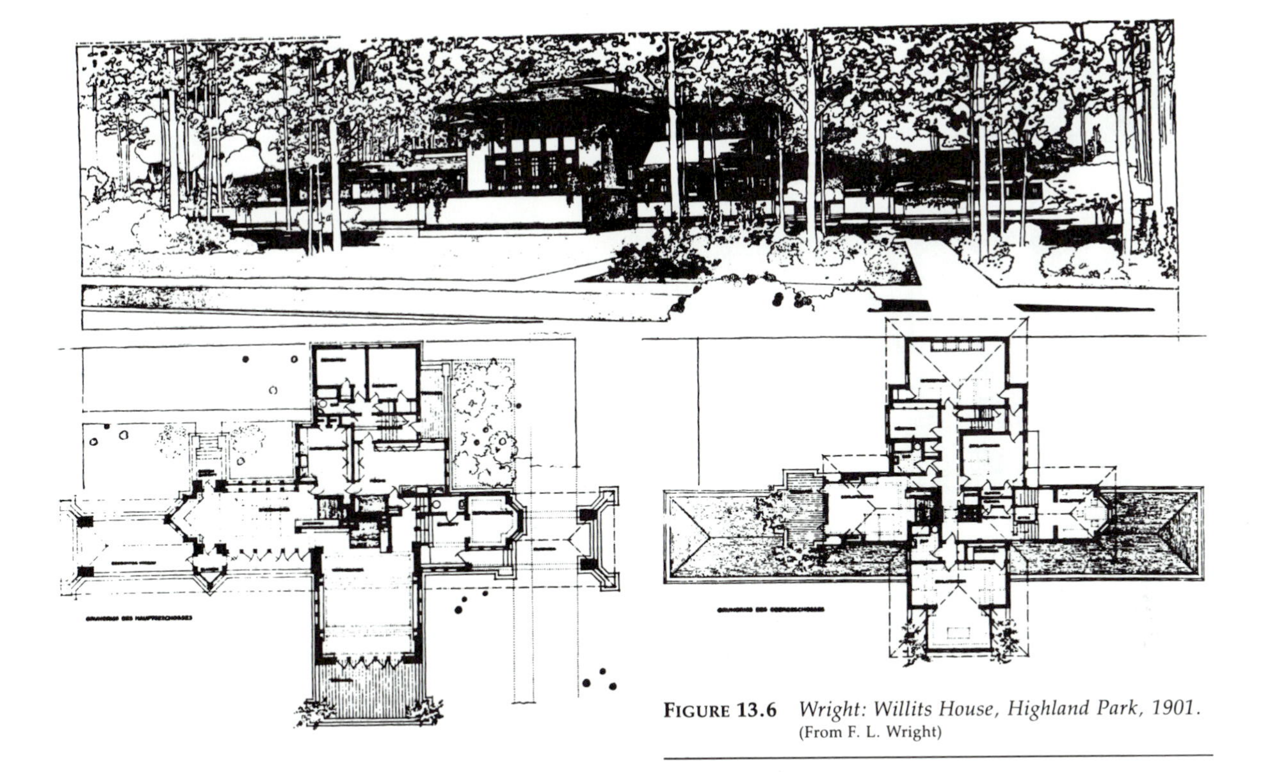

FIGURE 13.6 *Wright: Willits House, Highland Park, 1901.* (From F. L. Wright)

prevailing eclectic Victorian styles, which he had tried and discarded, Wright dismissed as "pimples" on the land. Wright was also challenged by the prevailing materials of construction, including brick and wood cut in standard sizes by sawmills, and he tried to devise uses for them that were sympathetic with the nature of the material and its modes of fabrication. Environmental factors also affected the designs. The broad overhanging eaves shielded the windows from the hot Chicago sun while permitting the lower winter rays to enter and warm the house. The central fireplace mass gave warmth to the heart of the home, both functionally and symbolically. All major rooms were oriented to provide cross-ventilation. Some of the most remarkable aspects of the Prairie houses are evident on the interior, where the living spaces of the house flow smoothly from one area to another, creating an integrated spatial experience that was to have profound influence on early modernist architects in Europe. Wright's Prairie houses are said to have "broken out of the box" because neither the external form nor the internal spaces are contained in tight rectangular units. Even the windows wrap around corners as if to deny the traditional structural corner post. The spatial freedom of the two-story living hall used by Richardson and Pugin has been extended to the entire interior, with corresponding freedom being given to the exterior as it embraces the landscape.

Wright incorporated all these features on even the most difficult of sites, such as the narrow suburban lot of Elizabeth Gale, an Oak Park neighbor for whom he designed a house in 1909 (Figure 13.7). Hemmed in by Victorian hulks on either side, the Gale House had little opportunity to spread out to the landscape, so Wright provided the visual link between interior and exterior with a series of balconies cantilevered off the major living spaces. He would return to this idea later when faced with the far more dramatic hillside site of the Kaufmann House (1935–1936).

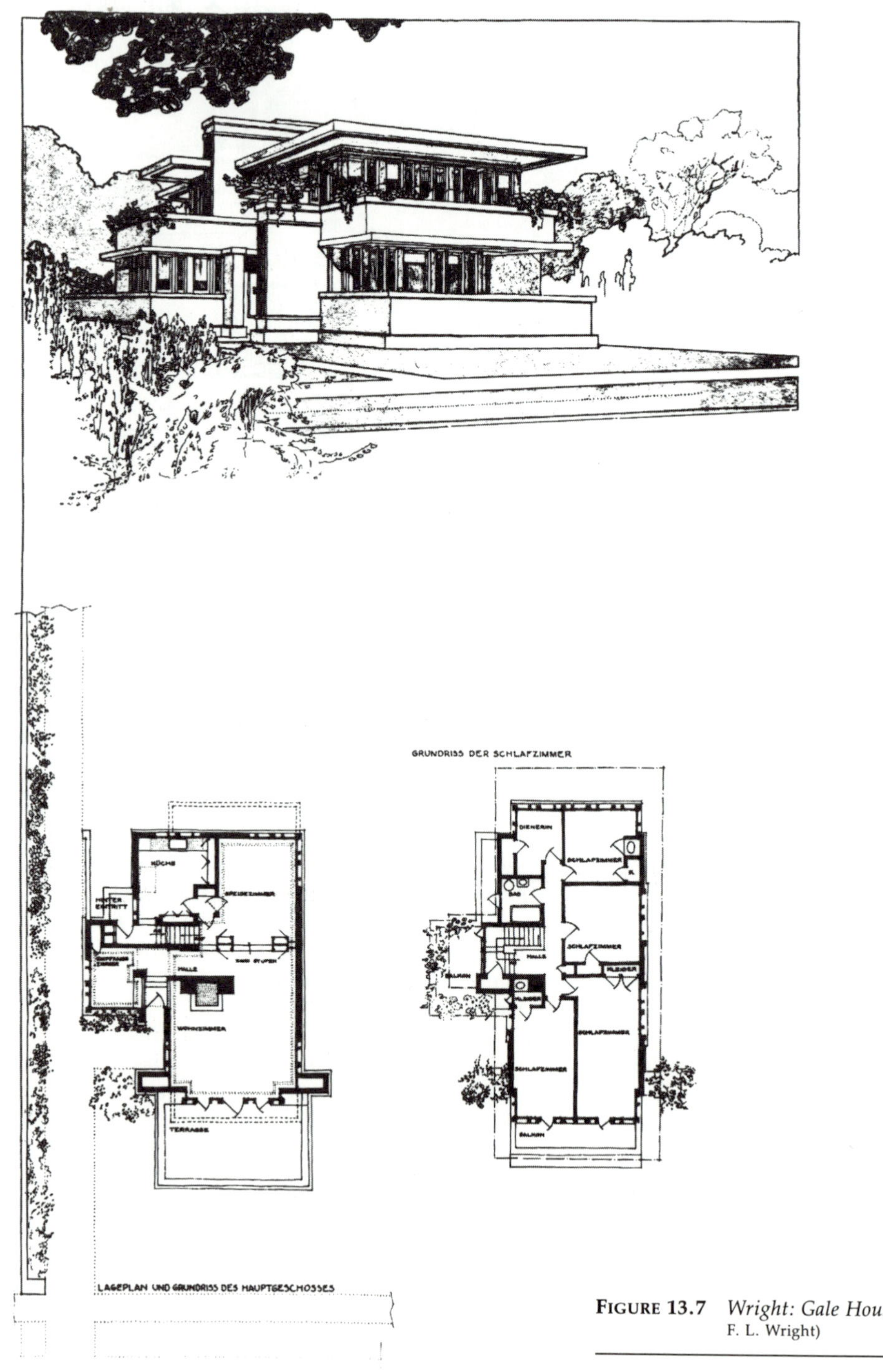

FIGURE 13.7 *Wright: Gale House, Oak Park, 1909.* (From F. L. Wright)

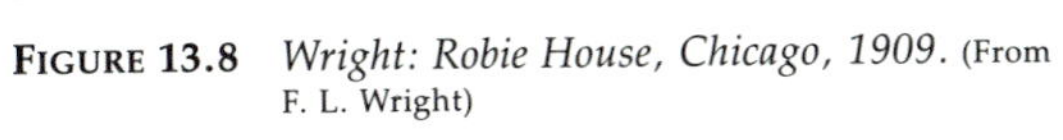

FIGURE 13.8 *Wright: Robie House, Chicago, 1909.* (From F. L. Wright)

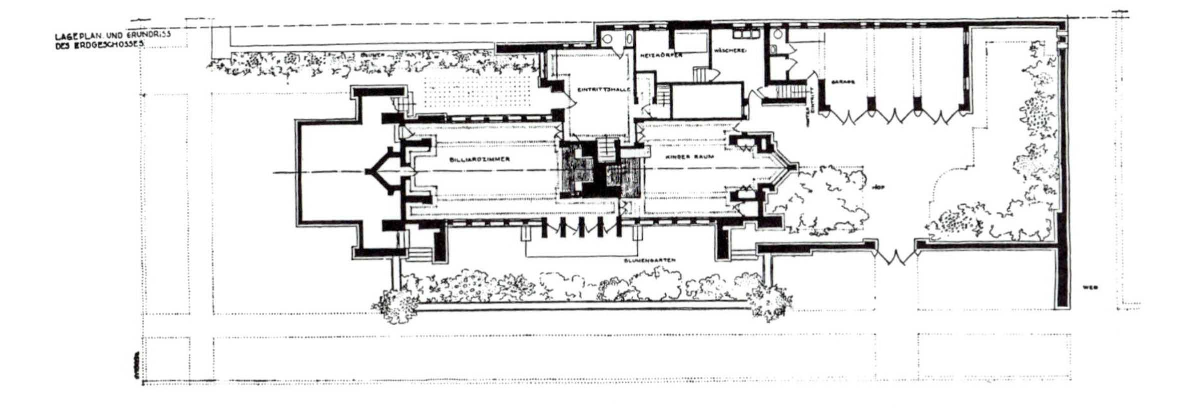

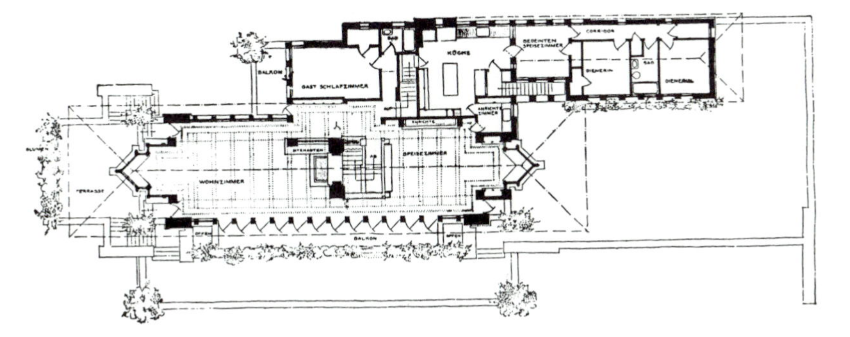

FIGURE 13.9 *Wright: Plans of the Robie House, Chicago.* (From F. L. Wright)

The last and by far the most celebrated of the early Prairie houses was built for Frederick Robie on two small corner lots in South Chicago in 1909 (Figures 13.8, 13.9). Robie was a self-made manufacturer who had an interest in engineering, and he and Wright got along exceedingly well. Robie requested a house where he could have privacy from the street and separation from the noise of his small children at play. Wright's response was a three-story design, with the garage, playroom, and service functions on the ground floor, the living and dining areas on the second floor, and bedrooms on the third. A wall extended around the ground floor to screen that floor from the view of passersby, and the elevated windows of the second floor, protected by a balcony, created the privacy Robie desired. A horizontal element was created by the long lines of the walls and balconies, but especially by the great roof of the second floor, which cantilevered daringly at either end of the house. Welded steel beams made this structural bravura possible, and their employment in the Robie House marked the first use of welded steel in residential construction. Bricks for the house, as for other Prairie houses, were custom-made in St. Louis. Shaped like the long, thin Roman bricks, they were laid with wide horizontal mortar joints that were sharply raked to cast a horizontal shadow.

In plan the house was organized around the chimney mass. The entrance was off the short side street frontage into the rear of the house, and the staircase that led to the second floor was integrated with the masonry of the chimney. The living room and dining room were in effect one continuous space, interrupted only partly by the fireplace, so that the great linear room, illuminated by long bands of windows on either side of the living space, was airy and integrated. Wright designed all the interior fittings to complement the space — the light fixtures, furniture, carpets, and even clothing for Mrs. Robie to wear when entertaining. All this was very much in the Arts and Crafts tradition, except for the fact that the designs, especially for the furniture, were based on primary geometric forms and crisp, uncompromising, right angles. This made the chairs and tables fit the space well, but all too often the furniture did not fit the nonorthogonal curves of the human body. Wright's furniture was designed to be correct visually rather than to accommodate the user.

Wright's early years as an architect were not entirely devoted to residential commissions. Two notable designs, the Larkin Building in Buffalo, New York, and Unity Church in Oak Park, illustrate his approach to public buildings. The Larkin Building (1904) (Figure 13.10) contained offices for a company that sold packaged soap with coupons printed on the labels. Consumers could save these coupons and redeem them for prizes, a practice ubiquitous today among merchants of breakfast cereals but novel at the turn of the century. The Larkin Building was populated with rows of young ladies handling clerical tasks and even more rows of filing cabinets holding the paperwork. For them Wright designed a frankly vertical six-story building with a full-height skylit atrium at the center (Figure 13.11). Banks of filing cabinets were placed in partitions or against the exterior wall with windows above them; light from the atrium balanced the illumination on each floor. Massed plantings at either end of the atrium introduced the natural environment to the work space, and uplifting moralizing inscriptions, such as "Honest labor needs no master. Simple justice needs no slaves," were cast in the spandrels and placed around the exterior fountains to inspire the workforce. The custom-designed metal furniture used throughout included chairs pivoted to the desks so that after hours the back would fold down on the seat and the entire chair would swing out of the way of the cleaning crew's mops. The exterior of the building was rather austere, rising as an uninterrupted vertical brick mass to the height of a thin string course carefully placed to mark the parapet wall around the rooftop recreation space. The stairs, located in all four corners, rose as towers distinct from the building mass, leaving the walls in between to be articulated by repetitive bands of windows. As an office building design, the Larkin Building was forward looking. Entirely ventilation-controlled, with filtered air intake and extract ducts in the stair towers, it was planned for modular furnishings and flexibility, while provisions made for employee recreation anticipate the corporate health clubs of the present day. It became one of Wright's most widely published designs, especially in Europe where it was emulated by various designers,

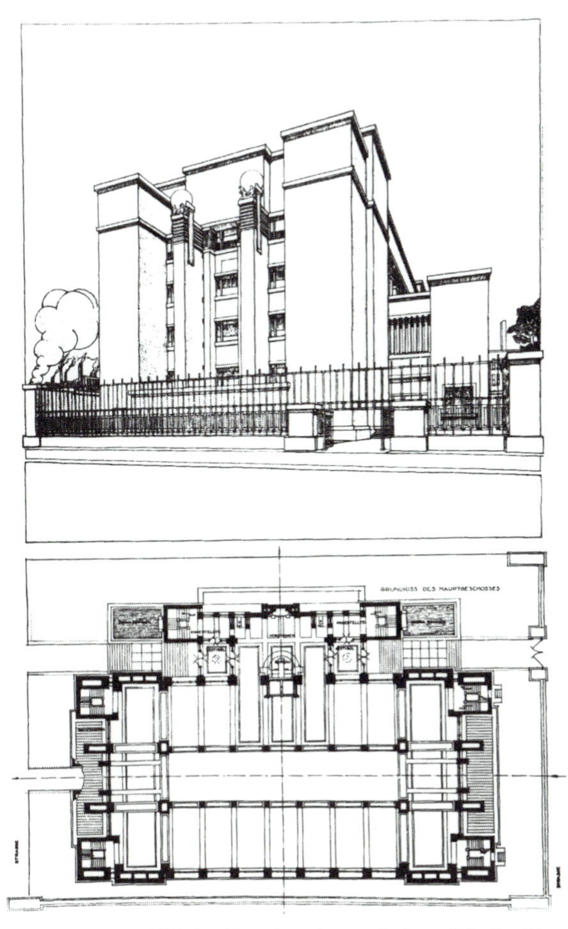

FIGURE 13.10 *Wright: Exterior view and plan of the Larkin Building, Buffalo, 1904.* (From F. L. Wright)

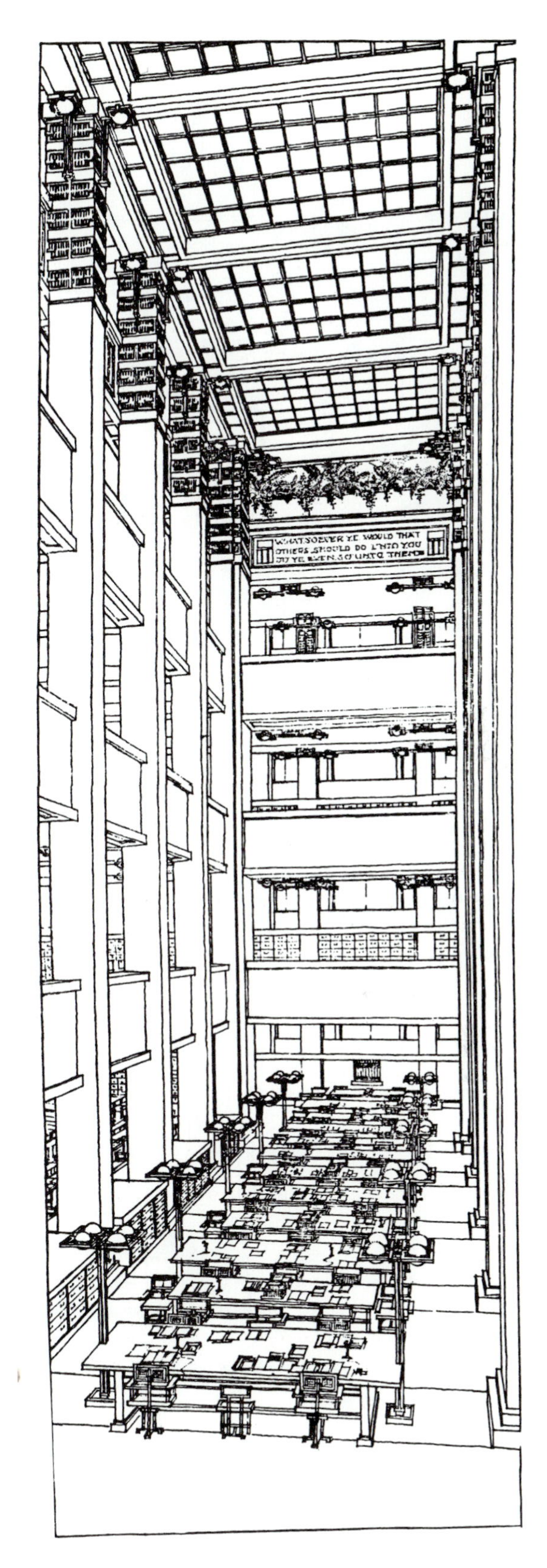

making it all the more unfortunate that the City of Buffalo demolished the building in 1949 to create a parking lot.

A happier fate has been the lot of Unity Church (Figures 13.12, 13.13), built in 1906 for the Unitarian-Universalist congregation of Oak Park. The site was on the corner of two particularly busy

FIGURE 13.11 *Wright: Interior atrium of the Larkin Building, Buffalo, 1904.* (From F. L. Wright) ▶

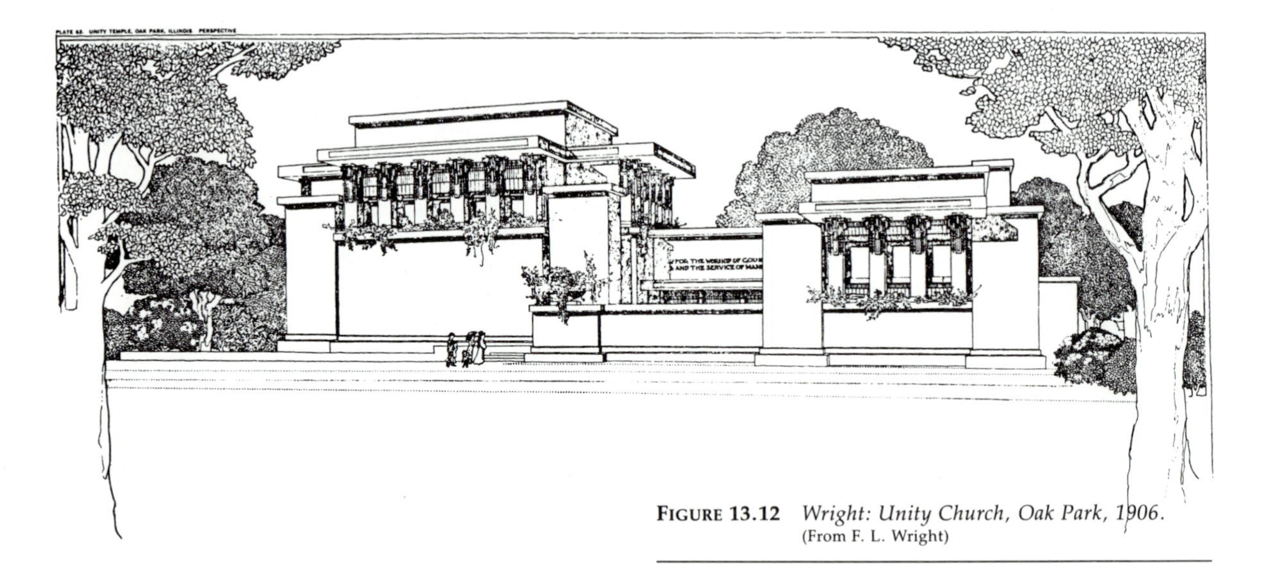

Figure 13.12 *Wright: Unity Church, Oak Park, 1906.* (From F. L. Wright)

Figure 13.13 *Wright: Plan of Unity Church, Oak Park.* (From F. L. Wright)

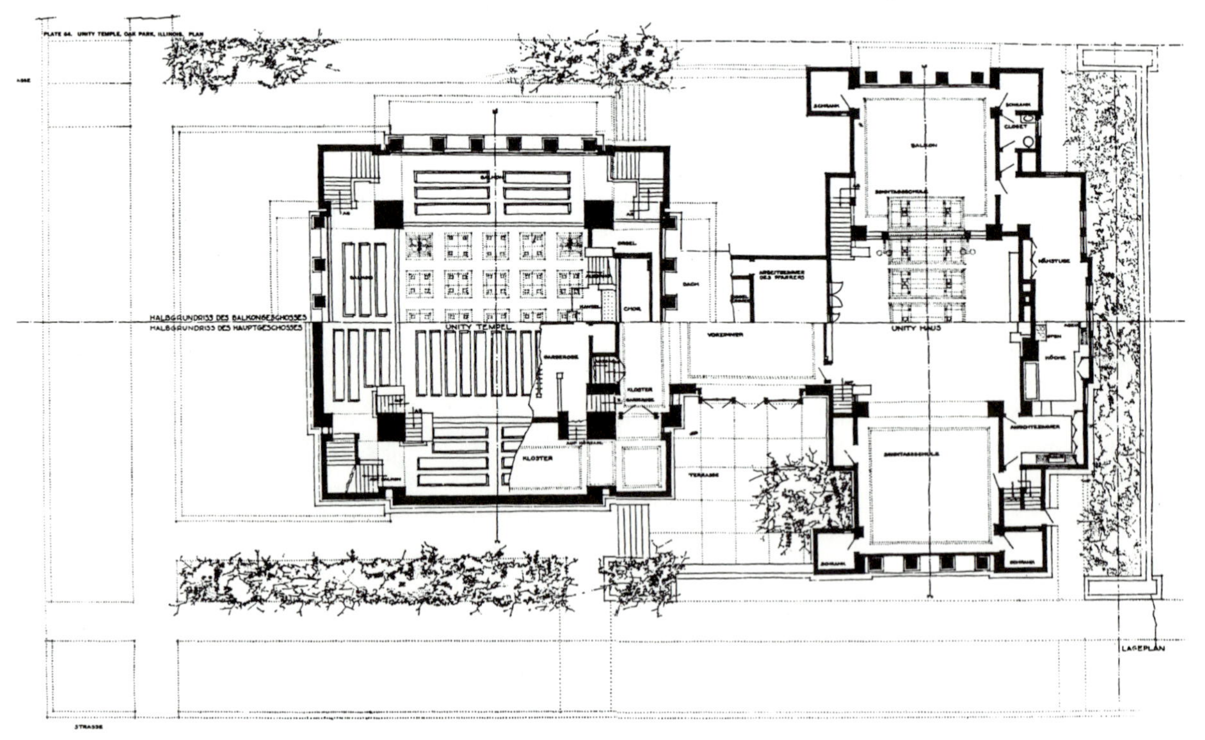

thoroughfares, and Wright turned the building inward to reduce the impact of street noise. The two major elements of the church, the worship space and the parish house, are connected by a vestibule, which they share equally, neatly solving at once the problems of entrance and separation of the noise of Sunday School classes from adult worship. Unity Temple, the worship space, was an articulated cube with two levels of balconies on three walls facing the pulpit on the fourth. It is a rich and glowing interior. Light from leaded glass windows high in the wall balances that from the deeply-coffered, amber-colored skylights over the major congregational seating in the center of the main floor. To the extent possible the interior trim conforms to orthogonal geometries composed of thin strips of wood. The lights, also designed by Wright, are either spheres or cubes of glass suspended from wooden frames.

Equally remarkable is the exterior, which is fabricated entirely in poured concrete. Unity Church was Wright's first essay in concrete, and it was also one of the first attempts anywhere to design straightforwardly with that material, instead of covering it or disguising the surface to resemble stone. Discrete geometric ornament was designed in the formwork of the piers between the high windows, and the same treatment was given the smaller and lower Unity House, which contained the parish house and Sunday School rooms. The church stands today, carefully restored, and still serving its original functions.

By 1909 Wright was well established as an architect, and his reputation had spread abroad. Public and professional acceptance did not bring happiness, however, and he felt increasingly hemmed in by family cares and office routine. When an offer came from Ernst Wasmuth, a prestigious Berlin publisher, to prepare a portfolio of his work for publication, Wright jumped at the chance to escape. Leaving behind his wife and six children, he took with him the wife of a client and neighbor, Mamah Borthwick Cheney, who left her husband and three children, and together they traveled to Europe in September of 1909. For the next twenty-five years, Wright's turbulent personal life seriously interfered with his professional work, and he built very little. The publications in 1910 and 1911 of the Wasmuth portfolios, *Ausgeführte Bauten und Entwürfe* (Executed Buildings and Projects), had enormous impact on European architects, but the press in the United States primarily covered the scandal in his private affairs.

In this difficult period the only major commission Wright received was for the Imperial Hotel in Tokyo (1916–1922) (Figure 13.14), remembered now chiefly for its ingenious foundations and cantilevered structural system. The very muddy subsoil conditions of the hotel site prompted Wright to float the foundations instead of digging further for bedrock. All of Japan is prone to earthquake hazard, so Wright sought to balance the building in sections on central concrete pile clusters with a cantilevered concrete slab on top, much as a waiter balances a tray on his raised fingertips. The hotel was designed around courtyards with a pool of water in front of the entrance, both for beauty and for fire fighting in case of earthquakes. Its form was complex and its decoration lavish with little of the spare qualities Wright so admired in Japanese woodblock prints. Indeed most of the decorative motifs and their manner of application owe more to the Aztec, Toltec, and Mayan cultures of central America than to anything Oriental. Decorative caprice aside, the structural system worked as intended in the severe earthquake of 1923, one of the few triumphs Wright could record for that unfortunate year. Over subsequent years, differential settlement, aided by a lowering of the water table under the area, caused large cracks in the building, and the demand for larger, air-conditioned hotel accommodations made Wright's scheme increasingly obsolete. It was demolished in the late 1960s to make room for a high-rise.

The architectural career of Frank Lloyd Wright was not over in 1920 for he would enter another phase of great productivity in the mid-1930s. Those works will be discussed later in this chapter along with projects of that same time period.

CONCRETE

Just as the development of metal-frame construction was one of the major engineering contributions of the nineteenth century, the development of reinforced concrete has been an important aspect of twentieth-century engineering. Although the idea

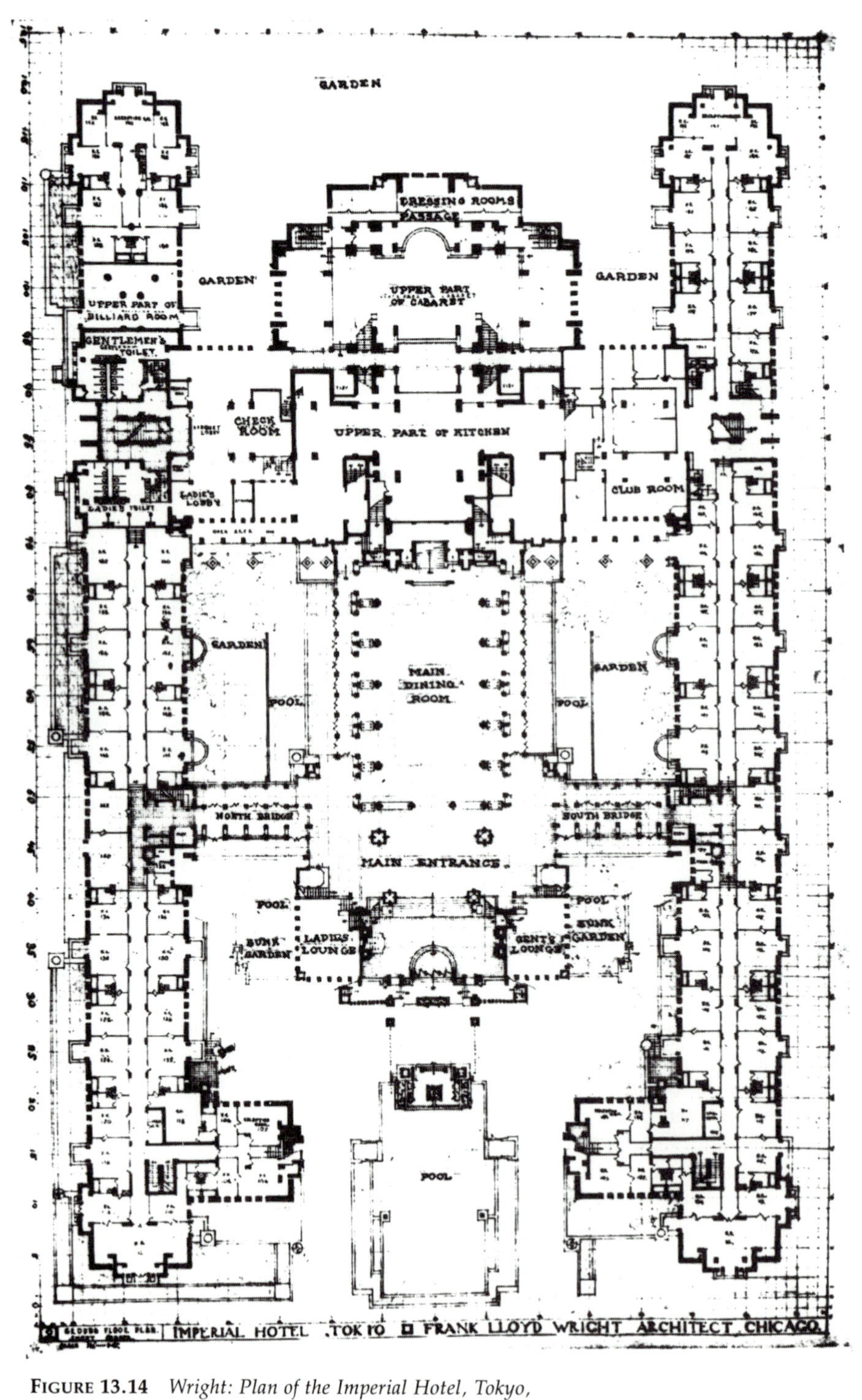

FIGURE 13.14 *Wright: Plan of the Imperial Hotel, Tokyo, 1916–1922.* (Courtesy *Architectural Record*)

of reinforcing concrete with metal rods originated in the late nineteenth-century, the technique was not extensively exploited for building construction until the twentieth century. Outstanding engineers, including Robert Maillart, Pier Luigi Nervi, and Felix Candela, contributed innovative bridge, shell, and frame constructions in concrete.

Concrete, a mixture of sand, gravel, water, and cement that hardens to a stonelike consistency, has proved to be a versatile building material in which the binding properties of the cement are most important. The Romans acquired from the Greeks a lime mortar made by burning finely broken limestone and grinding the result. By chance they discovered that adding the volcanic earth (pozzuolana) occurring near Naples improved the setting qualities of the mortar, enabling the resulting concrete to harden even if under water. They made wide use of this discovery, and Vitruvius reported on it in his *Ten Books on Architecture*: "There is also a kind of powder which, by nature, produces wonderful results. It is found in the neighborhood of Baiae and in the lands of the municipalities round Mount Vesuvius. This being mixed with lime and rubble, not only furnishes strength to other buildings, but also, when piers are built in the sea, they set under water." Many Roman buildings, including the Pantheon, were constructed of concrete with brick aggregate and marble facing.

The art of working with concrete declined with the Romans, however, and it remained for the inventors of the nineteenth century to devise a means of synthesizing the qualities of naturally occurring pozzuolana. Deposits of natural cements were exploited in Europe and the United States, but a reliable and easily manufactured artificial product was obviously required. In 1824 the Englishman Joseph Aspdin was granted a patent for his process, which involved heating a mixture of chalk and clay to 2550° Fahrenheit (the point of vitrification) and then grinding the result. He named his product Portland cement, because it resembled an especially strong limestone found around Portland, England. Portland cement is still the basis for modern concrete work.

Like stone, concrete is very good at carrying loads in compression, making it most useful for elements like foundations. The idea of incorporating iron in the mass to improve its qualities in tension was proposed as early as 1808, although widespread use of the idea awaited improvements in the cement. In 1854 Wilkenson patented a system of concrete floor slabs reinforced with wrought-iron bars, and a boat made of reinforced concrete was shown at the Paris Exhibition of 1855. Joseph Monier, a Paris gardener, obtained a patent in 1867 for his wire-mesh-reinforced flower pots, where the metal provided tensile strength and shape to the pot. He soon expanded to produce larger containers, pipes, and railroad ties, although the theoretical basis for the structural behavior of reinforced concrete had yet to be understood.

In the latter part of the nineteenth century François Hennebique (1843–1921) tested reinforced concrete as a material for construction and patented a system for constructing buildings from foundations to columns, floor slabs, and roof, all of reinforced concrete. After 1894, when Coignet and Tedesco published the results of their work, describing the elastic theory of concrete beams and providing an accurate scientific basis for engineering work in reinforced concrete, the use of the material for construction increased rapidly. By 1900 Hennebique alone had designed and built more than 3000 structures of plain or reinforced concrete, including over 100 bridges. Burnham and Root designed the first large all reinforced concrete building, the Montauk Building (1882–1883) in Chicago. It included spread foundations to prevent subsidence in the muddy soil of Chicago. Similar foundations were used in constructing the Hudson River Tunnel in New York (1875–1900) and in the base of the Statue of Liberty (1883–1886). Ernest L. Ransome, an engineer in San Francisco, designed buildings framed in reinforced concrete and built the first concrete-reinforced bridge in the United States in 1889 (Figure 13.15).

Robert Maillart (1872–1940), a Swiss engineer, further explored the possibilities of the material. He developed a construction system of mushroom or flared columns supporting flat slabs, thus eliminating the need for beams, and used it most notably in a warehouse at Zurich (1910). An American engineer, Claude A. P. Turner, independently developed the same idea and used it to construct the Johnson-Borey Building in Minneapolis (1905–

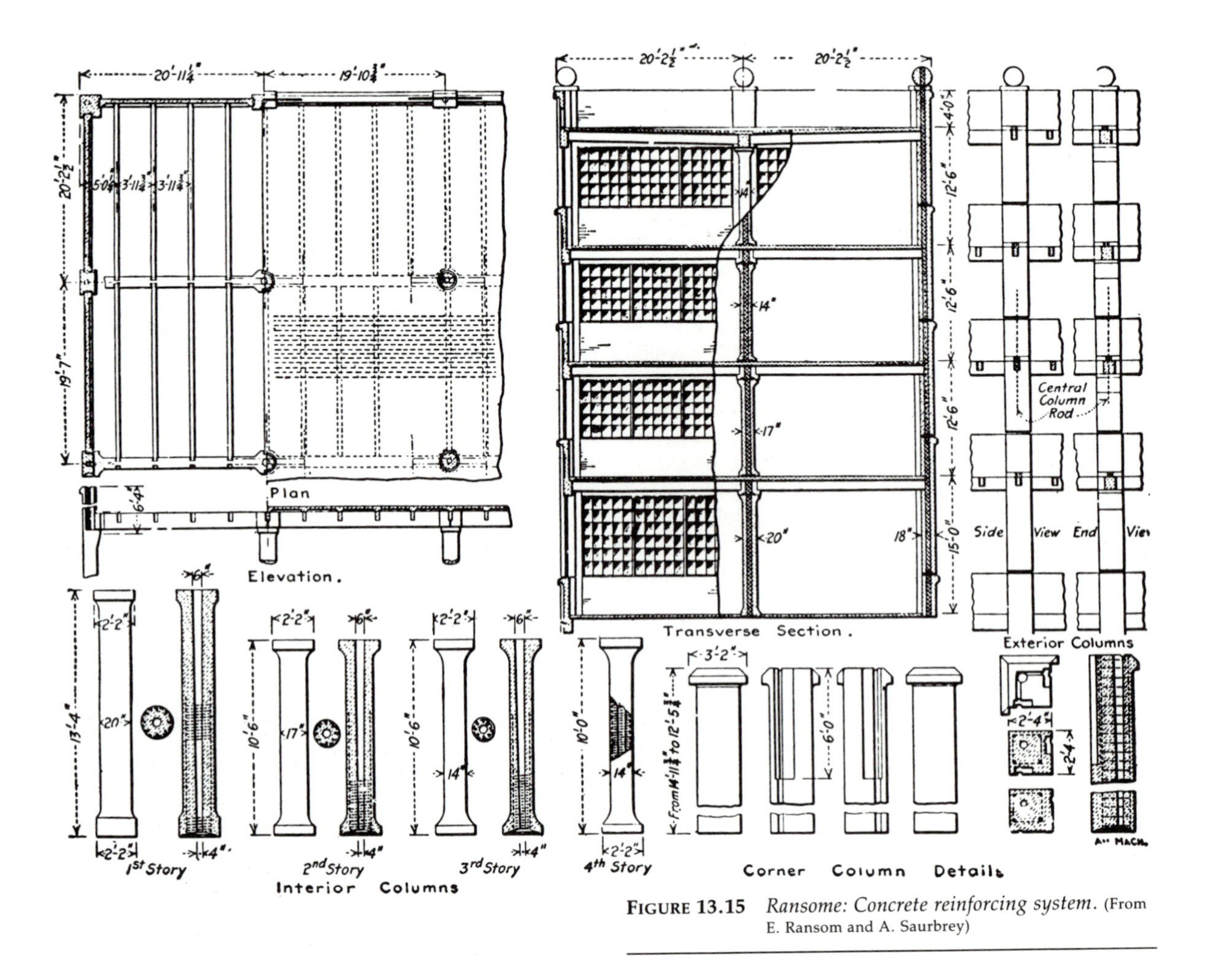

FIGURE 13.15 *Ransome: Concrete reinforcing system.* (From E. Ransom and A. Saurbrey)

1906); he obtained a patent on the system in 1908. Maillart is perhaps more famous for his reinforced concrete bridges, which combined the arch of the structure with the horizontal surface of the roadway in a single unitary design. His Tavanasa Bridge of 1905 (destroyed by a landslide in 1927) was the first to use this integration of parts, and he developed the theme further in later works, including most notably the Salginatobel Bridge of 1930 (Figure 13.16) near Schiers in eastern Switzerland. The bridge carries a small mountain road across a narrow valley, spanning 293 feet from steep sides. Maillart designed it as a three-hinged concrete arch, so the structure can rotate in response to small movements in the abutments. Also impressive is his design for the Schwandbach Bridge (1933), where a curved roadbed with arched supports is built in concrete slabs to create a graceful structure that appears to leap effortlessly across an alpine ravine. The curved roadbed allows uninterrupted traffic flow, and the design has taken into account the torsion loads created by moving vehicles on the road.

After designing the reinforcing bars to counter the stress of various loads, Maillart allowed the concrete to follow the shape of the internal steelwork. The form of the concrete thus followed the function

FIGURE 13.16 *Maillart: Salginatobel Bridge, Switzerland, 1930.* (Photo: Swiss National Tourist Office)

of the reinforcements, resulting in long, tenuous, diminishing horizontal slabs, with vertical slabs that tapered in height and broadened out again before merging into base foundations. Maillart also used naturalistic forms in his plastic, expressive concrete lines, for the potential of concrete is not realized in the limiting formalized shapes of rectangular columns, beams, and slabs. Even where the conventions of flat floors had to be maintained, Maillart often found ways to articulate the structural load-bearing functions, as in his customs warehouse at Chiasso, Italy, where the columns branch out to ribs, which in turn support trusses similar to the cross-sectional underside of a leaf.

In France Auguste Perret (1874–1954) built numerous apartment houses, commercial buildings, and churches, such as Notre-Dame-du-Raincy (1922–1923) (Figure 13.17), in reinforced concrete. His earliest notable work was the Paris apartment house at 25 bis rue Franklin (1902), in which the concrete frame allowed an irregular disposition of rooms to reflect the fact that the walls were not load

FIGURE 13.17 *Perret: Interior of Notre-Dame-du-Raincy, 1922–1923.* (Photo: Marburg)

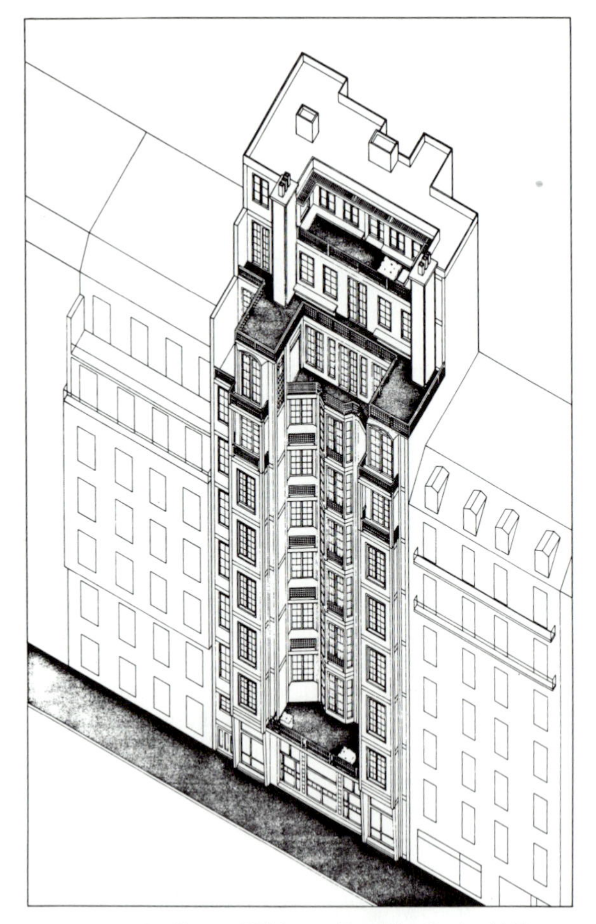

FIGURE 13.18 *Perret: 25* bis *rue Franklin, Paris, 1902.* (From R. Sherwood)

bearing (Figure 13.18). This same freedom is reflected in the disposition of the windows, which are closer together than would be possible in a structure with load-bearing walls. In response to neighborhood feelings about the "rudeness" of the material, the exterior concrete is scored to resemble stone. The young Le Corbusier worked for Perret and gained there his interest in and knowledge of reinforced concrete, a material he would use extensively throughout his career.

Another Frenchman, Eugène Freyssinet (1879–1962), explored in his work the techniques of prestressed and posttensioned concrete construction. Prestressed concrete involves stretching the reinforcing bars before pouring the concrete, so that when the concrete has set and the jacks maintaining the tension are released, the beam or girder has greater compressive and tensile strength. Posttensioning has much the same end effect, except the reinforcing here is stretched after the concrete is poured, and the steel ends (which pass through hollow cores in the concrete) are then restrained. Freyssinet is most famous for his two airship hangars at Orly (1916), which were constructed on a parabolic section with a folded surface, and provided a

FIGURE 13.19 *Nervi: Municipal stadium, Florence, 1929–1932.* (Photo: Alinari)

clear height of over 200 feet. Freyssinet also constructed numerous bridges.

Pier Luigi Nervi (1891–1975) and Felix Candela (b. 1910) have been the most innovative architect-engineers of our own day. Nervi built an impressive array of concrete structures, beginning with the Municipal Stadium in Florence (1929–1932), which has a dramatic cantilevered shell roof over the grandstand (Figure 13.19). Following the approach of Maillart, Nervi allowed his concrete shapes to reflect the structural stresses on the reinforcing inside, so the edge of the grandstand tapers to reflect the reduction in its structural load. In 1935 Nervi won a competition to build aircraft hangars for the Italian Air Force. The program required a clear interior space measuring 330 feet by 135 feet and an opening 165 feet wide on the long side. Model tests were used to confirm Nervi's almost intuitive structure, which could not then be calculated accurately. It involved a lamella-ribbed vault, analogous to the thin gill structure on the underside of a mushroom, with concrete struts supporting hollow tiles on the roof. (Later hangars employed a similar system with all the elements of precast concrete.) Buttresses extend from the corners to counter the thrust of the roof vault, and box beams span the entrances from one buttress to the next.

After World War II, Nervi experimented with what he termed *ferro-cemento,* a method of construction that involved spraying cement mortar on an existing form made of fine mesh steel (like chicken wire). Just slightly more than an inch of thickness was required of the cement to produce a strong structure. Nervi built himself a yacht hull this way (echoes of the Paris Exhibition of 1855!) and demonstrated its application to buildings in a warehouse for Rome (1945). Later works would see the use of ferro-cemento for large-span factories, sports facilities, and exhibition halls, where lightweight precast units were sprayed into shape without the complexity of wooden formwork. The lacy roof of the Palazzetto dello Sport (1960), erected for the Rome Olympics, was created this way (Figures 13.20, 13.21).

In contrast, the work of the Mexican engineer Felix Candela has concentrated on the structural possibilities of the hyperbolic paraboloid, a surface of double curvature for which it is difficult to calculate precise structural behavior. Candela has experimented with the form in a series of designs for

FIGURE 13.20 *Nervi: Palazzetto dello Sport, Rome, 1960.* (Photo: Marburg)

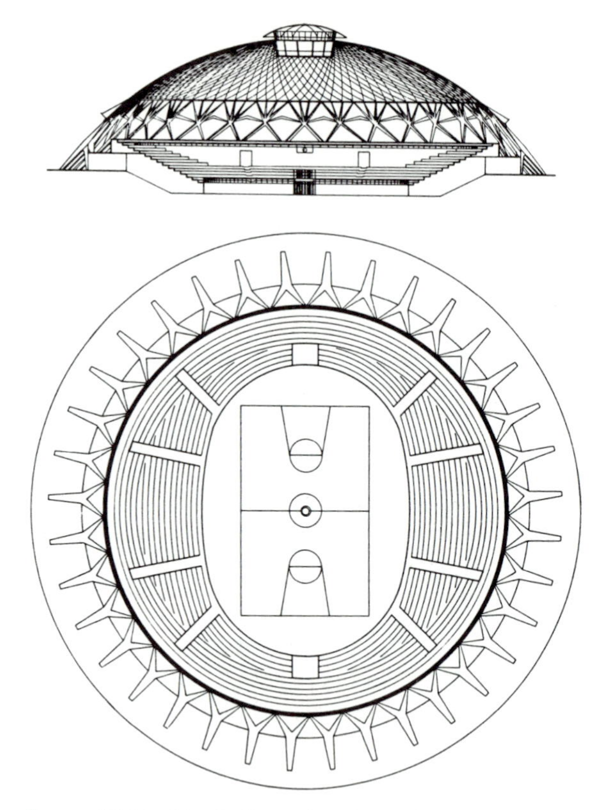

FIGURE 13.21 *Nervi: Plan and section of the Palazzetto dello Sport, Rome, 1960.* (From W. Blaser)

churches, warehouses, factories, and commercial buildings, basing his buildings on a standard single hyperbolic paraboloid supported at opposite corners or on a grouping of four of these into a monolithic umbrella supported on a central post. In the hands of masters like Nervi and Candela, reinforced concrete becomes one of the most intuitive, expressive, and exciting of materials.

FRANCE

Tony Garnier and the Industrial City

Tony Garnier, a designer in reinforced concrete, is more famous today for his scheme for an industrial city. Garnier (1869–1948) was an excellent student at the École des Beaux-Arts. In 1897 he came in second in the Grand Prix de Rome competition, and in 1899 he won the prize with a design for "A State Bank" that is still recognized as the epitome of Beaux-Arts planning and composition (Figure 13.22). During his four-year residence at the French Academy in Rome, Garnier began to turn away from the classical ideal espoused by the École, much to the distress of academic officials, who refused to accept the drawings, required annually of all scholars in Rome, that he first submitted because these were considered unworthy. In 1900 Garnier wrote, "Since all architecture rests on false principles, the architecture of antiquity was an error. TRUTH ALONE IS BEAUTIFUL. In architecture, truth is the product of the calculations made to satisfy known needs with known means." For a graduate of the École des Beaux-Arts this was nothing short of heresy! To pass the time in Rome Garnier embarked on academic reconstruction studies of Tusculum to satisfy academy requirements and, for his own inter-

FIGURE 13.22 *Garnier: "A State Bank," Grand Prix de Rome competition, 1899.* (From *Les Grandes Prix de Rome 1850-1900*)

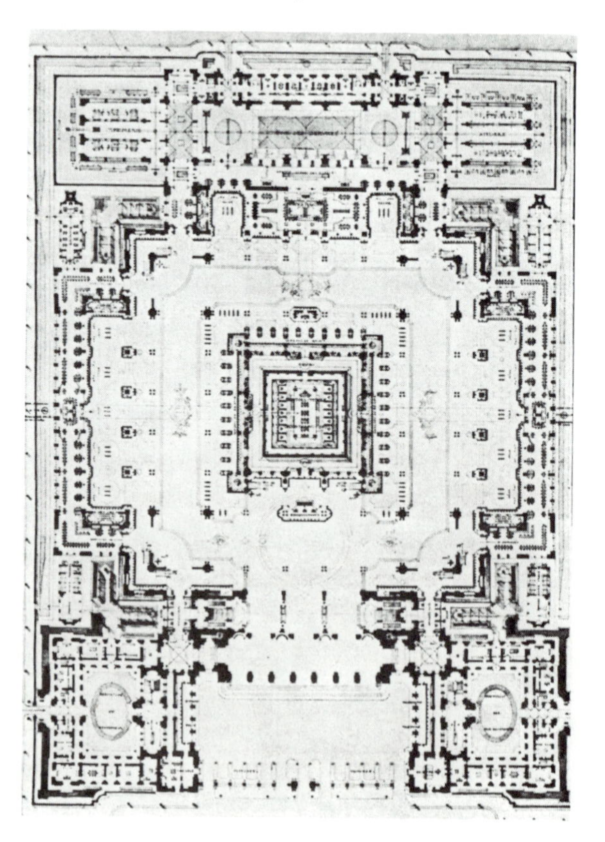

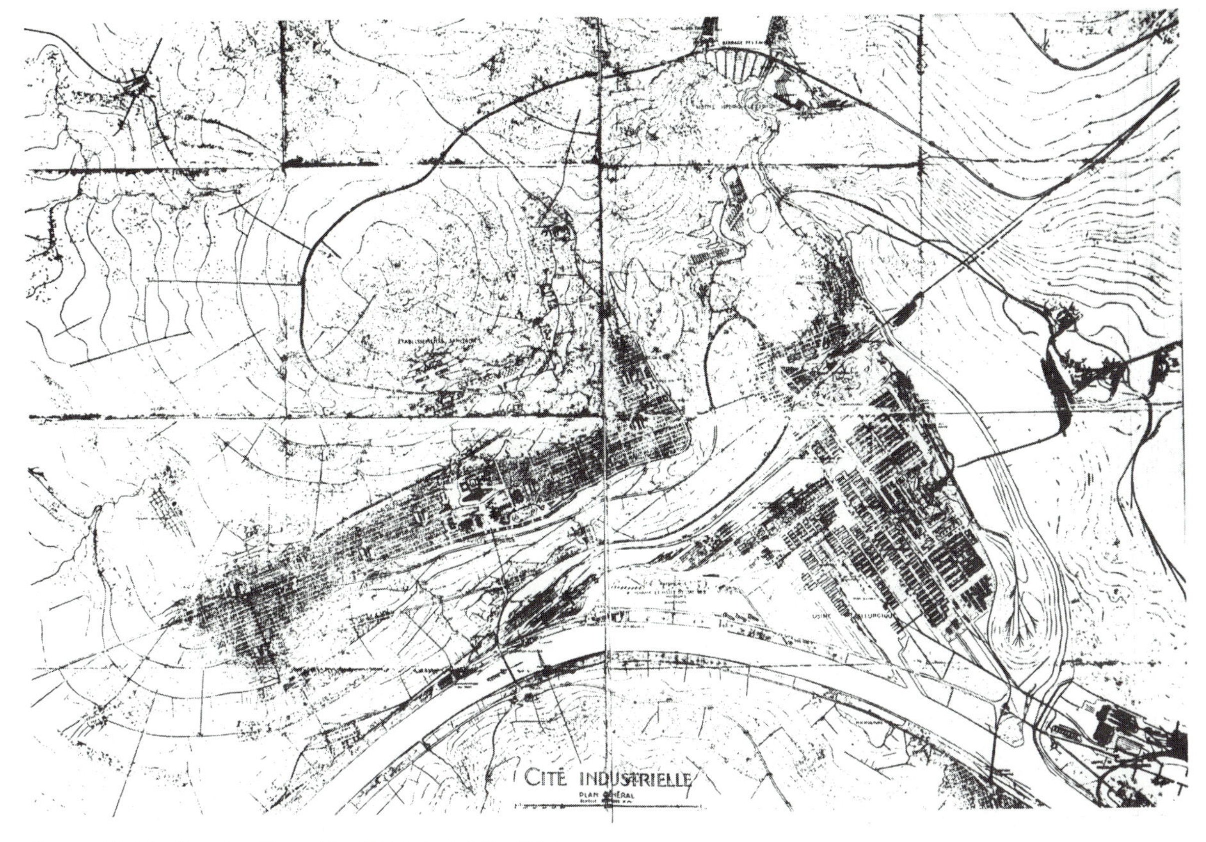

FIGURE 13.23 *Garnier: Plan of La Cité Industrielle, 1904–1917.* (From T. Garnier)

est, made plans for an ideal town he called *La Cité Industrielle.*

He chose an imaginary site for the town (Figure 13.23). The industrial quarter would be in the valley beside the river, laid out in orthogonal streets and provided with rail and waterway connections. A convenient ridge above would hold the residential and commercial districts, again deployed in an orderly grid, with a monumental civic open space surrounding the important governmental and cultural buildings in the city center. Greenery would be interspersed with houses in the residential sectors, for buildings there would be permitted to cover only 50 percent of the lot. The single family houses would be small and detached, with Roman atria and unornamented walls, flat roofs with garden terraces, and simple features (Figure 13.24). Construction would, of course, be in concrete, and Garnier emphasized the hygienic aspects of the design with such features as radius curves between floors and walls to eliminate the corners where dirt could accumulate. Sunlight and fresh air would penetrate all interior spaces. The strict zoning of industry (Figure 13.25) to the lowlands theoretically would remove its noises and odors from the town, although the single winding road connecting the industrial sector to the city proper would have encouraged traffic congestion.

Garnier's work was substantially complete in 1904, but he did not publish his Industrial City designs until 1917, then including designs of actual projects he had constructed as city architect for

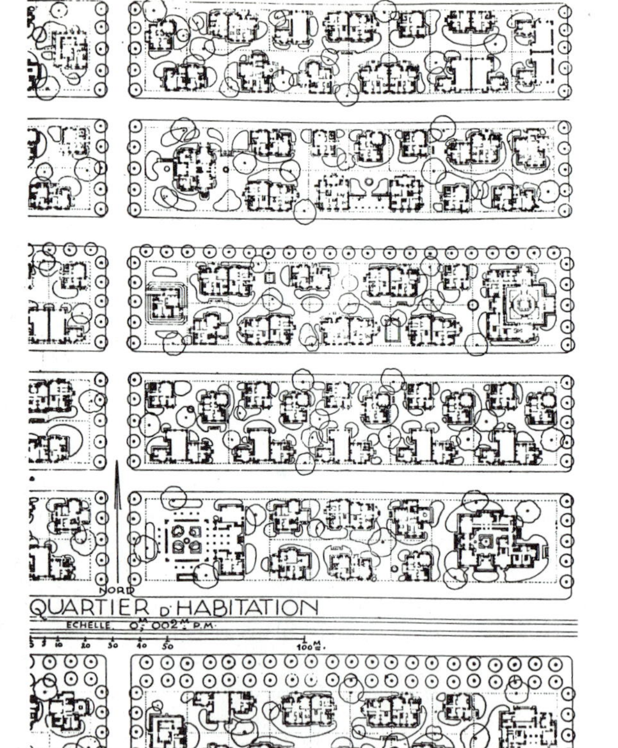

Figure 13.24 *Garnier: Plan and view of residential quarters in La Cité Industrielle.* (From T. Garnier)

Figure 13.25 *Garnier: View of the industrial sector of La Cité Industrielle.* (From T. Garnier)

Lyons. The great importance of his theoretical project was that an architect was actually considering the design of an industrial town at all, for the subject was not a common one for designers of his day. In the stress laid on healthful surroundings, the Industrial City links back to Chaux and forward to much subdivision construction in the twentieth century. In its use of concrete for residential construction, Garnier's designs anticipate the work of Le Corbusier, who would also employ flat roofs with garden terraces.

Le Corbusier

Charles Édouard Jeanneret-Gris, better known as Le Corbusier, is remembered for architectural mastery of form and light. Le Corbusier (1887–1964) was born in the Swiss watch-making town of La Chaux-de-Fonds, and he received his formal art instruction in the local arts and crafts school, which trained its students to do fancy engraving for watch cases. Recognizing his artistic talents his teachers encouraged him to consider more ambitious goals than a job in the watch industry. His architectural education came from experience in the offices of Auguste Perret (1908–1909) and Peter Behrens, sandwiched between sketching travels throughout the Mediterranean, including the Greek islands. He returned to La Chaux-de-Fonds in 1912, taught in the art school, and designed a few houses.

From Perret he acquired a firm understanding of reinforced concrete, and from Behrens he learned about designing for industry. He combined these two strains in his first noteworthy project, the Dom-ino House (1914), made in response to the First World War. Anticipating that destruction caused by the fighting would increase the demand for rebuilding when hostilities ended, Le Corbusier proposed a mass-produced housing scheme that reduced the components to a minimum: floor slabs, regularly spaced piers for vertical support, and stairs to connect the floors (Figure 13.26). Inherent in the design was the possibility of factory fabrication of these parts near the construction site and rapid erection of the frame by crane. The subdivision of the interior and precise weatherproof enclosure of the exterior would be left to the discretion of the builders so that local preferences could be observed.

In 1916 he moved to Paris and adopted the pseudonym Le Corbusier, a name from his mother's family, for his architectural projects. He continued to paint under his given name. With the war still raging, there was not much work for an unknown young Swiss architect, and Le Corbusier occupied his time with painting, writing, and drawing projects. In 1920 he and the poet Paul Dermée originated a small journal, *L'Esprit nouveau* (The New Spirit), which covered all the visual arts, music, and the aesthetic of modern life in its three years of publication. A collection of Le Corbusier's essays on architecture that first appeared in the pages of *L'Esprit nouveau* were reprinted as a book, *Vers une architecture* (Toward a New Architecture) in 1923. In it Le Corbusier's tendency for poetic overstatement is indulged in the best traditions of Romanticism, and the book is still illuminating to read for its flavor of the arts in Paris during the early 1920s. "Architecture is the masterly, correct, and magnificent play of masses brought together in light," he proclaimed, as he endorsed the design of buildings based on the aesthetics of the machine. In anticipation of eventual mass-production on a modular basis he also advocated the use of a common proportional system, based on the Golden Section and dimensioned by the height of man, for all elements in a building.

FIGURE 13.26 *Le Corbusier: Dom-ino House, 1914.* (Courtesy: Artemis Verlag)

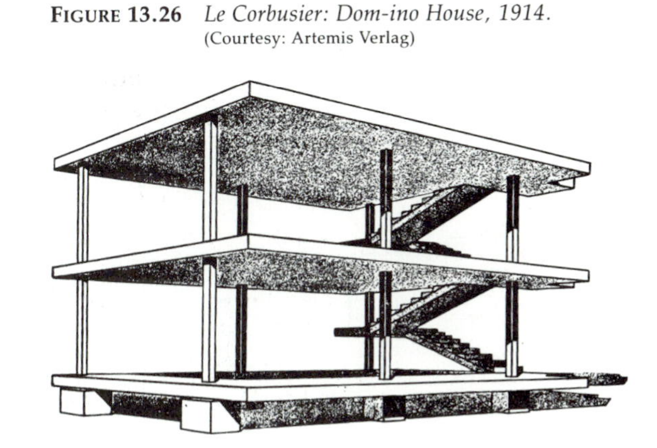

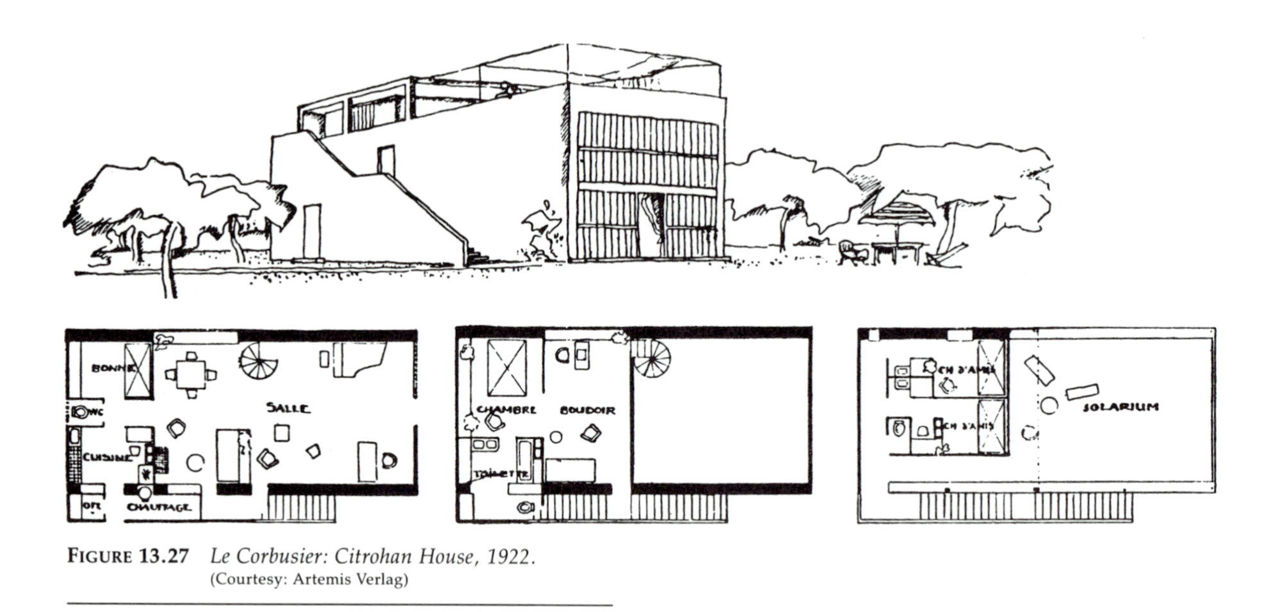

FIGURE 13.27 *Le Corbusier: Citrohan House, 1922.* (Courtesy: Artemis Verlag)

Among the projects illustrated in *Vers une architecture* was the Citrohan House (1922), Le Corbusier's attempt to design a modest dwelling that would be as affordable as the Citroen automobiles then being built in France (Figure 13.27). The house is built of reinforced concrete, raised off the ground by piers or **pilotis,** with a garage and service-storage rooms on the lowest level. The second floor, in the tradition of the piano nobile, has the living and dining rooms, maid's room, and kitchen; the third floor has the master bedroom overlooking the two-story living room; and children's rooms and a roof garden complete the fourth level. Many of Le Corbusier's later houses would incorporate a two-story living room with overlooking balcony. Fenestration consists of simple punched openings in the wall framing industrial windows, dividing the exterior into horizontal bands that extend continuously with little regard for the location of interior partitions.

Later in the decade, Le Corbusier was given the opportunity to build a number of modest and not-so-modest houses to test his design theories in practice. At Garches he designed the Villa Stein (1927) (Figure 13.28). As with the Citrohan House, the main living floor is at the piano nobile level, and an elegant terrace completes the roof. The regularly spaced structural piers permit freely curving interior partitions, while continuous bands of horizontal windows extend across both the north and south

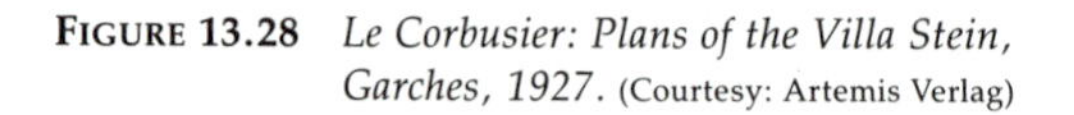

FIGURE 13.28 *Le Corbusier: Plans of the Villa Stein, Garches, 1927.* (Courtesy: Artemis Verlag)

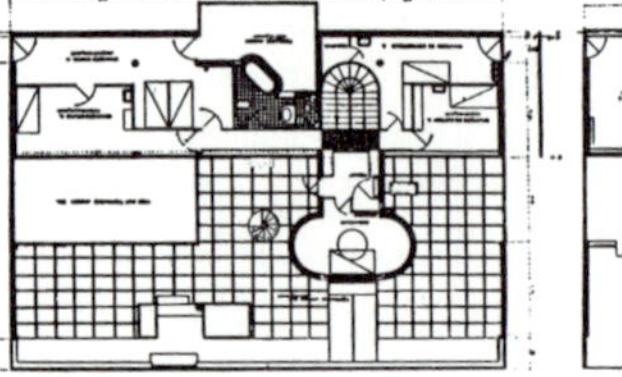

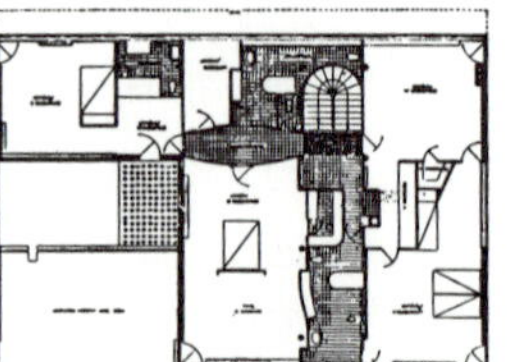

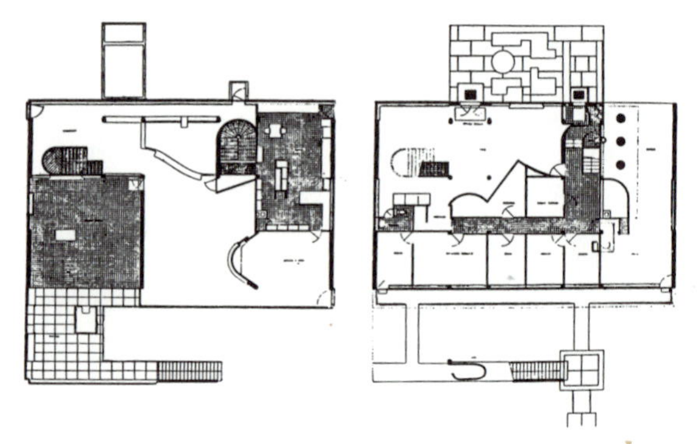

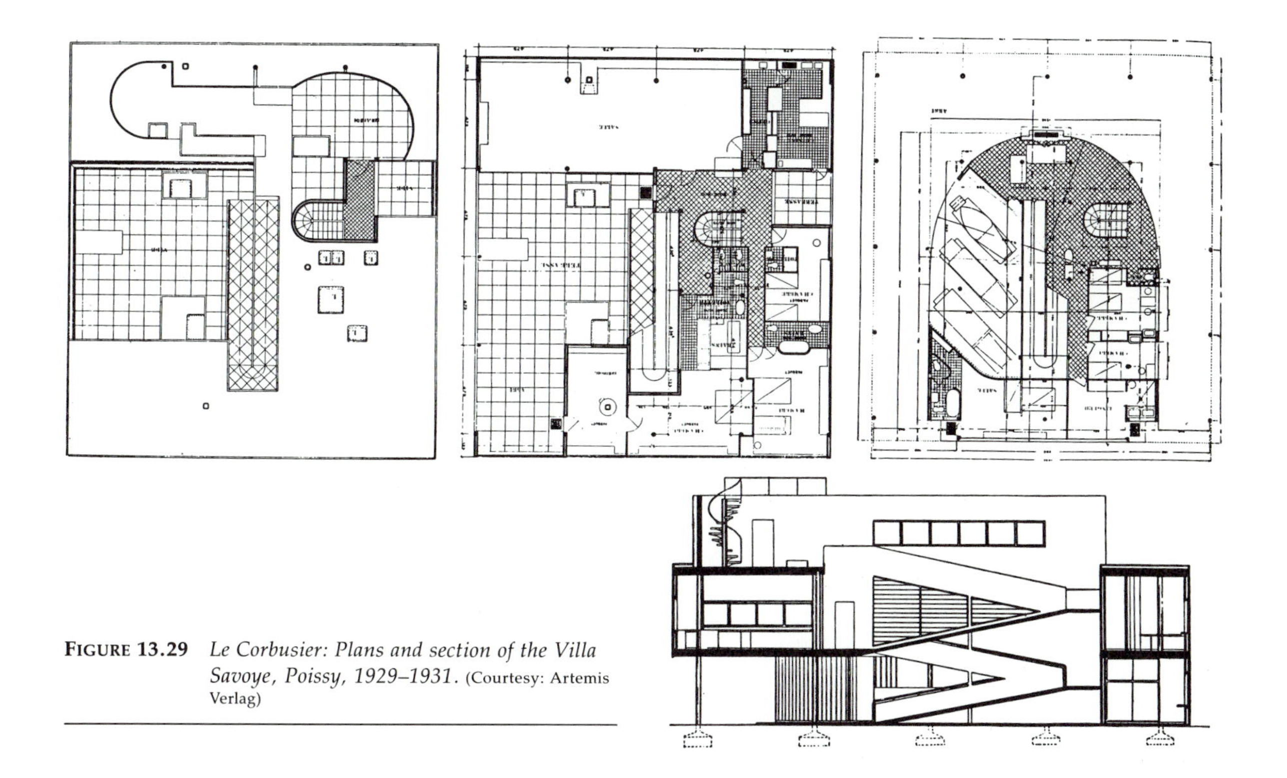

FIGURE 13.29 *Le Corbusier: Plans and section of the Villa Savoye, Poissy, 1929–1931.* (Courtesy: Artemis Verlag)

façades. (The end elevations are largely blank, for Le Corbusier was considering this as a prototype for rather narrow suburban lots, where the neighboring houses would curtail possibilities for light and view on the sides.) The major building proportions were based on Palladio and determined by the Golden Section, the "regulating traces" being included in the published elevation drawings.

More expressive was the Villa Savoye (1929–1931) at Poissy, outside Paris (Figure 13.29). Designed as a weekend house for an art-loving family, the curving ground floor wall is determined by the turning radius of the motor car that would convey the family out from Paris. The driveway extends under the house, between the pilotis, and continues past the main entrance to a three-car garage and the maid's quarters. From the ground-level entrance hall the visitor has the choice of climbing the sculptural stair or ascending the ramp (which links all three levels) to the second floor. Here, from the main living floor, one obtains an unobstructed view over the clearing in which the house sits to the forested hills enclosing the site. The large living room is separated by an enormous sliding glass door from the exterior patio and the ramp that continues to the upper level terrace with its sculptural windscreen walls. The appearance of regularity is carefully maintained on the exterior. All four elevations are essentially identical, consisting of a ribbon of windows and openings running the width of the façade at the second floor level, supported by regularly spaced pilotis. In fact the house is a good deal more complex than this simple exterior implies, for a close study of the plan reveals that the structural system is *not* a regular grid as both Le Corbusier's theoretical writings and the façade would lead one to believe. A regular spacing would have made it next to impossible to park cars in the garage, and it would have inconvenienced interior spaces on the second floor as well. Nevertheless, Le Corbusier scrupulously avoids having interior partitions coincide with columns.

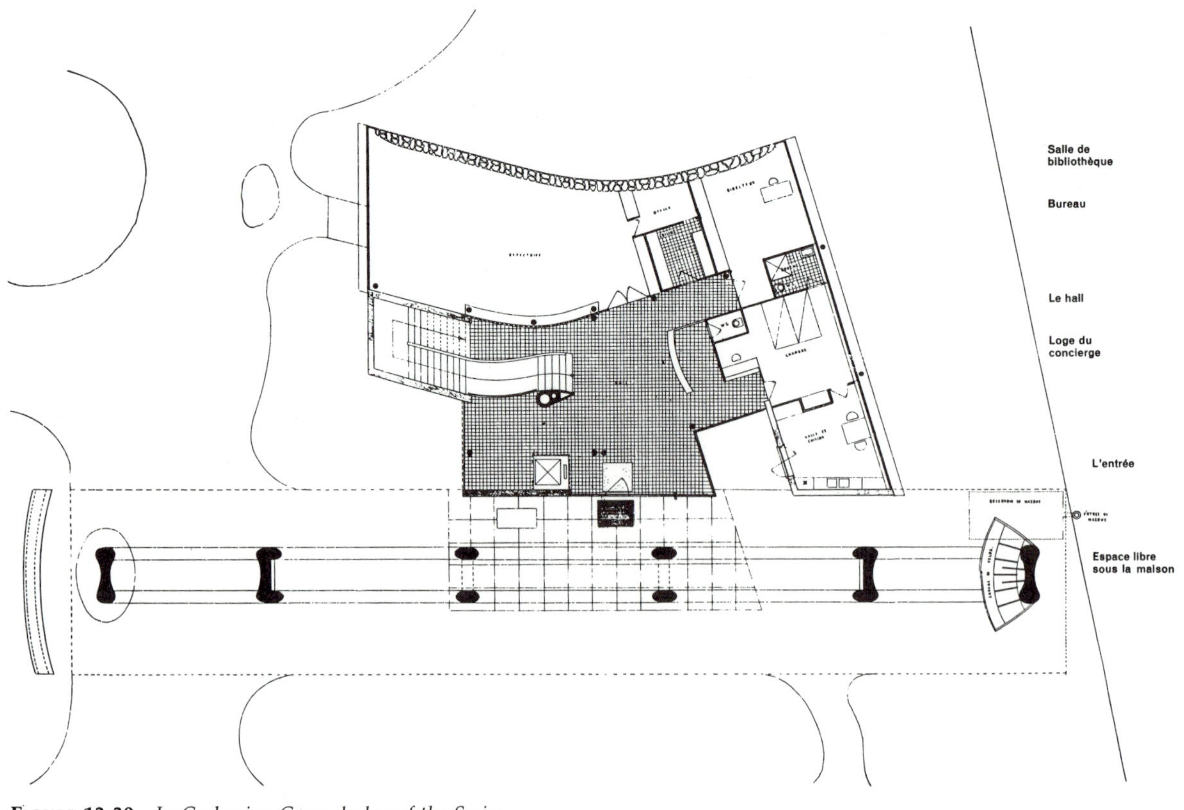

FIGURE 13.30 *Le Corbusier: Ground plan of the Swiss Pavillion, Cité Universitaire, Paris, 1930.* (Courtesy: Artemis Verlag)

Le Corbusier's choices of interior finishes and fittings reflect his enthusiasm for industrial products and his admiration for the functional aspects of ocean liners. The entrance hall alone has quarry tile flooring; simple pipe rails, painted black; a pedestal washbasin, freestanding in the hallway; and industrial light fixtures, directed upward to provide reflected light. Skylights, painted intense blue, provide softly colored lights to reflect on the white wall surfaces on the second floor, where the master bath has a particularly famous lounging recliner and tub in ceramic tile. The artful incorporation of varied spatial experiences and light within a simple geometric container testify to the mastery Le Corbusier had achieved by 1930.

At the Cité Universitaire of Paris, Le Corbusier was commissioned to design a dormitory for Swiss students, the Swiss Pavilion (1930). Here the four-story rectangular block of dormitory rooms is raised on the inevitable pilotis to provide a covered entrance to the lower block of common rooms, articulated separately in a sculptural free curve (Figure 13.30). Rather than using a uniform white finish for all surfaces, Le Corbusier allowed each material to express its own character. The concrete was unpainted and left with the board markings of the formwork, and natural stone was laid in random rubble on the exterior and interior end wall of the common room. Similarly the varied functions of the two sides of the dormitory block received different expressions: small punched openings illuminating the corridor on each floor and a window-wall of glass providing unrestricted views from each dormitory room.

Inherent in the Swiss dormitory were concepts of high-rise living that can be found in Le Corbusier's city-planning schemes dating back to 1922. His city of the future involved the construction of widely spaced towers, each allowing the apartment dwellers within to receive sunlight and fresh air, away from the dirt and noise of the typical urban street. Le Corbusier seems never to have appreciated the social function of the street, where crowds and varied sights, sounds, and smells contribute to the essence of urban life. As a Romantic and individualist Le Corbusier preferred solitude and natural surroundings, so he provided his buildings with rooftop gardens and raised them off the ground on pilotis, leaving the terrain unobstructed for recreational facilities or parks. By 1926 he had articulated "Five Points Towards a New Architecture:"

1. The supports are precisely calculated, spaced regularly, and used to elevate the first floor off the damp ground.
2. The flat roof is used for domestic purposes — gardening, play, relaxation — thereby recovering all the built-up area in cities.
3. The interior walls, independent of the support system, may be arranged in a free plan.
4. The horizontal windows, made possible by the support system, permit even illumination from wall to wall and provide eight times the amount of light as from a vertically placed window of equal area.
5. The façade, also independent of the structural supports, may be freely designed.

Some of these points do not make logical sense. Concerning point 4, for example, the amount of light coming through a given area of glass is the same regardless of window orientation, but other conditions in the room, such as color and reflective surfaces, do have a great deal to do with the spatial effect of light in a room. It is also unlikely that the rooftop recreation advocated in point 2 would be equivalent to being on the ground. All the points taken together, however, define a new aesthetic for building design, which Le Corbusier followed in most projects until the mid-1950s. His later works will be treated with contemporary developments later in this chapter.

GERMANY

Peter Behrens and the Deutscher Werkbund

Our discussion of the English Arts and Crafts movement mentioned the German Hermann Muthesius, who was sent to England from 1896 to 1903 to report on all aspects of English architecture, design, and manufacture, with the intent that his research would be useful in raising the design standards of German products. Muthesius's subsequent appointments of leading designers to leadership positions at German arts and crafts schools was one result of the reform process begun after his return to Germany. In 1907 Germany took another significant step toward improvement of the visual arts when Muthesius, together with concerned manufacturers and designers, formed the Deutscher Werkbund. (This German title does not translate easily. Perhaps "the German products association" would be an appropriate English equivalent.) The Werkbund encouraged fine design of industrially manufactured goods. The motive was primarily economic; Muthesius and others were very much concerned that German products would not be competitive in domestic or international markets unless they could equal the standards set by other countries, especially England. Just what artistic direction the Werkbund would take was the subject of considerable debate in the early years, but the word *quality* was used with great frequency. The Werkbund increasingly urged the merits of abstract forms for manufactured products, standardized parts for production ease, and aesthetic qualities evaluated separately from manufacturing quality. All these ideas were to be of great importance to postwar designers.

Another important event of 1907 was the hiring of Peter Behrens (1868–1940), a member of the Werkbund, by the Allgemeine Electricitäts-Gesellschaft (AEG), the German equivalent of General Electric. Behrens was responsible for all aspects of design for the firm — including the letterhead, electric light fixtures, and the architecture of production facilities — a job embracing the modern fields of graphic design, product design, and architecture (Figure 13.31). The man entrusted with this work

FIGURE 13.31 *Behrens: Poster design for AEG, 1908.*

FIGURE 13.32 *Behrens: Behrens House, Darmstadt, 1900.* (Photo: Marburg)

was originally trained as a painter, but he was also influenced by the arts and crafts teachings of Morris. The house he designed in 1901 for himself and his family at the Darmstadt artists' colony shows pronounced Secessionist tendencies in its furniture and decoration, while the oval curves of its dormers make a gesture to German Baroque (Figure 13.32).

The buildings Behrens designed for AEG show no hint of the Secession style. If anything, they have a quality of stripped classicism. In the main, they are forceful, bold statements, representing the first architectural attempts to deal with industrial facilities. The most famous is the Turbine Factory in Berlin (1909), where the polygonal profile of the roof truss over the large manufacturing assembly hall is reflected on the exterior (Figure 13.33). Behrens avoided applied ornament entirely and gave the structural materials direct expression. The steel frame is exposed along the side walls, where large windows span between the supports, while concrete panels, slightly battered and articulated in large rectangular coursings, dominate the end elevations. The large front window projects slightly forward of the concrete mass as if to emphasize its non-loading-bearing status. A lower two-story factory block to the left of the turbine hall has banks of vertical windows framed by a concrete surround closely modelled on classical proportions, but treated here without classical detail.

Perhaps because of his AEG work, Behren's office soon became known as one of the most progressive in Europe, and a number of the young designers who came to work for Behrens became the postwar leaders of the architectural profession. Walter Gropius met his first collaborator, Adolf Meyer, when both worked for Behrens; at other times both Mies van der Rohe and the young Le Corbusier were employed there before the outbreak of World War I.

Walter Gropius and the Bauhaus

Prior to World War I, thoughtful architects and designers in the United States, England, Austria, Italy, France, and Scotland were struggling with the problem of aesthetic expression appropriate to the industrial world. The war brought a temporary halt to

FIGURE 13.33 *Behrens: AEG Turbine Factory, Berlin, 1909.* (Photo: Marburg)

these investigations, but shortly after the termination of hostilities, an answer to the vexing problem of industrial production and artistic expression was proposed in the founding of the Bauhaus, a new school of design in Weimar, Germany. Its methods of teaching, students, faculty, and designs were to define the Modern Movement that spread worldwide.

Walter Gropius, the founder of the Bauhaus, was unusual among masters of the Modern Movement in being the product of a thoroughly academic architectural education at the universities of Berlin and Munich. The son of an architect, Gropius (1883–1969) obtained valuable practical experience from 1907 to 1910 in the office of Peter Behrens and then set up an independent practice with Adolf Meyer (1881–1929). Their first major project, the Fagus Shoe-Last Factory at Alfeld-an-der-Leine (1911), is still considered a landmark in the history of modern architecture because it used the elements later to characterize the International Style: glass curtain wall between expressed steel supports, corners left free of solid masonry, and simple rectangular massing with a flat roof (Figure 13.34). Having received the commission after a previous designer began construction on the complex, Gropius gave greatest design attention to one wing of the factory, where he was able to express his ideals most clearly.

FIGURE 13.34 *Gropius and Meyer: Fagus Shoe-Last Factory, Alfeld-an-der-Leine, 1911.* (Photo: Marburg)

FIGURE 13.35 *Gropius: Werkbund Model Factory, Cologne, 1914.* (Photo: German Information Center)

FIGURE 13.36 *Gropius and Meyer: Plan of the Werkbund Model Factory, Cologne.* (From *Deutsche Kunst und Dekoration*)

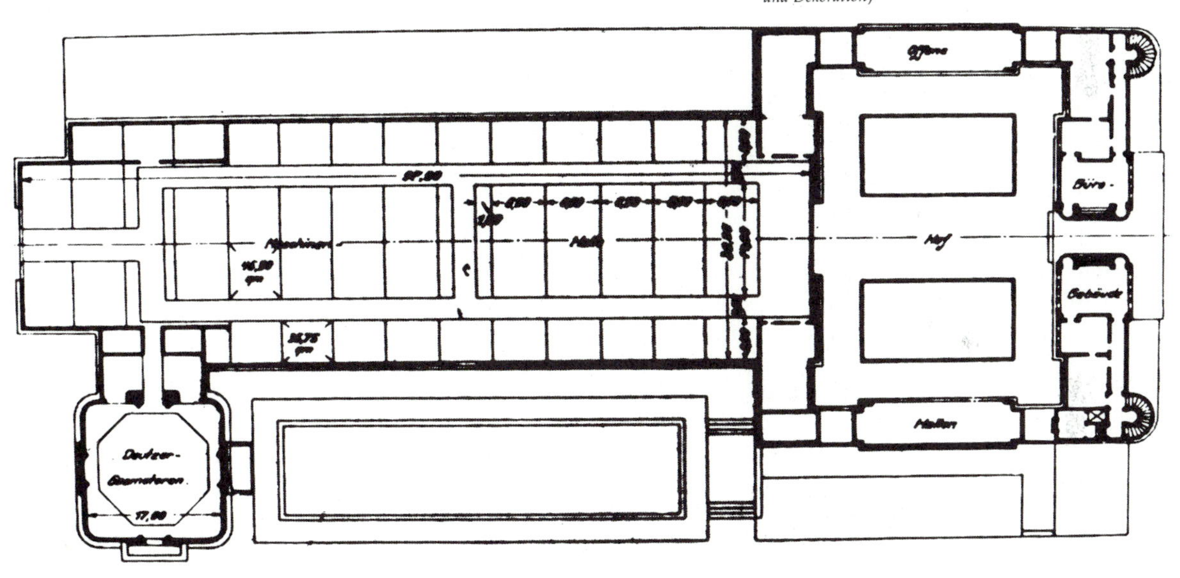

Like Behrens Gropius was a member of the Werkbund. For their exhibition in Cologne in 1914, Gropius and Meyer designed a model factory to demonstrate the possible architectural expression of a hypothetical manufacturing plant with an attached office block (Figures 13.35, 13.36). In consultation with local industry Gropius devised the building's program to answer the needs of a medium-sized industry. The rear of the office block was curtain-walled in glass, which extended dramatically around the sides to the circular stair towers on the front corners, while the front façade was windowless and clad with limestone made to look like brick. Symmetry governed the entire ensemble; the central entrance was placed on axis; and the stair cylinders were each overshadowed by a tower element containing a roof-level dance floor connected with a covered restaurant. Separating the office block from the manufacturing plant was a large open courtyard, which led axially to the industrial area, a large basilican hall, itself divided into thirds by the supports for its double-pitched skylit roof. It was a far more daring complex than anything currently constructed for German industry, and Gropius derived several design ideas from the European publications of Wright's work. The courtyard side of the office block, for example, relies on the elevation of the Mason City Hotel (1909) in Iowa, and the rooftop recreational facilities of the Larkin Building inspired similar accommodations in the Cologne factory. On the strength of this design, the Grand Duke of Sachsen-Weimar-Eisenach asked Gropius to assume direction of the ducal arts and crafts school.

The outbreak of World War I delayed implementation of the Grank Duke's invitation as Gropius served from 1914–1918 in the German Army on the western front. At the conclusion of the war the German nobility lost their domains, but the Grand Duke's recommendation was renewed through the new civic authorities, and in 1919 Gropius combined the former Grossherzoglich Sachsen Weimarische Hochschule für Angewandte Kunst and the Grossherzoghiche Kunstakademie in Weimar into the Staatliches Bauhaus Weimar. (Bauhaus might be translated House of Building, although the literal interpretation seems to be misleading in English.)

In joining the former ducal arts and crafts school with the fine arts academy, Gropius created a new institution dedicated to training students in all aspects of design, including architecture. In the early years most of the faculty were painters from Berlin and Vienna whom Gropius had known before the war. The model used for organizing the curriculum was the medieval guild; students were called apprentices and were graduated with journeyman's certificates. Gropius was firmly convinced that fine art came through mastery of craft, and he arranged the teaching program so that students were given manual instruction in one of the many craft workshops (wood, metal, weaving, pottery, mural painting) and theoretical studies in principles of form by separate instructors, most often painters. As Gropius wrote in an essay in 1923:

> By depriving handicrafts and industry of the informing services of the artist, the academies drained them of their vitality, and brought about the artist's complete isolation from the community. Art is not one of those things that may be imparted. Whether a design be the outcome of knack or creative impulse depends on individual propensity. But if what we call art cannot be taught or learnt, a thorough knowledge of its principles and of sureness of hand can be. Both are as necessary for the artist of genius as for the ordinary artisan.

Gropius, himself a product of the European academic system of architectural education, saw the curriculum of the Bauhaus as a sharp break with Beaux-Arts training, and he had harsh words for the older methods:

> The besetting vice of the academy schools was that they were obsessed by that rare "biological" sport, the commanding genius; and forgot that their business was to teach drawing and painting to hundreds and hundreds of minor talents, barely one in a thousand of whom could be expected to have the makings of a real architect or painter. In the vast majority of cases, this hopelessly one-sided instruction condemned its pupils to the lifelong practice of a purely sterile art. Had these hapless drones been given a proper practical training, they could have become useful members of society.

"The ultimate aim of all visual art is the complete building!" Thus began the 1919 prospectus advertising the Bauhaus to students. Through involvement in its workshops, students would become skilled in a craft, learn drawing and painting, and receive instruction in science and theory. It was envisioned that workshop projects would attract outside support, in the form of commissions or production licenses, and that the Bauhaus might soon become self-supporting. Collaboration was stressed from the first.

In 1921 Gropius received a commission from Adolf Sommerfeld to design a house, and he saw this as an opportunity to give practical (and paid) experience to some of his apprentices in the woodworking shop. Gropius (with Adolf Meyer) designed the architectural aspects, while the Bauhaus apprentices were given a rather free hand to design and furnish the interior. The result was an unusual house, to say the least. To get material for the house, Sommerfeld, a contractor, purchased a dismantled navy ship for the teakwood it contained, and this wood was used for almost everything because it was the only material available. (Postwar

Germany, saddled with enormous reparation payments to the Allies, had chronic shortages of just about everything.) In elevation the house has an affinity with Wright's Winslow House, with due allowance for the demands of its construction. The interior has been described as "a riot of styles and contemporary cliches," owing to Gropius's encouragement of individual approaches among his students.

As the Bauhaus matured, the thrust of its program, which began with the idea of handcraft as a means to art, shifted to handcraft as a means of making prototypes for industrial production. This adjustment had been made by 1923, partly in response to the outside pressure generated by growing skepticism toward some of the more flamboyant faculty artists, and partly because this shift enabled the school to fill a role more closely akin to Gropius's own interests in mass production. The anticipated support from trade groups or industrial concerns had not materialized, which left the Bauhaus in financial straits. If designs could be sold to manufacturers, the income would help alleviate the financial situation. More importantly, in placing emphasis on design for industrial production the Bauhaus had found an appropriate resolution of the relationship of art to the machine. Rather than seeing the two as adversaries, as Ruskin and the Arts and Crafts movement had done, the Bauhaus saw the integration of art with mechanized production as the essential challenge of the twentieth-century designer, and it organized its teaching to address this issue.

Despite these changes the position of the school in Weimar became increasingly difficult. Gropius removed the most eccentric faculty and requested that the students wear ordinary clothes, but the radio and newspaper attacks on the Bauhaus continued. At Easter in 1925 the progressive mayor of Dessau offered assistance in his city, and the Bauhaus moved to temporary quarters there. By December 1926 the school was established in a new home designed by Gropius, buildings that rank among the finest expressions of the emerging Modern Movement (Figure 13.37). The reinforced concrete buildings consist of four major elements, arranged freely on the flat site so that there is no "front" in the customary sense. The workshop wing, four stories tall, is the largest mass, containing behind its glass curtain wall the studio spaces for preliminary instruction and workshops for printing, carpentry, dyeing, sculpture, weaving, and wall painting, in addition to exhibition and lecture spaces. A road (added by Gropius) ran through the site beside the workshop building, requiring a bridge building to connect it to the (separately administered) trade school. In the

FIGURE 13.37 *Gropius: Bauhaus, Dessau, 1926.* (Photo: German Information Center)

bridge were administrative offices for the Bauhaus and Gropius's private architectural office. Parallel to the road and extending behind the workshop wing was the low dining hall and auditorium building, equipped with a stage between the two spaces and provided with movable walls for maximum flexibility. Beyond this was a five-story student dormitory with twenty-eight rooms and related facilities.

What made this building complex so remarkable? Several aspects can be identified. The asymmetrical, sprawling composition represented a break with the typical monumental disposition employed for educational facilities. Separate articulation was given to each element of the program, resulting in an abstract, sculptural treatment for the whole, and the introduction of a road and bridge reinforced the sense of free-moving space. Bauhaus workshops designed and executed all the interior finishing, with the metal workshop responsible for lighting fixtures and the tubular steel furniture (designed by Marcel Breuer), the printing workshop for graphics, and so on. The building was thus a total work of art, a unity of architecture and related crafts. Its industrial construction materials, concrete and glass, were used without ornament, and circulation was clearly expressed in the layout. Multiple viewpoints are required to appreciate the organization and composition of the whole.

Gropius also designed a series of seven dwelling units — one detached house and three duplex houses — for Bauhaus faculty. The duplex units were identical, yet by changing their orientation and making one the mirror image of the other, Gropius obtained the effect of three different designs. Standardization was thus combined with variety. Like the Bauhaus buildings, these houses were flat-roofed and painted white with industrial-looking pipe rail details on balconies.

The Bauhaus in Dessau continued to emphasize design for industrial production and licensed a number of products to German manufacturers. Gropius began to offer specific architectural instruction to advanced workshop students, marking the first time building design had been taught in the curriculum. Bauhaus designs, whether for architecture, graphic design, or products, tended to favor the primary geometric shapes and solids, coupled with linear elements, to achieve an appearance of simplicity. The forms of finished goods reflected both the nature of the material and the manufacturing process required for fabrication. Although Gropius always denied that there was a Bauhaus "style," there is a strong visual affinity in many of the student projects and faculty designs created at the Bauhaus.

These designs became widely known through exhibitions and publications, gaining general acclaim for the school throughout Europe. The facilities in Dessau provided workspace superior to anything the Bauhaus had had in Weimar, and it seemed that the turmoil that had marked the early years was past. This was not to be, however. Financial problems, while greatly reduced, were not entirely solved, and the reactionary political forces contributing to the rise of Naziism were gaining strength in the provinces around Dessau. In hopes of diminishing criticism of the Bauhaus, criticism he interpreted as being directed at him personally, Gropius resigned as head of the school in April 1928 and returned to his private architectural practice.

A young architect, Hannes Meyer, was appointed to succeed Gropius. Meyer set about enlarging the architectural program, adding courses in mathematics and engineering and emphasizing through lectures and studio projects the social responsibilities of architects. The other workshops were urged to increase production, and more designs than ever were licensed to industry, bringing increasing royalties to the school. But Hannes Meyer also encouraged students to become active in politics, not the wisest counsel in the deteriorating political climate of Germany, and in the summer of 1930 the authorities asked him to resign. His replacement was Mies van der Rohe, an architect long active in the Deutscher Werkbund, whose reputation was by then international.

Mies moved to stabilize the school by flatly prohibiting any political activity and insisting on the highest possible standards of work. More powerful political forces were gathering, however, and in 1932 the Nazi party gained control of Dessau. One of their first acts was to move against the Bauhaus, which to them symbolized Communism, decadence, and subversion; in October 1932 they closed the school. Shortly thereafter Mies managed to reopen the Bauhaus as a private institution in Berlin, but in April 1933 the building was raided by the Gestapo, and Mies finally closed the school in July 1933.

LUDWIG MIES VAN DER ROHE

The final director of the Bauhaus, Ludwig Mies van der Rohe (1886–1969), ranks as one of the leading architects of the twentieth century. He was the son of a stonemason, and he received a practical background in construction from his father, later working as an apprentice in the office of Bruno Paul. From 1908 to 1911 Mies worked in the office of Peter Behrens. His early designs as an independent architect show the strong effect of Schinkel, as can be seen in the projected house for Mrs. Kröller-Müller (1912), which was a symmetric rectangular solid with a stripped classical colonnade across the front.

After the First World War Mies worked on a series of projects that were to have enormous impact on later architecture even though they were never constructed. The first was a competition entry for an office building above the Berlin Friedrichstrasse station (1919), a twenty-story skyscraper completely sheathed in glass. In 1920–1921 Mies carried the concept of a glass skyscraper a step further in a project for a thirty-story tower, again encased entirely in glass, with a highly irregular perimeter and two circular elevator-stair cores (Figure 13.38). Mies's idea was to capitalize on the varying reflections possible with glass. The irregular curves of the walls were actually composed of short line segments, representing the width dimension of the curtain wall panels, so the entire building was to be a highly faceted, shimmering shaft. Its internal structure was provided by reinforced concrete slabs, cantilevered to a thin edge at the outside wall. (The state of material science and construction techniques in 1920 was inadequate to construct these designs, so the first all-glass façade building was not built until 1950–1952. It was Lever House on Park Avenue in New York City, designed by Gordon Bunshaft of Skidmore, Owings, and Merrill. A tower of the 1970s, the John Hancock Insurance Building in Boston designed by Henry Cobb of I.M. Pei and Partners, probably best embodies the character sketched by Mies in the 1919 competition.)

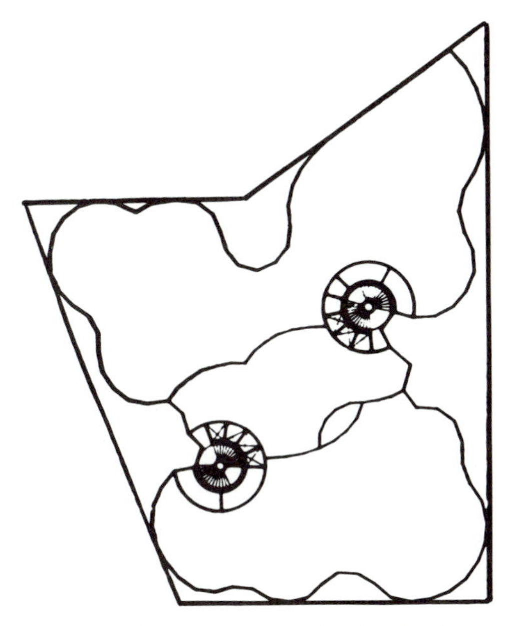

FIGURE 13.38 *Mies van der Rohe: Plan for glass tower, 1921.* (Courtesy *Architectural Record*)

Two other projects from the early 1920s show Mies was thinking about materials other than glass. His project for a concrete office block (1922) has seven floors, each a great horizontal tray cantilevered out from the reinforced-concrete structure. The height of the tray edge was determined by the vertical dimension of filing cabinets, those ubiquitous office furnishings; windows above ran in a continuous horizontal strip in a plane recessed from the outer edge of the concrete. If one recalls the Larkin Building, which had incorporated the same idea on its office floors, one can detect the influences of Wright's Wasmuth publications. The free plans and flowing spaces of the early Prairie houses also affected Mies's designs. His 1923 project for a brick country house, with its walls extending as vertical planes out into the landscape, seldom intersecting one another but defining space nonetheless, owes a debt to Wright. Some of this freedom would reappear in his 1929 masterpiece, the Pavilion of the Deutscher Werkbund for the International·Exposition in Barcelona.

The Barcelona Pavilion (Figure 13.39) has become one of the most celebrated architectural designs of the twentieth century, even though until recently it was known to most people only through photographs, since after the exposition was over, the building was dismantled and its materials sold at auction. (A replica of the pavilion has recently been built on the original site.) It is a small structure, and unlike most exhibition buildings, it contains no displays. Aside from the X-frame tables, stools, and chairs designed by Mies for the building (Figure 13.40), the only product on view was a sculpture of a dancing girl by Georg Kolbe, carefully

FIGURE 13.39 *Mies van der Rohe: German Pavilion, Barcelona, 1929.* (Photo: Moffett)

placed in a reflecting pool at one end of the building.

The importance of the Barcelona Pavilion lies not in what it contained but in the building itself. Mies aimed to have it stand for quality design, materials, and craftsmanship. The design is at once simple and sophisticated. Raised on a low podium (as if to elevate it above the rabble of the fair), the pavilion was a one-story jewel box (Figure 13.41). The greatest part of its ground plane was occupied by an exterior courtyard, dominated by a large reflecting pool lined with black glass. Eight cruciform columns supported a rectangular roof slab that appeared to hover like a great horizontal plane, floating independently of the vertical walls. Quite deliberately the walls were not incorporated in or aligned with the column grid, thereby expressing the separate functions of support and enclosure while conforming to the same orthogonal geometry. The columns were shiny chromium-plated steel; the walls were polished book-matched marble in deep colors of green and red, and the floors were Roman travertine; onyx and grey-tinted glass contributed to the feeling of exquisite taste and luxury. The Barcelona chairs were chrome-plated steel with white kid upholstery. Mies's collaborator, Lilly Reich, shares credit with him for the interior design, particularly for the deep red velvet curtain that hung over the front glass wall.

Sources for the Pavilion's architecture can be enumerated: Wright for the flowing spatial qualities and great horizontal sweep of the roof; Schinkel for the podium and basically symmetrical nature of the building proper; and de Stijl, the Dutch painterly movement for the almost abstract composition of solid, void, and line. The masterful integration of

FIGURE 13.40 *Mies van der Rohe: Interior of the German Pavilion, Barcelona.* (Photo: Moffett)

FIGURE 13.41 *Mies van der Rohe: Plan of the German Pavilion, Barcelona.* (Redrawn after P. Johnson)

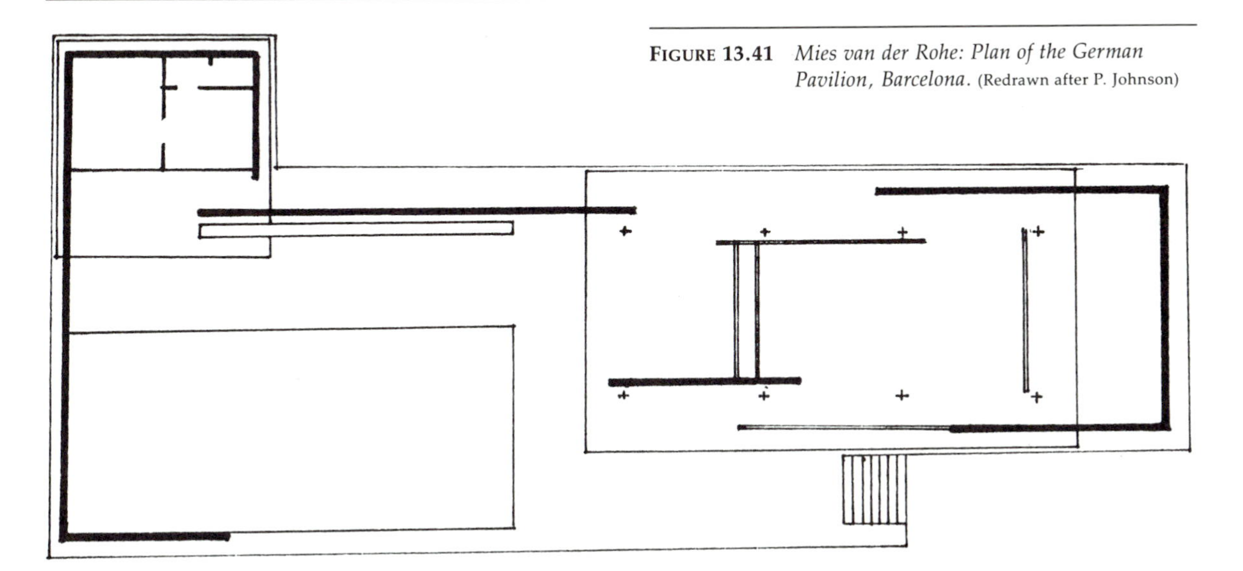

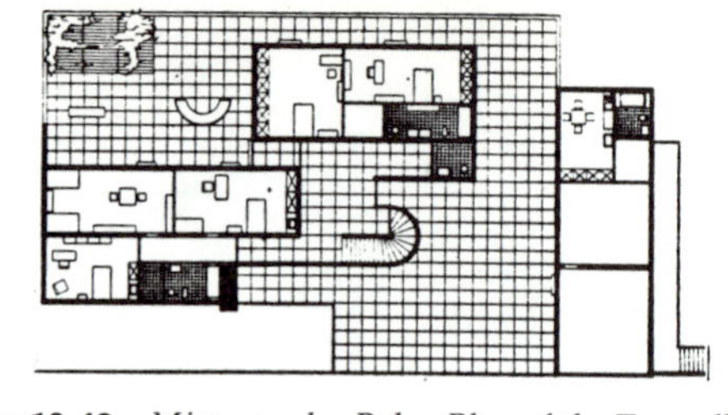

FIGURE 13.42 *Mies van der Rohe: Plan of the Tugendhat House, Brno, 1930.* (Courtesy *Architectural Record*)

these diverse influences into a new architectural synthesis remains the great accomplishment of Mies van der Rohe.

Concepts from the Barcelona Pavilion were used in a residential commission of 1930, the Tugendhat House (Figure 13.42) in Brno, Czechoslovakia. The same regular grid of chromium steel cruciform columns supports the roof, and polished slabs of marble serve as walls to define interior spaces in an open plan. Because of the hilly site, the Tugendhat House is two stories, set firmly within a series of terraces cut into the slope; but thanks to its largely glass walls, the predominant view is out to the natural landscape. Color on the interior is very much subdued, confined to the natural hues of the finish materials and a white linoleum floor, so that the changing light and palette of the outside world determines much of the color inside the house.

By the mid-1920s progressive architects in many European countries were working in a manner that reflected the varying influences on the time: a new admiration for industrial materials and products, respect for rational, straightforward architectural expression devoid of applied ornament, and an accompanying interest in the purity of simply geometric forms and planar surfaces. For want of a better term, this movement is still called Modern, although eventually we will need to develop a more descriptive label (perhaps even more than one) to reflect the diverse currents in architectural design since 1920.

THE WEISSENHOF SIEDLUNG AND THE INTERNATIONAL STYLE

In 1925 the Deutscher Werkbund proposed an exhibition be held in 1927 to demonstrate the latest architectural thinking in the area of housing design and display the state of the art in interior fittings and construction technology. The City of Stuttgart and various materials suppliers contributed land and money for the construction of thirty-three permanent buildings on a hillside on the outskirts of the city. Mies, as Vice-President of the Werkbund, was placed in charge of the enterprise, and he developed the master plan as well as contributing the design of a block of flats. With characteristic generosity Mies invited participation by sixteen leading architects across Europe, assigning them sites for detached houses, duplexes, or row houses. The permanent buildings became known as the Weissenhof Siedlung (or model housing development at Weissenhof) (Figure 13.43).

The concept behind the exhibition was to design modest scale, modern dwelling units suitable as prototypes for mass production. The variety of approaches taken by the individual designers was, in most cases, less important than the common factors shared by all. All the buildings were painted white; they had "functional" windows that emphasized the horizontal; and almost all the roofs were flat. (Some even featured garden terraces on the roof.) Industrialization was expressed in the cylindrical pipe railings on balconies, the major decorative element on the exterior. Window trim was minimal, and there were no cornices. In a manner recalling the Industrial City of Garnier, Mies had originally planned the layout to keep cars on the perimeter, with only pedestrian access in the housing area; but the city authorities, who wanted to resell the units as individual dwellings after the exhibition, requested the land be divided into plots with separate access. Mies was able to retain his basically sculptural conception of the overall form of the site, with the tallest and largest building, Mies's own four-story block of twenty-four flats, set on the highest portion of the hill (Figure 13.44). Within the tract of land, buildings were oriented with a view toward internal community and individual privacy for each unit, rather than following the geometry of the street.

A brief view of the principal buildings at the Weissenhof Siedlung illustrates the range of designs proposed. The building by Mies contained small apartments, arranged with certain standard elements (a kitchen-bathroom core, prefabricated partitions, and storage walls) that allowed each of the twenty-four units to be arranged differently in plan.

FIGURE 13.43 *Mies van der Rohe: Weissenhof Siedlung, Stuttgart, 1927.* (Photo: German Information Center)

FIGURE 13.44 *Mies van der Rohe: Block of flats at the Weissenhof Siedlung, Stuttgart, 1927.* (Photo: German Information Center)

FIGURE 13.45 *Le Corbusier: Steel double house at the Weissenhof Siedlung, Stuttgart.* (Photo: German Information Center)

Standardization and rational planning, together with a steel frame, made flexibility possible in the interior layout. The roof terrace provided recreational facilities, and each apartment had a small balcony. Horizontal strip windows facilitated cross-ventilation for each dwelling unit.

Walter Gropius built two detached houses. Continuing the approach being studied at the Bauhaus, he designed in close collaboration with several manufacturers, and both houses were constructed entirely of prefabricated panels. The module of the panels could readily be seen inside and out, and the interior was furnished with the products of Bauhaus workshops designed by Marcel Breuer. (After coming to the United States in 1937 Gropius continued his interest in prefabricated housing but failed to interest American manufacturers in the idea. When he built his own home at Lincoln, Massachusetts [1938], in collaboration with Breuer, Gropius turned instead to the building components already available in light industrial construction and artfully incorporated them for the major elements of the house.)

Le Corbusier also contributed two designs, one a single-family dwelling in reinforced concrete and the other a duplex in steel frame (Figure 13.45), a realization of the Citrohan concept. The latter was one of the most controversial of the exhibition, in part because of its unorthodox interior proportions. The main circulation spine was a corridor the length of the house, with dimensions and windows that suggested a train more than a residence, particularly as some bedrooms were narrow, like the sleeping compartments of European trains. Corbusier was, in fact, fascinated by the functional designs of ocean liners and airplanes, so it is possible that railway cars also inspired his architecture.

The common thread of rational or functional design could be detected in all buildings at the Weissenhof Siedlung, and the projects of German architects were not dissimilar to those of other countries in appearance. This aesthetic affinity and a book, *Internationale Architektur* (1925) by Walter Gropius, led Alfred H. Barr (of the Museum of Modern Art in New York) to call modern architecture of the late 1920s the International Style.

European architectural developments were a major focus of the show, "Modern Architecture: International Exhibition," organized by Henry-Russell Hitchcock and Philip Johnson for the Museum of Modern Art (MoMA) in 1932. For the first time the American public and American architects were made aware of postwar advances in Germany, France, Holland, and Belgium, as works like Gerrit Rietveld's Schroeder House (1924) in Utrecht were displayed alongside early Wright designs such as the Winslow House, and the abstract rationalism of de Stijl appeared alongside the work of Mies, Gropius, and Le Corbusier.

Hitchcock and Johnson published a book, *The International Style,* based on the material in the exhibition. According to the definition devised by Alfred H. Barr, the International Style was characterized by "emphasis upon volume — space enclosed by thin planes or surfaces as opposed to the suggestion of mass and solidity; regularity as opposed to symmetry or other kinds of obvious balance; and, lastly, dependence upon the intrinsic elegance of materials, perfection, and fine proportions, as opposed to applied ornament." Hitchcock later revised this statement to include the articulation of structure in the place of the section on ornament. Even allowing for these adjustments, it is already apparent that the architecture of the Weissenhof Siedlung was succinctly described by Barr's definition.

Only a handful of American buildings were included in *The International Style,* an indication of the strength of Beaux-Arts classicism and Art Deco in the United States in the 1920s. The largest International Style building included was the Philadelphia Saving Fund Society Building (1932) by Howe and Lescaze (Figure 13.46), which was cited for its clear articulation of sections by different surfacing materials, although it was acknowledged that "the relation of the base with its curved corner to the tower is awkward." The entire Market Street façade was cantilevered beyond the column line, allowing the windows to wrap in a horizontal band around the corner to glorify the freedom from structural constraint. No towers quite so bold as this would be built in the United States for the next decade, in part because of the Great Depression and World War II.

Smaller structures that were built according to the dictates of the International Style, or at least in imitation of it, were often seen as cheap because

FIGURE 13.46 *Howe and Lescaze: Philadelphia Saving Fund Society Building, Philadelphia, 1929–1932.* (Photo: Lawrence S. Williams/courtesy PSFS)

they lacked presumably expensive ornament. For a long time modern architecture was associated with inexpensive construction, a connection that was not entirely valid. One has only to recall the luxurious materials and costly craftsmanship essential to the Barcelona Pavilion, for example, to be reminded that the International Style did not always equate with low budgets.

LATER WORK OF MIES VAN DER ROHE

By making visible the modern architecture of Europe in the United States the MoMA show did much to increase awareness of the International Style on this side of the Atlantic. The impact would be far greater when the leading architects of Germany, fleeing Nazi intolerance of their work (called "Arab" by Hitler), emigrated to the United States. Walter Gropius came in 1937, after a period of professional practice in England, to direct the Department of Architecture at the Graduate School of Design at Harvard University; Marcel Breuer, a pupil and teacher at the Bauhaus, also taught under Gropius at Harvard; and Mies van der Rohe came to Chicago in 1938 to head the Architecture School at the Armour Institute of Technology (soon to merge with the Lewis Institute and become the Illinois Institute of Technology).

In his twenty years at IIT Mies had the opportunity to plan the new campus, design many of its buildings, and influence the architectural education of a whole generation of students. The curriculum laid down by him stressed clarity, rationality, intellectual order, and discipline and progressed from building in wood to stone, brick, concrete, and finally steel. Once students understood the materials, they studied problems of design. The highest standards of draftsmanship and precision were expected at all levels, and the essence of architecture was reduced to skin and bones — the glass spandrel panels or brickwork (skin) set in the structural frame (the bones).

The master plan made for IIT reflects the order and rationality of the curriculum. A square grid subdivides the rectangular site, and the buildings are all conceived as rectangular masses conforming to the grid, forming a continuous series of interlocked courtyards and exterior walks. Mies saw that steel was the major American industrial building material (labor costs for formwork often made concrete less economical), so he set about designing the purest, most elegant steel expressions achieved to that time. For the IIT campus he designed Crown Hall (1956) (Figures 13.47, 13.48) to house the School of Architecture. It is a one-story building raised above a high basement. Four deep panel

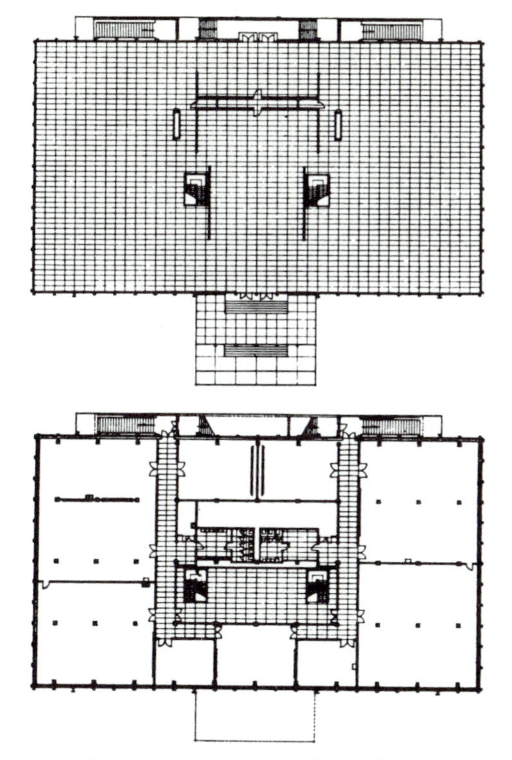

girders straddle the building, supporting the roof and leaving the entire interior free of columns. Except for the stairs and toilet rooms, which are fixed, the possible locations of subdividing walls are not hindered by the architectural container. As in his other projects, Mies was designing for flexibility and change, so that other, unforeseeable uses might easily be accommodated within the building at a later time.

In his office Mies designed a range of other types of projects. On a beautiful site in Chicago overlooking Lake Michigan, he built a pair of apartment towers known by their address, 860 Lake Shore Drive (1949–1951), the first glass and steel high-rise residential construction in the United States (Figure 13.49). Twenty-six stories tall, they are the realization of the concept first proposed in the glass tower schemes of 1919–1921. In the interval technological

FIGURE 13.47 *Mies van der Rohe: Plans of Crown Hall, IIT, Chicago, 1956.* (Courtesy *Architectural Record*)

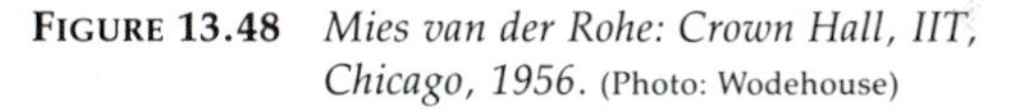

FIGURE 13.48 *Mies van der Rohe: Crown Hall, IIT, Chicago, 1956.* (Photo: Wodehouse)

FIGURE 13.49 *Mies van der Rohe: 860 Lake Shore Drive, Chicago, 1949–1951.* (Photo: Wodehouse)

capabilities had come up to the level required to construct a glass tower. The 860 Lake Shore Drive buildings are framed in steel, which of course must be fireproofed by a casing of concrete. Mies was able to express the actual structural material only by welding additional steel to the exterior of the frames afterward. To increase the vertical sense of the buildings, thinner I-beams run continuously up the building as window mullions. This exterior steel serves no structural function, of course, but it was necessary to have the building look right to Mies.

As early as 1946 Mies was at work designing an all-glass house for Dr. Edith Farnsworth, to be located on land near the Fox River in Plano, Illinois. Design and construction took six years, during which time Philip Johnson built a glass house for himself (1949) in New Canaan, Connecticut. The Farnsworth House (1950–1952), raised off the ground because the Fox River is known to flood over the site, sits as a simple white frame in the landscape, as elegant an expression of skin-and-bones architecture as could be desired (Figure 13.50). The glass walls can be screened with white curtains when privacy is desired, but the play of

FIGURE 13.50 *Mies van der Rohe: Farnsworth House, Plano, 1950–1952.* (Photo: Wodehouse)

FIGURE 13.51 *Mies van der Rohe: Seagram Building, New York City, 1956–1958.* (Photo: Roz Li)

light reflecting off the glass and the immediacy of the natural surroundings viewed through the walls are more effective unscreened. It is thus an expression of an architectural ideal rather than a model for everyday family living; it carries the concepts of the Tugendhat House to their logical conclusion, losing in the process a certain degree of practical function.

Mies evolved a thoroughly rational approach to architecture, designing "universal" spaces enclosed in rectangular containers, the most easily used of geometries. From the first, he designed for later modification and reuse with painstaking studies of the architectural expression to ensure a timeless and elegant character. Mies used one of several steel framing systems depending on the minimum clear span required. Short spans would use ordinary columns and beams, as in the Farnsworth House, 860 Lake Shore Drive, and the Seagram Building (1958) in New York City (Figures 13.51, 13.52); moderate spans would employ plate girders, as in Crown Hall; and the longest spans would have a steel space frame, as in the New Museum of Modern Art in Berlin (Figure 13.53). The Berlin building, completed in 1968, was the last project by Mies to be built before his death, and it is a fitting parallel to Schinkel's Altes Museum in the same city. Both are rectangular solids, raised on podiums and provided with axial stairs leading to a recessed central entrance. The buildings look entirely different, of course, because Mies was building with twentieth-century technology, whereas Schinkel was limited to the masonry bearing wall construction of the early nineteenth century. However, the same Neo-Classic ideals underlie both museums.

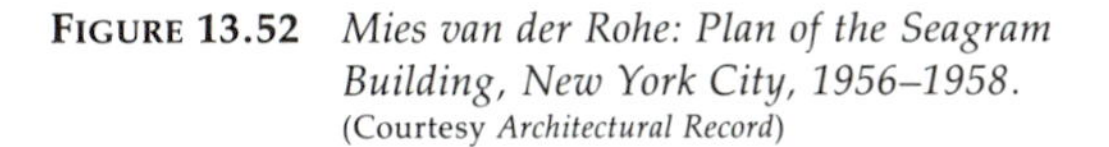

FIGURE 13.52 *Mies van der Rohe: Plan of the Seagram Building, New York City, 1956–1958.* (Courtesy *Architectural Record*)

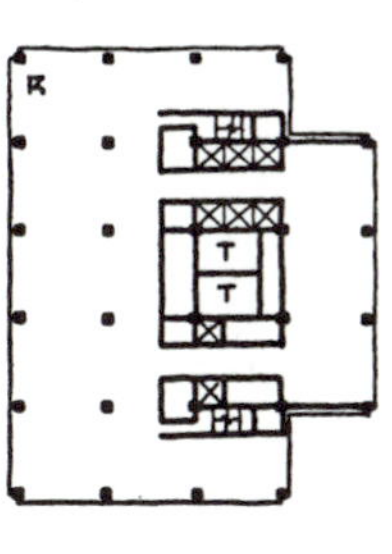

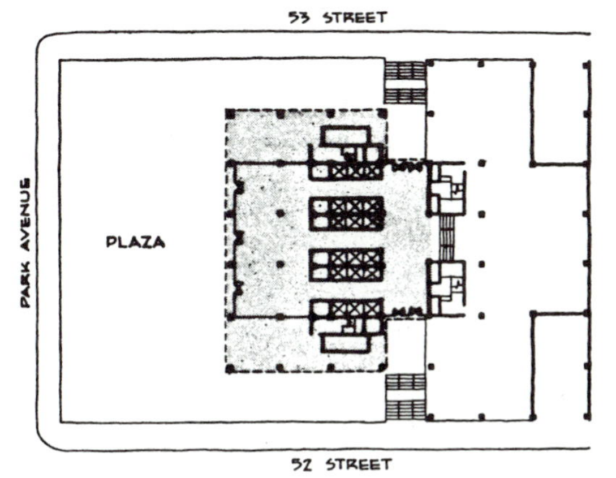

FIGURE 13.53 *Mies van der Rohe: New Museum of Modern Art, Berlin, 1968.* (Photo: German Information Center)

LATER WORK OF FRANK LLOYD WRIGHT

The previous discussion of Wright concluded with his design of the Imperial Hotel. While his architectural practice in the 1920s suffered because of his personal difficulties, he did manage to do some work, notably in California. There he built a series of so-called textile block houses, which were not of cloth but of patterned concrete block, laid in a stacked bond and held together by internal steel reinforcing bars. One such house, built in Pasadena for Alice Millard (1932), illustrates the group. The use of concrete block imposed an orthogonal geometry on the design, although Wright, as usual, created an open and flowing plan with balconies and terraces to link the house to its hillside site. The custom-designed pattern molded into each block contributes an overall texture to the exterior and reinforces the sense of surface integrity in both a structural and an artistic sense. As in the Imperial Hotel, one can detect influence from Mayan art in the massing and ornamental detail.

Toward the end of the decade, Wright's chaotic private life became more orderly. He was still hounded by the press and pursued by creditors (his home at Taliesin was almost sold for nonpayment of taxes), but in his third wife, Olgivanna Lazovich, he found a steadying spouse. To rescue him from financial pressures a group of loyal friends incorporated Wright and paid off the mortgages on Taliesin, counting on his future earnings to repay their investment. Wright formed the Taliesin Fellowship in 1932 for young men and women who wished to come and work under his tutelage, charging them a fee for the experience. It became a highly personal school of architecture, reflecting Wright's disdain for the formal trappings of educational enterprises. Students, called apprentices, participated in all aspects of life and work at Taliesin, from helping with farm and kitchen chores, constructing the ever-expanding physical plant, and performing in evening musicales or theatrical events, to assisting Wright in the drafting room. With Olgivanna's encouragement, Wright also began to write; the first edition of his *Autobiography* dates from 1932.

Just as Wright was again becoming a productive architect, the national economy took a nosedive into the Great Depression. There was little work for anyone to do, so Wright and his apprentices turned their attention to a utopian scheme that Wright christened Broadacre City. It illustrated many of Wright's ideals about the proper manner of living in America. The single-family house, set on about one acre of land, was the basic dwelling unit. Urban centers in the traditional sense were rather small and dispersed, for Wright anticipated that efficient communications and high-speed transportation would largely eliminate the need for the density and congestion associated with city life and business. (Heavy industry seems to have been conveniently overlooked.) In some respects Broadacre City looked backward to the nineteenth century and to the small, largely agrarian towns that characterized much of the United States then. Self-sufficient, small communities clustered around cultural and recreational facilities conjure up romantic visions of a past that probably never existed. In other respects Wright's scheme was farsighted, for it seemed to incorporate attitudes that are peculiarly American: a mistrust of bigness, a love of the land and open air, and the opportunity for individual expression. The phenomenal suburban growth around American cities after 1945 reflects in part the popular interpretation of concepts embedded in Broadacre City.

All of Wright's later actual buildings were designed to fit into Broadacre City. For residences, he developed the Usonian House as an ideal, and he constructed many actual examples across the country from the mid-1930s until the late 1950s. Usonian Houses differed from Prairie Houses in several respects. They were generally smaller, reflecting the reduced size of the American family and middle-class budgets, and they were designed for families without household servants. The design provides easy access to the house from the automobile, and the activity of the interior can be easily supervised from the kitchen, correctly identified as the principal workstation of the housewife. The interior opens up to outdoor spaces away from the street, either to the side or the rear of the lot. Wright was a master at site planning, generally managing to locate the house so that it appeared to rise naturally (organically, as he would describe it) from the land.

As has already been mentioned, buildings by Wright were included in the 1932 MoMA show on modern architecture, although not in the book illustrating the International Style. He had scathing comments to make about the leading Internationalists and their designs, remarking with characteristic humility to Henry-Russell Hitchcock, "Not only do I fully intend to be the greatest architect who has yet lived, but the greatest who will ever live. Yes, I intend to be the greatest architect of all time." But by International Style standards, Wright's work in the 1920s was loaded down with a superfluity of fussy detail and excessive ornament. Seeing the 1932 exhibition in New York must have influenced Wright to a certain degree, for several years afterward he designed in a much less ornate way, producing several masterpieces in the 1930s.

One of the young men who came to Taliesin as an apprentice was Edgar Kaufmann, Jr., son of a wealthy Pittsburgh department store owner. Hearing that his father was contemplating the construction of a vacation house in the mountains of western Pennsylvania, young Edgar persuaded E. J. Kaufmann, Sr., to employ Wright as architect. The result was Fallingwater (1935–1937), perhaps the most famous house not built for royalty anywhere in the world (Figures 13.54, 13.55). Wright took the major natural feature of the site, a rocky outcropping where a small stream fell over a series of ledges, and planted the house beside the stream, letting the reinforced concrete balconies cantilever like great trays over the stream. In order to see the waterfall, one must go outside, below the house, where the falls and the house can be seen together in the clas-

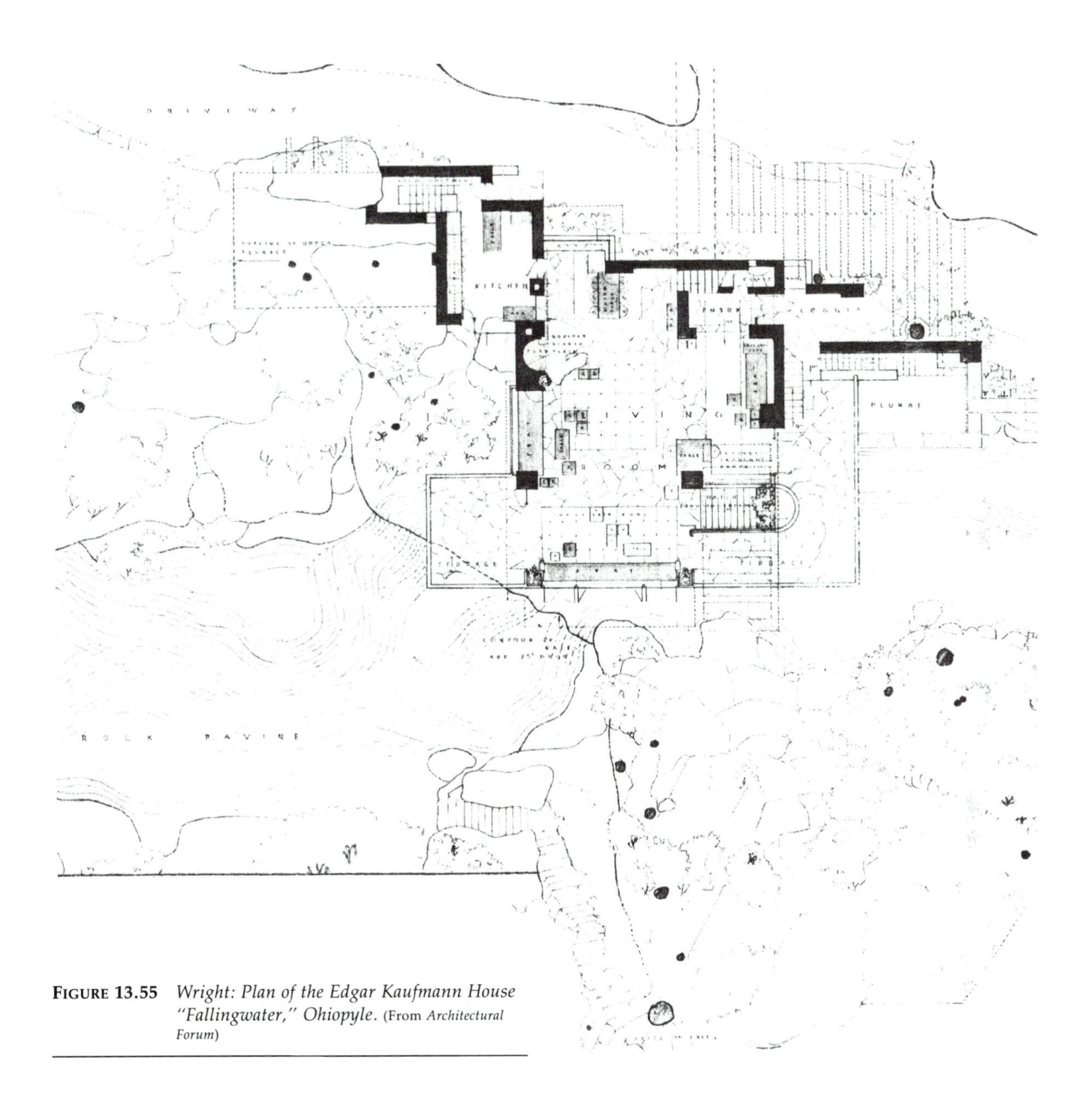

FIGURE 13.55 *Wright: Plan of the Edgar Kaufmann House "Fallingwater," Ohiopyle.* (From *Architectural Forum*)

sic view that Wright anticipated. (He did a rendering from just that point to measure the effect before construction.) At sixty-eight Wright's second period of great creativity was just beginning.

Stone quarried on the site was laid in irregular horizontal coursings to form the four great piers supporting the living room, the fireplace mass, and the remaining bearing walls. The balconies, which form the dominant and dramatic elements of the design, cantilever in two directions and are stiffened at their edges by the upturned parapet wall. Large expanses of glass float between slate floors and

◀ **FIGURE 13.54** *Wright: Edgar Kaufmann House "Fallingwater," Ohiopyle, 1935–1937.* (Photo: Western Pennsylvania Conservancy)

FIGURE 13.56 *Wright: Johnson Wax Company, Racine, 1936–1939; 1946–1949.* (Photo: Courtesy Johnson Wax Company)

FIGURE 13.57 *Wright: Plan of the Johnson Wax Company, Racine, 1936–1939.* (From W. Blaser)

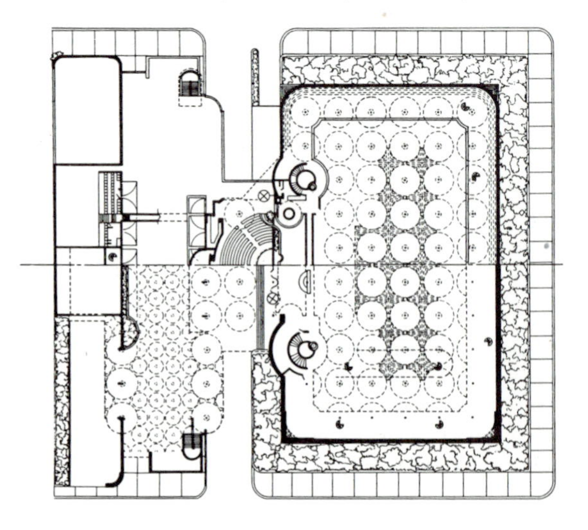

stuccoed ceiling, minimizing the distinction between interior and exterior. Fallingwater's planar treatment of surfaces and abstract fragmentation of volumes suggest a debt to the European modernists. It is Lewis Mumford's assessment that in Fallingwater, Wright "created a dynamic multidimensional composition that made Le Corbusier's buildings seem flat cardboard compositions." (Fallingwater is now open to the public under the trusteeship of the Western Pennsylvania Conservancy.)

Close on the heels of the Kaufmann House came a commission from the Johnson Wax Company of Racine, Wisconsin, for an administration building (1936–1939) (Figures 13.56, 13.57), later completed by a research tower (1946–1949) (Figure 13.58). Wright's growing interest in circular geometry materialized in this project. The brick walls sweep smoothly around radiused exterior corners, while the interior clerical area is covered by a skylit roof supported on tapering mushroom columns

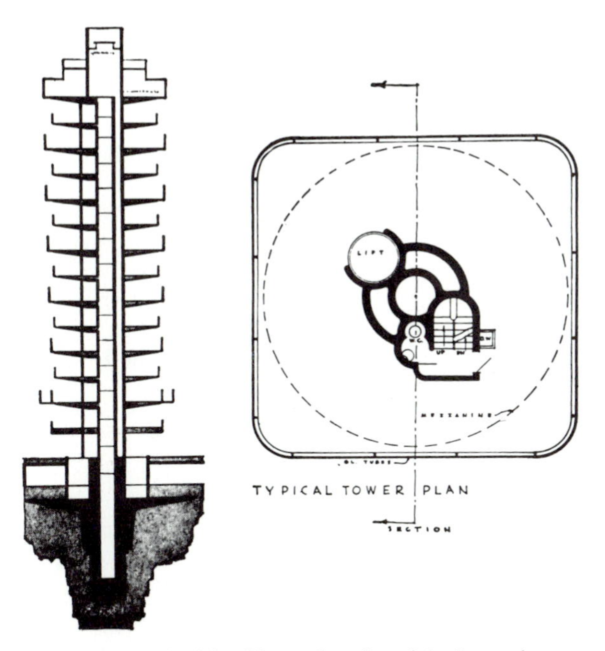

FIGURE 13.58 *Wright: Plan and section of the Research Tower, Johnson Wax Company, Racine, 1946–1949.* (From *Architectural Forum*)

with large circular tops. (Skeptical building officials doubted the structural integrity of these columns and required Wright to demonstrate their strength by test-loading a sample before they would issue building permits.) The circular motif continues in balconies, door pulls, and even in the secretarial furniture designed by Wright for the building. Curtain walls in the research tower and connecting walkways to the administration building are glazed with glass tubing laid in parallel rows. The light quality achieved is stunning, even though neither the original nor modern sealants can stop all the leaks.

Wright continued to explore the possibilities of circular forms, especially those involving continuous ramps. A project for an observatory atop Sugar Loaf Mountain in Maryland (1925) may have first set his mind to the idea, and the concept reappeared in the V.C. Morris Gift Shop (1949) in San Francisco (Figures 13.59, 13.60) in a parking garage proposed for Pittsburgh. Its full embodiment finally came in the Guggenheim Museum (1957–1959) in New York City (Figures 13.61–13.63), where a quarter-mile ramp spirals around a six-story interior sculpture court. The Guggenheim has extensive holdings of twentieth-century art, and it has been theorized that Wright was expressing his scorn for modern art by designing a museum with a continuously sloping floor and outward leaning, curving walls. Display possibilities are certainly restricted by the design, and no artist could single-handedly compete with the strong three-dimensional spatial experience Wright has created in the interior.

As he grew older, Wright preferred the warm weather of the desert southwest to the blustery cold

FIGURE 13.59 *Wright: V. C. Morris Gift Shop, San Francisco, 1949.* (Photo: Wodehouse)

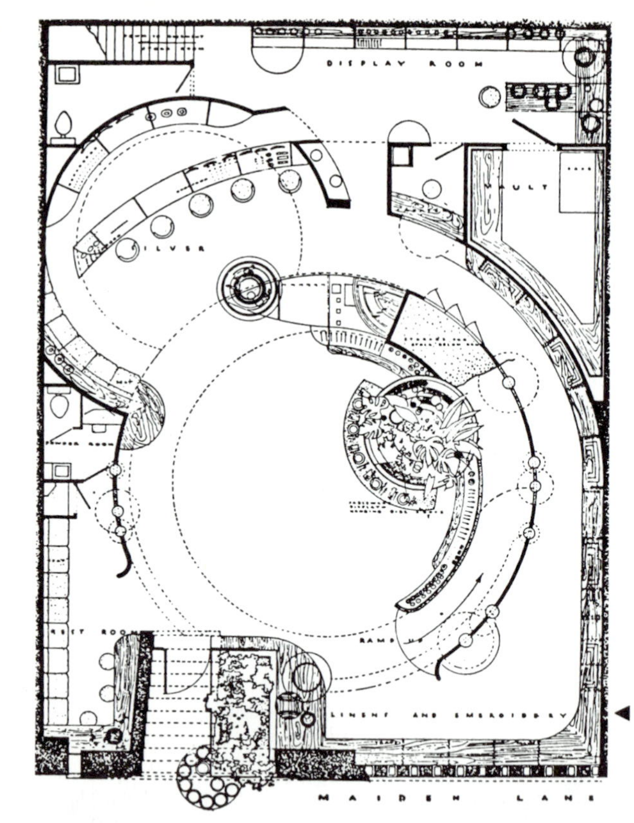

of Wisconsin winters, so the Fellowship moved south to avoid the cold, returning to Wisconsin in the spring. Near Phoenix, Arizona, construction began on Taliesin West (1938 onward), a sprawling encampment set in the rugged spareness of the desert to replace the wood-and-canvas Ocotillo Desert camp dating from 1927. Materials used were derived from the locale. Adobe and desert boulders, redwood beams, and canvas panels were combined to create a shaded interior that moderated the sun's heat and glare. As with Taliesin East in Spring Green, the construction was accomplished by the Fellowship apprentices.

◀ **FIGURE 13.60** *Wright: Plan of the V. C. Morris Gift Shop, San Francisco.* (From *Architectural Forum*)

FIGURE 13.61 *Wright: Guggenheim Museum, New York City, 1957–1959.* (Photo: Roz Li)

FIGURE 13.63 *Wright: Interior of the Guggenheim Museum, New York City.* (Photo: Robert Mates/ Guggenheim Museum) ▶

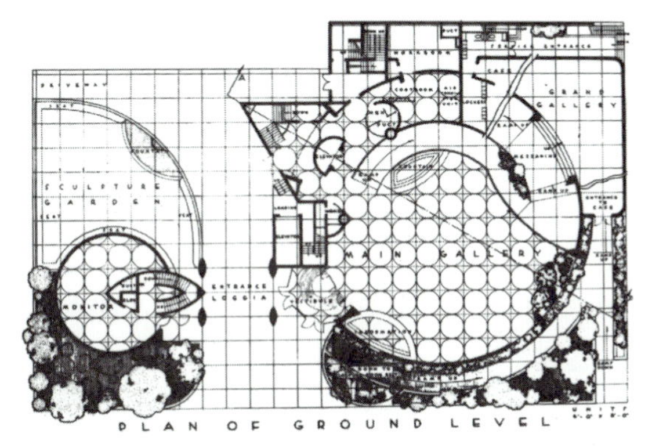

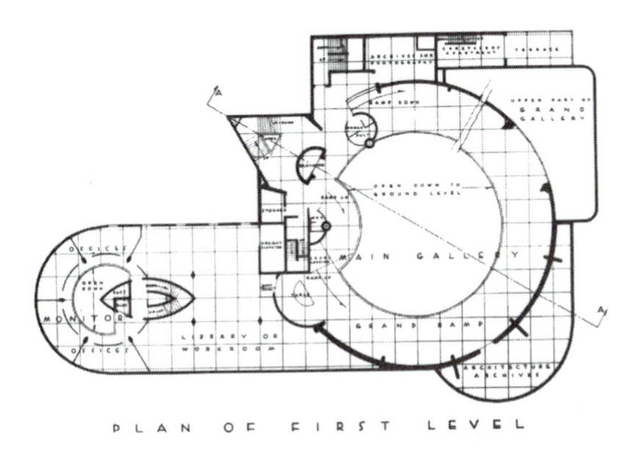

FIGURE 13.62 *Wright: Plans of ground and first level of the Guggenheim Museum, New York City.*
(Courtesy *Architectural Record*)

LATER WORK OF LE CORBUSIER

Just as Wright designed his later works to fit into Broadacre City, Le Corbusier conceived of his works as elements of an ideal city he called *La Ville Radieuse* (The Radiant City). The first opportunity he had to build an apartment tower came after the Second World War, when the Mayor of Marseilles invited Le Corbusier to construct the first Unité d'Habitation or Unified Dwelling House (1946–1952) (Figures 13.64–13.67). Some critics consider the Unité a masterpiece, both for its bold sculptural forms and its novel approach to the problems of apartment living. The Unité block is set in a green park and raised on pilotis. The apartments are ingeniously designed to have frontage on both east and west sides of the building, making possible cross-ventilation, a desirable trade-off for their long, thin shape. Balconies, integrated into **brise-soleil** (sun screens) give each side exterior living space. As a consequence of the apartment design, the elevator stops only on every third floor. The building features a two-story shopping floor (grocery store, beauty shop, repair services, etc.) halfway up, and the roof levels are devoted to extensive recreational and health facilities: a gymnasium, running track, movie theater, health club, nursery school, sun terraces, and the like. The concrete work throughout is forceful. Patterns resulting from the board marks of the carpentry formwork can be regarded as surface ornament disciplined by the fabrication process. Proportions based on the Modulor, which was the Golden Section reformulated by Le Corbusier to incorporate the average height of grown men, govern the entire design. Ship's imagery characterizes the rooftop ventilation stacks, elevator housing, and recreational facilities, for here Le Corbusier could exercise his formal repertoire rather freely. Above all the concept of sunlight, air, and green open space for all 1600 residents guided the design of this remarkable building.

Le Corbusier's critics have pointed out that the scheme is essentially antiurban, turning its back on the architectural and street patterns of Marseilles. Even the provision of shops (which were a financial failure) was attacked, because it meant the residents would have little need to associate with the commercial life of the town. (Grocery shopping, done daily in France, is a great socializing opportunity.) Rather than an affront to Marseilles, however, the Unité must be seen as a design in harmony with Le Corbusier's idealized city, a world that was quite different from any existing urban setting.

FIGURE 13.64 *Le Corbusier: Apartments in the Unité d'Habitation, Marseilles, 1946–1952.* (Photo: Moffett)

In the east of France not far from the Swiss border, Corbusier designed the famous pilgrimage chapel at Ronchamp, Notre-Dame du Haut (1951–1955) (Figures 13.68, 13.69), to replace a previous church destroyed by artillery fire during World War II. This small building allowed him to give maximum expression to the sculptural possibilities of architectural form. The rationalizations of earlier works were laid aside — no proportional system, no five points, no pilotis! — and a dramatic, highly symbolic design emerged. Even the structure is nonrational; metal frame is made to look like mas-

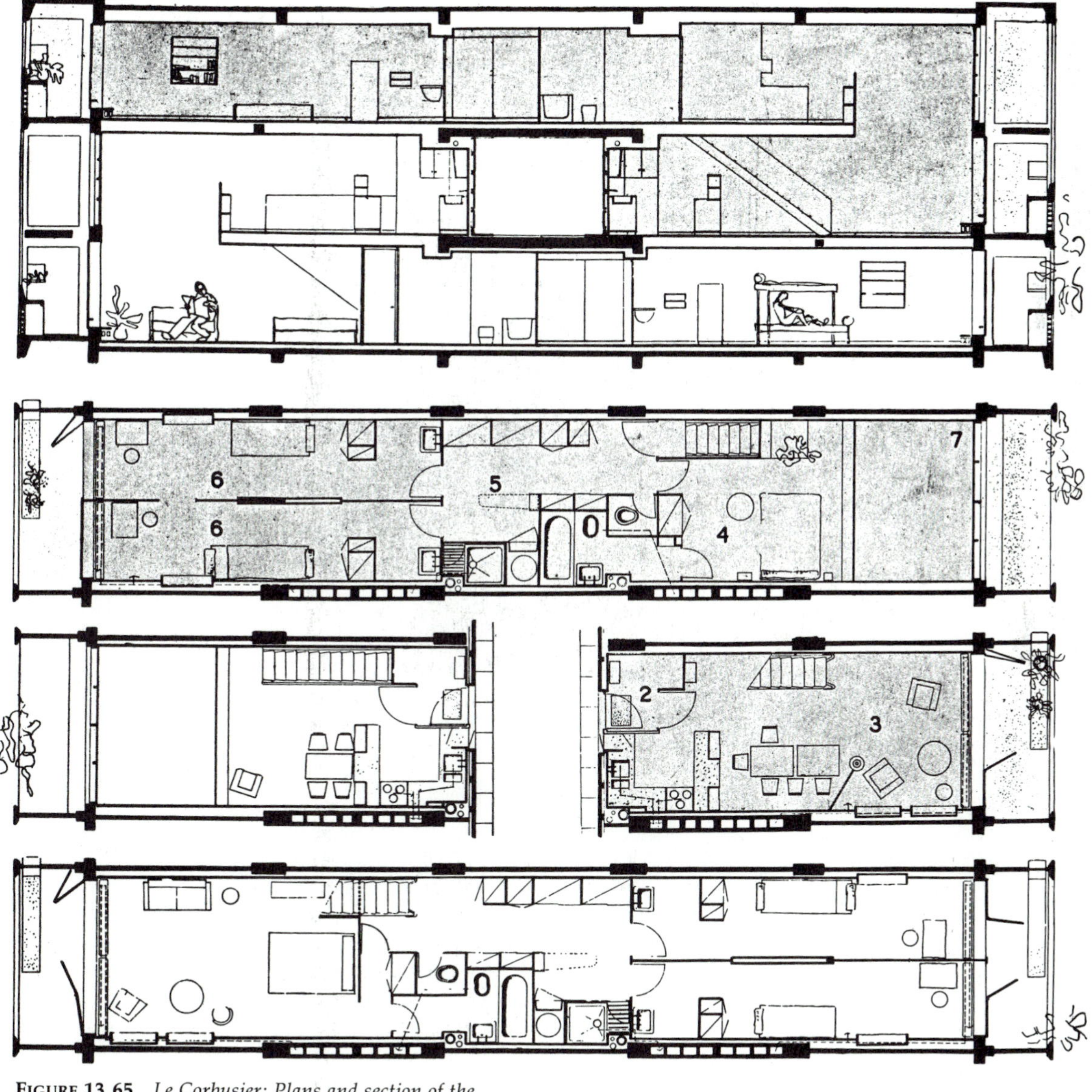

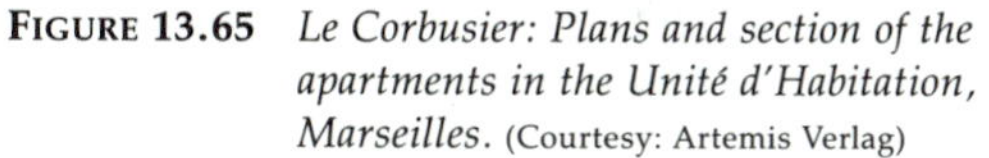

FIGURE 13.65 *Le Corbusier: Plans and section of the apartments in the Unité d'Habitation, Marseilles.* (Courtesy: Artemis Verlag)

◀ **FIGURE 13.66** *Le Corbusier: Section through the Unité d'Habitation, Marseilles.* (Courtesy: Artemis Verlag)

sive masonry. The walls are rough-textured stucco painted white, and the roof is a great billowing sail of board-formed concrete that rolls over the east wall to provide protection for the exterior pulpit. (Large crowds attend services out-of-doors, sitting on the lawn; the interior provides seats for only fifty people, although there is standing room for more.)

FIGURE 13.67 *Le Corbusier: Roof of the Unité d'Habitation, Marseilles.* (Photo: Moffett)

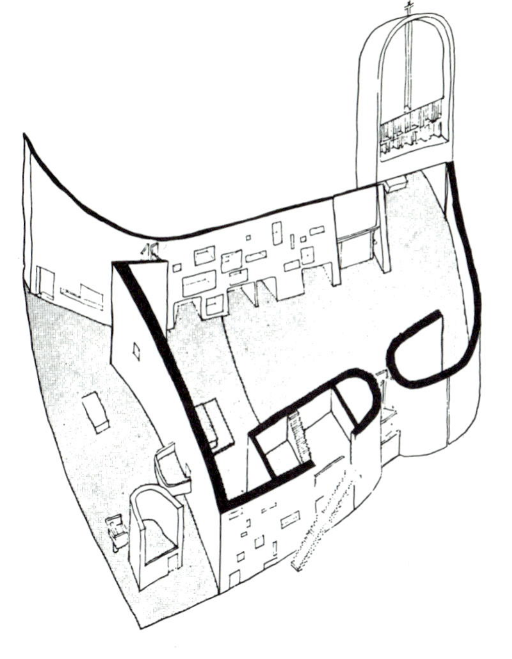

◀ **FIGURE 13.68** *Le Corbusier: Axonometric of Notre-Dame du Haut, Ronchamp, 1951–1955.* (From *Architectural Forum*)

The spectacular south wall has exaggerated thickness and an array of splayed windows inset with hand-painted colored glass. From the outside, it looks like an irregular series of small apertures, but from the interior, the wall is a glowing light sculpture, as moving in its way as the windows of Chartres (Figure 13.70). A very thin strip of clear

FIGURE 13.69 *Le Corbusier: Notre-Dame du Haut, Ronchamp, 1951–1955.* (Photo: Marburg)

glass intervenes between the roof and walls, seeming to defy the gravity load of the concrete ceiling. Meditation chapels underneath the towers have top illumination from high clerestories on the wall behind the worshipper. The light from an unseen source spilling softly over the rough-textured red stucco powerfully conveys a sense of man's essential loneliness.

Southwest of Lyon is the small town of Eveux, outside of which Le Corbusier was commissioned to design a Dominican monastery, Ste. Marie de la Tourette (1956–1960) (Figures 13.71, 13.72). Here he accomplished a modern reworking of the medieval monastic program. The church, a simple rectangular solid with sculptural subsidiary chapels in the crypt (Figure 13.73), is located on the west side of an open courtyard, criss-crossed by enclosed passageways connecting the church to other parts of

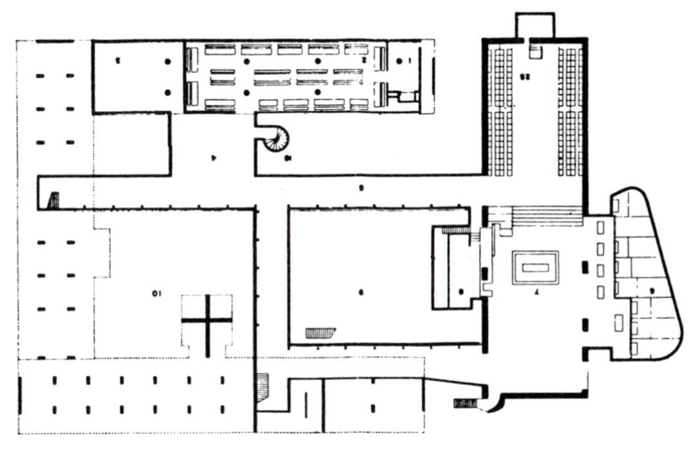

FIGURE 13.72 *Le Corbusier: Plan and section of Sainte-Marie de la Tourette, Eveux.* (Reprinted from *Architectural Record* July 1969 © 1969 by McGraw-Hill, Inc., with all rights reserved.)

FIGURE 13.71 *Le Corbusier: Sainte-Marie de la Tourette, Eveux, 1956–1960.* (Photo: J. Feuillie/ © C.N.M.H.S./ S.P.A.D.E.M.)

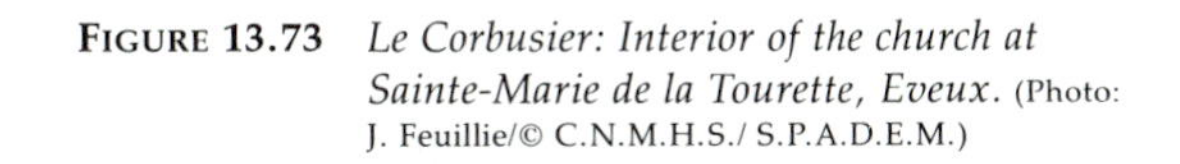

FIGURE 13.73 *Le Corbusier: Interior of the church at Sainte-Marie de la Tourette, Eveux.* (Photo: J. Feuillie/© C.N.M.H.S./ S.P.A.D.E.M.)

◀ **FIGURE 13.70** *Le Corbusier: Interior of Notre-Dame du Haut, Ronchamp.* (Photo: French Government Tourist Office)

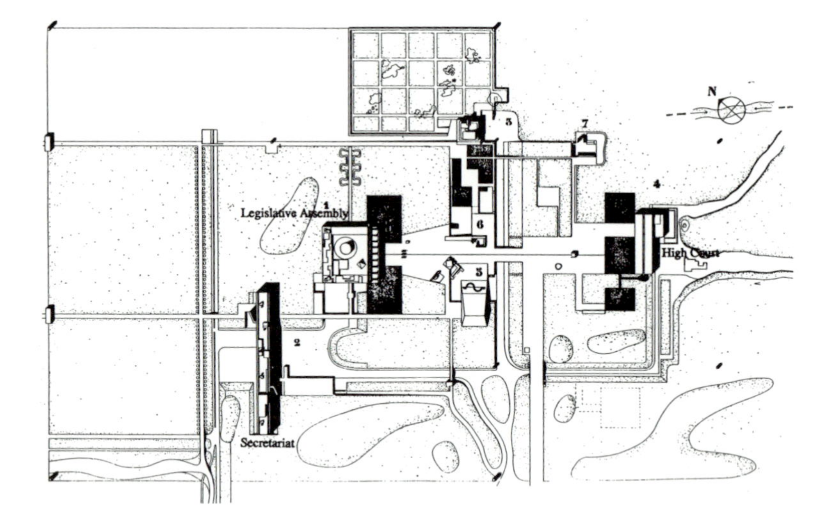

Figure 13.74 *Le Corbusier: Plan of the government buildings for the State Capitol of the Punjab, Chandigarh, 1951–1959.* (Courtesy: Artemis Verlag)

the monastery. The remaining monastic quarters are arranged in three wings: the refectory on the level of the church; the library, study rooms, and an oratory on the second level; and two floors of monks' cells around the upper levels.

All the work is in concrete. Le Corbusier returns to the use of pilotis and "regulating traces" of the Golden Section, although the sculptural freedom indulged on the chapel at Ronchamp is present here, too, in a more restrained fashion. With a master's hand Le Corbusier has manipulated light in dozens of different ways to enrich the experience of the basically simple forms within the building by the change and shift of the sun from day to day and season to season. Window mullions vary according to a harmonic rhythm; scoops catch the light and direct it through colored conic sections to focus on altars in the crypt; long horizontal ribbons provide even illumination for the corridors on the dormitory floor; each monk's room has a virtual wall of glass looking outward over the balcony brise-soleil to the distant horizon; and a truncated pyramid roof with a skylight provides an ethereal glow for the oratory. The monastery is a veritable encyclopedia of the architectural use of natural light.

For all the city planning projects he made, Le Corbusier was only once invited to design a town. In 1951 the government of India asked him to work on the layout and design of Chandigarh, the new capital of the State of Punjab in northern India. Le Corbusier's contribution to the planning was primarily the master plan itself, the design of actual sectors and buildings being left to others. Le Corbusier located the symbolic governmental buildings, designed by himself, on the highest land at the head of the scheme with the majestic foothills of the Himalayas beyond, in a manner recalling the acropolis in Athens (Figure 13.74). Four major buildings were grouped around a great ceremonial plaza: the palace of the governor (not built), the Secretariat (1951–1957), the Legislative Assembly Building (1956–1959), and the High Court (1951–1956). All of these buildings blend the rational discipline so evident in early works with the sculptural freedom enjoyed in later projects. The Legislative Assembly Building, for example, is virtually square in plan, with stacked rows of offices around two sides. The legislative chamber is circular, contained at the base of a truncated hyperbolic surface of revolution equipped with monitors at the top to filter the intense Indian sun. Control of light was of greatest importance, for with shade comes coolness. The brise-soleil were designed to exclude the direct sun but provide views. Concrete, Le Corbusier's favorite material, was well suited to the building task. It is inexpensive to manufacture and labor intensive to erect. Its mass also offered good buffering against the climatic extremes.

14.

Reactions to Modernism

The quite divergent styles of Mies and Le Corbusier are considered to define architecture of the Modern period, although it was the "glass box" designs of the International Style that inspired the largest corps of imitators, particularly in the United States after World War II. Schools of architecture adopted programs based on those of the Bauhaus, and the tenets of Modernism were reflected in the architectural work of the 1950s and 1960s. At best the results were efficient and spacious buildings, well-suited to their sites and functions; at worst Modernism produced dreary, repetitive buildings that established the popular image of modern design as almost a parody of the real thing. While Wright's designs for Broadacre City struck a responsive chord in countless American suburbs, corporate firms and real estate developers seized on the rationality and economy of curtain wall high-rise construction to house downtown offices. The "triumph" of International Style architecture, particularly in business districts across the country, led to increasing banality, and both architects and laymen began to excoriate Modernism's effect on the cityscape.

Most developments in architecture since 1945 have involved reactions to the International Style. Almost all architects came under its influence, but some eventually rejected the style and took other design approaches. This chapter is one attempt to understand the recent past, as architecture has questioned the ideals of Modernism and grown in different directions. Which of these directions will prove of lasting value is hard to say when we are still so close to the events themselves; significant trends are more easily seen from a distance.

MOVES AWAY FROM MODERNISM

The International Style had only limited impact on at least three of the twentieth century's most distinguished architects: Alvar Aalto, Eero Saarinen, and Louis Kahn. Although each did buildings that may be considered within Modernism, all three eventually discarded orthodoxy to explore other approaches.

Alvar Aalto (1898–1976) was a native of Finland and spent most of his career there. He studied architecture at the Helsinki Polytechnic Institute, graduating in 1921, and his early works show the influence of Neo-Classicism, which was the prevalent style in Scandinavia. He soon developed a functional approach that closely paralleled the German Werkbund architects of the same period, even though Aalto seems to have developed his approach independently. In 1927, he won the competition for a Municipal Library for Viipuri (now

FIGURE 14.1 *Aalto: Municipal Library, Viipuri, 1930–1935.* (Photo: Museum of Finnish Architecture)

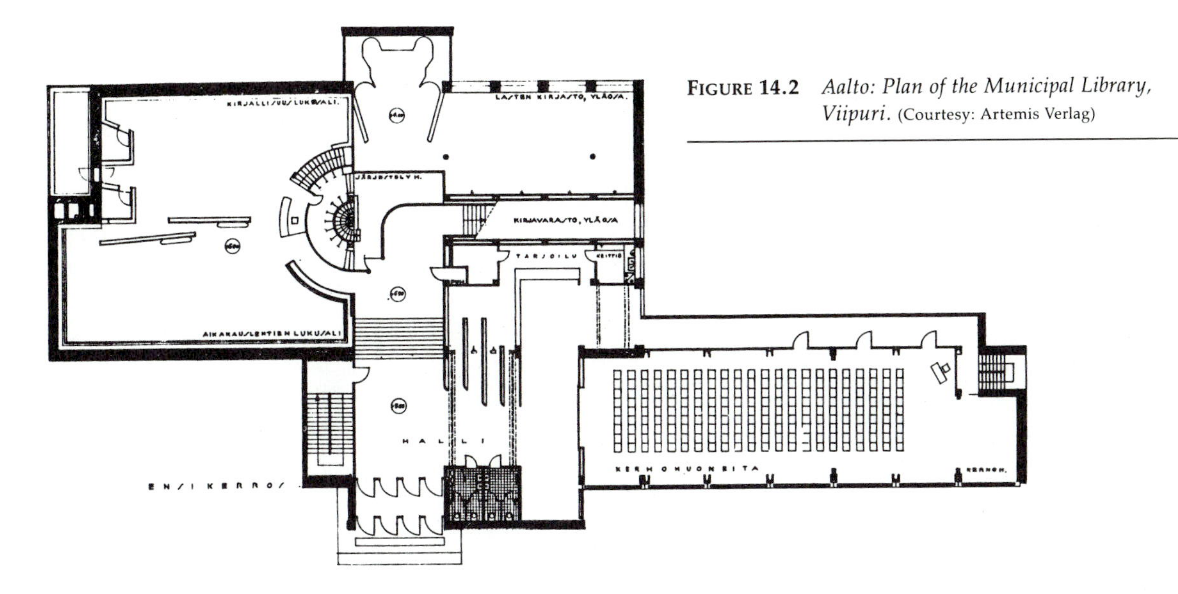

Figure 14.2 *Aalto: Plan of the Municipal Library, Viipuri.* (Courtesy: Artemis Verlag)

Vyborg, USSR) (Figures 14.1, 14.2) with such a thoroughly modern cast that conservative local forces delayed its construction until 1930–1935. The building includes an auditorium at ground level, which has a glazed wall overlooking parkland, and an undulating wooden ceiling to enhance acoustics. In the library proper, the walls are blank, with indirect lighting to prevent direct sunlight from annoying readers (Figure 14.3). The solid walls also helped to reduce noise.

Aalto's design for the Tuberculosis Sanatorium (1929–1933) at Paimio brought him international acclaim, both for its overall planning and its small-scale detail. Located on a hilltop surrounded with

Figure 14.3 *Aalto: Interior of the Municipal Library, Viipuri.* (Photo: Museum of Finnish Architecture)

FIGURE 14.4 *Aalto: Tuberculosis Sanatorium, Paimio, 1929–1933.* (Photo: Museum of Finnish Architecture)

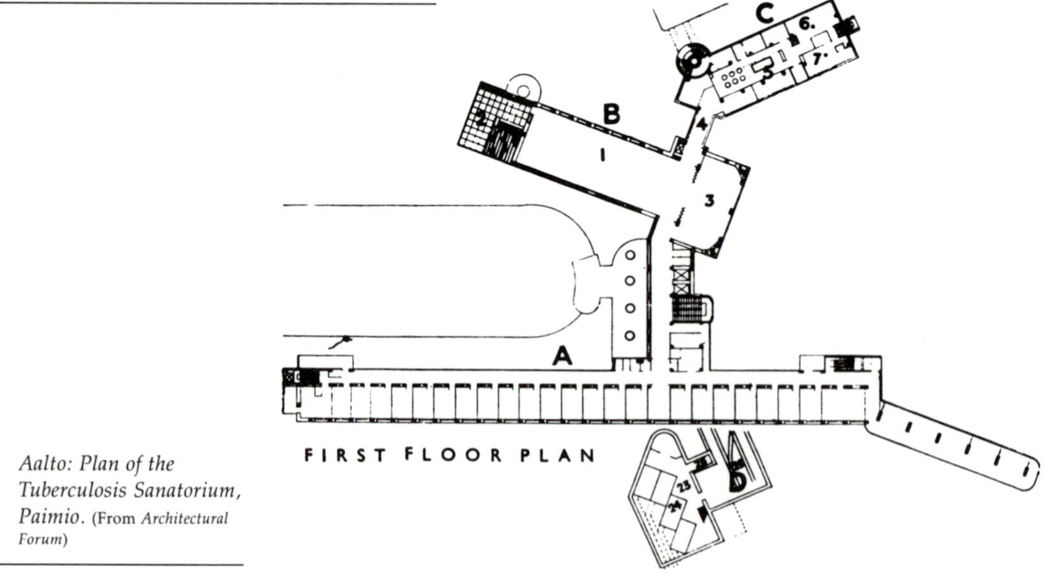

FIGURE 14.5 *Aalto: Plan of the Tuberculosis Sanatorium, Paimio.* (From *Architectural Forum*)

evergreens, the sanatorium rises dramatically in the landscape (Figures 14.4, 14.5). Like the Bauhaus buildings by Gropius, Aalto's design articulates each component of the hospital distinctly. The block of patient rooms, a long thin, six-story wing, dominates the grouping, connecting at angles via an entrance circulation wing to the public rooms, kitchen and services building, garage, and boiler house. To fit the hillside, the relationship between these units is not always orthogonal (as at the Bauhaus), introducing an expressive angularity to the site plan.

The interior details are just as impressive. All the ward rooms face south to receive maximum sunlight; balancing artificial light comes in from behind the patient's head, thereby reducing glare. Rooms are painted in soft tones with darker ceilings to create a restful effect. Carefully positioned insulation absorbs sound; wall-hung cabinets ease floor-cleaning; windows can be opened without creating drafts; tilted washbowls control splashing (Figure 14.6); and the door handles are shaped to fit the hand. Aalto custom-designed all the furniture, including the sanitary fittings, specifically for hospital use.

Furniture design interested Aalto throughout his career. Finland's greatest natural resource is wood, and Aalto used the material in innovative ways. Through experimentation he developed the technique of bending and laminating thin wood veneers to form plywood sheets of any desired curvature. In 1932 Aalto designed his first chair with a one-piece plywood seat and back supported on a tubular metal frame. Subsequent designs were fabricated entirely in wood, and many of these are still available on the commercial market.

In the 1930s Aalto's largest commission was for the Sunila Cellulose Factory (1936–1939, with later expansion 1951–1957) at Karhula, including the design of workers' housing nearby. The factory is a carefully composed array of repetitive rectangular forms, animated by the diagonal lines of conveyors and the vertical thrust of a smokestack (Figure 14.7). For employee housing situated well away from the factory's noxious fumes, Aalto built three-story blocks of apartments into the slope of a hill, so that each unit has its access at grade level (Figures 14.8, 14.9). The buildings are disposed on the site in a fan pattern in order to avoid monotony.

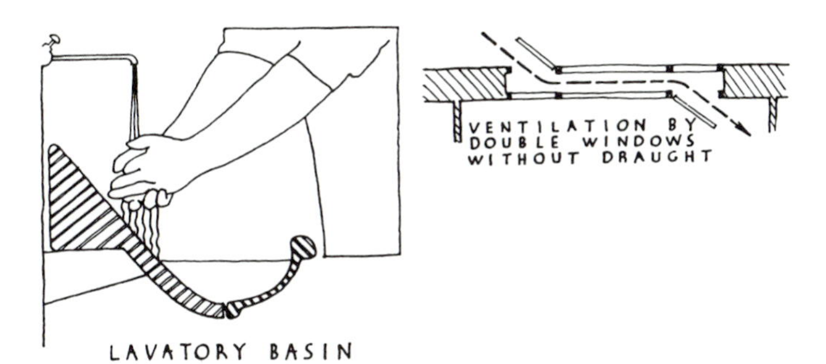

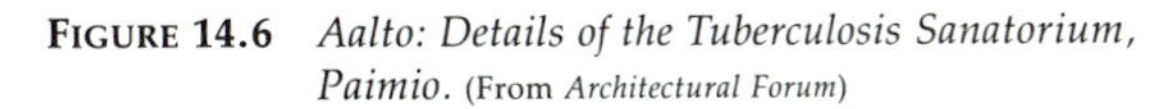

FIGURE 14.6 *Aalto: Details of the Tuberculosis Sanatorium, Paimio.* (From *Architectural Forum*)

FIGURE 14.7 *Aalto: Cellulose Factory, Sunila, 1936–1939.* (Photo: Museum of Finnish Architecture)

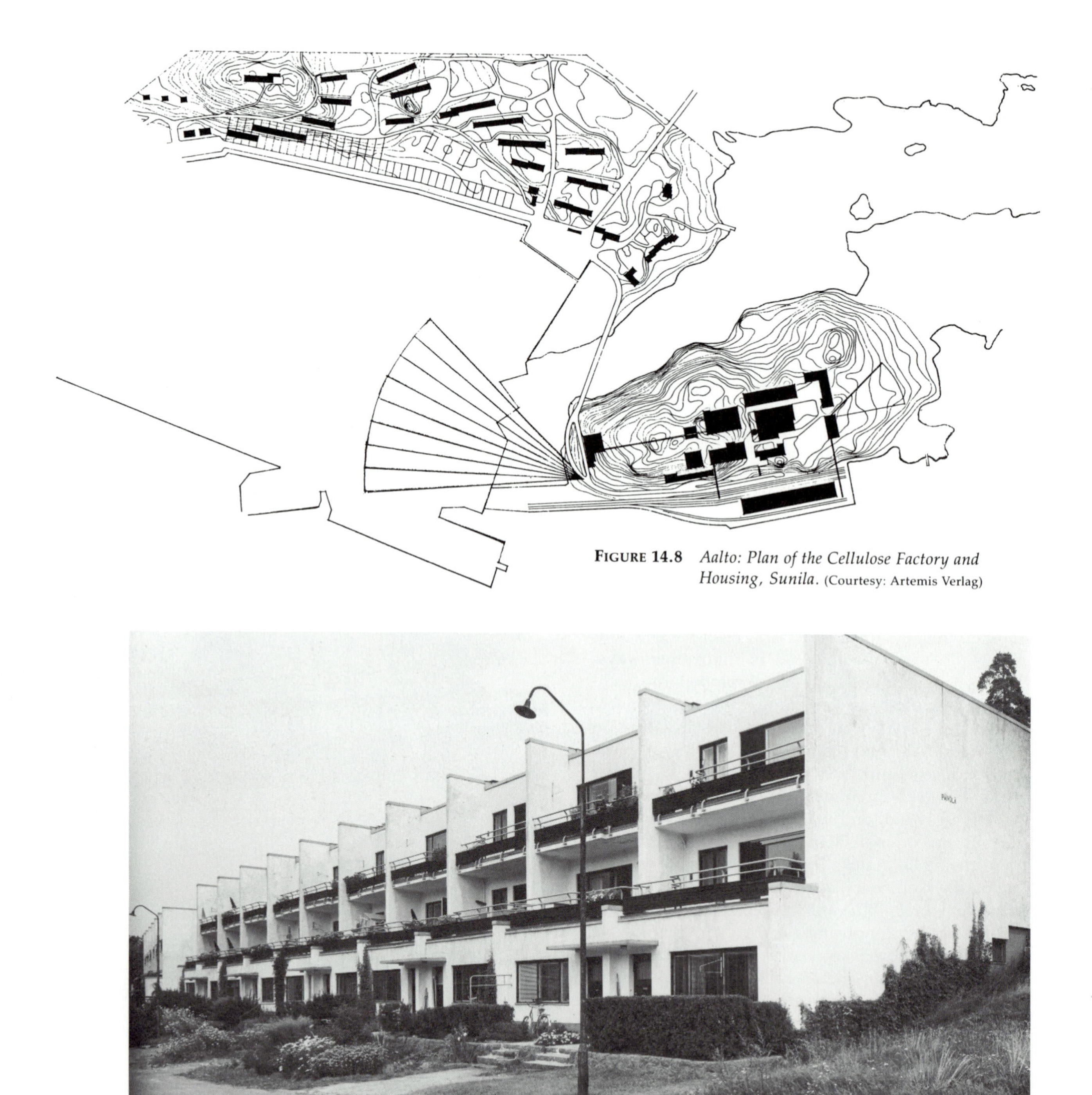

FIGURE 14.8 *Aalto: Plan of the Cellulose Factory and Housing, Sunila.* (Courtesy: Artemis Verlag)

FIGURE 14.9 *Aalto: Housing for the Cellulose Factory, Sunila.* (Photo: Museum of Finnish Architecture)

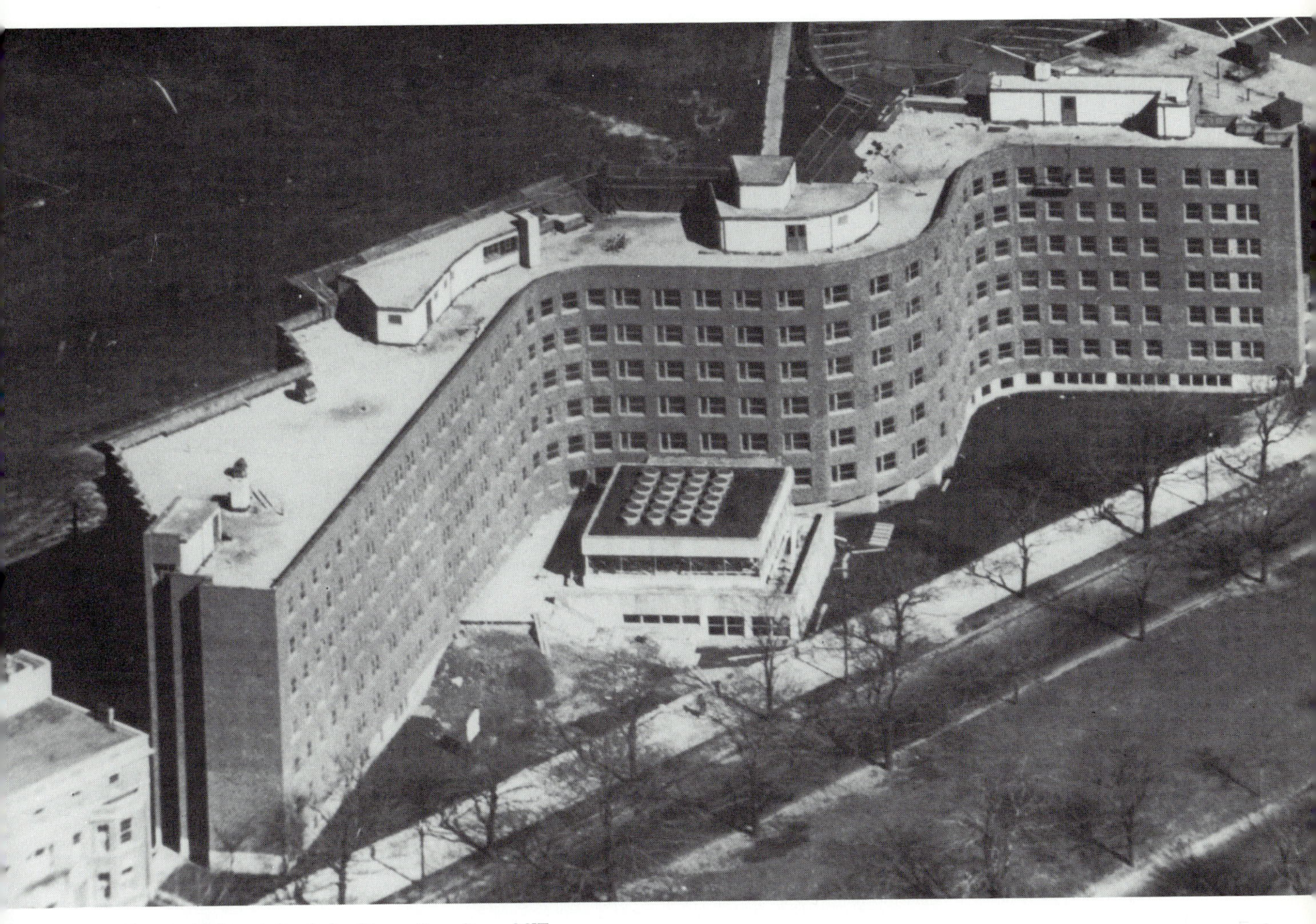

FIGURE 14.10 *Aalto: Baker House Dormitory, MIT, Cambridge, 1947–1949.* (Photo: Courtesy MIT)

After World War II, Aalto's mature style led him away from the white rectangular solids and pipe railings of International Style architecture, and he developed a characteristic building mode that does not follow postwar building trends or cliches. Brick and timber, covered with great copper roofs, became his favorite building materials, and he worked them into harmonious compositions that frequently included great curving walls, single-pitched roofs, and imaginative daylighting. During a teaching appointment at M.I.T. in the late 1940s he designed Baker House (1947–1949), a dormitory for the campus (Figure 14.10). Located on a site paralleling the Charles River, the brick dormitory has its riverfront rooms arranged in a sinusoidal curve in plan to permit oblique views up or down the river (Figure 14.11). To the extent possible, service and common rooms were kept at the rear on each floor, giving the

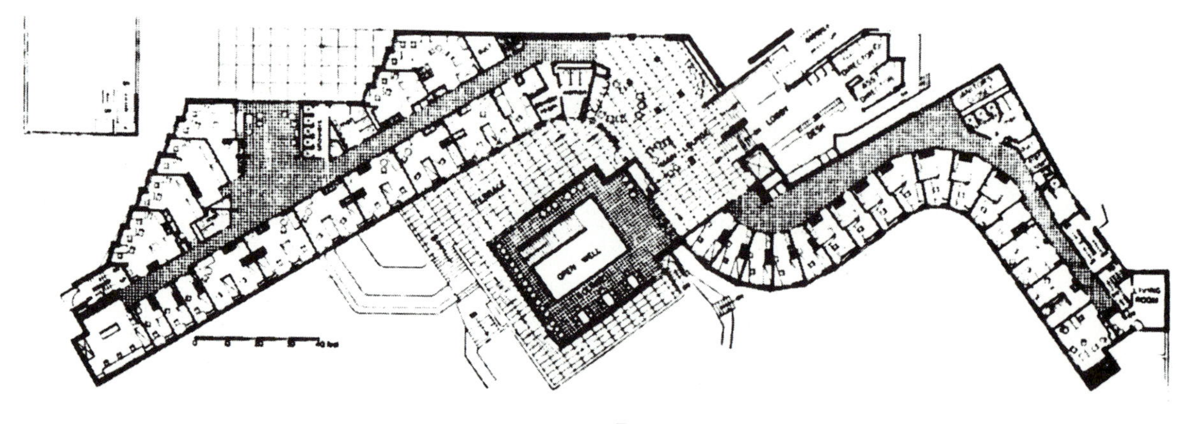

FIGURE 14.11 *Aalto: Plan of the Baker House Dormitory, MIT, Cambridge.* (From *Architectural Forum*)

FIGURE 14.12 *Aalto: Courtyard of the Town Hall, Säynätsalo, 1951–1952.* (Photo: Museum of Finnish Architecture)

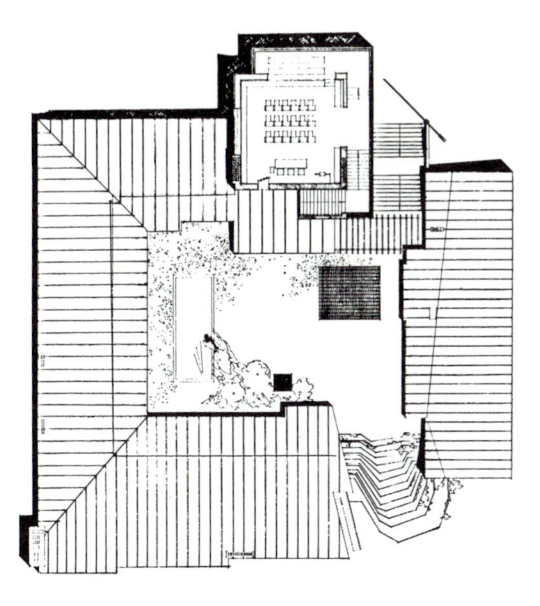

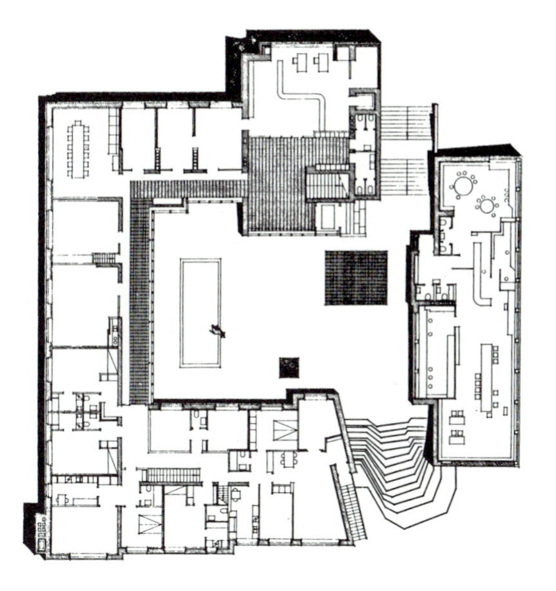

FIGURE 14.13 *Aalto: Plans of the Town Hall, Säynätsalo.* (Courtesy: Artemis Verlag)

individual dormitory rooms (singles, doubles, and triples) the desirable view. The dining hall and lounge are in a low wing at the front.

A more ambitious program was involved in the commission for a Town Hall for Säynätsalo (1951–1952), designed as a grouping of buildings around an open grassy courtyard (Figures 14.12, 14.13). It is in fact the civic center for this small community, housing the town offices, council chamber, public library, and retail shops in one composition, and it follows the scheme observed in most subsequent Aalto building complexes. Within a basically orthogonal pattern of buildings, one element is treated as a sculptural exception and is thereby given prominence. At Säynätsalo the brick volume of the council chamber dominates the ensemble, its sloped roof profile reflecting an intricate wooden fan truss inside (Figure 14.14). One enters the Town Hall by a set of brick or turf stairs; from either direction the sense of scale is exquisitely controlled. The building, which seems monumental in photographs, turns out in reality to be quite intimate in size. (One has this same sensation when visiting Fallingwater for the first time.)

A later project, illustrating the grouping of diverse buildings on a much larger scale, is the academic campus for the Otaniemi Technical Institute (1960–1965) outside Helsinki (Figures 14.15, 14.16). Here Aalto grouped the large lecture halls that would be used by all departments and made them

FIGURE 14.14 *Aalto: Interior of the Town Hall, Säynätsalo.* (Photo: Museum of Finnish Architecture)

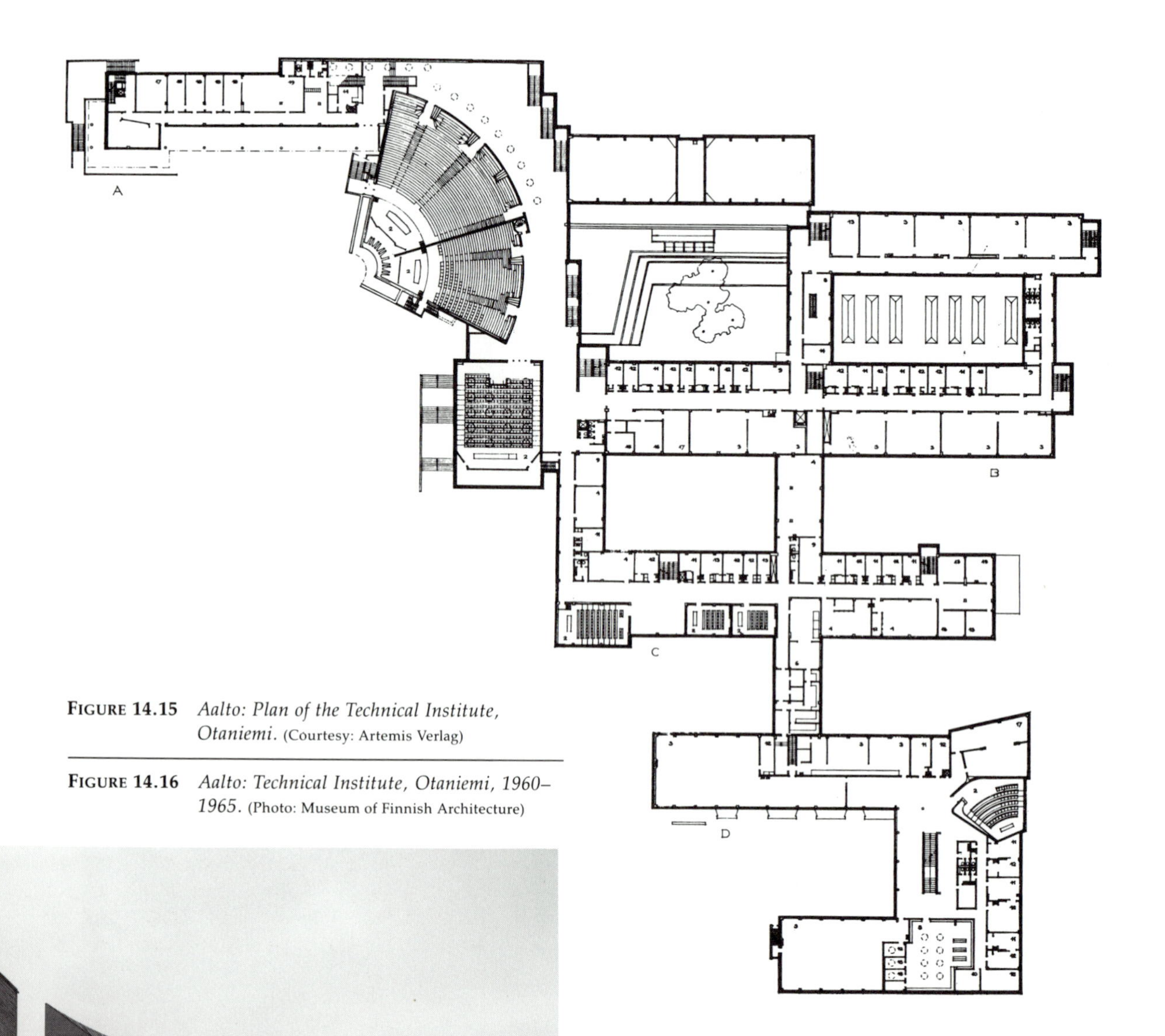

FIGURE 14.15 *Aalto: Plan of the Technical Institute, Otaniemi.* (Courtesy: Artemis Verlag)

FIGURE 14.16 *Aalto: Technical Institute, Otaniemi, 1960–1965.* (Photo: Museum of Finnish Architecture)

the focal point of the scheme, a quarter-cylinder volume with a steeply pitched roof defined by skylights. Inside the lecture halls, each a wedge shape with good acoustics and sight lines, great reinforced concrete arcs sweep across the ceiling in inverted L-shapes to diffuse daylight forward and downward, thus preventing the glare of direct sunlight. The remainder of the institute is accommodated in less-dazzling rectangular blocks organized around courtyards and interconnected for comfortable passage in the cold winter months. All are built in brick except the School of Architecture, which has marble facing on its exterior.

In all his work Aalto took a humanistic approach to architecture that is unmatched in the twentieth century. The vestiges of any movement or style are less important in his work than his concern for the experience of the individuals using the buildings. Some critics cite this as an excess of paternalism, and perhaps this is so. One should remember, however, that in an age where mechanization, industrial materials, and machine art were stimulating designers, Aalto never forgot that it was human beings, not machines, for whom he designed.

The works of Eero Saarinen (1910–1961) are eclectic, borrowing from a wider range of sources than those of Aalto. Saarinen was also of Finnish ancestry; his architect father, Eliel, had come to the United States in the 1920s because he hoped his approach to architectural design would be more readily accepted here than in Scandinavia. After studying sculpture in Paris and completing his architectural education at Yale in 1934, Eero practiced with his father until 1950. Saarinen considered architecture a fine art; it was the architect's role to be a form giver. In the General Motors Technical Center (1948–1956) at Warren, Michigan, Saarinen took a Miesian approach, setting modular glass-walled rectangular solids in a campuslike park; the grid theme is broken only by a circular auditorium and a sculptural water tower that gives a vertical thrust to the composition of horizontal mass-produced objects.

For the Trans World Airlines Terminal at Kennedy Airport in New York City, Saarinen created a fluid, sculptural design expressive of the idea of flight (Figure 14.17). The terminal's billowing roof resembles a great bird alighting, although others have noted its similarity to the swooping tail fins of 1959 Chevrolet automobiles, which Saarinen may have seen in developmental form at the General Motors Technical Center. On the interior the flow of space is dramatic but more intimate in scale than photographs suggest. Most fittings were custom designed to fit the spirit of the building, for ordinary furniture looks out of place in a building where curves dominate the walls and ceilings and ramps generate motion in the floor plane. A later design

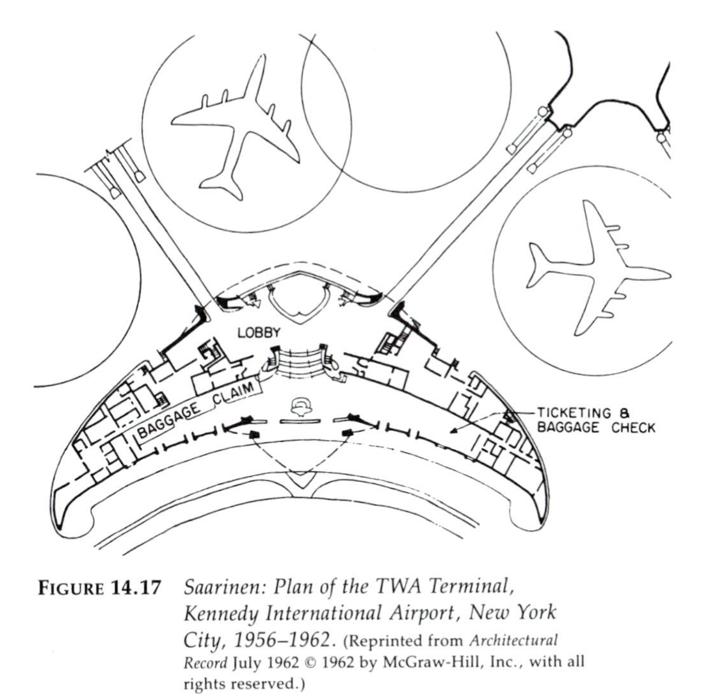

FIGURE 14.17 *Saarinen: Plan of the TWA Terminal, Kennedy International Airport, New York City, 1956–1962.* (Reprinted from *Architectural Record* July 1962 © 1962 by McGraw-Hill, Inc., with all rights reserved.)

for Dulles Airport (1958–1962) outside Washington, D.C., draws inspiration from early sketches done by the German Expressionist architect, Erich Mendelsohn (Figures 14.18, 14.19). Outward-leaning concrete pylons rise on the exterior to support the cable-hung roof, which provides a clear-span interior. The effect of the building in the landscape is noble, rather like the grand setting of Versailles, but the interior is a disappointment for the orthogonal clutter of partitions and a central roof drain that violates the untouched ceiling negate the curving geometries of the building's enclosure.

Saarinen drew on yet another form language in his designs for Morse and Stiles colleges (1958–1962) at Yale University (Figures 14.20, 14.21), finding inspiration for this commission in the irregular layouts and clustered massing of Italian hill towns, particularly the medieval towers of San Gimignano. Although Yale's other residential colleges were generally based on the more orthogonal shapes of medieval college quadrangles, Stiles and Morse colleges merge smoothly into the circulation patterns

FIGURE 14.18 *Saarinen: Plan of Dulles Airport, Chantilly, 1958–1962.* (Reprinted from *Architectural Record* July 1963 © 1963 by McGraw-Hill, Inc., with all rights reserved.) ▶

FIGURE 14.19 *Saarinen: Section through Dulles Airport, Chantilly.* (Reprinted from *Architectural Record* July 1963 © 1963 by McGraw-Hill, Inc., with all rights reserved.)

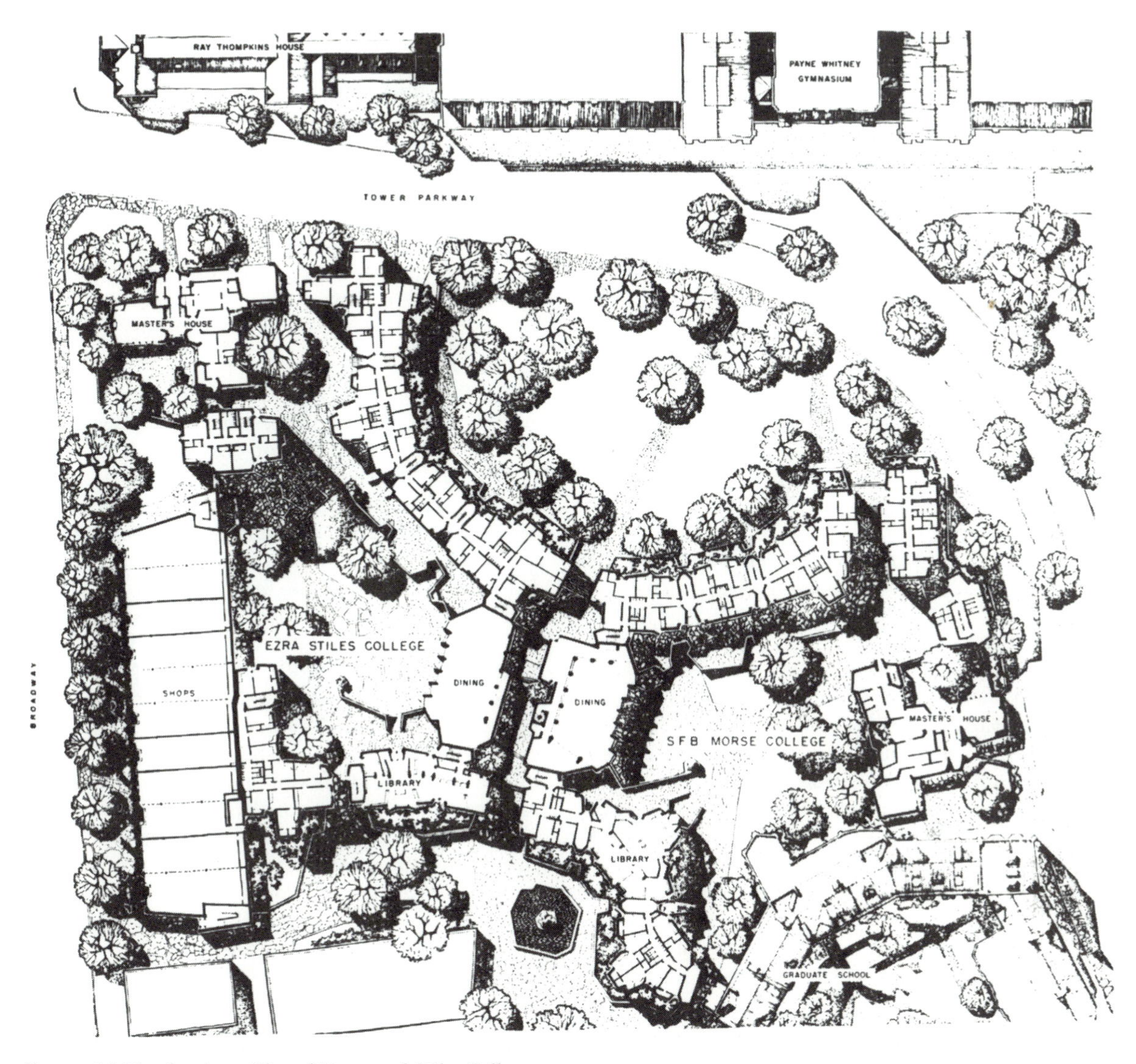

FIGURE 14.21 *Saarinen: Plan of Morse and Stiles Colleges, Yale University, New Haven.* (Reprinted from *Architectural Record* December 1962 © 1962 by McGraw-Hill, Inc., with all rights reserved.)

◀ **FIGURE 14.20** *Saarinen: Morse and Stiles Colleges, Yale University, New Haven, 1958–1962.* (Photo: T. Charles Erickson, Yale University)

of the campus and achieve a pleasant spatial variety appropriate to the academic setting.

Medieval vernacular forms from Italian hill towns also inspired Louis I. Kahn (1901–1974) in his design for the Richards Medical Research Building (1957–1961) at the University of Pennsylvania (Figure 14.22). In plan the building is a model of rationalism. The laboratories are square, open plan, glass-walled spaces stacked into multifloor units. Pairs of columns set on each side support the struc-

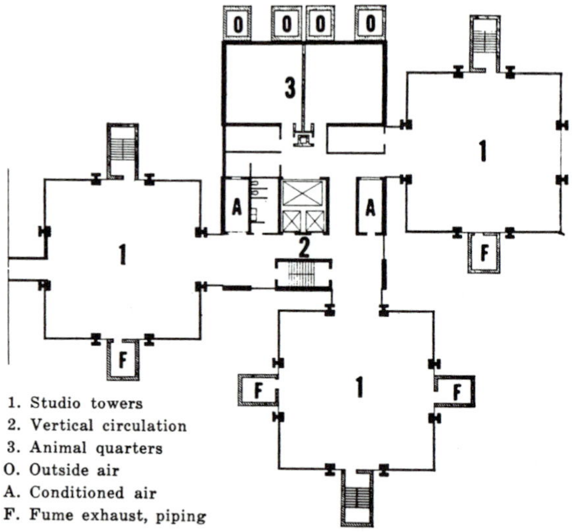

1. Studio towers
2. Vertical circulation
3. Animal quarters
O. Outside air
A. Conditioned air
F. Fume exhaust, piping

FIGURE 14.22 *Kahn: Plan of Richards Medical Building, University of Pennsylvania, Philadelphia, 1957–1961.* (Reprinted from *Architectural Record* August 1960 © 1960 by McGraw-Hill, Inc., with all rights reserved.)

tural grid of each floor, while ducts, mechanical services, elevators, and stairs are set in shafts, articulated on the exterior as vertical brick towers recalling San Gimignano. Kahn has thus wedded straightforward functional planning with a picturesque exterior to create one of the most influential architectural compositions of the 1960s. Purists note that one of the service shaft towers is a dummy, included for artistic effect rather than functional necessity, and scientists using the building have found the flexibility of lab spaces to be less than the designer imagined.

Kahn's work represents the fusion of seemingly contradictory sources. He obtained his architectural education at the University of Pennsylvania, then solidly based on Beaux-Arts programs, where he acquired the concept of served and servant spaces that would affect nearly all his buildings. In the Richards Medical Building the laboratories are the served spaces, and they are clearly distinguished in plan and reality from the servant functions of mechanical equipment and vertical circulation. But Kahn also absorbed principles of Modernism, particularly from the work of Le Corbusier; and he traveled in Europe, where Hadrian's Villa, vernacular townscapes, and the works of Brunelleschi created lasting impressions. The simple geometries of Neo-Classicism also influenced his architectural conceptions. Kahn admired the works of Boullée and Ledoux, considering them as important to architecture as Johann Sebastian Bach was to music. Among Kahn's writings, one finds the following:

> Spirit in will to express/ can make the great sun seem small./ The Sun is/ Thus the Universe./ Did we need Bach/ Bach is/ Thus music is./ Did we need Boullée/ Boullée is/ Did we need Ledoux/ Ledoux is/ Thus Architecture is.

The influence of Neoclassicism in general and Piranesi in particular is manifest in Kahn's designs for the National Assembly of Bangladesh in Dacca (1962–1974). The building is composed of circles and squares expressed volumetrically as prisms, and its masonry in brick and concrete features large circular openings for daylighting that recall buildings at Hadrian's Villa, while the interiors are as grand and sombre as images in the *Prisons* engravings. A similar treatment is found inside the Library of Phillips Exeter Academy (1967–1972) at Exeter, New Hampshire, where the essentially square building is dominated by a cubical volume at the center. Huge circular cutouts provide vistas into the library stacks on the surrounding floors in a manner reminiscent of Piranesi's *Prison with Rusticated Doorway surmounted by Large Circular Opening*. Individual study carrels surround the stacks on each floor, and their windows provide a regular articulation for the brick exterior, which is treated rather like nineteenth-century mill buildings of Manchester, New Hampshire.

In contrast to his contemporaries, Kahn was a late bloomer, emerging as an original voice in American architecture only in the late 1950s. His buildings reflect Beaux-Arts principles, tenets of Modernism, and a respect for historical values in a highly original synthesis. Both his works and his teaching at the University of Pennsylvania encouraged a generation of younger architects to explore alternatives to the orthodoxies of the International Style. His preference for articulating individual rooms in plan, rather than employing the space-flow characteristic of much Modern architecture, ties him to earlier eras, but his use of materials places him squarely in the twentieth century.

POST-MODERNISM

The 1960s saw the emergence of what has been called Post-Modernism, a new force in architecture that attempted to distance itself from the International Style. As has been the case with many twentieth-century artistic movements, Post-Modernism began with a treatise, published in 1966 as *Complexity and Contradiction in Architecture* and hailed by Vincent Scully as "the most important writing on the making of architecture since Le Corbusier's *Vers une Architecture* of 1923." The author, Robert Venturi (b. 1925), made the case for nonstraightforward architecture; using a style that echoed the phraseology of earlier manifestoes, he observed that

> Architects can no longer afford to be intimidated by the puritanically moral language of orthodox Modern architecture. I like elements which are hybrid rather than "pure," compromising rather than "clean," distorted rather than "straightforward," ambiguous rather than "articulated," perverse as well as impersonal, boring as well as "interesting," conventional rather than "designed," accommodating rather than excluding, redundant rather than simple, vestigial as well as innovating, inconsistent and equivocal rather than direct and clear. I am for messy vitality over obvious unity. I include the non sequitur and proclaim the duality.

The book extolled the mannerisms of Palladio, Michelangelo, Hawksmoor, Soane, Aalto, and Le Corbusier and glorified Baroque architecture generally. Venturi went on to equate the atmosphere, lighting effects, and theatrics of Las Vegas casinos with Counter-Reformation art. By celebrating the "ugly and ordinary" aspects of twentieth-century building, as exhibited in roadside strip developments, neon advertising signs, and billboards, Venturi discarded the orderly purity and tasteful character of Modernism in favor of pluralistic, anonymously designed, and eminently practical populist design, dubbed by some the New Banality. Venturi restated the Miesian dictum, "Less is more," as "Less is a bore." Roots for this shift in architectural thinking can be found in the cultural diversity manifested in political and social movements of the period; increased attention to vernacular architecture, stemming in part from Bernard Rudofsky's "Architecture without Architects" exhibition at the Museum of Modern Art in 1964; British "New Brutalism," which used large expanses of raw concrete as finish material in buildings; and the work of Venturi's mentor, Louis Kahn.

When *Complexity and Contradiction in Architecture* was published, Venturi had built very little, although he had placed well in architectural competitions. His largest completed commission was the ninety-one-unit Guild House (1960–1963) (Figure 14.23), Friends Housing for the Elderly in Philadelphia, in which common building elements were used in pragmatic yet unconventional ways. Double-hung windows were overscaled; a gold-anodized, roof-mounted, fake television antenna demarcated the central axis of the symmetrical façade; a single polished granite column denoted the entranceway and contrasted with the white glazed brick around the door, providing an institutionalized character to the building. Interiors were thoughtfully designed with the well-being of the tenants in mind. A majority of the apartments were oriented to the south and overlooked activity on the street, while the corridors were offset to avoid the institutional quality of long hallways.

More famous, perhaps, was the 1962 house for the architect's mother, Vanna Venturi, in Chestnut Hill, Pennsylvania (Figure 14.24). In this one modest dwelling, Venturi combined simplicity of external form with complexity of interior layout, conventional symbols and elements with contradictory arrangements. For example, the location of the central recess for the door was obvious, but the double-doors themselves were concealed and were much too grand for the cramped vestibule into which they opened. Stairs to the second floor were set behind the chimney mass and competed with it for space; they widen as they ascend, then abruptly narrow to a minimum passage around the firebox. The fireplace and mantle are overscaled for the size of the living room, and the furniture was of mixed ancestry rather than Bauhaus-inspired modern. On the outside the house presented a bold gable end to the street, in the manner of a Shingle Style house, yet its landlord-green color and stucco finish bore no resemblance to houses in that style. Most of the attributes praised in Venturi's book can be found in the Vanna Venturi house; his writings may ultimately prove more important than any of his buildings.

FIGURE 14.23 *Venturi: Guild House, Philadelphia, 1960–1963.* (Photo: courtesy Venturi, Rauch and Scott-Brown, Inc.)

FIGURE 14.24 *Venturi: Vanna Venturi House, Chestnut Hill, 1962.* (Photo: Rollin LaFrance/courtesy Venturi, Rauch and Scott-Brown, Inc.)

The architectural historian Robert A. M. Stern has summed up the essential attributes of Post-Modernism as contextualism, allusionism, and ornamentalism. Contextualism refers to connections between the building and its setting. Post-Modern architecture attempts to link the building with established patterns, geometries, and possibilities for future growth, rather than conceiving each design as an isolated object in the landscape. Allusionism stems from an interest in reexamining the past and making reference to previous historical periods in new works, so that the new is also familiar and comprehensible to both designers and users. Impetus for historical attributes has arisen in part from the concurrent emergence of preservation and adaptive reuse as valid and important aspects of contemporary architectural practice. Communities have taken renewed interest in their older buildings; developers have found that restored structures are sound investments; and by working on existing buildings architects have discovered historic design principles and details that were often not taught to them in Bauhaus-inspired school curricula. Constructing allusions generally involves ornamentalism, the third aspect of Post-Modern architecture. Arising in part as a reaction to Modernism's minimal use of surface decoration, the recognition that ornament plays an important role in creating scale, identity, and interest inside and outside buildings has encouraged designers to reinterpret historical motifs and devise new means of enriching wall surfaces.

Along with Venturi, two other architects, Richard Meier and Michael Graves, have been important in defining the development of Post-Modernism. Both were part of the "New York Five," who gained prominence in 1972 through the publication of their works in a book edited by Kenneth Frampton and Colin Rowe. Meier (b. 1934) would probably not consider himself as being a Post-Modernist but as continuing the early traditions of Modernism. While Meier's architecture owes an obvious debt to Le Corbusier's houses of the 1920s, he also claims to have been influenced by the spatial layering and light quality of Baroque interiors and by such works as Frank Lloyd Wright's Guggenheim Museum. Qualities abstracted from these and other sources include columnar systems of planning grids with a clearly expressed skin enclosing volumetric space; planar elements that slice through the building and penetrate one another; impeccable white panel exteriors derived from the late works of Hoffman and Wagner; and fundamentally cubical massing relieved by gentle curves.

The results of this approach can be seen in Meier's design for the Museum für Kunsthandwerk (Museum of Decorative Arts) in Frankfurt, which won a limited competition in 1980 and was completed in 1984 (Figures 14.25, 14.26). Although nominally an addition to an old villa containing the existing museum, Meier's building is nearly ten times larger than the Neo-Classic original, and, except for a second-floor glass-enclosed connector, it stands free of it in an L-shape. The position of the villa and the angle of the frontage road paralleling the Main River gave Meier the rationale to indulge in two overlapping grid systems set at an angle of 3½ degrees to one another. While such a minor shift is imperceptible in reality (unless the museum-goer commonly notes slight misalignments in normally orthogonal building materials), the two grids are distinctly seen in the plan drawings, and their interaction obviously inspired Meier to play with room shapes that otherwise would have seemed arbitrary. Le Corbusier-style regulating traces were scribed over elevation studies to show that both the villa and the new building have similar proportions; a module derived from the older building relates to basic quadrants in the addition. Square white porcelain-on-steel panels cover the exterior and align with square mullions in the generously sized windows. Interior circulation is organized by a system of switchback ramps linking axial corridors on all floors, while the exhibits are displayed in galleries created by partial-height walls set within the structural bays to establish a domestic scale appropriate to the museum's collections. Despite the clashing geometries of the building's plan, spaces merge gracefully into each other, and abundant natural light reflecting off shiny white surfaces is welcome in the habitually overcast Frankfurt weather.

Meier employed a similar vocabulary in the High Museum (1981–1984) designed for Atlanta, Georgia (Figures 14.27, 14.28). The continuous ramp of the Guggenheim Museum was abstracted here to become the dominant circulation path around the cir-

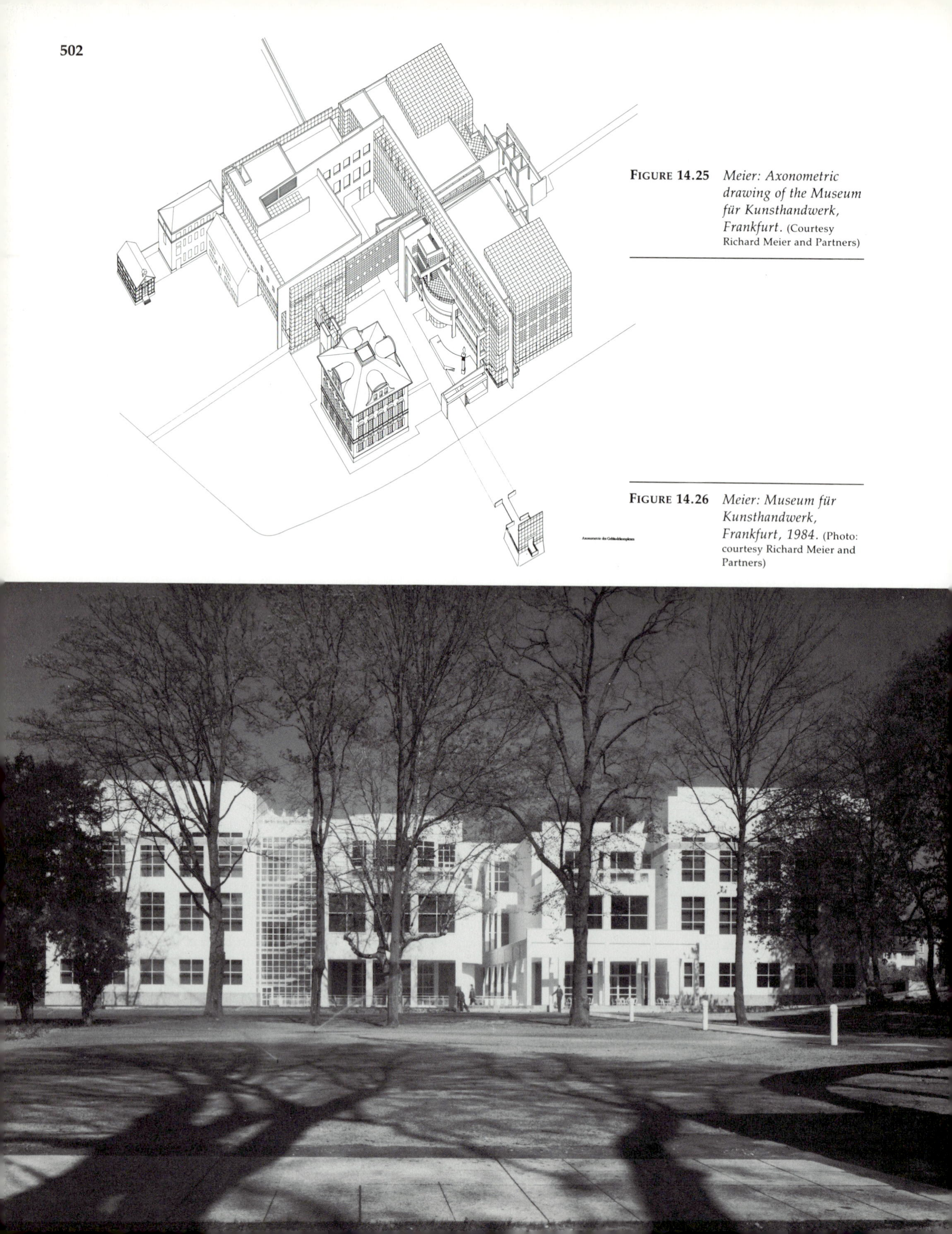

FIGURE 14.25 *Meier: Axonometric drawing of the Museum für Kunsthandwerk, Frankfurt.* (Courtesy Richard Meier and Partners)

FIGURE 14.26 *Meier: Museum für Kunsthandwerk, Frankfurt, 1984.* (Photo: courtesy Richard Meier and Partners)

Figure 14.27 *Meier: High Museum, Atlanta, 1981–1984.* (Photo: courtesy Richard Meier and Partners)

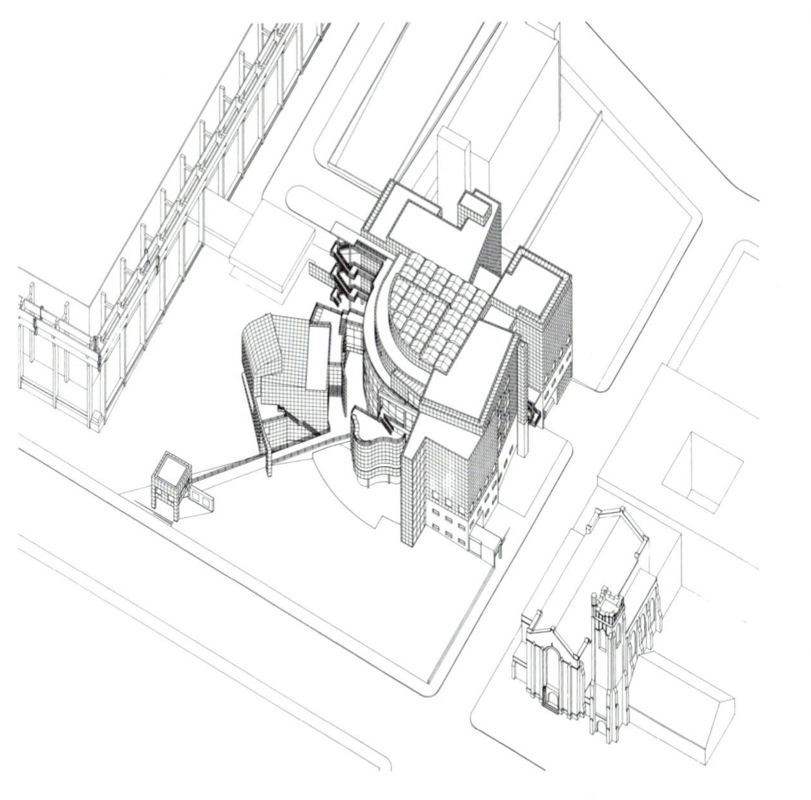

Figure 14.28 *Meier: Axonometric drawing of the High Museum, Atlanta.* (Courtesy Richard Meier and Partners)

cumference of a quarter-cylinder glass-enclosed atrium, off which more conventional orthogonal galleries with artificial illumination are arranged. Whereas the ramp in the Frankfurt museum is immediately adjacent to gallery displays, in the Atlanta museum their separation isolates the art from the building's most interesting architectural feature. The conditions most curators demand for the display of paintings are in part responsible. Strong sunlight quickly deteriorates pigments, so works of art need to be kept in controlled lighting conditions. In the High Museum, an exciting big space just happens to be attached to a museum for which it is inappropriate.

Another museum design, this one unbuilt, for the Fargo-Moorhead Cultural Center Bridge (1977) displays the architectural thinking of Michael Graves (b. 1934). This project comprises an art museum, concert hall, history museum, and broadcast facility to be set in Fargo, North Dakota, and Moorhead, Minnesota, joined by a bridge over the Red River, which separates the two cities. Imagery for the bridge element derives from Ledoux's design for the House at the Source of the Loue. Cylinders, pyramids, and long-radius curving planes merge in a design that is less rigid geometrically than Meier's work but no less rich in its allusions to precedent. Graves's "referential drawings" or thumbnail sketches for the Fargo-Moorhead project indicate the evolution of his ideas from many historic sources. After beginning as a neo-Corbusian, Graves has developed into an eclectic architect more heavily influenced by the color and ornament of Neo-Classicism and Beaux-Arts design. Axes, provided with interruptions, govern the plan, but the overall composition is not symmetrical, and assemblages of static, closed, heavy forms dominate the volumetric expression. Links to the surrounding landscape are implied by eroded fragmented terminations, as at the end of the history museum.

FIGURE 14.29 *Stirling: Engineering Building, Leicester University, Leicester, 1964.* (Photo: courtesy of James Stirling)

THE CRYSTAL PALACE AESTHETIC

The Crystal Palace was one of the most important nineteenth-century buildings, both for its construction methods and its sweeping interior space, and it is the common ancestor for two divergent architectural trends of the late twentieth century. In the first group are architects who employ industrial materials in somewhat unorthodox configurations to shape buildings that create the sensation of being outdoors in an interior space; the second group, which will be considered in the next section, design buildings that continue the Crystal Palace's unashamed celebration of technological progress.

In the 1960s the English architect James Stirling (b. 1926) used the theme of industrial assemblage in his commissions for the Engineering Building at Leicester University (1964) and the History Faculty Building at Cambridge University (1968), both of which were startling for their sculptural and unconcealed use of standard building materials. Aluminum-framed commercial greenhouse windows were set in the industrial-brick walls of the Engineering Building's office tower and were also employed to wrap completely the walls and ceiling of its attached laboratory wing, where sawtooth skylights are treated as prismatic solids when they

Figure 14.30 *Stirling: History Faculty Building, Cambridge University, Cambridge, 1968.* (Photo: courtesy of James Stirling)

terminate at the edge of the building (Figure 14.29). In the History Faculty Building (Figures 14.30, 14.31), which contains a library on the lowest levels and faculty offices in the L-shaped block that rises on two sides, industrial glazing systems are used to cover the library and enclose the long exterior walls of the offices. A giant cascade of glass brings abundant light (and solar greenhouse heat buildup in summer) to scholars working in the fan-shaped library. Stirling's conspicuous display of aluminum won him the $25,000 Reynolds Aluminum Award for architectural use of that material.

The well-lit atrium space of the History Faculty library links back to the aesthetics of the Crystal Palace, where Paxton had cleverly designed an expansive but inexpensive building using mass-produced glass and iron parts. A similar effect of spaciousness, without the reliance on ready-made components and their resulting economies, was manifest in the Ford Foundation Building (1963–

Figure 14.31 *Stirling: Section through the History Faculty Building, Cambridge University, Cambridge.* (Reprinted from *Architectural Record* February 1966 © 1966 by McGraw-Hill, Inc., with all rights reserved.)

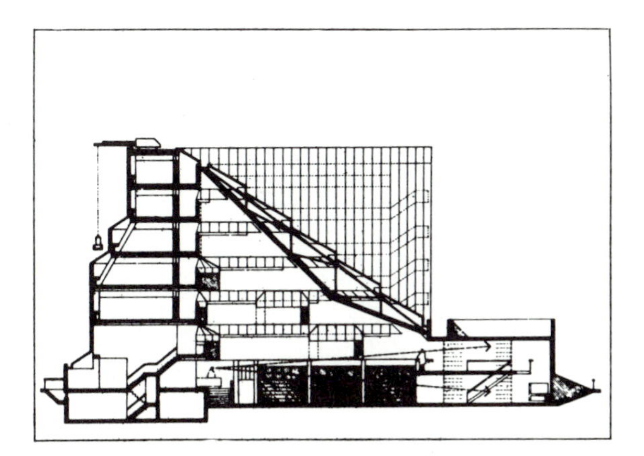

Figure 14.32 *Roche and Dinkeloo: Ford Foundation Building, New York City, 1963–1968.* (Photo: Roz Li)

Figure 14.33 *Roche and Dinkeloo: Context plan of the Ford Foundation Building, New York City.* (Reprinted from *Architectural Record* May 1968 © 1968 by McGraw-Hill, Inc., with all rights reserved.)

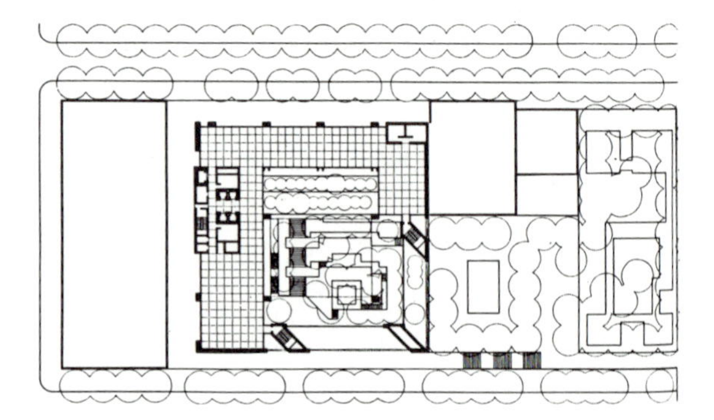

1968) (Figures 14.32, 14.33), designed by Kevin Roche (b. 1922) and John Dinkeloo (1918–1981), successors to the firm of Eero Saarinen. Set between Forty-Second and Forty-Third streets on a nearly square site within a Manhattan block near the United Nations Building, the Ford Foundation's offices enframe an eleven-story greenhouse that occupies about half the ground floor. Additional planted terraces on the third, fourth, and fifth floors extend the greenery above the entrance level, and the office spaces either share the view into the court or have outside windows. The building's major materials — weathering steel, granite, bronze, and glass — establish a neutral dark ground for the natural light and vegetation that characterize the interior. Richness and elegance, not cost-cutting, governed design decisions. The building's price — about sixteen million dollars for the 16,500 square feet of office space, plus common areas and the great atrium — works out to over $200 a square foot (in 1968 dollars).

Despite its extravagance, or perhaps because of it, the Ford Foundation headquarters became one of the most influential buildings of the third quarter of the twentieth century. Aside from providing a handsome working environment for the foundation's employees, it also created a pedestrian link through the long side of one of Manhattan's 200- by 400-foot blocks, and this idea of an enclosed walkway was taken up by the Office of Midtown Development as a solution to preserving pedestrian access within New York City. Zoning incentives encouraged developers to include ground-floor public passageways in new high-rise buildings. The idea was not new. The splendid nave of the Crystal Palace had inspired many glass-roofed commercial arcade buildings in Europe and the United States, of which the best-known example was the Galleria Vittorio Emanuelle (1865–1877) in Milan, Italy (Figure 14.34), designed by Giuseppe Mengoni (1829–1877) to connect the Piazza del Duomo to La Scala, the opera house a block away.

Major New York buildings that benefitted from these zoning incentives include the Citicorp Building (1974–1977), set between Fifty-third and Fifty-fourth streets on Lexington Avenue. Hugh Stubbins, the architect, designed a six-story podium building dedicated to retail shops opening off a cen-

FIGURE 14.34 *Mengoni: Galleria Vittorio Emanuelle, Milan, 1865–1877.* (Photo: Alinari)

◄ **FIGURE 14.35** *View of Manhattan looking east. Left to right: Trump Tower (Der Scutt, Swanke, Hayden and Connell), AT&T (Johnson/Burgee), and Citicorp (Hugh Stubbins Associates).* (Photo: Timothy Hursley/courtesy Johnson/Burgee)

tral atrium and then placed a fifty-nine-floor office tower astraddle a sunken plaza at the Lexington Avenue end. Citicorp's wedge-shaped top was once planned for solar collectors, which proved economically unfeasible, and the bold silhouette the building contributes to the skyline may well have inspired Philip Johnson to create a novel cap, in the form of the broken pediment often seen on Chippendale furniture, for the American Telephone and Telegraph Building (1980) on Madison Avenue. At the ground level, Johnson provided an enormous arcade, modeled after the form of Brunelleschi's Pazzi Chapel porch and furnished it with chairs and tables for public use. Behind the building is an enclosed shopping arcade that gives midblock passage

FIGURE 14.36 *Johnson and Burgee: Site plan, AT&T Building, New York City, 1980.* (Reprinted from *Architectural Record* May 1984 © 1984 by McGraw-Hill, Inc., with all rights reserved.)

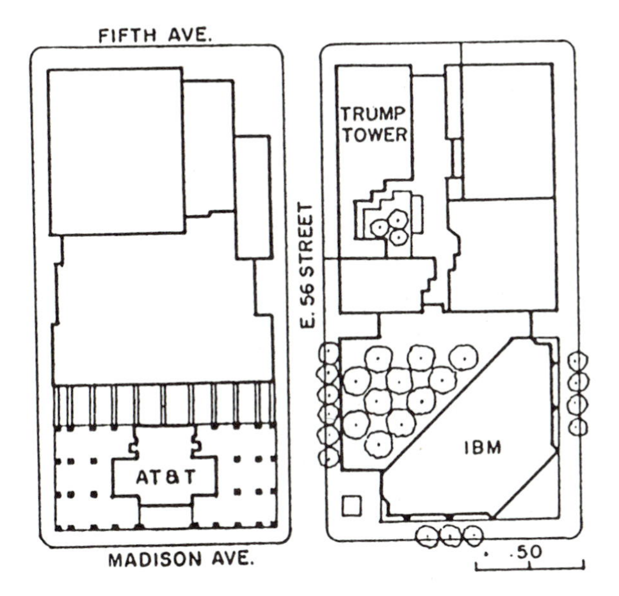

and additional life to the street. Rather than having only a pretentious corporate lobby (which the AT&T building has), the building also provides accommodation for passersby to shop or just pause for coffee and conversation. AT&T's new neighboring buildings, the IBM Center and Trump Tower (Figures 14.35, 14.36), also provide ground-level amenities with enclosed atrium spaces containing informal seating, food service, gallery displays, ornamental planting, and handsomely presented boutiques. All three developments humanize the environment by providing a respite from the hard and gritty world of midtown Manhattan.

LATE MODERN HIGH TECHNOLOGY

As has been recounted, industrial building technology was a contributing factor in the development of Modern architecture, becoming a part of the International Style because it represented functional efficiency. Le Corbusier praised the uncluttered design of ocean liners, while Mies adopted glass and steel construction as the significant architectural problem of the twentieth century. Walter Gropius's interest in prefabrication, developed during the Bauhaus years, continued into his tenure at Harvard where he tried without much success to interest American manufacturers in systems building. In designing his own house in Lincoln, Massachusetts, in 1937, Gropius used windows, stairs, and other fittings from the catalogs of light-commercial building suppliers. After World War II, Charles Eames, known primarily as a designer of furniture and graphics, built his house in California entirely from components available on the commercial market.

In the Post-Modern period this enchantment with using and expressing technology has been revived, particularly by European architects, and has led to designs in which the structural and mechanical aspects of building take precedence over formal issues. Unlike the atrium or galleria buildings of the Crystal Palace Aesthetic, which generally have sculptural form and internal spatial excitement, high-technology architecture concentrates on articulating and making visible all the building's components. An early example of high-tech architecture

FIGURE 14.37 *Foster: HongKongBank, Hong Kong, 1986.* (Photo: Ian Lambot/courtesy Foster Associates)

was the Pompidiou Center (1976) in Paris, designed by Renzo Piano and Richard Rogers in the Beaubourg area of Paris, not far from the former site of Les Halles. All the architectural interest hangs on the outside of the building, where the white web of diagonally braced steel framing, bright blue air-handling ducts, red exhaust stacks, and exterior escalator snaking up the front façade encase a multistory glass rectangular solid. The galleries contained inside are unremarkable when compared with the exterior, and the building's bristling mechanics are curiously out-of-place in its nineteenth-century neighborhood.

An even more spectacular tour-de-force is the international headquarters for the HongKongBank (1986) by Norman Foster Associates (Figure 14.37). Foster, a British architect, responded to the challenge of a site with splendid views of Hong Kong harbor (north) and Victoria Peak (south) with a forty-seven-story rectangular prism having its long sides oriented to the views while mechanical and service functions close off the short east and west elevations. The most public banking areas are housed in the third through twelfth floors, which are grouped around a central atrium lit by mirrors set in a south-facing sunscoop hung outside the building. Save for mechanical rooms, structure, and elevator lobbies, the ground level is devoted entirely to an open plaza from which paired escalators rise through a glass ceiling to the atrium above. Construction detail gives character to the exterior; eight steel-truss towers comprise the "legs" from which the floors are suspended in five modules of diminishing height. A column-free interior is thereby obtained with a structure that acts like five superimposed bridges suspended from horizontal trusses. Each horizontal truss occupies a double-height story containing meeting rooms, recreation areas, and food services, and each has exterior terraces that serve as refuge areas in case of fire. The truss floors divide the building into zoned layers housing related functional units of the bank, and floors within each zone are linked with escalators rather than elevators to establish spatial continuity. Setbacks at the upper levels conform to building codes, and a penthouse at the top provides space for the bank's officers and a future heliport.

The engineering and technology behind the HongKongBank is as impressive as it appears, with many details and components used here for the first time. Wind tunnel tests verified the building's structural response to typhoons and localized weather patterns, and full-sized mock-ups were built of such elements as the teller's counters, the prefabricated toilet room modules, and a typical office space complete with its underfloor services, flooring panels, and carpeting. Precision construction, including new techniques for shaping sheet aluminum into cladding for the structural steel and robot welding of its joints, governs the metal, glass, and concrete used in the bank. Both architects and engineers consciously sought to have the building's parts communicate their roles. Hangars, fasteners, supports, joints, and trusses are clearly expressed. Even the elevator mechanisms are enclosed in glass so that the works are visible.

As a spatial experience, the HongKongBank contains no surprises. Design efforts were almost exclusively expended on technological wizardry, and while the office floors are pleasantly light, open, and tastefully furnished, they are little different from what can be found in a building by Mies van der Rohe. If the building techniques and systems pioneered here advance the sophistication of building construction as much as predicted, however, the HongKongBank's impact on later architecture may place it with the Crystal Palace as a monument of its age.

Thus the architecture of the last quarter of the twentieth century is as dominated by mannerisms as design in the sixteenth century. Some Post-Modern architects continue in the traditions of the immediate past, as Palladio followed Alberti, while others seek new forms based on a widely divergent series of historic sources from many periods and styles. To some critics our period seems confused and eclectic, but just as the logic of the Baroque emerged from the plurality of Mannerist design, the rationality of the best early-twentieth-century architecture may combine with a renewed interest in the historical past to establish trends that can be exploited by innovative architects in a new tradition.

SELECTED BIBLIOGRAPHY

This bibliography primarily includes current books summarizing the whole of architectural history, the works of an individual architect, or buildings of a particular era. Save for a few isolated examples, all works cited are in English and should be available in larger libraries. Special mention should be made of two sets of books contained in this list:

1. The Pelican History of Art, published by Penguin under the general editorship of the late Sir Nikolaus Pevsner. These books reflect current scholarly thought although they are not always easy to read. The extensive bibliography contained in each volume provides a valuable guide to further resources. Pelican History of Art volumes are marked with an asterisk [*] in the list below.

2. The History of Architecture volumes published by Abrams under the editorship of the late Pier Luigi Nervi. These books are particularly recommended for their large and detailed illustrations. Rizzoli is now reissuing them in paperback editions with additional color photographs. Abrams History of World Architecture tiles are marked with a dagger [†] in the list below.

General Works

Benevolo, L. *The History of the City.* Cambridge: MIT Press, 1980.

Fleming, J., H. Honour, and N. Pevsner. *The Penguin Dictionary of Architecture.* Baltimore: Penguin, 1966.

Fletcher, B. *A History of Architecture.* London: Butterworths, 1987.
A virtual one-volume encyclopedia of architectural monuments worldwide, presenting brief stylistic descriptions and capsule summaries of individual buildings. Justifiably known for its distinctive plans and diagrams.

Janson, H. W. *The History of Art.* New York: Abrams, 1986.

Kostof, S. (ed.) *The Architect: Chapters in the History of the Profession.* New York: Oxford University Press, 1977.
A collection of essays describing architectural education and practice from antiquity to the École des Beaux-Arts.

Kostof, S. *A History of Architecture: Settings and Rituals.* New York: Oxford University Press, 1985.

Norberg-Schulz, C. *Meaning in Western Architecture.* New York: Praeger, 1974.

Pevsner, N. *An Outline of European Architecture.* Harmondsworth, England: Penguin, 1972.

Placzek, A. K. (ed.) *Macmillan Encyclopedia of Architects.* New York: Free Press, 1982.
A four-volume reference work containing biographical sketches of notable architects. Reference citations for each entry provide a useful bibliography.

Stierlin, H. *Encyclopedia of World Architecture.* New York: Van Nostrand Reinhold, 1983.
Contains clearly delineated plans and sections for hundreds of buildings. The text is minimal.

Trachtenburg, M., and I. Hyman. *Architecture from Prehistory to Post-Modernism: The Western Tradition.* Englewood Cliffs, N.J.: Prentice Hall, 1986.

Watkin, D. *A History of Western Architecture.* New York: Thames and Hudson, 1986.

Chapter One: The Beginnings of Architecture

Badawy, A. *Architecture in Ancient Egypt and the Near East.* Cambridge: MIT Press, 1966.

*Frankfort, H. *The Art and Architecture of the Ancient Orient.* Harmondsworth, England: Penguin, 1970.

Hawkes, J. *Atlas of Ancient Archaeology.* London: Heinemann, 1974.
A clear and useful summary of prehistoric sites, uniformly presented.

Hawkins, G. S. *Stonehenge Decoded.* Garden City, N.Y.: Doubleday, 1965.

Lauer, J-P. *Saqqara: The Royal Cemetery of Memphis.* New York: Scribner's Sons, 1976.
Summarizes archaeological work on the tomb complex of King Zoser as well as excavations of the much later shrines of the Apis bulls.

Mellaart, J. *Catal Hüyük: A Neolithic Town in Anatolia.* New York: McGraw-Hill, 1967.

Renfrew, C. *Before Civilization.* Harmondsworth, England: Penguin, 1973.

Smith, E. B. *Egyptian Architecture as Cultural Expression.* Watkins Glen, N.Y.: American Life Foundation, 1968.

*Smith, W. S. *The Art and Architecture of Ancient Egypt.* Harmondsworth, England: Penguin, 1981.

Chapter Two: The Second Millenium

Evans, A. J. *The Palace of Minos at Knossos.* London: Macmillan, 1921–1935.

Gurney, O. R. *The Hittites.* Harmondsworth, England: Penguin, 1961.

Woolley, C. L. *Ur of the Chaldees.* Harmondsworth, England: Penguin, 1954.

Chapter Three: The Greek World

Carpenter, R. *The Architects of the Parthenon.* Harmondsworth, England: Penguin, 1970.

*Lawrence, A. W. *Greek Architecture.* Harmondsworth, England: Penguin, 1973.

Martienssen, R. D. *The Idea of Space in Greek Architecture.* Johannesburg, South Africa: University of the Witwatersrand, 1964.

Robertson, D. S. *A Handbook of Greek and Roman Architecture.* Cambridge: Cambridge University Press, 1943.

Scully, V. *The Earth, The Temple, and the Gods.* New Haven, Conn.: Yale University Press, 1979.
Studies the specific relationship of individual Greek temples to their settings.

Wycherley, R. E. *How the Greeks Built Cities.* London: Macmillan, 1973.

Chapter Four: Roman Architecture

Boethius, A. *The Golden House of Nero.* Ann Arbor: University of Michigan Press, 1960.

Grant, M. *Cities of Vesuvius.* Harmondsworth, England: Penguin, 1976.

MacDonald, W. L. *The Architecture of the Roman Empire.* New Haven, Conn.: Yale University Press, 1982.

MacDonald, W. L. *The Pantheon: Design, Meaning, and Progeny.* Cambridge: Harvard University Press, 1976.

Vitruvius, M. *The Ten Books on Architecture.* New York: Dover, 1960.
English translation of the only complete surviving architectural treatise from antiquity.

*Ward-Perkins, J. B. *Roman Imperial Architecture.* Harmondsworth, England: Penguin, 1981.

Wheeler, R. E. M. *Roman Art and Architecture.* New York: Praeger, 1964.

Chapter Five: Early Christian and Byzantine Architecture

*Krautheimer, R. *Early Christian and Byzantine Architecture.* Harmondsworth, England: Penguin, 1981.

Krautheimer, R. *Rome: Profile of a City, 312–1308.* Princeton, N.J.: Princeton University Press, 1980.

†Mango, C. *Byzantine Architecture.* New York: Abrams, 1976.

MacDonald, W. L. *Early Christian and Byzantine Architecture.* New York: Braziller, 1962.

Rice, D. T. *The Art of Byzantium.* New York: Abrams, 1959.

Chapter Six: Islamic Architecture

Creswell, K. A. C. *A Short Account of Early Muslim Architecture.* Harmondsworth, England: Penguin, 1958.

†Hoag, J. D. *Islamic Architecture.* New York: Abrams, 1977.

Hoag, J. D. *Western Islamic Architecture.* New York: Braziller, 1963.

Rice, D. T. *Islamic Art.* New York: Praeger, 1965.

Chapter Seven: Early Medieval and Romanesque Architecture

*Conant, K. J. *Carolingian and Romanesque Architecture, 800–1200.* Harmondsworth, England: Penguin, 1974.

Conant, K. J. *Cluny: les églises et la maison du chef d'ordre.* Mâcon: Imprimerie Protat Frères, 1968.
The culmination of a lifetime's scholarly investigation. Although the text is in French, the extensive illustrations are universally understandable.

Focillon, H. *The Art of the West: Romanesque.* Ithaca, N.Y.: Cornell, University Press, 1980.

Horn, W., and E. Born. *The Plan of St. Gall.* Berkeley: University of California Press, 1979.
A model of modern research and scholarship, this three-volume work traces the impact of antique building on Carolingian architecture and the influence of the Plan of St. Gall on later buildings.

†Kubach, H. E. *Romanesque Architecture.* New York: Abrams, 1975.

Mâle, E. *Religious Art in France: The Twelfth Century.* Princeton, N.J.: Princeton University Press, 1978.

Stokstad, M. *Medieval Art.* New York: Harper and Row, 1986.

Chapter Eight: Gothic Architecture

Bony, J. *French Gothic of the 12th and 13th Centuries.* Berkeley: University of California Press, 1983.

Branner, R. (ed.) *Chartres Cathedral.* New York: Norton, 1969.

Branner, R. *Saint Louis and the Court Style in Gothic Architecture.* London: Zwemmer, 1965.

Braunfels, W. *Monasteries of Western Europe: The Architecture of the Orders.* Princeton, N.J.: Princeton University Press, 1972.

Bruzelius, C. A. *The 13th-century Church at St. Denis.* New Haven, Conn.: Yale University Press, 1985.

Crosby, S. *The Royal Abbey of Saint-Denis.* New Haven, Conn.: Yale University Press, 1987.
Published after Crosby's death, this work summarizes his investigations on Suger's work and previous churches on the site.

Focillon, H. *The Art of the West: Gothic.* Ithaca, Cornell University Press, 1980.

*Frankl, P. *Gothic Architecture.* Harmondsworth, England: Penguin, 1962.

†Grodecki, L. *Gothic Architecture.* New York: Abrams, 1977.

James, J. *Chartres: The Masons Who Built a Legend.* London: Routledge & Kegan Paul, 1982.

Leedy, W. C. *Fan Vaulting: A Study of Form, Technology, and Meaning.* Santa Monica, Calif.: Art & Architecture Press, 1980.
A short essay on fan vaults, elaborated by over 200 illustrations and a catalog of 130 surviving

fan vaults in churches, chapels, porches, and towers.
Mark, R. *Experiments in Gothic Structure.* Cambridge: MIT Press, 1982.
Mark, an engineer, has examined Gothic structural behavior through scale models, demonstrating the critical role played by loads carried in tension.
Salzman, L. F. *Building in England Down to 1540.* Oxford: Clarendon Press, 1952.
Simpson, O. von. *The Gothic Cathedral: Origins of Gothic Architecture and the Medieval Concept of Order.* Princeton, N.J.: Princeton University Press, 1974.
Stoddard, W. *Art and Architecture in Medieval France.* New York: Harper and Row, 1972.
Temko, A. *Notre-Dame of Paris.* New York: Viking Press, 1955.

Chapter Nine: Renaissance Architecture

Ackerman, J. S. *Palladio.* Baltimore: Penguin, 1966.
Ackerman, J. S. *The Architecture of Michelangelo.* Baltimore: Penguin, 1971.
Alberti, L. B. *On the Art of Building in Ten Books.* Cambridge: MIT Press, 1988.
A translation of Alberti's ideas and theories of architecture.
Argan, G. C. *The Renaissance City.* New York: Braziller, 1969.
*Blunt, A. *Art and Architecture in France, 1500–1700.* Harmondsworth, England: Penguin, 1957.
Burckhardt, J. *The Architecture of the Italian Renaissance.* London: Murray, 1985.
*Heydenreich, L. H., and W. Lotz. *Architecture in Italy, 1400 to 1600.* Harmondsworth, England: Penguin, 1974.
Hibbard, H. *Bernini.* Harmondsworth: Penguin, 1965.
Letarouilly, P. M. *Édifices de Rome moderne.* Princeton, N.J.: Princeton Architectural Press, 1982.
Lowry, B. *Renaissance Architecture.* New York: Braziller, 1967.
†Murray, P. *Renaissance Architecture.* New York: Abrams, 1971.
Murray, P. *The Architecture of the Italian Renaissance.* New York: Schocken Books, 1966.
Palladio, A. *The Four Books of Architecture.* New York: Dover, 1965.
Serlio, S. *The Five Books of Architecture.* New York: Dover, 1982.
Summerson, J. *Inigo Jones.* Harmondsworth, England: Penguin, 1966.
Wittkower, R. *Architectural Principles in the Age of Humanism.* London: Tiranti, 1962.
Theories of Renaissance architecture from Alberti to Palladio.

Chapter Ten: Baroque Architecture

†Norberg-Schulz, C. *Baroque Architecture.* New York: Abrams, 1971.
†Norberg-Schulz, C. *Late Baroque and Rococo Architecture.* New York: Abrams, 1971.
*Summerson, J. *Architecture in Britain 1530–1830.* Harmondsworth, England: Penguin, 1977.
Walton, Guy. *Louis XIV's Versailles.* Chicago: University of Chicago Press, 1986.
Whinney, M., and O. Millar. *English Art 1625–1714.* Oxford: Oxford University Press, 1957.
*Wittkower, R. *Art and Architecture in Italy, 1600–1750.* Harmondsworth, England: Penguin, 1958.

Chapter Eleven: The Eighteenth Century

Clark, K. *The Gothic Revival: An Essay in the History of Taste.* London: Constable, 1950.
Honour, H. *Neo-Classicism.* Harmondsworth, England: Penguin, 1968.
Rykwert, J. *On Adam's House in Paradise.* Cambridge: MIT Press, 1980.
Concentrates on the theories of the origins of architecture and the beginnings of the Romantic movement in the eighteenth century.

Chapter Twelve: Nineteenth-Century Developments

Benevolo, L. *History of Modern Architecture.* Cambridge: MIT Press, 1971.
Collins, P. *Changing Ideals in Modern Architecture.* London: Faber, 1965.

Condit, C. *American Building Art — The Nineteenth Century.* New York: Oxford University Press, 1960.

Condit, C. *The Chicago School of Architecture: A History of Commercial and Public Building in the Chicago Area, 1875–1925.* Chicago: University of Chicago Press, 1964.

Drexler, A. (ed.) *The Architecture of the École des Beaux-Arts.* Cambridge: MIT Press, 1977.
A reevaluation of all aspects of nineteenth-century French architectural instruction.

Germann, G. *Gothic Revival in Europe and Britain: Sources, Influences and Ideas.* London: Lund Humphries, 1972.

Giedion, S. *Space, Time, and Architecture.* Cambridge: Harvard University Press, 1967.

Hamlin, T. *Greek Revival Architecture in America.* New York: Oxford University Press, 1944.

*Hitchcock, H. R. *Architecture: Nineteenth and Twentieth Centuries.* Harmondsworth, England: Penguin, 1977.

Hitchcock, H. R. *Early Victorian Architecture in Britain.* New Haven, Conn.: Yale University Press, 1954.

Hitchcock, H. R. *The Architecture of H. H. Richardson and His Times.* Cambridge: MIT Press, 1966.

Pevsner, N. *Pioneers of Modern Design: From William Morris to Walter Gropius.* Harmondsworth, England: Penguin, 1974.
Essentially a study of the Arts and Crafts movement.

Scully, V. *The Shingle Style and the Stick Style.* New Haven, Conn.: Yale University Press, 1971.

Stanton, P. *Pugin.* New York: Viking, 1972.

Twombly, R. *Louis Sullivan: His Life and Work.* New York: Viking, 1986.
This is not the only book on Sullivan, but it is the most up to date and most thoroughly researched.

Chapter Thirteen: Twentieth-Century Modern

Banham, R. *The Architecture of the Well-Tempered Environment.* Chicago: University of Chicago Press, 1969.

Banham, R. *Theory and Design in the First Machine Age.* Cambridge: MIT Press, 1960.

Boesiger, W. (ed.) *Le Corbusier and Pierre Jeanneret: Oeuvre Complète.* Zurich: Girsberger, 1935–1965.
A detailed study of every major work by Le Corbusier, with his explanations of each project.

Collins, G. R. *Antonio Gaudi.* New York: Braziller, 1960.

Frampton, K. *Modern Architecture, A Critical History.* New York: Oxford University Press, 1985.

Hitchcock, H. R., and P. Johnson. *The International Style.* New York: Norton, 1932.

Hitchcock, H. R. *In the Nature of Materials: The Buildings of Frank Lloyd Wright, 1887–1941.* New York: Duell, Sloan, and Pierce, 1942.

Jacobus, J. *Twentieth-Century Architecture: The Middle Years 1940–1965.* New York: Praeger, 1966.

Jencks, C. *Le Corbusier and the Tragic View of Architecture.* Cambridge: Harvard University Press, 1973.

Jencks, C. *Modern Movements in Architecture.* New York: Doubleday, 1973.

Joedicke, J. *A History of Modern Architecture.* New York: Praeger, 1959.

Johnson, P. *Mies van der Rohe.* New York: Museum of Modern Art, 1978.

Jordy, W. H. *American Buildings and Their Architects. The Impact of European Modernism in the Twentieth Century.* New York: Doubleday, 1972.

Le Corbusier. *Towards a New Architecture.* London: Architectural Press, 1952.

Schulze, F. *Mies van der Rohe: A Critical Biography.* Chicago: University of Chicago Press, 1985.

Scully, V. *Frank Lloyd Wright.* New York: Braziller, 1960.

Scully, V. *Modern Architecture.* New York: Braziller, 1974.

Storrer, W. A. *The Architecture of Frank Lloyd Wright.* Cambridge: MIT Press, 1980.

Tafuri, M., and F. Dal Co. *Modern Architecture.* New York: Rizzoli, 1986.

Twombly, R. *Frank Lloyd Wright: His Life and His Architecture.* New York: Wiley, 1979.

Wingler, H. *Bauhaus: Weimar, Dessau, Berlin, Chicago.* Cambridge: MIT Press, 1969.
A heavily documented study of almost every aspect of the Bauhaus and all its participants.

Chapter Fourteen: Reactions to Modernism

Drexler, A. (ed.) *Five Architects: Eisenman, Graves, Gwathmey, Hejduk, Meier.* New York: Oxford University Press, 1975.

Jencks, C. *The Language of Post-Modern Architecture.* New York: Rizzoli, 1981.
It is difficult to write history at almost the same time that it is happening, but Jencks does this in a creditable manner. From 1977, when he invented the term *Post-Modernism,* to 1981, this book went through four editions, each one changing according to evolving interpretations.

Jencks, C. *Late Modern Architecture.* New York: Rizzoli, 1980.

Jencks, C. (ed.) *Post-Modern Classicism.* New York: Rizzoli, 1980.

Jencks, C., and W. Chaitkin. *Architecture Today.* New York: Abrams, 1982.

Venturi, R. *Complexity and Contradiction in Architecture.* New York: Museum of Modern Art, 1977.

GLOSSARY

abacus On a classical column the stone set directly over the capital.

acanthus A plant used as a model for decoration on Corinthian and Composite capitals.

acropolis Literally high city. In Greek city-states the acropolis was the location of the most important temples and religious shrines.

acroteria Upright ornaments placed at the apex and eaves of gabled roofs in Greek and Roman architecture.

agora In Greek cities the term applied to the area of markets and city government.

aisle In a basilican church the portion set parallel to the nave, generally separated from it by columns or piers.

ambulatory The curving passageway behind the choir of a church, often used to connect the radiating chapels of the east end.

apse The termination of the nave of a basilica or the choir in a basilican church.

aqueduct A pipe for conducting water under gravity flow. The term is often applied to the arched structure built to support the pipe across valleys.

arcade A series of arches carried on columns or piers.

arch A curved element that spans an opening and supports the structural loads above it. Most often, arches are made of small, wedge-shaped masonry elements called voussoirs. The profile of an arch may vary from semicircular to pointed to almost flat.

architrave In classical architecture the bottom portion of an entablature.

arris The intersection of two curved surfaces, most commonly applied to the line formed when the flutes of a Doric column join.

ashlar Smooth stone masonry laid so that the joints are visible.

atrium The central space of a Roman house, open to the sky and serving as a source of light and fresh air. In Early Christian churches the atrium was a large open courtyard, surrounded by covered galleries, which preceded the entrance to the church.

attic The story built above the cornice of a building, sometimes used to conceal the roof.

balcony A platform cantilevered from a wall, generally surrounded by a railing or balustrade.

baldacchino An elaborate canopy erected over an altar.

baptistry A building, generally octagonal, used for the Christian rite of baptism.

barrel vault A semicircular vault over a rectangular space.

base The lowest part of a column or pier, often broader than the sections above to spread the load to the foundation.

basilica Literally, king's hall. In Roman architecture a hall used for public administration. The term generally refers to a rectangular building having a central section with a higher roof (the nave) flanked by lower aisles on both long sides. A semicircular projection, the apse, was often set at one or both of the shorter ends. Early Christians adapted the form as a basis for church design, replacing one apse with the main entrance and establishing a processional axis the length of the building. The altar was placed in the apse at the end.

bay A building module defined by the repetition of an element such as a column or pier.

belfrey The tower or steeple in which bells are hung.

bouleuterion In classical Greek architecture a building used for senate or council meetings.

brise-soleil A screen attached to a building to shade windows from the sun.

buttress Masonry reinforcement applied to a wall to provide additional strength.

caldarium The hot bath chamber in Roman baths, or thermae.

campanile In Italy the name given to a free-standing bell tower.

capital In classical architecture the termination of a column, generally given decorative carving.

Carolingian The term applied to buildings constructed under the influence of the Emperor Charlemagne, who reigned from 792 to 814.

cartouche A boldly decorated frame hung above doorways.

caryatid A pier carved in the form of a standing woman and used in place of a column.

castellation A nonmilitary application of crenellations, generally decorative.

cathedral The church that serves as seat of a bishop. (The bishop's chair is called a cathedra.)

cella The shrine room in the center of a temple.

cement The binding component of concrete. Natural cements occur in areas of former volcanic activity, as around Puteoli, where the Romans exploited deposits they called pozzolana. Artificial cements have been made since 1824, when Joseph Aspdin discovered a process of heating limestone, clay, and sand to a very high temperature and then grinding the result.

chancel The east end of a church in which the main altar is placed.

chapter house An assembly room in a monastery, generally located off the cloister, where the monks and abbot would gather daily for reading a chapter of the Rule by which monastic life was governed.

clerestory Windows placed high in a wall, generally above lower roof elements.

coffers Ceiling recesses set in a geometric pattern.

column In classical architecture the upright structural element consisting of a base, shaft, and capital.

Composite A Roman order combining features of the Ionic and Corinthian.

concrete A plastic building material consisting of sand, water, cement, and aggregate, which hardens to a stonelike consistency.

console A bracket, generally decoratively curved, that supports a cornice or projecting element.

corbel Masonry that projects slightly from a wall and serves as a support.

Corinthian The order that features acanthus-leaf capitals atop a fluted shaft.

cornice The uppermost element of an entablature, which projects beyond the plane of the exterior wall; more generally, the overhanging molding at the top of any building.

cortile In Italian architecture the term applied to an open courtyard inside a building.

crenellation A fortification applied to the top of a wall with lower portions to provide space for throwing projectiles; sometimes called a battlement.

crockets Decorative budlike protrusions on the angles of Gothic stonework, especially on spires and towers.

crossing In a basilican church the space where transepts, nave, and choir intersect.

crypt The basement level of a church, originally used for burial.

cupola A dome; the term is also applied to the lantern on any roof structure, generally applied to the structure over the oculus of a dome.

curtain wall A nonstructural exterior surface hung from metal framing.

dentil A type of cornice molding, composed of

rectangular blocks set in a row like teeth; hence the name.

dome A continuously curved roof over a polygonal or circular plan, generally having a semicircular or elliptical section.

Doric The Greek order having a fluted shaft, no base, and an echinus molding supporting the abacus. Roman Doric columns have a base.

dormer A window that projects above the slope of a roof.

drum The cylindrical volume supporting a dome.

eave The edge of the roof plane that projects over the exterior wall of a building.

echinus The curved cushionlike molding that, together with the abacus, forms the capital in the Doric order.

entablature In classical architecture the horizontal elements supported by columns, consisting (in ascending sequence) of the architrave, frieze, and cornice.

entasis The slight outward curve of a column, which then tapers toward the top of the shaft.

exedra A semicircular niche for a seat of honor or placement of a statue.

façade The exterior elevation of a building.

fan vault In English Perpendicular Gothic buildings, vaults with ribs having the same curvature and radiating or fanning out from the springing of the vault.

fascia Horizontal bands in the architrave of the Ionic and Corinthian orders; more generally, the end board of a roof at the eaves.

fillet The flat vertical face between the flutings of a column shaft.

fluting Vertical grooves incised in the shaft of a classical column.

flying buttress In Gothic architecture the combination of external buttress pier and slender arch, which attaches to a wall just below the springing of the vaulting in order to resist thrust.

forum In Roman towns the open space near the center for trade and public business.

fresco Paintings executed on wall surfaces by working pigments into wet plaster.

frieze The horizontal element above the architrave and below the cornice in an entablature.

frigidarium Cold-water baths in a Roman thermae.

gable The pedimented end of a classical temple; more generally, the triangular space at the end of a double-pitched roof.

galilee A porch or chapel at the west end of medieval churches.

gallery The passage over the aisle in medieval churches.

gargoyle A decorative rainwater spout, often carved to resemble a fanciful animal.

groin vault The vault formed by two intersecting barrel vaults. Also known as a cross vault.

half-timbering Wall construction with heavy timber members carrying the structural load and made weathertight with infill materials.

hammerbeam A bracketed cantilevered beam used as support for a timber roof truss.

hypostyle hall A large hall composed of many columns placed closely together to support the roof.

insula A Roman apartment house.

intercolumniation The space between columns.

Ionic The order which features volutes in the capital; the shaft is usually fluted.

jetty A short wooden cantilever supporting an upper wall section, most commonly found on timber houses of the medieval period.

keep The central enclosed tower of a medieval castle.

keystone The central voussoir of an arch.

king post truss A triangular roof truss having a central vertical post.

lantern A tower with windows rising above the roofline or above the oculus of a dome.

lierne A decorative, nonstructural supplementary rib added to Gothic vaulting.

lintel Any horizontal member that spans an opening.

loggia An open porch, generally raised above the ground floor and covered by a roof.

long gallery A wide and long passageway in English and French Renaissance houses used for living purposes.

martyrium A building associated with the act or burial of a Christian martyr.

mastaba An Egyptian tomb with a flat top and sloping sides, built over a grave shaft.

mausoleum An elaborate tomb.

megaron In Mycenaean architecture a rectangular room having a central hearth and four columns supporting a roof with atrium opening. More generally the term applies to a single-cell house in the Aegean region.

metope An element of the Doric frieze, set alternately with triglyphs. Metope panels contain low relief carvings.

mihrab A directional niche in the qibla wall.

mimbar In a mosque the pulpit from which the imam leads prayers.

modillion Another word for console, sometimes applied to a series of ornamental brackets supporting a cornice.

mosaic Floor, wall, or ceiling decoration composed of small pieces of colored glass or stone that form designs.

narthex Entrance porch or chamber before the nave of a church.

nave The western arm of a basilican church.

niche A wall recess.

obelisk A stone monolith, square on plan, with tapering sides toward a pyramidal top.

oculus The circular opening at the apex of a dome.

order The trabeated systems of architecture developed by the Greeks and extended by Romans. The Greek orders — Doric, Ionic, and Corinthian — differ slightly in detail from Roman orders. The Romans developed the Tuscan and Composite orders.

Palladian motif An arched opening flanked by smaller rectangular-headed openings. Also known as a Serliana.

parapet A low wall at the perimeter of a roof.

pavilion A forward break in a wall plane generally used to mark the center and ends of a façade.

pediment The gable end of a temple, framed by cornices.

pendentive A spherical triangle that transforms a square bay into a circle for the springing of a dome.

peristyle A colonnaded court or garden.

piano nobile The main living floor of a house, generally raised a story above ground level.

pier A structural element, square or rectangular in plan, that supports an arch.

pilaster A rectangular column, engaged in a wall, which is articulated as an order.

pilotis Freestanding posts or supports for an upper-level structure; this term used most commonly by Le Corbusier.

plinth The base of a building or column.

polychromy The decorative use of colored stone, seen primarily in medieval architecture.

portico A colonnaded porch.

pylon A massive entrance to an Egyptian temple, with sloping walls and a central opening.

qibla The wall of a mosque that faces toward Mecca.

rib A raised molding applied to the arris of a vault.

rustication Rough stonework with exposed joints.

sahn An open arcaded courtyard in a mosque.

Serliana A Palladian motif first illustrated by Sebastiano Serlio.

shaft The vertical element above the base and below the capital in an architectural order.

skene The backdrop building in a classical theater.

soffit The underside of any projecting architectural element, usually applied to the eave.

squinch Corbeled arches that transform a square bay into an octagon for the springing of a dome.

stoa A covered market.

stylobate The base, usually having steps, on which a colonnaded temple sits.

tepidarium The warm water baths in a Roman thermae.

tholos A dome over a circular plan building, or more generally the building itself.

tierceron In Gothic vaulting a secondary rib extending from the support to the crown of the vault.

tracery The stonework divisions in Gothic windows.

transept The north and south arms of a basilican church.

triforium In Gothic churches the narrow passage below the clerestory corresponding to the lean-to roof over the aisle.

triglyph A channeled block set between metopes in a Doric frieze.

truss A structural frame composed of short elements, typically configured into triangles, used to form a bridge or span a roof.

tympanum A panel, generally semicircular, over the lintel and under the arch of a doorway. Also, the central triangle of a pediment.

vault An arched roof of brick or stone.

vestibule An antechamber before a major space.

volute A decorative spiral found in Ionic, Corinthian, and Composite capitals.
voussoir A wedge-shaped masonry unit set to form an arch.
westwerk The narthex, chapels, and towers set at the entrance end of churches of the Carolingian and later periods.
ziggurat A stepped pyramid form used in ancient Mesopotamia as a religious building.

INDEX

N.B. All names beginning with "Saint," whether written as S., SS., St., Saint-, Sainte-, or Sant', are listed alphabetically as if spelled out "Saint —."